"These war memoirs paint a new po
a persuasive one—of the leader of a lost cause, a man whose single-minded determination could not redeem France, but at least miti-gated the strain of war defeat and Vichy collaboration.... And in soaring language—on a par in its finest passages with Churchill's eloquence—the tale of tragedy and grandeur is told."
—*New York Times Book Review*

"This is a book which will have much to say to those who know and are interested in France and, especially, to those who still remember General Charles de Gaulle's heroic struggle in the name of his pros-trate mother-land."
—*Christian Science Monitor*

"From the literary standpoint, de Gaulle's memoirs...are the most distinguished of any war leader's with the exception of Churchill's.... With [his style's] commanding lucidity and logic, its classic periods, its patriotic eloquence and stately dignity, it is the style of a man who dwells on the remoter heights.... A valuable record of the French participation in the last period of the war and detailed reasons for General de Gaulle's actions in pursuit of his great objective, the re-establishment of his country as a major European power."
—*Atlantic Monthly*

"Endures as a historical monument. Vive de Gaulle!"
—*Kirkus Reviews*

"Written in bold, sometimes eloquent prose that serves as an admirable carriage for all the de Gaulle qualities: his soldier's self-lessness, his sometimes irritating sense of destiny, above all his incorruptible honesty."
—*Time Magazine*

THE COMPLETE WAR MEMOIRS OF
Charles de Gaulle

VOLUME I

THE CALL TO HONOUR

VOLUME II

UNITY

VOLUME III

SALVATION

CARROLL & GRAF PUBLISHERS, INC.
NEW YORK

Volume I. THE CALL TO HONOUR
Copyright © 1955 by Simon and Schuster, Inc.
Originally published in France under the title *L'Appel*.
Copyright © 1954 by Librairie Plon.

Volume II. UNITY
Copyright © 1959 by Simon and Schuster, Inc.
Originally published in France under the title *L'Unité*.
Copyright © 1956 by Librairie Plon.

Volume III. SALVATION
Copyright © 1959, 1960 by Charles de Gaulle
Originally published in France under the title *Le Salut*.
Copyright © 1959 by Librairie Plon.

First Carroll & Graf edition 1998

Carroll & Graf Publishers, Inc.
19 West 21st Street
New York, NY 10010-6805

Library of Congress Cataloging-in-Publication Data is available.
ISBN: 0-7867-0546-9

Manufactured in the United States of America

CONTENTS

VOLUME I

THE CALL TO HONOUR
1940-1942

Translated from the French by
JONATHAN GRIFFIN

VOLUME II

UNITY
1942-1944

Translated from the French by
RICHARD HOWARD

VOLUME III

SALVATION
1944-1946

Translated from the French by

RICHARD HOWARD

VOLUME I

THE CALL

TO HONOUR

1940-1942

Translated from the French by
JONATHAN GRIFFIN

CHAPTER 1

THE SLOPE

ALL MY LIFE I have thought of France in a certain way. This is inspired by sentiment as much as by reason. The emotional side of me tends to imagine France, like the princess in the fairy stories or the Madonna in the frescoes, as dedicated to an exalted and exceptional destiny. Instinctively I have the feeling that Providence has created her either for complete successes or for exemplary misfortunes. If, in spite of this, mediocrity shows in her acts and deeds, it strikes me as an absurd anomaly, to be imputed to the faults of Frenchmen, not to the genius of the land. But the positive side of my mind also assures me that France is not really herself unless in the front rank; that only vast enterprises are capable of counterbalancing the ferments of dispersal which are inherent in her people; that our country, as it is, surrounded by the others, as they are, must aim high and hold itself straight, on pain of mortal danger. In short, to my mind, France cannot be France without greatness.

This faith grew as I grew, in the environment where I was born. My father was a thoughtful, cultivated, traditional man, imbued with a feeling for the dignity of France. He made me aware of her history. My mother had an uncompromising passion for her country, equal to her religious piety. To my three brothers, my sister,

3

and myself a certain anxious pride in our country came as second nature. As a young native of Lille living in Paris, nothing struck me more than the symbols of our glories: night falling over Notre Dame, the majesty of evening at Versailles, the Arc de Triomphe in the sun, conquered colours shuddering in the vault of the Invalides. Nothing affected me more than the evidence of our national successes: popular enthusiasm when the Tsar of Russia passed through, a review at Longchamp, the marvels of the Exhibition, the first flights of our aviators. Nothing saddened me more profoundly than our weaknesses and our mistakes, as revealed to my childhood gaze by the way people looked and by things they said: the surrender of Fashoda, the Dreyfus case, social conflicts, religious strife. Nothing moved me so much as the story of our past misfortunes: my father recalling the fruitless sortie from Le Bourget and Stains, in which he had been wounded; my mother conjuring up the despair she had felt as a girl at the sight of her parents in tears: "Bazaine has capitulated!"

As an adolescent, the fate of France, whether as the subject of history or as the stake in public life, interested me above everything. I was therefore attracted, but also severely critical, towards the play which was performed, day in, day out, in the forum; carried away as I was by the intelligence, fire, and eloquence lavished upon it by countless actors, yet saddened at seeing so many gifts wasted in political confusion and national disunity. All the more so since at the beginning of the century the premonitory symptoms of war became visible. I must say that in my first youth I pictured this unknown adventure with no horror, and magnified it in anticipation. In short, I was convinced that France would have to go through gigantic trials, that the interest of life consisted in one day rendering her some signal service, and that I would have the occasion to do so.

When I joined the Army, it was one of the greatest things in the world. Beneath all the criticisms and insults which were lavished on it, it was looking forward with serenity and even a muffled hopefulness to the approaching days when everything would depend on it. After Saint-Cyr I went through my apprenticeship as officer with the 33rd Infantry Regiment, at Arras. My first colonel, Pétain, showed me the meaning of the gift and art of command. Then, as the hurricane swept me off like a wisp of straw through the shocks of war—my baptism of fire, the calvary of the trenches, attacks, bombardments, wounds and captivity—I was privileged to see France, though deprived of part of her necessary means of defence by an insufficient birth-rate, by hollow ideologies, and by the negligence of the authorities, extract from herself an incredible effort, make up by measureless sacrifices for all she lacked, and bring the trial to an end in victory. I was privileged to see her, in the most critical days, pull herself together morally, at first under the ægis of Joffre, at the end of the drive of the "Tiger." I was privileged to see her, later, though exhausted from losses and devastation, with her social structure and moral balance overthrown, resume with tottering steps her march towards her destiny, while the regime, taking once more its former shape and repudiating Clemenceau, rejected greatness and returned to confusion.

During the years which followed, my career passed through various stages: special duty and a campaign in Poland, a professorship of history at Saint-Cyr, the Ecole de Guerre, attachment to a marshal's personal staff, command of the 19th Battalion of Chasseurs at Trèves, and General Staff service on the Rhine and in the Levant. Everywhere I noted the renewal of prestige which her recent successes had earned for France and, at the same time, the doubts about the future which were being awakened by the erratic behaviour of her rulers. In spite of everything, I found in the soldier's trade the powerful interest it has to offer to the mind and to the heart. In the Army, though a mill without grist, I saw the instrument of the great actions which were approaching.

It was clear, in fact, that the outcome of the First World War had not established peace. Germany was reverting to her ambitions, in proportion as she recovered her strength. While Russia isolated herself in her revolution; while America held aloof from Europe; while England treated Berlin gently in order that Paris might have need of her; while the new states remained weak and disunited—it was on France alone that the burden fell of containing the Reich. She did in fact try, but disjointedly. And so it came about that our policy first applied constraint under the leadership of Poincaré, then attempted reconciliation at the instigation of Briand, and finally sought refuge in the League of Nations. But Germany was growing big with menaces. Hitler was nearing power.

At this period I was detailed to the Secrétariat Général de la Défense Nationale, a permanent body at the disposal of the Premier for preparing the state and the nation for war. From 1932 to 1937, under fourteen governments, I found myself involved, in a planning capacity, in the whole range of political, technical, and administrative activity concerning the country's defence. I had, in particular, to be familiar with the plans for security and for limitation of armaments presented by André Tardieu and Paul-Boncour, respectively, at Geneva; to supply the Doumergue Cabinet with the elements for its decisions when it chose to adopt a different course after the arrival of the Führer; to weave the Penelope-web of the bill for the wartime organization of the nation; and to go into the measures involved by the mobilization of the civil departments, of industry, and of public services. The work I had to do, the discussions at which I was present, the contacts I was obliged to make, showed me the extent of our resources, but also the feebleness of the state.

For the disjointedness of government was rife all over this field. Not—certainly—that the men who figured there lacked intelligence or patriotism; on the contrary, I saw men of incontestable value and sometimes of great talent come to the head of the ministries. But the political game consumed them and paralysed them. As a reserved but passionate witness of public affairs, I watched the constant repetition of the same scenario. Hardly had a Premier taken office when he was at grips with innumerable demands, criticisms, and bids for favour, which all his energy was absorbed in warding off without ever contriving to master them.

Parliament, far from supporting him, offered him nothing but ambushes and desertions. His Ministers were his rivals. Opinion, the press, and sectional interests regarded him as the proper target for all complaints. Everyone, indeed—and he first of all—knew that he was there for only a short time; in fact, after a few months, he had to give place to another. As regards national defence, such conditions prevented those responsible from achieving that organic whole of continuous plans, matured decisions, and measures carried to their conclusion, which we call a policy.

For these reasons the military, who received from the state no more than spasmodic and contradictory impulses, continued to defer to doctrine. The Army became stuck in a set of ideas which had had their heyday before the end of the First World War. It was all the more inclined that way because its leaders were growing old at their posts, wedded to errors that had once constituted their glory.

Hence the concept of the fixed and continuous front dominated the strategy envisaged for a future action. Organization, doctrine, training, and armament derived from it directly. It was understood that, in case of war, France would mobilize the mass of her reserves and would build up the largest possible number of divisions, designed not for manœuvring, attacking, and exploiting, but for holding sectors. They would be placed in position all along the French and Belgian frontiers—Belgium being then explicitly our ally—and would there await the enemy's offensive.

As for the means: tanks, aircraft, mobile and revolving guns—which the last battles of the First World War had already shown to be capable of effecting surprise and the breakthrough, and whose power had since been growing without cease—were to be used only for reinforcing the line and, at need, restoring it by local counterattacks. The types of weapons were established with this in mind: heavy tanks armed with light, short pieces and intended for escorting infantry, not for rapid, independent action; interceptor aircraft designed for defending areas of sky, beside which the Air Force could muster few bombers and no divebombers; artillery designed to fire from fixed positions with a narrow horizontal field of action, not to push ahead through all sorts of country and fire at all angles. Besides, the front was traced in advance by the works of the Maginot Line, prolonged by the Belgian fortifications. Thus the nation in arms would hold a barrier, behind which it would wait—so it was thought—for the blockade to wear the enemy down and the pressure of the free world to drive him to collapse.

Such a conception of war suited the spirit of the regime. Condemned by governmental weakness and political cleavages to stagnation, it was bound to espouse a static system of this kind. But, in addition, this reassuring panacea corresponded too well to the country's state of mind for anyone desirous of being elected, applauded, or given space in print not to be tempted to approve it. Public opinion did not care for offensives, yielding to the illusion that by making war against war the bellicose would be prevented from making war, remembering many ruinous attacks, and failing to discern the revolution in military strength produced since then by the internal-combustion engine. In short, everything converged to make passivity the very principle of our national defence.

To my mind, such an orientation was as dangerous as could be. I considered that, from the strategic point of view, it handed the initiative over to the enemy, lock, stock, and barrel. From the political point of view, I believe that by proclaiming our intention to keep our armies at the frontier, Germany was being egged on to act against the weak, who were from that moment isolated: the Sarre, the Rhineland, Austria, Czechoslovakia, the Baltic states, Poland, and so on; that Russia was being discouraged from forming any bond with us; and that Italy was being assured that, whatever she might do, we would not impose any limit to her malevolence. Lastly, from the moral point of view, it seemed to me deplorable to make the country believe that war, if it came, ought to consist, for it, in fighting as little as possible.

To tell the truth, the philosophy of action, the inspiration and use of armies by the state, the relations between government and

High Command, had preoccupied me for a long time. I had already laid bare my thinking on these subjects by means of several publications: *La Discorde chez l'ennemi, Le Fil de l'épée,* and a certain number of articles in reviews. I had given lectures in public, at the Sorbonne, for instance, on the conduct of war. But in January 1933 Hitler became master of the Reich. From that moment, things could only move headlong. If no one proposed anything that would meet the situation, I felt myself bound to appeal to public opinion and bring forward my own plan. But as the matter was likely to have consequences, I must expect a day to come when the spotlights of public life would settle on me. It was hard for me to make up my mind to this after twenty-five years spent under military rules.

Under the title *Vers l'armée de métier,*[1] I launched my plan and my ideas. I proposed the creation, as a matter of urgency, of an army of manœuvre and attack, mechanized, armoured, composed of picked men, to be added to the large-scale units supplied by mobilization. In 1933 an article in the *Revue politique et parlementaire* served me as starting point. In the spring of 1934 I brought out the book, which set forth my reasons for and my conception of the instrument it was necessary to construct.

Why? Dealing first with the defence of France, I showed that geography (which canalizes the invasion of our territory through the north and the northeast), the nature of the German people (which inclines it to vast ambitions, attracts it westwards, and marks out as its direction Paris through Belgium), and the character of the French people (which lays it open to surprise at the start of each conflict), imposed on us the need to hold a fraction of our forces always on the alert, ready to deploy in its entirety at any moment. "We cannot," I wrote, "rely on a hasty defensive by uncertain formations to bear the first shock. The moment has come to add to the mass of our reserves and of our recruits, which is the principal element of the national resistance but is slow to

[1] English edition published in 1940 (London and Melbourne: Hutchinson) under the title *The Army of the Future.* (Translator's note.)

gather and cumbrous to set to work, an instrument of manœuvre capable of acting without delay—that is to say, permanent, coherent, and accustomed to arms."

I then argued from technical developments. Since the machine has dominated the military order, as it has everything else, the quality of those who must work the machines used in war has become an essential element in the effectiveness of the equipment. How true this was, above all, for the new weapons—tanks, aircraft, ships— which had been engendered by mechanical power, were being perfected very rapidly and were reviving mobility! I noted: "It is henceforward a fact that on land, on sea, and in the air a carefully chosen personnel, able to get the most out of extremely powerful and varied matériel, possesses a terrible superiority over more or less confused masses." I quoted Paul Valéry: "We shall see the development of enterprises carried out by chosen men, acting in crews and producing, in a few moments, at a time and place unforeseen, shattering results."

Turning to the conditions imposed by politics upon strategy, I observed that the latter could not limit itself to the strict defence of the territory since the former must extend its field of action beyond the frontiers. "Whether we like or not, we form part of a certain established order, all of whose elements are interdependent. . . . What becomes, for example, of Central and Eastern Europe, of Belgium or of the Sarre, touches us vitally. . . . With how much blood and tears did we pay for the error of the Second Empire in letting Sadowa happen without moving the army to the Rhine? . . . We must then be ready to act abroad, at any time, on any occasion. How are we to do so in practice, if in order to undertake anything whatever we have got to mobilize our reserves? . . ." Besides, in the competition which was reviving between Germany and France for military strength, we could not fail to be outdistanced as far as numbers were concerned. On the other hand, "given our gifts of initiative, adaptation, and pride, it depended entirely on us to win the upper hand in quality." I concluded this section on the "Why?" as follows: "A weapon for preventive and repressive action—that is what we must provide for ourselves."

How? The internal-combustion engine supplied the basis of the answer—"the internal-combustion engine which is ready to carry whatever one wants, wherever it is needed, at all speeds and distances; . . . the internal-combustion engine which, if it is armoured, possesses such a fire power and shock power that the rhythm of the battle corresponds to that of its movements." Going on from there, I fixed the aim to be attained: "Six divisions of the line and one light division, motorized throughout, armoured in part, will constitute the sort of army to bring about decisions."

The way in which this army ought to be composed was laid down clearly. Each of the divisions of the line was to include an armoured brigade of two regiments, one of heavy tanks, the other of medium tanks, and a battalion of light tanks; a brigade of infantry comprising two regiments plus a battalion of chasseurs, all with caterpillared transport; a brigade of artillery, supplied with all-angle guns and formed of two regiments serving respectively short- and long-range pieces, and completed by an anti-aircraft group. To second these three brigades, the division would also have a reconnaissance regiment, a battalion of engineers; a signals battalion; a camouflage battalion, and sundry services. The light division, designed for scouting purposes and to prevent surprise, would be equipped with faster machines. In addition, the army itself would have its own general reserves: tanks and very heavy guns, engineers, signals, camouflage. Finally, a strong force of reconnaissance aircraft, interceptors, and fighters would be integrated with this large corps—a group for each division, a regiment for the whole—without prejudice to the combined operations that would be carried out by the mechanized air army in conjunction with those of the mechanized ground army.

But in order that the army of shock troops might be in a position to get the best possible results out of the complex and costly matériel with which it would be equipped, in order that it might be able to act suddenly, in any theatre, without waiting to be supplemented or learning instead of doing, it would have to be composed of professionals. Total effectives: a hundred thousand men. These troops would therefore be made up of regulars. Serving for six years in the crack corps, they would be moulded in that time by technical skill, emulation, and *esprit de corps*. They would later supply cadres to the *contingents* and reserves.

After this came a description of how this strategic battering ram was to be used to break down a well-established resistance. Positions taken up without warning, in a single night, this being made possible by the motorization of all elements, by their ability to move in any sort of country, and by the use of active and passive camouflage. Attack launched by three thousand tanks, disposed in several echelons on an average front of fifty kilometres, followed and supported closely by the decentralized artillery, and rejoined at the successive objectives by the infantry, who would be transported together with their means of fire power and of ground organization, the whole being articulated in two or three *corps d'armée* and kept informed and sustained by the air force belonging to the divisions and to the army. Rate of advance of the whole system attaining normally about fifty kilometres in a day's fighting. After which, and if the enemy was still putting up a continuous resistance, a general regrouping, with a view either to enlarging the breach laterally, or to resuming the effort to advance, or to holding the ground gained.

But the wall once pierced, larger possibilities might suddenly lie open. The mechanized army would then deploy fanwise to exploit its gains. On this subject I wrote: "Often, after a success, we shall rush to gather its fruits and to thrust out into the zone of prizes. We shall see the exploitation of gains become a reality, where formerly it was only a dream. . . . Then will lie open the road to great victories, to those victories which, by their deep and rapidly extended effects, lead to a general collapse among the enemy, as the smashing of a pillar sometimes brings down a cathedral. . . . We shall see fast troops range far and wide in the enemy's rear, strike at his vital points, throw his dispositions into confusion. . . .

Thus will be restored that strategic extension of tactical results which once used to constitute the supreme end and, as it were, the nobility of the art. . . ." But the hostile people and state might, when their distress and the annihilation of their apparatus of defence reached a certain point, themselves collapse.

All the more so, and the more quickly, since "this aptitude for surprise and for the breakthrough harmonized perfectly with the properties, from now on vital, of air forces." I pictured the air army preparing and prolonging by its bombardments the operations carried out on the ground by the mechanized army and, vice versa, the latter conferring an immediate strategic utility upon the destructive actions of the air squadrons by erupting into the zones just ravaged.

So profound an evolution of the art made necessary a similar evolution of the command. After bringing out the fact that henceforward radio communications would provide the means of binding together the elements of the army of the future, I ended the work by showing what methods the Command must employ in order to handle the new instrument. It would no longer be the job of leaders to direct, by anonymous orders, from dug-in posts, a distant human matériel. On the contrary, to be there, see for oneself and set an example, would become once again essential in the midst of that shifting drama, filled with unforeseen hazards and split-second opportunities, which the warfare of mechanized forces would be. The personality of the leader would be much more important than codified recipes. "If," I asked, "evolution were destined thus to favour the rise of those who, in the tragic hours when the storm sweeps away conventions and habits, are the only ones to remain on their feet and to be, therefore, necessary, would not that be all to the good?"

In conclusion, I appealed to the state. The Army, no more than any other body, would in practice transform itself unaided. Since the specialized corps was bound to bring with it profound changes in military ways, as well as in the technique and politics of warfare, it was to the government that the burden of creating it fell.

To be sure, there would be need, once again, of a Louvois or a Carnot. At the same time such a reform could be only one part of a whole, one element in the effort towards a renovation of the country. "But in the fact that this national recasting must begin with the Army there would be nothing that would not be in harmony with the natural order of things. In that case, in the hard toil which is needed to rejuvenate France, her Army will serve her as stand-by and as ferment. For the sword is the axis of the world, and greatness is not divisible."

In working out this comprehensive project I had naturally made use of the lines of thought already set going, all over the world, by the appearance of the fighting internal-combustion engine. General Estienne, apostle and first Inspector of Tanks, envisaged, as early as 1917, bringing a good number of them into action at a great distance in advance of those escorting the infantry. That was why, at the end of 1918, enormous machines weighing sixty tons were beginning to come from the factories. But the armistice stopped their manufacture and confined the theory within the formula of the concerted action completing the escorting action. The British, who had shown themselves pioneers by engaging the Royal Tank Corps at Cambrai in 1917 in a massive action of deep penetration, continued to keep alive the idea of the autonomous operation by armoured detachments—an idea whose advocates were General Fuller and Captain Liddell Hart. In France, in 1933, the High Command brought together some scattered elements at Suippes camp and put to the test an embryo light division for preventing surprise and for scouting.

Others had even larger views. General von Seeckt, in his work *Thoughts of a Soldier*,[2] which appeared in 1929, depicted the possibilities which an army of quality (meaning the Reichswehr with a hundred thousand men on long-term service) had as opposed to masses without cohesion—he was thinking of those of the French. The Italian general Douhet, calculating the effects

---

[2] English version by Gilbert Waterhouse, with introduction by General Sir Ian Hamilton (London: Ernest Benn, 1930). (Translator's note.)

which bombardments from the air could produce on the centres of industry and life, estimated that an air army could win a decision unaided. Lastly, the "Maximum Plan," advocated at Geneva by M. Paul-Boncour in 1932, proposed placing under the League of Nations a professional force, which would have disposal of all the tanks and all the aircraft in Europe and would be charged with maintaining collective security. My plan aimed at building into a single whole, and for the benefit of France, these fragmentary but converging views.

My book aroused interest at first, but no deep feeling. As long as *Vers l'armée de métier* seemed to be merely a book that set going some ideas of which the hierarchy would make what use it chose, people were willing to see in it an original theory. It entered nobody's head that our military organization might be modified in consequence. If I had felt that there was no hurry, I would indeed have been content to advocate my thesis in specialist circles, sure that, with evolution on their side, my arguments would make their way. But Hitler was not the man to wait.

In October 1933 he broke with the League of Nations and automatically assumed his freedom of action in the matter of armaments. The years 1934 and 1935 saw the Reich deploy an immense effort in manufacture and in recruitment. The National-Socialist regime made no secret of its determination to smash the Treaty of Versailles by conquering its "Lebensraum." For this policy an offensive military machine was necessary. Hitler was, to be sure, preparing the *levée en masse*. Not long after gaining power he instituted labour service and, later, conscription. But in addition he needed a means of intervention in order to cut the Gordian knots at Mainz, Vienna, Prague, and Warsaw, and in order that the Germanic lance, when given a sharp point, might be capable of piercing at one stroke to the heart of France.

The well-informed, indeed, were not unaware that the Führer intended to stamp his mark upon the new German Army; that he listened gladly to the officers formerly grouped around General von Seeckt, such as Keitel, Rundstedt, and Guderian, who were partisans of manœuvre, speed, and quality, and therefore was attracted towards mechanized forces; and finally that, adopting the theories of Göring, he wanted an air force whose action could be directly linked with the battle on the ground. I was soon told that he himself had had my book read to him, since his advisers attached importance to it. In November 1934 it was learned that the Reich was creating the first three Panzer divisions. A book published at that time by Colonel Nehring of the General Staff of the Wehrmacht specified that their composition would be, practically speaking, identical with that which I was suggesting for our armoured divisions of the future. In March 1935 Göring announced that the Reich was providing itself with a powerful air force, and that this would include, besides many interceptors, numerous bombers and a strong force of divebombers. And indeed, although these measures were so many flagrant violations of the treaties, the free world was content to oppose to them a platonic protest from the League of Nations.

I could not bear to see the enemy of tomorrow endowing himself with the means of victory while France was still without them. And yet, in the incredible apathy in which the nation was plunged, no voice in authority was lifted to demand the required action. The stake was so great that it did not seem to me permissible to maintain my reserve, slight as were my importance and my fame. Responsibility for national defence belonged to the government. I resolved to carry the debate there.

I began by allying myself with André Pironneau, news editor of the *Echo de Paris,* and then editor of *l'Epoque.* He made it his task to make known the plan for a mechanized army and to keep the authorities on the move by the goad of a great newspaper. Tying his campaign up with the news, André Pironneau published forty main articles which made the subject familiar. Every time events turned the attention of the public towards national defence, my friendly helper demonstrated in his paper the need for creating the specialized corps. Since it was known that Germany was concentrating the essential part of her armaments effort towards the engines of attack and of follow-up, Pironneau uttered cries of alarm—but they were obstinately stifled by the general indiffer- ence. He proved, twenty times over, that the German armoured mass, supported by the air force, could quickly demolish our defences and produce among our population a panic from which it would not recover.

While André Pironneau was doing his good work, other journa- lists and critics were at least raising the question. Such were Rémy Roure and General Baratier in *Le Temps,* Pierre Bourget and Generals de Cugnac and Duval in the *Journal des Débats,* Emile Buré and Charles Giron in *L'Ordre,* André Lecomte in *L'Aube,* Colonel Emile Mayer, Lucien Nachin, and Jean Auburtin in va- rious reviews, and so on. Nevertheless the established order of things and ideas was too compact to be affected merely by articles in the press. The political rulers of the country had to be made aware of the problem.

M. Paul Reynaud seemed to be pre-eminently marked out for this undertaking. His intelligence was fully capable of absorbing the arguments; his talent, of putting them effectively; his courage, of fighting them through. In addition, though already an estab- lished figure, M. Paul Reynaud gave the impression of being a man who had his future in front of him. I saw him, convinced him, and from then on worked with him.

At the tribune of the Chambre des Députés, on March 15, 1935, he made an arresting speech, showing why and how our military organization must be completed by a mechanized army of quality. Not long afterwards, when the government asked Parliament to vote the two years' service, M. Paul Reynaud, while agreeing to this, submitted a bill for "the immediate creation of a specialized corps of six divisions of the line, one light division, and general reserves and services, formed of regulars, and to be brought com- pletely up to strength by April 15, 1940, at the latest." During the next three years M. Paul Reynaud affirmed his position in several speeches, which stirred the parliamentary dough pro- foundly, in a book called *Le problème militaire français,* in vigorous articles and interviews, and finally by conversations on the subject with important politicians and military men. He thus took on the appearance of an innovating and resolute statesman, marked out by nature for the exercise of power in case of serious difficulties.

As I thought it good that the melody should be played on various instruments, I applied myself to drawing other public men in. M. Le Cour Grandmaison, attracted by the aspects of a professional army—which answered to our traditions—nobly made himself its apostle. Three left-wing deputies—Philippe Serre, Marcel Déat, and Léo LaGrange, whose talent was of the right kind for throwing into relief the revolutionary aspect of the new proposal—agreed to join us. The first did so in fact, and with such brilliance that he gained recognition as a great orator and shortly afterwards entered the government. The second, the one on whose gifts I counted most, was seduced into an opposite course after his failure in the 1936 election. The third was prevented, by the party of which he was a member, from stating his conviction. But soon men as considerable as M. Paul-Boncour in the Chambre and President Millerand in the Senate gave me to understand that they too were in favour of the reform.

Meanwhile, however, the official bodies and their unofficial supporters, rather than recognize obvious necessities and accept the change subject to modification of its formula and application, clung to the system in force. Unfortunately they did so in so categorical a manner that they closed against themselves the way towards learning better. To fight the idea of the mechanized army they set to work to misrepresent it. To fly in the face of technical development they busied themselves denying it. To resist events they affected to be unaware of them. I verified, on this occasion, that the clash of ideas, as soon as it involves the established errors and the men in office, assumes the uncompromising mood of theological dispute.

General Debeney, a glorious army commander in the First World War, who in 1927, in his capacity as Chief of the General

Staff, had worked out the laws dealing with military organization, condemned the project formally. In the *Revue des Deux Mondes* he explained authoritatively that any European conflict would have its decisive phase on our northeast frontier, and that the problem consisted in holding this solidly. He therefore saw nothing to change either in the laws or in practice, and merely insisted that the system resulting from them should be reinforced. General Weygand intervened in his turn, likewise in the *Revue des Deux Mondes*. Admitting, a priori, that my idea would separate the army into two portions: "Two armies—not at any price!" he protested. As for the function I assigned to the specialized corps, he did not deny its interest but stated that it could be fulfilled by elements already formed. "We have," he explained, "a mechanized, motorized, and mounted reserve. There is nothing to create, everything exists." On July 4, 1939, speaking in public at Lille, General Weygand was to proclaim yet again that we lacked nothing.

Marshal Pétain thought it right to join in. He did so in a preface to General Chauvineau's book, *Une invasion est-elle encore possible?* The Marshal there claimed that tanks and aircraft did not modify the basic factors of warfare, and that the principal element of French security was the continuous front buttressed by fortification. *Le Figaro* published, under the signature of Jean Rivière, a series of inspired and reassuring articles: "Tanks Are Not Invincible," "The Weakness of the Tanks," "When the Politicians Go Wrong," and so on. In the *Mercure de France* a French general who hid his identity under a signature consisting of three stars rejected even the principle of motorization. "The Germans," he declared, "being naturally aggressive, must naturally have Panzer divisions. But France, being pacific and defensive, is bound to be anti-motorization."

Other critics had recourse to ridicule. The critic of one of the big literary reviews wrote: "One is hard put to it to assess, with the courtesy one would wish, ideas which touch the fringe of delirium. Let us simply say that Monsieur de Gaulle was anticipated, some years ago, by the Père Ubu, who was likewise a great tactician with modern ideas. 'When we are back from Poland,' he used to say, 'we will imagine, with the aid of our physical science, a wind machine for transporting the whole army.'"

If the conventionality of the conservative elements came out in fundamental hostility, that of the party of progress was no better disposed. In *Le Populaire,* during November and December 1934, Léon Blum expressed uncompromisingly the aversion and uneasiness inspired in him by the plan. In several articles—"Professional Soldiers and Professional Army," "Towards a Professional Army?" "Down with the Professional Army!"—he too took his stand against the specialized corps. He did so not on grounds of national defence, but in the name of an ideology which he styled democratic and republican and which was traditionally determined to see in everything military a menace to the regime. Léon Blum pronounced the anathema, therefore, against a body of professionals whose composition, spirit, and weapons would, if he was to be believed, automatically endanger the republic.

Thus buttressed to right and left, the official bodies set their faces against all change. M. Paul Reynaud's plan was rejected by the Army Committee of the Chambre. The report on this subject, presented by M. Senac and drawn up with the cooperation of the Army General Staff, concluded that the proposed reform "was useless, undesirable, and had logic and history against it." At the tribune of the Assemblée, General Maurin, Minister for War, said in answer to the orators who favoured the corps of manœuvre: "When we have devoted so many efforts to building up a fortified barrier, is it conceivable that we would be mad enough to go ahead of this barrier, into I know not what adventure?" He added: "What I have just told you is the government's view, and it, at least in my person, is perfectly familiar with the war plan." These words, which settled the fate of the specialized corps, at the same time let those in Europe who had ears to hear know in advance that, whatever happened, France would undertake nothing beyond manning the Maginot Line.

As could be foreseen, ministerial reprobation extended to me personally. Nonetheless this happened in episodic bursts, not by condemnation in due form. Thus it was that at the Elysée, at the end of a meeting of the Conseil Supérieur de la Défense Nationale, whose secretary I was, General Maurin addressed me sharply: "Good-bye, de Gaulle! Where I am there's no place for you!" In his office he would shout at visitors who mentioned me: "He has got himself a tame writer—Pironneau—and a gramophone—Paul Reynaud. I shall send him to Corsica!" While making the thunder rumble, however, General Maurin had the magnanimity not to launch the thunderbolt. Shortly afterwards M. Fabry, who replaced him at the Rue Saint-Dominique, and General Gamelin, who succeeded General Weygand as Chief of the General Staff while remaining head of the Army staff, adopted the negative policy of their predecessors towards the scheme and the same embarrassed and irritated attitude towards me.

At bottom the men in office, although they maintained the *status quo,* could not help being secretly sensitive to my arguments. They were, indeed, too well aware of what was going on to believe entirely in their own objections. When they declared exaggerated the ideas I was spreading about what a mechanized force could do, they were nevertheless uneasy about the one the Reich was forging for itself. When they pretended to supply the place of the seven shock divisions by as many large-scale ordinary units of the defensive type, and when they called these "motorized" because they would be transported in lorries, they knew, better than anyone, that that was only a play upon words. When they alleged that by adopting the specialized corps we would be cutting our army in two, they were affecting not to recognize that the two years' service, which had been voted since my book had come out, made it possible, if need be, to introduce into the *corps d'élite* a certain proportion of soldiers from the contingents; that there already existed a navy, an air force, a Colonial army, an Africa army, a police force, and a *garde mobile,* which were specialized without the cohesion of the whole having suffered damage; and, finally, that what makes the unity of the various national forces is not the identity of their equipment and of their recruitment, but the fact of serving the same country, under the same laws, and under the same flag.

It made me sad, therefore, to see those eminent men, in virtue of a sort of upside-down loyalty, constitute themselves not exactly guides but reassuring spokesmen. Nevertheless, beneath their apparent conviction, I could feel their wistfulness for the horizons now open to them. This was the first episode in a long series of events, in which a part of the French *élite,* condemning all the ends I would be led to pursue, and yet, deep down in itself, miserable at remaining ineffective, was to grant me, beyond its strictures, the melancholy homage of its remorse.

Destiny followed its course. Hitler, knowing now what to expect from us, opened his series of *coups de force.* Already, in 1935, over the Sarre plebiscite, he had created an atmosphere so menacing that the French government threw in its hand before playing it, and then the people of the Sarre, attracted and intimidated by the Germanic fury, voted in a body for the Third Reich. Mussolini, on his side, braving the Geneva sanctions—thanks to the Laval government's support and the Baldwin Cabinet's tolerance—moved on to the conquest of Ethiopia. Suddenly, on March 7, 1936, the German army crossed the Rhine.

The Versailles treaty forbade the troops of the Reich access to the territories on the left bank, which the Locarno agreement had, in addition, neutralized. In strict law, we could reoccupy them as soon as Germany repudiated her signature. If the specialized corps had existed even in part, with its fast machines and its personnel ready to march on the instant, the natural force of things would have at once directed it to the Rhine. As our allies, Poles, Czechs, and Belgians were ready to support us and since the British were committed in advance, Hilter would certainly have drawn back. He was, in fact, at the beginning of his rearmament effort and still in no condition to face a general conflict. But such a check, inflicted by France at this period, on this ground, could have disastrous consequences for him in his own country. By such a gamble he could have, at one go, lost everything.

He won everything. Our organization, the nature of our armaments, the very spirit of our national defence, tempted to inaction an administration which had all too much tendency that way and prevented us from marching. Because we were ready only to hold our frontier and had imposed on ourselves a self-denying ordinance against crossing it in any case, there was no riposte to be expected from France. The Führer was sure of this. The whole world took note of the fact. The Reich, instead of finding itself compelled to withdraw the troops it had adventured, established them without a blow in the whole of the Rhineland territory, in direct contact with France and Belgium. After that, M. Flandin, Minister for Foreign Affairs, could indeed travel to London with bleeding heart to inform himself of England's intention; M. Sarraut, the Premier, could indeed declare that the Paris government "would not admit that Strasbourg should be within range of German guns"; French diplomacy could indeed obtain a theoretical censure of Hitler from the League of Nations: these were only gestures and words in face of the accomplished fact.

To my way of thinking, the emotion aroused by the event could be salutary. The authorities had a chance to use it with a view to filling some deadly gaps. Although people in France were absorbed by the elections and by the social crisis which followed them, everyone was agreed on the need to reinforce the country's defences. If the effort were concentrated upon the creation of the instrument we lacked, what was essential might be saved. Nothing of the kind occurred. The considerable military credits which were opened in 1936 were used to complete the existing system, not to modify it.

I had some hope, all the same. In the great unrest which then agitated the nation and was canalized politically in an electoral and parliamentary coalition known as the Popular Front, there was, it seemed to me, the psychological factor which made it possible to break with passivity. It was not inconceivable that, in the presence of National Socialism triumphing at Berlin, fascism reigning at Rome, and falangism advancing on Madrid, the French Republic might be willing simultaneously to transform its social structure and to reform its military power. In October, Léon Blum, the Premier, invited me to come and see him. It happened that our meeting took place on the very afternoon of the day that the King of the Belgians publicly put an end to the alliance with France and with Great Britain. The King alleged that, if his country were attacked by Germany, this alliance would not protect it. "In practice," he proclaimed, "given what modern mechanized forces are capable of doing, we would in any case be alone."

Léon Blum assured me warmly of the interest he took in my ideas. "And yet," I said to him, "you have opposed them." "One gets a different perspective," he replied, "when one becomes head of the government." We talked first of what would happen if, as was to be foreseen, Hitler marched on Vienna, Prague, and Warsaw. "It's very simple," I pointed out. "According to circumstances, we shall have a limited call-up or a full mobilization. Then, peering between the battlements of our fortifications, we shall watch the enslavement of Europe."

"What's that?" cried Léon Blum. "Would you have us send an expeditionary force to Austria, to Bohemia, to Poland?" "No!" I said. "But if the Wehrmacht advances along the Danube or the Elbe, why shouldn't we go to the Rhine? While it is debouching on the Vistula, why shouldn't we enter the Ruhr? Besides, the mere fact of our being capable of these ripostes would no doubt prevent the acts of aggression. But our present system forbids us to stir. The armoured corps, on the contrary, would induce us to do so. Isn't it true that a government may find a certain relief in feeling that its direction is set in advance?"

The Premier agreed to that with good grace but declared: "It would be deplorable, certainly, if our friends in Central and Eastern Europe were temporarily submerged. All the same, in the last resort, nothing would have been achieved for Hitler as long as he had not crushed us. How would he manage that? You will agree that our system, ill adapted though it is to attack, is excellent for defence."

I showed that it was by no means so. Reminding him of the declaration made public that morning by Leopold III, I pointed out that it was the inferiority in which the absence of a *corps d'élite* placed us in relation to the Germans that was costing us the Belgian alliance. The head of the government did not dispute this, although he thought the attitude of Brussels had other than merely strategic motives. "In any case," he said, "our defensive front and our fortifications would protect our territory." "Nothing is less certain," I answered. "Already in 1918 there was no longer such a thing as an impregnable front. Well, look at the progress made since then by tanks and aircraft! Tomorrow the concentrated action of a sufficient number of machines will be capable of smashing, in a chosen sector, any defensive barrier whatever. Once the breach is open, the Germans will have a chance of thrusting far behind our lines a fast-moving armoured mass supported by their Air Force. If we have the same, all can be repaired. If not, all will be lost."

The Premier told me that the government, with the support of Parliament, had decided on a great programme of expenditure on national defence over and above the ordinary budget, and that a considerable part of the credits was to be devoted to tanks and the Air Force. I drew his attention to the fact that almost all the aircraft whose construction was envisaged were to be designed for interception, not for attack. As for the tanks, nine-tenths of them would be Renaults and Hotchkisses of the 1935 type, modern of their kind but heavy, slow, armed with short-range guns, made for cooperation in the infantry battle, but not at all for forming an autonomous whole with large-scale units. Besides, we had no such idea. Our organization would therefore remain what it was. "We are going," I remarked, "to build as many machines and spend as much money as would be needed for a mechanized army, and we shall not have that army." "The way in which the credits allotted to the War Department are used," observed the Premier, "is the affair of M. Daladier and of General Gamelin." "No doubt," I answered. "Allow me, though, to think that national defence is the government's responsibility."

During our conversation the telephone had rung ten times, deflecting Léon Blum's attention to petty parliamentary or administrative questions. As I took my leave and he was again called, he made a great, tired gesture. "Judge," he said, "if it is easy for the head of the government to hold to the plan you have outlined when he cannot remain five minutes with the same idea!"

I soon learned that the Premier, though struck by our interview, was not going to pull down the columns of the temple and that the old plan was to be applied as it was. From that moment our chance of counterbalancing the Reich's new strength before it was too late seemed to me heavily compromised. I was convinced, in fact, that Hitler's character, his doctrine, his age, and even the impulse he had given to the German people, made it impossible for him to wait. Things would now move too fast for France to be able to make up for the time she had lost—even if her rulers had been willing.

On May 1, 1937, a complete Panzer division, with hundreds of aircraft flying over it, marched through Berlin. The impression produced on the spectators, and first and foremost on M. François-Poncet, the French ambassador, and on our military attachés, was of a force that nothing could stop—except a similar force. But their reports produced no modification in the arrangements made by the Paris government. On March 11, 1938, Hitler carried out the Anschluss. He launched against Vienna a mechanized division, the mere sight of which rallied the general consent, and with it, that very evening, he entered the Austrian capital in triumph. In France, far from learning the lesson of this rough demonstration, efforts were made to reassure the public by an ironic description of the breakdown of a few German tanks in the course of this forced march. There was no greater willingness to be enlightened by the lessons of the Spanish Civil War, in which the Italian tanks and German divebombers, few as they were, played the principal part in every battle in which they appeared.

In September the Führer, with the complicity of London and then of Paris, executed Czechoslovakia. Three days before Munich the Chancellor of the Reich, speaking at the Sportspalast in Berlin, had dotted the *i*'s, in the midst of joyous laughter and hurrahs of enthusiasm. "Now," he shouted, "I can admit publicly what you all know. We have acquired an armed force such as the world has never seen." On March 15, 1939, he extracted from President Hacha a formal abdication and entered Prague the same day. After which, on September 1, he hurled himself upon Poland. In these successive acts of one and the same tragedy, France played the part of the victim that awaits its turn.

As for me, I watched these events without surprise but not without pain. After having, in 1937, taken part in the work of the Centre des Hautes Etudes Militaires, I had been given command of the 507th Tank Regiment at Metz. My duties as colonel and the distance from Paris deprived me of the opportunities and contacts required for carrying on my great controversy. And in the spring of 1938, M. Paul Reynaud joined the Daladier Cabinet, first as Minister of Justice, then of Finance. Apart from the fact that he was now bound by ministerial solidarity, the re-establishing of our economic and monetary equilibrium was a task so pressing that it completely occupied all his time. Above all, the obstinacy of the authorities in cultivating a static military system while Germany's dynamic force was deploying over Europe, the blindness of a regime which went on with its absurd games in face of a Reich that was ready to spring upon us, and the stupidity of the boobies who acclaimed the Munich surrender, were really only the effects of a profound national renunciation. Against that I could do nothing. Nevertheless in 1938, feeling the tempest rising, I published *La France et son armée.* In it I showed how, from century to century, the soul and the fate of the country were constantly reflected in the mirror of its Army: the final warning which, from my modest place, I addressed to my country on the eve of the cataclysm.

When, in September 1939, the French government followed the
British Cabinet's example and consented to join in the conflict already begun in Poland, I had not the least doubt that it did so
with the illusion that, in spite of the state of war, we would not
fight all-out. It was therefore without astonishment that, as commander of the tanks of the Vth Army, in Alsace, I saw our mobilized forces settle down into stagnation, while Poland was struck
down in two weeks by the Panzer divisions and the air squadrons.
It is true that the Soviet intervention hastened the crushing of the
Poles. But in Stalin's decision to make common cause with Hitler
one could discern his conviction that the French would remain
stationary, that the Reich therefore had its hands free, and that it
was better to share its prey than to be its prey. While the enemy
forces were almost all being used on the Vistula, we did nothing
really, apart from a few token actions, by way of placing ourselves on the Rhine. We did nothing, either, to check Italy by giving her the choice between a French invasion and the pledges for
her neutrality. We did nothing, lastly, to realize immediately the
junction with Belgium by gaining Liége and the Albert Canal.

Once more the dominant school tried to view this wait-and-see
policy as a fruitful strategy. Over the radio the members of the government—first among them the Premier—and in the press many
notable people, did their best to vaunt the advantages of immobility, thanks to which, so they said, we were maintaining the integrity
of our territory without losses. M. Brisson, editor of *Figaro,* when
he asked me my opinion during a visit he paid me at Wangenbourg
and heard me deploring the passivity of our forces, exclaimed:
"Don't you see that we have already *gagné la Marne blanche*
[won a platonic Battle of the Marne]?" When I visited Paris in
January and dined at M. Paul Reynaud's flat in the Rue Rivoli, I
met Léon Blum. "What's your prophecy?" he said to me. "The
problem," I answered, "is whether in the spring the Germans will
attack westwards to take Paris or eastwards to reach Moscow."
"Do you think so?" said Léon Blum, astonished. "The Germans
attack to the east? But why should they go and lose themselves

in the depths of Russian territory? Attack to the west? But what could they do against the Maginot Line?" When President Lebrun visited the Vth Army, I presented my tanks for his inspection. "I am familiar with your ideas," he told me amiably. "But it does seem too late for the enemy to apply them."

It was too late for us. And yet, on January 26, I made a last attempt. I addressed to the eighty chief persons in the government, the High Command, and politics a memorandum whose aim was to convince them that the enemy would take the offensive with a very powerful mechanized force, on the ground and in the air; that our front might therefore be broken through at any moment; that if we had not ourselves equivalent units of riposte, we were in great danger of being annihilated; that the creation of the required instrument ought to be decided on at once; that, besides pushing the necessary manufacture, it was urgent to gather into one mechanized reserve those units, already existing or in course of formation, which could, if need be, form part of it.

I concluded: "The French people should not, at any price, fall into the illusion that the present military immobility might be in harmony with the nature of the present war. The opposite is the truth. The internal-combustion engine endows modern means of destruction with such force, speed, and range that the present conflict will be marked, sooner or later, by movements, surprises, breakthroughs and pursuits the scale and rapidity of which will infinitely exceed those of the most lightning events of the past. . . . Let us make no mistake about it! The conflict which has begun might well be the most extended, the most complex, the most violent of all those that have ravaged the earth. The political, economic, social, and moral crisis from which it has issued is so profound and so ubiquitous that it is bound to end in a complete upheaval of both the condition of the peoples and the structure of states. And the obscure harmony of things is providing this revolution with the military instrument—the army of machines— exactly proportioned to its colossal dimensions. It is high time for France to draw the conclusion."

My memorandum produced no shock. However, the ideas expressed and the proofs exhibited were at last having some effect. At the end of 1939 there were two light mechanized divisions in existence and a third was being formed. These were, however, only scouting units, which would have been very useful for guiding the manœuvres of an armoured mass, but would be capable of very little as long as there was no such mass. On December 2, 1938, the Conseil Supérieur de la Guerre, at the insistence of General Billotte, had decided on the creation of two armoured divisions. One of them was formed by the beginning of 1940. The other was due to be formed in March. These divisions would be armed with some thirty-ton Type B tanks, of which the first examples had been in existence for fifteen years, and three hundred were being—at last!—made. But each of them, whatever the quality of its machines, would be a very long way from having the power I had proposed. It would comprise 120 tanks: I would have liked 500. It would have made use of only one battalion of infantry transported in lorries: to my mind, seven were required, in caterpillar vehicles. It would possess two artillery groups: seven groups supplied with all-angles pieces were what I judged necessary. It would have no reconnaissance group: to my mind, it needed one. Lastly I could only conceive of mechanical units being employed in the form of an autonomous mass, organized and commanded in the way appropriate to this. All that was envisaged, on the contrary, was to attach the armoured divisions to various *corps d'armée* of the old type—in other words, to fuse them into the general arrangement.

The same faint stirrings of change which, in place of purpose, were appearing on the military plane were beginning to show in the political field. The sort of euphoria which the "phony war" had at first maintained among the men in office was beginning to fade. By mobilizing millions of men, devoting industry to the manufacture of arms, and undertaking enormous expenditure, the nation was being subjected to upheavals whose effects were already becoming apparent to the alarmed politicians. Besides, there was nothing to indicate that progressive weakening of the enemy which was expected from the blockade. Without any other war policy— for which there were not the means—being suggested out loud, everyone nonetheless turned his uneasiness and bitterness against the one which was being carried out. As usual, the regime, being incapable of adopting the measures that would have saved the situation, but seeking to throw dust in its own eyes and in those of public opinion, started a ministerial crisis. On March 21 the Chambre overthrew the Daladier Cabinet. On the 23rd, M. Paul Reynaud formed the government.

Summoned to Paris by the new Premier, I drew up at his request a short, clear statement which he accepted without change for reading out to Parliament. Then, with intrigues already rustling in the corridors, I went to the Palais-Bourbon to witness from one of the galleries the scene of its presentation.

This was appalling. After the government's statement of policy had been read out by its head to a sceptical and apathetic House, hardly anyone was to be heard in the debate but the spokesmen of those groups or men who considered themselves injured by the new coalition. The danger in which the country stood, the necessity of a national effort, the cooperation of the free world, were mentioned only to adorn claims and complaints. Léon Blum alone, although he had no place offered him, spoke with greatness. Thanks to him, M. Paul Reynaud won through, though by an extremely narrow margin. The government received a vote of confidence by a majority of one. "And indeed," M. Herriot, the President of the Chambre, was to tell me later, "I'm not very sure that it had that."

Before rejoining my post at Wangenbourg, I remained for a few days with the Premier, who now had his quarters at the Quai d'Orsay. That was enough to show me how far the demoralization of the regime had gone. In all the parties, in the press, in the administration, in business, in the trade unions, there were influential groups openly favouring the idea of stopping the war. The well-informed said that this was the opinion of Marshal Pétain, our ambassador at Madrid, and he was supposed to know, through the Spaniards, that the Germans would gladly lend themselves to an arrangement. "If Reynaud falls," it was everywhere being said, "Laval will take power with Pétain at his side. The Marshal is, in fact, in a position to make the High Command accept an armistice." A leaflet was circulating in thousands of copies: it bore on its three pages pictures of the Marshal, first as victorious leader in the First World War with the legend: "Yesterday, a great soldier!"; then as ambassador: "Today, a great diplomat!"; and then as a huge, indistinct figure: "Tomorrow?"

It must be said that some circles were more inclined to see Stalin as the enemy than Hitler. They were much more concerned with the means of striking at Russia, whether by aiding Finland, or by bombarding Baku, or by landing at Istanbul, than with how to cope with the Reich. Many quite openly professed their admiration for Mussolini. Some, even in the government, were working to get France to buy the good graces of the Duce by ceding to him Jibuti, the Chad, a share in a condominium over the Tunisian Regency. The Communists, on their side, having noisily rallied to the national cause as long as Berlin was opposed to Moscow, started cursing the "capitalist" war as soon as Molotov and Ribbentrop had reached agreement. As for the mass of the people, it was bewildered and, feeling that nothing and nobody at the head of the state was capable of dominating events, wavered in doubt and uncertainty. Clearly a serious reverse would cause in the country a wave of astonishment and alarm which might very well sweep everything away.

In this pernicious atmosphere M. Paul Reynaud endeavoured to establish his authority. This was all the more difficult because he was in perpetual conflict with M. Daladier, whose successor he was as Premier, but who remained in the government as Minister of National Defence and War Minister. This strange situation could not be modified, for the Radical party, without whose forbearance the government would have fallen, insisted that its leader should remain in it, while waiting to regain the leadership

at the first opportunity. At the same time M. Paul Reynaud, in his
anxiety to enlarge his tiny majority, was trying to melt the prejudices of the moderates against him. A delicate operation this, for
a large fraction of the Right desired peace with Hitler and an
entente with Mussolini. The Premier thus found himself obliged
to summon to his side as Undersecretary of State M. Paul Baudouin, who was very active in these circles, and to appoint him
secretary of the War Committee which he had just set up.

In reality M. Paul Reynaud had thought of entrusting this work
to me. The War Committee, which handled the conduct of the
war and brought together, for this purpose, the principal Ministers
as well as the Army, Navy, and Air commanders-in-chief, might
play a decisive part. Its secretary's job was to prepare its discussions, be present at its meetings, communicate its decisions, and
see that they were carried out. Many things might depend on the
way this was done. But while M. Paul Reynaud seemed to wish
that it should be done by me, M. Daladier would not agree. To
the Premier's messenger who came to the Rue Saint-Dominique
to make this wish known to him, he replied straight off: "If de
Gaulle comes here, I shall leave this office, go downstairs, and
telephone M. Paul Reynaud to put him in my place."

M. Daladier was in no way hostile to me personally. He had
proved it, some time back, by himself, as Minister, taking the initiative of inscribing me on the list for promotion, when the clerks'
cabal was trying to keep me off it. But M. Daladier, who had
borne the responsibility for national defence for several years, had
wedded himself to the system in force. Feeling that events were
going to speak, sooner or later, assuming in advance the consequences of their judgment, and reckoning that, in any case, it was
too late to change the organization, he was more than ever determined on the positions he had taken up. But for me to act as
secretary to the War Committee in spite of the opposition of the
Minister of National Defence was manifestly impossible. I left
again for the front.

Before this, I had been to see General Gamelin, who invited

me to his headquarters in the Château de Vincennes. There he was, in a setting which suggested a convent, attended by a few officers, working and meditating without mixing in day-to-day duties. He left General Georges to command the northeastern front—an arrangement which might work as long as nothing was happening, but would certainly become untenable if battle were joined. As for General Georges, he was installed at La Ferté-sous-Jouarre with part of the staff, while other officers were functioning at Montry, under the direction of General Doumenc as chief of staff. In fact the organism of the supreme command was cut up into three sections. In his ivory tower at Vincennes, General Gamelin gave me the impression of a savant testing in a laboratory the chemical reactions of his strategy.

He told me, first of all, that he meant to raise the number of armoured divisions from two to four, and informed me of his decision to give me command of the 4th, which would be formed as from May 15. Whatever my general feelings about our perhaps irremediable lateness in respect to mechanized forces, I felt very proud at finding myself called upon, as a colonel, to command a division. I said so to General Gamelin. He replied simply, "I understand your satisfaction. As for your misgivings, I don't believe they are justified."

The generalissimo then spoke to me of the situation as he saw it. Unfolding a map which showed the enemy's positions and our own, he told me he expected a German attack in the near future. It would be directed, according to what he foresaw, mainly against Holland and Belgium, and its aim would be the Pas-de-Calais, with a view to cutting us off from the British. Various signs led him to think that the enemy would first carry out a covering operation or diversion towards the Scandinavian countries. He himself seemed not only confident of his own arrangements and of the value of his forces, but satisfied and even impatient to see them put to the test. Listening to him, I was convinced that, by dint of carrying about with him a certain military system and applying his labour to it, he had made of it a faith. I felt too that referring himself to the example of Joffre, whom he had assisted at close quarters and to some extent inspired in the early days of the First World War, he had persuaded himself that, at his level, the essential thing was to fix one's purpose, once for all, upon a well-defined plan and then not to let oneself be deflected from it by any avatar. This man, in whom intelligence, fineness of perception, and self-control attained a very high degree, had certainly no doubt that in the coming battle he was bound in the end to win.

It was with respect, but also a certain uneasiness, that I took leave of this great leader, as he made ready in his cloister to assume all of a sudden an immense responsibility, staking everything for everything on a move I judged to be wrong.

Five weeks later the storm broke. On May 10 the enemy, having first laid hands on Denmark and almost the whole of Norway, began his great offensive. This was destined to be carried out, from one end to the other, by mechanized forces and air power, mass following movement without there ever being any need to engage it fully. In two groups—the Hoth group and the Kleist group—ten armoured and six motorized divisions rushed westwards. Seven of the ten Panzers crossed the Ardennes and reached the Meuse in three days. On May 14 they had got across it at Dinant, Givet, Monthermé, and Sedan, while four big motorized units supported and covered them. Divebombers cooperated with them ceaselessly, and the German bombers, striking at railways and road junctions behind our lines, paralysed our transport. On May 18 these seven Panzers were regrouped around Saint-Quentin, ready to swoop either on Paris or on Dunkerque, having crossed the Maginot Line, smashed our positions, and annihilated one of our armies. During this time the other three, accompanied by two motorized divisions and operating in the Low Countries and Brabant, where the Allies had the Dutch army, the Belgian army, the British army, and two French armies, threw this total of 800,000 fighting men into a confusion which was to prove irreparable. It can be said that in a week our fate was sealed. Down the fatal slope to which a fatal error had long committed us, the

Army, the state, France, were now spinning at a giddy speed.

There were, however, 3000 up-to-date French tanks and 800 motorized machine-guns. The Germans had no more. But ours were, according to plan, distributed up and down the sectors of the front. Also, they were not, for the most part, built or armed to form part of a mass for manœuvre. Even the few large mechanized units included in the order of battle were engaged piecemeal. The three light divisions, which had been thrown towards Liége and towards Breda for scouting purposes, were quickly forced back and were then spread out to hold a front. The 1st Armoured Division, restored to a *corps d'armée* and launched alone in a counterattack on May 16 to the west of Namur, was enveloped and destroyed. On the same day the 2nd, having been transported by rail in the direction of Hirson, had its elements, as they were disentrained, swallowed up one by one in the general confusion. On the day before, to the south of Sedan, the 3rd Division, which had just been formed, was immediately split up between the battalions of an infantry division and was engulfed, fragment after fragment, in an abortive counterattack. Had they been grouped together beforehand, these mechanized units, for all their deficiencies, would have been able to deal the invader some formidable blows. But, isolated one from another, they were nothing but shreds six days after the German armoured groups had begun to move. As for me, as I discerned the truth through the scraps of news, there was nothing I would not have given to have been wrong.

But battle, even if disastrous, takes a soldier out of himself. This one seized hold of me in my turn. On May 11 I received the order to take command of the 4th Armoured Division—which indeed did not exist, but whose elements, coming from far distant points, were to be placed at my disposal gradually. From Vésinet, where my post was fixed to begin with, I was summoned on May 15 to GHQ to be given my instructions.

These were communicated to me by the chief of staff. They were wide. "The High Command," General Doumenc told me, "wishes to establish a defensive front on the Aisne and Ailette to bar the way to Paris. The VIth Army, commanded by General Touchon and formed of units mustered in the east of France, will deploy there. With your division, operating alone in advance in the region of Laon, you are to gain the time necessary for this taking-up of positions. General Georges, commander-in-chief on the northeast front, leaves it to you to decide on the means to be used. You will indeed depend solely and directly on him. Commandant Chomel will ensure liaison."

General Georges, when he received me, was calm, cordial, but visibly overwhelmed. He confirmed what he expected of me and added: "There, de Gaulle! For you who have so long held the ideas which the enemy is putting into practice, here is the chance to act." The administrative services then did their best to get the elements earmarked for me up towards Laon as soon as possible. I observed that the staff, though submerged by the innumerable problems of movement and transport that were raised everywhere by the surprise and disorder suffered during these terrible days, was doing its job as well as possible. But one could feel that hope was departing and that the spring was broken.

I hastened to Laon, set up my headquarters at Bruyères to the southeast of the town, and made a tour of the surroundings. By way of French troops in the district there were only a few scattered elements belonging to the 3rd Cavalry Division, a handful of men holding the citadel of Laon, and the 4th independent Artillery Group, which had instructions to resort to chemical warfare in certain contingencies and had been forgotten there by chance. I annexed this group, formed as it was of fine men armed only with carbines, and disposed them, against surprise, along the Sissonne Canal. Already, that very evening, the enemy patrols made contact.

On the 16th I was joined by the embryo of my staff. I carried out reconnaissance and collected information. The impression I gained was that large German forces which had debouched from the Ardennes through Rocroi and through Mézières were march-

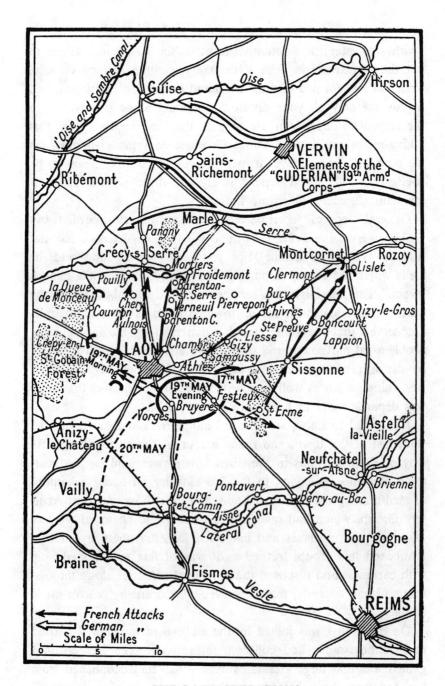

THE LAON OPERATIONS

ing, not southwards, but westwards, to reach Saint-Quentin, covering their left with flank guards extending to the south of the Serre. Miserable processions of refugees crowded along all the roads from the north. I saw, also, a good many soldiers who had lost their weapons. They belonged to the troops routed by the Panzers during the preceding days. Caught up, as they fled, by the enemy's mechanized detachments, they had been ordered to throw away their arms and make off to the south so as not to clutter up the roads. "We haven't time," they had been told, "to take you prisoners!"

Then, at the sight of those bewildered people and of those soldiers in rout, at the tale, too, of that contemptuous piece of insolence of the enemy's, I felt myself borne up by a limitless fury. Ah! It's too stupid! The war is beginning as badly as it could. Therefore it must go on. For that, the world is wide. If I live, I will fight, wherever I must, as long as I must, until the enemy is defeated and the national stain washed clean. All I have managed to do since was resolved upon that day.

To begin with, I would attack next morning with whatever forces might have reached me. Advancing some twenty kilometres northeastwards, I would try to reach Montcornet on the Serre, the junction of the roads to Saint-Quentin, Laon, and Reims. I would thus cut the first of these, so that the enemy could not use it in his march westwards, and I would bar the other two, which otherwise would lead him straight to the VIth Army's thinly held front. By dawn on May 17 I had received three battalions of tanks: one of Type B (the 46th Battalion), strengthened by a company of D2s and belonging to the 6th Half-Brigade; the other two of Renault 35s (the 2nd and 24th Battalions), forming the 8th Half-Brigade. I threw them forward as soon as daylight appeared. Sweeping away on their path the enemy units which were already invading that piece of country, they reached Montcornet. Till evening they fought on the outskirts of the place and within it, reducing many nests of snipers and shelling the German convoys that tried to pass. But on the Serre the enemy was in force. Obviously our tanks, with nothing to support them, could not cross it.

In the course of the day there arrived the 4th Battalion of Chasseurs. It was hardly there when I used it to reduce an enemy advance guard near Chivres, which had let our tanks go by and revealed itself later. This was soon done. But from north of the Serre the German artillery was firing on us. Our own was far from being in position. All afternoon the Stukas, swooping out of the sky and returning ceaselessly, attacked our tanks and lorries. We had nothing with which to reply. Finally German mechanized detachments, more and more numerous and active, began skirmishing in our rear. We were lost children thirty kilometres in advance of the Aisne; we had to put an end to the situation that was, to say the least, risky.

When night came I placed in contact with the enemy the reconnaissance regiment, the 10th Cuirassiers, which had just reached me, and I brought the tanks and chasseurs back towards Chivres. There were several hundred German dead and plenty of burned-out lorries on the field. We had taken 130 prisoners. We had lost less than two hundred men. In the rear, on the roads, the refugees had ceased to flee. Some were even on their way back. For the rumour was rife, in their sad columns, that the French troops had advanced.

And now it was no longer to the northeast but to the north of Laon that we must act; for important enemy forces, coming from Marle and going westwards, were moving on La Fère, hugging the course of the Serre. At the same time the German flank guards were beginning to spread out to the south and threatening to reach the Ailette. The 4th Armoured Division used the night of May 18-19 to get into position on the northern outlets of Laon. Meanwhile I had received reinforcements: the 3rd Cuirassiers, or two squadrons of Somua tanks, and the 322nd Artillery Regiment with its two groups of 75s. In addition, General Petiet, commanding the 3rd Light Cavalry Division, had promised me the support of his guns from positions close to Laon.

It was true that of the tanks—about 150—I now had at my

disposal, only 30 were of Type B and armed with 75s, 40 or so were D2s or Somuas with little 47 mm. guns, and the rest were Renault 35s, having only short-range guns of 37 mm., effective at six hundred metres at the very most. It is true that each of the Somua crews consisted of a tank leader who had never fired the gun and a driver who had done only four hours' driving. It is true that the division included only a single battalion of infantry, and this transported in buses and therefore extremely vulnerable when on the move. It is true that the artillery had only just been formed out of detachments furnished by many different depots and that many officers were literally meeting their men for the first time on the field of battle. It is true that we had no radio network and that I could command only by dispatching motorcyclists to the subordinate echelons and—above all—by going to see them. It is true that all the units were badly short of the transport, replacements, and victuals they should normally have included. And yet, already, an impression of general enthusiasm was emerging from this improvised body. Come! The springs are not dried up.

On the 19th, at dawn, forward! The tanks of the division, through a succession of objectives, were launched against Crécy, Mortiers, and Pouilly. They were to reach the bridges there and cut the enemy's path to La Fère. The artillery accompanied them. To the right, the reconnaissance regiment and the battalion of chasseurs gave them cover along the Baranton River, and a probe was made towards Marle. The morning went well. We reached the Serre after putting to flight various enemy elements that had been infiltrating into the region. But north of the river the enemy was in position. He held the crossings in force and destroyed those of our tanks that tried to tackle them. His heavy artillery got to work. In fact we were in contact with the large German units crowding towards Saint-Quentin. To be able to cross the watercourse and push our tanks farther forward we needed infantry, which we had not got, and more powerful artillery. During those difficult hours I could not help imagining what the mechanized army of which I had so long dreamed could have done. If it had been there that day, to debouch suddenly in the direction of Guise, the advance of the Panzer divisions would have been halted instantly, serious confusion caused in their rear, and the northern group of armies enabled to join up once more with those of the centre and the east.

But there were only very poor resources to the north of Laon. So it was the Germans who crossed the Serre. They had been doing so since the day before, at Montcornet, where we no longer were. From noon onwards they were crossing also at Marle. With armoured cars in plenty, motor-driven canon, motor-borne mortars, motorized infantry, they attacked our right along the river Baranton and our rear at Chambry. And now came the Stukas! Till nightfall they were to bombard us, with formidable effect on our vehicles unable to leave the roads and our artillery out in the open. Early in the afternoon General Georges sent me the order not to go on. The deployment of the VIth Army had been completed and my division must be used immediately for other tasks. I decided to delay the enemy for yet another day, by regrouping the division for the night around Vorges, ready to attack his flank if he tried to push on from Laon against Reims or Soissons, and not retreating across the Aisne till the day after.

The movement was carried out in good order, although the enemy tried to hold us up everywhere. At the exits from the cantonments skirmishing went on all night. On May 20 the 4th Armoured Division made for Fismes and for Braine, literally in the midst of the Germans, who swarmed wherever they went, held many strong points, and attacked our columns with plentiful armoured cars. Owing to the tanks, which cleaned up the roads and their approaches as we went along, we reached the Aisne without serious mishap. Even so, at Festieux the 10th Cuirassiers, the reconnaissance regiment which formed the rearguard with a battalion of tanks, disengaged only with difficulty; and on the plateau of Craonne the division's transport was roughly handled and forced to leave behind some lorries on fire.

While the 4th Division was operating in the Laon district, events farther north were following their course at the rapid rate of the Panzer divisions' march. The German Command, having decided to liquidate the Allied armies in the north before finishing with those of the centre and the east, was pushing its mechanized forces towards Dunkerque. These took the offensive again, starting from Saint-Quentin, in two columns: one going straight for the objective via Cambrai and Douai, the other slipping up the coast via Etaples and Boulogne. Meanwhile two Panzer divisions seized Amiens and Abbeville and established there, south of the Somme, bridgeheads which were to prove useful later on. On the Allied side, by the evening of May 20, the Dutch army had disappeared, the Belgian army was retreating westwards, and the British army and Ist French Army saw themselves cut off from France.

Certainly the French Command showed the intention of restoring contact between the two fragments of its forces by attacking with the northern group of armies from Arras towards Amiens, and with the left of the centre group of armies from Amiens towards Arras. Those were General Gamelin's orders on the 19th. General Weygand, who replaced him on May 20 and was to visit Belgium next day, took over the idea. Theoretically the plan was logical. But for it to be carried out, it would have been necessary for the High Command still to have hope and the will to win. The crumbling of the whole system of doctrines and organization, to which our leaders had attached themselves, deprived them of their motive force. A sort of moral inhibition made them suddenly doubtful of everything, and especially of themselves. From then on the centrifugal forces were to show themselves rapidly. The King of the Belgians was not slow to contemplate surrender; Lord Gort, re-embarkation; General Weygand, the armistice.

While the Command was dissolving in disaster, the 4th Armoured Division was marching westwards. First there was question of making it cross the Somme to take the lead in the projected attack northwards. But the idea was given up. Then it was pro-

posed to use it, with other forces, to drive back the Germans
who had crossed the Somme at Amiens. But the idea of giving it
a share in this attempt was abandoned, although one of its tank
battalions was taken from it for the purpose. Finally, during the
night of May 26-27, the division's commander—promoted general
two days earlier—received from General Robert Altmayer, in
command of the Xth Army now grouping together the forces that
were being hastily brought up to the lower Somme, the order to
make for Abbeville without delay and attack the enemy, who had
set up a solidly held bridgehead to the south of the city.

At that moment the division was resting round about Grand-
villiers. Starting on May 22, and passing through Fismes, Soissons, Villers-Cotterets, Compiègne, Montdidier, and Beauvais, it
had covered a hundred and eighty kilometres in five days. It is
fair to say that, from its birth in the fields of Montcornet, it had
never stopped fighting or marching. The condition of the tanks
showed it. Thirty or so were left behind on the way. On the other
hand, valuable supplements had reached us as we went: a battalion of Type B tanks (the 47th Battalion); a battalion of D2s
(the 19th Battalion), equipped with twenty-ton machines, which
I was unfortunately forced to part with before Amiens; the 7th
Regiment of motorized dragoons; an artillery group with 105s; an
anti-aircraft battery; and five batteries of 47 mm. anti-tank guns.
Except the battalion of D2s, all these were improvised units. But
as soon as they arrived they were caught up in the atmosphere
of keenness which hung over the division. Finally, for the operation which had just been allotted to me, the 22nd Colonial Infantry Regiment and the artillery of the 2nd Cavalry Division were
placed at my disposal. In all, a hundred and forty tanks in working order and six infantry battalions, supported by six artillery
groups, were to assault the southern front of the bridgehead.

I decided to attack that very evening. For the enemy aircraft
were watching the division all the time, and the only chance of
obtaining some effect of surprise was to advance zero hour. The
Germans were, in fact, ready for us. For a week they had held,

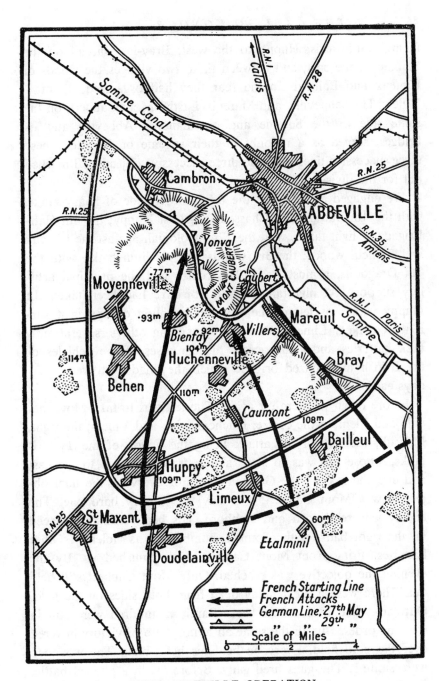

R.N.1 Calais

R.N.28

Somme Canal

Cambron

ABBEVILLE

R.N.25

R.N.25

R.N.35
Amiens →

Yonval

Moyenneville

·77m

MONT CAUBERT

Caubert

Mareuil

Somme

·93m

·92m

Bienfay

Villers

R.N.1 Paris

·104m

Huchenneville

Bray

·114m

Behen

110m

Caumont

108m

Bailleul

Huppy

109m

Limeux

60m

R.N.25

St Maxent

Doudelainville

Etalminil

French Starting Line
French Attacks
German Line, 27th May
     "   "   29th
Scale of Miles

0   1   2   4

THE ABBEVILLE OPERATION

facing southwards, Huppy to the west, Bray-les-Mareuil on the Somme to the east, and between these two villages the woods of Limeux and Bailleul. In the rear they had organized: Bienfay, Villers, Huchenneville, and Mareuil. Lastly, Mont Caubert, on the same side of the Somme and commanding Abbeville and its bridges, served as a redoubt in their scheme of defence. These three successive lines were the three successive objectives I marked out for the division.

We engaged at six p.m.: the 6th Half-Brigade of heavy tanks, with the 4th Battalion of Chasseurs, against Huppy; the 8th Half-Brigade of light tanks, with the 22nd Colonial, against the Limeux and Bailleul woods; the 3rd Cuirassiers, medium tanks, with the 7th Dragoons, against Bray. The centre had the principal artillery support. At nightfall the first objective had been taken. In Huppy what was left of the German battalion occupying it surrendered. Near Limeux we captured, among others, several anti-tank batteries and came across the carcasses of the vehicles of the British mechanized brigade which they had destroyed a few days earlier.

Before dawn we were off again. The left was to take Moyenneville and Bienfay; the centre, Huchenneville and Villers; the right, Mareuil; the key of the attack being the action of the Type B tanks, whose job was to slant across from the west to the east and clip the rear of the German line. For everyone the final objective was Mont Caubert. The day was a very hard one. The enemy was reinforced and stubborn. His heavy artillery, placed on the right bank of the Somme, bombarded us violently. Other batteries, firing from Mont Caubert, also punished us. By the evening the objective was reached. Only Mont Caubert still held out. There were a great many dead from both sides on the field. Our tanks had been sorely tried. Barely a hundred were still in working order. But all the same an atmosphere of victory hovered over the battlefield. Everyone held his head high. The wounded were smiling. The guns fired gaily. Before us, in a pitched battle, the Germans had retired.

In his book, *Abbeville* (a history of the German Blümm Division, which was holding the bridgehead), Major Gehring was to write, some weeks later:

What, in fact, happened on May 28? The enemy had attacked us with powerful armoured forces. Our anti-tank units had fought heroically. But the effects of their blows had been considerably reduced by the value of the armour. The enemy had therefore managed to break through with his tanks between Huppy and Caumont. Our anti-tank defences had been crushed, the infantry had withdrawn. . . .

When the alarming news poured in to divisional HQ and, under the incessant fire of the French artillery, there was no means of communicating with any of the battalions in the line, the general commanding the division went forward himself. . . . He encountered the routed troops, regrouped them, and led them to prepared defensive positions some kilometres to the rear of the first lines. . . .

But a profound terror of the tanks had got into the bones of our soldiers. . . . Losses were heavy. . . . There was, practically speaking, nobody who had not lost cherished comrades. . . .

However, reinforcements reached the Germans. During the night of the 27th-28th they succeeded in relieving all their units in the line. Corpses and prisoners gave us proof of this. During the night of the 28th-29th a fresh relief. So it would be fresh troops we would encounter, on the third day as well as the second. Nothing reached us. And yet we needed so little to achieve success. Never mind! On May 29, as we were, we would attack once more.

On that day, the attack on Mont Caubert. Our principal effort was directed across its western slope. From Moyenneville and Bienfay the last of our Type B tanks were to start, with the Somuas transferred from the right to the left. The battalion of chasseurs reduced by more than a half, the reconnaissance regiment diminished by two-thirds, and a battalion of dragoons, were to follow them. Our remaining Renaults, with the 22nd Colonial, were to be launched from Villers. To aid us, General Altmayer had ordered the 5th Light Cavalry Division, which was stretched out along the Somme upstream from the bridgehead, to push forward its right against Cambron. But it would in fact be unable to make progress. He had asked for bombers to help by acting against the exits from Abbeville. But the aircraft were elsewhere. Five p.m. was our zero hour. The slopes of the hill were reached, but the crest remained to the enemy. When night fell the Germans, with powerful artillery support, made a counterattack on the villages of Moyenneville and Bienfay but did not succeed in recapturing them.

On May 30, the 51st Scottish Division under the command of General Fortune, having recently arrived in France, came, all fresh and spruce, to relieve the 4th Armoured Division. This regrouped near Beauvais. With me, Colonels Sudre, Simonin, and François for the tanks, de Ham for the reconnaissance regiment, Bertrand for the chasseurs, Le Tacon for the colonials, de Longuemare for the dragoons, Chaudesolle and Ancelme for the artillery, and Chomel for the staff, evaluated the results of the operation. We had not managed to liquidate the Abbeville bridgehead, but it had been reduced by three-quarters. As it now was, the enemy could not debouch from it in force without first reconquering it. Our losses were heavy; less, however, than those of the other side. We were bringing five hundred prisoners to be added to those of Montcornet, and a large quantity of arms and matériel which had fallen into our hands.

Alas! In the course of the Battle of France, what other ground had been or would be won, except this strip fourteen kilometres deep? Apart from the crews of aircraft shot down in our lines, how many other Germans were to be made prisoner? Instead of one poor division, weak, incomplete, unprovided, and isolated, what results would not have been obtained during these last days of May by an armoured *corps d'élite?*—for which many of the elements did indeed exist, though deformed and dispersed. If the state had played its part; if, while there was time, it had directed its military system towards enterprise, not passivity; if our leaders had in consequence had at their disposal the instrument for shock and manœuvre which had been often suggested to the politicians and to the High Command; then our arms would have had their chance, and France would have found her soul again.

But on May 30 the battle was virtually lost. On the day before, the Belgian King and army had capitulated. At Dunkerque the British army was beginning to re-embark. What was left of the French troops in the north was trying to do the same—a retreat that was bound to be disastrous. Before long the enemy would start the second, southward phase of his offensive against an adversary reduced by a third and more than ever unprovided with the means of countering the German mechanized forces.

In my cantonment in Picardy I had no illusions. But I was determined not to abandon hope. If the situation could not, after all, be restored in the homeland, it must be re-established elsewhere. The Empire was there, offering its refuge. The fleet was there, to protect it. The people were there, doomed in any case to suffer invasion, but capable of being roused by the republic to resistance, that terrible occasion for unity. The world was there, able to give us fresh weapons and, later, powerful aid. One question dominated everything: would the government have the sense, whatever happened, to place the state out of range, to preserve independence and safeguard the future? Or was it going to surrender everything in the panic of the collapse?

This—as I was not sorry to realize—would depend largely on the attitude of the High Command. If the High Command refused to lower the flag as long as, according to military regulations, "all the means commanded by duty and honour have not been exhausted," in short, if it adopted, in the last resort, the African solution, it could become the rescue buoy for the shipwrecked state. If, on the contrary, untrue to itself, it were to urge an unstable government to surrender, what an argument it would supply for the degradation of France!

These reflections haunted my mind as, on June 1, I went to see General Weygand, who had summoned me. The Commander-in-Chief received me at the Château de Montry. The gift of clarity and the simplicity of manner characteristic of him were, as usual, in evidence. He began by complimenting me on the Abbeville operation, about which he had just given me a most laudatory mention. Then he asked my opinion on what it would be best to do with the modern tanks—1200 or so—which we still had at our disposal.

I told the generalissimo that, in my view, these tanks should be brought together without delay into two groups: the main one, north of Paris; the other, to the south of Reims; the remains of the armoured divisions would provide the nuclei. To command the first, I suggested General Delestraint, Inspector of Tanks. To these groups would be attached, respectively, three and two infantry divisions, provided with transport, and with a doubled artillery. We would thus have a *moyen d'infortune* to act against the flank of any of the German mechanized corps whenever, pushing on in their direction of advance after breaking through our front, they were more or less uncoordinated in breadth and stretched in depth. General Weygand took note of these proposals. After which he spoke to me of the battle.

"I shall be attacked," he said, "on June 6 on the Somme and on the Aisne. I shall have on my hands twice as many German divisions as we have ourselves. That means that the prospects are poor. If things don't go too fast; if I can recover, in time, the French troops who have escaped from Dunkerque; if I have arms to give them; if the British army comes back to take part in the struggle after being re-equipped; if the Royal Air Force consents to engage its whole resources in the fighting on the Continent— then we still have a chance." And the Commander-in-Chief added, shaking his head: "If not . . ."

I knew now. I left General Weygand with heavy heart.

At one go there had fallen on his shoulders a crushing burden he was not built to bear. When, on May 20, he had taken over the supreme command, it was too late, without any doubt, to win the Battle of France. It seems likely that the realization was a surprise to him. As he had never considered the real possibilities of mechanized force, the immense and sudden effects produced by the enemy's resources had stupefied him. To face the disaster effectively he would have had to renew himself; to break, from one day to the next, with ideas, a rate of action, a set of methods which no longer applied; to wrench his strategy out of the narrow frame of the French mainland; to turn the deadly weapon back against the enemy who had launched it; and to take into his own hand the trump card of great spaces, great resources, and great speeds by including distant territories, alliances, and oceans. He was not the man to do it. His age, no doubt, was against it, as well as his turn of mind—but, above all, his temperament.

Weygand was, in fact, by nature a brilliant second. In this capacity he had served Foch admirably. In 1920 he had made Pilsudski adopt a plan which saved Poland. As Chief of the General Staff he had intelligently and courageously represented to several Ministers, under whose authority he was, the vital interests of the Army. But if the qualities demanded for staff service and those required by command are in no way contradictory, they should not be confused. To take action on one's own responsibility, to want no mark upon it but one's own, to face destiny alone—the harsh, exclusive passion characteristic of a chief—for these Weygand had neither the inclination nor the preparation. Besides, whether this was due to his own tendencies or to a combination of circumstances, he had not, in all his career, ever exercised command. No regiment, no brigade, no division, no *corps d'armée,* no army, had seen him at its head. To choose him for the taking of the greatest risk that had ever occurred in our military history, not because he was known to be up to it but on the pretext "that he was a banner," was a fruit of the error—habitual in our political life—which is called "taking the line of least resistance."

At any rate, as soon as it was recognized that General Weygand was not the man for the position he ought to have left it, either by asking to be relieved, or by the government's taking the decision as a matter of course. Nothing of the kind happened. From then on the generalissimo, carried away by a current he was no longer trying to master, was bound to seek the solution within his reach: capitulation. But as he did not intend to assume the responsibility for this, his action would consist in steering the government towards it. In this he found an ally in the Marshal, who, for different reasons, was demanding the same solution. The regime, having neither faith nor vitality, decided in favour of the worst surrender. The price, for France, was thus to be not only a disastrous military armistice, but the enslavement of the state. So true it is that, face to face with the great perils, the only salvation lies in greatness.

On June 5 I heard that the enemy was resuming the offensive. In the course of the day I went to ask for orders from General Frère, in command of the VIIth Army, in whose zone my division was. As alarming reports were being opened all round him and doubts and reticences could be seen under the outward professional calm, that excellent soldier said to me: "We're sick. Rumour has it that you're to be Minister. It's certainly late in the day for a cure. Ah! At least let's save our honour!"

CHAPTER 2

THE FALL

IT WAS DURING the night of June 5-6 that M. Paul Reynaud, in reshuffling his government, brought me in as Undersecretary of State for National Defence. I was told the news in the morning by General Delestraint, Inspector of Tanks, who had heard it broadcast. A few moments later an official telegram brought me confirmation of it. After saying good-bye to my division, I set off for Paris.

When I arrived at the Rue Saint-Dominique I saw the Premier. He was, as usual, assured, lively, incisive, ready to listen, quick to make up his mind. He explained to me why he had thought it necessary, some days earlier, to take Marshal Pétain into his cabinet, when neither of us had any doubt that he was the screen for those who desired an armistice. "It's better," said Paul Reynaud, using the customary formula, "to have him inside than out."

"I'm afraid," I answered, "you may be forced to change your opinion. All the more so since events are now going to move very fast, and defeatism may easily submerge everything. The disproportion between our forces and the Germans' is so great that, barring a miracle, we have no longer any chance of winning in Metropolitan France, or even of holding there. Besides, the High Command has been overwhelmed by surprise and will not pull

53

itself together. Lastly, you know better than anyone with what an atmosphere of abandon the government is surrounded. The Marshal and those behind him are going to have things their way from now on. At the same time, if the war of '40 is lost, we can win another. Without giving up the fight on European soil as long as it is possible, we must decide on and prepare for the continuation of the struggle in the Empire. That implies a policy to fit: the transport of resources to North Africa, the choice of leaders qualified to direct the operations, and the maintenance of close relations with the British, whatever grievances we may have against them. I propose to you that I should deal with the measures to be taken for the purpose."

M. Paul Reynaud gave me his consent. "I want you," he added, "to go to London as soon as possible. In the interviews I had on May 26 and 31 with the British government, I was able to make them realize that we were not excluding the possibility of an armistice. But now what is needed is, on the contrary, to convince the English that we will hold out, whatever happens, even overseas if necessary. You will see Mr. Churchill and you will tell him that the reshuffling of my Cabinet and your presence by my side are the signs of our resolution."

Apart from this general message, I was to do, in London, what I could, in my turn, to get the Royal Air Force—particularly the fighter aircraft—to continue to take part in the operations in France. Lastly, I was to ask, as the Premier had already done, for information about the time it would take to rearm the British units that had escaped from the Dunkerque disaster and to send them back to the Continent. The answer to these two questions involved technical data, which the staffs were competent to supply, but also decisions depending on Mr. Winston Churchill in his capacity as Minister of Defence.

While the liaison bodies were arranging for the meetings I was to have in the British capital, I went on June 8 to make contact with General Weygand at the Château de Montry. I found the Commander-in-Chief calm and master of himself. But a few moments of conversation were enough to make me realize that he was resigned to defeat and resolved upon an armistice. Here, almost word for word, is our dialogue, whose terms have—with good reason!—remained engraved on my mind.

"You see," the Commander-in-Chief said, "I was not mistaken when I told you, a few days ago, that the Germans would attack on the Somme on June 6. They are in fact attacking. At this moment they are crossing the river. I can't stop them."

"All right! They're crossing the Somme. And then?"

"Then? The Seine and the Marne."

"Yes. And then?"

"Then? But that's the end!"

"How do you mean? The end? And the world? And the Empire?"

General Weygand gave a despairing laugh. "The Empire? But that's childish! As for the world, when I've been beaten here, England won't wait a week before negotiating with the Reich."

And, looking me in the eyes, the Commander-in-Chief added, "Ah! if only I were sure the Germans would leave me the forces necessary for maintaining order!"

Discussion would have been useless. I left, after telling General Weygand that his way of looking at things was the opposite of the government's intentions. The government would not give up the struggle even if the battles went badly. He made no fresh observation and was most courteous when I took my leave.

Before starting back to Paris I chatted for some time with acquaintances of mine among the officers from various staffs who had come that morning to a conference with General Weygand. They confirmed my impression that in the upper echelons of the Command the game was considered lost and that everyone, while carrying out his duties mechanically, was suggesting in whispers, and would soon be proposing out loud, that an end be put, somehow or other, to the Battle of France. To steer men's minds and courage towards the continuation of the war in the Empire, a categorical intervention by the government was immediately necessary.

I stated this, as soon as I got back, to M. Paul Reynaud and urged him to take away the command from General Weygand, who had given up trying to win. "It's impossible for the moment," the Premier replied. "But we must think of a successor. What's your view?"

"As regards a successor," I said, "the only one I can see now is Huntziger. Although he is not ideal, he is capable, in my opinion, of rising to the level of a world strategy."

M. Paul Reynaud approved my suggestion in principle but was not, all the same, willing to put it into practice at once.

Resolved, however, to raise the question again, and soon, I harnessed myself to work out the plan for transporting all possible units to North Africa. Already the Army General Staff, in liaison with the Navy and the Air Force, had begun preparing the evacuation of everything not engaged in the battle to the other side of the Mediterranean. This meant, in particular, the two classes of recruits who were being trained in the depots of the west and south of France and those fractions of the personnel of the mechanized forces which had managed to escape from the disaster in the north; in all, five hundred thousand men of good quality. Later, as the debris of our armies was driven back towards the coasts, many fighting elements could no doubt be embarked. In any case, the remains of the bomber air force, the range of whose machines would enable them to cross the sea, the survivors of the fighter groups, the ground staff, the men at the naval bases, and finally and above all our fleet itself, would have to stand out for Africa. The Navy, whose job it was to carry out this transportation, estimated at five hundred thousand tons the extra merchant shipping required in addition to the French vessels already at its disposal. It was England that would have to be asked for this assistance.

Early on June 9 an airplane took me to London. I had with me my aide-de-camp, Geoffroy de Courcel, and M. Roland de Margerie, the Premier's *chef du cabinet diplomatique*. It was Sunday. The English capital had a look of tranquillity, almost indifference. The streets and parks full of people peacefully out for a walk, the long queues at the entrances to the cinemas, the many cars, the impressive porters outside the clubs and hotels, belonged to another world than the one at war. Certainly the newspapers allowed the real situation to pierce through, in spite of the diluted news and puerile anecdotes with which, as in Paris, semi-official optimism filled them. Certainly the notices people were reading, the digging of shelters, the carrying of masks, suggested the great dangers in the offing. Nonetheless it was obvious that the mass of the population had no idea of the gravity of events in France, so fast had been their pace. It was plain, in any case, that to English feelings the Channel was still wide.

Mr. Churchill received me at Downing Street. It was my first contact with him. The impression he gave me confirmed me in my conviction that Great Britain, led by such a fighter, would certainly not flinch. Mr. Churchill seemed to me to be equal to the rudest task, provided it had also grandeur. The assurance of his judgment, his great culture, the knowledge he had of most of the subjects, countries, and men involved, and finally his passion for the problems proper to war, found in war their full scope. On top of everything, he was fitted by his character to act, take risks, play the part out-and-out and without scruple. In short, I found him well in the saddle as guide and chief. Such were my first impressions.

What followed only confirmed them and revealed to me, in addition, the eloquence which was Mr. Churchill's own and the use he knew how to make of it. Whatever his audience—crowd, assembly, council, even a single interlocutor—whether he was before a microphone, on the floor of the House, at table, or behind a desk, the original, poetic, stirring flow of his ideas, arguments, and feelings brought him an almost infallible ascendancy in the tragic atmosphere in which the poor world was gasping. Well tried in politics, he played upon that angelic and diabolical gift to rouse the heavy dough of the English as well as to impress the minds of foreigners. The humour, too, with which he seasoned his acts and words, and the way in which he made use now of graciousness, now of anger, contributed to make one feel what a mastery he had of the terrible game in which he was engaged.

The harsh and painful incidents that often arose between us, because of the friction of our two characters, of the opposition of some of the interests of our two countries, and of the unfair advantage taken by England of wounded France, have influenced my attitude towards the Prime Minister, but not my judgment. Winston Churchill appeared to me, from one end of the drama to the other, as the great champion of a great enterprise and the great artist of a great history.

That day I explained to the British Prime Minister what the French Premier had instructed me to tell him as regards our government's will to continue the struggle even, if need be, in the Empire. Mr. Churchill showed the lively satisfaction which this determination gave him. But would it be carried out? He left me with the impression that he was not convinced. In any case, he no longer believed in the possibility of a re-establishment of the front in Metropolitan France, and he made this clear to me by refusing categorically the assistance of his air force.

Since the re-embarkation of the British army at Dunkerque, the Royal Air Force had no longer been cooperating in the battle, save in an episodic fashion. Indeed, with the exception of a fighter group which still followed the fortunes of our Air Force, the British squadrons, being based in Great Britain, were too far away to be of use to a front continually withdrawing southwards. To my pressing request that he should transfer at least a part of the British army cooperation air force to the airdromes south of the Loire, Mr. Churchill gave a formal refusal. As for the land forces, he promised to send to Normandy a Canadian division, which was arriving from its country, and to keep with us the 51st Scottish Division as well as the debris of the mechanized brigade which was still fighting at our side. But he stated that he could not indicate, even approximately, towards what date the expeditionary corps, which had just escaped destruction in Belgium—but had left there its equipment—would be able to return to the battle.

So, therefore, strategic unity between London and Paris was practically broken. A reverse on the Continent had been enough to make Great Britain desire to absorb herself in her own defence. That meant the success of the Germanic plan, of which Schlieffen, beyond death, was still the inspiration and which, after the German failures in 1914 and 1918, was at last achieving its object—to separate the French and British forces and, simultaneously, to divide France and England. It was only too easy to imagine what conclusions would be drawn by defeatists at home.

Apart from this interview with Mr. Churchill, I had made contact the same day with Mr. Eden, Minister of War, Mr. Alexander, First Lord of the Admiralty, Sir Archibald Sinclair, Air Minister, and General Sir John Dill, Chief of the Imperial General Staff. I had also conferred with M. Corbin, our ambassador, M. Monnet, "chairman" of the Franco-British committee for the coordination of purchases of war matériel, and the heads of our military, naval, and air missions. It was clear that in London, if calm reigned over the crowd, the minds of the well-informed were, on the contrary, filled with forebodings of disaster and doubt as to the firmness of the French government. In the evening the airplane took me uneasily back to Le Bourget, whose airdrome had just been bombarded.

During the night of June 9-10, M. Paul Reynaud had me summoned to his home. Grave information had just reached him. The enemy had reached the Seine below Paris. In addition, everything suggested that, at any moment, the German armoured forces would pass to the decisive attack in Champagne. The capital was therefore immediately threatened from the west, east, and north. Lastly, M. François-Poncet announced that he was expecting at any moment to receive from the Italian government its declaration of war. In face of these bad tidings, I had only one suggestion to make: to take the line of maximum effort and go as soon as possible to Africa, and embrace, with all its consequences, a war of coalition.

In the few fractions of day and night which I spent at the Rue Saint-Dominique, I found only too many reasons to reinforce my conviction that there was nothing else to be done. Things were going too fast for it to be possible to regain control of them there. Every scheme at once took on a character of unreality. Recourse was had to precedents from the 1914–18 war, which no longer applied at all. The pretence was made of thinking that there was still a front, an active Command, a people ready for sacrifices; those were only dreams and memories. In fact, in the midst of a prostrate and stupefied nation, behind an Army without faith and without hope, the machine of government was turning in irremediable confusion.

Nothing made me feel this more clearly than the rapid formal visits I paid to the principal figures of the republic: first, President Lebrun, to whom I was presented together with the new Ministers, then the Presidents of the Assemblies, and finally the members of the government. All made a show of calm and dignity. But it was clear that, in the setting where custom placed them, they were now only supers. In the middle of the cyclone, the Cabinet meetings—instructions being sent down, reports being sent up—public statements, and the procession of officers, civil servants, diplomats, members of Parliament, and journalists—all with something to report on or to ask—gave the impression of a sort of phantasmagoria without aim or effect. On the assumptions and in the surroundings where we were now engaged, there was no way out except capitulation. Unless we resigned ourselves to that—as some were already doing, and those not nonentities—we must at all costs change our surroundings and assumptions. The so-called "Marne recovery" was possible, but on the Mediterranean.

June 10 was a day of agony. The government was to leave Paris that evening. The retreat of the front was accelerating. Italy was declaring war. The obvious fact of collapse was now borne in on all minds. But at the top of the state the tragedy was being played through as though in a dream. At certain moments one might even have thought that a sort of terrible humour was seasoning the fall of France, as she rolled from the crest of history down to the deepest hollow of the abyss.

So it was that, that morning, the Italian ambassador, M. Guariglia, came to the Rue Saint-Dominique on a somewhat strange visit. He was received by Baudouin, who reported what the diplomat said as follows: "You will see that the declaration of war will in the end clarify relations between our two countries! It creates a situation from which, when all is said and done, much good will come. . . ."

Shortly afterwards, when I went to see M. Paul Reynaud, I found Mr. William Bullitt there. I supposed that the United States ambassador was bringing some encouragement for the future from Washington. But no! He had come to say good-bye. The ambassador was remaining in Paris with the intention of intervening, if need be, to protect the capital. But, praiseworthy as was the motive which inspired Mr. Bullitt, the fact remained that during the supreme days of crisis there would be no American ambassador to the French government. The presence of Mr. A. J. Drexel Biddle, responsible for relations with the refugee governments, would not, whatever the qualities of this excellent diplomat, remove the impression on our officials that the United States no longer had much use for France.

However, as M. Paul Reynaud was hastily preparing a statement which he was to broadcast and on which he was consulting me, General Weygand arrived at the Rue Saint-Dominique. Hardly had he been announced when he burst into the Premier's office. When the Premier expressed some astonishment, the Commander-in-Chief answered that he had been sent for. "Not by me!" said M. Paul Reynaud. "Nor by me!" I added. "Then it's a misunderstanding!" General Weygand went on. "But the mistake is a useful one, for I have something important to say." He sat down and began to explain the situation as he saw it. His conclusion was obvious. We must, without delay, ask for an armistice. "Things have reached the point," he declared, laying a document on the table, "where everyone's responsibilities must be clearly established. That's why I have put my opinion on paper and am handing you this note."

The Premier, though hard pressed by the necessity of very soon delivering the broadcast which had been announced, decided to dispute the generalissimo's opinion. The latter gave no ground. The battle in Metropolitan France was lost. We must capitulate.

"But there are other prospects," I said at one point.

General Weygand said mockingly, "Have you something to suggest?"

"The government," I replied, "has not suggestions to make, but orders to give. I am sure it will give them."

In the end M. Paul Reynaud showed the Commander-in-Chief out, and we separated in a most heavy atmosphere.

The last hours of the government's presence in the capital were filled with the arrangements which such an exodus involved. It was true that many things had been prepared under a withdrawal plan worked out by the Sécretariat Général de la Défense Nationale. But there remained all the unforeseen factors. At the same time the imminent arrival of the Germans beneath the walls of Paris raised cruel problems. I myself, as soon as I took up my post, had advocated that the capital should be defended and had asked the Prime Minister, as Minister of National Defence and for War, to appoint a resolute leader as governor for this purpose. I suggested General de Lattre, who had just distinguished himself at the head of a division in the fighting round about Rethel. But soon afterwards the Commander-in-Chief declared Paris an "open city," and the Cabinet approved this. Nonetheless it was necessary to organize, quite suddenly, the evacuation of a mass of things and a crowd of people. I worked at this till evening, while everywhere cases were being packed, last-minute visitors filled the building from top to bottom with rumour, and desperate telephones rang without cease.

Towards midnight M. Paul Reynaud and I got into the same car. The journey was slow, along a crammed road. At dawn we were at Orléans and went into the prefecture, where contact was made by telephone with GHQ, now being set up at Briare. Shortly afterwards General Weygand rang up and asked to speak to the Premier. He took up the telephone and, to his great surprise, was told that Mr. Winston Churchill would be arriving that afternoon. The Commander-in-Chief, through military liaison channels, had begged him to come urgently to Briare.

"Mr. Churchill must, indeed," added General Weygand, "be directly informed about the real situation at the front."

"What?" I said to the head of the government. "Are you allowing the generalissimo to invite the British Prime Minister like this, on his own authority? Don't you see that General Weygand is pursuing, not a plan of operations at all, but a policy, and that it is not yours? Is the government going to leave him still in command?"

"You are right!" answered M. Paul Reynaud. "This situation must cease. We spoke of General Huntziger as a possible successor to General Weygand. Let's go at once and see Huntziger!"

But when the cars came up, the Premier told me, "Thinking it over, it's better that you should go alone to see Huntziger. I shall prepare for these interviews with Churchill and the English. We will meet again at Briare."

I found General Huntziger, who was in command of the centre group of armies, at Arcis-sur-Aube, his command post. At that very moment this group of armies was being attacked and broken through on the Champagne front by Guderian's armoured corps. Nonetheless I was struck by Huntziger's coolness. He informed me of the bad situation he was in. I gave him an up-to-date picture of affairs as a whole. In conclusion I said, "The government sees plainly that the Battle of France is virtually lost, but it means to continue the war by transporting itself to Africa with all the resources that can be got across. That implies a complete change in strategy and in organization. The present generalissimo is not the man to be able to carry it out. Would you be the man?"

"Yes!" answered Huntziger simply.

"Well! You will be receiving the government's instructions."

To reach Briare I went via Romilly and Sens, in order to make contact with the commands of various large units. Signs of disorder and panic were in evidence everywhere. Everywhere sections of units were retreating southwards, mixed pell-mell with the refugees. My modest suite was held up for an hour near Méry, so badly blocked was the road. A strange fog—which many took for a gas cloud—increased the terror of that military throng, which was like a shepherdless flock.

At the Briare GHQ I sought out M. Paul Reynaud and told him of Huntziger's answer. But I could see that for the Premier the immediate replacement of Weygand was no longer actual and that he had once more adopted the idea of travelling the war road with a generalissimo who wanted to take the peace road. As I entered the gallery I saluted Marshal Pétain, whom I had not seen since 1938.

"You're a general!" he said to me. "I don't congratulate you. What good are ranks in defeat?" "But you yourself, Monsieur le Maréchal, received your first stars during the 1914 retreat. A few days later there was the Marne." Pétain grunted. "No comparison!" In that, he was right.

Mr. Churchill was arriving. We went into conference.

During that meeting the ideas and passions which were to dominate the new phase of the war confronted one another openly. All that had served up to then as a basis for action and for attitudes now belonged only to the past. The solidarity of England and France, the strength of the French Army, the authority of the government, the loyalty of the High Command, were ceasing to be factors that could be counted on. Already each of those taking part was behaving no longer as a partner in a game played in common, but as a man who, from now on, takes his own course and plays his own game.

General Weygand made it clear that what he wanted was to liquidate the battle and the war as quickly as possible. Drawing support from the reports of Generals Georges and Besson, he unrolled before the conference the picture of a hopeless military situation. The Commander-in-Chief, who had in addition been Chief of the General Staff from 1930 to 1935, set forth the causes of the defeat of the armies under his orders in the staid, though aggressive tones of one who attaches the blame without bearing the responsibility. His conclusion was that the ordeal must be brought to an end, for the military organization might collapse suddenly and give a free run to anarchy and revolution.

The Marshal intervened to reinforce pessimism.

Mr. Churchill, wishing to ease the atmosphere, said to him jovially, "Come, come, Monsieur le Maréchal! Remember the Battle of Amiens in March 1918, when things were going so badly. I visited you then at your HQ. You outlined your plan to me. A few days later the front was re-established."

Then the Marshal answered harshly, "Yes, the front was re-established. You, the English, were done for. But I sent forty divisions to rescue you. Today it's we who are smashed to pieces. Where are your forty divisions?"

The Premier, while repeating that France would not withdraw from the struggle and while pressing the British to send the bulk of their Air Force to our aid, made it plain that he would not part with Pétain and Weygand, as if he hoped to see them rally to his policy one day. Mr. Churchill appeared imperturbable, full of vitality, yet to be confining himself to a cordial reserve towards the French at bay, and to be preoccupied already—not, perhaps, without an obscure satisfaction—by the terrible and magnificent prospect of an England left alone in her island, waiting for him to lead her in her struggle towards salvation. As for me, thinking of what was to come, I had a full sense of how empty and conventional those palavers were, since they were not directed towards the one valid solution: to re-establish ourselves overseas.

After three hours of discussion, which reached no result, we sat down to dinner at the same table. I was next to Churchill. Our conversation fortified my confidence in his strength of purpose. He himself, no doubt, went away with the feeling that de Gaulle, though without means, was no less resolute.

Admiral Darlan, who had not shown up during the conference, appeared after the meal. Pushing in front of him General Vuillemin, the Air Chief of Staff, he came up to M. Paul Reynaud. The object of his visit was decidedly ominous. A combined operation of naval and air bombardment had been prepared against Genoa. According to the plan, it was to begin that night. But Darlan, having changed his mind, wished to countermand it, using as cover the anxieties of General Vuillemin, who was afraid of Italian reprisals against the Berre petrol dumps. All the same, the admiral was asking for the government's agreement.

"What do you think?" M. Paul Reynaud asked me.

"Having got so far," I answered, "the most sensible course is, on the contrary, to show no tenderness. The operation must be carried out as planned."

Darlan won, however, and the counterorder was given. Genoa was, all the same, bombarded later by a small naval detachment three days after the date planned. This incident made me understand that Darlan too was now playing his own game.

During the 12th, while staying at the Château de Beauvais, the property of M. Le Provost de Launay, I worked with General Colson on the plan for transportation to North Africa. To tell the truth, the events I had witnessed the day before and the isolation in which I was now left made me fear that the spirit of abandon had gained too much ground and that the plan would never be put into practice. However, I was determined to do all that was in my power to get the government to adopt it and impose it on the High Command.

Having completed the main part of it, I went over to Chissay, where M. Paul Reynaud was living. It was late. The Premier, emerging from the Cabinet meeting which had been held at Cangey and to which I was not invited, arrived towards eleven in the evening, accompanied by Baudouin. While they were dining with their entourage, I took a seat near the table and bluntly raised the question of North Africa. But my interlocutors would talk of only one problem—a related one, indeed, and a very urgent one—

which the Cabinet had just brought up. What should be the government's next destination? In fact the Germans, having crossed the Seine, would soon reach the Loire. Two solutions were contemplated: Bordeaux or Quimper? There followed, over the plates, a discussion that was confused and agitated by fatigue and irritation. No formal decision was taken, and M. Paul Reynaud retired, giving me an appointment for the morning.

I was naturally for Quimper. Not that I had any illusions about the possibility of holding out in Brittany; if the government did withdraw there, sooner or later there would be no alternative except to put to sea. Since the Germans would necessarily have to occupy the peninsula in order to act against the English, there could be no "free zone" in Brittany. Once embarked, the Ministers would in all probability make for Africa, either directly or after a halt in England. In any case, Quimper was a stage on the way to decisions of energy. Also, as soon as I had joined the government, when M. Paul Reynaud had spoken to me of the "Breton redoubt" plan, I had supported it. Conversely, it was for motives inspired by their policy and not—whatever they may claim—by military art, that it was opposed by those who, like Pétain, Weygand, and Baudouin, were working for capitulation.

Early on the 13th I returned to Chissay. After a long debate and in spite of my arguments, the Premier took the decision to transfer the government to Bordeaux, alleging that that was the view expressed by the Ministers the night before. This merely made me more persistent in demanding, at least, the signature of an order telling the Commander-in-Chief to envisage and prepare for transportation to Africa. That was really, I knew, M. Paul Reynaud's ultimate intention. But so pressing and exhausting were the contrary intrigues and influences with constant access to him that I could see this last hope dwindling, hour by hour.

The Premier did, however, sign, towards noon that day, a letter addressed to General Weygand, in which he defined for him what the government thenceforward expected of him. First: "to hold out as long as possible in the Massif Central and in Brittany."

Next: "if we should fail, . . . to install ourselves and organize the struggle in the Empire, making use of the freedom of the seas." This letter assuredly showed a salutary intention. But it was not, in my view, the categorical order that the circumstances demanded. Besides, after being signed, it was queried again behind the scenes and was not actually sent till the next day.

During the same morning of the 13th, M. Jeanneney, President of the Senate, and M. Herriot, President of the Chambre, had come to Chissay. The former, exhibiting a resolute bearing in the midst of all the agitation, invoked the example of Clemenceau, with whom he had collaborated directly and closely in the government during the great moments of 1917 and 1918. The latter, affable and accomplished, expressed with eloquence the many and various emotions by which he was swept. Both of them showed themselves favourable to the Premier, opposed to capitulation, and entirely ready to cross over to Algiers with the administration. It seemed to me, once again, that M. Paul Reynaud, whatever the defeatist cabals on all sides of him, could remain master of the game, provided he made no concessions.

I was at Beauvais at the beginning of the afternoon when M. de Margerie, M. Paul Reynaud's *chef du cabinet diplomatique,* rang me up. "A conference is about to start in a moment, at the prefecture at Tours, between the Premier and Mr. Churchill, who has just arrived with several of his Ministers. I am warning you in haste, as I myself was warned. Although you are not invited, I suggest you should come. Baudouin is at work, and I don't like the look of it." Such was M. de Margerie's communication.

I drove towards Tours, well aware of all the disquieting possibilities of this unexpected meeting, which the Premier, with whom I had just spent several hours, had not thought fit to mention to me. The courtyard and corridors of the prefecture were filled with a crowd of members of Parliament, civil servants, and journalists whom the news had attracted and who formed, as it were, the tumultuous chorus of a tragedy nearing its catastrophe. I entered the office where M. Paul Reynaud was enclosed, between Baudouin and de Margerie. The conference was adjourned. Margerie told me rapidly that the British Ministers, now in conclave in the garden, were about to give their reply to this question, put to them by the French: "In spite of the agreement of March 28, 1940, which excludes any separate laying-down of arms, would England consent to France asking the enemy what would be, for her, the terms of an armistice?"

Mr. Churchill sat down, Lord Halifax, Lord Beaverbrook, and Sir Alexander Cadogan took their places, also General Spears who accompanied them. There was a moment of crushing silence. The Prime Minister began to speak, in French. In an even, sad voice, rocking his head, with his cigar in his mouth, he began by expressing his commiseration, that of his government, and that of his people, for the lot of the French nation. "We see plainly," he said, "how things are with France. We understand how you feel cornered. Our friendship for you remains intact. In any case, be sure that England will not retire from the struggle. We shall fight to the end, no matter how, no matter where, even if you leave us alone."

Coming to the prospect of an armistice between French and Germans, which I expected would provoke an explosion from him, he expressed, on the contrary, a compassionate understanding. But suddenly, moving on to the question of the fleet, he became very precise and very firm. Obviously the British government was so afraid of seeing the French fleet handed over to the Germans that it was inclined, while there was still time, to barter its renunciation of the March 28 agreement for guarantees about the fate of our ships. This was, in fact, the conclusion which emerged from that abominable conference. Mr. Churchill, before leaving the room, asked in addition, insistently, that if France ceased to fight she should first hand over to England the four hundred German airmen who were prisoners. This was immediately promised him.

The British were then led by M. Paul Reynaud into the adjoining room, where the Presidents of the Assemblies and several

Ministers were waiting. There the tone was very different. M. Jeanneney, M. Herriot, and M. Louis Marin in particular spoke only of continuing the war. I went over to M. Paul Reynaud and asked him, somewhat forcibly, "Is it possible that you are thinking of France's asking for an armistice?" "Certainly not!" he told me. "But we must give the British a shock, to get more help out of them." I could not, obviously, take this reply as a valid one. After we had separated, in the midst of the confusion in the courtyard of the prefecture, I went back to Beauvais, overwhelmed, while the Premier telegraphed to President Roosevelt to entreat him to intervene, letting it be understood that, without that, all was lost for us. That evening M. Paul Reynaud stated in a broadcast: "If a miracle is needed to save France, I believe in a miracle."

It seemed to me a foregone conclusion that all would soon be over. Just as a besieged fortress is near surrender as soon as the governor talks of one, so France was heading for an armistice because the head of her government officially contemplated one. My presence in the Cabinet, secondary though my position might be, was going to become an impossibility. That night, however, at the very moment when I was about to dispatch my letter of resignation, Georges Mandel, who had been warned by my *chef de cabinet,* Jean Laurent, sent me a request to go and see him.

André Diethelm took me in to the Minister of the Interior. Mandel spoke to me in a tone of gravity and resolution which impressed me. He was convinced, just as much as I was, that the independence and honour of France could be safeguarded only by continuing the war. But it was because of this national necessity that he recommended me to stay on in the post where I was. "Who knows," he said, "whether we shall not finally get the government, after all, to go to Algiers?" He described to me what had happened in the Cabinet after the departure of the British; firmness had prevailed there in spite of the scene which Weygand had come to make. He gave me the news that, at that moment, the first German troops were entering Paris. Then, pointing to the future, he added, "In any case we are only at the beginning of a world war. You will have great duties to fulfil, General! But with the advantage of being, in the midst of all of us, an untarnished man. Think only of what has to be done for France, and consider that, in certain circumstances, your present position may make things easier for you." I must say that this argument persuaded me to wait before resigning. On this perhaps depended, physically speaking, what I was able to do later on.

June 14: withdrawal of the government! I said my good-byes to my hosts, the Le Provost de Launays. *They* would not leave and, surrounded by those of their people who were neither mobilized nor mobilizable, they would await in their home the battles of the retreat and then the arrival of the invader. Towards the end of the afternoon, after a gloomy journey along the road crammed with processions of refugees, I reached Bordeaux and had myself taken to the seat of the military commander, where M. Paul Reynaud was to reside. The deputy and mayor of the town, M. Marquet, was there and gave me the first-fruits of the discouraging thoughts he was getting ready to express to the Premier.

When the Premier arrived I said to him, "In the last three days I have realized the speed with which we are rushing towards capitulation. I have given you my modest assistance, but it was for making war. I refuse to submit to an armistice. If you stay here, you will be submerged by the defeat. You must get to Algiers as quickly as possible. Are you—yes or no—resolved on that?" "Yes!" answered M. Paul Reynaud. "In that case," I went on, "I must go to London at once myself to arrange for the British to help us with the transport. I will go tomorrow. Where shall I rejoin you?" The Premier replied, "You will rejoin me at Algiers."

It was agreed that I should leave that night and on the way stop in Brittany to see what could be embarked there. M. Paul Reynaud asked me, lastly, to summon Darlan to see him next morning. He wanted, he told me, to speak to him about the fleet.

Darlan was on his way to La Guéritoulde. I caught him on the telephone that evening and gave him the appointment. A peevish voice answered me. "Go to Bordeaux tomorrow? I don't know what the Premier thinks he is doing there. But I've a command, I have, and I've no time to waste." At length he submitted. But the tone adopted by Darlan opened up depressing vistas. A few minutes later I gauged the evolution of certain minds in the course of a short conversation with Jean Ybarnegaray, Minister of State, who till then had shown himself a partisan of war to the end. He came over to me at the Hotel Splendide, where I was swallowing my dinner in the company of Geoffroy de Courcel. "For me, as an ex-soldier," he said, "nothing counts except obeying my chiefs— Pétain and Weygand!" "Perhaps you will see one day," I answered, "that for a Minister the safety of the state should override all feelings." I went in silence over to Marshal Pétain, who was dining in the same room, to present my respects. He shook me by the hand without a word. I was not to see him again, ever.

What a current was carrying him along, and towards what an ineluctable destiny! The whole career of that exceptional man had been one long effort of repression. Too proud for intrigue, too forceful for mediocrity, too ambitious to be a time-server, he nourished in his solitude a passion for domination, which had long been hardened by his consciousness of his own value, the setbacks he had encountered, and the contempt he had for others. Military glory had already lavished on him its bitter caresses. But it had not satisfied him, since it had not loved him alone. And here, suddenly, in the extreme winter of his life, events were offering to his gifts and pride the opportunity—so long awaited!—to expand without limits; on one condition, however: that he should accept disaster as his elevation's scutcheon and should adorn it with his glory.

It must be said that, in any case, the Marshal considered the game lost. This old soldier, who had put on the harness in the aftermath of 1870, was naturally inclined to view the struggle as no more than another Franco-German war. Beaten in the first one, we had won the second—that of 1914–1918—with allies, certainly, but allies who played a secondary part. We were now losing

the third. It was cruel but normal. After Sedan and the fall of
Paris, the only thing was to end it, negotiate, and, if the case arose,
crush the Commune, just as, in the same circumstances, Thiers
had already done. In the old Marshal's judgment the world character of the conflict, the possibilities of the overseas territories,
and the ideological consequences of Hitler's victory hardly entered
into account. Those were not things he was in the habit of considering.

In spite of everything, I am convinced that in other times Marshal Pétain would not have consented to don the purple in the
midst of national surrender. I am sure that, in any case, as long
as he remained himself, he would have taken to the road of war
again as soon as he could see that he had been wrong, that victory was still possible, that France would have her share in it. But
alas! under the outer shell the years had gnawed his character.
Age was delivering him over to the manœuvres of people who
were clever at covering themselves with his majestic lassitude. Old
age is a shipwreck. That we might be spared nothing, the old age
of Marshal Pétain was to identify itself with the shipwreck of
France.

That is what I was thinking of as I drove through the night towards Brittany. At the same time I fortified my resolution to continue the war, wherever that might lead me. Reaching Rennes on
the morning of June 15, I saw General René Altmayer, who was
in command of the various elements engaged to the east of
Mayenne, General Guitry, commanding the military region, and
the Préfet of Ille-et-Vilaine. All three were doing their best in
their respective fields. I endeavoured to organize the coordination
of their efforts and resources for the defence of that part of the
country. Then I went on to Brest, overtaking some British convoys on their way there to re-embark. At the Préfecture Maritime
I studied, with Admiral Traub and Admiral de Laborde (who
was the "Amiral-Ouest"), the shipping available and shipping required for the embarkation of troops at the Brittany ports. In the
afternoon I went aboard the destroyer *Milan,* which was to take

me to Plymouth together with a mission of chemists headed by
General Lemoine, who were being sent by M. Raoul Dautry,
Minister of Armaments, to place the "heavy water" in safety in
England. As we left the Brest roadstead, the *Richelieu,* which
stood ready to sail for Dakar, gave me the salute. From Plymouth
I set off for London, where I arrived on the 16th at dawn.

A few minutes later M. Corbin and M. Monnet came into my
room at the Hyde Park Hotel, where I was washing. The ambassador told me, first, that the various appointments I was to have
with the British, to discuss the matter of transport, had been arranged for the morning. It was also understood that, unless France
asked Germany for an armistice, Mr. Churchill would meet M.
Paul Reynaud at Concarneau next day in the morning, to lay down
jointly how the embarkations should be carried out. Then my visitors passed on to another subject.

"We know," they said, "that at Bordeaux the mood of surrender is making rapid progress. Indeed, while you were on your
way here the French government confirmed by telegram the request made orally on the 13th to Mr. Churchill by M. Paul Reynaud with a view to the release of France from the March 28
agreement. We do not yet know what reply the British will give—
it is to be sent this morning. But we think they will consent, in
return for guarantees regarding the fleet. So we are nearing the
last moments. All the more so as there is to be a Cabinet meeting
at Bordeaux in the course of the day, and, in all probability, this
meeting will be decisive."

"It has occurred to us," added M. Corbin and M. Monnet,
"that some sensational stroke, by throwing a new factor into the
situation, might be what is needed to change the state of mind
and, in any case, to strengthen M. Paul Reynaud in his intention
to go to Algiers. We have therefore worked out with Sir Robert
Vansittart, Permanent Undersecretary at the Foreign Office, a
plan which does seem striking. It would consist of a proposal for
the union of France and England, to be solemnly addressed by the
London government to the Bordeaux government. The two coun-

tries would decide on the fusion of their administrations, the pool-
ing of their resources and losses—in short, a complete linking of
their respective destinies. In face of such a proposal, made in
such circumstances, it is possible that our Ministers may wish to
think again and, at least, postpone surrender. But we still have to
get the plan adopted by the British government. You alone can
obtain that from Mr. Churchill. It is arranged that you will lunch
with him. That will be the supreme opportunity—if, of course,
you approve of the idea."

I examined the text which was put before me. It was clear
to me at once that the grandeur of the thing in any case made its
rapid realization impossible. It was obvious that one could not,
by an exchange of notes, even in principle fuse England and
France together, including their institutions, their interests, and
their Empires, supposing this were desirable. Even the points in
the proposal that were capable of being settled practically—for
instance, the sharing of war damage—would demand complex
negotiations. But the offer addressed by the British government
to ours did involve a manifestation of solidarity which might take
on a real significance. Above all, I thought, like M. Corbin and
M. Monnet, that the proposal was of a nature to provide M. Paul
Reynaud, in the supreme crisis in which he was plunged, with an
element of comfort and, vis-à-vis his Ministers, an argument for
tenacity. I consented, therefore, to do what I could with Mr.
Churchill to get him to adopt it.

The morning was a full one. I began by settling the destination
of the *Pasteur,* carrying a cargo of a thousand 75s, some thousands of machine-guns, and quantities of ammunition, all from
the United States. On the advice of our military mission, the
ship, which was still at sea, was diverted by my orders from Bordeaux, whither she was bound, to a port in Great Britain. Given
the turn of events, this cargo, then invaluable, had to be prevented
from falling into the hands of the enemy. In fact the guns and
machine-guns brought by the *Pasteur* helped to rearm the British,
who had lost at Dunkerque nearly all their matériel.

As for the question of the transports, I found the British sincerely anxious to strengthen our means of getting our troops away and protecting the convoys; the machinery for carrying this out was being set up by the Admiralty in liaison with our naval mission under Admiral Odend'hal. But there was evidently little belief in London that official France would pull itself together. The contacts I made showed that the measures contemplated by our allies in the various fields were based on the assumption of our imminent renunciation of the struggle. Over and above everything the fate of our Navy literally haunted their minds. During these tragic hours every Frenchman could feel weighing on him the mute or explicit question from every Englishman he met: "What is going to become of your fleet?"

The British Prime Minister also was thinking of that when I came, with M. Corbin and M. Monnet, to lunch with him at the Carlton Club. "Whatever happens," I said to him, "the French fleet will not be willingly surrendered. Pétain himself would not consent to that. Besides, the fleet is Darlan's fief. A feudal lord does not surrender his fief. But for it to be possible to be sure that the enemy will never lay hands on our ships, it would be necessary for us to remain at war. Well, I am obliged to tell you that your attitude at Tours came as an unpleasant surprise to me. You appeared there to attach little value to our alliance. Your attitude of resignation plays into the hands of those among us who favour capitulation. 'You can see perfectly well we have no choice,' they say. 'The British themselves are giving us their consent.' No! What you have to do to encourage us in the frightful crisis in which we are is something quite different."

Mr. Churchill seemed disturbed. He conferred for a moment with Major Morton, his private secretary. I supposed that he was making, *in extremis,* the necessary arrangements to modify a decision already taken. Perhaps that was the cause of the fact that at Bordeaux, half an hour later, the British ambassador came and withdrew from M. Paul Reynaud's hands the note he had brought him in which the British government consented in principle to

France's asking Germany what would be the terms of an armistice if it came to that.

I then raised with Mr. Churchill the proposal for the union of the two peoples. "Lord Halifax has spoken to me about it," he told me. "But it's an enormous mouthful." "Yes," I answered. "That means that its realization would involve a great deal of time. But the gesture can be immediate. As things are now, nothing must be neglected by you that can support France and maintain our alliance."

After some discussion the Prime Minister fell in with my view. He at once summoned the British Cabinet and went to Downing Street to preside at its meeting. I went with him and, while the Ministers were deliberating, waited with the French ambassador in an office adjoining the Cabinet Room. I had meanwhile telephoned to M. Paul Reynaud to warn him that I was hoping to send him, before the end of the afternoon and with the British government's agreement, a most important communication. He answered that he was putting off his Cabinet meeting till five p.m. on this account. "But," he added, "I shan't be able to postpone it longer."

The meeting of the British Cabinet lasted for two hours, during which, from time to time, one or another of the Ministers came out to clear some point with us. Suddenly they all came in, led by Mr. Churchill. "We are agreed," they exclaimed. And in fact, details apart, the text they produced was the same as the one we had proposed to them. I immediately telephoned to M. Paul Reynaud and dictated to him the document. "It's very important!" said the Premier. "I shall use it at the meeting that is about to start." In a few words I told him all the encouraging things I could. Mr. Churchill then took the telephone. "Hullo, Reynaud! De Gaulle is right! Our proposal may have great consequences. You must hold out!" Then, after listening to the reply, he said, "Well, see you tomorrow! At Concarneau."

I said good-bye to the Prime Minister. He lent me an airplane in which to go back at once to Bordeaux. We agreed that the machine should remain at my disposal in case of events which might lead me to return. Mr. Churchill himself had to catch a train in order to board a destroyer for the journey to Concarneau. At nine-thirty p.m. I landed at Bordeaux. Colonel Humbert and Auburtin, from my office, were waiting for me at the airdrome. They told me that the Premier had resigned and that President Lebrun had asked Marshal Pétain to form a government. That meant certain capitulation. My decision was taken at once. I would leave as soon as morning came.

I went to see M. Paul Reynaud. I found him with no illusions about what the consequences would be of the Marshal's taking power, and, on the other hand, like one relieved of an intolerable burden. He gave me the impression of a man who had reached the limit of hope. Only those who were eyewitnesses of it can measure what the ordeal of being in power meant during that terrible period. All through days without respite and nights without sleep, the Premier could feel the entire responsibility for the fate of France weighing upon him personally. For a leader is always alone in face of ill fortune. He it was who received in their full force the reverses that marked the stages of our fall: the German breakthrough at Sedan, the Dunkerque disaster, the flight from Paris, the collapse at Bordeaux. Yet he had assumed the leadership only on the very eve of our misfortunes, with no time in which to confront them and after having, for a long time, advocated the military policy which could have averted them. He faced the storm with a steadfastness which did not waver. Never, during those days of drama, did M. Paul Reynaud cease to be master of himself. Never was he seen to lose his temper, give way to anger, or complain. The spectacle of that man's high value, ground down unjustly by a too great weight of events, was a tragic one.

At bottom, the personality of M. Paul Reynaud was the right one for conditions where it would have been possible to conduct the war within a state in running order and on the basis of traditionally established data. But everything was swept away! The head of the government saw the system collapsing all around him,

the people in flight, the Allies withdrawing, and the most illustrious leaders failing. From the day when the government left the
capital, the very business of exercising power became merely a
sort of agony, unrolling along the roads amid the dislocation of
services, disciplines, and consciences. In such conditions M. Paul
Reynaud's intelligence, his courage, and the authority of his office
were, so to speak, running free. He had no longer any purchase
upon the fury of events.

To seize the reins once more he would have had to wrench
himself out of the whirlwind, cross over to Africa, and start everything afresh from there. M. Paul Reynaud saw this. But it involved
extreme measures: changing the High Command, getting rid of
the Marshal and half the Ministers, breaking with certain influences, resigning himself to the total occupation of Metropolitan
France—in short, striking out at all costs from the ordinary framework and procedure in a situation without precedent.

M. Paul Reynaud did not think fit to take upon himself decisions so far outside the normal and calculated orbit. He tried to
attain the aim by manœuvring. That explains, in particular, the
fact that he envisaged a possible examination of the enemy's
armistice conditions, provided England gave her consent. No
doubt he judged that even those who were pushing towards an
armistice would recoil when they knew its terms, and that then
there would come into play the regroupment of all men of value,
to make war and save the country. But the tragedy was too harsh
to be resolved. Either make war without sparing anything, or surrender at once: there was no alternative, only these two extremes.
M. Paul Reynaud, through failing to identify himself wholly with
the first, gave place to Pétain, who completely adopted the second.

It has to be said that at the supreme moment the regime offered
to the head of the last government of the Third Republic nothing
to fall back upon. Assuredly many of the men in office looked
upon capitulation with horror. But the authorities, shattered by
the disaster for which they felt themselves responsible, did not
react at all. At the time when they were faced by the problem on

which, for France, all the present and all the future. depended, Parliament did not sit, the government showed itself incapable of adopting as a body a decisive solution, and the President of the Republic abstained from raising his voice, even within the Cabinet, to express the supreme interest of the country. In reality this annihilation of the state was at the bottom of the national tragedy. By the light of the thunderbolt the regime was revealed, in its ghastly infirmity, as having no proportion and no relation to the defence, honour, and independence of France.

Late in the evening I went to the hotel where Sir Ronald Campbell, the British ambassador, was residing, and informed him of my intention to leave for London. General Spears, who came and joined in the conversation, declared that he would accompany me. I sent word to M. Paul Reynaud. He made over to me the sum of a hundred thousand francs, on the secret funds. I begged M. de Margerie to send at once to my wife and children, who were at Carantec, the necessary passports for reaching England, which they could just do by the last boat leaving Brest. On June 17, at nine in the morning, I flew off, with General Spears and Lieutenant de Courcel, in the British airplane which had brought me the evening before. There was nothing romantic or difficult about the departure.

We flew over La Rochelle and Rochefort. Ships set on fire by German aircraft were burning in these ports. We passed over Paimpont, where my mother lay very ill. The forest was all smoking with the munition dumps which were being destroyed there. After a stop at Jersey, we reached London in the early afternoon. While I was taking rooms and Courcel was telephoning to the Embassy and the missions and finding them already reticent, I seemed to myself, alone as I was and deprived of everything, like a man on the shore of an ocean, proposing to swim across.

CHAPTER 3

FREE FRANCE

Go ON WITH THE WAR? Yes, certainly! But to what end and within what limits? Many, even among those who approved of the undertaking, wanted it to be no more than aid given by a handful of Frenchmen to the British Empire, still standing and in the fight. Not for a moment did I look at the enterprise in that way. For me, what had to be served and saved was the nation and the state.

I thought, in fact, that it would be the end of honour, unity, and independence if it were to be admitted that, in this world war, only France had capitulated and that she had let the matter rest there. For in that case, whatever might be the issue of the conflict—whether the country, after decisive defeat, would one day be rid of the invader by foreign arms, or would remain enslaved—its self-disgust and the disgust it would inspire in others would poison its soul and its life for many generations. As for the immediate future, in the name of what were some of its sons to be led out to a fight no longer its own? What was the good of supplying with auxiliaries the forces of another power? No! For the effort to be worth while, it was essential to bring back into the war not merely some Frenchmen, but France.

That was bound to involve the reappearance of our armies on

81

the battlefields, the return of our territories to belligerence, participation by the country itself in the effort of its fighting men, and recognition by the foreign powers of the fact that France, as such, had gone on with the struggle—in short, to bring our sovereignty out from disaster and from the policy of wait-and-see, over to the side of war and, one day, of victory.

What I knew of men and things left me with no illusions about the obstacles to be surmounted. There would be the power of the enemy, which could be broken only by a long process of wearing down and would have the help of the French official machine in opposing the belligerent recovery of France. There would be the moral and material difficulties which a long and all-out struggle would inevitably involve for those who would have to carry it on as pariahs and without means. There would be the mountain of objections, insinuations, and calumnies raised against the fighters by the sceptics and the timorous to cover their passivity. There would be the so-called "parallel" but in fact rival and opposing enterprises, to which the French passion for disputation would not fail to give rise, and of which the policy and services of the Allies would make use, in the customary way, in order to control them. There would be, on the part of those whose aim was subversion, the determination to side-track the national resistance in the direction of revolutionary chaos, to result in their dictatorship. There would be, finally, the tendency of the great powers to take advantage of our weakness in order to push their interests at the expense of France.

As for me, with a hill like that to climb, I was starting from scratch. Not the shadow of a force or of an organization at my side. In France, no following and no reputation. Abroad, neither credit nor standing. But this very destitution showed me my line of conduct. It was by adopting without compromise the cause of national recovery that I could acquire authority. It was by acting as the inflexible champion of the nation and of the state that it would be possible for me to gather the consent, even the enthusiasm, of the French and to win from foreigners respect and consideration. Those who, all through the drama, were offended by this intransigence were unwilling to see that for me, intent as I was on beating back innumerable conflicting pressures, the slightest wavering would have brought collapse. In short, limited and alone though I was, and precisely because I was so, I had to climb to the heights and never then to come down.

The first thing to do was to hoist the colours. Broadcasting was to hand for that. Already in the afternoon of June 17 I outlined my intentions to Mr. Winston Churchill. Washed up from a vast shipwreck upon the shores of England, what could I have done without his help? He gave it me at once, and to begin with put the BBC at my disposal. We agreed that I should use it after the Pétain government had asked for the armistice. That very evening the news came that it had done so. Next day, at six p.m., I read out at the microphone the well-known text:

APPEAL BY GENERAL DE GAULLE TO THE FRENCH
June 18, 1940

The leaders who, for many years past, have been at the head of the French armed forces, have set up a government.

Alleging the defeat of our armies, this government has entered into negotiations with the enemy with a view to bringing about a cessation of hostilities. It is quite true that we were, and still are, overwhelmed by enemy mechanized forces, both on the ground and in the air. It was the tanks, the planes, and the tactics of the Germans, far more than the fact that we were outnumbered, that forced our armies to retreat. It was the German tanks, planes, and tactics that provided the element of surprise which brought our leaders to their present plight.

But has the last word been said? Must we abandon all hope? Is our defeat final and irremediable? To those questions I answer—No!

Speaking in full knowledge of the facts, I ask you to believe me when I say that the cause of France is not lost. The very factors that brought about our defeat may one day lead us to victory.

For, remember this, France does not stand alone. She is not isolated. Behind her is a vast Empire, and she can make common cause with the British Empire, which commands the seas and is continuing the struggle. Like England, she can draw unreservedly on the immense industrial resources of the United States.

This war is not limited to our unfortunate country. The outcome of the struggle has not been decided by the Battle of France. This is a world war. Mistakes have been made, there have been delays and untold suffering, but the fact remains that there still exists in the world everything we need to crush our enemies some day. Today we are crushed by the sheer weight of mechanized force hurled against us, but we can still look to a future in which even greater mechanized force will bring us victory. The destiny of the world is at stake.

I, General de Gaulle, now in London, call on all French officers and men who are at present on British soil, or may be in the future, with or without their arms; I call on all engineers and skilled workmen from the armaments factories who are at present on British soil, or may be in the future, to get in touch with me.

Whatever happens, the flame of French resistance must not and shall not die.

As the irrevocable words flew out upon their way, I felt within myself a life coming to an end—the life I had lived within the framework of a solid France and an indivisible army. At the age of forty-nine I was entering upon adventure, like a man thrown by fate outside all terms of reference.

It was nonetheless my duty, while taking the first steps in this unprecedented career, to make sure that no authority better qualified than mine was willing to step forward to bring France and the Empire back into the struggle. As long as the armistice was not in force it was possible to imagine, though against all probability, that the Bordeaux government would at the last moment choose war. Even if there was only the feeblest chance, it must be encouraged. That is why, as soon as I reached London the afternoon of the 17th, I telegraphed to Bordeaux to offer my services in carrying on in the British capital the negotiations I had begun on the day before about the war matériel from the United States, the German prisoners, and the transport for North Africa.

The reply was a dispatch summoning me to return at once. On June 20 I wrote to Weygand, who had taken, in the midst of capitulation, the astonishing title of Minister of National Defence, to urge him to place himself at the head of the resistance and to assure him of my entire obedience if he did so. But this letter was to be returned to me by him, some weeks later, with a comment of which the least one can say is that it expressed his ill will. On June 30 the so-called "French Embassy" notified me of the order to surrender myself prisoner at the Saint-Michel prison in Toulouse, there to be tried by the Conseil de Guerre. This condemned me, first, to a month's prison. Then—upon an appeal *a minima* demanded by the "Minister," Weygand—it condemned me to death.

Discounting indeed, and rightly, this attitude on the part of Bordeaux, I had already addressed myself to our authorities overseas. As early as June 19 I had telegraphed to General Noguès, commander-in-chief in North Africa and Resident-General in Morocco, to place myself at his orders if he should reject the armistice. That same evening, in a broadcast, I urged "the Africa of Clauzel, of Bugeaud, of Lyautey, of Noguès, to refuse the enemy conditions." On June 24, by telegram, I renewed my appeal to Noguès, and addressed myself also to General Mittelhauser and to M. Puaux, respectively commander-in-chief and High Commissioner in the Levant, as well as to General Catroux, Governor-General of Indochina. I suggested to these high authorities that they should form an organization for the defence of the Empire, and that I could immediately assure its liaison with London. On June 27, being apprised of a rather warlike speech made by M. Peyrouton, the Resident-General in Tunisia, I urged him too to join the "Defence Committee," at the same time renewing my offers to General Mittelhauser and to M. Puaux. On the same day, in case of need, I booked places for myself and my officers on board a French cargo boat preparing to leave for Morocco.

All I received by way of answer was a message from Admiral de Carpentier, in command of the Navy in the Levant, telling me that M. Puaux and General Mittelhauser had telegraphed to General Noguès to the same effect as I. In addition, one of General Catroux's sons, who was then in London, brought me a telegram from his father, addressed to him, encouraging him to fight and bidding him assure me of his father's sympathetic approval. But at the same time the British, who had sent a minister, Mr. Duff Cooper, together with General Gort, to North Africa to offer Noguès the assistance of their forces, saw their delegation return to London without even having been received. Finally, General Dillon, head of British military liaison in North Africa, was asked to leave Algiers.

And yet Noguès' first impulse had been to hoist the flag. As is known, on June 25, having seen the German terms, he had telegraphed to Bordeaux to let it be known that he was ready to continue the war. Using an expression I myself had used in a broadcast six days before, he referred to "the panic in Bordeaux" as making it impossible for the government "to appreciate objectively North Africa's possibilities of resistance." He invited General Weygand "to reconsider his orders concerning the carrying out of the armistice," and protested that, if these orders were maintained, "he could not carry them out without blushing." It is clear that if Noguès had chosen the path of resistance the whole of the Empire would have followed him. But it soon became known that he himself and the other residents, governors, and commanders-in-chief were obeying the summonses of Pétain and Weygand and were consenting to the armistice. Only General Catroux, Governor-General of Indochina, and General Legentilhomme, in command of our troops on the Somali coast, maintained their opposition. Both of them were replaced, without their subordinates doing much to support them.

But indeed this sort of collapse of most of the "proconsuls" coincided with a total political breakdown at home. The papers that reached me from Bordeaux, and then from Vichy, displayed their acceptance and that of all the parties, groups, authorities, and institutions. The National Assembly met on July 9 and 10 and gave Pétain full powers, almost without debate. Actually eighty of the members present voted courageously against this abdication. Also those parliamentarians who had embarked for North Africa aboard the *Massilia* bore witness, by so doing, that for them the Empire had not given up the struggle. Nevertheless it is a fact that not one public man raised his voice to condemn the armistice.

Moreover, even though the collapse of France had plunged the world into stupefaction, even though ordinary people all over the world watched with terror the destruction of that great light, even though this poem by Charles Morgan and that article by François Mauriac brought tears to many eyes, states were not slow to accept accomplished facts. No doubt the governments of the countries at war with the Axis did recall their representatives from France, whether they did so spontaneously, as in the cases of Sir Ronald Campbell or General Vanier, or were asked to do so by the Germans. But there remained, all the same, in London, installed in the building of the French Embassy, a consul who was in communication with Metropolitan France, while Mr. Dupuis, the Canadian consul-general, remained accredited to the Marshal, and the Union of South Africa left its representative there. Above all, an imposing diplomatic corps could be seen assembling at Vichy around Monsignor Valerio Valeri, the papal nuncio, M. Bogomolov, the Soviet ambassador and, soon, Admiral Leahy, the United States ambassador. That was enough to cool the ardour of those personalities whose first impulse might have driven them towards the Cross of Lorraine.

Thus, among the French as within the other nations, the immense convergence of fear, interest, and despair caused a universal surrender in regard to France. Though there were many feelings still loyal to her past and many interests eager to take advantage of the shreds yet left to her by the present, no responsible man anywhere acted as if he still believed in her independence, pride, and greatness. That she was bound henceforward to be enslaved, disgraced, and flouted was taken for granted by all who counted in the world. In face of the frightening void of the general renunciation, my mission seemed to me, all of a sudden, clear and terrible. At this moment, the worst in her history, it was for me to assume the burden of France.

But there is no France without a sword. To set up a fighting force was more important than anything. I began work on that at once. There were some military elements in England. First of all, there were the units of the Alpine Light Division, which, after some brilliant campaigning in Norway under General Béthouart, had been brought back to Brittany in the middle of June and re-embarked there along with the last British troops. There were also some ships belonging to the Navy—nearly a hundred thousand tons in all—which had escaped from Cherbourg, Brest, and Lorient with many individuals and auxiliaries on board beside their crews, the whole totalling at least ten thousand sailors. There were, in addition, several thousand soldiers who had been wounded in Belgium and brought to hospital in Great Britain. The French military missions had organized the command and administration of all these elements with a view to keeping them under the orders of Vichy and preparing their general repatriation.

The mere act of making contact with these many dispersed fractions involved great difficulties for me. To begin with, I had only a very small number of officers, nearly all subalterns, full of immense good-will but powerless to storm the machinery of the hierarchy. What they could do—and did—was propaganda among those officers and men whom they managed to meet. The yield was bound to be small. A week after my appeal of June 18 the number of volunteers encamped in Olympia, which the British had lent us, amounted to only a few hundred.

It must be said that the British authorities did little to help our efforts. Certainly they had distributed a leaflet advising members of the French forces that they could choose between repatriation, joining General de Gaulle, and serving in His Majesty's forces. Certainly the instructions given by Churchill and the activities of Spears, whom the Prime Minister had made responsible for liaison between Free France and the British services, did sometimes succeed in vanquishing inertia or opposition. Certainly the press, the wireless, many associations, and countless individuals gave our enterprise a warm welcome. But the British High Command, which from one day to another expected the German offensive and perhaps invasion, was too much absorbed by its preparations to busy itself with a task which in its eyes was secondary. Besides, it was inclined by professional decorum and habit to respect the normal order of things—that is to say, Vichy and its missions. Finally, it looked with some mistrust upon these Allies of yesterday, humiliated by misfortune, dissatisfied with themselves and with others, and loaded with complaints. What would they do if the enemy gained a bridgehead? Wasn't the most sensible course to ship them away as quickly as possible? And what, after all, was the use of the few battalions without cadres and the crews without officers which General de Gaulle claimed he could rally?

On June 29 I went to Trentham Park, where the Light Mountain Division was encamped. The general commanding the division was himself anxious to return to France, though with the firm intention of getting back into the line one day—which indeed he was destined to do, effectively and with glory, later. But he had arranged for me to see the whole of each unit. This made it possible for me to rally a large part of the two battalions of the 13th Half-Brigade of the Foreign Legion with their leader, Lieutenant-Colonel Magrin-Verneret, known as Monclar, and his number two, Captain Koenig, two hundred Chasseurs Alpins, two-thirds of a tank company, some elements of gunners, engineers, and signals, and several staff and administrative officers, including Commandant de Conchard and Captains Dewavrin and Tissier. This in spite of the fact that, after I had left the camp, the British Colonels de Chair and Williams, sent by the

War Office, had in turn had the troops paraded in order to tell them literally this: "You are perfectly free to serve under General de Gaulle. But it is our duty to point out to you, speaking as man to man, that if you do so decide you will be rebels against your government. . . ."

Next day I wanted to visit the camps at Aintree and at Haydock, where several thousand French sailors were assembled. As soon as I arrived the British admiral in command at Liverpool told me that he was opposed to my seeing the men because this might be prejudicial to order. I had to return empty-handed. I was luckier at Harrow Park a few days later. In spite of everything, a stream of enlistments was starting among our sailors. A few resolute officers who had joined me at once, such as Capitaines de Corvette d'Argenlieu, Wietzel, Moulec, and Jourden, were putting their heart and soul into it. The officers and crews of three small warships had declared themselves at once: the submarine *Rubis* (Commandant Cabanier), then cruising near the Norwegian coast; the submarine *Narval* (Commandant Drogou), which left Sfax immediately after my appeal and reported at Malta, later to be sunk in action in the Mediterranean; and the trawler and patrol craft *Président Honduce* (Commandant Deschatres). The arrival of Vice-Admiral Muselier, who had set many elements in the Navy against him by the incidents of his career and the features of his personality, but whose intelligence and knowledge of the world offered advantages at that adventurous period, made it possible for me to give this embryo of our naval forces a centre and a technical head. At this time also some dozens of airmen, whom I went to see in camp at St. Atham, grouped themselves around Captains de Rancourt, Astier de Villatte, and Becourt-Foch, until Commandant Pijeaud was given command of them.

Meanwhile isolated volunteers were reaching England daily. They came mostly from France, brought by the last ships to have left there normally, or escaping in small boats which they had managed to seize, or, again, having with great difficulty got across Spain, evading its police which shut up in the camp at Miranda those it caught. Some airmen saved their machines from the control of Vichy and contrived to get away from North Africa and reach Gibraltar. Some merchant seamen, placed outside French ports by the chances of navigation or, sometimes, by the escape of a ship—as, for example, the *Capo Olmo* (Commandant Vuillemin)—asked to be enrolled as combatants. Some Frenchmen resident abroad came and demanded to serve. Having called a meeting at the White City of two thousand men who had been wounded at Dunkerque and were convalescing in British hospitals, I got two hundred enlistments. A Colonial battalion, which happened to be in Cyprus, detached from the Armée du Levant, rallied spontaneously under its leader, Commandant Lorotte. In the last days of June a flotilla of fishing boats reached Cornwall, bringing over to us all the able-bodied men from the island of Sein. Day after day the enrollment of these lads, so splendid in their keenness, many of whom had performed exploits to get to us, strengthened our determination. Messages from all parts of the world piled up on my table, bringing me, from individuals or from small groups, moving requests for enlistment. My officers and those of the Spears mission expended prodigies of ingenuity and obstinacy to arrange their transport.

Suddenly a lamentable event occurred to stop the stream. On July 4 the radio and the newspapers announced that on the previous day the British Mediterranean fleet had attacked the French squadron at anchor at Mers-el-Kébir. At the same time we were informed that the British had occupied by surprise the French warships which had taken refuge in British ports and had taken ashore and interned—not without some bloodshed—their officers and crews. Finally, on the 10th, the news was made public of the torpedoing, by British aircraft, of the battleship *Richelieu,* at anchor in Dakar roads. In London the official communiqués and the newspapers tended to present this series of aggressions as a sort of naval victory. It was clear that, in the British government and Admiralty, the fear caused by the danger they were in, the stale reek of an old naval rivalry, the resentments accumulated since the beginning of the Battle of France and brought to the point of paroxysm with the armistice concluded by Vichy, had exploded in one of those dark bursts by which the repressed instinct of this people sometimes smashes all barriers.

It had never, though, been likely that the French fleet would of itself open hostilities against the British. Ever since my arrival in London I had stressed this, both to the British government and to the Admiralty. Besides, it was certain that Darlan, quite apart from all the obvious patriotic motives, would not of his own accord go and surrender to the Germans his own wealth—the Navy —as long as it was under his control. At bottom, if Darlan and his advisers renounced the chance of playing the magnificent part offered them by events and becoming the last resort of France at a time when, in contrast to the Army, the fleet was intact, it was because they thought they were certain of keeping their ships. Lord Lloyd, the British Minister for Colonies, and Admiral Sir Dudley Pound, the First Sea Lord, when they came to Bordeaux on June 18, had obtained from Darlan his word of honour that our ships would not be handed over. Pétain and Baudouin, for their part, had given formal undertakings. Lastly, contrary to what the British and American agencies had at first suggested, the terms of the armistice included no direct provision entitling the Germans to lay hands on the French fleet.

On the other hand it must be recognized that, faced by the capitulation of the Bordeaux authorities and the prospect of future flinchings on their part, England might well fear that the enemy would one day manage to gain control of our fleet. In that case Great Britain would have been mortally menaced. In spite of the pain and anger into which I and my companions were plunged by the tragedy of Mers-el-Kébir, by the behaviour of the British, and by the way they gloried in it, I considered that the saving of France ranked above everything, even above the fate of her ships, and that our duty was still to go on with the fight.

I expressed myself frankly about this on July 8, in a broadcast. The British government, on the advice of its Minister of

Information, Mr. Duff Cooper, was clever enough, and elegant enough, to let me use the BBC microphone, however disagreeable for the British the terms of my statement may have been.

But it was a terrible blow to our hopes. It at once showed in the recruitment of volunteers. Many of those, military or civilian, who were preparing to join us turned on their heels then. In addition, the attitude adopted towards us by the authorities in the French Empire and by the naval and military elements guarding it changed for the most part from hesitation to opposition. Vichy, of course, did not fail to exploit the event to the utmost. The consequences were destined to be grave as regards the rallying of the African territories.

Still, we resumed our task. On July 13 I went so far as to announce, "Frenchmen! Realize this! You have still a fighting army." On July 14, in Whitehall, in the midst of a deeply moved crowd, I reviewed our first detachments and then went at their head to place a Tricolour wreath at the foot of the statue of Marshal Foch. On July 21, at my request, several of our airmen took part in a bombardment of the Ruhr, and I announced that the Free French had resumed the fight. Meanwhile all our troops, in accordance with an idea put forward by d'Argenlieu, adopted as their badge the Cross of Lorraine. On August 24, King George VI came to visit our little army. To see it, one could well believe that "the stump of the blade" would be toughly tempered. But God! how short it was!

At the end of July the number of our effectives was barely seven thousand. That was all we would be able to recruit in Great Britain itself: those French troops who had not joined us had now been repatriated. With great difficulty we were recovering the arms and matériel they had left behind, seized often either by the English or by other allies. As for the ships, we were only able to man some of them, and it was heartbreaking to see the others sailing under a foreign flag. Little by little, in spite of everything, our first units took shape, equipped with an odd assortment of weapons, but formed of resolute men.

These were, in fact, of that strong type to which the fighting men of the French resistance, wherever they might be, were bound to belong. A taste for risk and adventure pushed to the pitch of art for art's sake, a contempt for the cowardly and the indifferent, a tendency to melancholy and so to quarreling during the periods without danger, giving place to an ardent cohesion in action, a national pride sharpened to its extreme by their country's ill fortune and by contact with well-equipped allies, and, above all, a sovereign confidence in the strength and cunning of their own conspiracy—such were the psychological characteristics of this elite, which started from nothing and was to grow, gradually, until it drew after it the whole nation and the whole of the Empire.

While we were trying to forge some forces of our own, the need to define our relations with the British government became imperative. The British government was indeed ready for this, not so much from a taste for juridical definitions as from its desire to see a practical settlement, in His Majesty's territory, of the rights and obligations of those sympathetic but somewhat disconcerting people, the Fighting French.

From the very beginning I had let Mr. Churchill know of my intention to promote, if possible, the formation of a National Committee to direct our war effort. To help towards this, the British government made public two statements on June 23. The first denied that the Bordeaux government possessed independence. The second took note of the proposal to form a French National Committee and expressed, in advance, the intention of recognizing it and dealing with it on all matters relative to the carrying-on of the war. On June 25 the British government issued a communiqué acknowledging the will to resist shown by several high authorities of the French Empire and offering them its assistance. Then, as no response came from any quarter, the London Cabinet found itself once more face to face with General de Gaulle alone, and took the decision, on June 28, to recognize him publicly as "leader of the Free French."

It was therefore in this capacity that I opened the necessary conversations with the Prime Minister and the Foreign Office. The point of departure was a memorandum which I had myself sent to Mr. Churchill and to Lord Halifax on June 26. The result was the agreement of August 7, 1940. Several clauses to which I attached importance gave rise to delicate bargaining between the negotiators: Mr. Strang, on behalf of our allies, Professor René Cassin on ours.

Bearing in mind, on the one hand, the hypothesis that the fortunes of war might bring England to a compromise peace, and considering, on the other, that the British might perhaps be tempted by this or that overseas possession of ours, I insisted that Great Britain should guarantee the re-establishment of the frontiers of Metropolitan France and of the French Empire. The English in the end consented to promise "the integral restoration of the independence and greatness of France," but without any commitment as regards the integrity of our territories.

Although I was convinced that given the proportion between the resources, the joint military operations, on land, on sea, and in the air, should normally be directed by British commanders, I reserved for myself in all cases the "supreme command" of the French forces and accepted for them only "the general directives of the British High Command." In this way their purely national character was established. I also had it laid down—not without objections on the part of the British—that in no case would the volunteers "bear arms against France." That did not mean that they were never to fight against Frenchmen. The contrary, alas, had to be foreseen, Vichy being what it was and not being—far from it—France. But the clause aimed at guaranteeing that Allied military action, with which our own was merged, should not, even when it came up against the forces of official France, be used against the real France and injure its patrimony or its interests.

Although the expenses relating to the forces of Free France were bound, under the agreement, to fall provisionally upon the British government, seeing that at the start we had no financial resources, I insisted on having it formulated that these were only advances, to be repaid one day, account being taken of what we furnished in return. The complete repayment did in fact take place, even before the end of the war, so that on balance our war effort remains in no way a charge upon England.

Finally, in spite of the thirst for tonnage by which—all too legitimately—the British were devoured, we made them agree, with some difficulty, that a "permanent liaison" should be established between their services and ours to settle "the use to be made of French merchant ships and their crews."

It was at Chequers that Churchill and I signed the document together.

The August 7 agreement had considerable importance for Free France, not only because it got us out of immediate material difficulties, but also because the British authorities, having now an official basis for their relations with us, no longer hesitated to make things easier for us. Above all, the whole world knew that a new beginning of Franco-British solidarity had been made in spite of everything. The consequences soon made themselves felt in certain territories of the Empire and among the French residents abroad. But in addition other states, when they saw Great Britain proceeding to a beginning of recognition, took some steps in the same direction. This happened, first of all, with the refugee governments in England, who possessed, no doubt, little in the way of forces but had retained their international representation and influence.

For in the case of each of the European nations submerged by Hitler's armies the state had carried its independence and sovereignty across to free shores. It was to be the same for those whose territory was later occupied likewise by Germany or Italy. Not one government consented to submit to the invader's yoke, not a single one except, alas, that which called itself the government of France and yet had under its control a vast Empire guarded by large forces and one of the principal navies of the world!

In the course of the disasters of June, Great Britain had seen arrive upon her soil the sovereigns and Ministers of Norway, Holland, and Luxembourg, then the President of the Polish Republic and the Polish Ministers, and, after some delay, the Belgian Cabinet. The Czechoslovaks were busy organizing themselves. The King of Albania was making certain contacts. It was from both generous and interested motives that England offered hospitality to these refugee states. However denuded they might be, they had always something left. Several of them brought the gold and foreign exchange of their banks. The Dutch had Indonesia and a by no means negligible fleet; the Belgians had the Congo; the Poles a small army; the Norwegians, a good many merchant ships; the Czechs—or more exactly Beneš—intelligence networks in Central and Eastern Europe and active American relations. Moreover, England did not exactly suffer in prestige by appearing as the last rampart of the old world in ruin.

To these exiles, Free France, which had nothing, was an interesting experiment. But it above all attracted the most anxious and the most unhappy among them, such as the Poles and the Czechs. In their eyes, we who remained faithful to the traditions of France represented, by that very fact, a hope and a pole of attraction. In particular Sikorski and Beneš, suspicious though they were in the midst of the intrigues and susceptibilities which complicated their plight, established constant and sustained relations with me. Perhaps never better than at the bottom of that gulf have I felt what the vocation of France meant to the world.

While we endeavoured to obtain for France the beginnings of an international hearing, I was trying to get going the embryo of a political machinery and administration. Almost unknown and wholly without resources as I was, it would have been ridiculous of me to call the elementary organization which I was forming around me a "government." Besides, although I was convinced that Vichy would go on from fall to fall till it reached total degradation, and although I had proclaimed the illegitimacy of a regime which existed at the enemy's discretion, I wished to avoid prejudicing the possibility of the state machinery being recast in the mould of war, should the occasion ever present itself. And so I refrained as long as possible from setting up, even as a matter of terminology, anything which might in any circumstances embarrass the regrouping of the state. All I had suggested to the holders of authority in the Empire was that they should unite for its defence. Then, when their failure had been verified, I decided that I myself would form, as soon as possible, a simple National Committee.

It was necessary, however, that some sufficiently representative people of eminence should be willing to support me. During the first days certain optimists thought these could easily be found. From hour to hour it was announced that such and such a well-known politician, famous general, or revered academician had passed through Lisbon or landed at Liverpool. But the denial soon followed. Even in London, with few exceptions, those well-known Frenchmen who happened to be there, whether on service or by chance, did not join Free France. Many had themselves repatriated. Some stayed where they were but professed obedience to Vichy. As to those who took sides against the capitulation, some organized their life in exile on their own, either in England or in the United States, others placed themselves at the service of the British or American government. The "proved men" who ranged themselves under my banner were few.

"You are in the right!" I was told, for instance, by M. Corbin, the French ambassador. "I who have devoted the best part of my career to the cause of the Franco-British alliance have taken sides openly by sending in my resignation the very next day after your appeal. But I'm an old civil servant. For forty years I've lived and worked within a regular framework. Outlawry is too much for me."

"You are wrong," M. Jean Monnet wrote to me, "to set up an organization which might appear in France as though created under the protection of England. . . . I wholly share your determination to prevent France from abandoning the struggle. . . . But London is not the place from which the effort at insurrection can start."

"I must go back to France," M. René Mayer let it be known, "in order not to separate my fate from that of the people of my religion who are going to be persecuted there."

"You have my approval," M. Bret assured me. "As for me, whether in France or in the Empire, I shall do all I can to help the recovery of France."

"We are going to America," I was informed by M. André Maurois, M. Henri Bonnet and M. de Kérillis. "That is where, indeed, we shall be able to be of most use to you."

"I have been appointed consul-general at Shanghai," M. Roland de Margerie announced to me, "and I am passing through London not to join you but to reach China. I shall serve the interests of France there, as you are doing here."

On the other hand, M. Pierre Cot, overcome by what had happened, begged me to use him at no matter what task, "even sweeping the staircase." But he was too conspicuous for that to be desirable.

All in all, whatever the reasons for it, this well-nigh general abstention of Frenchmen of note certainly did not heighten the credit of my enterprise. I had to put off the formation of my Committee till later. The fewer eminent people came, the fewer wished to come.

Some, however, were immediately at my side, and brought to the duties which they assumed extempore an ardour and an energy thanks to which, in spite of everything, the ship was launched and proved seaworthy. Professor Cassin was my assistant—and what a valuable one!—with regard to all those agreements and other documents upon which, starting from nothing, our internal and external structure was established. Antoine had to run the administration of our first civilian services, a thankless task in that period of improvisation. Lapie, Escarra, and then Hackin— the latter doomed soon to perish at sea, together with his wife, while on a mission—kept in touch with the various departments of the Foreign Office and with the European governments in exile. They also made contact with the Frenchmen resident abroad to whom I had appealed. Pleven and Denis had charge of our minute finances and worked on the conditions under which the colonies could live when they rallied to us. Maurice Schumann acted as the spokesman of Free France on the radio. Massip studied the press and kept it informed about us. Bingen settled with our allies the use of French merchant shipping and seamen.

On the strictly military side, Muselier assisted by d'Argenlieu, Magrin-Verneret by Koenig, and Pijeaud by Rancourt, organized, respectively, the various naval, land, and air units. Morin was in charge of supply. Tissier, Dewavrin, and Hettier de Boislambert formed my staff. Geoffroy de Courcel acted as my *chef de cabinet,* aide-de-camp, interpreter, and—often—wise adviser. Such were the members of that "entourage" which opposing propaganda denounced as a collection of traitors, mercenaries, and adventurers. But they, exalted by the grandeur of the task, stuck to me for better and for worse.

To the British services, whose cooperation was then indispensable to us, our affairs were presented by General Spears. He did so with a tenacity and a dexterity of which it is my duty to say that they were, at these harsh early stages, more than valuable—essential. Yet even he did not find things at all easy on the British side. The conventionality of the official hierarchies made them distrust this man who, as Member of Parliament, officer, businessman, diplomat, and author, belonged to many categories at once without becoming classifiable in any of them. But to speed up routine he brought into play his intelligence, the fear inspired by his biting sallies of wit, and, lastly, the charm he knew how to display on occasion. In addition, he had for France, which he knew as well as a foreigner can know her, a sort of uneasy, dominating love.

At a time when so many others considered my enterprise an encumbering adventure, Spears had immediately understood its nature and its scope. It was with ardour that he had taken up his mission to deal with Free France and its leader. But his wish to serve them only made him the more jealous of them. If he approved of their independence towards all the others, he resented it painfully when it rose up before him. That is why, in spite of all that he did to help us at the start, General Spears was destined one day to turn away from our enterprise and to begin fighting against it. In the passion he brought to this, was there not regret at not having been able to lead it and sadness at having left it?

But at its birth Free France did not yet meet with the kind of adversaries which success arouses. It merely struggled among the afflictions which are the lot of the weak. My assistants and I worked in St. Stephen's House on the Embankment, in a flat furnished with a few tables and chairs. Later the British administration placed at our disposal a more convenient building in Carlton Gardens, and there our principal centre was installed. There it was that the daily wave of disappointment broke upon us. But there, too, the flood of encouragements came to raise us above our normal level.

For testimony was flowing in from France. By the most ingenious routes, sometimes with the connivance of the censors, simple people were sending us letters and messages. For instance, that photograph taken on July 14 in the Place de l'Etoile as the Germans arrived there, showing a group of women and men, sunk in grief, around the tomb of the Unknown Soldier, and sent on July 19 with these words: "De Gaulle! we have heard you. Now we shall wait for you!" Or again, that picture of a grave covered with innumerable flowers put there by passers-by—the grave was that of my mother, who had died at Paimpont on July 16, offering up her sufferings to God for the salvation of the country and her son's mission.

And so we were able to measure the resonance our refusal to accept the defeat was arousing in the recesses of the people. At the same time we had proof that, all over the country, people were listening to the London broadcasts, and that through them a powerful means of war was at our disposal. Indeed, the French who resided abroad returned the same echo of the national feeling. Many placed themselves in contact with me, as I had asked them to do, and formed groups to help Free France. Malglaive and Guéritte in London, Houdry and Jacques de Sieyès in the United States, Soustelle in Mexico, Baron de Benoist at Cairo, Godard at Teheran, Guérin in the Argentine, Rendu in Brazil, Piraud in Chile, Géraud Jouve at Constantinople, Victor at Delhi, Levay at Calcutta, Barbé at Tokyo, and others, took the first initiatives in this respect. I could soon be certain that in spite of pressure from the Vichy authorities, of the calumnies of their propaganda, and of the weakness of a great many, it was to Free France that the people turned what remained to it of pride and hope. The thought of what this supreme appeal from the nation laid upon me has never left me since then for an instant in all I have had to undertake and to endure.

In England itself the Free French were surrounded by esteem and sympathy. The King, first of all, was quick to give proof of these. Each of the members of his family did the same. The Ministers and authorities, for their part, lost no opportunity of expressing their good wishes. But it would be impossible to imagine the generous kindness which the English people everywhere showed towards us. All sorts of charities were formed to help our volunteers. The people who came to offer us their services, their time, and their money could not be counted. Every time I had to appear in public, it was in the midst of the most comforting demonstrations. When the London papers announced that Vichy was condemning me to death and confiscating my property, quantities of jewels were left at Carlton Gardens anonymously and dozens of unknown widows sent their wedding rings in order that the gold might serve the work of General de Gaulle.

It should be said that a tense atmosphere enveloped England at that time. The German offensive was expected from one moment to the next, and, faced by this prospect, everyone entrenched himself in exemplary steadfastness. It was a truly admirable sight to see each Englishman behaving as if the safety of the country depended on his own conduct. This universal feeling of respon-

sibility seemed the more moving because in reality everything was
going to depend on the air force.

If ever the enemy managed, indeed, to seize the mastery of
the sky, England would be done for! The fleet, bombarded from
the air, would not prevent the German convoys from crossing
the North Sea. The army, whose strength was a bare dozen divisions sorely tried by the Battle of France and without equipment,
would be incapable of beating back the troops that had been
landed. After which the large German units would have little
trouble in occupying the whole land, in spite of the local resistance
organized by the Home Guard. Certainly the King and the government would have left for Canada in time. But the well-informed
whispered the names of politicians, bishops, writers, and businessmen who, in this event, would come to terms with the Germans
to assure, under their thumb, the administration of the country.

But those were speculations which did not touch the mass of
the people. The British as a whole were getting ready to fight to
the bitter end. Each man and each woman joined the network
of defence. Everything to do with the building of shelters, the distribution of weapons, tools, and implements, work in the factories
and fields, services, duties, and rationing left nothing to be desired
as regards ardour and discipline. The only thing lacking was equipment, in this country which, like ours, had long neglected to take
precautions. But everything went on as if the English intended
to make up by devotion for whatever they lacked. Humour, too,
was not lacking. One newspaper cartoon showed the formidable
German army already in Great Britain, but held up on the road,
with its tanks, its guns, its regiments, and its generals, in front of
a wooden barrier. A notice indicated, in fact, that to pass it one
must pay a penny. Not having received from the Germans all the
required pennies, the Englishman in charge of the toll-gate, a little
old man, courteous but inflexible, was refusing to raise the barrier,
in spite of the indignation which ran the whole length of the invaders' monstrous column.

Meanwhile, at the alert on its airdromes, the Royal Air Force was ready. Among the people many, in their desire to emerge from an almost unbearable tension, went so far as to say out loud that they wished the enemy would risk the attack. Foremost among them, Mr. Churchill found the waiting hard to bear. I can still see him at Chequers, one August day, raising his fists towards the sky as he cried, "So they won't come!" "Are you in such a hurry," I said to him, "to see your towns smashed to bits?" "You see," he replied, "the bombing of Oxford, Coventry, Canterbury, will cause such a wave of indignation in the United States that they'll come into the war!"

I expressed some doubt about that, reminding him that two months earlier the distress of France had not made America emerge from her neutrality. "That's because France was collapsing!" stated the Prime Minister. "Sooner or later the Americans will come, but on condition that we here don't flinch. That's why I can't think of anything but the fighter air force." He added, "You see, I was right to refuse it to you at the end of the Battle of France. If today it was destroyed, all would be lost for you, as well as for us." "But," said I in my turn, "the intervention of your fighters, if on the contrary that had happened, might perhaps have given new life to the alliance and brought about, in France, the continuation of the war in the Mediterranean. In that case the British would be less threatened and the Americans more tempted to engage themselves in Europe and in Africa."

Mr. Churchill and I agreed modestly in drawing from the events which had smashed the West this commonplace but final conclusion: when all is said and done, Great Britain is an island; France, the cape of a continent; America, another world.

CHAPTER 4

AFRICA

B Y AUGUST, Free France had some resources, the beginnings of an organization, a certain popularity. I had to make use of them at once.

In other respects I may have been assailed by perplexities, but there was no doubt in my mind as to the immediate action to be undertaken. Hitler had managed to win the first round, in Europe. But the second was about to begin, and it would be on a world scale. One day the opportunity might come of winning a decision where one was possible—that is to say, on the soil of the old Continent. Meanwhile it was in Africa that we French must continue the struggle. The course into which I had tried in vain, a few weeks before, to draw the government and High Command was the one I naturally intended to follow, as soon as I found that all that had remained in the war—of both of them—was embodied in me.

In the vast spaces of Africa, France could in fact re-create for herself an army and a sovereignty, while waiting for the entry of fresh allies at the side of the old ones to reverse the balance of forces. When that happened Africa, being within reach of the peninsulas of Italy, the Balkans, and Spain, would offer an excellent base for the return to Europe, and it would be French. What was more, the national liberation, if accomplished one day thanks to the forces of the Empire, would establish links of solidarity between Metropolitan France and the overseas territories. If, on the contrary, the war were to end without the Empire having made any effort to save the mother country, that would be the end, without a doubt, of the work of France in Africa.

It was also to be foreseen that the Germans would carry the war across the Mediterranean, either to cover Europe, or to acquire some territory there, or to help their Italian associates—and possibly Spanish ones too—to increase theirs. Indeed, there was fighting going on already. The Axis aimed at reaching Suez. If we remained passive in Africa, our adversaries would sooner or later annex some of our possessions, while our allies would be led to lay hands, in the course of operations, on such of our territories as were necessary to their strategy.

To take part in the Battle of Africa with French forces and territories was to bring back, as it were, a fragment of France into the war. It was to defend her possessions directly against the enemy. It was, as far as possible, to deflect England—and perhaps one day America—from the temptation to make sure of them on their own account, for their fighting needs and for their advantage. It was, lastly, to wrench Free France free from exile and install her in full sovereignty on national territory.

But where should we start upon Africa? I could expect nothing positive in the immediate future from the Algeria-Morocco-Tunisia block. It was true that at first many messages of adhesion from municipalities, associations, officers' messes, and bodies of ex-servicemen had been addressed to me. But resignation had come quickly, while at the same time penalties and censorship were extending, and the tragedy of Mers-el-Kébir stifled the last schemes of resistance. On the spot, too, it was realized, with a certain "cowardly relief," that the armistice left North Africa outside the occupation. French authority was visibly maintained there in a military and unequivocal form which reassured the French residents and yet did not displease the Moslems. Lastly, certain aspects of what Vichy called "the national revolution"—the appeal to men of substance, the importance given to administration, the parades of ex-servicemen, the display of anti-Semitism—answered to many people's inclinations. In short, without ceasing to imagine that North Africa might one day "do something," people were settling down to wait and see. No spontaneous movement in the interior was to be counted on. As for seizing power there by an action coming from outside, obviously I could not think of it.

Coloured Africa presented quite other possibilities. In the first days of Free France the demonstrations which occurred at Dakar, Saint-Louis, Ouagadougou, Abidjan, Konakry, Lomé, Duala, Brazzaville, and Tananarive, and the messages which reached me from those places, showed that for these new territories where the spirit of enterprise was dominant the continuation of the war appeared self-evident. No doubt the attitude of resignation finally adopted by Noguès, the unfavourable impression produced by the Oran affair, and the activity of Boisson (at first Governor-General of Equatorial Africa and then High Commissioner at Dakar) who dissipated in ambiguity the enthusiasm of those under his rule, had diminished the seething of the Africans. Still, the fire was smouldering in most of our colonies.

It was chiefly in the block of our Equatorial territories that prospects were opening. In the Cameroons especially, the movement of opposition to the armistice extended to all classes. The population, both French and native, of this active and lively country was indignant at the capitulation. Indeed, no doubt was felt there that the victory of Hitler would bring back the German domination suffered before the First World War. General emotion was caused when tracts were passed round in which some of the former German colonists, who had retired not long before to the Spanish island of Fernando Po, announced their imminent return to positions and plantations. A committee of action had set itself up under M. Mauclère, the director of public works, and had given me its adherence. It was true that the Governor-General, Brunot, bewildered by the turn of events, was refusing

to take sides. But it was possible to suppose that a resolute intervention from outside would bring the solution.

In the Chad conditions seemed better still. The Governor, Félix
Eboué, had reacted immediately in favour of resistance. This man
of intelligence and heart, this coloured man so ardently French,
this humanist philosopher, revolted with his whole being against
the submission of France and the triumph of Nazi racial intoler-
ance. From the moment of my first call, Eboué, in agreement
with Laurentie, his secretary-general, had made his decision in
principle. The French elements and the population inclined to the
same side. For many, after all, the promptings of courage were
also those of reason. The soldiers, who were at their posts, in
contact with Italian Libya, kept the war spirit intact and longed
for the reinforcements which de Gaulle might bring them. The
French civil servants and traders, like the African chieftains,
thought anxiously of what would become of the economic life of
the Chad if its normal market, British Nigeria, were suddenly
closed to it. Informed of this situation by Eboué himself, I telegraphed him on July 16. He sent me in reply a detailed report,
announcing his intention to join us publicly, explaining the conditions governing the defence and the life of the territory which
France had entrusted to him to guard, and finally asking what I
was in a position to do to make it possible for him to carry out
his responsibilities under the Cross of Lorraine.

In the Congo the situation appeared more obscure. Boisson,
the Governor-General, had resided at Brazzaville up to the middle
of July. Then, having installed himself at Dakar but reserving a
right of supervision over the whole Equatorial block, he had left
there as his successor General Husson, an estimable soldier but
prisoner of a mistaken notion of discipline. Husson, in spite of
the grief into which the disaster had plunged him, would certainly
not free himself from obedience to Vichy. In Ubangi, where many
elements were opting for resistance, the issue depended solely on
the attitude of the Congo. On the other hand, in the Gabon, an
old and conventional colony traditionally inclined to regard itself

as distinct from the other territories of the group, certain circles maintained an enigmatic reserve.

Reviewing the situation of Coloured French Africa, I resolved to attempt first of all, and with the shortest possible delay, to rally the Equatorial block. I felt sure that the operation would not require a real engagement of forces, except probably in the Gabon. Next, if this first undertaking was a success, I would venture on action in West Africa. But that was an undertaking I could not think of starting on except with prolonged effort and considerable resources.

The first problem was to go for Fort-Lamy, Duala, and Brazzaville. The whole thing would have to be done at one blow and without loosening grip. For Vichy, having control of the ships, aircraft, and troops at Dakar, and being able, at need, to call on the forces in Morocco and even on the fleet at Toulon, had all the resources required for intervening rapidly. Admiral Platon had indeed been sent by Pétain and Darlan to the Gabon and the Cameroons on a tour of inspection, and had influenced certain military and civilian elements in Vichy's favour. I therefore hurried things on. Lord Lloyd, the British Minister for Colonies, to whom I outlined my plan, understood very well its importance, especially in regard to the security of the British possessions— Nigeria, the Gold Coast, Sierra Leone, and Gambia. He gave his governors the instructions I desired, and, when the day came, placed an airplane at my disposal to transport my team of "missionaries" from London to Lagos.

These were Pleven, Parant, and Hettier de Boislambert. They would be required to settle with Eboué, the Governor, the conditions under which the Chad was to join us, and to carry out, with the help of Mauclère and his committee, the *coup d'état* in Duala. Just as they were leaving I was able to add to the team a fourth, whose efficiency the future was to show. This was Captain de Hauteclocque. He had just arrived from France through Spain, with his head bandaged, having been wounded in Champagne, and pretty tired. He came to report to me, and when I

saw what sort of a man I was dealing with I settled his destination at once. It should be the Equator. He had just time to
assemble his kit, and under the name of Commandant Leclerc
flew off with the others.

But while hoisting the Cross of Lorraine over the Chad and
the Cameroons it would also be necessary to rally to us the three
colonies of the Lower Congo, Ubangi, and Gabon, and this would
mean, essentially, seizing Brazzaville, the capital of Equatorial
Africa, the seat and symbol of authority. This was the task I assigned to Colonel de Larminat. That brilliant and keen officer
was then in Cairo. At the end of June, as chief of staff of the
French Army of the Middle East, he had attempted, without success, to persuade his chief, General Mittelhauser, to continue the
struggle, and then had himself organized the departure for Palestine of those elements who did not accept the armistice. But Mittelhauser had succeeded in making them turn back—helped, indeed, by General Wavell, the British commander-in-chief in the
Middle East, who was afraid that this exodus might, all in all,
bring him more troubles than advantages. Only a few fractions
had persevered and reached the British zone. Larminat had been
arrested but had escaped. After making his way to Jibuti, he
there seconded General Legentilhomme in his vain efforts to keep
the French Somali Coast in the war, and then retired to Egypt.

There the order to proceed to London reached him. But on
his way he received the further order to proceed to Léopoldville.
In the Belgian Congo he met with discreet but determined support
from the Governor-General, Ryckmans, with sympathy from public opinion, and, lastly, with active support from the French citizens established in that territory, who were morally grouped together under Dr. Staub. According to my instructions, Larminat
was to prepare—from one bank of the Congo to the other—his
establishment in Brazzaville and to coordinate action over the
whole Equatorial block.

When all was ready, Larminat, Pleven, Leclerc, and Boislambert, together with Commandant d'Ornano, who had come from

the Chad by devious ways, met at Lagos. Sir Bernard Bourdillon, the Governor-General of Nigeria, gave the Free French his active and intelligent support on this occasion, as he was always to do. It was agreed that the Chad should join us to begin with. Next day the Duala business would be carried out. The day after that, that of Brazzaville.

On August 26, at Fort-Lamy, Eboué, the Governor, and Colonel Marchand, who commanded the troops in the territory, solemnly proclaimed that the Chad was joining General de Gaulle. Pleven had arrived the day before by air, to ratify the event in my name. I announced it myself in a broadcast from London and held up the Chad as an example to the Empire.

On the 27th Leclerc and Boislambert succeeded brilliantly with the *coup de main* in the Cameroons, as planned. And yet they had set out with minute resources. I had at first hoped to obtain for them a military detachment, which would make things easier. We had discovered in a camp in England a thousand coloured sharpshooters, who had been sent from the Ivory Coast during the Battle of France to reinforce certain Colonial units, and, having arrived too late, were stationed in England, awaiting repatriation. I had agreed with the British that the detachment should go to Accra, where Commandant Parant was to take command of it. It was legitimate to suppose that the return of these coloured troops to Africa would not alarm Vichy. As it turned out, they were landed on the Gold Coast. But they looked so fine that the British officers could not refrain from incorporating them in their own troops. Leclerc and Boislambert, therefore, had at their disposal only a handful of soldiers and a few colonists who were refugees from Duala. Even so, just as they were leaving Victoria, they received from General Giffard, the British commander-in-chief, who had suddenly begun to fear the consequences of the operation, an order forbidding them to carry it out. In full agreement with me—I had telegraphed them that they must act on their own—they disregarded it and, thanks to the understanding of the British at Victoria, left in native canoes for Duala.

The small band arrived there in the course of the night. A certain number of Gaullists, who had hastened to the house of Dr. Mauze at the first signal, received it as arranged. Leclerc, having become, as by enchantment, colonel and governor, simply occupied the Palais du Gouvernement. Next day, escorted by two companies of the Duala garrison, he arrived by train at Yaunde, where the authorities were. The "transmission" of powers took place there painlessly.

At Brazzaville the business was equally well managed. On August 28, at the appointed time, Commandant Delange proceeded to the Palais du Gouvernement at the head of his battalion and invited the Governor-General, Husson, to yield. He did so without resistance, though not without protest. The garrison, civil servants, colonists, and natives, whose opinion had for the most part been settled in advance under the influence of Médecin-Général Sicé, the Intendant Souques, Colonel of Artillery Serres, and Air Lieutenant-Colonel Carretier, accepted the fact with joy. General de Larminat crossed the Congo and immediately took over, in my name, the functions of High Commissioner of French Equatorial Africa, with civil and military powers. The same boat which had brought him returned to Léopoldville with General Husson on board.

As for Ubangi, de Saint-Mart, the Governor, who was only waiting for that, telegraphed his adhesion as soon as he was notified of what had happened at Brazzaville. However, the commander of the troops and certain military elements shut themselves up in their barracks and threatened to fire on the town. But Larminat at once came to Bangui by airplane and brought these honestly misled men back to their duty. A few officers were nonetheless segregated and sent at their own request to West Africa.

And so the greater part of the Equatorial Africa-Cameroons block was attached to Free France without a drop of blood having been shed. Only the Gabon remained detached from the whole. And yet this colony also nearly joined us. At Libreville on August 29 the Governor, Masson, when advised by Larminat of the

change of authority, had replied by telegraphing his adhesion. At
the same time he publicly proclaimed that the territory was joining
us and notified the commander of the troops.

But at Dakar the Vichy authorities had reacted quickly. Under
orders from them, the naval commander at Libreville, who had
a sloop, a submarine, and several small craft, opposed the Governor and announced the arrival of a squadron. M. Masson then
changed his attitude and declared that the decision of the Gabon
to join Free France had been the result of a misunderstanding. A
naval flying-boat, coming and going between Libreville and Dakar,
deported to West Africa those men of note who had "compromised" themselves and brought to the Gabon officials devoted to
Vichy. The situation had been reversed. A hostile enclave, difficult for us to reduce because it gave on the sea, was thus created
within the block of the Equatorial territories. To take advantage
of it, Vichy sent to Libreville Air Force General Têtu, with the
title of Governor-General of Equatorial Africa and with instructions to re-establish authority all over it. At the same time several
Glenn Martin bombers landed on the airdrome, and General Têtu
put it about that they were only the advance guard of what would
soon follow.

Yet on the whole the result was favourable. I drew from it
the hope that the second part of the plan for rallying Coloured
Africa would likewise succeed.

To tell the truth, this new phase bid fair to be much more
arduous. In West Africa the established authority was strongly
centralized and, what was more, closely linked with that of North
Africa. The military resources there were still considerable. The
fortress of Dakar, well armed, equipped with modern works and
batteries, supported by several squadrons of aircraft and serving
as the base for a naval squadron, including in particular some
submarines and the powerful *Richelieu,* whose officers' one dream
had been vengeance since the British torpedoes had damaged the
ship, constituted a redoubtable defensive and offensive entity.
Finally, Governor-General Boisson was a man of energy, whose

ambition—greater than his discernment—had made him choose
to play on the Vichy side. He proved it as soon as he reached
Dakar in the middle of July, by imprisoning Louveau, the admin-
istrator-in-chief of the Upper Volta, who had proclaimed the adherence of that territory to Free France.

With our resources as they were, therefore, I could not think
of tackling the place direct. Besides, I considered it essential to
avoid a large-scale collision. Not that—alas—I indulged in illusions about the possibility of achieving the liberation of the country without blood ever being shed between Frenchmen. But at
such a moment and on that particular ground, for us to engage
in a big battle would, whatever its outcome, have gravely diminished our chances. The course of the Dakar affair cannot be
understood if it is not realized that that was the conviction which
dominated my mind.

My initial plan therefore ruled out direct attack. The idea was
to land at a great distance from the fortress a resolute column,
which would proceed towards the objective, rallying, as it went,
the territories through which it passed and the elements which it
encountered. One might hope that in this way the forces of Free
France, growing by contagion, would reach Dakar by land. Konakry was the place where I thought of landing the troops. From
there one would have the use of a continuous railway and road
for the march on the capital of West Africa. But, to prevent the
Dakar naval squadron from annihilating the expedition, it was
necessary for this to be covered from the sea. I was bound to
ask the British fleet for this cover.

I had confided what I had in mind to Mr. Churchill in the
last days of July. He gave me no positive answer straightaway,
but sometime afterwards invited me to come and see him. I found
him, on August 6, as usual, in that large room in Downing Street
which is used, by tradition, both as the Prime Minister's office
and as the place where the government meets. On the enormous
table which fills the room he had had some maps laid out, before
which he paced up and down, talking with animation.

"We must," he said to me, "together gain control of Dakar. For you it is capital. For if the business goes well, it means that large French forces are brought back into the war. It is very important for us. For to be able to use Dakar as a base would make a great many things easier in the hard Battle of the Atlantic. And so, having conferred with the Admiralty and the Chiefs of Staff, I am in a position to tell you that we are ready to assist in the expedition. We mean to assign to it a considerable naval force. But we would not be able to leave this force on the coast of Africa for long. The necessity of bringing it back to help in covering England, as well as in our operations in the Mediterranean, demands that we should do things very quickly. That is why we do not agree with your proposal for landing at Konakry and proceeding slowly across the bush—which would oblige us to keep our ships in the neighbourhood for months. I have something else to propose to you."

Then Mr. Churchill, colouring his eloquence with the most picturesque tints, set to work to paint for me the following picture: "Dakar wakes up one morning, sad and uncertain. But behold, by the light of the rising sun, its inhabitants perceive the sea, to a great distance, covered with ships. An immense fleet! A hundred war or transport vessels! These approach slowly, addressing messages of friendship by radio to the town, to the navy, to the garrison. Some of them are flying the Tricolour. The others are sailing under the British, Dutch, Polish, or Belgian colours. From this Allied force there breaks away an inoffensive small ship bearing the white flag of parley. It enters the port and disembarks the envoys of General de Gaulle. These are brought to the Governor. Their job is to convince him that if he lets you land the Allied fleet retires, and that nothing remains but to settle, between him and you, the terms of his cooperation. On the contrary, if he wants a fight, he has every chance of being crushed."

And Mr. Churchill, brimming over with conviction, described and mimed, one by one, the scenes of the future, as they spurted up from his desire and his imagination.

"During this conversation between the Governor and your representatives, Free French and British aircraft are flying peacefully over the town, dropping friendly leaflets. The military and the civilians, among whom your agents are at work, are discussing passionately among themselves the advantages offered by an arrangement with you and the drawbacks presented, on the contrary, by a large-scale battle fought against those who, after all, are the allies of France. The Governor feels that, if he resists, the ground will give way under his feet. You will see that he will go on with the talks till they reach a satisfactory conclusion. Perhaps meanwhile he will wish, 'for honour's sake,' to fire a few shots. But he will not go further. And that evening he will dine with you and drink to the final victory."

Stripping Mr. Churchill's idea of the seductive ornaments added to it by his eloquence, I recognized, on reflection, that it was based on certain solid data. Since the British could not divert important naval forces to the Equator for long, a direct operation was the only means to be envisaged for making myself master of Dakar. This, short of taking on the character of a full-dress attack, was bound to involve some mixture of persuasion and intimidation. At the same time I judged it probable that the British Admiralty would be led, one day or another, with or without the Free French, to settle the question of Dakar, where the existence of a great Atlantic base and the presence of the *Richelieu* could not fail to arouse in it both desire and uneasiness.

I concluded that, if we were present, there would be some chance of the operation's becoming an adherence, though perhaps a forced one, to Free France. If, on the contrary, we abstained, the English would want, sooner or later, to operate on their own account. In this case the place would resist vigorously, using the fortress guns and the artillery of the *Richelieu,* while the Glenn Martin bombers, the Curtiss fighters, the submarines—very dangerous for ships which were not, at that time, provided with any means of detection—would hold any transport armada at their mercy. And even if Dakar, crushed by shellfire, were finally forced to surrender with its ruins and its wrecks to the British, there would be reason to fear that the operation would end to the detriment of French sovereignty.

After a short delay I returned to Mr. Churchill to tell him that I accepted his suggestion. I worked out the plan of action with Admiral Sir John Cunningham who was to command the British squadron, and whom I was to find, during this painful affair, sometimes troublesome to work with, but an excellent sailor and a man of feeling. At the same time I organized the resources—very meagre they were!—which we French would be able to engage in the enterprise. They consisted of three sloops—the *Savorgnan de Brazza,* the *Commandant Duboc,* and the *Commandant Dominé*—and two armed trawlers—the *Vaillant* and the *Viking.* There were also—on board two Dutch liners, the *Pennland* and *Westerland,* since we had none, at the time, that were French—a battalion of the Foreign Legion, a company of recruits, a company of marines, the personnel of a tank company, that of an artillery battery, and finally some embryo services: in all, a couple of thousand men. There were, in addition, the pilots of two air squadrons. There were, lastly, four French cargo boats—the *Anadyr, Casamance, Fort-Lamy,* and *Nevada*—carrying the heavy matériel: tanks, guns, Lysander, Hurricane, and Blenheim aircraft in cases, vehicles of various kinds, and some victuals.

As for the British, their squadron was not destined to include all the ships of which Mr. Churchill had spoken at first. It was finally composed of two old-fashioned battleships—the *Barham* and the *Resolution*—four cruisers, the aircraft carrier *Ark Royal,* some destroyers, and a tanker. In addition, three transports would bring, in case of need, two battalions of marines under the command of Brigadier Irwin, with apparatus for landing. On the other hand, a Polish brigade, which at first was to have taken part in the affair, had been dropped. It looked as if the General Staff, less convinced than the Prime Minister of the importance, or else of the chances, of the enterprise, had whittled down the resources envisaged at the start.

A few days before we set sail a bitter discussion was raised by the British about what, in case of success, I intended to do with a very important stock of gold which was at Bamako. This was bullion deposited there by the Bank of France on its own account and for the Belgian and Polish national banks. The reserves and deposits of the Bank of France had in fact, at the moment of the German invasion, been in part evacuated to Senegal, while another portion had been placed in safety in the vaults of the Federal Reserve Bank, and the balance was on its way to Martinique. Through blockade, across frontiers, between guard posts, the Bamako gold was being watched attentively by the Intelligence services of the various belligerents.

The Belgians and the Poles desired, very legitimately, that their share should be given to them, and I gave M. Spaak and M. Zaleski the appropriate assurances. But the British, who of course laid no claim to the ownership of any of it, intended nonetheless to use this gold as a means of paying directly for their purchases in America, alleging that they were doing so in the interests of the coalition. At this period, in fact, the United States was selling nothing to anybody that was not paid for in cash. In spite of the insistence of Spears, and even of his threat that I might see the British give up the expedition which had been agreed on, I rejected this claim. In the end it was conceded, as I had suggested from the first, that the French gold at Bamako should be used to cover only that part of the purchases in America which England would be obliged to make on behalf of Fighting France.

Before we embarked, the news of the adherence of the Chad, the Cameroons, the Congo, and Ubangi had come, just in time to enliven our hopes. Even should we not succeed in laying hold of Dakar, at least we counted on organizing in the centre of Africa, thanks to the reinforcements we were bringing, a base for action and sovereignty for belligerent France.

The expedition left Liverpool on August 31. I myself, with part of the French units and a small staff, was on board the *Westerland,* which flew the French flag beside the Dutch, and

whose commander (Captain Plagaay), officers, and crew were to
prove, like those of the *Pennland,* models of friendly devotion.
Spears accompanied me, delegated by Churchill as liaison officer,
diplomat, and informant. In England I left our forces in course
of formation under the orders of Muselier, an embryo administration under the direction of Antoine, and in the person of Dewavrin
an element of liaison and direct information. In addition, General
Catroux was expected shortly from Indochina; and in a letter
which was to be handed to him as soon as he arrived I explained
to him my projects as a whole and what I had in mind for him. I
reckoned that, in spite of my absence, and provided it did not
last long, the reserves of wisdom accumulated by my companions
would prevent internal quarrels and intrigues from outside from
shaking the still very fragile edifice too profoundly! Nonetheless,
on the deck of the *Westerland,* after leaving the port in the middle
of an air-raid warning with my small troop and my tiny ships, I
felt crushed, as it were, by the dimensions of duty. Out in the
open, in black night, on the swell of the ocean, a poor foreign
ship, with no guns, with all lights extinguished, was carrying the
fortunes of France.

Our first destination was Freetown. According to the plan, we
were to regroup there and collect the latest information. We did
not arrive there till September 17, having sailed at the slow speed
of our cargo boats and made a wide detour into the Atlantic to
avoid German aircraft and submarines. During the voyage radio-
grams received from London had given us a piece of news about
the Vichy forces which might well lead to everything's being reconsidered. On September 11 three large modern cruisers—the
Georges Leygues, Gloire, and *Montcalm*—and three light cruisers
—the *Audacieux, Fantasque,* and *Malin,* having started from
Toulon, had passed the Strait of Gibraltar without being stopped
by the British fleet. They had then touched at Casablanca and
reached Dakar. But hardly had we anchored at Freetown when a
new and grave piece of information completed our perplexity. The
squadron, reinforced at Dakar by the cruiser *Primauguet,* had

just weighed anchor and was heading southwards at full speed. A British destroyer, detached to watch it, was keeping in touch with it at a distance.

I could have no doubt that this powerful naval force was bound for Equatorial Africa, where the port of Libreville was open to it, and where it would find it easy to retake Pointe-Noire and Duala. If such a thunderclap did not suffice to reverse the situation in the Congo and Cameroons, these magnificent ships could easily cover the transport and landing of forces of repression from Dakar, Konakry, or Abidjan. The hypothesis was confirmed, indeed, almost immediately, when the cargo vessel *Poitiers,* coming from Dakar and bound for Libreville, having been hailed by the British, was scuttled by her captain. It was clear that Vichy was starting a large-scale operation to re-establish itself in the territories which had rallied to Free France, and that the dispatch of seven cruisers towards the Equator was conceivable only with the full consent, if not at the orders, of the Germans. Admiral Cunningham fell in with my view that the Vichy squadron must be stopped at once.

We agreed that the intruders should receive the injunction to return, obviously not to Dakar, but to Casablanca. Failing this, the British squadron would open hostilities. We felt sure, indeed, that the threat would suffice to make these errant ships change course. For if the speed of the British ships—which was notably inferior—did not permit them to intercept those of Vichy, their power—which was double—would assure them the advantage over the others, as soon as these were obliged to moor in some Equatorial roadstead undefended by any battery. The aggressor would then have either to give in or to accept battle in unfavourable conditions. The chances that the leader of the expedition would let himself be reduced to such a choice were slight.

In fact, the British cruisers which made contact with Admiral Bourragué, the commander of the untimely squadron, had no difficulty in making it change course when its leader learned, to his complete surprise, of the presence of a Franco-British fleet in the region. But the Vichy ships, defying all pursuit, made straight for Dakar. Only the cruisers *Gloire* and *Primauguet,* which were slowed down by engine trouble, and with which Commander Thierry d'Argenlieu, now on board the destroyer *Ingerfield,* got into direct touch on my behalf, submitted to the terms and went to Casablanca, after declining my offer of repairs at Freetown.

In this way Free French Africa escaped a very great danger. This fact alone justified over and over again the expedition we had fitted out. At the same time the behaviour of the squadron that had come from Toulon, setting course for the Equator as if we were not there, then renouncing its mission the moment it perceived that we were, suggested that Vichy was not sure of our real destination. But after congratulating ourselves on having made our adversaries' plan come to nothing, we had to admit that our own was gravely compromised. In fact the Dakar authorities were henceforward on their guard and had received a most valuable reinforcement of ships. We learned almost at once, through our Intelligence agents, that to serve the shore batteries naval gunners had been substituted for the men of the Colonial artillery, who were considered less reliable. In short, our chances of occupying Dakar appeared, from now on, very small.

In London, Mr. Churchill and the Admiralty reckoned that, in these circumstances, it was better to do nothing. They had telegraphed this to us as early as September 16, proposing that the fleet should simply escort our vessels as far as Duala and then move on elsewhere. I must say that to give up in this way seemed to me the worst possible solution. In fact, if we left everything at Dakar as it was, all Vichy would have to do, to resume its attempt on Equatorial Africa, would be to wait for the British ships to return northwards, as they soon would. With the sea open to them, Bourragué's cruisers would swoop once more towards the Equator. In this way the combatants under the Cross of Lorraine, including General de Gaulle, would sooner or later be mewed up in these distant territories and, even if they did not succumb to it, absorbed by a sterile struggle carried on against other Frenchmen in the bush and forest. No prospect for them, in these conditions, of fighting Germans or Italians. I had no doubt that those were the intentions of the enemy, of which the Vichy puppets inevitably made themselves the instruments, conscious or not. It seemed to me that, at the stage things had now reached, we ought in spite of everything to try to enter Dakar.

Besides, I must admit that the adherences already obtained in Africa had filled me with a secret hope, confirmed by the good news which, since we had left London, had come from elsewhere. On September 2 the French Settlement of Oceania, under the provisional government of M. Ahne, M. Lagarde, and M. Martin, had joined Free France. On September 9, Governor Bonvin proclaimed that the French Settlements in India were taking up position at our side. On September 14, at Saint Pierre and Miquelon, the Ex-Servicemen's General Assembly sent me its formal adhesion, after which the British government urged the Canadian government to support their movement. On September 20, Governor Sautot, having himself brought New Caledonia over on July 18, had gone by my orders to Nouméa. There the "de Gaulle Committee," presided over by Michel Verges, had made itself master of the situation with the enthusiastic support of the population, and this allowed Sautot to take over the government. Lastly, I had seen Bourragué's squadron turn about at the first summons. Who could be sure that we would not find at Dakar that mood of consent to which the most formal instructions adjust themselves? In any case, we must try.

Admiral Cunningham reacted in the same sense. We telegraphed to London, arguing, most pressingly, that we should be allowed to attempt the operation. Mr. Churchill, as he told me later, was surprised and enchanted by this insistence. He willingly consented and the action was decided on.

Before starting, however, I was subjected to an energetic intervention by Cunningham, who claimed to take me and my modest forces under his orders, and offered me, in compensation, hospitality on his flagship, the *Barham*. I declined, of course, both the demand and the invitation. That evening there were some stormy passages on board the *Westerland,* where the interview took place. In the course of the night the admiral wrote me a note full of cordiality, giving up his claims. We weighed anchor on September 21. At dawn on the 23rd, in the midst of a very thick fog, we were before Dakar.

The fog was bound to compromise our enterprise seriously. In particular, the moral effect which, according to Churchill, the sight of our fleet was to produce upon the garrison and population would not come into play at all, since not a thing was to be seen. But postponement was obviously impossible. The plan as prepared was therefore put into execution. At six o'clock I addressed the Navy, the troops, and the inhabitants by radio, announcing our presence and our friendly intentions. Immediately afterwards two small Lucioles, French touring aircraft, unarmed, took off from the deck of the *Ark Royal;* they were to land at the airdrome of Ouakam and there set down three officers—Gaillet, Scamaroni, and Soufflet—with a fraternization mission. In fact, I quickly learned that the Lucioles landed without difficulty and that the signal "Success!" was displayed on the airfield.

Suddenly ack-ack fire was heard at various points. Some of the guns of the *Richelieu* and of the fortress were firing at the Free French and British machines which were beginning to fly over the town, dropping friendly leaflets. And yet, sinister though this cannonade might be, it seemed to me to have something hesitant about it. I therefore gave the order to the two pinnaces with the spokesmen on board to enter the port, while the Free French sloops, together with the *Westerland* and *Pennland,* approached in the mist as far as the entrance to the roads.

There was at first no reaction. Commander d'Argenlieu, Major Gotscho, Captains Becourt-Foch and Perrin, and Sub-Lieutenant Porges ordered their boats to be moored, landed on the quay, and asked for the port commander. When he presented himself, d'Argenlieu told him that he was the bearer of a letter from General de Gaulle for the Governor-General, which letter he was instructed to deliver personally. But the port commander, with unconcealed embarrassment, informed the spokesmen that he had orders to have them arrested. At the same time he showed his intention of calling the guard. Seeing which, my envoys returned to the pinnaces. As these drew away, some machine-guns opened fire on them. D'Argenlieu and Perrin were brought on board the *Westerland,* seriously wounded.

Thereupon the Dakar batteries began aiming at the British and French ships an intermittent fire, which for several hours remained without reply. The *Richelieu,* having been moved within the harbour by tugs so that its guns might be put to better use, began firing in its turn. Towards eleven, the cruiser *Cumberland* having been badly hit, Admiral Cunningham addressed this message by radio to the fortress: "I am not firing on you. Why are you firing on me?" The reply was: "Retire to twenty miles' distance!" Upon which the British in their turn sent some broadsides. Meanwhile time was passing without a sign, on one side or the other, of real fighting ardour. No Vichy airplane had taken off up to midday.

From these indications as a whole I did not draw the impression that the place was determined on a desperate resistance. Perhaps the Navy, garrison, and Governor were waiting for something to happen which could serve them as pretext for conciliation? Towards noon Admiral Cunningham sent me a signal to let me know that this was his feeling too. Certainly there could be no thought of getting the squadron into the harbour. But would it not be possible to land the Free French somewhere near the fortress, which they would then attempt to approach by land? This alternative had been considered in advance. The small port of Rufisque, outside the range of most of the works, seemed suitable for the operation, provided always that this did not meet with determined resistance. In fact, while our sloops could reach Rufisque, our transports could not, because of their draught. The troops would therefore have to be disembarked by lighter, which would deprive them of their heavy weapons and make complete peace essential. However, having received from Cunningham the assurance that he was covering us from the sea, I set all in motion towards Rufisque.

Towards three p.m., still in the fog, we arrived at the spot. The *Commandant Duboc,* with a section of marines on board, entered the port and sent some sailors ashore in a boat to prepare the berthing. On shore a crowd of natives was already running up to welcome the patrol when the Vichy troops in position in the neighbourhood opened fire on our sloop, killing and wounding several men. A few moments earlier two Glenn Martin bombers had flown over our little force at a low altitude, as if to show it that they held it at their mercy—which was indeed the case. Lastly, Admiral Cunningham signalled that the cruisers *Georges Leygues* and *Montcalm* had left Dakar roads and were in the mist at a mile's distance from us, and that the British ships, occupied elsewhere, could not protect us from them. Decidedly the affair was a failure! Not only was the landing not possible, but, what was more, a few shots fired by the Vichy cruisers would be enough to send the whole Free French expedition to the bottom. I decided to make for the open again, which was done without further incident.

We passed the night on tenterhooks. Next morning the British fleet, having received from Mr. Churchill a telegram inviting it to push on actively with the affair, addressed an ultimatum to the Dakar authorities. They replied that they would not surrender the place. From then on the day was spent by the British in exchanging a rather lively cannonade with the shore batteries and ships in the roads, firing blind in the mist, which was thicker than ever. By the end of the afternoon it seemed evident that no decisive result could be obtained.

As evening fell, the *Barham* came up quite close to the *Westerland,* and Admiral Cunningham asked me to come and see him, to discuss the situation. On board the British battleship the atmosphere was gloomy and strained. They were sorry, certainly, not to have succeeded. But the dominant feeling was that of surprise. The British, being practical people, could not understand how and why the authorities, naval forces, and troops at Dakar expended such energy upon fighting against their compatriots and against their allies, at a time when France lay beneath the invader's boot. As for me, I had from that moment given up being astonished at it. What had just happened showed me, once for all, that the Vichy rulers would never fail to misuse, against the interests of France, the courage and discipline of those who were in subjection to them.

Admiral Cunningham summed up the situation. "Given," he declared, "the attitude of the place and of the squadron supporting it, I do not think bombardment can result in a solution." General Irwin, who commanded the landing units, added "that he was ready to send his troops ashore to assault the fortifications, but that it must be clearly understood that this would mean a great risk for each boat and each soldier." Both of them asked me what would become of the Free France "movement" if an end were put to the expedition.

"Up to now," I said, "we have not made an all-out attack on Dakar. The attempt to enter the harbour peaceably has failed. Bombardment will decide nothing. Lastly, a landing against opposition and an assault on the fortifications would lead to a pitched battle, which, for my part, I desire to avoid and of which, as you yourselves indicate, the issue would be very doubtful. We must therefore, for the moment, give up the idea of taking Dakar. I propose to Admiral Cunningham that he should announce that he is stopping the bombardment at the request of General de Gaulle. But the blockade must be maintained in order not to allow the ships now at Dakar their liberty of action. Next, we shall have to prepare a fresh attempt by marching against the place by land, after disembarking at undefended or lightly defended points, for instance, at Saint-Louis. In any case, and whatever happens, Free France will continue."

The British admiral and general fell in with my view as regards the immediate future. In the falling night I left the *Barham* on board a launch which danced on the waves, while the officers and crew, drawn up along the hand rails, sadly gave me a ceremonial send-off.

But during the night two facts were to make Admiral Cunningham go back on what we had agreed. First, a fresh telegram from Mr. Churchill expressly called upon him to pursue the enterprise. In it the Prime Minister showed astonishment and irritation at the idea of the affair coming to nothing—the more so because, already, political circles in London and, above all, in Washington, were beginning to grow agitated, impressed by the Vichy and Berlin radios. At the same time the fog was lifting, and this at once seemed to give the bombardment another chance. The fighting therefore began again at dawn—this time without my having been consulted—with an exchange of gunfire between the fortress and the British. But toward evening the battleship *Resolution,* torpedoed by a submarine and in danger of sinking, had to be taken in tow. Several other British ships had been badly hit. Four aircraft from the *Ark Royal* had been shot down. On the other side, the *Richelieu* and various other ships had taken some hard punishment. The destroyer *Audacieux,* the submarines *Persée* and *Ajax* had been sunk; a British destroyer had managed to pick up the latter's crew. But the stalwarts of the fortress still went on firing. Admiral Cunningham decided to cut the losses. I could but agree. We headed for Freetown.

The days which followed were cruel for me. I went through what a man must feel when an earthquake shakes his house brutally and he receives on his head the rain of tiles falling from the roof.

In London a tempest of anger, in Washington a hurricane of sarcasms, were let loose against me. For the American press and many English newspapers it was immediately a matter of course that the failure of the attempt was due to de Gaulle. "It was he," the echoes repeated, "who thought of this absurd adventure, misled the British by imaginative reports on the situation at Dakar, and insisted, out of Don Quixotism, that the place be attacked when the reinforcements sent by Darlan made any success impossible. Besides, the cruisers from Toulon had come only as the result of the incessant indiscretions of the Free French, which had put Vichy on the alert. Once for all, it was clear that no reliance could be placed on people incapable of keeping a secret." Soon Mr. Churchill too was roughly handled for having, so it was said, so easily let himself be carried away. Spears, with a long face, kept bringing me telegraphed reports from his correspondents, suggesting it as probable that de Gaulle in despair, abandoned by his partisans, dropped by the British into the bargain, would renounce all activity, while the British government would take up afresh with Catroux or Muselier, on a much more modest scale, the recruitment of French auxiliaries.

As for the Vichy propaganda, it triumphed without restraint. The Dakar communiqués gave the impression that the thing had been a great naval victory. Innumerable messages of congratulation, addressed to Governor-General Boisson and to the heroic fighters of Dakar, were published and commented upon by the newspapers of both zones and by the so-called "French" radios. And I, in my narrow cabin, in a harbour crushed by the heat, was completing my education in what the reactions of fear could be, both among adversaries taking revenge for having felt it and among allies suddenly alarmed by a setback.

However, it very soon became clear to me that, in spite of their reverse, the Free French remained unshakeable. Among the men of our expedition—and I visited them as soon as we had anchored—not one wished to leave me. On the contrary, all of them had been hardened by the hostile attitude of Vichy. So it happened that, when an airplane from Dakar came and flew over our ships at anchor, a furious fusillade greeted it from every vessel, which would certainly not have been the case a week before. Soon warm telegrams came from Larminat and Leclerc, to tell me that, for them and those about them, resolute loyalty was less than ever in doubt. From London no defection was reported to me, in spite of the tumult of bitter reproaches now breaking

against our people. This confidence on the part of all those who
were linked to me gave me powerful comfort. It meant that the
foundations of Free France were indeed solid. Come! We must
go on! Spears, his serenity somewhat restored, quoted to me Victor Hugo: *"Le lendemain, Aymeri prit la ville."*

It must be said that in London, if ill will was active, the government on the contrary had managed to avoid it. Mr. Churchill,
although he himself was being strongly harassed, did not disown
me any more than I disowned him. On September 28, in the
House of Commons, he gave an account of what had happened,
with all the objectivity that could be expected, and declared that
"all that had happened had only strengthened His Majesty's Government in the confidence it extended to General de Gaulle." It
is true that at that moment the Prime Minister knew, although he
was unwilling to say, how the squadron from Toulon had managed
to pass the Strait of Gibraltar. He told me himself when, two
months later, I returned to England.

A telegram sent from Tangier by Captain Luizet, a French
Intelligence officer who had secretly joined Free France, had
given London and Gibraltar news of the movement of the Vichy
ships. But this message had arrived at a time when the bombing
of Whitehall by German aircraft kept the personnel in the cellars
for hours on end and so led to a prolonged dislocation of the
work of the staff. The deciphering of the message took place too
late for the First Sea Lord to be able to warn the fleet at Gibraltar
in time. Much worse! When the Vichy naval attaché at Madrid
had himself, in all innocence(?), warned the British attaché, and
the admiral in command at Gibraltar had thus been given the
alarm from two different sources, nothing had been done to stop
the dangerous ships.

The Prime Minister's public attitude towards the Gaullists
helped greatly to allay the agitation in Parliament and in the newspapers. But in spite of everything the Dakar affair was destined
to leave in the hearts of the British a wound which remained raw,
and in the minds of the Americans the idea that, if one day they

themselves had to land on territory held by Vichy, the action should be carried out without Free French and without British.

In the short run, in any case, our British allies were determined not to renew the attempt. Admiral Cunningham told me expressly that we must give up the idea of resuming the affair in any way whatever. All he himself could do now was to escort me as far as the Cameroons. We headed for Duala. On October 8, when the French vessels were about to enter the estuary of the Wouri, the British saluted them and made for the open.

The enthusiasm, however, which broke over the town as soon as the *Commandant Duboc,* on board which I had made the passage, entered the port of Duala, was extreme. Leclerc was there, waiting for me. After the review of the troops I went to the Palais du Gouvernement, while the elements that had come from England were disembarking. The civil servants, French colonists, and native leaders, with whom I made contact, were swimming in a full tide of patriotic optimism. They forgot, however, no part of their special problems, of which the chief one was that of keeping up the export of the territory's produce and bringing in what was required to live on and was not to be found there. But, above anxieties and differences of opinion, the moral unity of the Free French, whether they had joined up in London or rallied to the cause in Africa, was instantly apparent.

This identity of nature between all those who took their stand beneath the Cross of Lorraine was to be, from then on, a sort of permanent factor of the enterprise. No matter where, and no matter what happened, one could now know in advance, to all practical purposes, for certain, what the Gaullists would think and how they would behave. For example, the enthusiastic emotion I had just encountered: I was to find it again, always, in all circumstances, as soon as the crowd was present. I must say that for me its result was to be a perpetual bondage. The fact of embodying for my comrades the fate of our cause, for the French multitude the symbol of its hope, and for foreigners the image of a France indomitable in the midst of her trials, was to dictate my bearing and to impose upon my personality an attitude I could never again change. For me this meant, without respite, a stubborn self-supervision as well as an extremely heavy yoke.

For the moment, what counted was to keep the whole of French Equatoria going and mobilize it to take part in the Battle of Africa. My intention was to establish, on the borders of the Chad and Libya, a Sahara theatre of operations, ready for the day when the evolution of events would permit a French column to seize the Fezzan and debouch from there upon the Mediterranean. But because of the desert and the unparalleled difficulties of communication and supply, it would not be feasible to devote to this more than limited and specialized effectives. I therefore wished at the same time to send to the Middle East an expeditionary force, which would join up with the British there. The distant objective for everyone was French North Africa. However, it was first necessary to liquidate the hostile enclave in the Gabon. At Duala, on October 12, I gave the necessary orders.

While this painful operation was preparing, I left the Cameroons to visit the other territories. I went first to the Chad, after a short stop at Yaunde. The career of the leader of Free France and of those accompanying him nearly came to an end in the course of this journey. For the Potez 540 which was taking us to Fort-Lamy had engine trouble, and it was a marvel that it managed to land, without too much damage, in the middle of a swamp.

In the Chad I found an atmosphere of tense excitement. Everyone had the feeling that the beam of history had just lighted upon this land of merit and suffering. Nothing, certainly, could be achieved there except by supreme effort, so heavy were the servitudes imposed by the distances, by isolation, by the climate, by lack of means. But, to make up for this, that heroic mood in which great actions germinate was already abroad there.

Eboué received me at Fort-Lamy. I could feel he was giving me his loyalty and confidence, once for all. At the same time I noted that he was sufficiently large-minded to embrace the vast plans with which I wanted to associate him. He formulated views full of common sense, yet never raised objections to the risk or effort involved. And yet, for the Governor, nothing less was involved than undertaking an immense job of creating communications, to make the Chad capable of receiving from Brazzaville, Duala, and Lagos, and then of transporting right to the frontiers of Italian Libya, all the matériel and all the supplies which the Free French forces would require for carrying on active warfare. The territory would have, by its own means, to blaze or to maintain four thousand miles of tracks. In addition, it would be necessary to develop the country's economy, in order to feed the fighting men and workers and to export produce to cover the costs. The task was all the more difficult because a good many of the colonists and civil servants were going to be mobilized.

With Colonel Marchand, commander of the troops in the Chad, I flew as far as Faya and the desert posts. There I found troops who were resolute but terribly short of supplies. There were, by way of mobile elements, only some camel units and a few motorized sections. And so, when I told the officers that I was counting on them to seize the Fezzan one day and reach the Mediterranean, I could see stupor plain upon their faces. Some German and Italian raids, which they would have plenty of trouble in repulsing if they came, seemed to them much more probable than the far-reaching French offensive whose prospect I outlined. Not one of them, indeed, showed any hesitation about continuing the war, and already the Cross of Lorraine had been hoisted everywhere.

Meanwhile, farther to the west, in the territories of the Niger and the Sahara oases, the comrades of these officers, of the same stuff as they were, and posted, like them, on the borders of Libya, but not having above them, anywhere in the hierarchy, a single leader who dared break the spell, were holding themselves ready to fire on anyone who should claim to lead them to fight against the enemies of France! Among all the moral torments inflicted on me by the culpable errors of Vichy, none made me suffer more than the spectacle of this stupid sterility.

To set against this, I was to find, on my return to Fort-Lamy, a signal encouragement. It was brought to me by General Catroux. When he had arrived in London, after my departure for Africa, certain experts on ulterior motives imagined that the British would try to make themselves an alternative trump card out of this full general accustomed to big posts, while certain sticklers for etiquette wondered if he himself would consent to serve under a mere brigadier. He had seen Churchill more than once, and there was much chatter about these interviews, in the course of which it did seem that the Prime Minister had in fact suggested to him that he should take my place—doubtless not with the idea that he should try his hand at it, but with the classic objective of dividing in order to rule. A few days before Dakar, Churchill had all of a sudden telegraphed me that he was sending Catroux to Cairo to work upon the Levant, where there was hope of some favourable opportunity arising. I had reacted sharply, not against the idea, which certainly did not seem to me a bad one, but because the initiative required my approval first. Churchill had then given a satisfactory explanation, on the ground of urgency.

And now here was Catroux, arrived from Cairo. At the meal I raised my glass in honour of this great leader, for whom I had always had feelings of deferential friendship. He answered, in a very noble and very simple way, that he placed himself under my direction. Eboué and all those present recognized, not without emotion, that, for Catroux, de Gaulle was from now on outside the ladder of rank and invested with a duty that knew no hierarchy. No one made any mistake about the weight of the example thus given. When, after determining with him his mission, I parted from General Catroux near the aircraft which was taking him back to Cairo, I felt he was going away greater than he had come.

At Brazzaville, where I arrived on October 24, things were looked at, on the whole, with as much conviction as at Duala and at Fort-Lamy. But they were looked at level-headedly. That was natural for the "capital." The administration, the general staff, the services, business circles, and the missions measured the difficulties which the Equatorial territories—the poorest in the whole Empire—would have to surmount in order to live for years cut off from the mother country and to support the war effort. Some of their products—oil, rubber, timber, cotton, coffee, hides—would indeed be easy to sell to the British and the Americans. But as there were no factories, nor indeed any minerals apart from a little gold, the total exports would not make it possible to balance all that would have to be bought abroad.

To second Larminat in this field, I appointed Pleven secretary-general. When he had got the machine running, he would go to London and Washington to settle the question of exchange and payments. His capabilities, supported by Larminat's authority, turned out to be most efficient. Administrators, planters, traders, and carriers, seeing that there was a great deal to do and that it was worth while, started upon that period of intense activity which was to transform the life of the Equatorial territories profoundly, even in the midst of war. The journey I made at the end of October to Ubangi, where I was welcomed by Governor de Saint-Mart, and then the one which took me to Pointe-Noire, administered by Daguin, made it possible for me to give, on the spot, the impulse for which all were waiting.

Finally, on October 27, I went to Léopoldville, where the authorities, army, and people, as well as the French residents in the Belgian Congo, gave me a most moving reception. Governor-General Ryckmans, who, like me, was cut off from his native land but wanted his country to take part in the war, was in sympathy with Free France. And indeed Free France was a protection to the Belgian Congo against the spirit of capitulation which had come near to investing it from the north. Ryckmans was destined, all the way through, to maintain close relations with his French neighbour on the other bank of the Congo. It may be noted that it was the same with their British colleagues—Bourdillon in Nigeria and Huddleston in the Sudan. Instead of the rivalries and intrigues which had formerly set the neighbours at loggerheads, there was established between Lagos, Duala, Brazzaville, Léopoldville, and Khartoum a personal solidarity among governors, which was a weighty factor in favour of the war effort and the maintenance of order in Africa.

Meanwhile all had been made ready for ending the Gabon affair. Before my arrival at Duala, Larminat had already taken the first steps. Under the orders of Commandant Parant a few troops, raised in the Congo, had advanced as far as Lambaréné, on the Ogowe. But they had been stopped by resistance from the Vichy forces. At the same time a small column, sent from the Cameroons and commanded by Captain Dio, was besieging the post at Mitzic. At Lambaréné and Mitzic, Gaullists and Vichyists were in contact and were exchanging a few shots—and plenty of arguments. Sometimes a Glenn Martin from Libreville would come and drop a few bombs and a great many leaflets on our men. A Bloch 200 from Brazzaville would do the same, next day, to the other side. These dragging, aching hostilities offered no solution.

As soon as I had arrived I had decided to have Libreville captured directly and had determined the plan of action. There could unfortunately be no doubt that serious resistance would be put up to our forces. General Têtu, whose headquarters were at Libreville, had at his disposal four battalions, some artillery, four up-to-date bombers, the sloop *Bougainville,* and the submarine *Poncelet.* He had mobilized a certain number of colonists. Besides, the instructions he had received obliged him to fight. To prevent him from receiving reinforcements, I had to ask Mr. Churchill if he would agree to warn Vichy that, if this happened, the British fleet would oppose it. Following my telegram, Admiral Cunningham had come to see me at Duala. We had settled that his ships should not take part directly in the Libreville operation, but that they should station themselves out at sea to prevent the Dakar people from again sending their cruisers, if this should by any chance be their intention. For our part, we looked forward to the affair with heavy hearts, and I announced, in the midst of a general assent, that there would be no mentions in dispatches for anyone on this painful occasion.

On October 27 the post at Mitzic was taken. On November 5

the garrison at Lambaréné laid down its arms. Immediately afterwards the vessels carrying the column bound for Libreville left Duala. Leclerc was in over-all command; Koenig was at the head of the land troops—a Legion battalion and a mixed Colonial battalion of Senegalese and colonists from the Cameroons. The landing took place at La Mondah Point during the night of November 8, and some rather violent fighting broke out on the 9th in the approaches to the town. On the same day, under the direction of Commandant de Marmier, several of the Lysander aircraft, which we had brought in cases from England and which had been hastily assembled at Duala, flew over the field and dropped some bombs. It was then that d'Argenlieu, on board the *Savorgnan de Brazza,* followed by the *Commandant Dominé,* entered the roadstead where the *Bougainville* lay. In spite of messages of friendship, repeated many times by our men, the *Bougainville* opened fire. The *Brazza*'s reply set her on fire. During this time the Legion was breaking the resistance of the Vichy elements on the irdrome. D'Argenlieu having conveyed to General Têtu a essage urging him to stop fighting, the surrender was concluded. Koenig occupied Libreville. Parant, whom I had appointed Governor of the Gabon, took up his post. There were, alas, some twenty killed.

On the previous day the submarine *Poncelet,* having left Port-Gentil and met with one of Cunningham's cruisers out at sea, had fired a torpedo at it. Attacked with depth-charges, the submarine surfaced, and while the crew was being picked up by the British, her commander, Capitaine de Corvette de Saussine, scuttled his ship and went down bravely with her.

There remained the task of occupying Port-Gentil. This was done on November 12, after long discussions but without resistance from the fortress. The only victim of this final operation was Governor Masson, who, after having brought the Gabon over to us in August, had later gone back on it. The poor man, in despair at this error and its consequences, had taken up his quarters on board the *Brazza* after the capture of Libreville, and had landed at Libreville in order to ask the administrator and garrison not to

open, on their side, a fratricidal struggle. This action had helped
to prevent calamity. But M. Masson, worn out by the nervous torments he had just been through, hanged himself in his cabin in
the course of the return journey.

I went to Libreville on November 15, and to Port-Gentil on the
16th. The dominant feeling among the population was satisfaction
at being out of an absurd situation. At the hospital I visited the
wounded of both sides, who were being cared for side by side.
Then I had the cadres of the Vichy units presented to me. A few
elements joined Free France. The majority, who had been made
by their chief to give their word that they would "remain faithful
to the Marshal," preferred internment. They waited for the re-
entry of North Africa into the war before going back to service,
and from that moment, like many others, did their duty valiantly.
General Têtu was entrusted to the hospitality of the Fathers of the
Holy Spirit and later transferred to the hospital at Brazzaville.
From there, in 1943, he too left for Algiers.

The Dakar, Vichy, and Paris radio indulged in furious insults,
after having, a few weeks earlier, exaggerated its cries of triumph.
I was accused of having bombarded, burned, and pillaged Libreville, and even of having shot the notables, beginning with the
bishop, Monseigneur Tardy. It seemed to me that, by inventing
such lies, the Vichy people wished to cover some infamous action.
At the time of the Dakar affair they had arrested the three Free
French airmen who had been landed unarmed on the Ouakam airfield, and then Boislambert, Bissagnet, and Kaouza, whom I had
sent secretly into the town, together with Dr. Brunel, to spread the
good word there. Of these "missionaries" Brunel alone had managed, after the fighting, to get out again into British Gambia. The
accusations hurled by Dakar made me think that perhaps the
people there were proposing to take vengeance on the prisoners.
The more so since when, with the necessary discretion, I had a
proposal conveyed to Boisson for exchanging these against Têtu
and his officers, the Dakar broadcasts had immediately made my
move public, with many outrageous and provocative statements.

I then warned the Vichy High Commissioner that I had enough of his friends in my hands to answer for the life of those Free French whom he held in prison. The tone of the opposing radio was lowered instantly.

For the rest, various signs revealed the disorder into which the Vichy rulers were being thrown by what had happened. The sort of base optimism into which the armistice had plunged them had rapidly dispersed. Contrary to what they had announced in order to justify their capitulation, the enemy had not finished off England. At the same time the rallying of several colonies to de Gaulle, then the Dakar affair, and finally that of the Gabon, made it evident that even if Free France did know how to use the radio, it was something quite other than "a handful of mercenaries grouped round a microphone." All at once people in France were beginning to catch sight of a refuge that was truly French, while the Germans were compelled to include in their calculations the growing difficulties which would be caused for them by resistance. Deep in Africa, I could perceive the jolts which this state of affairs was already giving to the behaviour of the Vichy people.

On the morrow of Dakar violence had been their first reaction. Aircraft from Morocco had dropped bombs on Gibraltar. But immediately afterwards an attempt was made at appeasement. Telegrams from Mr. Churchill and Mr. Eden informed me of conversations which had been opened, on October 1 at Madrid, by M. de la Baume, the ambassador, with his British colleague, Sir Samuel Hoare. The object was to persuade the British to let cargoes coming from Africa pass over to France, on the strength of a guarantee that the Germans would not get hold of them. But in addition M. de la Baume declared, on behalf of Baudouin, that "if the enemy seized these supplies, the government would be transferred to North Africa, and France would resume the war by the side of the United Kingdom."

While noting the disarray revealed by such declarations, I had put the British on their guard. It was hard to see how people who had themselves placed the state under the enemy's law, and

condemned those who wanted to fight, could suddenly become
the champions of resistance because the invader helped himself
to a few supplies over and above those which he was taking every
day. In fact, in spite of the efforts made by the London government to encourage Vichy in the good intentions of which it was
making a display, in spite of the personal messages addressed to
the Marshal by the King of England and by the President of the
United States, in spite of the contacts made by the British with
Weygand, now installed at Algiers, and with Noguès, still in
Morocco, all illusion was soon to disappear under German pressure. On October 24 there took place the meeting between Pétain
and Hitler at Montoire. Vichy's collaboration with the enemy was
officially proclaimed. Finally, in the first days of November,
Vichy put an end to the Madrid negotiations.

From now on, obvious reasons ordained that I should deny to
the Vichy rulers, once for all, the right of legitimacy, should constitute myself the trustee of the interests of France, and should
exercise in the liberated territories the attributes of a government.
The republic was the source of this provisional power, as also the
objective assigned to it, and I proclaimed my obedience and responsibility towards the sovereign people, engaging myself solemnly to
render account to it as soon as it should have regained its liberty.
I determined this national and international position on October
27 at Brazzaville, in French territory, by means of a manifesto,
two ordinances, and an "organic declaration," which, taken together, were to constitute the charter of my activity. I believe I
never departed from it until the day, five years later, when I remitted to the representatives of the nation the powers I had assumed. At the same time I set up the Defence Council of the
Empire, designed to aid me with its advice, and made members
of it, at the start, Catroux, Muselier, Cassin, Larminat, Sicé,
Sautot, d'Argenlieu, and Leclerc. Finally, I laid down, once for all,
in a note addressed to the British government on November 5,
the attitude which Free France was adopting, and which she invited her allies to take, towards both the Vichy government and

its proconsuls, such as Weygand and Noguès, of whom some obstinate optimists were trying to believe that they would one day move over into action against the enemy.

On the whole, if our African enterprise had not attained all the results at which it had aimed, at least the basis of our war effort was solidly established, from the Sahara to the Congo, and from the Atlantic to the basin of the Nile. In the first days of November I set up the command which was to direct activities there. Eboué, appointed Governor-General of French Equatorial Africa, had his headquarters at Brazzaville, with Marchand as commander of the troops. Lapie, summoned from London, became governor of the Chad, and Administrator Cournarie, governor of the Cameroons, where he replaced Leclerc. The latter, in spite of the objections dictated to him by his desire to go on with what he had begun at Duala, was sent to the Chad to command the Sahara operations, in which he was destined to make the harsh and disturbing acquaintance of glory. Finally, Larminat, as High Commissioner with civil and military powers, was to guide the whole.

Before leaving for London, I laid down with him the plan of action for the next months. Our aim was, on the one hand, to set in motion the first motorized and air raids against Murzuk and Kufra. We aimed, at the same time, at sending to Eritrea a mixed brigade and also a bomber group, which would take part in the fighting against the Italians. This latter expedition would be the beginning of French intervention in the Middle East campaign. But it was also necessary to recruit, officer, and arm the elements which would go, as and when ready, to reinforce these advance guards, both in the Sahara and on the Nile. It is impossible to imagine what efforts were to be required, in the immensities of central Africa, under the Equatorial climate, for the mobilization, training, equipping, and transport of the forces which we meant to create and send into battle at colossal distances. It is impossible to measure, either, what prodigies of activity all concerned were to bring to this.

On November 17 I left Free French Africa for England, via Lagos, Freetown, Bathurst, and Gibraltar. As, under the autumnal rain, the aircraft skimmed the ocean, I pictured the incredible detours by which, in this strange war, the Fighting French must henceforth pass to get at the Germans and the Italians. I sized up the obstacles which barred their way, and the greatest of which, alas, were raised against them by other Frenchmen. But at the same time I encouraged myself with the thought of the ardour which the national cause was exciting among those who were free to serve it. I thought of all there was to exalt them in an adventure whose dimensions were those of the earth. Harsh though the realities might be, perhaps I would be able to master them, since it was possible for me, in the phrase of Chateaubriand, "to lead the French there by dreams."

CHAPTER 5

LONDON

I**N LONDON**, as that winter began, fog had settled about men's minds. I found the British strained and depressed. Certainly they thought with pride of how they had just won the air battle, and how the risks of invasion had greatly diminished. But, as they cleared their ruins, other terrors were swooping down upon them and upon their poor allies.

The submarine war was raging. With growing anxiety the British people saw German submarines, aircraft, and raiders effecting the destruction of the ships on which depended the course of the war and even the level of rations. For the Ministers and services the one question was "shipping." Tonnage became an obsession, a tyrant dominating everything. The life and glory of England were staked, every day, upon the sea.

In the East active operations were beginning. But the Mediterranean, owing to Vichy's defection, was becoming inaccessible to the slow British convoys. The troops and matériel which London was sending to Egypt had to go round the Cape, following a sea route as long as halfway round the world. What was sent there from India, Australia, and New Zealand likewise arrived only after interminable journeys. At the same time the mass of raw materials, armaments, and foodstuffs—sixty million tons in 1941—

which Great Britain imported for her industry, her armies, and her population, could no longer come to her except from a long way away, from America, Africa, or Asia. It required a colossal tonnage, sailing in zigzags over immense distances, ending up in the narrow neck of the Mersey or the Clyde, and demanding considerable escort forces.

British uneasiness was all the heavier because on no side did happy prospects lie open. Contrary to what many English people had hoped, the bombing of their towns and the victory of the Royal Air Force did not decide America to come in. Certainly public opinion in the United States was hostile to Hitler and Mussolini. At the same time President Roosevelt, as soon as he was re-elected on November 5, strengthened his efforts to draw America towards intervention both by his diplomatic activity and by his public statements. But the official attitude of Washington was still neutrality, which, indeed, was imposed by law. Therefore, during this dark winter, the British had to pay for their purchases in the United States in gold and foreign exchange. Even such indirect help as the President's casuistic cleverness contrived to give them was the object of lofty reprobation in Congress and in the press. In short, the British, at the rate of payments imposed by their needs, saw the moment approaching when, for want of cash, they would no longer be able to receive what they required for fighting.

As regards Soviet Russia, no crack was to be seen in the bargain which bound her to the Reich. On the contrary, after two journeys by Molotov to Berlin, a Germano-Russian trade agreement, concluded in January, was to give powerful aid in the feeding of Germany. Meanwhile, in October 1940, Japan had signed the Tripartite Pact, and so proclaimed her menacing solidarity with Berlin and Rome. At the same time the unity of Europe under German hegemony seemed to be becoming a reality. Hungary, Rumania, and Slovakia adhered to the Axis in November. Franco met Hitler at San Sebastián and Mussolini at Bordighera. Lastly Vichy, unable to maintain even the fiction of independence granted to it by the armistice, was entering into effective collaboration with the invader.

With the horizon dark outside, very heavy burdens were pressing on the British people within. Mobilization was sending off twenty million men and women to the armies, to the factories, to the land, to the public services, and to passive defence. For everybody consumption was rigorously limited, and the courts dealt with the black market, as and when it arose, with extreme severity. At the same time the enemy's air activity, though no longer aiming at decisive results, continued, nevertheless, harassing the ports, industry, and railways, all of a sudden crushing Coventry, the City of London, Portsmouth, Southampton, Liverpool, Glasgow, Swansea, Hull, and so on, keeping the inhabitants on the alert night after night, wearing out the first-aid and defence teams, compelling a multitude of poor people to leave their beds and go down to the cellars, to the shelters and even, in London, to the underground stations. At the close of 1940 the British, besieged in their island, felt that they were at the darkest part of the tunnel.

The many trials that the British were undergoing did not make our relations with them easier. Concentrated as they were on their own preoccupations, our special problems seemed to them ill timed. Indeed, the fact that we complicated things for them made them all the more inclined to absorb us. It would, in fact, have been more convenient for them, from the administrative as well as from the political point of view, to treat the Free French as elements incorporated in the British forces and services rather than as allies full of ambitions and claims. Besides, during this period when the war was settling down and at the same time destitution threatened, there was not much inclination, in governing circles in London, to innovate, or even to settle, anything. In the midst of pressing but insoluble problems, general staffs and ministries fell naturally into the system of pending questions and disputed functions, while the government, under fire from critics in Parliament and in the press, had difficulty in taking agreed decisions. "You know," Churchill said to me one day, "what a coalition is. Well! the British Cabinet is one."

Nevertheless Free France had need of everything, and urgently. After the improvisations of the summer and autumn, and before the fresh enterprises which I had decided to set going in the spring, we had to obtain from the British what was indispensable, while maintaining towards them a resolute independence. From this state of things frequent friction was bound to arise.

All the more so since the shifting and composite character of our organization justified, to some extent, the circumspection of the British, while at the same time it made their attempts to interfere easier. It was inevitable that Free France, recruited in haste, man by man, should not at once find its internal balance. In London each of its categories—Army, Navy, Air, finance, foreign affairs, colonial administration, information, liaison with France— formed itself and functioned with a strong desire to do well. But experience and cohesion were cruelly lacking. Besides, the adventurous spirit of certain individuals, or simply their inability to conform to the rules and obligations of a public service, gave the machine some rude jolts. So it was that, during my absence in Africa, André Labarthe had left our administration, and Admiral Muselier had fallen foul of the other services. Some bitter personal conflicts and office tragi-comedies had arisen at Carlton Gardens, scandalizing our volunteers and worrying our allies.

As soon as I got back at the end of November I set to work to put people and things in their place. But hardly had I begun this reorganization when I found myself up against a startling error on the part of the British government, itself led astray by Intelligence.

The siege fever with which England was then afflicted made information and security organizations increase and multiply there. Intelligence, which to the British is a passion quite as much as a service, had obviously not failed to thrust out antennae in the direction of Free France. On this it employed both some who were well inspired and others who were not. In short, at the instigation of certain undesirable agents, the British Cabinet was suddenly to inflict on Free France a wound which just missed being disastrous.

In the evening of January 1, when I was in Shropshire with my family, Mr. Eden sent me a request to come and see him urgently at the Foreign Office, where he had recently replaced Lord Halifax, now appointed ambassador to the United States. I went straight there the next morning. As he welcomed me, Eden showed signs of being deeply disturbed. "Something lamentable," he said, "has occurred. We have just had proof that Admiral Muselier is secretly in touch with Vichy, that he attempted to transmit the plan of the Dakar expedition to Darlan at the moment when it was being prepared, and that he is planning to hand over the *Surcouf* to him. The Prime Minister, as soon as he heard, gave the order to arrest the admiral. It has been approved by the Cabinet. Muselier is therefore in prison. We have no illusions about the impression this dreadful affair will make on your people and on ours. But it was impossible for us not to act without delay."

Mr. Eden then showed me the documents on which the accusation was based. They consisted of typed notes on the headed paper and with the stamp of the French Consulate in London— still occupied by a Vichy official—and apparently signed by General Rozoy, formerly head of the Air Mission and recently repatriated. These notes gave an account of information allegedly supplied by Admiral Muselier to Rozoy. The latter was supposed to have passed them on to a South American legation in London, from which they were to reach Vichy. But on their way, according to Mr. Eden, certain clever Intelligence agents had intercepted the documents. "After a thorough inquiry," he added, "the British authorities were, alas, forced to believe in their authenticity."

Though dumbfounded at first, I immediately had the feeling that "it was laid on a bit too thick" and that it could only be a huge mistake arising from some machination. I said so clearly to Mr. Eden and told him that I was going to see for myself what there might be in it, and that, meanwhile, I would treat this extraordinary affair with every possible reserve.

Not however, at first, going so far as to imagine that the affair could have been staged under cover of a British service, I attributed it to Vichy. Might not some of Vichy's henchmen have manufactured and left in England this delayed-action bomb? After forty-eight hours of inquiry and reflection, I went to see the British Minister and said to him, "The documents are ultra-suspect, both in their context and in their supposed source. In any case, they are not proofs. Nothing justifies the shocking arrest of a French vice-admiral. Besides, he has not been heard. I myself am not allowed to see him. All this is unjustifiable. For the moment, at the very least, Admiral Muselier must come out of prison and be treated honourably until this dark business has been cleared up."

Mr. Eden, though disconcerted, did not consent to give me satisfaction, alleging the seriousness of the inquiry made by the British services. In a letter, then in a memorandum, I confirmed my protest. I visited Admiral Sir Dudley Pound, First Sea Lord, and invoking the admirals' international code, invited him to intervene in this dishonouring quarrel picked with one of his peers. As the result of the steps I had taken, the attitude of the British authorities showed some hesitation. And so I obtained permission, as I had demanded, to go and see Muselier at Scotland Yard, not in a cell but in an office, without guard and without witnesses, in order to demonstrate to everyone, and to tell him, that I rejected the imputation of which he was victim. Finally, certain indications having led me to think that two individuals, who had been incorporated in our own "security service" during my time in Africa, in French uniform but at the insistence of the British, had had something to do with the affair, I sent for them and became convinced, at the sight of their terror, that this was decidedly an "Intelligence business."

To General Spears, summoned by me on January 8, I formally confirmed my certainty. I told him that I gave the British government twenty-four hours in which to set the admiral free and make reparation to him, failing which all relations between Free France and Great Britain would be broken off, whatever might be the consequences. That same day Spears came, crest-fallen, to tell me that the error was admitted, that the documents were simply fakes, that the men to blame had confessed, and that Muselier was coming out of prison. Next day the Attorney-General visited me, told me that legal proceedings were being instituted against the authors of the machination, in particular several British officers, and asked me to appoint someone to follow the inquiry and the trial in the name of Free France, which I did.

That afternoon at Downing Street, Mr. Churchill and Mr. Eden, obviously much put out, expressed to me the British government's excuses and its promise to repair, in regard to Muselier, the insult which had been done him. I must say this promise was kept. Indeed, the reciprocal change of attitude on the part of the British and of the admiral was so complete that it soon turned out to be excessive, as will be seen later.

I will not conceal that this lamentable incident, by setting in relief the element of precariousness always present in our situation relative to our allies, did not fail to influence my philosophy on the question of what should definitely be our relations with the British state. However, the immediate consequences of the trouble were not all bad. For the British, no doubt desirous of making up for their error, showed themselves more disposed to discuss with us the matters awaiting settlement.

So it was that, on January 15, I signed with Mr. Eden a "jurisdiction" agreement concerning the Free French in British territory and especially our own courts, which would operate "in accordance with the national military legislation." At the same time we were able to open negotiations with the British Treasury with a view to a financial, economic, and monetary agreement. Cassin, Pleven, and Denis were charged, on our side, with these negotiations, which achieved their aim on March 19.

The problems which we had to resolve in this connection were such that it was essential for us to break out from the practice of hand-to-mouth expedients. How were we to make viable, as a whole, the territories which had rallied to us in Africa and Oceania—we who had not yet a bank, or a currency, or transport or communications, or commercial representation recognized abroad? How keep up the forces of Free France, dispersed as they were all over the world? How balance the value of the matériel and services supplied to us by our allies and that of those we supplied to them? Under the terms of the agreement it was understood that every payment, whatever its purpose, should be effected in London between the British government and General de Gaulle, and not arranged haphazard with the local French authorities. The rate of exchange adopted was 176 francs to the pound—that is to say, the same as that which was in force before the armistice concluded by Vichy.

Pursuing the same policy, we were led, a little later, to set up the Caisse Centrale de la France Libre. This bank was to disburse all payments—clearances, salaries, purchases, and so on— and to receive all payments—contributions from our territories, advances from the British Treasury, gifts from French people abroad. It became, at the same time, the only bank of issue for Free France, anywhere in the world. Thus, while their rallying to de Gaulle bound all our elements together morally, their administration also was now strongly centralized. Because there were in our midst no budgetary and economic fiefs, any more than there were political and military ones, and because at the same time England forbade all local intervention by financial means, unity was established over the whole, improvised and dispersed though it was to the last degree.

And yet, while consolidating our overseas base, it was of Metropolitan France that we were chiefly thinking. What to do there? How? With what? We had at our disposal no means of action in France and could not even see where to start on the problem, but this did not prevent us from being obsessed by vast schemes, in the hope that the country would support them massively. And so we had in mind nothing less than an organization which would enable us, at one and the same time, to give light to the Allied operations by means of our intelligence about the enemy, to rouse within the country resistance in all fields, to equip forces there which, at the right time, would take part in the battle for liberation at the enemy's rear, and, finally, to prepare the national regrouping which, after victory, would set the country going again. In addition we wanted this manifold contribution by Frenchmen to the common war effort to be made so as to benefit France, and not be divided up into services rendered directly to the Allies.

But clandestine action was a field entirely new to us all. No preparations had ever been made in France with a view to the situation into which the country had been hurled. We knew that the French Intelligence service was still active to some extent at Vichy. We were not unaware that the Army staff was trying to keep certain stocks of matériel out of the hands of the armistice commissions. We suspected that various military elements were trying to make arrangements on the assumption that hostilities might be resumed. But these fragmentary efforts were being carried on apart from us, on behalf of a regime whose *raison d'être* consisted precisely in not using them, and without the authorities' seeking or accepting the least contact with Free France. In short, there was nothing in Metropolitan France to which our action could attach itself. The service which was to operate on this special field of battle would have to be drawn out of the void.

There was not, certainly, any shortage of applicants round about me. By a sort of obscure foresight of nature's, it happened that in 1940 part of the adult generation was set, in advance, towards clandestine action. Between the two wars the young had shown a marked taste for stories of the Deuxième Bureau, secret service, detection, and even sabotage and conspiracy. Books, newspapers, the theatre, and the cinema had devoted themselves largely to the adventures of more or less imaginary heroes who were prodigal of shadowy exploits in the service of their country. This psychology was destined to make recruitment for special missions easier. But it involved, also, the risk of introducing into them romanticism,

irresponsibility, and sometimes fraud, and these would be the most
dangerous reefs. In no field were there to be more applications
for jobs, or more need for those in responsible positions to show
themselves sober as well as bold.

Luckily there were some good ones. Commandant Dewavrin,
known as Passy, was their chief. Passy had had no preparation
for this unprecedented mission. But in my eyes this was preferable. As soon as he was appointed, indeed, a sort of cold passion
for his job took hold of him, which was destined to sustain him
along a dark road where he was to be mixed up with both the
best there was and the worst. All through that daily drama, the
action within France, Passy, seconded by Manuel and later by
Vallon, Wybot, Pierre Bloch, and others, kept the ship afloat
in face of a succession of alarms, intrigues, and disappointments.
He himself proved capable of resisting his disgust and guarding
against conceit, the familiar demons of this kind of activity. That
is why, whatever changes the Bureau Central de Renseignements
et d'Action (BCRA) had to undergo in the light of experience, I
kept Passy where he was, through thick and thin.

The most urgent thing was to install an embryo organization
within the national territory. The British, for their part, would
have liked to see us simply send over agents with instructions to
gather, in isolation, information about the enemy with reference
to defined objectives. Such was the method used for espionage.
But we meant to do better. Since the action in France would be
carried on in the midst of a population which would, we thought,
be teeming with well-wishers, we meant to set up networks. By
binding together hand-picked elements and communicating with
us through centralized means, these would give the best return.
The first experiments were made by d'Estienne d'Orves and Duclos, who landed on the Channel coast; by Fourcault, who went
in through Spain; and by Robert and Monnier, who came from
Tunisia to Malta and were sent on into North Africa. Shortly
afterwards Rémy, in his turn, began that career of secret agent in
which he was to show a kind of genius.

Then began the struggle on this hitherto unknown battlefield. Month after month, or rather moon after moon, for many operations were dependent on the luminary of night, the BCRA set its work in motion: recruitment of fighters for the clandestine war; orders to be given to the missions; reports to be gone through; transport by trawler, submarine, aircraft; routes through Portugal and Spain; parachute landings; making contact with those ready to help in France; comings and goings for inspection and liaison; radio communications, couriers, and agreed signals; work with the Allied services which formulated the requests from their staffs, supplied the material, and made things easier or complicated them as the case might be. Later on, this action was to grow wider and to include the armed groups within the country and the resistance movements with their multiple activities. But we were not yet at that stage during this dark winter.

Meanwhile we had to work out a *modus vivendi* with the English, which would make it possible for the BCRA to operate and at the same time to remain national. That was indeed a tricky business. Certainly the British understood the advantages to be gained from the help given by the French from the Intelligence point of view—the only one which interested them at first. But direct contacts were what the British bodies concerned were chiefly seeking. A regular competition therefore started immediately, with us appealing to the moral and legal obligation of Frenchmen not to join a foreign service, and the British using the means at their disposal to try and gain for themselves agents, and then networks, of their own.

As soon as a Frenchman arrived in England, unless he was somebody well known, he was confined by Intelligence in the "Patriotic School" buildings and invited to join the British secret services. It was only after a whole series of remonstrances and requests that he was allowed to join us. If, however, he had yielded, he was kept away from us and we would never see him. Even in France the English used equivocation to recruit their auxiliaries. "De Gaulle and Great Britain are the same thing!"

was the line. As for the material means, for which we were almost entirely dependent on our allies, we sometimes obtained them only after obstinate bargaining. To what friction this behaviour led is obvious. It is true that, if the British often went near the limit, they never went beyond it. At the right moment they put the brake on and yielded, at least partially, to our firmness. Then would follow a period of useful collaboration—until suddenly fresh storms rumbled.

But what we were trying to do could be of some value, in this respect as in the others, only if French opinion was with us. On June 18, when I broadcast for the first time in my life, and imagined, with a certain dizziness, the women and men who were listening in, I realized what a part was going to be played in our enterprise by broadcast propaganda.

The British, among other merits, had that of immediately discerning, and of using in masterly fashion, the effect which a free radio was capable of producing upon imprisoned peoples. They had at once begun to organize their French propaganda. But in that as in everything else, although they sincerely desired to reinforce the national response aroused by de Gaulle and Free France, they also meant to profit from it while keeping the control in their own hands. As for us, we intended to speak only on our own account. For my part, it goes without saying that I never admitted any supervision, nor even any foreign advice, over what I had to say to France.

These different points of view shook down together into a practical compromise, according to which Free France had the use of the waves for five minutes twice every day. At the same time, and independently of us, the well-known team "Les Français parlent aux Français" worked under the direction of M. Jacques Duchesne, a Frenchman employed by the BBC. Several Free French, such as Jean Marin and Jean Oberlé, took part in it with my approval. It was, indeed, understood that the team would keep in close liaison with us, which was in fact for a long time the case. I must say that the talent and effectiveness of this group decided us to give it all the help we could. We did as much, indeed, for the review *France Libre,* which owed its existence to the initiative of M. Labarthe and M. Raymond Aron. We treated in the same way the Agence Française Indépendante and the newspaper *France,* run respectively by Maillaud (known as Bourdan) and by M. Comert, with the direct support of the British Ministry of Information but without their being in any way attached to us.

Things went on like this, with a few incidents, as long as the interests and policies of England and Free France remained parallel. Later there arose crises in which the propagandists of "Les Français parlent aux Français," the Agence Française Indépendante, and the newspaper *France* did not take up our quarrel. It is true that through the wireless station at Brazzaville we always had the means of making public what appeared to us useful. Our modest African radio had, in fact, functioned actively from the beginning, and I myself used it often. But we wanted to enlarge it and increase its coverage. The necessary apparatus was ordered in America. To get it we had not only to wait a long time and pay a great many dollars, but also to outwit a great deal of intrigue and forced bidding in the United States. It was not until the spring of 1943 that the small installation belonging to the heroic beginnings was relieved, on the Congo, by the big Fighting France station.

The importance we attached to our brief broadcasts from London will be understood. Every day the man who was to speak in our name entered the studio imbued by the sense of his responsibility. As is well known, it was Maurice Schumann who spoke most often; with what talent is also well known. About once a week I spoke myself, with the moving impression that I was accomplishing, for the millions who were listening to me in dread through frightful jamming, a sort of priestly duty. I based my broadcasts on very simple elements: the course of the war, which was demonstrating the error of the capitulation; the national pride, which, on contact with the enemy, was stirring men's souls profoundly; and lastly, the hope of victory and of a new greatness for "our lady France."

And yet, favourable though the effect produced might be, we were forced to recognize that, in both zones, opinion inclined to passivity. Certainly people listened in to "the London radio" with satisfaction, often even with fervour. The Montoire interview had been criticized severely. The students' demonstration in Paris, when they went on November 11 to the Arc de Triomphe in procession behind two rods—*deux gaules*—and were broken up by the Wehrmacht with rifle and machine-gun fire, sounded a moving and encouraging note. The temporary dismissal of Laval looked like an official impulse towards recovery. On January 1, as I had asked, a large part of the population, above all in the occupied zone, had stayed at home, emptying the streets and squares, for an hour—"the hour of hope." But no sign led one to suppose that French people in appreciable numbers were re- solved on action. The enemy, wherever he was, ran no risk in our country. As for Vichy, few were those who contested its authority. The Marshal himself remained very popular. A film, which had reached us, of his visits to the principal towns of the centre and of the south gave obvious proofs of this. At bottom, the great majority wanted to believe that Pétain was playing a deep game and that, when the day came, he would take up arms again. The general opinion was that he and I were secretly in agreement. In the last resort, propaganda had, as always, only slight value in itself. Everything depended on events.

For the moment, what mattered was the Battle of Africa. Free France was beginning to figure in it. As early as July 14 I had got into direct touch with General Wavell, British commander-in- chief, Middle East, to ask him to group the French elements in his zone into properly formed units and to send them as reinforce- ments to General Legentilhomme at Jibuti. Then, when it be- came clear that the French Somali Coast was submitting to the armistice, I obtained Wavell's agreement that the Marine Infantry Battalion, which had joined us in Cyprus in June and had been completed by some of the French in Egypt, should take part in the first offensive carried out by the English in Cyrenaica in the direction of Tobruk and Derna. In France and outside, many patriots had thrilled when they heard that, already on December 11, Commandant Folliot's brave battalion had distinguished itself in the battle of Sidi Barrâni. But the great effort, now, was to bring a division—alas, a light one—to the Red Sea from Equatorial Africa, and to arrange for it to take part, as such, in the operations.

It was in Eritrea and Ethiopia that the British command wished to bring force to bear, in the spring, so as to liquidate the army of the Duke of Aosta before starting anything else on the shores of the Mediterranean. Whatever the distances, I intended that a first French echelon should take part in the action. On December 11 and 18 I had given Larminat and Catroux the necessary instructions. They involved the Foreign Legion half-brigade, a Senegalese battalion from the Chad, a company of marines, a tank company, an artillery battery, and some rearward services, the whole to be under the orders of Colonel Monclar. Already a squadron of Spahis, brought from Syria in June 1940 by Commandant Jourdier, and a few airmen, some of whom had come from Riyaq with Captain Dodelier, the others from Tunisia with Lieutenants Cornez and de Maismont, were fighting side by side with the British. I had had arrangements made for transporting the Legion brigade to Port Sudan, with Wavell's agreement; the tanks and artillery were to follow, likewise by sea. As for the Chad battalion, it had left Khartoum quite simply by field tracks, using small local lorries. It was, indeed, destined to arrive without trouble, in spite of the ominous predictions of experienced Africans, and, as early as February 20, to be engaged near Kubkub under Commandant Garbay and to win a signal success. Later four other Senegalese battalions joined these leading elements and formed, with them, an appreciable battle unit. At the same time a French bombardment group, equipped with Blenheim machines which we had brought from England, was to be sent to Khartoum. Lastly, the gallant sloops *Savorgnan de Brazza* and *Commandant Duboc* were on their way to the Red Sea.

How much more important the French part in the battle of Abyssinia could have been if the French Somali Coast, with its garrison of ten thousand well-armed men and its port of Jibuti, railhead of the Addis Ababa railway, had become belligerent again! Therefore, while pressing on with the dispatch of troops towards Ethiopia, I wanted to try to bring this French colony over. Now at Jibuti, after some thought of refusing the armistice, they had submitted to Vichy's orders. But would perhaps the fact that, in that very region, a battle was being joined with the enemy, and that Frenchmen were arriving to take part in it, bring about a change of attitude? If so, Jibuti was the place where the troops of Free France should be landed, in order to combine them with the garrison there. From that moment a really important French force would be able to take the offensive, starting from there and joining its efforts with that of the British. If, on the contrary, the Somali Coast did not consent to rally, the Free French expedition would fight alone, side by side with the English.

In London our allies agreed to this programme. I instructed General Legentilhomme to try to bring his old troops at Jibuti into the fight, and in any case to command those that were being or would be sent to the Red Sea from Equatorial Africa. He left at once for Khartoum. To General Catroux and General Wavell I defined the conditions within which Legentilhomme and the forces under his orders were to act. At the same time I begged Mr. Churchill to make the best of the French initiative, of which at first he appeared to be fighting shy.

While we were trying to reinforce the action of the British forces in the Middle East, we were opening on the frontiers of the Chad and Libya a strictly French front—this, to tell the truth, with very feeble resources and over immense expanses. But we could depend only on ourselves there, and I regarded it as essential that it should be so.

Since his arrival in the Chad, Leclerc, under the orders of High

Commissioner Larminat, who gave him all he could, had been preparing with extreme activity the first operations ordered in the desert. In January, with Lieutenant-Colonel d'Ornano, who was killed in this affair, he thrust out a brilliant reconnaissance, in which a British patrol from the Nile had joined, as far as the Italian post at Murzuk. At the end of January, at the head of a carefully formed column supported by our aircraft, Leclerc hurled himself at the Kufra Oases, a thousand kilometres away from his bases. During several weeks of manœuvring and fighting, he attacked the Italians in their posts, repelled their mobile troops, and on March 1 made the enemy surrender.

At the same moment the rapid advance of the British in Libya seemed able to offer us still larger prospects. This is why, on February 17, I ordered General de Larminat to prepare for the conquest of the Fezzan. The later course of events in Libya was destined to prevent us from carrying this out at the time. But Leclerc and his Saharans were, from now on, keyed up towards this main objective. I had been led, meanwhile, to define the position of France in relation to that of the British concerning the future of Kufra and the Fezzan. We would remain at Kufra, although the Oases had formerly been attached to the Anglo-Egyptian Sudan. One day, when the Fezzan had been conquered by us, and provided that England recognized our right to stay there, we would be able to evacuate Kufra.

And yet whatever the British, and with them the Free French, might do, the strategic initiative still belonged to the enemy. The direction taken by the war depended on him. In default of being able to invade England, would he come flooding over North Africa through Suez and Gibraltar? Or would he wish to settle accounts with the Soviets? In any case there were signs that he was about to start one or other of these enterprises. Whatever might happen, the arrangements we had drawn up made it possible, we thought, for Free France to engage profitably what forces she had. But in addition, and in spite of the terrible weakness amid which we struggled, I was determined, in face of each of the problems which the new offensive by Germany and her allies would set the world, to speak in the name of France and to do so suitably.

In November 1940 Italy had attacked Greece. On March 1, 1941, the Reich forced Bulgaria to join the Axis. In the first days of April German troops were to enter Greece and Yugoslavia. By thus laying hands on the Balkans the enemy might equally well be aiming at debouching towards the Middle East and at denying the British any bridgehead in the rear of the Wehrmacht should it penetrate into Russia. Right at the start of the Italian offensive in Greece I had telegraphed to General Metaxas, Hellenic Prime Minister, that it might be known publicly on which side were the prayers and the loyalty of France. The reply from Metaxas showed that he had understood. Nevertheless I was unable to get the British to agree to the transport to Greece of a small detachment which I was anxious to send there as a token. It must be said that Wavell, absorbed by the operations in Libya and Eritrea, was not himself, at that time, sending any of his own forces to Greece.

At the beginning of February we had learned of the arrival in Syria of the German mission of von Hintag and Roser. The agitation which this mission was bound to stir up in the Arab countries might serve either to prepare for the eruption of the forces of the Axis or to create a diversion there which would be useful in case of an attack by those forces in the direction of Kiev and Odessa.

At the same time, in the Far East, the Japanese menace was becoming definite. Certainly it was impossible to make out whether we had to deal with a fixed determination by the Japanese to enter the war in the near future, or simply with pressure intended to tie up in Southeast Asia the largest possible proportion of British forces and American precautions while Germany and Italy deployed their strength either towards Moscow or across the Mediterranean. But in any case the Japanese wanted to make sure of the control of Indochina at once. In addition, if they should come in, New Caledonia, our archipelago in the Pacific, the French Settlements in India, and even Madagascar, would be threatened.

In Indochina, Japanese intervention had begun as soon as it was clear that France was losing the battle in Europe. In June 1940 General Catroux, the Governor-General, had considered himself forced to give satisfaction to the first Japanese demands. Before making up his mind to this, he had had the British and Americans sounded and had concluded that no help from outside could be expected. Thereupon Vichy had replaced Catroux by Decoux. As for me, not being in a position either to arouse in Indochina a movement capable of taking matters in hand, or to smash on the spot the Japanese intervention which such a movement would not have failed to provoke, or to decide the Allies to oppose Japanese encroachments there, I found myself forced to sit and wait till further notice. It is easy to guess with what feelings I had telegraphed, from Duala on October 8, to Inspector-General of Colonies Cazaux, Director of Finance at Saigon, in reply to a moving message in which he informed me of the sympathy of a large part of the population towards the Free French, but also of the impossibility of Indochina's acting as she desired. To me, steering a very small boat on the ocean of war, Indochina seemed like a great ship out of control, to which I could give no aid until I had slowly got together the means of rescue. As I saw her move away into the mist, I swore to myself that I would one day bring her in.

At the beginning of 1941 the Japanese were pressing Siam to take possession of both banks of the Mekong, and even of Cambodia and Laos. At the same time they were increasing their own demands, claiming for themselves, to begin with, a sort of economic control over Indochina, and then military occupation of the essential points. I was informed of the developments of this grave affair not only by the British and the Dutch in London, but also by the representatives Free France had at the principal centres of the world: Schompré, then Baron and Langlade, at Singapore; Garreau-Dombasle at Washington; Egal at Shanghai; Vignes at Tokyo; Brénac at Sydney; André Guibaut, then Béchamp at Chungking; Victor at New Delhi. It seemed to me that the various policies were, in point of fact, as unsure as they were complex, but that in any case no one would do anything to help Indochina to resist the Japanese. Free France obviously had not the means. Vichy, which had them but had handed them over to the Germans, was denied by these the chance of using them. The British, although they felt that the storm would one day reach Singapore, wanted only to gain time, and their representative at Bangkok showed himself above all desirous of keeping friendly relations with Siam, whatever might be the fate of the Mekong territories. As for the Americans, who were not ready either materially or morally to face conflict, they did not intend to intervene.

In these conditions what we could do, and what was done, consisted first of all in notifying everyone that Free France would hold as null and void any abandonment in Indochina to which Vichy might agree. It consisted also—without our friends going over to the policy and doctrine of Vichy—in not embarrassing by any internal movements the resistance which the local authorities might wish eventually to put up against the Japanese and Siamese. It consisted, again, in concerting our action in the Pacific with that of other threatened powers and trying—but in vain—to obtain a joint mediation by England, the United States, and Holland in favour of Indochina. It consisted, lastly, in organizing the defence of New Caledonia and Tahiti, in common with Australia and New Zealand.

In this last connection I saw the Australian Prime Minister, Mr. Menzies, when he passed through London in March, and settled the essential points with this man of great good sense. After which Governor Sautot negotiated and concluded in my name a detailed agreement with the Australians, all precautions being taken that there should be no encroachment on French sovereignty.

We soon heard that the Thailanders were attacking on the Mekong and that, after suffering some serious setbacks on land and sea, they were nonetheless gaining possession of the coveted territories, thanks to merciless pressure by the Japanese at Saigon

and at Vichy, under the name of "mediation." Later Japan herself
was to impose her control on Indochina. There was no opposition,
not even any protest, on the part of any other power interested
in the Pacific. From that moment it was clear that the entry of
the Japanese into the world war would be only a question of time.

As the reasons for common action increased in detail, relations
between French and British multiplied. And indeed, as the days
went by, we had got to know each other. It is my duty to say
that, as those of the British who were running their country had
my wholehearted esteem, so, it appeared to me, did they personally bestow theirs on me. First of all, the King, who was exemplary
and always informed, the Queen, and each of the members of
their family sought out many occasions on which to show it.
Among the Ministers, it was clearly with Mr. Churchill that I was
chiefly in contact, public and private. But I saw also, at this
period, whether on business or at friendly gatherings, principally
Mr. Eden, Sir John Anderson, Mr. Amery, Sir Edward Grigg,
Mr. Alexander, Sir Archibald Sinclair, Lord Lloyd, Lord Cran-
borne, Lord Hankey, Sir Stafford Cripps, Mr. Attlee, Mr. Duff
Cooper, Mr. Dalton, Mr. Bevin, Mr. Morrison, Mr. Bevan, and
Mr. Brendan Bracken. Among the leading high officials, civil and
military, it was most often Sir Robert Vansittart, Sir Alexander
Cadogan, Mr. Strang, Mr. Morton, General Sir John Dill, General
Ismay, Admiral Sir Dudley Pound, and Air Marshal Portal whom
I had to meet. But whether they were members of the government,
military leaders, high officials, or personalities from Parliament,
the press, or the business world, all displayed a striking and imposing loyalty and assurance with regard to British interests.

Not, certainly, that these men were in any way devoid of critical sense, or even of idiosyncrasies. How often, indeed, have I
savoured the humour with which, overworked though they were,
they judged men and events in the midst of the drama which was
sweeping us all about as the sea sweeps the pebbles! But there
was in each of them a devotion to the public service, and between
all of them a community of aims, which bound them together.

The whole gave the impression of a cohesion among those in authority which I very often envied and admired.

But of which I had also to suffer the grip. For to resist the British machine, when it set itself in motion to impose something, was a severe test. Without having experienced it oneself, it is impossible to imagine what a concentration of effort, what a variety of procedures, what insistence, by turns gracious, pressing, and threatening, the English were capable of deploying in order to obtain satisfaction.

First of all there would be allusions, poured out on this hand and on that but striking in their agreement, to put us on the alert and subject us to a methodical preparation. Suddenly, in the course of a meeting called with due decorum, the right person would produce the British request, or demand. If we did not consent to go down the proposed paths—and I must say that this was frequent—there began the trial of "pressure." Everyone around us got to work on it, in all ways, at all levels. There were official conversations, or informal ones, in which men of the most diverse positions invoked friendship, interest, or fear, according to the occasion. There was the action of the press, skilfully restrained as regards the subject of the dispute itself, but creating an atmosphere of criticism and gloom about us. There was the attitude of the people with whom we were in personal touch, who all, instinctively in agreement, endeavoured to persuade us. Everywhere, in mass and all at once, there would be remonstrances, complaints, promises, and signs of anger.

Our British partners were aided in this by the natural propensity of the French to yield to foreigners and become divided. Among those of us who, in their careers, had had to do with foreign affairs, whether from afar or close to, concession was most often a habit, if not a principle. To many, from having lived under a regime devoid of consistency, it was practically an understood thing that France never said No. Therefore, at those moments when I was holding out against the British demands, I could see signs, even in my own circle, of astonishment, uneasiness, anxiety.

I could hear people whispering behind my back and could read in people's eyes the question: "Where does he think he's going?" As if it were inconceivable that one should go anywhere but towards acceptance. As for those French émigrés who had not rallied to us, they took sides against us almost automatically. Most of them followed the bent of their school of politics, for which France was always in the wrong as soon as she asserted herself. And all disapproved of de Gaulle, whose firmness, which they called dictatorial, appeared to them suspect in relation to the spirit of surrender, which they had the arrogance to confound with that of the republic!

After these manifold influences had been given full play, suddenly silence spread. A sort of void was created around us by the British. No more interviews or correspondence; no more visits or lunches. Questions remained pending. Telephones no longer rang. Those of the British with whom chance brought us nonetheless in contact were sombre and impenetrable. We were ignored, as if for us the page of the alliance, and even that of life, had henceforth been turned. In the heart of concentrated and resolute England, an icy coldness enveloped us.

Then would come the decisive attack. A solemn Franco-British meeting would take place unexpectedly. At it, all means would be brought to bear; all the arguments produced; all the complaints given utterance; all the tunes chanted. Although among the responsible British there were different degrees of dramatic skill, each one of them played his part like an artist of distinction. For hours on end heart-rending and alarming scenes followed one another. It would break up on a solemn warning of what would happen if we did not yield.

A little while more and there would come the epilogue. Various British sources would give out signals for an easing of tension. Intermediaries would come and say that there had doubtless been a misunderstanding. Suitable people would ask how I was. Some benevolent paragraph or other would appear in the newspapers. Thereupon there would arrive a British proposal for accommodation over the disputed question, with a good deal of resemblance to what we ourselves had proposed. The terms becoming acceptable, the matter would be quickly settled, at least in appearance. The rounding-off would be done at a friendly party, not without our partners' attempting, at a venture, in the midst of the optimism arising from restored understanding, to obtain some advantage by surprise. Then relations would become as close as before; the basis of things, however, remained undetermined. Because, for Great Britain, there was no such thing as a case tried and done with.

At the beginning of March 1941 I felt beyond doubt that the war was on the point of confronting us, in the Middle East and in Africa, with great trials in face of the enemy, obstinate opposition from Vichy, and grave dissensions with our allies. I would have to take the necessary decisions on the spot. I decided to go there.

Before leaving, I spent the week-end with the Prime Minister at Chequers, and he told me two things, besides saying good-bye. On March 9 at dawn, Mr. Churchill came and woke me up to tell me, literally dancing with joy, that the American Congress had passed the Lend-Lease bill, which had been under discussion for several weeks. There was indeed matter of comfort there for us, not only from the fact that the belligerents were from now on assured of receiving from the United States the matériel necessary for fighting, but also because America, by becoming, in Roosevelt's phrase, "the arsenal of democracy," was taking a gigantic step towards war. Then, wishing no doubt to profit by my good humour, Mr. Churchill formulated his second communication. "I know," he said, "that you have some complaints against Spears as head of our liaison with you. However, I am most anxious for you to keep him on and to take him with you to the Middle East. It is a personal service you will be doing me." I could not refuse, and on that we parted.

As I flew towards the Equator on March 14 I felt, this time, that Free France possessed a serviceable framework. Our Empire Defence Council, dispersed though its members were, formed a valuable and coherent whole, recognized indeed, since December 24, 1940, by the British government. In London our central administration had gained in strength; men of quality, like Cassin, Pleven, Palewski, Antoine, Dejean, Alphand, Dennery, Boris, Antier, and others, formed the bones of it. At the same time, from the military point of view, several valuable officers—such as Colonels Petit, Angenot, Dassonville, and Brosset, who had come from South America where they had been *en mission;* Bureau, transferred from the Cameroons; Capitaine de Frigate Auboyneau, who had hurried to us from Alexandria; and Colonel de l'Air Valin, who was joining us from Brazil—were giving our staffs a firmer consistency. In the Middle East, Catroux, in Africa, Larminat, had things well in hand. Under the drive coming from Garreau-Dombasle for the United States, Ledoux for South America, Soustelle for Central America, and d'Argenlieu and Martin-Prevel for Canada, our delegations were planting themselves all over the New World. Our committees abroad were developing all the time, in spite of the activity exercised on the spot by the representatives of Vichy, the ill will of most of the French notables, and the quarrels usual among our compatriots. The Order of Liberation, which I had instituted at Brazzaville on November 16, 1940, and established in London on January 29, 1941, was arousing emulation in the best sense among the Free French. At last we could feel, across the sea, France looking towards us.

These gains by Free France in resources and solidarity were apparent to me already, along my route, in the attitude of the British governors with whom I broke the journey, at Gibraltar, Bathurst, Freetown, and Lagos. I had found them cordial before; I now found them full of consideration. Next, as I passed through the French Equatorial block, I nowhere felt anxiety or uncertainty. Everyone, assured now in his faith and in his hope, had his eyes fixed on the outside world and was ambitious to see our strength emerge from its distant cradle, grow by fresh rallyings, strike at the enemy, draw near to France.

CHAPTER 6

THE MIDDLE EAST

TOWARDS THE COMPLEXITIES of the Middle East I flew with simple ideas. I knew that, in a welter of intricate factors, a vital game was being played there. We therefore had to be in it. I knew that, for the Allies, the key was the Suez Canal, whose loss would lay Asia Minor and Egypt open to the Axis, but whose retention would, on the contrary, make it possible one day to act from the east westwards upon Tunisia, Italy, and the South of France. That meant that everything commanded us to be present at the battles of which the Canal was the stake. I knew that between Tripoli and Baghdad, passing through Cairo, Jerusalem, and Damascus, and between Alexandria and Nairobi, passing through Jidda, Khartoum, and Jibuti, political, racial, and religious passions and ambitions were being sharpened and drawn tenser under the excitement of the war, that France's positions there were sapped and coveted, and that there was, on any hypothesis, no chance of her keeping any of them if, for the first time in history, she remained passive when everything was in the melting pot. My duty, then, was to act, there as elsewhere, in place of those who were not doing so.

As for the resources which belonged to France in this part of the world, there were, to begin with, those of which I already disposed: combat troops and reserves in course of formation, but also the Chad territory, which put us in a position to act in Libya from the south and, in addition, gave the Allied air forces the advantage of bringing their aircraft by air direct from the Atlantic to the Nile instead of transporting them by sea all the way round the Cape. There were, at the same time, the assets which Vichy was busy losing: the presence of France in the Levant States, where she had an army and where the petrol debouched; our colony at Jibuti; and our naval squadron at Alexandria. While, for tactical reasons or from necessity, I could consider leaving one or other of these elements outside the war for a time, while I could measure how far the temporizing of the subordinates was often excusable and their obedience explicable, I was nonetheless resolved to bring them all to heel as soon as possible. At the moment of leaving London I had, indeed, collected the opinions of the members of the Defence Council on what it would be best to do if, faced by some direct threat from the Germans, England and Turkey decided to make sure of the Syrian and Lebanese territories. In short, I was arriving in the Middle East determined to let no considerations stand in the way of extending the action of France and of safeguarding all that could be safeguarded of her position.

I landed first at Khartoum, the base for the battle of Eritrea and the Sudan. This was being directed—extremely well—by General Platt, an alert and dynamic leader, who had in fact just taken the Italians' principal line of defence on the Keren heights. Colonel Monclar's brigade and Commandant Astier de Villatte's air group had taken a brilliant part in this. As for the troops at Jibuti, although General Legentilhomme had made some contacts with them, they had not decided to come over, and Governor Noailhetas was repressing by every means, including the death penalty, the stirrings which showed themselves in favour of rallying.

To bring Jibuti back into the war, it would be wrong, therefore, to count on a spontaneous adhesion. At the same time I did not think it right to go in by force of arms. There remained blockade, which was certainly capable of bringing to its right mind a colony whose subsistence came to it by sea from Aden, Arabia, and Madagascar. But we never managed to induce the English to do all that was necessary.

Certainly their military command was favourable in principle to an adhesion which would result in reinforcements. But other British influences were less keen. "If," they probably thought, "the competition which has set Great Britain, France, and Italy at loggerheads near the sources of the Nile for the last sixty years ends in a strictly British triumph; if, when the Italians have been finally crushed, it is apparent that the French have remained passive and impotent, what an unparalleled situation England will have thenceforth in the whole area—Abyssinia, Eritrea, Somaliland, and the Sudan! For the sake of a few battalions which Jibuti might engage in a battle already virtually won, is it right to forgo such a result?" This state of mind, more or less widespread among the British, explains, in my opinion, why the Vichy authorities succeeded, for two years, in feeding the colony and thereby maintaining it in pernicious obedience.

Their default only rendered more meritorious the services of the French troops that did fight in Eritrea. I went to spend the days of March 29 and 30 with them. A French airplane having brought me to the Agordat airfield, I reached the area to the east of Keren, where our brigade, joined onto an Indian division, formed the left of the Allied position. Our troops were magnificent. After Kubkub they had taken a notable part in the victory of Keren, by smashing and overrunning the right flank of the Italians. Lieutenant-Colonel Génin, who had distinguished himself in the operation, was presented to me. To join us from Algiers, he had just crossed Africa and, no sooner arrived, had rushed into the fight. "You've seen now, Génin. What do you think?" "Ah! if they could all see, on the other side, there'd be no more question!"

On the morrow of my visit, while General Platt started the

follow up, the commander of the French brigade led his men towards Massawa, the capital and redoubt of Eritrea. Once Montecullo and the Umberto fort had been stormed by our men, on April 7, the Legion entered Massawa like a whirlwind, pell-mell along with a rabble of routed Italians, rushed to the port, seized the Admiralty, and gave Colonel Monclar the honour of receiving the surrender of the commander of the enemy fleet in the Red Sea. In all, the French detachment had taken more than four thousand prisoners in battle and received at Massawa the surrender of ten thousand more.

Henceforth the fragments of the Italian forces, thrown back into Abyssinia, no longer operated except in sporadic actions. But the fact that French Somaliland remained outside the struggle baulked France of the decisive part which her forces might have played by marching directly along the railway from Jibuti to Addis Ababa, whither the Negus was to return. I could only accept the deplorable consequences. It was elsewhere that the Free French forces would now have to be brought to bear—both those that had just been engaged and those that were rushing up to be so. Palewski would remain on the spot as political and military delegate, keeping at his disposal a battalion and a few aircraft.

Cairo, where I landed on April 1, was where the heart of the war was beating—but a shaky heart. The situation of the British and their allies there was indeed clearly unstable, not only because of military events, but also since they were on soil undermined by political currents, in the midst of populations who were watching, without taking part in, the battle between Western nations and were ready, whatever happened, to profit from the spoils of the vanquished.

These conditions gave a most complex character to the conduct of the war in the Middle East. General Wavell, the British commander-in-chief, by good fortune very highly gifted both with judgment and with coolness, moved in the midst of multiple contingencies, many of which had only an indirect relation to strategy. Besides, this strategy itself was as uneasy as could be. At the beginning of April, Wavell was carrying on a battle on three fronts painfully supplied over immensely long lines of communications.

In Libya, after handsome successes which had brought the British to the threshold of Tripolitania, it had been necessary to withdraw. Cyrenaica, except Tobruk, was about to be lost. The command, for all its value, the troops, for all their courage, had not yet finished their apprenticeship in this desert struggle, so mobile and rapid over vast spaces without cover, so exhausting with the chronic thirst and fever, under the fiery sun, in the sand, among the flies. Rommel was busy reversing fortune at the very moment when the London government was ordering Wavell to strip his battle corps by sending an important fraction of his forces to Greece. On the Hellenic front things were not going well either. It is true that the victories in Eritrea and Abyssinia brought some consolation. But alarming signs were making their appearance in the Arab countries. Iraq was growing restless. Egypt remained enigmatic. On the subject of Syria the Germans were opening disquieting dealings with Vichy. In Palestine the latent conflict between Arabs and Jews made many precautions necessary.

To the many difficulties accumulated round Wavell, there was added that of interference. There were the telegrams from London. For Mr. Churchill, impatient and expert, never ceased to ask for explanations and give directives. Apart from the visits of Mr. Eden, first as Minister for War and then, in April 1941, when I met him in Cairo, as Secretary of State for Foreign Affairs, there were the interventions of the ambassador, Sir Miles Lampson, who was invested, in virtue of his qualities and of the force of circumstances, with a sort of permanent coordination mission. There was the fact that the army in the Middle East consisted largely of contingents from the Dominions—Australia, New Zealand, South Africa—whose governments watched jealously the use made of their forces, and also of the Indian troops, which it was necessary to use without seeming to abuse. In short, Wavell exercised his command only through all sorts of political trammels.

I must say that he suffered them with a noble serenity. To the point of keeping his headquarters in Cairo, where they hemmed him in on all sides. It was in the heart of that teeming city, in the tumult and dust, between the walls of a small office overheated by the sun, that he was continually assailed by interventions outside his normal domain as a soldier. And here came I, troublesome and pressing, fully determined to resolve on behalf of France problems which involved the British and, first of all, their commander-in-chief.

I went over our prospects with General Catroux. The essential thing for us was what would happen to Syria and in the Lebanon. Sooner or later we would have to go there. As soon as we were there, France would have a chance of bringing an important contribution to the common effort. Otherwise, with this chance lost, the position of France would likewise be lost. For, supposing that the Axis won, it would dominate there as elsewhere. If the opposite happened, the English would take our place. The authority of Free France must therefore be extended to Damascus and to Beirut as soon as events should offer the opportunity.

But when I reached Cairo the opportunity was not in sight. There was no hope of the authorities and army of the Levant themselves breaking the maleficent spell which held them enchained. The movement which, at the end of June 1940, was thrusting whole columns in the direction of Palestine had changed to a waiting game. Besides, the demobilization of many officers and men, decreed by Vichy after its armistice, had brought them back to France. In addition, among the military and civil servants who remained active, Vichy had repatriated, or even placed under arrest, a number of Gaullists. In short, the movement hoped for at the time of General Catroux's arrival in Cairo had not materialized, and our informants in Beirut and Damascus did not lead us to think that it was likely to materialize very soon.

The same inclination to give in was silting up the French squadron at Alexandria. Ever since Admiral Godfroy had concluded the agreement with Andrew Cunningham neutralizing his ships, the battleship *Lorraine,* the cruisers *Duguay-Trouin, Duquesne, Suffren,* and *Tourville,* the destroyers *Basque, Forbin,* and *Fortuné,* and the submarine *Protée,* had remained at anchor in the port. A few from among the officers and crews joined us at intervals. But the others, obeying Vichy's orders, spent this time of war in proving to one another that the best way of serving invaded France consisted in not fighting. One April day, as I crossed the harbour of Alexandria to visit Admiral Cunningham on his flagship, I was able to see—and it wrung my heart—the fine French ships somnolent and useless in the midst of the British fleet with its decks cleared for action.

Unable, however, to admit that the course of the battle in the Mediterranean might have no effect on the state of mind of the leaders in Africa and the Middle East, we had tried to make contact with them. In November, Catroux sent Weygand a neighbourly letter. Slight as were my illusions, I had approved this step. I myself broadcast several explicit appeals, declaring in particular, on December 28, 1940: "All French leaders, whatever their mistakes, who may decide to draw the sword which they have sheathed, will find us at their side with no desire to exclude them and no ambition. If French Africa arises—at last!—to make war, we shall join it with our part of the Empire."

In January, having consulted the members of the Defence Council about the attitude we would have to take if by chance Vichy should re-enter the struggle, I found them, like me, in favour of union. On February 24 I had written to General Weygand in the same sense, in spite of the disagreeable fate to which he had consigned me and the discourteous reception he had given to my preceding missive. I urged Weygand to seize the last opportunity which was being offered him to resume the struggle. I proposed that we should unite, making it plain to him that, if he consented, he could count on my respect and cooperation. At the same time Catroux missed no chance of sending tempting signals to Admiral Godfroy. Lastly, in November, he had written to M.

Puaux, High Commissioner in the Levant, to General Fougère, over-all commander of the troops, and to General Arlabosse, his second in command, if only to make the beginnings of some sort of liaison with them.

But these many attempts had produced no result. To our emissaries Weygand replied, now "that de Gaulle ought to be shot," now "that he himself was too old to make a rebel," now "that with two-thirds of France occupied by the enemy and the remaining third by the Navy—which was even worse—and with Darlan having him perpetually spied upon, he could do nothing even if he had wanted to." As for Admiral Godfroy, he received General Catroux's messages with politeness but did nothing about them. Lastly, from Beirut, Arlabosse sent Catroux an impeccable but chilling reply. Besides, at the end of December, after the air accident to Chiappe, Ambassador Puaux was replaced by General Dentz, an extremely conventional general officer who was ready to apply strictly the orders given him by Darlan. Not long afterwards Fougère in his turn was relieved, and the command of the troops passed to General de Verdilhac.

In these conditions we could not think of entering Syria unless the enemy himself was setting foot there. Meanwhile the only thing to be done was to collect Legentilhomme's troops and place them at the disposal of Wavell, for him to engage them in Libya. That is what I arranged with the British commander-in-chief. At the same time I settled with Air Marshal Longmore the organization and use of our small air force.

I must say that our soldiers, as they gradually arrived, made the best possible impression. In that quivering Middle East, where age-long echoes reverberated the renown of France, they felt that they were champions. The Egyptians, as it happened, gave them a particularly warm welcome—not, perhaps, free from the intention that their graciousness towards the French should contrast with the coldness they were displaying to the British. I had myself made agreeable contacts with Prince Mohammed Ali, the King's uncle and heir, as well as with Hussein Sirry Pasha, the head of the government, and with several of his Ministers. As for the Frenchmen resident in Egypt—scientists, members of the teaching profession, specialists in antiquities, churchmen, businessmen, traders, engineers, and employees of the Canal—most of them were warmhearted and active in aiding our troops. Already on June 18 they had, on the initiative of Baron de Benoist, Professor Jouguet and M. Minost and M. Boniteau, formed an organization which at once became one of the pillars of Free France. Nevertheless some of our compatriots were holding aloof from the movement. Sometimes, in the evening, when I went for a short walk in the Cairo zoological gardens and passed in front of the French Legation which stood opposite them, I could see, appearing at the windows, the strained faces of those who were not joining us, yet whose gaze followed General de Gaulle.

Thus, during the two weeks spent in the Sudan, Egypt, and Palestine, certain things had been made clear. But the main thing remained to be done, and for the moment I could do nothing about it. I then went back to Brazzaville. It was in fact necessary, in any case, to push on with the organization of our Equatorial block. If the Middle East were destined to be lost, that would become the breakwater of Allied resistance; if not, we would have there a base for some future offensive.

My tour of inspection took me once more to Duala, Yaunde, Marua, Libreville, Port-Gentil, Fort-Lamy, Moussoro, Faya, Fada, Abéché, Fort-Archambault, Bangui, and Pointe-Noire. Many things were lacking there, but order and good will were not among them. The governors—Cournarie in the Cameroons, Lapie in the Chad, Saint-Mart in Ubangi, Fortuné in the Middle Congo, Valentin-Smith in the Gabon (where he had just replaced Parant, killed on service in an air accident)—were commanding and administrating in that atmosphere in which no doubts are felt, and which envelops the French whenever by chance they are at one in serving a great cause. In the military field it was to the preparation of Leclerc's Saharan column that I gave first priority. I had him sent from England all the officers and NCOs still there, as well as all the appropriate matériel that the English consented to supply. But from the end of April it was clear to me beyond doubt that, from one day to the next, it was in the Levant that we would have to act.

In fact, the Germans were debouching upon the Mediterranean. On April 24 Anglo-Hellenic resistance collapsed, while the Yugoslavs also had just succumbed. Doubtless the British would try to hang on in Crete. But would they be able to hold? It seemed to me obvious that, starting from the shores of Greece, the enemy would, in the near future, bring to bear on Syria air squadrons at least. Their presence in the midst of the Arab countries would arouse there an agitation which might serve as a prelude to the arrival of the Wehrmacht. At the same time, from the airfields of Damascus, Riyaq, and Beirut, three hundred miles from Suez and Port Said, the German aircraft would easily bombard the Canal and its approaches.

In this matter Darlan was powerless to reject Hitler's demands. But I did indulge in the hope that, should the leaders and soldiers of the Levant see the machines of the Luftwaffe landing on their bases, many of them would refuse to submit to their presence and to cover it with their arms. In this case we would have to be ready to give them a hand at once. I therefore worked out my directives about the action to be undertaken. It would involve thrusting General Legentilhomme's small division straight at Damascus, as soon as the appearance of the Germans should provoke among our compatriots the movement which seemed probable. Catroux for his part prepared to make, on this hypothesis, all the contacts possible, with Dentz himself if need be, so as to establish the common front of Frenchmen against the invader of France and Syria.

But these plans did not meet with the agreement of the British. General Wavell, absorbed by his three battle fronts, did not intend to see a fourth opened for him, at any price. Also, not wishing to believe the worst, he said he was sure, on the strength of the reports of the British consul-general at Beirut, that Dentz would resist the Germans if the case arose. At the same time the London government was making efforts to coax Vichy. So it was that, in February, the British Admiralty had, in spite of my protests, accorded free passage to the steamer *Providence,* which was transporting from Beirut to Marseille some compulsorily repatriated Gaullists. So it was that, at the end of April, a commercial treaty was concluded with Dentz, assuring food supplies to the Levant. So it was that negotiations, opened by Governor Noailhetas with a view to the same result for Jibuti, were going on at Aden.

The information reaching us from France led me to think that American influence had something to do with these attempts at "appeasement." It was reported to me that Pétain and Darlan were prodigal of their seductions towards Admiral Leahy, the ambassador at Vichy, while at the same time they were secretly agreeing to Hitler's demands. Roosevelt, influenced in his turn by Leahy's telegrams, was pressing the English to be lenient. The more necessary it seemed to me to prepare for action in the Levant, the less our allies were disposed to it. On May 9 Spears advised me, from Cairo, that no operation there was "contemplated for the moment" for the Free French, that there would be "disadvantage" in my coming to Egypt, and that the best thing would be to go back to London.

Convinced that temporization might well cost us dear, I thought it my duty to impress the English in my turn. On May 10 I telegraphed to Cairo, to the British ambassador and to the commander-in-chief, to protest on the one hand against the "unilateral decisions taken by them on the subject of the supply of foodstuffs to the Levant and Jibuti," on the other hand against the "delays caused to the concentration of the Legentilhomme division within reach of Syria at a time when the arrival of the Germans there was daily more probable." I made it plain that, in these conditions, I had no intention of going to Cairo in the near future, that I was letting matters there follow their course, and that it was in the Chad that I would henceforth bring the French effort to bear. Then I let London know that I was recalling General Catroux from Cairo, since his presence there was becoming useless. Finally, as the excellent Mr. Parr, the British consul-general at Brazzaville, brought me messages sent by Mr. Eden to justify the policy of appeasement towards Vichy, I dictated to him a reply condemning this policy, with all the more vigour because I had just heard of the interview between Darlan and Hitler at Berchtesgaden, of the conclusion of an agreement between them, and finally of the landing of German airplanes at Damascus and Aleppo.

For the enemy too was playing for high stakes. At his instigation Rashid Ali al-Gailani, the head of the Iraqi government, opened hostilities in the first days of May. The English were besieged on their airfields. On May 12 the Luftwaffe machines arrived in Syria and from there reached Baghdad. On the day before, the Vichy authorities had sent to Tel Kotchek, on the Iraqi frontier, the war matériel which the Italian armistice commission had previously made them place under its control. These arms were evidently intended for Rashid Ali. Dentz, from whom the British demanded an explanation, answered evasively, without, however, denying the facts. He added that if he received the order from Vichy to let the German troops disembark, he would not fail to obey—which amounted to saying that the order had already been given. It has since become known, in fact, that the beaches where the enemy was to land had already been assigned.

The London Cabinet judged that, in these conditions, it was better to come round to my way of thinking. The reversal was sudden and complete. As from May 14, Eden, on the one hand, and Spears, who was still in Egypt, on the other, told me so straight out. Finally, a message from Mr. Churchill asked me to go to Cairo and not to withdraw Catroux, seeing that action was imminent. Very satisfied with the attitude adopted by the British Prime Minister, I answered him warmly and, for once, in English. I could not, however, fail to draw the unavoidable conclusions about the behaviour of our allies in this affair. As for General Wavell, his government had ordered him to undertake the action planned by us in Syria. I found him resigned to doing so, when I arrived in Cairo on May 25. It is true that the loss of Crete and the disappearance of the Greek front lightened, for the moment, the burdens of the commander-in-chief.

Meanwhile in Syria itself things were not turning out as we had hoped. Catroux had, for one moment, believed that he could carry out our plan and march on Damascus with the Free French forces alone. But it soon became necessary to realize that the collusion between Vichy and the enemy was arousing no mass movement among the Levant troops. On the contrary, these were taking up positions on the frontier, to resist the Free French and the Allies, while behind them the Germans could move about as they wished. As Dentz had available more than thirty thousand men, well provided with artillery, aircraft, and armour, without counting the Syrian and Lebanese troops, our first project of marching on Damascus with our six thousand infantrymen, our eight guns and our ten tanks, supported by our two dozen aircraft and taking advantage of the help we dreamed of finding on the spot, could not be applied as it was. The British would have to join in, and a pitched battle lay ahead.

At least we were anxious to reduce its desperate character and its length as far as possible. It was a question of the resources used. Our friends at Beirut and Damascus sent word to us: "If the Allies enter Syria from all directions and in large numbers, there will only be a show of resistance for honour's sake. If, on the contrary, the Levant troops find themselves up against forces that are mediocre in numbers and matériel, their professional pride will come into play and the battles will be harsh." Accompanied by General Catroux, I had many interviews on this subject with Wavell. We pressed him to go into the Levant not only from the south, starting from Palestine, but also from the east, starting from Iraq, where, in fact, the British were engaged in reducing Rashid Ali. We asked the commander-in-chief to operate with four divisions, one of them armoured, and to deploy a large section of the Royal Air Force in the Syrian sky. We insisted that he should give

Legentilhomme's troops what they chiefly lacked: means of transport and artillery support.

General Wavell was certainly not without strategical intelligence. In addition, he wanted to satisfy us. But, absorbed as he was by the Libya operations and harassed, no doubt, by Mr. Churchill's comminatory telegrams in which he saw the effect of our own insistence, he met our plain speaking with a negative courtesy. Nothing could persuade him to devote more than a strict minimum of forces to the Syrian affair. All he would put into the field, under General Wilson's orders, was an Australian division and a cavalry brigade marching along the Tyre-Sidon coastal road, an infantry brigade making for El Kuneitrah and Merd-jayoun, and a Hindu brigade lent to Legentilhomme, who was to bear down on Damascus through Dera. Wavell added, later, two Australian battalions. Lastly, a Hindu detachment eventually, as a last resort, went into action from Iraq. The whole was supported by about sixty aircraft, while various warships accompanied the land operations along the coast. In all, the Allies engaged less forces than would be opposed to them. And yet on these inadequate bases we had to act and go through with it. The final decision was taken. The tragedy was about to begin.

On May 26 I had been to inspect the Free French troops at Kistina, concentrated now, but still ill provided. Legentilhomme paraded for me seven battalions, a tank company, a battery, a squadron of Spahis, a reconnaissance company, and supporting services. It was on this occasion that I bestowed the first Crosses of Liberation earned in Libya and Eritrea. In making contact with the officers and men, I realized that they were in exactly the same state of mind as I was: grief and disgust at having to fight Frenchmen, indignation with Vichy for leading astray the discipline of the troops, and conviction that it was necessary to march, to make sure of the Levant and turn it against the enemy. On May 21 Colonel Collet, who commanded the group of Circassian squadrons, an officer of high value and legendary bravery, crossed the frontier and joined us with part of his troops. On June 8 Free

French and British advanced, waving the Allied flags, with orders, given jointly by Wavell and Catroux, to use their weapons only against those who should fire on them. A radio station had been set up in Palestine and for weeks had been broadcasting, with the voices of Captains Schmittlein, Coulet, and Repiton, friendly exhortations to our compatriots, in whom we hoped, from the bottom of our hearts, not to find adversaries. Nonetheless we had got to get through. In a public declaration I left no doubt on this point.

I was, indeed, all the more resolved to push things to a conclusion, and quickly, since many signs led us to expect an offensive by Vichy, and perhaps by the Axis, against Free French Africa. According to our information, Hitler had demanded of Darlan, during their interviews at Berchtesgaden on May 11 and 12, not only that the Syrian airdromes and ports should be placed at Germany's disposal, but also that his troops, aircraft, and ships should be able to use Tunis, Sfax, and Gabès, and, moreover, that the Vichy forces should reconquer the Equatorial territories. Certainly, our informants added that Weygand had refused to allow the Germans access to Tunisia and to start an offensive against the Free French territories, alleging that his subordinates would not obey him. But if Hitler's plan was firmly decided on, what weight would a protest from Weygand possess, when in the last resort, and failing the willingness to fight, all he would have to put against it, in the Marshal's councils, was an offer of resignation?

We were therefore holding ourselves in readiness to reply to an attack. Larminat, taking advantage of the impression made by the arrival of German aircraft in Syria upon certain elements in the Ivory Coast, Dahomey, Togoland, and the Niger, was preparing to march in at the first opportunity. I had myself given him instructions on the line of conduct to follow. At the same time the British government, when I asked it what it would do if Vichy, with or without immediate assistance from the Germans, were to attempt to act, for instance, against the Chad, replied in a message to me from Mr. Eden that it would help us to resist by all means in its power. Lastly, we had done the necessary to interest the Americans directly in the security of Free French Africa. On June 5 I handed to the United States minister in Cairo a memorandum bringing out the fact that Africa would one day have to be an American base for the liberation of Europe and proposing to Washington that it should without delay establish air forces in the Cameroons, the Chad, and the Congo. Four days later the United States consul at Léopoldville went to see Larminat, asked him on behalf of his government if he considered that French Equatorial Africa was threatened, and, on the High Commissioner's affirmative answer, invited him to let him know what direct aid he would wish America to give him, especially in armaments. In spite of everything, and of all the precautions we had managed to take to defend the Equatorial bastion in case of need, I was very impatient, faced by the prospect of a major effort by the Axis and its collaborators in Africa, to see the Levant shut against the Germans and cut off from Vichy.

While British and Free French were preparing to act together there on the military field, their political rivalry was taking shape behind the façade. In Allied staff circles, around the Cairo Embassy, in close touch with the British High Commissioner's office at Jerusalem, in the communications made by the Foreign Office to Cassin, Pleven, and Dejean and passed on by them from London to me, and through the columns of the inspired newspapers, notably the *Palestine Post,* we could perceive the quivering activity of a specialized personnel which saw opening—at last—in Syria the prospect of realizing plans of action long since prepared. Events were about to put Great Britain in possession of such a hand of trumps, political, military, and economic, that she would certainly not refrain from playing them on her own account.

All the more since, once installed at Damascus and Beirut, it would be impossible for us even to maintain the *status quo ante* there. The shocks caused by the disaster of 1940, Vichy's capitulation, and the activity of the Axis made it imperative for Free France to take up towards the Levant States a new position, answering to developments and to the forces emerging. It seemed to us, indeed, that once the war was over France would not keep the mandate. Even if she still wished to do so, it was clear that the movement of the Arab peoples and international necessities would not allow her to do so. Now, only one regime could, *de jure* and *de facto,* be substituted for the mandate, and that was independence—historical precedence and the interests of France being, however, safeguarded. That had, indeed, been the purpose of the treaties concluded by Paris in 1936 with the Lebanon and Syria. These treaties, although their ratification had been postponed, constituted facts which good sense and the circumstances forbade us to ignore.

We had therefore decided that, at the moment of going into Syrian and Lebanese territory, Free France would declare its determination to put an end to the regime of the mandate and to conclude treaties with the now sovereign states. As long as the war lasted in the Middle East, we would naturally keep the mandatory's supreme power in the Levant, together with its obligations. Lastly, since the territory of Syria and the Lebanon was part and parcel of the Middle East theatre of operations, over which the English possessed, compared to us, an enormous superiority in resources, we would consent that the British military command should exercise the strategic direction over the whole against the common enemy.

But it was at once evident that the English would not be content with that. Their game—settled in London by firmly established services, carried out on the spot by a team without scruples but not without resources, accepted by the Foreign Office, which sometimes sighed over it but never disavowed it, and supported by the Prime Minister, whose ambiguous promises and calculated emotions camouflaged what was intended—aimed at establishing British "leadership" in the whole Middle East. British policy would therefore endeavour, sometimes stealthily and sometimes harshly, to replace France at Damascus and at Beirut.

The procedure to be employed by this policy would be that of going one better—letting it be thought that every concession granted by us to Syria and the Lebanon was granted thanks to England's good offices, egging the local rulers on to formulate increasing demands, and, lastly, supporting the acts of provocation to which it was bound to lead them. At the same time efforts would be made to use the French as foils—to raise up local and international opinion against them, and so to divert popular reprobation from British encroachments in the other Arab countries.

Hardly had the decision to go into Syria been taken in common when already the British let their intentions be seen. As Catroux was preparing his declaration announcing independence, Sir Miles Lampson requested that the proclamation should be made both in the name of England and in that of Free France. I opposed this, naturally. The ambassador then insisted that the text should mention the British guarantee given to our promise. I rejected this request on the ground that the word of France had no need of a foreign guarantee. Mr. Churchill, when he telegraphed me on June 6 to express his friendly wishes on the eve of the advance, insisted on the importance of this famous guarantee. I replied to these good wishes, but not to this claim. It was easy to see that our partners wanted to create the impression that, if the Syrians and Lebanese received independence, they would owe it to England, and so to place themselves in the position of arbiters between us and the Levant States in the next phase. In the end Catroux's declaration was as it should be. But as soon as it had been made the London government published another, separately and in its own name.

The memories evoked in me by the campaign we had been obliged to open are cruel ones. I can still see myself coming and going between Jerusalem, where I had fixed my headquarters, and our brave troops as they advanced towards Damascus, or else going to visit the wounded in the Franco-British ambulance unit of Mrs. Spears and Dr. Fruchaut. As I heard, gradually, how many of our men, and of the best, were left on the field—how, for instance, General Legentilhomme had been severely wounded, how Colonel Génin and Capitaine de Corvette Détroyat had been killed, how Commandant de Chevigné, de Boissoudy, and de Villoutreys had been badly hit—and how, on the other side, many good officers and men were falling bravely under our fire—how, on the Litani on June 9 and 10, before Kiswa on the 12th, and round about El Kuneitrah and Izra on the 15th and 16th, violent fighting had mingled the French dead from both camps and those of their British allies, I felt towards those who were opposing us on a point of honour mixed emotions of esteem and commiseration. At a time when the enemy held Paris under his boot, was attacking in Africa, and was infiltrating into the Levant, this courage shown and these losses borne in the fratricidal struggle imposed by Hitler upon leaders who had fallen under his yoke made on me an impression of horrible waste.

But the tighter sorrow gripped, the firmer I grew in the determination to go through with it. The same was true, indeed, of the soldiers of Free France, of whom, practically speaking, none was to weaken. The same was true, likewise, of all our compatriots in Egypt, who, meeting in Cairo for the first anniversary of June 18, responded to my address with unanimous acclamations.

On that day there was reason to believe that Dentz was on the point of putting an end to this odious struggle. Already, indeed, it no longer offered him any hope. In fact, Benoist-Méchin, sent by Vichy to Ankara to obtain permission for reinforcements to be sent to the Levant across Turkey, had met with a refusal. At the same time the rout of Rashid Ali in Iraq and his flight to Germany on May 31 opened to the Allies the gates of Syria by way of the desert and the Euphrates. All at once the Germans seemed no longer in a hurry to get fresh forces through into Arab countries. On the contrary, the aircraft they had sent there were brought back to Greece. The only reinforcements that had reached the Levant since the start of the fighting were two French air squadrons, which had come from North Africa via Athens, where the Germans had welcomed them and refuelled them. And now there reached us from Washington the news that M. Conty, political director of the Levant High Commissioner's office, had on June 18 begged the American consul-general at Beirut to ask the British, as a matter of urgency, what terms they themselves and the Gaullists would require for a cessation of hostilities.

As early as June 13, foreseeing what would follow and by way of precaution, I had made known to Mr. Churchill what were the bases on which, in my view, the future armistice should be concluded. In the course of the meeting held on June 19 at Sir Miles Lampson's, at which Wavell and Catroux were present, I drew up in the same sense the text of the terms which appeared to me acceptable for ourselves and suitable for those who were fighting against us. "The arrangement," I wrote, "must be based on honourable treatment for all members of the armed forces and all officials; a guarantee given by Great Britain that, as far as she is concerned, the rights and interests of France in the Levant will be maintained; and the representation of France in the Levant to be the responsibility of the Free French authorities." I specified that "all members of the armed forces and officials who may desire it shall be able to remain, and likewise their families, the others being repatriated later." But I added that "all possible steps should be taken by the Allies that this choice may be really free." Finally, in order to counter the rumours which Vichy was spreading, I declared that "never having brought to judgment those of my army comrades who have fought against me in obedience to orders received by them, I had no intention of doing so in the present case." These are, in essence, the provisions which, adopted there and then by the British, were at once telegraphed to London to be passed on to Washington and, from there, to Beirut.

I was disagreeably impressed, therefore, next day, when I came to know the exact text which the British government had finally sent, and which did not resemble the one to which I had subscribed. Free France was not even mentioned in it, as though it were to England that Dentz was being asked to hand over Syria! There was not a word, either, about the precautions which I was anxious to take to prevent the members of the armed forces and officials in the Levant from being repatriated wholesale and compulsorily; and it was vital for me to hold on to these as much as possible. I therefore sent Mr. Eden a formal protest and warned him that for my part I was adhering to the conditons of June 19 and not recognizing any others. This reservation was to have its importance, as will be seen later.

Why did the Vichy authorities wait more than three weeks before carrying out their own intention of negotiating the end of the struggle? Why was it necessary, on this account, to go on for so long with fighting which could alter nothing except the total of losses? The only explanation I can find is in the start of the German offensive in Russia. On June 22, the morrow of the day on which the United States consul at Beirut handed Great Britain's reply to the High Commisioner, Hitler launched his armies in the direction of Moscow. He had an obvious interest in the largest possible fraction of the forces opposed to him being tied up in Africa and Syria. Rommel was looking after this on one side. It was necessary that the unfortunate French forces of the Levant should do as much on the other.

Meanwhile, on June 21, after a sharp engagement at Kiswa, our troops entered Damascus. Catroux proceeded there at once. I arrived there on the 23rd. In the night that followed, German aircraft came and bombarded the town, killing some hundreds of people in the Christian quarter and demonstrating in this way their cooperation with Vichy. But hardly were we on the spot before there reached us, from all sides—notably from the Hauran, the Jebel ed Druz, Palmyra, and Jezireh—disquieting news about the behaviour of the British. There was no time to be lost if we wished to show that Vichy's discomfiture did not mean the retirement of France, and to affirm our authority.

On June 24 I appointed General Catroux delegate general and plenipotentiary in the Levant and defined for him, by letter, the purpose of his mission: "To direct the re-establishment of an internal and economic situation as close to the normal as the war may permit; to negotiate, with the qualified representatives of the population groups, treaties instituting the independence and sovereignty of the states, and at the same time the alliance of these states with France; to ensure the defence of the territory against the enemy, and to cooperate with the Allies in the operations of war in the Middle East." Until such time as the future treaties would enter into force, General Catroux was assuming "all the powers and all the responsibilities of the High Commissioner of France in the Levant." As for the negotiations to be opened, they were to be so "with governments approved by assemblies really representative of the populations as a whole, and called together as soon as possible; the point of departure for the negotiations being the treaties of 1936." Thus "the mandate entrusted to France in the Levant would be brought to its due conclusion and the work of France continued."

During my stay at Damascus I received all the political, religious, and administrative notabilities who were there, and there were many. Through the usual oriental prudence it was possible to see that the authority of France was without dispute, recognized in us personally, that the failure of the German plan for gaining a footing in Syria was put down largely to our credit, and finally that everyone expected from us, and from no one else, the re-starting of the machinery of state and the setting up of a new government. General Catroux, who had a profound knowledge of men and things in that country, saw to it that order, food supplies, and health services were ensured, but took his time over appointing ministers.

The tragedy, indeed, was ending. On June 20 Legentilhomme, who in spite of his severe wound had never given up commanding his troops, seized En Nebk and, on the 30th, repulsed a final counterattack there. A Hindu column from Iraq crossed the Euphrates on July 3 by the Deir ez Zor bridge, left intact through some chance which I can safely call well arranged, and made progress towards Aleppo and towards Homs. Along the coastal road the British reached Damour on the 9th, and farther to the east, Jezzin. On July 10 Dentz sent his warships and aircraft to

Turkey, where they were interned. He then asked for a cease fire, which was granted immediately. It was agreed that the plenipotentiaries should meet three days later, at Saint John of Acre.

Many signs led me to think that the outcome of this meeting would not be in conformity with the interests of France. It was true that I had warned Mr. Churchill on June 28 "of the extreme importance which England's behaviour towards us in the Middle East would have from the point of view of our alliance." It was true that I had obtained agreement that General Catroux should be present at the negotiations. It was true that our delegates in London had received from myself clear indications as to the way in which our authority should be established in the Levant, for them to make use of in their conversations. But the terms already formulated by Mr. Eden for the armistice with Dentz, the mood which prevailed in the British services, and the fact that the loyal Wavell had just left Cairo, having been appointed Viceroy of India, and that his successor, Auchinleck, was not yet installed there—which left the field clear for the passions of the "Arabophiles"—made it impossible for me to doubt that the arrangement would leave much to be desired. In point of fact the armistice was to be concluded by Wilson with Verdilhac. My only means of limiting the damage was to gain space and height, to reach some cloud and from there swoop down upon a convention which would not bind me, and which I would tear up as far as I could.

The cloud was Brazzaville. I stayed there, while at Saint John of Acre the act was drawn up, whose substance and form went beyond my worst fears.

In fact, the text of the agreement amounted to a pure and simple transference of Syria and the Lebanon to the British. Not a word about the rights of France, either for the present or for the future. No mention of the Levant States. Vichy was abandoning everything to the discretion of a foreign power and sought to obtain only one thing: the departure of all the troops, and likewise of the maximum number of French officials and nationals. In this way de Gaulle would be, as far as possible, prevented from increasing his forces and from preserving the position of France in the Levant.

By signing this capitulation Vichy showed itself faithful to its wretched vocation. But the English were apparently lending themselves to it with all their ulterior motives. Obviously ignoring, even in matters of form, their Free French allies, whose initiative and cooperation had powerfully helped them to gain the strategic aim, they seemed to be taking advantage of Vichy's supineness in order to try to gather under the grasp of their military command the authority which Dentz was handing over to them at Beirut and at Damascus. They were, moreover, ready to let the Levant troops go as soon as possible. These, according to the convention, would be concentrated under the orders of their leaders and embarked on the ships which Darlan would send. What was more, the Free French were forbidden to make contact with them and to try to win them over. The matériel which they would leave behind would be handed over to the English alone. Finally, the so-called "special,"—that is to say, Syrian and Lebanese— troops, which had always showed themselves faithful to France, so much so that Vichy had not dared to use them against us in the recent engagements, were to be placed, without more ado, under British command.

Before I even knew the details, and taking as my basis the naturally sugared indications given by the London radio, I let it be known that I repudiated the Saint John of Acre convention. After which, I left for Cairo, making it plain to the British governors and military leaders at each stage of my journey how serious the matter was. I did so at Khartoum to General Sir Arthur Huddleston, the excellent and friendly Governor-General of the Sudan, at Kampala to the Governor, at Wadi Halfa to the Manager of the Club, so as to have myself preceded by alarming telegrams. On July 21 I made contact with Mr. Oliver Lyttelton, Minister of State in the British government, who had just been sent by it to Cairo, there to group under his authority all British affairs in the Middle East.

Captain Lyttelton, an amiable and thoughtful man with a lively and open mind, had manifestly no desire to begin his mission with a catastrophe. He welcomed me with some embarrassment. I tried to avoid explosions and, casing myself in ice, told him, in substance, this:

"Thanks to a campaign which we have just carried through together, we have managed to gain ourselves a notable strategic advantage. The mortgage which, in the Levant, Vichy's subordination to Germany made such a burden on the eastern theatre of operations is now liquidated. But the agreement you have just concluded with Dentz is, I must tell you, unacceptable. The authority in Syria and the Lebanon cannot pass from France to England. It belongs to Free France, and to her alone, to exercise it. She must render account for it to France. At the same time I need to bring over as many as possible of the French troops who have just been fighting against us. Their rapid and wholesale repatriation, as also the fact of their being kept all together and in isolation, deprive me of all means of acting upon them. In short, the Free French cannot consent to be kept away from a French source of reinforcements, and, above all, they do not admit that our common effort should end in establishing your authority at Damascus and Beirut."

"We have no such intention," replied Mr. Lyttelton. "Great Britain is pursuing no aim in Syria and the Lebanon other than to win the war. But that implies that the internal situation there should not be troubled. Therefore it seemed to us necessary that the Levant States should receive independence, which England has guaranteed to them. At the same time, as long as the war lasts, the military command has overriding powers as regards public order. Decisions on the spot therefore belong to it in the last resort. As for the technical conditions adopted by General Wilson and General de Verdilhac for the withdrawal and embarkation of the French troops, they also answer to our anxiety to see that things pass off in an orderly fashion. Lastly, we do not understand why you should not trust us. After all, our cause is common."

"Yes," I resumed, "our cause is common. But our position is not, and our action may cease to be. In the Levant, France is the mandatory power, not Great Britain. You speak of the independence of the states. But we alone are qualified to give it to them, and in fact are giving it them, for reasons and on terms of which we are alone judge and alone responsible. You can certainly give us your approval from outside. It is not for you to meddle with it inside. As for public order in Syria and the Lebanon, that is our affair, not yours."

"All the same," said Mr. Lyttelton, "you recognized the authority of the British High Command by our agreement of August 7, 1940."

"I have," I replied, "in fact recognized the right of that command to give directives to the Free French forces, but only in strategic matters and against the common enemy. I never intended that this prerogative should extend to sovereignty, policy, or administration in territories for which France has the responsibility. When, one day, we land on French soil proper, will you invoke the rights of the High Command in order to claim to govern France? Also, I must repeat to you that I am anxious to have contacts made with the elements who were under Vichy's orders. This, indeed, is to your advantage as well. For it would be strictly absurd to send back, without more ado, troops that have been warmed up by fighting and that we shall meet again one day, in Africa or elsewhere. Lastly, the war matériel and the command of the special troops must belong to Free France."

"You have made known to me your point of view," Mr. Lyttelton then said. "As regards our reciprocal relations in Syria and the Lebanon, we can discuss them. But as far as the armistice convention is concerned, it is signed. We must apply it."

"That convention does not bind Free France. I have not ratified it."

"Well, what do you intend to do?"

"This. To obviate all ambiguity as regards the rights which the British Command seems to wish to exercise in Syria and the

Lebanon, I have the honour to inform you that the Free French forces will no longer be dependent on that command as from July 24—that is, in three days' time. Moreover, I am ordering General Catroux to take in hand immediately the authority over the whole extent of the territory of Syria and the Lebanon, whatever opposition he may meet with from any quarter. I am giving the Free French forces the order to enter into contact, as best they may, with all other French elements and to take control of their war matériel. Finally, the reorganization of the Syrian and Lebanese troops, which we have already begun, will be actively pursued."

I handed Captain Lyttelton a note prepared in advance, laying down these conditions. As I took my leave I said to him, "You know what I myself and those who follow me have done and are doing for our alliance. You can therefore measure how great our regret would be if we were forced to see it deteriorate. But neither we nor those who, in our country, turn their hopes towards us, could admit that the alliance should work to the detriment of France. If, by ill fortune, the case should arise, we would prefer to suspend our engagements with regard to England. In any event, indeed, we shall pursue the fight against the common enemy with the means in our power. I intend to proceed to Beirut in three days. Between now and then I am ready for any negotiation which might seem to you desirable."

I left Lyttelton, who, under a cool exterior, seemed to me disturbed and uneasy. I was myself somewhat deeply moved. That afternoon I confirmed to him by letter that the subordination of the Free French forces to the British Command was ceasing on the 24th at midday, but that I was ready to settle with him the new lines for military collaboration. Finally I telegraphed Churchill as follows: "We regard the Saint John of Acre convention as being opposed, in its substance, to the military and political interests of Free France, and as being, in its form, extremely painful to our dignity. . . . I hope you may feel personally that such an attitude on the part of Great Britain, in a matter which is vital for us, aggravates my difficulties considerably and will have consequences, which I consider deplorable, from the point of view of the task I have undertaken."

It was England's turn to speak. She did so in the direction of concession. That very evening Mr. Lyttelton, having asked to see me again, spoke to me in the following terms: "I agree that certain appearances may have given you the idea that we wanted to take the place of France in the Levant. I assure you that it is mistaken. To dispel this misunderstanding, I am ready to write you a letter guaranteeing our complete disinterestedness in the political and administrative fields."

"That," I replied, "would be an auspicious statement of principle. But there remains the Saint John of Acre convention, which goes against it in an unfortunate way and which, what is more, threatens to lead to incidents between your people, who are applying it, and mine, who do not accept it. There remains also your proposed extension of the competence of your military command in the Levant, an extension incompatible with our position."

"Would you perhaps have some proposal to make to us on these two questions?"

"On the first I can see no issue other than an immediate agreement between us on the subject of the 'application' of the armistice convention, correcting in practice what is vicious in the text. As for the second question, what is necessary and urgent is that you should undertake to limit the competence of your command in Syrian and Lebanese territory to the military operations against the common enemy."

"Give me a chance to think it over."

The atmosphere was improving. After various to-ings and fro-ings we reached, to begin with, on July 24, an agreement "interpretative" of the Saint John of Acre convention—an agreement negotiated by General de Larminat and Colonel Valin on our behalf. In it the English declared themselves ready to let us make contacts with the Levant troops so as to find those among them who would come over to us, recognized that the war matériel belonged to the Free French forces, and gave up the claim to take the Syrian and Lebanese troops under their control. It was also understood that "if a substantial violation of the armistice convention by the Vichy authorities became a fact, the British forces and the Free French forces would take all measures they might consider useful to bring the Vichy troops over to Free France." As several "substantial violations" had already been reported, there was reason to believe—as Mr. Lyttelton himself assured me—that in the end the whole matter of the destination of the troops would be reconsidered.

I had no doubt of the British Minister's good will. But what were General Wilson and his Arabophile team going to do, in spite of the agreements concluded? To try to make sure that they would behave properly I telegraphed afresh to Mr. Churchill, urging him "not to let an entire army, with its units as formed, be handed over again to Vichy, to dispose of." "I must report to you," I added, "that it seems to me in accordance with elementary security to suspend the repatriation of Dentz's army, and to let the Free French proceed as they mean to do in order to bring back into the path of duty these poor troops led astray by enemy propaganda."

Next day, the 25th, Mr. Oliver Lyttelton, Minister of State in the British government, wrote to me, in the name of his country: ". . . We recognize the historic interests of France in the Levant. Great Britain has no interest in Syria or the Lebanon except to win the war. We have no desire to encroach in any way upon the position of France. Both Free France and Great Britain are pledged to the independence of Syria and the Lebanon. When this essential step has been taken, and without prejudice to it, we freely admit that France should have the dominant privileged position in the Levant among all European nations. . . . You will have seen the recent utterances of the Prime Minister in this sense, and I am glad to reaffirm them now."

In the same letter Mr. Lyttelton declared his acceptance of the text of an agreement which I had given him, concerning co-operation between the British and French military authorities in the Middle East. It said in effect that the English would have no call to interfere in the political and administrative fields in the Levant, in return for which we agreed that their command should exercise the strategic leadership—under certain well-defined conditions, indeed.

That same day I left for Damascus and Beirut.

At the solemn entry of the leader of Free France into the Syrian capital, that great city, which till then had been concerned to show its coldness towards the French authority on every occasion, was moved by an enthusiasm plain to see. A few days later, speaking in the university precincts to the country's most eminent men, who were there together with the members of the Syrian government, I met with obvious assent as I defined the aim which France, from that time on, had set before herself in the Levant.

It was on July 27 that I arrived at Beirut. The French and Lebanese troops lined the streets, while the population, massed in the open, applauded without stint. Passing through the Place des Canons, which rang with enthusiasm, I proceeded to the Petit Sérail, where I ceremonially exchanged speeches full of optimism with the head of the Lebanese government, M. Alfred Naccache. Then I moved on to the Grand Sérail, where the leading Frenchmen were assembled. The majority had given their support, and often their confidence, to the system established by Vichy. But as I made contact with them I realized, once more, how strongly accomplished facts, when they have right behind them, influence men's attitudes and even their convictions. Officials, notables, and churchmen all assured me of their loyalty and promised me to bring unreserved devotion to the service of the country under the new authority. I must say that, with few exceptions, this undertaking was kept. Almost all the Frenchmen who remained in the Lebanon and in Syria continued to show themselves—in the midst of the most difficult circumstances—ardently united within Free France, fighting as it was to liberate the country and at the same time to assume the rights and duties of France on the spot.

It was in fact most urgent to assert these rights and duties. Hardly had I reached Beirut when I realized, without surprise, how little account General Wilson and the political agents assisting him under cover of uniform took of the agreements concluded by me with Lyttelton. As regards both the carrying-out of the armistice and the behaviour of the British in Syria and the Lebanon, everything was going on as though nobody owed us anything.

Dentz, in full agreement with the English, had concentrated his troops in the region of Tripoli. He was still commanding them. The units, with their leaders, their arms, and their flags, were encamped side by side, showered by Vichy with decorations and mentions in dispatches, receiving no information except what came to them through the channel of the hierarchy, and basking in an atmosphere of imminent repatriation. Indeed, the ships, which were to take them away wholesale, were already announced from Marseille, for Darlan was not wasting a day before getting them on their way, nor the Germans before letting them leave. Meanwhile, in obedience to Dentz's orders, which the British armistice commission and the police posts were enforcing integrally, the officers and ranks found themselves forbidden to have any relations with their Free French comrades, nor had these any chance of getting in touch with them. In such conditions few came over. Instead of the honest influence which we claimed the right to exercise on the mind and conscience of men placed, as individuals, in a position to hear us and to choose, there would merely be an operation of collective embarkation applied to an army still in formation, kept in an atmosphere of rancour and humiliation and with no desire other than to leave, as soon as possible, the theatre of its useless sacrifices and bitter efforts.

While the undertakings made to us by the British government about the interpretation of the Saint John of Acre armistice remained thus a dead letter, it was exactly the same with regard to Great Britain's political disinterest in Syria and the limits of its military command's authority. While at Damascus and Beirut the encroachments kept a certain appearance of discretion, they displayed themselves openly, on the contrary, in the most sensitive regions, at which the ambitions of England or of her Husseinite vassals had always aimed.

In Jezireh, Commandant Reyniers, General Catroux's delegate, was treated as a suspect by the British forces on the spot and prevented from re-forming the Assyro-Chaldean battalions and the Syrian squadrons, which had been provisionally dispersed. At Palmyra and in the desert, Mr. Glubb, known as Glubb Pasha, the English commander of the Transjordanian Force, was rampant, endeavouring to win the Bedouin tribes over to Emir Abdullah. In the Hauran the English agents were bringing pressure upon the local chieftains to make them also recognize the authority of Abdullah and pay taxes to him. Alarming reports came from Aleppo, as also from the tribal state of the Alawis.

But it was in the Jebel ed Druz, above all, that the British showed their intentions openly. And yet no fighting had taken place there, and it had been agreed between Catroux and Wilson that the Allied troops should not penetrate there before a joint decision had been taken. It is easy to judge of our state of mind when we heard that a British brigade was installing itself there, that the Druz squadrons were being compulsorily taken in charge by the English, that certain chieftains, who had been summoned and promised immunity by Mr. Bass, known as Commodore Bass, were declaring that they rejected French authority, that at Es Suweida the Maison de France, the residence of our delegate, had been made by force into the seat of the British Command, and, finally, that the latter had, in the presence of the troops and population, hauled down the Tricolour flag on it and hoisted the Union Jack.

It was essential to react at once. General Catroux, with my agreement, gave Colonel Monclar on July 29 the order to proceed immediately to Es Suweida with a solid column, retake possession of the Maison de France, and recover the Druz squadrons. Wilson, duly warned, sent me a somewhat threatening message urging me to stop the column. I answered "that it had already reached its destination, . . . that it was open to him, Wilson, to settle with Catroux—who had proposed this to him—the question of the stationing of British and French troops in the Jebel ed Druz, . . . that I considered his menacing allusions regrettable, . . . but that, while I remained ready for frank military cooperation, the sovereign rights of France in Syria and the Lebanon and the dignity of the French army must be kept free from all injury."

At the same time Monclar, having arrived at Es Suweida, was told by the commander of the British brigade that "if there had to be a fight, they would fight," and replied with an affirmative. Things did not go so far. On July 31 Monclar was able to install himself at the Maison de France, ceremonially replace the Tri-colour upon it, quarter his troops in the town, and re-form the group of Druz squadrons under the orders of a French officer. Shortly afterwards the British forces left the region.

But, to set against one incident that was settled, many others kept arising everywhere. Wilson even announced that he was go-ing to establish what he called "martial law" and take over all powers. We warned him that, in this case, we would oppose our powers to his, and it would mean rupture. Lyttelton, though kept posted, abstained from intervening. On hearing the rumour that Catroux was about to open discussions at Beirut and Damascus with a view to the future treaties, the British Minister of State even wrote to him direct to ask, as something to be taken for granted, that Spears should be present at these negotiations. This persistent claim to meddle in our affairs, and the incessantly mul-tiplying encroachments, were now reaching the limit of what we could tolerate. On August 1, I telegraphed Cassin to go and see Mr. Eden and tell him, from me, "that meddling by England was leading us to the gravest complications, and that the doubtful advantages which British policy could derive, in the Levant, from this forgetfulness of the rights of France would be decidedly mediocre in comparison with the major disadvantages which would result from an open quarrel between Free France and England."

Open quarrel? London did not want that. On August 7 Mr. Lyttelton came to visit me at Beirut and spent the day at my residence. This was the occasion of a conference which one might have thought decisive—if anything, in the Middle East, ever was so for the British. The Minister agreed frankly that the British military were not carrying out our agreements of July 24 and 25. "In that there is no more," he affirmed, "than a delay, to be attributed to faults of transmission and, perhaps, of understanding, which I keenly regret and to which I mean to put an end." He appeared surprised and displeased at the incidents created by the English agents, of which Catroux gave chapter and verse. He declared that Vichy was violating the armistice convention; that, for example, the fifty-two British officers who had been made prisoner in the recent fighting and were supposed to be given up without delay, had not yet been so, and that it was not even known where they had been put; that, in consequence, Dentz was about to be transferred to Palestine, and that all facilities would henceforth be given us for winning people over.

I did not conceal from Lyttelton that we were outraged by the manner in which our allies were practising cooperation. "Rather than continue like this, we prefer," I told him, "to go our own way while you go yours." When he complained, in his turn, citing the obstacles we were creating for the British Command, I replied, on the lines of what Foch in person had once taught me, that there could be no such thing as a valid interallied command that was not disinterested, and that whatever he, Lyttelton, might say to me or write to me in all good faith, that was not the case here with the British. As for invoking, as Wilson was doing, the necessity of the defence of the Levant in order to usurp authority in the Jezireh, at Palmyra, and in the Jebel ed Druz, this was merely a bad excuse. The enemy was now a long way away from the Jebel ed Druz, from Palmyra, from the Jezireh. If it was wise to provide for the possibility of the Axis menace weighing on Syria and the Lebanon anew, the proper way to prepare for that was a common defence plan between French and

British, not an English policy of encroachments on our domain.

Mr. Lyttelton, anxious to end his visit on some note of harmony, caught the "defence plan" ball. He suggested bringing in General Wilson, whom I had been unwilling to have come to our meeting, to discuss it. I replied in the negative but agreed that Wilson should see Catroux outside Beirut to get a draft worked out. Their meeting took place next day. Practically nothing came of it: a proof that, on the English side, as far as the Levant was concerned, something quite other than an offensive by the Germans was in mind. However, the Minister of State, to mark his good will, had handed me, before leaving, a letter which repeated the assurances already given on the subject of Great Britain's political disinterestedness. In addition, Mr. Lyttelton had stated to me verbally that I would be satisfied by the practical results of our interview.

As so many shocks had not shattered Free France, I was prepared to believe that one might, in fact, count on a respite from our difficulties. Nonetheless I had seen enough to be sure that, sooner or later, the crisis would begin again. But sufficient unto the day is the evil thereof. To formulate the conclusion of this temporarily overcome trial, I sent to the delegation in London, which was alarmed at my attitude, messages recapitulating its phases and drawing this moral: "Our greatness and our strength consist solely in intransigence concerning the rights of France. We shall have need of this intransigence up to the Rhine, inclusive."

At any rate, from that moment things took a different turn. Larminat was able, with his staff, to visit those units which were not yet embarked and to make the last-moment appeal to officers and men. Catroux had the opportunity of seeing certain officials whom he personally wanted to keep. I myself received many visits. In the end those who came over amounted to 127 officers and about 6000 NCOs and men, or one-fifth of the strength of the troops in the Levant. In addition, the Syrian and Lebanese elements, totalling 290 officers and 14,000 men, were at once reconstituted. But 25,000 officers, NCOs, and men of the French Army and Air Force were finally torn away from us, whereas the great majority would, without any doubt, have decided to join us if we had had the time and the means to enlighten them. For those Frenchmen who were regaining France with the permission of the enemy, so giving up the possibility of returning there as fighters, were, I knew, submerged in doubt and sadness. As for me, it was with my heart wrung that I gazed at the transports sent by Vichy in the harbour and saw them, once loaded, disappear out to sea, taking with them one of the chances of our country.

At least those that remained to it on the spot could now be made to yield results. General Catroux applied himself to this most actively. Possessing the sense of the greatness of France and the taste for authority, skilful at handling men, especially those of the Middle East, whose subtle and passionate games he readily saw through, as sure of his own value as he was devoted to our great enterprise and to the man at its head, he was destined to guide the policy of France in the Levant with much dignity and distinction. If I came to think that his desire to charm and his leaning towards conciliation did not always answer to the kind of sword play which was imposed on him, if, in particular, he was late in discerning the full depths of malice of the British design, I never ceased to recognize his great merits and his high qualities. In a situation rendered exceptionally unpromising by appalling initial conditions—the lack of resources and the obstacles reared up on every side—General Catroux did France good service.

He had, to begin with, to organize from top to bottom the representation of France, which the departure of most of the "authoritative" officials and of the majority of the political officers had suddenly and everywhere reduced almost to nothing. Catroux took as his secretary-general Paul Lepissié, who had come to us from Bangkok, where he was French minister. He delegated General Collet and M. Pierre Bart, respectively, to the Syrian and

Lebanese governments. At the same time M. David, and later M. Fauquenot, at Aleppo, M. de Montjou at Tripoli, M. Dumarçay at Sidon, Governor Schoeffler, and later General Montclar, among the Alawis, and Colonels Brosset in the Jezireh, des Essars at Homs, and Oliva-Roget in the Jebel ed Druz, were to ensure our presence and our influence in each of the regions.

I must say that the populations showed warm approval of us. They saw in Free France something gallant, surprising, and chivalrous, which seemed to them to correspond to what was, in their eyes, the ideal persona of France. Besides, they felt that our presence warded off the danger of a German invasion of their territory, assured them of a future in the economic field, and imposed a limit on the abuses of their feudal lords. Lastly, our generous announcement of their independence never ceased to move them. The same manifestations which had occurred at the moment of my entry into Damascus and Beirut were renewed, a few days later, at Aleppo, at Latakia, at Tripoli, and in many towns and villages of that marvellous land, where every site and every locality, in its drama and poetry, is, as it were, a witness of history.

But while the feelings of the people showed themselves clearly favourable, the politicians yielded less frankly. Here, what was most urgent, in each of the two states, was to invest a government capable of assuming the new duties we were about to transfer to it, especially in the fields of finance, economics, and public order. We intended, in fact, to reserve to the mandatory authority merely the responsibility for defence, for foreign relations, and for the "interests common" to the two states: currency, customs, supply—all fields in which it was as impossible to hand over at once as it was to separate Syria and the Lebanon on the spur of the moment. Later, when the evolution of the war made it possible, elections would be held, from which complete national authorities would issue. Pending this stage, the setting-to-work of governments with enlarged prerogatives was already bringing clan passions and personal rivalries to the boiling point.

In Syria the situation, from this point of view, was particularly complicated. In July 1939, when Paris finally refused to ratify the 1936 treaty, the High Commissioner had been led to set aside the President of the Republic, Hashim al-Atassi, and to dissolve Parliament. We found in the saddle at Damascus, under the direction of Khaled Bey Azem, who indeed was a valuable and well-thought-of man, a ministry which confined itself to dispatching business without taking on the character of a national government. I had at first hoped to be able to re-establish in Syria the previous state of things. At first President Hashim al-Atassi and, with him, the head of his last government, Djemil Mardam Bey, and M. Fares el Koury, president of the dissolved House, had shown themselves ready in principle for this in the course of the conversations I had with them in the presence of General Catroux. But although they were all three experienced politicians, patriots devoted to their country, and men desirous of conciliating French friendship, they did not seem to discern in all its amplitude the historic opportunity, now presented to them, of setting Syria on the road to independence in full agreement with France and by overcoming misgivings and grievances in one great impulse. I found them too careful, to my way of thinking, of juridical formalities, and too sensitive to the suggestions of a punctilious nationalism. However, I invited General Catroux to pursue the conversations with them and to turn towards a different solution only if their reservations were really preventing us from getting anywhere.

In the Lebanon we were able to move faster, though what we met with was not the ideal. The President of the Republic, Emile Eddé, an unshakeable friend of France and a seasoned statesman, had voluntarily resigned three months before the campaign which brought us to Beirut. He had not been replaced. At the same time the duration of the Parliament's mandate had long expired. From the point of view of principles and of the Constitution, we had a clean slate before us. But the same could not be said of the struggles of the political clans. A desperate rivalry set against Emile Eddé another eminent Maronite, M. Bechara el Koury. Inured to the twists and turns of Lebanese affairs, he grouped around him numerous partisans and various interests. "Eddé has had the position already," M. Koury told me. "It's my turn to be President!" Lastly, Riad Solh, the passionate leader of the Sunnite Moslems, waving the standard of Arab nationalism round about the mosques, alarmed the two competitors without, however, making them agree.

We judged, in these circumstances, that it was better to raise to the supreme rank the man whom we found in the saddle at the head of the government—M. Alfred Naccache, who was less brilliant than any of the other three, but capable, esteemed, and a man whose presence at the head of the state in a transitional situation ought not, it seemed to us, to provoke vehement opposition. That, indeed, was only partly true. For while Emile Eddé adapted himself generously to our momentary choice and Riad Solh avoided embarrassing the man who was carrying the burden, M. Koury went at him full tilt with intrigues and cabals.

Pending the free consultation of the people, this political situation at Damascus and Beirut was in no way disquieting in itself. Public order was in no danger. The administration did its job. Opinion accepted straightaway the postponement of the elections due to the *force majeure* of war. In short, the transition period between the mandate regime and that of independence could and would, no doubt, pass off very peacefully, if British intervention did not systematically seek in it pretexts and opportunities.

Now, while Mr. Lyttelton, at Cairo, absorbed himself in the problems raised by the supplying of the Middle East, and while General Wilson disappeared, together with his martial law and direct encroachments, Spears was installing himself at Beirut as head of the British liaison services, to become, in January, British minister plenipotentiary to the Syrian and Lebanese governments. He had some incomparable trump cards: the presence of the British army; the multifarious activity of the Intelligence agents; the mastery of the economic relations of the two countries, which lived on exchanges; support in all capitals from the leading diplomatic service in the world; great propaganda resources; official backing from the neighbouring Arab states—Iraq and Transjordania, where Husseinite princes reigned; Palestine, whose British High Commissioner constantly displayed alarm as to the repercussions among the Arabs in his territory of the "oppression" suffered by their Syrian and Lebanese brothers; and, lastly, Egypt, where the stability of the Ministers in power and the ambition of those who aspired to reach it had alike no real chance except with British blessing.

In the permeable, intrigue-ridden, venal medium which the Levant laid open to England's plans, the game, with such cards, was easy and tempting. Only the prospect of a rupture with us and the necessity of conciliating the feelings of France could impose on London a certain moderation. But the same prospect and the same necessity similarly restricted our own freedom of action. The moral and material damage which separation from Great Britain would entail for us was bound, obviously, to make us hesitate. Besides, would not Free France, as she grew larger, lose some of that concentrated firmness which had made it possible for her to win this time by staking all on one throw? How, lastly, could we reveal to the French people the behaviour of its allies when, in the abyss where it was plunged, nothing was more vital than to arouse its confidence and hope in order to lead it into the fight against the enemy?

In spite of everything, the fact that our authority was being set up in Syria and the Lebanon brought considerable reinforcement to the camp of liberty. From now on, the Allies' rear in the Middle East was solidly protected. It was no longer possible for the Germans to get a footing in the Arab countries, unless by undertaking a large-scale and dangerous expedition. Turkey, whom Hitler hoped to harass sufficiently to make her join the Axis and serve it as a bridge between Europe and Asia, was no longer in danger of being invested and would therefore grow firmer. Finally, Free France was in a position to put increased forces into the field.

In this connection we decided to hold the Levant territories with the Syrian and Lebanese troops, a fixed coastal defence entrusted to our Navy, and a reserve formed by a French brigade, the whole placed under the orders of General Humblot. At the same time we organized two strong mixed brigades and an armoured group with the corresponding services, to go and fight elsewhere. General de Larminat, replaced in his function of High Commissioner at Brazzaville by Médecin-Général Sicé, was given command of this mobile entity, whose effectives, alas, were limited, but whose fire-power was great, thanks to the war matériel we had just taken in the Levant. On my way back through Cairo I saw General Auchinleck, the new commander-in-chief. "As soon as our forces are ready," I told him, "we shall place them at your disposal, provided it is to fight." "Rommel," he replied, "will certainly see to it that I shall find the opportunity."

But while in the Mediterranean the war was about to become concentrated on the borders of Egypt and Libya, in conditions better for us and for our allies, it was setting fire to immense expanses of Europe from the Baltic to the Black Sea. The German offensive in Russia was progressing with immense rapidity. And yet, whatever the initial successes of Hitler's armies, Russian resistance was strengthening, day after day. On the political plane as on the strategic, these were events of incalculable bearing.

Because of them, America saw offered to her a chance for decisive action. No doubt it had to be expected that Japan would soon undertake in the Pacific a diversion of great scope which would reduce and retard the intervention of the United States. But this intervention, aimed at Europe and at Africa, was henceforth certain, since a gigantic adventure now absorbed the main part of the German strength in the distances of Russia, since at the same time the British, with the help of the Free French, had been able to make sure of solid positions in the Middle East, and since, finally, the turn taken by the war was bound to awaken hope, and so a fighting spirit, in the oppressed peoples.

What I had to do now was, as far as possible, to influence Washington and Moscow, to push on towards the development of French resistance, to inspire and guide the mobilization of our resources throughout the world. For that, I needed to return to London, the centre of communications and capital of the war. I arrived there on September 1, foreseeing, after my recent experiences, what the ordeals of the enterprise would be like down to the last day, but convinced, from now on, that victory lay at the end.

CHAPTER 7

THE ALLIES

I N THE WORLD'S EYES Free France, at the approach of its second
winter, was no longer the astonishing escapade which had
been received at first with irony, pity, or tears. Its reality—political, martial, and territorial—was now to be seen on all sides.
From now on, what it needed was to debouch onto the diplomatic
plane, clear the space which belonged to it in the midst of the
Allies, appear there as belligerent and sovereign France, whose
rights must be respected and whose share of victory reserved.
In these matters I was prepared to submit to periods of transition. But I was neither willing nor able to concede anything as
regards the substance. Besides, I was impatient to reach results
and to acquire the position before the decisive collision should
have settled the outcome of the war. There was therefore no time
to lose, especially with the great powers: Washington, Moscow,
and London.

The United States brings to great affairs elementary feelings
and a complicated policy. This was the case in 1941 with their
attitude towards France. While in the depths of American opinion
the enterprise of General de Gaulle aroused passionate response,
the whole fringe of officialdom persisted in treating it with coldness or indifference. As for the officials, they kept their relations

with Vichy unchanged, claiming thus to be wresting France from German influence, preventing the fleet from being handed over, maintaining contact with Weygand, Noguès, and Boisson, whom Roosevelt expected one day to open to him the gates of Africa. But, with an astonishing self-contradiction, the policy of the United States, while keeping diplomatic relations with Pétain, held aloof from Free France on the pretext that it was impossible to prejudge what government the French nation would give itself when it was liberated. At bottom, what the American policy-makers took for granted was the effacement of France. They therefore came to terms with Vichy. If, nonetheless, at certain points of the world they contemplated collaborating with this or that French authority as the struggle might dictate, they intended that this should be only by episodic and local arrangements.

These conditions made agreement with Washington difficult for us. Besides, the personal equation of the President affected the problem with a factor that was the opposite of favourable. Although Franklin Roosevelt and I had not yet been able to meet, various signs made me aware of his reserve towards me. I wanted, nonetheless, to do everything possible to prevent the United States, then about to enter the war, and France, for whom I was ready to answer that she had never left it, from following divergent paths.

As for the form of the relations to be established—a subject which the politicians, diplomats, and publicists were to discuss to their hearts' content—I must say that to me at that time it was almost a matter of indifference. I attached much more importance to the reality and content of the relations than to the successive formulas which the jurists of Washington would drape about the "recognition." At the same time, in face of America's enormous resources and the ambition of Roosevelt to make law and dictate rights throughout the world, I felt that independence was well and truly at stake. In short, while I wanted to try to reach an understanding with Washington, we had to do so on practical foundations and yet standing on our own feet.

During the heroic period of the first months of Free France, Garreau-Dombasle and Jacques de Sieyès had served me most usefully as spokesmen. It was now a matter of negotiating. I instructed Pleven to begin the approaches. He knew America. He was skilful. There was nothing he did not know of our own affairs. As early as May 1941 I had laid down this mission for him as follows: "Settling the establishment of our permanent and direct relations with the State Department, the economic relations of Free French Africa and Oceania with America and the direct purchases by us of matériel useful for the war; setting on foot our information and our propaganda services in the United States; forming our committees there and organizing the assistance of American well-wishers." Pleven had left at the beginning of June and was not arriving empty-handed. In fact we were offering the United States, immediately, the possibility of installing their air forces in the Cameroons, the Chad, and the Congo, Africa being marked out in advance to serve them as a base for approaching Europe when the day came on which they would have to take armed action. In addition, in face of the Japanese menace, the assistance of the Pacific islands over which the Cross of Lorraine was flying would have considerable importance for them.

In fact, the American government was not slow to ask for the right to use certain of our African bases, and then those in the New Hebrides and New Caledonia, for its aircraft. Not being yet belligerent, it did so on behalf of Pan-American Airways, but without there being any possible doubt as to the significance of its step.

As the United States saw approaching them the date when war would fall due, Washington showed us more attention. In August a liaison mission directed by Colonel Cunningham was sent to the Chad. In September, Mr. Cordell Hull stated publicly that there was a community of interests between the United States and Free France. "Our relations with this group," he added, "are very good in all respects." On October 1 Pleven was received officially at the State Department by the Undersecretary of State, Sumner

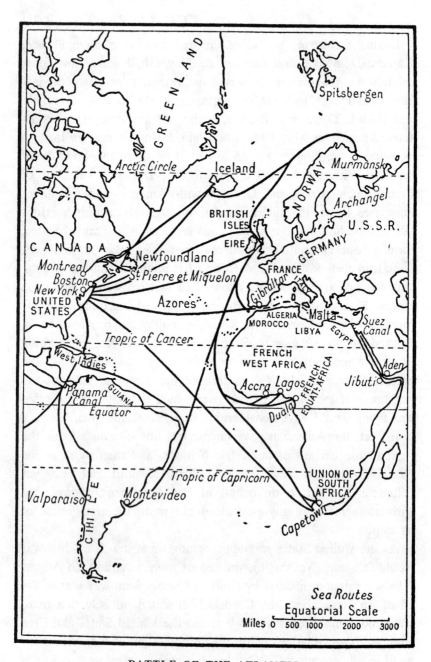

BATTLE OF THE ATLANTIC

Welles. On November 11 President Roosevelt, in a letter to Mr. Stettinius, extended the benefit of Lend-Lease to Free France because "the defence of the territories rallied to Free France was vital for the defence of the United States." At the end of the same month Weygand, recalled from Algiers, took with him an American illusion, and Washington did not yet know by what other to replace it. Meanwhile, Pleven having returned to London to serve as a member of the National Committee which I had just set up, Adrien Tixier, the director of the International Labour Office, became head of our delegation, in agreement with the State Department. Lastly, in London itself, regular relations had been established between us and Mr. Drexel Biddle, ambassador of the United States to the refugee governments in Great Britain.

While the first official relations were thus being drawn together, various changes became noticeable in the press and radio, hitherto malevolent about us, when not silent. At the same time there were signs among the French émigrés, some of whom were men of note, of the desire to link themselves with those who were upholding the flag. So it was that when Professor Focillon founded the Ecole Libre des Hautes Etudes at New York, grouping together the leading scientists, historians, and philosophers, he obtained the agreement of his colleagues that he should ask General de Gaulle to recognize its establishment by decree.

On December 7 the attack on Pearl Harbor hurled America into the war. One might have thought that, from that moment, American policy would treat as allies the Free French who were fighting its own enemies. Nothing of the sort happened, however. Before Washington finally made up its mind to do so, many painful ups and downs would have to be endured. So it was that, on December 13, the American government requisitioned in its ports the liner *Normandie* and thirteen other French ships, without consenting to treat with us, or even to talk with us, about the use to be made of them or the arming of them. A few weeks later the *Normandie* went up in flames, in lamentable circumstances. On January 1, 1942, the Declaration of the wartime United Nations was signed by twenty-six governments, of whom we were not one. The strange, not to say troubling, nature of the attitude of the United States towards us was to be revealed, indeed, by an incident almost insignificant in itself but which was given serious importance by the official reaction of Washington. Perhaps, on my side, I had provoked it in order to stir up the bottom of things, as one throws a stone into a pond. This was the rallying of Saint Pierre and Miquelon.

We had thought of this since the beginning. It was indeed scandalous that, quite close to Newfoundland, a small French archipelago, whose population was asking to join us, should be kept in obedience to Vichy. The British, haunted by the idea that, right on the route of the big convoys, the German submarines might one day receive assistance thanks to the radio station at Saint Pierre, wished it to be rallied. But, according to them, Washington's agreement was necessary. As for me, I considered this agreement desirable but not indispensable, since this was merely an internal French affair. Indeed I was all the more determined to gain control of the archipelago when I saw Admiral Robert, Vichy's High Commissioner for the Antilles, Guiana, and Saint Pierre, treating with the Americans—the end of which could only be the neutralization of these French territories under Washington's guarantee. Hearing in December that, in point of fact, Admiral Horne had been sent by Roosevelt to settle with Robert the terms for the neutralization of our possessions in America, and of the ships there, I decided to act at the first opportunity.

This opportunity presented itself in the form of Admiral Muselier. As he was to go to Canada to inspect the submarine cruiser *Surcouf,* then stationed at Halifax, together with the French corvettes on convoy escort duty, I arranged with him that, in principle, he should carry out the operation. In fact, on December 12, having grouped the corvettes *Mimosa, Aconit,* and *Alysse* around the *Surcouf,* he held himself ready to move on to Saint Pierre and Miquelon. But he thought it right, on his own, to ask the Canadians and Americans at Ottawa for their assent beforehand. The secret was thus out. I found myself obliged to warn the British in order to avoid the appearance of concealment. To Muselier, Washington sent the answer No! through its minister at Ottawa, and the admiral assured him that from that moment he was giving up the idea of going to the islands. To me the London government wrote that, for its part, it raised no obstacle, but that, given the American opposition, it requested that the operation should be postponed. In these circumstances, and barring some new fact, we would have to resign ourselves to this.

But the new fact did arise. A few hours after replying to me the Foreign Office let us know—was that intentional?—that the Canadian government, in agreement with the United States, if not at their instigation, had decided to land at Saint Pierre, with consent or by force, the staff necessary to take over the radio station. We at once protested in London and Washington. But as soon as foreign intervention on French territory was in question, no hesitation seemed to me permissible. I gave Admiral Muselier the order to win Saint Pierre and Miquelon over at once. He did so on Christmas Eve, in the midst of the greatest enthusiasm from the inhabitants, without a shot having to be fired. A plebiscite gave Free France a crushing majority. The young people at once joined up. The men in their prime formed a detachment to ensure the defence of the islands. Savary, appointed as administrator, replaced the Governor.

One might have thought that this small operation, carried out so happily, would have been ratified by the American government without any shock. The most to be normally expected was a little ill humour in the offices of the State Department. But no, it was a real storm that broke in the United States. Mr. Cordell Hull himself began it with a communiqué in which he announced that he was interrupting his Christmas holidays and returning in haste to Washington. "The action taken by three so-called Free French ships at Saint Pierre–Miquelon," the Secretary of State added, "was an arbitrary action contrary to the agreement of all parties and certainly without the prior knowledge or consent of the United

States government." He ended by declaring that his government had "inquired of the Canadian government as to the steps that government is prepared to take to restore the *status quo* of these islands."

In the United States, for three weeks, the tumult in the press and the emotion of public opinion went beyond all imaginable limits. This was because the incident suddenly offered the American public the opportunity of manifesting its preference between an official policy which was still based on Pétain and the feeling of many which was inclining towards de Gaulle. As for us, the end having been attained, we now aimed at bringing Washington to a more just understanding of things. As Churchill was at Quebec, in conference with Roosevelt, I telegraphed to the Prime Minister to warn him of the bad effect produced on French opinion by the State Department's attitude. Churchill replied that he would do all he could to see that the affair was settled, although he referred to favourable developments as being held up by it. At the same time Tixier, on my behalf, handed appeasing messages to Mr. Cordell Hull, while Roussy de Sales used his credit with the American press for the same purpose and we tried to enlist Mr. Bullitt, the last United States ambassador to the Republic, who was then in Cairo.

The Washington government, faced by much criticism in its own country and tacit disapproval from England and Canada, could in the end only accept the accomplished fact. However, before consenting to this, it tried intimidation, using the British government as intermediary. But this intermediary was itself not very convinced. Mr. Eden saw me twice on January 14 and put up a show of insisting that we should agree to the islands being neutralized, to the administration being independent of the National Committee, and to a control by Allied officials being established on the spot. As I refused such a solution, Mr. Eden announced to me that the United States was thinking of sending a cruiser and two destroyers to Saint Pierre. "What will you do then?" he asked me. "The Allied ships," I answered, "will stop at the limit of territorial waters, and the American admiral will come to lunch with Muselier, who will be delighted." "But if the cruiser crosses the limit?" "Our people will summon her to stop in the usual way." "If she holds on her course?" "That would be most unfortunate, for then our people would have to open fire." Mr. Eden threw up his arms. "I can understand your alarm," I concluded with a smile, "but I have confidence in the democracies."

The only thing to do was to turn over the page. On January 19 Mr. Cordell Hull received Tixier and explained to him without bitterness the reasons for the policy he had pursued up to then. Not long afterwards he took cognizance of the reply I had had conveyed to him. On the 22nd, Mr. Churchill, back in England, sent to ask me to call on him. I went with Pleven. The Prime Minister, with Eden beside him, proposed to us on behalf of Washington, London, and Ottawa an arrangement according to which everything at Saint Pierre and Miquelon would remain as we had ordered it. In exchange, we were to let the three governments publish a communiqué which would to some extent save the face of the State Department. "After which," the British Ministers told us, "no one will meddle in the business." We accepted the arrangement. In the end nothing was published. We kept Saint Pierre and Miquelon, and none of the Allies bothered about it any more.

Moreover, whatever might be Washington's juridical position and feeling towards us, the entry of the United States into the war obliged them to cooperate with Free France. This was the case, immediately, with the Pacific, where, by reason of the lightning advance of the Japanese, our possessions—New Caledonia, the Marquesas, Tuamotu, the Society Islands, and even Tahiti— might from one day to the next become vital to Allied strategy. Some of them were already being used as naval and air stopping places. In addition, New Caledonia's nickel was of great importance for armaments manufacture. The Americans soon saw the advantage which an understanding with us would present. This was true reciprocally, for if the need arose we would not be capable of defending our islands by ourselves. It was thus of set policy that our National Committee had decided in advance to give satisfaction to what the Americans would ask of us as regards our possessions in the Pacific Ocean, on the sole condition that they on their side would respect French sovereignty and our own authority there.

It was necessary, however, that this authority should be exercised on the spot in a satisfactory way. This would certainly not be easy in view of the extreme remoteness and dispersion of our islands, the shortage of resources, and the character of the populations—who were certainly very attached to France and had proved it by rallying, but were on the other hand unstable and accessible to the intrigues that were being stimulated by local or foreign interests. Moreover, many of the best of the elements that had been mobilized had, on my orders, left Oceania to come and fight in the Free French forces in Africa. Thus the fine and gallant Pacific Battalion, together with other small units, had been sent to the Middle East under the command of Lieutenant-Colonel Broche. This contribution by Oceania to the fighting for the liberation of France had high significance. But it made the direct defence of our settlements more precarious. Lastly, the state of war was disorganizing the economic life of these remote possessions. In short, there was imperious need of an authority as strong and centralized as possible in Oceania.

As early as the spring of 1941 I had thought it wise to send Governor-General Brunot, who had become available when Leclerc had liberated the Cameroons, on a tour of inspection. But Brunot had come up, often violently, against officials who attributed to him, not without apparent reason, the intention of installing himself and his friends there in their place. Papeete had been the scene of tragi-comic incidents. The Governor, the Secretary-General, and the consul for Great Britain there had been placed under arrest at M. Brunot's orders, while at Nouméa, Governor Sautot made no secret of his mistrust of the inspector.

Exceptional measures were necessary. In July 1941 I appointed Captain—later Admiral—Thierry d'Argenlieu as High Commissioner in the Pacific, with full civil and military powers and, as mission, "to re-establish definitively and without half-measures the authority of Free France, to render operative for war all the resources which are there, and to assure there, against all the dangers which are possible and perhaps imminent, the defence of the French territories in union with our allies."

I had confidence in d'Argenlieu. His lofty character and firmness gave him the moral qualifications to dominate intrigues. His capabilities as a leader made me feel sure that our resources would be used with vigour but also with deliberation. His diplomatic talents would find scope. For while his nature and, if I may say so, his vocation,[1] led him to conceive of the action of Free France as a crusade, he thought, and rightly, that this crusade could perfectly well be skilful. The light cruiser *Le Triomphant* and the sloop *Chevreuil* were placed at the disposal of the High Commissioner in the Pacific. He began by putting things in order once more in Tahiti. Orselli was appointed governor there, while Brunot and his "victims" came to state their case in London. At the same time, with the situation in the Far East becoming graver day by day, d'Argenlieu saw his original mission augmented by that of coordinating the activities of our representatives in Australia, New Zealand, and China, as well as at Hong Kong, Singapore, Manila, and Batavia. At the same time Escarra, who was already well known among the Chinese as an international jurist, proceeded to Chungking to make contact with Marshal Chiang Kai-shek and prepare for the establishment of official relations.

Suddenly, at the beginning of December, the Pacific caught fire.

[1] After serving in the French Navy during the First World War, he joined the Carmelite Order in 1920. In 1932 he was chosen as Provincial of the Carmelite Order. In August 1939 he was again called to the service of France and was placed on the staff of the Cherbourg sector. In June 1940 he played an active part in the defense of the arsenal and was made prisoner. Having escaped to the French coast from the convoy taking him to Germany, he crossed the Channel and joined General de Gaulle. (Translator's note.)

After the terrible surprise at Pearl Harbor, the Japanese landed in British Malaya, in the Netherlands East Indies, and in the Philippines, and seized Guam, Wake, and Hong Kong. By the beginning of January they were blockading a British army at Singapore, and it was soon forced to capitulate. At the same time they took Manila. MacArthur was besieged in the Bataan peninsula. What I knew of this general made me esteem him highly. One day I went to call on John Winant, United States ambassador in London, a diplomat of great intelligence and feeling, and spoke as follows: "As a soldier and an ally, I must tell you that the disappearance of MacArthur would be a great misfortune. There are only a few first-class military leaders in our camp. He is one of them. He must not be lost. But he is lost unless his government gives him the order personally to leave Bataan by some combination of motorboat and flying boat. I think this order ought to be given him and am asking you to make General de Gaulle's opinion on this subject known to President Roosevelt." I do not know whether my approach did or did not contribute to the decision which was taken. In any case it was with great satisfaction that I heard, some time afterwards, that General MacArthur had managed to reach Melbourne.

As early, then, as the end of December, New Caledonia was threatened—and all the more so since it flanked Australia, a principal enemy objective. On December 22, indeed, Vichy, foreseeing the occupation of our islands in Oceania by the Japanese and wishing, no doubt, to try to regain authority there under cover of the invader, appointed Admiral Decoux as High Commissioner for the Pacific. By means of the Saigon radio he ceaselessly incited the population of New Caledonia to revolt against Free France. Meanwhile, d'Argenlieu, struggling in the midst of anxieties and difficulties, was sending me reports full of determination but free from any illusion. As for me, while assuring him of my certainty that he would save honour at least, I dispatched to Nouméa the few reinforcements available: cadres, naval guns, the auxiliary cruiser *Cap des Palmes,* and, lastly, the *Surcouf,* whose submarine usefulness and wide radius of action would, it was hoped, find scope for themselves in the Pacific. Alas! On the night of February 19, near the entrance to the Panama Canal, this submarine—the largest in the world—was run down by a cargo boat and sank with her commander, Capitaine de Corvette Blaison, and her crew of 130 men.

Meanwhile, under the pressure of events, cooperation with our allies was beginning to get organized. On January 15 the State Department sent our Washington delegation a memorandum laying down the undertakings into which the United States were entering with reference to "respect for our sovereignty in the French islands of the Pacific; the fact that the bases and installations which they would be authorized to establish there would remain the property of France; the right of reciprocity which would be recognized as belonging to France if the American bases were kept there after the war." On January 23 Mr. Cordell Hull telegraphed me that "the American and British chiefs of staff appreciated the importance of New Caledonia and were taking steps to ensure its defence in accordance with the conditions laid down in the memorandum of January 15." The Secretary of State graciously expressed "his hope that the splendid assistance and the cooperation offered in the past by the French High Commissioner would be continued in the future."

Practical measures followed these excellent moves. On February 25 I was able to announce to d'Argenlieu that General Patch, who had been appointed commander of the American land forces in the Pacific, had received orders from his government to go to Nouméa and there to reach agreement with him "directly and in the most friendly spirit" on the organization of the command. On March 6 the French National Committee was invited to send its representative to the Pacific War Committee, which had been set up in London and on which delegates from Great Britain, New Zealand, Australia, and the United States sat for the purpose of exchanging information and suggestions. On March 7 the American government asked us for, and obtained, authorization to establish bases in the Tuamotu Archipelago and the Society Islands. Lastly, on March 9, General Patch arrived at Nouméa, followed by considerable forces.

The French possessions in the Pacific had, from that moment, some chance of escaping invasion. However, before cooperation between our allies and us could work on the spot as it should, a serious crisis was to arise and require surmounting. At first, certainly, harmony reigned between Patch and d'Argenlieu. But soon the presence of American forces, dollars, and secret services, in the midst of populations disturbed by siege fever, was to aggravate the latent causes of agitation. Part of the militia, stirred by local ambitions, stole away from the High Commissioner's authority and placed itself under that of Patch, who committed the error of covering this insubordination. At the same time Governor Sautot, who found it hard to endure being subordinated to d'Argenlieu, sought to acquire a personal popularity of which he might make use. When, after exercising patience for some time, I summoned Sautot to London to give him a different post—and indeed one suitable to the services he had rendered—he decided at first to obey, but then, giving as his reason "the discontent caused among the population by the order he had received," he took it upon himself to "postpone his departure."

Governor Sautot was nonetheless shipped away—with the proper formalities and the requisite firmness—to answer my summons, Montchamp being sent from the Chad to replace him, and Colonel de Conchard dispatched from London to command the troops. But there followed, at Nouméa and in the bush, violent demonstrations openly encouraged by the attitude of the Americans. Having a foreboding of some unfortunate move, I had warned Washington, and at the same time let Patch know, that "we could not accept his interference in a French matter." But simultaneously I invited d'Argenlieu "to make the greatest efforts to re-establish personal relations of confidence with Patch and to show, if possible, some good nature towards a population which is obviously disturbed." After three days of incidents, good sense resumed its sway and d'Argenlieu all the levers of command. Indeed it was urgent, for on May 6 at Corregidor and on the 10th at Mindanao the last American forces in the Philippines had capitulated, while in the Coral Sea, which washes Australia on the northeast, a battle was beginning on which all depended, between the fleets of Japan and the United States. From one moment to another, Nouméa might be attacked.

In face of the imminent peril, the population, condemning the recent disorders, drew together about the French authority. Various turbulent individuals were sent off to serve in Syria. Patch, on his side, went to see d'Argenlieu to excuse himself for the "misunderstandings" in which he had become involved. I telegraphed the American general that he had my confidence and that of Free France, provided he marched hand in hand with the High Commissioner of France. After which, Americans and French went off, together and resolutely, to take up their battle stations. As things happened, indeed, they did not have to defend themselves. For at that very moment the Japanese, beaten in the Coral Sea, were obliged to give up the idea of attacking Australia and New Caledonia.

In this way the war was forcing the United States to entertain closer and closer relations with us. It must be said that, in their own country, the national mood favoured this. At a time when the American people were inspired by instinctive idealism to a crusading fervour and had decided to impose upon themselves an immense and magnificent armament and mobilization effort, the fighters of Free France could not fail to be popular. Politics were bound to feel the effects. In February 1942 we were in a position to complete our delegation in Washington by a military mission, which I entrusted to Colonel de Chevigné. On March 1, in a public statement, America recognized that "the French Islands in the Pacific were under the effective control of the French National Committee, and that it was with the authorities exercising this control that the government of the United States was dealing and would continue to deal." As for Equatorial Africa, the State Department declared in a communiqué dated April 4, that there too it recognized the authority of Free France, while a United States consul-general was being appointed to Brazzaville with our exequatur. Since the United States were asking us for the right to use the airdrome at Pointe-Noire for their heavy bombers, we gave them the authorization on condition that they should first supply us with the eight Lockheed aircraft indispensable to our own communications. After a close negotiation the Lockheeds were delivered to us, and this made it possible for Colonel de Marmier to establish a French line between Brazzaville and Damascus and for the American aircraft to land and take off at Pointe-Noire. Between America and us the air had been cleared without our having ceased—far from it—to stand up for France.

While we were, step by step and not without trouble, reducing tl e diplomatic distance that separated Washington from Free France, we managed, in one leap, to create a relationship of alliance with Moscow. It must be said that, in this respect, the attack launched by Hitler simplified the procedure by placing Russia in mortal peril. At the same time the Soviets realized the absurdity of the policy by which they had, in 1917 and in 1939, treated with Germany and turned their back on France and England. In the extreme disarray into which the invasion was plunging them, the rulers of the Kremlin were now seen to reverse their attitude immediately and without reserve. Whereas the Moscow radio had not ceased to hold forth against the "English imperialists" and "their Gaullist mercenaries" up to the very moment when the German tanks crossed the Russian frontier, the Moscow wave lengths were heard pouring forth encomia on Churchill and de Gaulle literally an hour afterwards.

In any case, for crushed France the fact that Russia was now thrown into the war opened up the greatest hopes. Unless the Reich succeeded in rapidly liquidating the army of the Soviets, the latter would make the enemy suffer a constant and terrible attrition. I had no doubt, obviously, that a victory in which the Soviets would have taken a major share might well, *ipso facto,* face the world with other perils later. These would have to be taken into account even as we fought at their side. But I considered that, before philosophizing, one must live—that is to say, win. Russia offered the chance of doing so. At the same time her presence in the Allied camp brought Fighting France a balancing element over against the Anglo-Saxons, of which I was determined to make use.

It was at Damascus, where I had gone after the entry of our troops into the town, that I heard, on June 23, 1941, of the opening of hostilities between Russians and Germans. My decision was made at once. As early as the 24th, I telegraphed the delegation in London the following instructions: "Without consenting to discuss at present the vices and even crimes of the Soviet regime, we must proclaim—like Churchill—that we are very frankly with the Russians, since they are fighting the Germans. . . . It is not the Russians who are crushing France, occupying Paris, Reims, Bordeaux, and Strasbourg. . . . The German aircraft, tanks, and soldiers which the Russians are destroying and will destroy will no longer be there to prevent us from liberating France." Such is the tone I ordered to be given to our propaganda. At the same time I invited our delegation to go to M. Maisky, the Soviet ambassador in London, and tell him in my name: "The French people are with the Russians against Germany. We desire, therefore, to organize military relations with Moscow."

Cassin and Dejean saw M. Maisky, who immediately showed himself as well disposed as could be wished. As for practical consequences, the rupture of relations between Vichy and Moscow, a rupture exacted by Hitler from Vichy, was soon to make things easier. From Beirut, on August 2, I invited Cassin and Dejean, therefore, to ask M. Maisky "if Russia would be disposed to entertain direct relations with us, . . . and if she would contemplate addressing a declaration to us on the subject of her intention to help restore the independence and greatness of France—adding to those words, if possible, the word 'integrity.' "

The conversations resulted, on September 26, in an exchange

of letters between M. Maisky and myself. The ambassador of the USSR declared, in the name of his government, that it "recognized me as Leader of all the Free French, . . . that it was ready to enter into relations with the French Empire Defence Council over all questions relative to collaboration with the overseas territories placed under my authority, . . . that it was disposed to lend aid and assistance to the Free French for the common struggle, . . . and that it was resolved to ensure the full and entire restoration of the independence and greatness of France. . . ." Nonetheless the Soviets did not—any more than Great Britain had done in the agreement of August 7, 1940—mention our territorial integrity.

Shortly afterwards the Soviet government accredited M. Bogomolov as its representative to the National Committee. M. Bogomolov came from Vichy, where for the last year he had been ambassador to Pétain. He adapted himself without any embarrassment to the—to say the least—novel conditions in which he was to serve. Never, however, did I hear from his mouth any malevolent personal remark about those—Marshal or Ministers—to whom he had just been representing his government. In one of our conversations he even went out of his way to tell me this: "At Vichy I had leisure, and used it to wander incognito through the countryside, chatting with the good people. A peasant, who was ploughing, said to me one day, 'It's very sad that the French should have been beaten at the start. But look at this field! I can till it because they've managed to fix things up so that the Germans let me keep it. You'll see, soon they'll manage to fix it up so that they clear out of France.' " I supposed that, by this fable in illustration of the theory of the shield and the sword, M. Bogomolov meant to show me that he had understood the French situation thoroughly and, at the same time, to explain to me the reasons for Soviet Russia's successive attitudes.

From that time onwards I saw M. Bogomolov often. In the steps he took and the things he said, to the utmost extent to which the crushing rigidity imposed on him allowed him to show himself human, he did so. Stiff, on his guard, all of a piece, when he was making or receiving an official communication, this man of real culture showed himself, in other circumstances, winning and relaxed. In his judgments of people and things he could be humorous, even going so far as to smile. I must say that by my contact with him I became convinced that, while the Soviet rule encased the personality of its servants in an iron mask without a chink, it was unable to prevent there being still a man underneath.

For our part, we had sent General Petit to Moscow as military liaison. The Soviets had at once shown that they were predisposed to treat him graciously and with consideration: staff conferences, a visit to the front, reception by Stalin himself. I had occasion, indeed, to wonder, later, if the purpose of their advances to Petit was merely professional. In any case the reports which came from various sources gave the impression that the Russian armies, at first broken by the German offensive, were gradually recovering, that the people, in their deep recesses, were arising for resistance, and that Stalin, in the national peril, was endeavouring, by appointing himself field marshal and never appearing out of uniform, to seem not so much the mandatory of the regime as the leader of everlasting Russia.

The map of the vast battle was spread out on the walls of our offices. There the gigantic effort of the Germans could be seen developing. Their three groups of armies—von Leeb, von Bock, and von Rundstedt—had in four months penetrated to the heart of the Russian lands, taken several hundred thousand prisoners, and seized an enormous booty. But in December, round about Moscow, the vigorous activity of Zhukov, powerfully aided by a harsh and premature winter, checked the invader, then made him draw back. Leningrad had not fallen. Sebastopol was still holding out. It seemed that Hitler had not succeeded in imposing on the German High Command the only strategy that could have been decisive, that is, the grouping of all its mechanized forces solely in the direction of the Soviet capital, so as to strike straight at the enemy's heart. In spite of the model victories of the campaigns in Poland, France, and the Balkans, the Führer had this time had to offer up sacrifices to the time-honoured errors, distribute the shock resources between his three marshals, deploy a front instead of launching a battering ram. Surprise once past, the Russians, over immense expanses, would make him pay dearly for it.

Meanwhile we tried to furnish a direct contribution, however modest, to the eastern front. Our corvettes and our cargo boats took part in the Allied convoys which were carrying war matériel to Murmansk through the Arctic Ocean, under the hardest conditions. As I could not succeed at first in getting the British to agree that the two light divisions formed in the Levant by Larminat should be engaged in Libya, I gave General Catroux in February the order to prepare the transfer of one of them to Iran and the Caucasus—which enchanted the Russians and worried the English. Later, when Larminat's troops were after all detailed for the battle against Rommel, I sent to Russia the Normandie fighter group (later the Normandie-Niémen Air Squadron), which was to do magnificent service there and was the only western force fighting on the eastern front. Inversely, we saw arrive in London, under the leadership of Captain Billotte, a detachment of about fifteen officers and two hundred men, who, having escaped from German prison camps, had managed to reach Russia, only to be interned there. Released shortly after the beginning of the Germano-Soviet war, they reached us via Spitzbergen, on board a convoy returning from Archangel.

On January 20, 1942, in a broadcast, I paid tribute to Russia's military recovery and affirmed the alliance we had made with her for the present and for the future. In February, Roger Garreau, who till then had been minister plenipotentiary at Bangkok and now had joined Free France, was sent to Moscow as delegate of the National Committee. For three years Garreau was to represent France in Russia effectively and intelligently, make all the contacts allowed by the regime, and keep us well informed. As soon as he reached his post he saw M. Molotov and M. Vishinsky, respectively Commissar and Vice-Commissar for Foreign Affairs, and also M. Lozovsky, Vice-Minister. All three expressed to him with insistence their government's intention of creating the closest possible relations with Fighting France.

In May, M. Molotov came to London. On the 24th I had a very thorough conversation with him. He was accompanied by Bogomolov and I by Dejean. That day, as afterwards, I found in M. Molotov a man who seemed both physically and mentally— lock, stock, and barrel—made to fill the office which had been delegated to him. His tone serious, his gestures rare, his politeness thoughtful but stiff, his gaze directed within himself, the Soviet Minister for Foreign Affairs said what he had to say evenly and listened with attention. But he let nothing escape him that appeared spontaneous. Nothing would move him, make him laugh, or irritate him. Whatever problem was raised, one felt that he knew the file about it, that he was registering faultlessly the new elements added to it by the conversation, that he was formulating his official position exactly, but that he would not depart from what had been prepared and decided elsewhere. He had certainly, in the past, brought to concluding the German-Soviet agreement with Ribbentrop the same assurance that he brought to negotiating, now, the Western pacts. In Molotov, who was and wanted to be merely a perfectly adjusted cog in an implacable machine, I thought I had identified a complete success of the totalitarian system. I paid tribute to its greatness. But however much of what was at the bottom might remain hidden from me, I could feel the melancholy of it.

In the course of our conversation in London the Soviet Minister for Foreign Affairs reached agreement with me on what his government and the National Committee should do for each other in the immediate future. Free France would urge the American and British allies to open a second front in Europe as soon as possible. At the same time she would aid, by her diplomatic and public attitude, in doing away with the isolation to which Soviet Russia had long been relegated. The latter, on her side, would support us in Washington and London in our effort to re-establish the unity of the Empire and national unity by fighting. This would apply to the administration of our territories—for instance, Madagascar—to the so-called parallel, but in reality separatist, enterprises which the Anglo-Saxons were encouraging, and finally to the resistance movements in France—about which Moscow recognized that no foreign government, even that of the Soviets, had the right to turn any of them from obedience to General de Gaulle. As for the future, it was agreed that France and Russia should work together over the shaping of the peace. "My government," M. Molotov told me, "is the ally of those in London and Washington. It is essential for the war that we should collaborate closely with them. But, with France, Russia desires to have an independent alliance."

The effort of Free France to widen its relations in the directions of Washington and Moscow did not prevent its centre from still functioning in London, or its affairs—military activity, liaison with Metropolitan France, propaganda, information, finance, economic life of the overseas territories—from being, by the force of things, dovetailed, as it were, with those of the British. The consequence, for us, was the obligation to maintain closer relations with them than ever. But their encroachments were more painful to us as we grew bigger. And yet the entry of Russia and America into the war, which involved for England, in her turn, the heavy servitude of an alliance with giants, might well have led her to bring her policy closer to ours and to practise a frank solidarity with us, covering action in Europe, the Middle East, Africa, and the Pacific. We would have lent ourselves willingly to such a change, and we sometimes had the impression that certain British leaders were also ready for it.

Anthony Eden, for instance. This British Minister, though as British and as ministerial as could be, showed an openness of mind and a sensitiveness that were European rather than insular, human rather than administrative. This favoured child of British traditions—Eton, Oxford, Conservative party, House of Commons, Foreign Office—was nonetheless accessible to what seemed to be spontaneous and to break new ground. This diplomat entirely devoted to his country's interests did not despise those of others, and remained careful of international morality in the midst of the cynical brutalities of his time. I often had to deal with Mr. Eden. Many questions that we had to discuss were frankly disagreeable. On most of these occasions I admired not only his brilliant intelligence, his knowledge of affairs, and the charm of his manners, but also the art he had of creating and maintaining around the negotiation a sympathetic atmosphere which favoured agreement when that was possible and avoided wounds when it was not. Above all, I am convinced that Anthony Eden felt a special affection for France. From her he had derived a large part of his culture. To his political brain she seemed clearly indispensable to the balance of a world assailed by every sort of barbarism. Lastly, this man with a heart did not fail to be sensitive to the plight of a great nation.

However, Mr. Eden's good intentions were not able to make the alliance a rose without thorns. I recognize that he was often thwarted in his efforts by the spiked and touchy qualities he met with in us. But it was chiefly from the British side that the difficulties arose: the suspiciousness of the Foreign Office, ambitions of the Colonials, prejudices of the military, intrigues of Intelligence. At the same time political society in London, though on the whole favourable to Free France, was subject to influences that were not always so. Certain conservative circles eyed frowningly these Cross of Lorraine Frenchmen who talked of revolution. Various labour people wondered, on the contrary, whether de Gaulle and his companions had not a tendency towards fascism. I can still see Mr. Attlee coming softly into my office, asking for the assurances needed to relieve his conscience as a democrat, and then, after he had heard me, withdrawing with a smile on his face.

In the last resort everything depended on the Prime Minister. He, deep down, could not bring himself to admit the independence of Free France. What was more, Mr. Churchill, each time we came into collision on account of the interests for which we were respectively responsible, treated our disagreement as a personal thing. He was hurt by it and grieved, in proportion to the friendship which bound us to each other. This attitude of mind and sentiment, added to the devices of his political tactics, plunged him into fits of anger which gave our relationship some rude shocks.

Other reasons, besides, converged to make this great man irascible at that time. The English, while pouring forth meritorious and glorious exertions throughout that period, notably in the submarine struggle, sometimes suffered reverses that were all the more galling because the enemy who inflicted them had not always the material superiority. On December 10, 1941, at sea off Malaya, the magnificent battleship *Prince of Wales* and the battle cruiser *Repulse* were sunk by Japanese aircraft before being able to fire a shot. On February 15, 1942, 73,000 British soldiers capitulated at Singapore after a brief resistance. In June, in spite of the considerable resources accumulated in the Middle East by the English, Rommel broke the VIIIth Army front and drove it back to the gates of Alexandria, while the 33,000 men who were supposed to hold Tobruk gave themselves up to the Germans with a haste difficult to justify. Mr. Churchill measured, better than anyone, the consequences of these reverses as regards the conduct of the war. But, above all, he suffered as an Englishman and as a soldier.

It must be added that some people in governing circles did not hesitate to impute to him, discreetly, part of the blame for the British failures. Although England as a whole cherished Winston Churchill as the apple of her eye, the papers printed, Parliament heard, the committees muttered, and the clubs spread, judgments about him that were sometimes hostile. The result of all this was that Mr. Churchill was not, during the first months of 1942, in the mood to soften or be at ease, especially towards me.

Finally, and perhaps chiefly, the Prime Minister had made for himself a rule to do nothing important except in agreement with Roosevelt. Though he felt, more than any other Englishman, the awkwardness of Washington's methods, though he found it hard to bear the condition of subordination in which United States aid placed the British Empire, and though he bitterly resented the tone of supremacy which the President adopted towards him, Mr. Churchill had decided, once for all, to bow to the imperious necessity of the American alliance. He therefore did not mean to adopt towards Free France an attitude that would conflict with that of the White House. Since Roosevelt showed himself distrustful towards General de Gaulle, Churchill would be reserved.

At the time of my arrival in London in September 1941, his ill humour was great. The Prime Minister had difficulty in accepting what had happened in Syria and the Lebanon between us and England. On September 2 he went so far as to write to me that, in view of my attitude, he did not think there was any point in his meeting me at present. In the Commons, on September 9, he made a disquieting statement. True, he recognized that "among all the nations of Europe the position of France in Syria is one of special privilege," but he took it upon himself to add that "there is no question of France maintaining the same position in Syria which she exercised before the war," and that "there must be no question, even in wartime, of a mere substitution of Free French interests for Vichy interests." As usual, Mr. Churchill's displeasure was accompanied by a systematic tension in Franco-British relations. The London government affected, for several days, to have no business to discuss with us and to close its doors to us—which led me, on my side, to suspend all participation by the Free French in broadcasting from London. However, in accordance with the usual swing of the pendulum, a resumption of relations soon followed these vexations. On September 15 I had a conversation with Mr. Churchill which ended well after a bad beginning. He assured me, in conclusion, that his government's policy relative to the Levant remained as it had been defined in our Cairo agreements.

Wishing to clear the matter up, I saw Mr. Eden several times in October and November. We reached an agreement which laid down the essential points. England recognized that the French mandate was still in existence and was exercised by General de Gaulle, until it should be replaced by treaties duly ratified in accordance with the legislation of the French Republic—that is to say, in fact, after the war. She admitted that the proclamation of the independence of Syria and the Lebanon by Free France did not modify this position in law. It was also established that the Lyttelton-de Gaulle agreements remained the charter of Franco-British relations in the Middle East.

In fact, when General Catroux instituted on September 27 the independence and sovereignty of the Syrian Republic under the presidency of Sheik Tageddine, and, on November 26, of the Lebanese Republic under the presidency of M. Alfred Naccache, England, although she had disputed these decisions in advance, accepted them as soon as they had been taken and recognized the two republics together with the two heads of state resulting from them. At the same time I notified the Secretariat-General of the League of Nations on November 28, and on November 29 the American government and all the other Allied states, together with Turkey, of the arrangements which had just been made in my name in Syria and the Lebanon. "These arrangements," the notes stated, "do not affect the juridical situation which results from the Mandate Act and must continue to exist until the conclusion of new international acts." The British government made no objection to these communications. What is more, it had itself suggested them.

It might therefore have been thought that the question was settled, at least until the peace. Circumspect though I was, I even wrote, myself, to our delegation in the Middle East that, in my opinion, "in face of the difficulties that England was encountering in the Arab countries, she was, like us, anxious to see the mean rivalries of the past succeeded by a feeling of solidarity between the two greatest Moslem powers." The directive I gave to our delegation was "to avoid everything that might increase the difficulties of our allies and to neglect nothing to facilitate their task by a genuine collaboration, while at the same time maintaining intact the position and rights of France." I was counting, unfortunately, on something that did not exist. In reality British policy, without contesting the legal position in theory, was still to snap its fingers at it in practice.

In fact, repeated incidents were destined to keep the Franco-British quarrel alive in the Middle East. There was the recruitment—illegal—by the English of Druze cavalry. There was their claim—rejected of course—to proclaim on their own account the state of siege—that is to say, to take power—in the Jezireh, where disorders had broken out in consequence of the revolt in Iraq. There was their unwarranted interference in the operations of the Grain Office set up by us in the Levant, in which they demanded to be represented with the aim of meddling in the local administration. There was the threat—vain indeed—made by General Wilson to have certain French officials, who were not amenable to him, expelled. There was the attitude of Spears, who used hostile and threatening language and constantly intervened in the relations between our delegation and the governments at Damascus and Beirut.

General Catroux steered his ship between the reefs. Although he was inclined to compromise and conceded more to the English than I would have wished, he found himself at every moment faced by fresh intrusions. Whence, ceaseless unrest in the Levant, and in London some snarling negotiations.

In May 1942 British pressure busied itself with trying to have elections take place in Syria and the Lebanon without delay. Our National Committee was naturally not opposed to a consultation of the people, from which fully representative governments would issue. Those we had set up were there only for the transition. This was particularly the case at Damascus, and I for my part was sorry that President Hashim had not resumed his functions. But we considered that, to hold elections, it would be best to wait for the end of the war—that is to say, for a moment when the two states would be once more under normal conditions, when our responsibilities as mandatory power and as defenders would be lightened, and when the English would no longer be there to influence the voting. However, General Catroux, under energetic pressure from Mr. Casey, who had replaced Mr. Lyttelton in Cairo as British Minister of State, made him a promise of elections in the near future, which the newspapers immediately made public. I had to acquiesce in this arrangement, though I ordered its date to be postponed. But it was easy to foresee that it would form, thenceforward, a copious source of Franco-British friction.

There were to be others. Over Jibuti our allies were playing a double game. While allowing our small force—Commandant Bouillon's battalion and the camel corps—to continue the blockade by land, they themselves had stopped the blockade by sea. From Aden in Arab small craft, and from Madagascar in submarines or in the sloop *d'Iberville,* the supplies required to nourish the policy of wait-and-see were reaching the colony. But the English meanwhile were negotiating with the Negus the treaty which set up their tutelage over Ethiopia. Their activity at Addis Ababa explains their inaction over Jibuti. For if, thanks to their help, Free France had been able rapidly to win French Somaliland over and to possess herself, in consequence, of the port, the railway, and a considerable force, she would have been in a position herself to offer Addis Ababa the outlet and the security of which it stood in need. On the contrary, as long as Vichy occupied the place, the British held the fate of the Emperor and of his states in their hands alone.

That is why Gaston Palewski was unable to get the colony effectively blockaded. He could not succeed, either, in bringing the British and Abyssinians to conclude a tripartite agreement instead of one between the two of them. Nonetheless his activity and that of his assistants—Lieutenant-Colonel Appert, commanding the detachment, and Chancel, a young diplomat accredited to Nairobi—were a useful preparation for what followed. The links established by them with various French elements in Jibuti and with the natives, the propaganda which they carried on by leaflets and broadcasts, and their relations with General Platt, resulted in the rallying of Somaliland being a mere formality when the day came. At the same time they made French representation reappear at Addis Ababa. Our rights over the railway were reserved, our religious and lay charities, at one time closed by the Italian occupation, could resume their activity, and the French Legation reopened its doors. Though I deplored the delays, I could see the fruit ripening on the shores of the Red Sea.

But suddenly the intervention of the English in another part of the Empire brought my uneasiness and irritation to their peak. On May 5, 1942, a telephone call from a press agency at three in the morning informed me that a British squadron was landing troops at Diégo-Suarez. Our allies were occupying a French possession by force without even having consulted us!

Ever since Pearl Harbour I had tried, by many means of approach, to discuss the rallying of Madagascar with the British government: a conference with General Brooke, chief of the Imperial General Staff, on December 10; a letter sent to Mr. Churchill on the 16th; a plan for operations handed on February 11 to the Prime Minister, to General Brooke, and to the High Commissioner of the Union of South Africa; a fresh letter to Mr. Churchill on February 19; finally, on April 9, a pressing note to Mr. Eden. In all these documents I proposed swift action by a Free French brigade, which would be landed at Majunga and would make for Tananarive with, if by chance it should be necessary, British air support, while our allies would create a diversion by blockading Diégo-Suarez from the sea. At the same time I claimed the administration of the island for the National Committee.

Meanwhile, since the Union of South Africa seemed to me directly interested in this affair, I inquired as to the plans, if any, of the Pretoria government. As early as the end of 1941 I had sent Colonel Pechkoff there as delegate of Free France. Personally, Colonel Pechkoff had won the liking of General Smuts, and I expected that, if the Union meant to come in, its Prime Minister would not conceal this from my skilful and loyal representative.

Lastly, in March, Médecin-Général Sicé, the High Commissioner at Brazzaville, visited South Africa. From his conversations with Smuts and the Ministers he gained the impression that the Union would not itself take action over Madagascar. It was therefore in London that I deployed my efforts, in the conviction that there were no scruples to be conciliated.

In point of fact, the entry of Japan into the war was threatening Madagascar. It had to be foreséen that Vichy would, sooner or later, be constrained by the Germans at least to allow Japanese raiders and submarines to use the Madagascar bases and paralyse Allied navigation off South Africa.

We were well enough informed on the state of people's minds in the island by volunteers who, from time to time, managed to escape from there, and by the crews of ships that called there. The 1940 armistice had at first been badly received. Governor-General de Coppet would not have had any trouble, at the time, in joining Free France if he had followed up his own declarations. But he had not made up his mind. Vichy had almost immediately replaced him by Cayla, who, assisted by Air General Jeaunaud, had applied himself to lulling the spirit of resistance to sleep, before yielding place himself to Governor-General Anet. Pétain would be obeyed if he ordered that the Japanese be allowed to do as they liked in Madagascar. He would also be obeyed if he ordered resistance to an Allied landing. One day or another the Anglo-Saxons would want to make sure of the island. But in that case, given the traditional impulses of British policy, everything made it imperative for Free France to be present at the operation.

It can therefore be understood into what anxieties the action and proceedings of the English plunged us. All the more so since, on the very day of the Diégo-Suarez attack, Washington published a communiqué stating that "the United States and Great Britain are in accord that Madagascar will, of course, be restored to France after the war or at any time that the occupation of Madagascar is no longer essential to the common cause of the United Nations." But did that mean, then, that meanwhile Madagascar

THE ALLIES

would be taken away from France? To what power, other than Anglo-Saxon, would she be attached? What would be the participation of the French there in the war? What would be left of the authority of France there in the future?

We had to play a cautious game. I waited on purpose for six days before making the contact with Mr. Eden for which he asked. The British Minister, in the conversation I had with him on May 11, showed a certain embarrassment. "I give you my guarantee," he said to me, "that we have no designs on Madagascar. We want the French administration to continue to function there." "What French administration?" I asked. From what Mr. Eden said I gathered that the English planned to negotiate with Governor-General Anet to establish a *modus vivendi* that would leave everything in Madagascar as it was, and in exchange the Allies would remain at Diégo-Suarez and supervise the rest of the island.

I told Mr. Eden that we were opposed to this plan. "Either it will come off," I said to him, "and the result will be the neutralization of a French territory under Allied guarantee—which we will never accept. Or it will not come off, and in a few weeks' time you will have to undertake alone, in the interior of the island, an expedition which will begin to look like a conquest. It seems to me, indeed, very probable that this second hypothesis is the one that will be realized, for the Germans will be able to force Vichy to fight you." "We are engaged," Mr. Eden recognized, "upon an enterprise which in fact may well lead to many complications. But I am in a position to assure you that my government desires and expects that it shall be you who finally will establish your authority in Madagascar. We are ready to state this publicly." It was agreed that the London Cabinet should publish a communiqué in this sense, which it did on May 13, stating: "It is the intention of His Majesty's Government that the Free French National Committee should play its due part in the administration of the liberated French territory, since the National Committee is cooperating with the United Nations as the representative of Fighting France."

That constituted an important undertaking on the part of England. I took cognizance of it on the radio next day. In exchange, in my broadcast, I expressed confidence that the Allies would keep their word. But I publicly rejected any compromise about Madagascar, declaring that it was the will of France that her Empire should be neither divided nor neutralized. "What France wants," I added, "is that Fighting France should in her name direct and organize the French war effort in all its forms and in every field, represent her rights vis-à-vis the Allies in the same way as it defends them against the enemy, and uphold and administer French sovereignty in those of her territories which have been, or will be, set free." On the same day I ordered the commander of the troops in Equatorial Africa to get ready a mixed brigade to proceed to Madagascar.

But the British government's promises and my own statements as to the future role of the National Committee were assuming as solved a problem which was not. Vichy, in point of fact, was still master of practically the whole island. It was soon learned that the British, confining their effort to the capture of Diégo-Suarez, were entering into negotiations with Governor-General Anet. At the same time the Intelligence service in East Africa was sending to the spot a group of agents led by Mr. Lush. These measures were opposed to what Free France wanted. The re-entry of Madagascar into the war was being retarded by them, Anet's authority reinforced and the division of the Empire prolonged. In addition I was afraid of the possible activities of the British political team, which we had had a chance of seeing at work in the Middle East, at Jibuti and in Abyssinia. We were provided with a sinister sign straight away. Pechkoff, whom I wished to send to Diégo-Suarez to inform me of what was happening, found himself prevented from leaving.

Thus, towards the beginning of June 1942, heavy clouds were spreading over Franco-British relations. To all the many alarming or disobliging actions of the English in Syria, Somaliland, and Madagascar, there were added other measures that confirmed our grievances. In the Gold Coast a British mission, directed by Mr. Frank, was making mysterious contacts with the populations of the French territories in the loop of the Niger. At the same time General Giffard, commander-in-chief in West Africa, warned the Free French missions at Bathurst and Freetown that they must leave. When I myself was making ready to proceed to Libya to inspect our troops there, I received from the British government a pressing request to postpone my journey, which meant that the means for it would not be given me. In London the members of the government, the Ministries, and the British general staffs enclosed themselves in a thick atmosphere of secrecy, not to say mistrust.

It was evident that the Anglo-Saxons were busy working out the plan for a vast operation in the western theatre. General Marshall, Chief of Staff of the American Army, and Admiral King, commander-in-chief of the Atlantic Fleet, had spent some time in London in May and had avoided seeing me. And yet, in what the Allies were manifestly planning to do, France, by virtue of her possessions, her populations, and her forces, would be essentially implicated. But no doubt the idea was to keep out of it, as far as possible, her active element, Free France, to dispose of her lands and substance fragment by fragment, perhaps even to take advantage of this dispersal to allot to themselves, here and there, parcels of her property. It was time to react. The Allies must be shown that Free France was in their camp to embody France there, but not to act there as cover, against the French nation, for the abuses and encroachments they might commit to its detriment. The National Committee, after a moving and careful discussion, was unanimous in thinking so.

On June 6 I charged Mr. Charles Peake, the faultlessly distinguished diplomat whom the Foreign Office had attached to us, with making our position known to Mr. Churchill and Mr. Eden. "If it should happen," I told him, "that in Madagascar, in Syria, or elsewhere, France was forced, by the action of her allies, to lose any part whatsoever of what belongs to her, our direct co-operation with Great Britain and eventually with the United States would no longer have any justification. We would have to put an end to it. That would amount, in practice, to concentrating ourselves in the territories that are already rallied or will be, and to pursuing the struggle against the enemy to the limit of our strength but alone and on our own account." That same day I telegraphed to Eboué and Leclerc on the one hand, on the other to Catroux and Larminat, to let them know of this decision and to invite them to prepare. I ordered them also to warn the Allied representatives attached to them that such was our determination.

The effect was not long in coming. On June 10 Mr. Churchill asked me to come and see him. We spent a packed hour together. After warm compliments on the French troops who were covering themselves with glory at Bir Hakeim, the Prime Minister launched into the question of Madagascar. He admitted frankly that Fighting France had reason to be offended at the way in which the operation had been undertaken. "But we have," he stated, "no ulterior motive about Madagascar. As for what we mean to do there, we have no idea as yet. The island is very large. We should like to come to some arrangement so as not to get lost in it." "What we want," I said, "is for Madagascar to join Free France and come back into the war. For that we are ready today, as I have proposed to you before, to engage troops there." "You are not my only ally," the Prime Minister answered. He thus gave me to understand that Washington was opposed to our taking part. To tell the truth, I had no doubt of it.

I drew Mr. Churchill's attention insistently to the danger caused to our alliance by a certain way of proceeding with regard to the French Empire and—perhaps in the near future—to France herself. He protested his good intentions. Then, suddenly jumping to his feet, "I am the friend of France!" he cried. "I have always wanted, and I want, a great France with a great army. It is necessary for the peace, order, and security of Europe. I have never had any other policy!" "That's true!" I replied. "You even had the merit, after Vichy's armistice, of continuing to play the card of France. That card is called de Gaulle. Don't lose it now! It would be all the more absurd since you have reached the moment when your policy is succeeding and when Free France has become the soul and frame of French resistance."

We spoke of Roosevelt and of his attitude towards me. "Don't rush things," said Churchill. "Look at the way I yield and rise up again, turn and turn about." "You can," I remarked, "because you are seated on a solid state, an assembled nation, a united Empire, large armies. But I! where are my resources? And yet I, as you know, am responsible for the interests and destiny of France. It is too heavy a burden, and I am too poor to be able to bow." Mr. Churchill brought our conversation to an end with a demonstration of emotion and friendship. "We still have some stiff obstacles to get over. But one day we shall be in France; perhaps next year. In any case we shall be there together!" He accompanied me out as far as the street, repeating, "I shan't desert you. You can count on me."

Three days later Mr. Eden in his turn set himself to give me renewed and satisfactory assurances as to British disinterestedness about the French Empire in general and Madagascar in particular. He announced to me that "Brigadier" Lush had been recalled and that Pechkoff would be able to leave. "Believe me," he said warmly, "we desire to go forward hand in hand with you to prepare the western front."

Provisionally, then, things remained in suspense. However, the warning we had given had been heard. It was from now on unlikely that British arbitrariness about our Empire would go beyond a certain limit. There were chances that there would be some respite in the Syrian affair, that Somaliland would be encouraged to rally, and that one day the Cross of Lorraine would fly over Madagascar. What was more, I felt more clearly than ever that in the last resort England would not give up her alliance with us.

Among the most keenly interested spectators of the diplomatic drama in which, through a hundred contrasting acts, Free France was to be seen taking up afresh the place of France, were the refugee governments in Great Britain. In 1941 their circle was enlarged by the arrival of the Greek King and Ministers, and then of the Yugoslav King and Ministers. For both of them what was happening to France was a major subject of anxiety. Betrayed and vilified at home by the quislings who were usurping their place, they were fundamentally hostile to Vichy, whose attitude served the collaborators in their countries as an argument. At the same time, and although their sovereignty was not contested by the Allied great powers, they were nonetheless suffering the painful lot of the weak given over to the discretion of the strong. Lastly, they had no doubt that the recovery of France was the condition for equilibrium in Europe and for their own future. It was therefore with secret delight that they watched the action carried on by Free France to establish her independence. The audience we found in them left nothing to be desired.

On our side we did not fail to cultivate relations with these governments, which, though deprived of territories, possessed official representation and an appreciable influence everywhere in the free world. Dejean and his colleagues on the National Committee kept in touch with their Ministers and officials. Our staffs and services met theirs. I myself saw the heads of states and principal members of these governments.

We derived honour and profit from these visits and conversations, for these were men of worth with whom we had to deal. But underneath the externals of etiquette we could discern the dramas caused in their souls by defeat and exile. Certainly these governments, still deploying the ceremony of authority, made a brave show of serenity. But deep down among the anxieties and sorrows in which they were all plunged, each one in shadow lived through his own heart-rending tragedy.

The truth was that since the entry of Russia and the United States into the war the leaders of the Western countries no longer doubted that their respective countries would be liberated. But in what state? That was what was obsessing those with whom I spoke—Dutch, Belgians, Luxembourgers, Norwegians. The noble

Queen Wilhelmina; her Prime Minister, Professor Gerbrandy; her Minister for Foreign Affairs, the enterprising M. van Kleffens; Prince Bernhard of the Netherlands: all with despair saw the Empire of the Indies disappearing, in spite of the magnificent efforts of Admiral Helfrich's fleet and the resistance carried on in the bush by General ter Poorten. M. Pierlot, M. Gutt, and H. Spaak, who together formed a team of wisdom, ardour, and skill in the service of Belgium, were submerged in sadness when they mentioned the question of their king. As for the Grand Duchess Charlotte, her husband Prince Félix de Bourbon-Parma, and their happily perpetual Minister, M. Bech, they never ceased imagining the material and moral consequences that Nazi domination might well have in Luxembourg. Lastly, King Haakon VII, exemplary in his confidence and firmness, and M. Trygve Lie, who exerted an indefatigable activity in all fields, grieved as they watched their merchant ships disappearing: "It is our national capital that is sinking," the Norwegians kept saying.

Far more tragic still was the situation of Greece, of Yugoslavia, of Czechoslovakia, and of Poland. For while Moscow's entry into the war guaranteed them the defeat of Germany, it involved other threats for them. Their heads of states and Ministers spoke of these openly. King George II of Greece and M. Tsouderos, the head of the government, described to me the appalling misery into which the invasion was plunging the Hellenic people, the resistance they were putting up, in spite of everything, against the enemy, but also the saturation of the starving and of the fighters by the Communist party. At the same time, around the young King Peter II of Yugoslavia and inside the Cabinet presided over, successively, by General Simovich, M. Yovanovich, and M. Trifunovich, I could perceive the shocks produced by the events that were dislocating their country: the erection of Croatia into a separate kingdom of which the Duke of Spoleto was proclaimed king; the annexation by Italy of the Slovene province of Ljubljana, and also of Dalmatia; and the competition and, soon, hostility of Tito towards General Mikhailovich, who nonetheless was pursuing, in Serbia, the struggle against the invader.

It is true that President Beneš and his Ministers, Monsignor Šramek, M. Masaryk, M. Ripka, and General Ingr gave, on the contrary, the impression that they were confident about the future behaviour of the Soviets. Through the intermediary of M. Bogomolov they entertained apparently good relations with the Kremlin. Their representative at Moscow, M. Fierlinger, seemed to be in favour there. A Czechoslovak corps, recruited from among the Czechs taken prisoner by the Russians in the ranks of the Wehrmacht, was placed on a war footing by the Soviet High Command. It could be seen that whatever might be his aversion from the Soviet regime, it was mainly on Russia that President Beneš was counting for his own return to Prague and the restoration of the Czechoslovak state.

Conversations with Beneš consisted of lofty lessons in history and politics, which he taught at length without either the listener or the master ever tiring of them. I can still hear him citing, in our conversations, the fortunes of the state over whose destinies he had presided for twenty years. "This state," he would say, "cannot continue to exist without the direct support of Moscow, since it is essential to incorporate in it the Sudeten region with its German population, Slovakia, over whose loss Hungary is inconsolable, and Těšin, which is coveted by the Poles. France is too uncertain for us to be able to trust ourselves again to her good will." "In the future," concluded the President, "we might be able to avoid the hazards of an exclusive alliance with the Kremlin, but only on condition that France resumes in Europe the rank and role which ought to be hers. Meanwhile, what choice have I?" So M. Beneš reasoned—not without my being aware of the anxiety that was always there, deep down in him.

As for the Poles, they had no doubt. In their eyes the Russian was an adversary even when he found himself forced to fight the common enemy. In the view of the President of the Republic, M. Raczkiewicz, of General Sikorski, the head of the government and of the army, and of the Ministers, M. Zaleski, M. Raczynski, and General Kukiel, Soviet expansion would inevitably follow the German defeat. On the question of how to dam the ambitions of Moscow when Berlin had been vanquished the Poles were divided between two tendencies. Sometimes they were dominated by a sort of doctrine of the worst, from which their despair derived intoxicating illusions, as the music of Chopin draws dreams from grief. At others they cherished the hope of a solution that would extend Poland to the west, concede part of the Galician and Lithuanian territories to Russia, and obtain her agreement to refrain from ruling in Warsaw by imposing a Communist government there. But when they did contemplate an agreement, their psychology was so passion-ridden that it produced rivalry among themselves, uncertainty among the Allies, and irritation in the Soviets.

Nevertheless, risky though conciliation might be, General Sikorski was resolved to try it. This man of great character was the right person for his country's destiny. For, having been in the past opposed to Marshal Pilsudski's policy and then to the cocksureness of Bech and Smigly-Rydz, he had found himself, since the disaster, invested with all the authority a state in exile can possess.

As soon as the German armies had entered Russia, Sikorski had not hesitated to re-establish diplomatic relations with the Soviets, in spite of the passions accumulated in Polish hearts. As early as July 1941 he signed an agreement with the Soviets declaring null and void the partition of Poland effected by Russia and Germany in 1939. In December he had gone himself to Moscow to negotiate the liberation of the prisoners and their transfer to the Caucasus, whence, under the command of General Anders, they would be able to reach the Mediterranean. Sikorski had had long discussions with Stalin. On his return, in a description of their conversations, he depicted to me the master of the Kremlin as plunged in the abysses of anguish, but with his lucidity, ruthlessness, and cunning in no way impaired. "Stalin," Sikorski told me, "has stated that in principle he favours an *entente*. But what he will put into it and force us to put into it will depend solely on the forces confronting one another—in other words, on the support we shall, or shall not, find in the West. When the moment comes, who will help Poland? It will be France, or no one."

And so the anxious chorus of the refugee governments made a muted accompaniment to the progress of Free France. All of them had, like the English, recognized the National Committee in terms full of reserve. But they all considered General de Gaulle as the Frenchman qualified to speak in the name of France. They showed it, for example, by signing with me a common declaration about war crimes, which was done on January 12, 1942, in the course of a conference of heads of governments. In all, our relations with the refugee states and the reputation they helped to create for us aided us on the diplomatic plane and gained for us the assistance of many imponderable factors in public opinion.

During the world tragedy, to be sure, the great men carried Anglo-Saxon public opinion along with them; but public opinion in its turn, and in spite of wartime censorships, guided the governments. We therefore tried to bring it into play on our side. I myself endeavoured to do so by taking advantage of the sympathy and curiosity which our enterprise aroused. I regularly addressed the British and American public. Following the classic procedure, I chose, from among the associations that invited me to make myself heard, some gathering that suited the moment and the subject. As guest of honour at the luncheon or dinner organized for the occasion, I could see, at the end of the meal, many professionals in the information world or privileged persons, who came for the speech, joining the guests and discreetly filling up the room. Then, having been complimented by the chairman in accordance with British custom, I would say what I had to say.

Not, alas, knowing English well enough, I generally spoke in French. But afterwards Soustelle would go into action. My speech, translated in advance, was circulated as soon as I had made it.

The press and radio of Great Britain and the United States made it their business to publish its main points. As regards objectivity, I venture to say that that of the American papers seemed to me relative, for they would stress certain phrases taken out of their context. These phrases, at any rate, "got across." The English papers, though often unrestrained in their criticism, hardly ever distorted the text. It should be added that the Latin-American press, out of friendship for France, esteem for Gaullism, and, perhaps, desire to counterpoise the attitude of the United States, did not fail to give prominence to my own statements. In short, except during a few crises when "military necessities" were invoked to stifle my voice, I always found the Allied democracies respectful of freedom of expression.

Before going to the Levant in the spring of 1941, I had made speeches to several British audiences, in particularly to the Foyles Literary Luncheon Club and to the Anglo-French Parliamentary Group. After my return to London in September and up to the month of June following, I was successively heard by the Allied press representatives, the workers and then the directors and staff of the English Electric, a tank factory at Stafford, the Royal African Society, the Foreign Press Association, the Oxford University French Club, the English-Speaking Union, the City Livery Club, the National Defence Public Interest Committee, the municipality and principal citizens of Edinburgh, and a meeting organized in the Parliament building for members of the House of Commons. In May 1942 I held a press conference for the first time. On July 14, 1941, when I had been at Brazzaville, the National Broadcasting Company in America had relayed over all its stations an appeal which I addressed by radio to the United States. On July 8, 1942, the Columbia Broadcasting System carried throughout America, from a special mass meeting in Central Park, called by Mayor La Guardia of New York, a speech in English by "our friend and ally, General de Gaulle." On the 14th, for the French national festival, a fresh message to the Americans. To these main occasions there were added others on which, though obliged to speak without preparation, I still met with a worthwhile response: for example, at receptions given for me by the towns of Birmingham, Leeds, Liverpool, Glasgow, Hull, and Oxford, by Edinburgh University, by the Admiralty at Portsmouth, by the Brigham and Cowan Naval shipbuilding yards, the Talbot works, the Harmelin factories, the *Times* newspaper and, lastly, many clubs, all of them kind and well disposed.

But while I varied the tone it was always the same ideas and feelings that I cast to the mercy of foreign echoes. I gave as explanation for the defeat suffered by France at the start the outworn military system prevalent in all the democracies at the beginning of the war, of which my country had been the victim because she had no oceans to protect her and because she had been left alone to act as advance guard. I affirmed that the French nation was still, underneath oppression, living on with a deepseated and sturdy life, and would reappear, resolved upon exertion and recovery. I gave as proof of this the Resistance, which was growing within and without. But I depicted the French people as all the more sensitive to the way in which its allies behaved towards it because it was plunged in misfortune and humiliation, because Hitler's propaganda kept waving before its eyes prospects of recovery if only it would cross over into the totalitarian camp, and because Vichy was only wrong—was I not obliged to use every argument?—insofar as the democracies respected the rights of France.

So it was that on April 1, 1942, I made a speech that dotted the *i*'s in this respect and led to keen controversy. "Let it not be supposed," I declared, "that the kind of miracle, which Fighting France is, is a thing given once for all. . . . The basis of the whole matter is this: that Fighting France means to stand by her allies on condition that her allies stand by her. . . ." Referring directly to relations which the United States were still entertaining with Vichy and to the dark dealings they were carrying on with its proconsuls, I added: "For the democracies to lean towards men who have destroyed all freedom in France and who seek to model their regime on fascism or a caricature of it, would be to introduce into politics the principles of the poor simpleton who threw himself into the sea for fear of getting wet in the rain. . . ." To set the thunder rumbling I added: "There is here a grave failure to recognize a fact which dominates the whole French question and is known as revolution. For it is a revolution, the greatest in her history, that France, betrayed by her ruling and privileged classes, has begun to accomplish." And I uttered this cry: "It would not be tolerable if the self-styled realism that, from one Munich to another, has led liberty to the very edge of the abyss were to continue to impose upon ardour and to betray sacrifice . . ."

The positions had been taken up. Free France had succeeded in winning recognition, both in the feelings of the public and in the assent of the chancelleries, not only as the sword bearer of France but also as the unshakeable trustee of her interests. This result was attained in the nick of time. For at the beginning of the summer of 1942 conditions had combined to enable the war to take a decisive turn. Russia had remained standing and was now passing to the offensive. England, while sending numerous reinforcements to the Middle East, had considerable forces available on her territory. The United States was ready to bring to the West its entirely fresh units and immense war matériel. Lastly, France, crushed and enslaved though she was in the home country and passive throughout a large part of her overseas territories, was still in a position to engage in the final struggle important military forces, her Empire, and her resistance. Just as one unfurls the banner at the edge of the field of battle, I had, in the spring of 1942, given the name "Fighting France" to what, till then, was "Free France," and had notified the Allies of this new title.

For the destiny of France would be at stake in the coming collision. Territory of hers—North Africa or the home country—would serve as a theatre of operations. What she did, or failed to do, in face of the enemy would determine her share in the victory. But it would be on the behaviour of the Allies that her rank in the world, her national unity, and her imperial integrity would depend. I could have no doubt that some, and not the least important, meant to see to it that on this supreme occasion the guiding French body should be as dependent and fluid as possible and that Fighting France should be absorbed, if not set aside. But the situation she had acquired in the world was now solid enough for it to be impossible to break her from outside.

On condition that she herself held firm, and that she had the support of the nation in proportion as this emerged in its reality. While carrying on our fight, I thought of nothing else. Would Fighting France, in the coming test, have enough keenness, courage, and vigour not to split within? Would the French people, exhausted, misled, and torn as it was, be willing to listen to me and follow me? Could I unite France?

CHAPTER 8

FIGHTING FRANCE

WHILE, between the summer of 1941 and that of 1942, Fighting France was extending her diplomatic campaign, she was herself ceaselessly growing. Although the present account sets forth the development of these two efforts successively, they were nonetheless simultaneous and connected. But the fact that the field of action was continuously enlarging made it necessary for me to place an adequate organism at the head of the enterprise. De Gaulle could no longer direct everything single-handed. The number and dimensions of the problems made it essential to bring points of view and persons of competence face to face before decisions were taken. Steps for putting them into action had to be decentralized. Lastly, since in all states power took the collegiate form, we should be helping to get ourselves recognized diplomatically by adopting it for ourselves. By an ordinance of September 24, 1941, I instituted the National Committee.

As a matter of fact, I had been thinking of this constantly from the beginning. But the fact that, in the space of one year, I had had to spend eight months in Africa and the Middle East, and, above all, the shortage of so-called "representative" men, had constrained me to postpone it. On my arrival in London after the Syrian affairs I could, on the contrary, look forward to a long phase of organization. Also, while most of the individuals who had joined me early on were not, at the start, very well known, some had become so. I could therefore give the Committee a membership that would count. For Fighting France, the National Committee would be the directing organ gathered around me. In it the "Commissioners" would debate all our affairs collectively. Each of them would be required to direct one of the "departments" in which our activity was exercised. All would bear responsibility for the decisions taken. In short, the Committee would be the government. It would have the prerogatives and structure of one. It would not, though, have the title. I was keeping that in reserve for the day, however far off it might still inevitably be, when an authority with the dimensions of French unity could be formed. It was with the same prospect in view that my ordinance provided for the formation, later, of a Consultative Assembly, "with the task of furnishing the Committee with as wide as possible an expression of national opinion." A good deal of time, however, was to go by before this assembly saw the light of day.

As was to be expected, my decision caused eddies within the small French groups which, on the pretext of being political, were more or less astir in Great Britain and in the United States. They were willing that de Gaulle should act as a soldier and provide the Allies with the reinforcement of a contingent. But they would not admit that the leader of the Free French should take upon him governmental responsibilities. Not having rallied to me, they rejected my authority and preferred to entrust to foreigners—that is, in fact, to Roosevelt, Churchill, and Stalin—the future of France.

I agree that there was a genuine antinomy between the ideas of these circles and my own. For me, in the national tragedy, policy had to be action in the service of a powerful and simple idea. But they, pursuing the same chimeras they had always cherished, would not consent that it should be anything but a choreography of attitudes and groupings, executed by a company of professional mimes, from which nothing would ever emerge but newspaper articles, speeches, platform performances and allocations of office. Although this regime had been swept away by events, although it had cost France a disaster from which it was possible to doubt that she would ever rise again, although these intoxicated people were now deprived of the usual means for their agitation—Parliament, congresses, ministerial offices, and editorial desks—they were continuing their game in New York or in London, striving to involve in it, for lack of others, the Anglo-Saxon Ministers, Members of Parliament, and journalists. The origin of the troubles caused for Free France by her own allies and of the campaigns carried on against her by their press and radio lay, often, in the influence of certain French émigrés. They could not fail to disapprove of the sort of political promotion which the institution of the National Committee meant for Fighting France, and they would certainly attempt to counteract the operation.

Admiral Muselier was the man who served them as instrument. The admiral had a kind of double personality. As a sailor he gave proof of capacities which deserved high consideration and to which the organization of our small naval forces was largely due. But he was periodically possessed by a sort of fidgets, which impelled him to intrigue. As soon as he knew of my intention to form the Committee, he wrote to me posing as champion of understanding with the Allies and of democracy, which, according to him, my policy might well endanger. That these might both thenceforth be safeguarded, he proposed that I should place myself in an honorary position and leave the reality of the powers to him. As for the means he employed in the attempt to force my consent, this was nothing less than the threat of secession by the Navy which, he told me on the telephone, "is becoming independent and continuing the war."

My reaction was clear and the discussion was short. The admiral yielded, alleging a misunderstanding. For reasons of sentiment and expediency, I made a show of letting myself be convinced, took cognizance of his undertakings, and appointed him

Commissioner for the Navy and Merchant Marine in the National Committee.

It included: in charge of Economy, Finance, and Colonies, Pleven; of Justice and Public Education, Cassin; Foreign Affairs, Dejean; War, Legentilhomme; Air, Valin; action in Metropolitan France, Labour, and Information, Diethelm, who had just arrived from France. Catroux and d'Argenlieu, at that time posted abroad, became members of the Committee without portfolio. I allotted to Pleven the burden of ensuring the administrative coordination of the civil departments: rank, salaries, distribution of staff, accommodation, and so on. I had wanted from the start, and later tried several times, to widen the membership of the Committee by bringing into it some of the eminent Frenchmen who were in America. In pursuance of this I asked M. Maritain and M. Alexis Léger for their help. The replies were courteous but negative.

The National Committee was working satisfactorily when Muselier brought on a fresh crisis. Back in London after the Saint Pierre expedition, for which he had received our unanimous congratulations, he declared, at a sitting of the Committee on March 3, that things were not going to his liking in Free France, tendered his resignation as national commissioner, and wrote to me to confirm it. I accepted this resignation, put the admiral on the reserve of officers, and replaced him by Auboyneau, who was recalled from the Pacific. But Muselier then declared that, while ceasing to be a member of the National Committee, he was keeping the supreme command of the naval forces for himself, as though what was in question was a fief of which he was the owner. This could not be allowed, and the matter was settled in advance when, suddenly, the intervention of the British government began.

This intervention had been prepared for a long time, the instigators being a few hotheads of the emigration and certain elements in the Commons and in the British Navy. The conspirators had found a helper in Mr. Alexander, First Lord of the Admiralty. They represented to him, as Minister, that if Muselier went, the Free French Navy would dissolve, so depriving the Royal Navy of a by no means negligible auxiliary. They persuaded him, as a Labour man, that de Gaulle and his Committee had tendencies toward fascism and that the Free French naval forces must be separated from their policy. The British Cabinet, for reasons that had to do with its internal balance and also, probably, with the intention of making de Gaulle easier to deal with by weakening him, adopted Alexander's thesis. It decided to require of me the maintenance of Muselier in his post as commander-in-chief of the Free French naval forces.

On March 5 and 6 Mr. Eden, flanked by Mr. Alexander, notified me of this demand. For me, from that moment, the case was judged. At whatever cost, the National Committee's decision must be carried out just as it was, and England must give up meddling in this French matter. On March 8 I wrote to Eden that I myself and the National Committee had decided that Muselier was no longer commander-in-chief of the Navy and that we were not accepting the interference of the British government on this subject. I added: "The Free French consider that what they are doing at the side of the British and for the same cause implies that they must be regarded and treated as allies and that the support of the British must not be given to them on conditions incompatible with their own *raison d'être.* . . . If this were not the case, General de Gaulle and the National Committee would cease to slave at a task which had become impossible. They hold it, in fact, essential, as regards the future of France as well as the present, to remain faithful to the aim which they have set themselves. This aim consists in raising France up once more and reconstituting national unity in war at the side of the Allies, but without in any degree sacrificing French independence, sovereignty, and institutions."

I received no reply for the moment. No doubt, before going any further, the English were waiting to see what would happen inside our Navy. There was no movement of dissidence on any ship, in any training depot or any of our establishments. On the contrary, all the elements of the Free French naval forces drew closer to de Gaulle with an ardour proportionate to the difficulties that had been created for him. Only a few officers, forming a group about the admiral, organized an unseemly demonstration at his staff headquarters, where I had gone to speak to them in person. I then ordered Admiral Muselier to reside for a month in a place that would keep him away from all contact with the Navy. I invited the British government, in accordance with the jurisdiction agreement of January 15, 1941, to ensure the carrying-out of this measure, since it was taken on British territory. Then, as the necessary assurances were long in reaching me, I went away to the country, prepared for anything, expecting anything, and leaving in the hands of Pleven, Diethelm, and Coulet a sort of secret testament which entrusted them with the mission of informing the French people in case I should be obliged to give up pursuing what I had undertaken and should not be in a position to explain the matter myself. Meanwhile I had let our allies know that, to my great regret, I would not be able to resume my relations with them until they themselves had applied the agreement which bound them.

This was done on March 23. Mr. Peake came to visit me. He handed me a note informing me that his government was not insisting that Muselier should remain commander-in-chief and would see that, for a month, the admiral was unable to make contact with any element in the French naval forces. The British government, however, recommended him to my benevolence for some mission suitable to his services. Thereupon Auboyneau, who had arrived from the Pacific, took in hand the administration and command of the Navy. In May, wishing to offer Admiral Muselier a chance of serving still, I invited him to come and see me to settle the terms of a mission of inspection I proposed to entrust to him. He did not come. A few days later this admiral, who had done much for our Navy, notified me that his collaboration with Free France was finished. I was sorry for his sake.

After this painful incident nothing further happened to prevent the regular functioning of this "London Committee," which various sources of hostile propaganda—not confined to that of the enemy and that of Vichy—represented sometimes as a group of greedy politicians, sometimes as a team of fascist adventurers, sometimes as a rabble of communist fanatics, but for which, I bear witness, nothing mattered in comparison with the welfare of the country and of the state. The National Committee met at least once a week, with some ceremony, in a large room at Carlton Gardens, known as the Clock Room. In conformity with its rules of procedure, it heard the report of each of the Commissioners on the business of his department or on any question that one or another of them thought it his duty to raise. Cognizance was taken of documents and information, things were discussed thoroughly, and the proceedings ended with decisions drawn up at the sitting in the form of minutes, later notified to the forces and departments. No important step was ever taken without the Committee having deliberated on it first.

I always received valuable assistance and loyal support from the National Committee as a collective organ, as also from each of its members. Certainly I was still obliged to go personally into everything that was sufficiently important. But the burden on me was less heavy from the fact that I was aided and surrounded by men of worth. No doubt these Ministers, none of whom had embarked on public life before, were to some extent lacking in authority and reputation. These, however, they proved able to acquire. All, in addition, had their own experience and individual qualities. The whole which they formed laid open to Fighting France avenues of influence that otherwise would have remained closed to it. I might often encounter, from these collaborators, not indeed opposition, but objections, even contradictions, to my plans and acts. In the difficult moments, when I was usually inclined towards vigorous solutions, several members of the Committee had a leaning towards compromise. But, taken all in all, it was better that way. In the last resort, indeed, after he had enlightened me, no national commissioner disputed my final word.

In fact, while opinions might be divided, my responsibility nonetheless remained entire. In the struggle for liberation the one who answered for everything was still, in the last resort, my poor self. Inside France especially, those who were beginning to turn in growing numbers towards active resistance looked in the direction of de Gaulle. There was a more and more distinct response there to my appeals. There was also a convergence of feelings there, which seemed to me as necessary as it was moving. For, realizing that the propensity of the French to divide and the dispersal imposed on them by oppression tended to brand their rebellion with an extreme diversity, I was dominated by the anxiety to bring about the unity of the resistance. This was in fact the condition for its warlike effectiveness, its national value, and its weight in the opinion of the world.

From the summer of 1941 onwards, what was happening at home was known to us soon after it happened. Independently of what one could read between the lines of the newspapers or hear underneath the words of the radio of both zones, a complete harvest of intelligence was constantly brought to us by the evidence from our networks, the reports of certain well-placed men who were already taking up positions, the testimony of the volunteers who were reaching us daily from France, the indications supplied by diplomatic posts, the statements made by the émigrés on their way through Madrid, Lisbon, Tangier, and New York, and the letters sent to Free Frenchmen by their families and friends and passed through by dint of a thousand tricks. I therefore had in my mind a picture kept always up to date. How many times I was privileged to realize, as I talked with compatriots who had just left the country but had there been more or less confined within their trade or their locality, that, thanks to innumerable efforts at collecting, transmitting, and collating information by an army of devoted people, I was as well aware as anyone of French affairs!

What emerged from all this was the degradation of Vichy. The illusions of the regime were being finally dispelled. In the first place the victory of Germany, which had been proclaimed as certain in order to justify the capitulation, became unlikely as soon as Russia was engaged in the struggle, the United States came in in their turn, and England and Free France held firm. The claim to be "saving the furniture from the burning house" at the cost of servitude was clearly ridiculous, in view of the facts that our 1,500,000 prisoners were not coming back, that the Germans were practically annexing Alsace and Lorraine and keeping the north of the country cut off administratively from the rest, that the levies made by the occupier in money, raw materials, and farm and industrial products were exhausting our economy, and that the Reich was forcing a growing number of Frenchmen to work for it. The assertion that the Empire was being defended "against no matter whom" could no longer deceive anyone from the moment when the Army and Navy were forced to fight against Allies and Gaullists at Dakar, in the Gabon, in Syria, and in Madagascar, while the Germans and Italians of the armistice commissions did as they pleased at Algiers, Tunis, Casablanca, and Beirut, while the aircraft of the Reich were landing at Aleppo and Damascus, while the Japanese were occupying Tonkin and Cochin-China. In the eyes of all, from now on, it was Fighting France that represented the chance of recovering the overseas territories one day, by making sure, one by one, of Equatorial Africa, the islands of Oceania, Pondichéry, the Levant, Saint Pierre, Madagascar, and French Somaliland, and extending its unyielding shadow before it over North Africa, West Africa, the Antilles, and Indochina.

As for the "national revolution" by which Vichy was attempting to make up for its own capitulation, the impression it gave was of a waste of reforms, some of which in themselves had their value but which were compromised and discredited by the fact of being associated in men's minds with disaster and enslavement. Vichy's claim to a moral renovation and to a restoration of authority, and even its indisputable effort at economic and social organization, resulted, outwardly only, in the processions of the legionaries, the hagiography of the Marshal, and the proliferation of committees, and, as to substance, in base persecutions, in domination by police and censorship, in privileges, and in the black markets.

And so, even within the regime, the signs of disarray began to be manifest. From the end of 1940 to the summer of 1942 there were, in succession, the dismissal of Laval; the foundation in Paris, by Déat, Deloncle, Luchaire, Marquet, Suarez, and others, of the Rassemblement National Populaire, which, with the direct support of the Germans, abused those in office and carried on a noisy campaign of going one better in favour of collaboration; the incessant alterations of Darlan's prerogatives; resignations of members of the Cabinet—Ybarnegaray, Baudouin, Alibert, Flandin, Peyrouton, Chevalier, Achard, and others—who declared, one after the other, that the task was impossible; the strange and sudden cessation of the Riom trial; the retirement of Weygand; Colette's attempt to assassinate Laval; the latter's appointment as head of the government. The Marshal himself made public his distress. "From several regions of France," he said on the radio in August 1941, "I can feel an evil wind blowing. Unrest is taking hold of people's minds. Doubt is seizing their souls. The authority of the government is being called in question. Orders are being carried out badly. A real uneasiness is striking at the French people." In June of the following year, on the second anniversary of his request for an armistice, he stated in a broadcast: "I do not conceal from myself the poorness of the response my appeals have met with."

As the pomp and the works of Vichy declined, nuclei of resistance began to form here and there in Metropolitan France. The activities in question were, of course, most diverse, often ill defined, but all inspired by the same intentions. In one place a propaganda sheet was being edited, printed, and distributed. In another the enemy was being spied on to keep a network informed. A few determined men were setting up action groups for the most diverse purposes: raids, sabotage; receiving and distributing war matériel, either parachuted or transported; welcoming or sending off agents; passing from one zone to the other; crossing a frontier, and so on. Some were forming embryo movements whose members were bound together by rules or simply by acceptance of one and the same state of mind. In short, underneath the passive and slowed-down appearance displayed by life in Metropolitan France, resistance was starting its ardent, secret life. Fighters at home were now thinking how to strike blows at the enemy through the tight-drawn nets of police and informers.

In September 1941 the series of isolated attacks on German soldiers began. A major coming out of an underground station, the commander of the garrison at Nantes, an officer at Bordeaux, and two soldiers in Paris, in the rue Championnet, were the first to be killed. Other executions followed. By way of reprisals, the enemy shot hostages in hundreds, threw thousands of patriots into prison and later deported them, and crushed under the weight of fines and servitudes the towns where his men fell. It was with sombre pride that we heard of these acts of war accomplished individually, at the price of immense risks, against the occupier's army. At the same time the death of the Frenchmen who served as victims to Germanic vengeance threw our soul into mourning, but not into despair, for it was equivalent to the sacrifice of the soldiers on the battlefields. Yet for elementary reasons of war tactics we considered that the struggle ought to be directed, and that indeed the moment had not come for starting open fighting at home. The harassing of the enemy, then the engagement of our home forces at chosen points, and finally the national rising, which we hoped to obtain one day, would be powerfully effective, on condition that they formed a whole and were coordinated with the action of the armies of liberation. But in 1941 resistance was barely beginning, and at the same time we knew that literally years would go by before our allies would be ready for the landing.

On October 23, therefore, I declared in a broadcast: "It is absolutely natural and absolutely right that Germans should be killed by Frenchmen. If the Germans did not wish to receive death at our hands, they had only to stay at home. . . . Since they have not succeeded in bringing the world to its knees, they are certain to become, each one of them, a corpse or a prisoner. . . . But there are tactics in war. War must be conducted by those entrusted with the task. . . . For the moment, my orders to those in occupied territory are not to kill Germans there openly. This for one reason only: that it is, at present, too easy for the enemy to retaliate by massacring our fighters, now, for the time being, disarmed. On the other hand, as soon as we are in a position to move to the attack, the orders for which you are waiting will be given."

While trying to limit our losses, which in such circumstances were excessive for far too slender results, it was nevertheless necessary to use the emotion caused by German repression in the interests of national vitality and solidarity. On October 25, the day after the invader had massacred fifty hostages at Nantes and fifty at Bordeaux, I announced by radio: "By shooting our martyrs, the enemy thought he would frighten France. France is about to show him that she is not afraid of him. . . . I invite all Frenchmen and all Frenchwomen to cease all activity and remain motionless, each wherever he happens to be, on Friday, October 31, from four to four-five, . . . for this gigantic warning, this immense national strike, will show the enemy the threat enveloping him and will be a proof of French fraternity." On the evening before the appointed day I renewed my appeal. In point of fact, the demonstration was impressive in many places, above all in the factories. I was reinforced by it in my determination to prevent the resistance from turning into anarchy, but to make of it, on the contrary, an organized whole—without, however, breaking the initiative which was its mainspring or the partitioning without which it might well have disappeared altogether, at one blow.

In any case its constituent elements, the movements, were now in existence, very resolute in many respects but suffering gravely from the lack of military cadres. Where they could and should have found them—that is to say, in what remained of the army— Vichy barred their way. And yet the first acts of resistance had come from soldiers. Some officers belonging to the army and regional staffs were saving war matériel from the armistice commissions. The Intelligence service continued in shadow to carry out measures of counterespionage and, at intervals, transmitted information to the English. Under the impulse of Generals Frère, Delestraint, Verneau, Bloch-Dassault, and Durrmeyer, and by making use, in particular, of the rankers clubs, mobilization measures had been prepared. General Cochet inaugurated active propaganda against the spirit of the capitulation. Many of the monitors of the Chantiers de Jeunesse,[1] who included a number of ex-soldiers, were training themselves and the others with a view to taking up arms. In what remained of the established units, nearly all the officers, NCOs, and men showed unconcealed hope of returning to the fight.

The public, indeed, thought that a very good thing. A news film from France, which I had shown to me privately in London, gave me a striking example of this. In it Pétain was to be seen, in the course of a visit to Marseille, on the balcony of the Hôtel de Ville in front of troops and a crowd astir with patriotic ardour. Yielding to the immense power of suggestion that rose from this mass of people, he could be heard shouting suddenly: "Don't forget that you are all of you still mobilized!" One witnessed the unchaining of enthusiasm which those words aroused in that civil and military assembly, laughing and crying with emotion.

Thus the Army, in spite of the captivity or death of most, and often the best, of its people, was showing itself spontaneously disposed to officer the national resistance. But that is what the so-called government, to which its obedience subjected it, did not want. Vichy, practising first the fiction of neutrality, and then collaboration, prevented it from responding to its own vocation and shut it up in a moral blind alley from which no one could emerge without breaking with a formal discipline. Although many military men had nonetheless crossed the barrier—in particular those of them who were members of the networks—those, too,

---

[1] A youth movement formed by Marshal Pétain in 1940; voluntary at first, but made compulsory in January 1941. (Translator's note.)

who were to enter the secret army, and lastly those who later formed the Organisation de Résistance de l'Armée—it is a fact that, at the start, the movements had to improvise their own cadres.

In the so-called free zone, Combat, of which Captain Frenay had taken the lead; Libération, in which Emmanuel d'Astier de la Vigerie was playing the chief part; and Franc-Tireur, whose directing organ was presided over by Jean-Pierre Lévy, were developing a considerable propaganda activity and recruiting paramilitary formations. At the same time what was left of the old trade-union movement—the Confédération Générale du Travail and the Confédération Française des Travailleurs Chrétiens—was spreading a state of mind favourable to resistance. It was the same with a few groups that issued from the old political parties, especially the Socialists, the Popular Democrats, and the Republican Federation. Since the Germans were not occupying the zone, it was of course to Vichy that opposition was being put up, it was with its police and courts that there was a bone to pick. The leaders, indeed, while preparing forces that could, if need be, be used against the enemy, were thinking of the seizure of power, and saw in the resistance not only an instrument of war but also the means of replacing the regime.

The political character of the movements in the southern zone certainly helped to render them alive and active, to attract into their ranks people of influence, and to give their propaganda a touch of passion and topicality which struck the public mind. But at the same time good understanding and, later, common action between the directing committees inevitably suffered from it. It must be said that the mass of the members and sympathizers hardly worried about the programme which the resistance might apply later, or about the conditions in which it would one day take power, or about the choice of those who would then be called upon to govern. In the general feeling, the only thing was to fight, or at least to prepare for that. To acquire weapons, find hiding places, work out and sometimes carry out raids—that was the business. For that it was necessary for people who knew one another to organize on the spot, find a few resources, and keep their activities to themselves. In short, while within the movements the inspiration was relatively centralized, action was divided up, on the contrary, into separate groups, each of which had its own leader and operated on its own, and all competing against one another for the terribly limited resources in weapons and money.

In the occupied zone this rivalry disappeared in face of the immediate danger, but the physical dispersion of people and efforts was even more necessary there. They were there in direct and overwhelming contact with the enemy. It was with the Gestapo that they had to deal. No means of moving about, corresponding, or choosing a place of residence without running the gantlet of strict controls. Any suspect went to prison until deported. As for active resistance, it exposed the fighters to torture and to execution without mercy. Activity, in these circumstances, was extremely dispersed. On the other hand, the presence of the Germans kept in existence an atmosphere that urged men on to struggle and encouraged connivance. And so the movements in this zone took on a tensely warlike and conspiratorial character. The Organisation Civile et Militaire, founded by Colonel Touny, Ceux de la Libération, headed by Ripoche, Ceux de la Résistance, recruited by Lecompte-Boinet, Libération-Nord, which Cavaillès had brought into being, and lastly, in the Hainaut, in Flanders, in the mining country, La Voix du Nord, directed by Houcke, formally rejected any political tendency, thought of nothing but the fight, and produced swarms of small clandestine groups isolated from one another.

At the end of 1941 the Communists came into action in their turn. Up to then their leaders had adopted a conciliatory attitude towards the occupier, making up for it by abuse of Anglo-Saxon capitalism and its lackey Gaullism. But their attitude changed suddenly when Hitler invaded Russia and when they themselves had had time to find hiding places and to set up the liaison arrangements indispensable to the clandestine struggle. They were prepared for this, indeed, by their organization in cells, the anonymity of their hierarchy, and the devotion of their cadres. They were therefore destined to take part with courage and skill in the national war, being certainly sensitive—especially some of modest station—to the appeal of their country, but never, as an army of revolution, losing sight of the objective, which was to establish their dictatorship by making use of the tragic situation of France. Hence they tried ceaselessly to keep their freedom of action. But also, exploiting the tendencies of the fighters who—their own people included—wanted only one single fight, they obstinately attempted to permeate the whole of the resistance in order to make of it, if possible, the instrument of their ambition.

So it was that, in the occupied zone, they formed the Front Nationale, a group that was purely patriotic in aspect, and the Francs-Tireurs et Partisans, a force that seemed intended only for the struggle against the Germans. So it was that into these they attracted many elements that were non-Communist but, from that very fact, might serve as cover for their designs. So it was that they camouflaged some of their own people and pushed them into the directing organs of all the other movements. So it was that they were soon to offer me their assistance, though never ceasing to mutter against the "de Gaulle myth."

And I wanted them to serve. There were no forces that should not be employed to beat the enemy, and I reckoned that theirs had great weight in the kind of war imposed by the occupation. But they would have to do so as part of a whole and, to be quite frank, under my control. Firmly counting on the power of national feeling and on the credit given me by the masses, I had from the first decided to assure them of their place within the French resistance —even, one day, in its guiding body. But I was quite as decided not to let them ever gain the upper hand, by-pass me, or take the lead. The tragedy in which the fate of our country was being played out offered these Frenchmen, who had been separated from the nation by the injustice which roused them and the error which misled them, the historic opportunity of coming back into the national unity, even if only for the duration of the fight. I wanted to do what was needed to prevent this opportunity from being lost forever. So, once again, "Long live France!" would then have been the cry uttered, at the moment of dying, by all those who had given their lives for her, no matter how, no matter where. In the ceaseless movement of the world, all doctrines, all schools, all rebellions, have only one time. Communism will pass. But France will not pass. I am sure that in the end it will count for much in her destiny that, in spite of everything, she will, at the moment of her liberation—a fugitive instant, yet decisive in her history—have been a single, reunited people.

In October 1941 I heard of the presence in Lisbon of Jean Moulin, who had arrived from France and was seeking to come to London. I knew who he was. I knew, in particular, that as prefect of the Eure-et-Loir Department at the moment when the Germans entered Chartres, he had shown exemplary firmness and dignity, that the enemy, after maltreating him, wounding him, and throwing him into prison, had in the end set him free with apologies and expressions of esteem, and that Vichy, having replaced him in his post, had since been keeping him in the wilderness. I knew he wanted to serve. I therefore asked the British services that this man of calibre should be sent to England. I had to wait two months before being given satisfaction. Intelligence, in fact, was trying to win Moulin for itself. He, on the contrary, was asking to be sent to me. By dint of a pressing letter to Mr. Eden I managed to get the loyal voyager to his destination. I was later to have equal trouble in obtaining his return to France.

In the course of December I had long conversations with him. Jean Moulin, before leaving for London, had made numerous contacts with each of the resistance movements and had at the same time taken soundings in various political, economic, and administrative circles. He knew the ground on which I planned to engage him first. He made clear proposals and formulated precise requests.

This man, still young but with an experience already formed by responsibility, was kneaded from the same dough as the best of my companions. Filled to his soul's brim with a passionate love for France, convinced that Gaullism must be not only the instrument of the fight but also the motive power of a complete renovation, and penetrated by the feeling that the state was embodied in Free France, he aspired to great undertakings. But at the same time, being full of judgment and seeing things and people as they were, he would be watching each step as he walked along a road that was undermined by adversaries' traps and encumbered with obstacles raised by friends. Being a man of faith and calculation, with no doubts but general mistrust, an apostle and at the same time a minister, Moulin was to accomplish, in eighteen months, a major task. He was to bring the resistance in Metropolitan France, which had still merely the outline of a symbolic unity, to practical unity. Later betrayed, made prisoner, and tortured appallingly by an enemy who had no honour, Jean Moulin was to die for France, like so many good soldiers who, under the sun or in shadow, sacrificed a long, empty evening the better to "fill their morning."

We had agreed that he should bring his efforts to bear first on the movements in the south zone, to resolve them to form, under his presidency, a common body that would be directly tied to the National Committee, would make union a reality, issue watchwords, and settle internal disputes. That done, he would tackle the north zone and would try to set up a council of all the resistance, attached to Fighting France, for the territory as a whole. But as soon as it was a matter of capping with one organism all participants in the struggle within Metropolitan France, two questions arose: that of the political parties and that of the military forces at home.

Given the representative, but by no means directive, character which I wished to see the future council take on—and which it would in fact take on—I did not expect to be able to exclude the parties. That some should exist was inevitable. To my mind, indeed, our misfortunes had come not from their existence, but from the fact that, under cover of decadent institutions, they had wrongly arrogated to themselves the powers of government. Therefore, while reserving them their place, I did not intend that they should now capture the resistance movement. This, after all, by no means arose from their spirit or from their activity, since all of them, without exception, had given way at the decisive moment. But, struck down yesterday by disaster, they were now beginning to pull themselves together. Some of their members, while joining the resistance movements, were at the same time regrouping within the old frameworks.

It is true that, having no longer a following to flatter or coalitions to operate or portfolios to haggle over, they believed and made believe that they were returning to the noble sources from which they had their origins: the will for social justice, the cult of national traditions, the spirit of lay rationalism, the Christian flame. Their respective organisms, now thoroughly purged, had no aim, so it seemed, but to bring an immediate contribution to the struggle by mobilizing this or that tendency in public opinion. Public opinion, indeed, was once more becoming in some degree responsive to the cunning of these familiar groups, all the more so since they abjured their errors. Lastly, the Allies were naturally attentive to the attitude of the party men. These were facts which I could not underestimate if I wanted to build up French unity. I therefore instructed Moulin to introduce into the council that was to be formed, when the day came, delegates of the parties side by side with those of the movements.

While I meant in this way to see some degree of unity established in the political action in France, I wished it to be the same with the military action. The first difficulty in regard to this came from the movements themselves, for, having recruited fighting groups, they claimed to keep them as their own. What was more, except in a few mountainous or very well-wooded regions, these groups could not exist except in small bands. This applied especially to the Maquis, composed as they were chiefly of outlaws who had always to keep to the country. The only kind of warfare to be expected of them, therefore, was guerrilla warfare. But this could be very effective indeed if the detailed actions formed part of a concerted whole. The problem then was, while letting the various fractions operate autonomously, to bind them together by a flexible but efficient frame which would be attached directly to me. In this way it would be possible to lay down for them, in the form of plans established in agreement with the Allied High Command, groups of objectives against which they could take action as circumstances developed, and especially when—at last—the landing of the armies came. I made Moulin responsible for leading the movements to this elementary cohesion among their military people. I had to wait, however, for several months before being able to set up a command for the secret army in the person of General Delestraint.

Jean Moulin was dropped by parachute in the south during the night of January 1. He carried credentials from me appointing him as my delegate for the non-occupied zone of Metropolitan France and instructing him to ensure unity of action among the elements of the resistance there. This would mean that his authority would not, in principle, be disputed. But he would have to exercise it, and I would have to support him. It was therefore agreed that it was he who would be the centre of our communications in France, first with the south zone, then, as soon as possible, with the north zone; that he would have the means of transmission under his authority; that our envoys would be attached to him; that he would be kept posted as to movements of personnel, matériel, and mail effected on our behalf from England to France and *vice versa;* and finally that he would receive and distribute the funds sent by us to various bodies operating in Metropolitan France. Thus provided with prerogatives, Moulin set to work.

Under his drive, supported by pressure from base, the heads of the movements in the south zone soon formed between them a sort of council, of which the National Committee's delegate assumed the presidency. In March they published, under the heading "One single fight, one single leader," a common declaration in which they committed themselves to united action and proclaimed that they were carrying on the struggle under the authority of General de Gaulle. Order began to reign in the various activities.

In the paramilitary field, preparations for fusion were going ahead. At the same time, with help from us, Moulin equipped his delegation with centralized services.

So it was that the service called Opérations Aériennes et Maritimes received direct from Colonel Dewavrin the instructions relative to the comings and goings of aircraft and boats. Every month, during the nights when there was a moon, Lysanders or bombers, guided by pilots such as Laurent and Livry-Level, who were specialized in these courageous performances, landed on the chosen terrain. Men who were each time staking their lives carried out the signalling, the reception or embarkation of the travellers and matériel, the protection of everything and everybody. Often "containers," parachuted at designated points, had to be collected, hidden, and passed on. The Service Radio, which Julitte had begun to organize on the spot, likewise worked under the delegate's authority, sending to London and receiving hundreds, and later thousands, of telegrams each month, ceaselessly moving its stations, which the enemy's detector apparatus tracked down, and replacing as they occurred the heavy losses it suffered. Moulin had also set up the Bureau d'Information et de Presse, directed by Georges Bidault, which kept us posted as to the state of people's minds, especially among intellectuals, workers on social questions, and politicians. The Comité Général des Etudes, attached to the delegate, and with Bastid, Lacoste, de Menthon, Parodi, Teitgen, Courtin, and Debré working on it, elaborated plans for the future. Bloch-Laine directed financial operations on the delegation's behalf and banked the funds received from London. In this way Moulin, keeping the essential instruments in his hands, made the action of our government felt in practice. As early as the first months of 1942, witnesses arriving from France brought us proofs of this.

One of them was Rémy. He returned from Paris one night in February, bringing bundles of documents for our services, and for my wife a potted azalea he had bought in the Rue Royale. His network, Confrérie Notre-Dame, was working at full spate.

For example, not a single German surface boat arrived at or left Brest, Lorient, Nantes, Rochefort, La Rochelle, or Bordeaux without London's being warned by telegram. Not a single military work was built by the enemy on the Channel or Atlantic coasts, particularly in the submarine bases, without its situation and plan being at once known to us. Rémy had in addition organized contacts methodically, either with other networks, with the movements in the occupied zone, or with the Communists. The latter had got in touch with him shortly before his departure and had charged him with telling me that they were ready to place themselves under my orders and to send a representative to London to hold himself at my disposal there.

In March, Pineau, one of the leaders of Libération-Nord and a man trusted by the trade unionists, came and worked most usefully with us for three months. In April there arrived Emmanuel d'Astier, fully armed with proposals and also with interested schemes, and whom I thought it well to send, before he went back to France, to the United States with some definite information about the resistance. The next to join us was Brossolette, who was prodigal of ideas, could rise to the highest planes of political thought, could measure the full depth of the abyss in which France lay gasping, and placed his hopes of a recovery in Gaullism, which he erected into a doctrine. He was to play a large part in inspiring our movement at home. Then one day, having fallen into the hands of the enemy while doing his duty, he was to hurl himself to death to avoid the risk of weakening. Roques too had come, bearing messages from a certain number of parliamentarians. Later he was to be executed by the Gestapo. Paul Simon landed in his turn, sent from the occupied zone by the Organisation Civile et Militaire to establish liaison. Simon brought to bear his keen intelligence and cold determination, and was to render signal services. He was to be killed by the enemy on the eve of liberation. Lastly Philip, Charles Vallin, Viénot, Daniel Mayer, and yet others asked to be brought to London.

My interviews with these men, for the most part young, all of them seething with ardour and tense in their fighting spirit and ambition, helped to show me to what extent the regime under which the French people had been living at the moment of the disaster was discredited in its mind. The resistance was not only the rebound of our self-defence reduced to extremities: it was also arousing the hope of a national revival. Provided it did not disperse after victory, one might hope that it would serve as the lever for a profound change of system and for a vast national effort. As I saw its leaders pass before me, having come in answer to my call, I thought that those of them who survived would perhaps form around me the directing team of a great human and French achievement. But this would be on condition that, once the danger was passed, they would still accept that disciplining of minds and claims without which nothing is worth anything and which had, for once, united them.

The moment had come, in any case, for me to proclaim, in agreement with the whole of the resistance and in its name, the purpose we wished to attain. This purpose was liberation in the full sense of the word—that is to say, that of man as well as of the country. I did so in the form of a manifesto adopted in National Committee, after having asked the opinions, in France, of the movements and the delegation. In it I declared our intention that the liberty, dignity, and security, which we had resolved to assure to France in the world through the crushing of the enemy, should be obtainable by each man and woman in our country in his or her life through a change from the bad regime that had denied them to many. I condemned "that moral, social, political, and economic regime which had abdicated in the midst of defeat" at the same time as "the one which emerged from a criminal capitulation." And I affirmed: "While the French people is uniting for victory, it is assembling for a revolution." The manifesto was published on June 23, 1942, in all the clandestine papers of both zones, as well as broadcast by the radios of Brazzaville, Beirut, and London.

These conditions governing action at home were what chiefly

made it essential for me, during this period, to keep the seat of the National Committee in London. And yet the idea of establishing it on French territory, for example, at Brazzaville, often occurred to me. This was so, in particuar, every time a crisis arose in our relations with England. But I was forced then to return myself this answer: "How, from the depths of Africa, communicate with our country, make myself heard by it, influence the resistance? In Great Britain, on the contrary, there are the means required for liaison and information. Again, our diplomatic action upon the Allied governments implies relations and an atmosphere which the English capital offers us and of which, quite obviously, we would be deprived on the bank of the Congo. Lastly, I must keep contact with those of our forces which can be based only in the British Isles."

After my return from the Middle East, therefore, I established my residence in London. I was to remain there for ten months.

I can see again my life at that time. Easy to believe that it was packed. To simplify it, I lived at the Connaught Hotel. In addition I took a country house, first at Ellesmere in Shropshire, and then at Berkhamsted near the capital, where I spent the weekends with my wife and our daughter Anne. Later we were to make our home in London, at Hampstead. Philippe, after passing through the Ecole Navale, was sailing and fighting in the Atlantic on board the corvette *Roselys,* and later in the Channel as second-in-command of motor-torpedo boat 96. Elisabeth was a boarder with the Dames de Sion, preparing to enter Oxford. The ordinary people round about us observed a sympathetic discretion. The attitude of the English when they saw me with my family passing along a street, taking a walk in a park, or going into a cinema was as kindly reserved as the demonstrations were fervent when I appeared in public. So I was able, to my advantage, to verify that, among this great people, each one respects the liberty of the others.

Most often my day was spent at Carlton Gardens. It was there that François Coulet (who had become my *chef de cabinet* since

Courcel left to command an armoured-car unit in Libya) and Billotte (my chief of staff in succession to Petit, now on the mission to Moscow, and to Ortoli, who was commanding the *Triomphant*) presented me with reports, letters, and telegrams. It was there that Soustelle summarized for me the day's intelligence, Dewavrin brought me the reports from France, and Schumann received my directives for what he was going to say at the microphone. It was there that I settled business with the national commissioners and heads of services, received visitors or persons sent for, gave orders and instructions, and signed decrees. Often luncheon, and sometimes dinner, brought me together with eminent Allied persons or else with Frenchmen with whom I desired to talk. As for the great labour involved, for me, by the composition of my speeches, I did it at home, in the evenings or on Sundays. Whatever happened, I tried not to upset the functioning of the departments by a badly arranged timetable. In principle, work was not done at night at Carlton Gardens, except in the cipher office.

I had indeed to pay many visits outside. Apart from conversations with British Ministers, staff conferences, and ceremonies to which I was invited by the British government or by some other of our allies, I used to go, whenever occasion arose, to one of the centres of French life in London. The Institut Français, which had rallied to me literally from the first moment in the person of its director, Professor Saurat, supplied our compatriots with valuable educational resources and an active intellectual circle. The Alliance Française was continuing its work under the driving force of Thémoin and Mademoiselle Salmon. The Maison de l'Institut de France, up to the day when it was bombed to pieces together with its administrator, Robert Cru, produced from its library documentation of which our services had need. The Amis des Volontaires Français, a group directed by Lord Tyrrell, Lord De la Warr and Lord Ivor Churchill and composed chiefly of British, and in Scotland the Comité de Co-ordination de la France Combattante, under the friendly chairmanship of Lord Inverclyde, poured forth for our fighters an assistance that was as intelligent as it was generous. The French Chamber of Commerce played its part in fostering trade between Great Britain and the territories that had rallied to us. The Centre d'Accueil de la France Libre received the people who came from France. The French Hospital looked after a good number of our wounded. In associating myself with these various institutions my aim was to tighten in England, as I was trying to do elsewhere, national solidarity.

The Association des Français de Grande-Bretagne helped me actively in this. By it, in particular, were organized certain big meetings to which civilians and military flocked, making it possible for me to meet the mass of French people, for those present to demonstrate their feelings and heighten their convictions, and for the people at home to hear us, thanks to the radio, which retransmitted the speeches and the stirrings of the audience. Already on March 1, 1941, at the Kingsway Hall, before some thousands of listeners, I had defined our mission and affirmed our hopes. On November 15, in the midst of an assembly that filled the huge space of the Albert Hall, I solemnly formulated the three articles of our policy.

"Article One," I said, "is to wage war—that is to say, to give the French effort in the conflict the greatest possible extent and power. . . . But this effort is being made by us only at the call and in the service of France." Then, condemning at the same time the prewar regime and that of Vichy, I declared: "We hold it to be necessary that a rumbling and cleansing wave should arise from the depths of the nation and sweep pell-mell before it the causes of the disaster together with the whole superstructure built on the capitulation. For this reason Article Two of our policy is to restore to the people the power to make itself heard as soon as events shall permit it freely to make known what it wants and what it will not have." Lastly, under Article Three, I outlined the foundations we wished to give to the renewed institutions of France. "These foundations," I said, "are defined by the three mottoes of the Free French. We say, 'Honour and Country,' meaning thereby that the nation can live again only by victory and continue to exist only through the cult of her own greatness. We say, 'Liberty, Equality, Fraternity,' because our determination is to remain faithful to democratic principles. We say, 'Liberation,' for if our efforts cannot conceivably cease before the defeat of the enemy, it must result, for every Frenchman, in conditions making it possible for him to live and work in dignity and security."

The audience on this occasion, by its visible emotion and hurricane of shouting, gave a demonstration which rang out far beyond the precincts of the Albert Hall.

Such meetings were rare. I went on the other hand frequently, under the outward form of a military inspection, to see our volunteers. Our land, sea, and air forces, small and dispersed though they were, and although we could only make them of bits and pieces, now formed a coherent whole which was continuously consolidating. The plan of organization which I had laid down for 1942 for the War, Navy, and Air commissioners, was being carried out as provided for. I saw this for myself as I visited the units based in Great Britain. On these occasions the men, as they saw, close to, the man whom they called *le grand Charles*,[2] offered him, through their gaze, their bearing and their keenness, at the exercises, the homage of loyalty that would never compromise.

For our small army fighting in Africa and in the Middle East there were on English soil no more than training centres. But these were instructing a large part of the cadres. In camp at Camberley, Colonel Renouard paraded for me the battalion of chasseurs, the artillery group, the armoured squadron, the engineers' detachment, and the signals unit, from which there emerged, every six months, NCOs and specialists. I moved on to the Artillery Park, which, under Commandant Boutet, was putting into condition the French matériel that had been brought to Great Britain by the base services of the Norway expedition or by the warships arrived from France since the invasion. Arms, ammunition, and vehicles were being sent to equip the new formations, concurrently with the

[2] This nickname, of course, carries the two senses of "great Charles" and "tall Charles." (Translator's note.)

matériel supplied either by the English under the terms of the agreement of August 7, 1940, or by the Americans under Lend-Lease. The negotiations and executive decisions required by this major task fell to the Service de l'Armement. It acquitted itself of it under the direction of Colonel Morin, until that excellent officer was shot down in the air in the course of a long-distance mission. Commandant Hirsh was his successor. In London itself I sometimes saluted the Compagnie des Volontaires Françaises, which had as its captain Mademoiselle Terré, following in the footsteps of Madame Mathieu, and was training well-deserving young girls to become drivers, nurses, and secretaries. From time to time I visited the Cadets de la France Libre at Malvern, and later at Ribbersford. I had set up the school in 1940 for the sake of students and college boys who had come over to England. We had soon made of it a nursery garden of cadets. Commandant Baudoin was in charge of the Cadet School. Five batches were to come from it, in all, 211 section or group leaders; 52 were to be killed in action. Nothing gave so much comfort to the leader of the Free French as the contact with these young people; that jewelled spray of hope added to the darkened glory of France.

While the units of the land forces stationed in Great Britain carried out the training of elements intended for fighting elsewhere, it was from British ports that the majority of our naval forces took part—in the Atlantic, the Channel, the North Sea, and the Arctic—in the battle of communications. To do so it was essential for us to take advantage of the Allied bases. We had, in fact, no means of our own of repairing, maintaining, and supplying our ships. Still less could we equip them with the new resources—anti-aircraft defence, asdic, radar, and so on—required by the evolution of the struggle. Lastly, over the vast theatre of maritime operations of which England was the centre, technical and tactical unity was necessary.

Therefore, while the ships manned by us belonged entirely to us, whatever their origin, while the only flag they flew was the tricolour, while the officers and crews acknowledged French discipline alone, and while they carried out missions solely on orders from their leaders—in short, while our Navy remained purely national—we had conceded that, apart from episodes that might lead us to make direct use of it, it formed part, as regards the use made of it, of the total naval activity carried on by the British. This, after all, placed it within an admirably competent, disciplined, and active system, which had an effect on its own value. The English, on their side, were highly appreciative of this help and lent the Free French naval forces large material support. Their arsenals and their services set all their wits to the conditioning and equipping of our ships, in spite of the differences of types and armament. The new apparatus used by the British Navy were supplied to ours without delay. New ships—corvettes and motor-torpedo boats, and later on frigates, destroyers, and submarines—were offered to us as soon as built. If our small fleet succeeded in playing a part and in upholding the honour of France upon the seas, this was due to Allied aid as well as to the merits of our sailors.

I realized this every time I went to see some fraction of it at Greenock, Portsmouth, Cowes, or Dartmouth. Given the character of the struggle, given also the limited numbers available to us, we manned only small ships. But on board those of Free France keenness was pushed to the limit of what is possible.

Naturally we first manned ships that had come from France. In the spring of 1942 there remained, of our first five submarines, the *Rubis,* the *Minerve,* and the *Junon,* which were busy in Norwegian, Danish, and French waters, attacking ships, laying mines, and landing commandos; the *Narval* had disappeared off Malta in December 1940, and the *Surcouf* had sunk with all hands in February 1942. The destroyers *Triomphant* and *Léopard* and the torpedo boats *Melpomène* and *Bouclier* had for months been escorting convoys in the Atlantic and the Channel. Then the *Triomphant* left for the Pacific. The *Léopard* went to South Africa; later she brought Réunion over to us; in the end she was to be wrecked off Tobruk. The *Melpomène* moved to the North Sea.

The *Bouclier* became one of our training ships. Of our five sloops, three—the *Savorgnan de Brazza,* the *Commandant Duboc,* and the *Commandant Dominé*—were cruising off the coasts of Africa; the *Moqueuse* was helping to protect cargo boats in the Irish Channel; and the *Chevreuil,* in Oceania, was patrolling from Nouméa and on May 27, 1942, brought the Wallis and Futuna Islands over to Free France. Two minesweepers, the *Congre* and the *Lucienne-Jeanne,* carried out their hard task in the approaches to the harbours of Great Britain. Ten submarine chasers took part in the cover given to Allied cargo boats between Cornwall and the Pas-de-Calais. There were now only eight of them, for two had gone to the bottom. Six patrol trawlers were put into service: the *Poulmic,* sunk off Plymouth in November 1940; the *Viking,* sunk off Tripolitania in April 1942; the *Vaillant, Président Honduce,* and *Reine des Flots,* which were still scouring the seas; and the *Léonille,* used as a depot for the merchant marine. The auxiliary cruiser *Cap des Palmes* did shuttle service between Sydney and Nouméa. Four base ships—the *Ouragan, Amiens, Arras,* and *Diligente*—completed the "naval unit" at Greenock and the *Bir Hakeim* crew depot at Portsmouth, where our sailors were trained. The old battleship *Courbet* was a centre for the passage of recruits, a group of workshops, and a depot for ammunition and stores; anchored in Plymouth roads, she gave support with her artillery to the air defence of the great harbour.

Many other ships, supplied by the English, formed part of our small fleet. There were, in the first place, corvettes, built since the beginning of the war for convoy protection, sailing the seas between England, Iceland, Newfoundland, and Canada without respite. Nine were handed over to us: the *Alysse,* sunk in action in March 1942; the *Mimosa,* sunk three months later with the commander of the little division, Capitaine de Frégate Birot, on board; the *Aconit, Lobelia, Roselys, Renoncule, Commandant d'Estienne d'Orves, Commandant Drogou,* and *Commandant Détroyat.* Next, there were the eight motor-torpedo boats of the 28th Flotilla, ploughing the Channel at high speed to attack the enemy cargo boats that crept along the coast of France by night and the warships that escorted them. There were also eight motor launches making up the 20th Flotilla and seconding, in the Channel, our French-built chasseurs. We were, besides, preparing for the manning of some brand-new ships. Among the frigates which were emerging from the British arsenals, several, only just launched, were offered us by our allies. We kept four of these: *La Découverte, L'Aventure, La Surprise,* and *La Croix de Lorraine.* We also earmarked for ourselves the torpedo boat *La Combattante* and the submarines *Curie* and *Doris,* whose construction was being completed. We would have liked many more, which would increase the total of submarines, cargo boats, and enemy escorting craft sunk by our ships, and of the aircraft brought down by them. But it was the shortage of manpower, certainly not the lack of ships, that limited our size and our part.

By June 1942, 700 Free French sailors had already died for France. Our naval forces contained 3600 sailors in service at sea. There should be added the battalion of marines, commanded by Amyot d'Inville after the death of Détroyat on the field of honour. There should also be added certain isolated men of the naval air force, who, not being enough to form a unit, were serving in the Air Force. Lastly, there should be added the commando unit, training in Great Britain under the orders of Lieutenant de Vaisseau Kieffer. In May I settled with Admiral Lord Mountbatten, whom the English had put in charge of "combined operations," the conditions in which this very resolute troop would be used. This meant that it would soon take part in the raids on the French coast.

These effectives had been, for the most part, recruited from among the elements of the Navy who were in England in 1940. Some had rallied to us, after having fought us in the Gabon and the Levant. The same was the case with the crews of the submarine *Ajax,* sunk off Dakar, the submarine *Poncelet,* scuttled off Port-Gentil, and the sloop *Bougainville,* which we had been forced to put out of action in Libreville harbour. A few elements from the active list joined us from time to time from Metropolitan France, North Africa, Alexandria, the Antilles, and the Far East. The Navy enlisted all the young Frenchmen it could in England, America, the Levant, Egypt, and Saint Pierre. Lastly, the merchant ships gave the naval forces a large part of their manpower.

The most difficult problem for the naval commissioner's department was to form the ships' complements of officers. They had to be made up of extremely varied, not to say disparate, elements, by doing violence to the rules of specialization. We had few officers from the active list. We were therefore training young ones. Under Capitaines de Frégate Wietzel and Gayral, who successively commanded the "division des écoles," the Free France Naval School worked actively on board the *Président Théodore Tissier* and the schooners *Etoile* and *Belle Poule*. There came from it, in four batches, eighty cadets who were to bring to the French Navy a sense of vocation saturated, from the start, in grief, battle, and aspiration. At the same time the reserve officers, whom we found on board trading ships or among the Suez Canal personnel, formed a large part of the cadres of our naval forces. Two hundred cadets recruited in this were to keep watch on board the frigates, corvettes, chasseurs, vedettes, and trawlers for a total of over a million hours.

In spite of these raids on its manpower, the fraction of the French merchant fleet serving in the camp of the Allies made an appreciable contribution to their convoys. Out of the 2,700,000 tons—or 660 liners and cargo boats—possessed by France at the beginning of the conflict, 700,000 tons—or 170 ships—were to carry on with the war effort after the "armistices." Our merchant marine service, directed by Malglaive and Bingen, and later by Smeyers and Andus-Fariz, arranged for the manning of the greatest possible number of ships by French crews. They also had their say in the use made of the other ships, of which the British took charge. In that case, the Union Jack was flown beside the Tricolour on the poop or at the masthead of these exiled ships. In spite of everything, 67 merchant ships, totalling 200,000 tons, were manned by us. Twenty had been or were to be lost. Concerned in maintaining this service were 580 officers and 4300 sailors. By the spring of 1942 over a quarter had already perished at sea.

The liners were acting as troop transports. So it was that the *Ile de France,* the *Félix Roussel,* and the *Président Paul Doumer* brought to the Middle East the British reinforcements from Australia or from India. The cargo boats, carrying raw materials, arms, and ammunition where they were wanted, ordinarily sailed in convoys. Sometimes one of them had to cross the ocean alone. They reached port only to sail again. Even then, they would be bombed while in harbour. On the high seas the service was as exhausting as it was dangerous. It meant keeping watch night and day, observing strict rules, perpetually rushing to action stations. Often it meant fighting, firing the ship's gun, and manœuvring desperately to avoid the torpedo or the bomb. The ship might sink and a man might find himself struggling in the oily and icy water, with his comrades drowning all around. He might also have the terrible joy of watching the bomber's fall or of staring at the patch of oil beneath which the enemy submarine was going down. One of these ships might even, though a mere cargo boat, be the cause of it, like the *Fort-Binger,* which in May 1942, off Newfoundland, sent a German submarine to the bottom.

One day, at Liverpool, Admiral Sir Percy Noble, who from headquarters there directed navigation and fighting over the whole Atlantic expanse, took me to the underground reinforced-concrete Operations Room. On the walls, great charts indicated the position, kept up to date hour by hour, of all the Allied convoys, all the warships, and all the aircraft that were out, as well as the detected or supposed position of the German submarines, aircraft, and raiders. A telephone exchange, connected with the outside world, with the radio stations, and with the cipher office, and served by calm teams of women—operators, stenographers, and messengers—transmitted with barely a murmur the orders, messages, and reports sent by the command to the remote regions of the sea or reaching it from them. Everything was recorded instantly on luminous surfaces. So the immense battle of communications was at every moment outlined and formulated with all its swaying changes.

After having considered the whole, I looked on the maps to see where ours were. I saw them in the good places—that is to say, the most honourable. The salute of the leader of the Free French went out, by wireless, to reach them. But then, as I measured how small, numerically—and for that reason absorbed in a foreign system—was the share they represented; as I imagined, over there, the ships wasted in inaction at Toulon, Casablanca, Alexandria, Fort-de-France, and Dakar; and as I remembered the historic occasion this war was offering to the maritime vocation of France, I felt sadness flooding through me. It was with heavy steps that I climbed the stairs from the subterranean shelter.

A similar sentiment mingled with my pride when I made contact with our airmen at one or other of the British air bases. When I saw their worth and, at the same time, thought what could have been done from North Africa, the Levant, or England by the French Air Army if only it had been allowed to fight, I could feel a great chance for the nation being thrown away. But it only made me the more intent on making sure that the efforts of those who had managed to join me should be credited to France. While I of course admitted that everyone in our forces who flew from bases in Great Britain in aircraft supplied by the English must form part of the British air system, I was anxious that our combatants in the air should also constitute a national element.

This was not easy. At the start our allies were hardly interested in a Free French Air Force. Going straight for what was most practical and most pressing, they welcomed some of our pilots into their units. But all they offered us was to incorporate our air volunteers into the Royal Air Force. I could not agree to that. And so, for nearly a year, the destination of our men remained undetermined. Some, grouped in extemporized French squadrons, had been able to take part in the air battles of Eritrea and Libya. Others, provisionally adopted by British squadrons, took part in the Battle of Britain.

But the majority, for lack of machines, organization, and training, were kicking their heels on the edge of the air bases in Great Britain or in Egypt.

The problem, however, was solved in its turn. In the spring of 1941 I managed to settle the questions of principle with Sir Archibald Sinclair, the British Air Minister. An understanding and generous man, he was willing to recognize that the existence of a French Air Force would not be without interest. He agreed, as I asked, that we should form units—actually groups modelled on the squadrons—the British lending us what we lacked in the way of ground staff and carrying out the training of our recruits in their schools. Any pilots we had in excess were to serve in British units. But their position there would be that of seconded French officers, subject to French discipline and wearing French uniform. I wrote to Sir Archibald from Cairo on June 8, 1941, to confirm the agreement negotiated on this basis by Colonel Valin. From that moment he had, in carrying it out, the constant support of Air Marshals Portal in London and Longmore, later Tedder, in the Middle East.

So it was that at the end of 1941 we set up in England the fighter group Ile de France. Its commander was Scitivaux. When he was brought down over France—whence, indeed, he was to return—he was succeeded by Dupérier. On the morrow of the Syrian campaign, the fighter group Alsace was formed in Egypt: it fought at first in Libya under Pouliguen and then moved to Great Britain, where Mouchotte took command, to be killed in action in the following year. The Lorraine bomber group was born in the Levant, under the command of Pijeaud. He, after being shot down behind the enemy lines a few weeks later, managed to regain ours, only to die there. Corniglion-Molinier replaced him. The Bretagne mixed group was formed in the Chad, with Saint-Péreuse as its leader, to give support to our Saharan operations. In the spring of 1942 the elements that were to constitute the Normandie group—later regiment—in Russia were brought together, partly in London, partly at Riyaq. Tulasne and Littolf were to be successively at its head. After their deaths it would be Pouyade. Lastly, some of our pilots were, by my orders, placed at the disposal of the Royal Air Force. Morlaix, Fayolle, and Guedj commanded squadrons within it. The two last were killed in action. Glory is costly in the battles of the sky. The Free French Air Force lost, in all, twice as many killed as its effective flying strength.

But while the world character of the war made me determined to see that French forces were engaged in all theatres of operations, I set myself to concentrate the principal effort on the one that interested France most directly—that is to say, North Africa. Once the Italian army in Ethiopia was annihilated, access to Syria forbidden to the Germans, and Vichy's schemes for action against Free French Africa stifled at birth, Libya was where we had to act.

In November 1941 the British had taken the offensive there once more. If they succeeded in reaching the Tunisian frontier, it was essential that we should be there with them, having first helped to beat the enemy. If, on the contrary, he managed to drive them back, we ought to do everything to aid them in stopping him before he could overrun Egypt. In any case, it was the moment to deploy the full effort of which we were capable, but by playing our own part in order to win a success that would be truly a French one.

We had two possibilities of action: to push up from the Chad towards the Fezzan the Saharan column, which Leclerc had long been preparing, or to engage in Libya, side by side with the English, the mobile forces perfected by Larminat. I decided to do both, but to do so in such a way that the action of our soldiers should directly benefit France.

The conquest of the Fezzan and, after that, the march on Tripoli would be an operation that could be hazarded only once for all. If, in fact, the business did not succeed, it could not be undertaken again for a long time, given the unheard-of difficulties involved by the formation, equipment, and supply of the Chad column. This column should therefore act to the full only if the

British, having retaken Cyrenaica, entered Tripolitania. Otherwise it would have to confine itself to harassing the Italians by deep, swift raids.

At the same time I intended that the Chad front—if one can go so far as to use this name for a group of inevitably discontinuous actions—should remain a French front. Certainly the start of our Saharan enterprise would have to be coordinated with the march of the British VIIIth Army. That was a matter of liaison with Cairo. But for the rest Leclerc would continue to be responsible only to me, until the day when, having effected his junction with our allies on the shores of the Mediterranean, it would become logical to place him under their direction. I attached the more importance to this autonomy since the conquest of the Fezzan would place in our hands a guarantee as regards the later settlement of the fate of Libya.

In the course of November and December the British, fighting hard and bravely, penetrated into Cyrenaica. In preparation for their eruption into Tripolitania, Leclerc, with the support of General Serres, at that time over-all commander of the troops in Free French Africa, made his arrangements for launching out at the Fezzan. As for me, my optimism about this was reserved. Knowing that Rommel had managed to disengage himself from the grip of the English and that, Weygand having been recalled from North Africa, the application of the Hitler-Darlan agreement would make it possible for the enemy to supply himself through Tunisia, I was not relying on a rapid progress by the Allies towards Tripoli. On the contrary, an enemy counterattack seemed to me more likely. That is why, while allowing the offensive to be prepared, I kept for myself the right to order its start. As, at the same time, the liaison mission which Leclerc had sent to Cairo had let itself be drawn into accepting his subordination to the British High Command, I made it clear to General Ismay that nothing of the sort was the case, and put the minds of the "Chadians" right as to how things should be in this matter.

In fact our allies did not enter Tripolitania. For both adversaries the first months of 1942 were a period of stabilization. Once that was clear, the proper thing for our troops in the Chad was to carry out tip-and-run raids only. Leclerc was burning to do so. On February 4 I gave the authorization. He acted, rushing through the Fezzan, in the course of March, with his combat patrols supported by his aircraft, destroying several enemy posts, taking many prisoners, and capturing war matériel. He then returned to his base, having suffered only the smallest losses. To extend this exceptionally valuable leader's zone and resources for action, I gave him command, in April, of all the forces in Free French Africa. Once again I had to overcome protests from his rigorous modesty. From that time he and his troops felt certain that they would capture the Oases as soon as events in Libya took a decisive turn for the good. However, they would have to wait ten long months more, under a torrid heat, among the stones and sand, before grasping victory and coming to wash off their dust in the Mediterranean.

But while in the Chad it was necessary for us to postpone the decisive stroke, we were about to find in Cyrenaica, on the contrary, the long awaited opportunity for a brilliant feat of arms. And yet we had had to overcome a great many obstacles before getting the Allies to agree that large French units should be engaged on this ground.

The two light divisions and the armoured regiment formed in Syria under the orders of Larminat had, in fact, not been expected by the British High Command to take part in the offensive started at the end of October. And yet the two large-scale units were solid and well armed. Each of them was motorized and comprised five infantry battalions, an artillery regiment, an anti-tank defence company, an anti-aircraft defence company, a reconnaissance group, an engineers' company and park, a signals company, a transport company, a general staff company, and services. These units, comprising all arms and therefore capable of playing a special tactical part, were real divisions. Although they were certainly "light," I was set on giving them the name they deserved.

Larminat, using the arms left behind by Dentz or else gathered from the magazines where the Italian armistice commissions had impounded them, equipped each section with a formidable armament, which our keen and alert volunteers would know how to handle—none better. So it was that, independently of the divisional artillery, each battalion had six 75 mm. guns of its own. It was also very powerfully provided with mortars and automatic weapons. The troops would have to be lightened for an attack, if the occasion arose. But if holding ground was what was wanted, they had an altogether exceptional fire-power at their disposal.

Having on September 20 approved the composition of the two light divisions, I sent Mr. Churchill, on October 7, a note to inform him of our desires and our resources. At the same time I wrote to General Auchinleck, commander-in-chief, Middle East, to remind him of how anxious we were that our troops should fight in Libya. I made it clear to Mr. Churchill and to General Auchinleck that, for these operations, I was ready to place the whole of the Larminat group under the orders of the British High Command and that at the same time Leclerc, though acting autonomously, could be launched against the Fezzan at the date they might ask us. On October 9 I went to see Mr. Margesson, the British Minister for War, and asked him to intervene. Lastly, on October 30, I indicated to General Catroux the conditions under which it would be right for our forces to be engaged—that is to say, as large-scale units.

It was not till November 27 that I received the British reply. It was sent to me by General Ismay, the War Cabinet's and Mr. Churchill's Chief of Staff. His letter amounted to a dismissal of my request, as courteous as it was explicit. To explain their refusal our allies alleged "the dispersal of the French units at various points in Syria," the fact that "they were not trained to act as divisions or brigades," and lastly "the insufficiency of their equipment." They expressed, however, the hope that the future might make it possible to reconsider the question.

Obviously the British command was counting on achieving the conquest of Libya and overcoming Rommel without the help of the French. It is true that it had on the spot considerable land and air forces and that it believed Admiral Cunningham—who was a magnificent leader and sailor—to be in a position to do more than a miracle and cut the enemy's communications between Italy and Tripolitania.

The disappointment which the English reply caused me can be imagined. I could not tolerate that our troops should remain standing at ease indefinitely while the fate of the world was being decided in battle. Rather than accept that, I preferred to take the risk of a change of front. I therefore sent for M. Bogomolov and begged him to let his government know that the National Committee desired that French forces should take part directly in the Allied operations on the eastern front if the North Africa theatre should be closed to them. I made, of course, no mystery of my request in London. But even before Moscow's reply reached me, the British intentions had changed. On December 7 Mr. Churchill wrote me a warm letter to tell me that he had "just heard from General Auchinleck that he is most anxious to use a Free French brigade immediately in the Cyrenaican operations." "I know," the Prime Minister added, "this will be in accordance with your wishes, and how eager your men are to come to grips with the Germans."

I answered Mr. Churchill that I approved of the project and was giving General Catroux the necessary orders. In fact the English, apart from the annoyance that might be caused to them by the possible transfer of the French forces to Russia, were beginning to measure the military advantage that would be involved by our assistance in the battle of Cyrenaica. They realized, indeed, that the enemy there was yielding ground only step by step, that their own troops were suffering heavy losses, and that they would have to reorganize on the spot a command ill adapted to mechanized operations. Giving up the idea of carrying the offensive into Tripolitania, they now expected Rommel to take the initiative again, and soon. This prospect made them glad for us to lend them a hand.

In Cairo, then, Catroux settled with Auchinleck the movement of the 1st Light Division towards Libya, and Koenig, instructed to negotiate the details, obtained from our allies a useful complement in anti-tank weapons, anti-aircraft guns, and means of transport. In January this division had a few brilliant engagements with some elements of Rommel's, who were encircled at Salum and Bardia and soon gave themselves up. When they saw the processions of German prisoners they had helped to take, our troops felt as though they had had an electric shock. It was most cheerfully that they moved westwards. In the course of February, when the English placed their principal forces at the heart of Cyrenaica, in the so-called "Gazala" position, composed of several zones of resistance, ours were given that of Bir Hakeim, the most southerly. When they were still organizing themselves there, they opened an active contest of skirmishes and patrols in the deep no-man's-land that separated them from the bulk of the enemy.

But while the 1st Light Division was thus being given its chance, nothing was being done for the 2nd, which was eating its heart out in the Levant. I meant that it too should take part in the operations. And indeed, on December 10, M. Bogomolov had come to tell me that my project for sending French troops to Russia met with warm agreement from his government, and that it was ready to supply our forces on the spot with all the necessary matériel. I therefore contemplated sending to the east not only the Normandie air group, but also the 2nd Light Division. Starting from Syria and passing through Baghdad, it would cross Persia in lorries and then, from Tabriz, be transported by rail to the Caucasus. This was the route taken from the Iranian ports by the convoys of war matériel which the Allies were sending to Russia. On December 29 I wrote to General Ismay to warn him of my intentions and gave General Catroux the required instructions. The 2nd Division would leave on March 15 for the Caucasus if it had not, before that, been allowed into Libya.

The British High Command raised all the possible objections to the transfer of this unit to Russia. But at Moscow, on the contrary, the Soviets gave it great importance. Molotov, speaking to Garreau, and General Panfilov to Petit, pressed us to carry it out. Mr. Eden, being informed, joined in and wrote to me to support the view of the British military. I could only stick to mine, and it was to mine that the Allied Command consented to come round, at the end of February. Ismay let me know. Auchinleck asked Catroux to put the 2nd Division at his disposal. Leaving Syria, it arrived in Libya in the last days of March.

Larminat, from now on, had his group where it could act: Koenig in the line at Bir Hakeim with the 1st Division; Cazaud in reserve with the 2nd. The armoured regiment, commanded by Colonel Rémy, was in the rear, having been given new matériel. A company of parachutists, which I had sent from England, was now training at Ismailia, ready to carry out the raids for which it would receive orders. In all, 12,000 fighting men, or about a fifth of the total strength which the Allies were putting into action simultaneously. The Alsace fighter group and the Lorraine bomber group had been fighting in the skies of Cyrenaica since October. Several of our sloops and trawlers were helping to escort the convoys along the coast. Thus an important French force had been gathered in time in the principal theatre. In his justice, the God of Battles was about to offer the soldiers of Free France a great fight and great glory. On May 27 Rommel took the offensive. Bir Hakeim was attacked.

In enterprises in which one risks everything, there usually comes a moment when the person responsible feels that fate is being determined. By a strange convergence the thousand trials in the midst of which he is struggling seem suddenly to blossom into a decisive episode. If it turns out well, fortune will be in his hands. But if it works to the leader's confusion, the whole is lost. While the drama of Bir Hakeim was being enacted round about the polygon of sixteen square kilometres held by Koenig and his men, I in London, reading the telegrams, listening to the commentaries, and seeing now shadow, now light, in people's expressions, could measure what consequences depended on what was happening out there. If those 5500 fighting men, who carried each one with him his grief and his hope, who had come of their own free will from France, Africa, the Levant, and the Pacific, and who had been gathered where they were at the cost of so many difficulties, were to undergo a sad reverse, our cause would be indeed compromised. On the contrary, if, at this moment, on that ground, they achieved some striking feat of arms, then the future was ours!

The first engagements left nothing to be desired. On May 27 I learned that, while the enemy's main body was passing south of Bir Hakeim to turn the Allied position, the Italian mechanized division Ariete had launched some hundred of its tanks against the French position and had lost forty of them, leaving their wrecks on the approaches. On the 28th and 29th, our detachments, making sweeps in all directions, destroyed fifteen machines more and took two hundred prisoners. On the 30th General Rommel, having failed to settle with the British mechanized formations at the first blow, decided to retire in order to prepare a new manœuvre. Two days later a French column, commanded by Lieutenant-Colonel Broche, made a dash for Rotonda Signali, over thirty miles to the west, and captured the position. On June 1 Larminat inspected our troops in the field. His report was full of optimism. In the world at large a mood was forming. Some people, in fact, felt it in their bones that this action might well go far beyond military tactics. Praise for the French troops and their leaders began to appear guardedly in conversation, in veiled phrases on the radio, with a certain caution in the newspapers.

Next day Rommel seized the initiative. This time he pushed straight at the centre of the position held by General Ritchie, to whom Auchinleck had entrusted the command of the fighting front. The Germans overwhelmed a British brigade at Got-el-Skarab, crossed at this point the big minefield with which the Allies were covering themselves from El Gazala to Bir Hakeim, and, to widen the breech, sent a division of the Afrika Korps against our troops. For the first time since June 1940, full-scale contact was made between French and Germans. This at first took the form merely of skirmishes, in which we took a hundred and fifty prisoners. But very quickly the front was established for a battle. To the two enemy spokesmen who asked if we were willing to surrender, Koenig sent word that he had not come for that.

The following days saw the adversary tighten his hold. Batteries of heavy calibres, including 155s and 220s, opened an intensifying fire on our men. Three, four, five times a day the Stukas and Junkers attacked them in squadrons of a hundred machines. Supplies were coming up in small quantities only. At Bir Hakeim stocks of ammunition were visibly getting lower, food rations diminishing, water rations being cut. Under the burning sun, in the midst of the sandstorms, the defenders were perpetually on the alert, living with their wounded, burying their dead close by them. On June 3 General Rommel summoned them, in his own handwriting, to lay down their arms "on pain of being annihilated like the British brigades at Got-el-Skarab." On June 5 one of his officers came and renewed this ultimatum. It was our artillery that replied. But at the same time, in many countries, public attention was awakening. The French of Bir Hakeim were interesting the spoken or printed news bulletins more and more. Opinion was getting ready to judge. The question was whether glory could still smile on our soldiers.

On June 7 the investment of Bir Hakeim was complete. The 90th German Division and the Italian Trieste Division, supported by about twenty batteries and by some hundreds of tanks, were ready to start the assault. "Hold out for six days longer," the Allied Command had ordered Koenig on the evening of June 1. The six days had passed. "Hold out for another forty-eight hours," General Ritchie asked. The fact had to be faced that the losses and confusion inflicted on the VIIIth Army by the blows of the enemy were such that any operation for relief or aid was thenceforward impossible. As for Rommel, he was in a hurry to rush on towards Egypt, taking advantage of the disarray he detected among the British, and was impatient at this resistance at his rear, dragging on and upsetting his communications. Bir Hakeim had become his chief anxiety and his main objective. He had already come several times to look at the field. He was to come again to urge the assailants on.

Powerful attacks started on the 8th. Several times the enemy infantry, with great artillery and tank reinforcements, attempted, bravely but in vain, to overrun this or that sector of our lines. The day was a very hard one for our men. So was the night, spent in putting the wrecked positions in order again. On the 9th the assaults resumed. The enemy artillery had been still further reinforced with heavy calibres, against which the 75s of Colonel Laurent-Champrosay could not hold their own. Our men were being given no more than just two litres of water every twenty-four hours, which is cruelly insufficient in such a climate. Yet it was essential to hold on still, for with the disorder that was gradually gaining the various elements of the British Army, Koenig's resistance now took on a capital importance. "Heroic defence by the French!" "Magnificent feat of arms!" "The Germans beaten in front of Bir Hakeim!" all the trumpets of the news in London, New York, Montreal, Cairo, Rio, and Buenos Aires announced at full blast. We were drawing near the aim we had had in mind in obtaining for the Free French troops—limited though their numerical strength might be—a great role on a great occasion. To the whole world the guns of Bir Hakeim announced the beginning of the recovery of France.

But what now obsessed me was the safety of the defenders. I knew they would not for long be able to smash attacks supported by such crushing resources. True, I was certain that in any case the division would not surrender, that the adversary would be deprived of the satisfaction of seeing a long column of French prisoners pass before Rommel, and that, if our troops remained where they were, he would have, if he wanted to finish with them, to destroy them group by group. But the thing was to rescue them, not to resign oneself to their glorious extermination. I had great need, for what was to come, of these hundreds of excellent officers and NCOs and these thousands of very good soldiers. Their exploit being established, they must now accomplish another, blaze themselves a way through the assailants and minefields, rejoin the bulk of the Allied forces.

Although I was careful not to intervene directly in the conduct of the battle, I could not help letting the British Imperial General Staff know, on June 8 and 9, in the most pressing manner, how important it was that Koenig should receive, before it was too late, the order to attempt to break out. I repeated this on June 10 to Mr. Churchill, with whom I was discussing the question of Madagascar. In any case the denouement was approaching, and I telegraphed to the commander of the 1st Light Division: "General Koenig, know, and tell your troops, that the whole of France is looking at you and you are her pride!" At the end of that same day General Sir Alan Brooke, the Chief of the Imperial General Staff, informed me that since dawn the enemy had raged against Bir Hakeim without ceasing, but that Ritchie had ordered Koenig to move to a new position if he found this possible. The operation was planned for that night.

Next morning—June 11—the broadcast and press commentaries were dithyrambic and funereal. Not knowing that the French were trying to disengage, everyone evidently expected their resistance to be overwhelmed from one moment to another. But behold, that evening, Brooke sent me word: "General Koenig and a large part of his troops have reached El Gobi, out of reach of the enemy." I thanked the messenger, told him he could go, shut the door. I was alone. O heart throbbing with emotion, sobs of pride, tears of joy!

Of the 5500 men, roughly, who comprised the 1st Light Division before Bir Hakeim, Koenig, after fourteen days of fighting, was bringing back nearly 4000 uninjured. It had been possible to transport to the rear a certain number of wounded as well as the units. Our troops left on the field 1109 officers and men, killed, wounded, or missing. Among the killed, three were senior officers: Lieutenant-Colonel Broche, Commandants Savey and Bricogne. Among the wounded left behind: Commandants Puchois and Babonneau. Some war matériel, first carefully destroyed, had had to be abandoned. But we had inflicted on the enemy three times the losses we had suffered.

On June 12 the Germans announced that they had "taken Bir Hakeim by storm" the day before. Then the Berlin radio published a communiqué declaring: "The white and coloured Frenchmen made prisoner at Bir Hakeim, since they do not belong to a regular army, will be subject to the laws of war and will be executed." An hour later I had the following note put out in all languages by the BBC: "If the German army were so far to dishonour itself as to kill French soldiers taken prisoner when fighting for their country, General de Gaulle announces that to his profound regret he would find himself obliged to inflict the same fate on the German prisoners who have fallen into the hands of his troops." The day was not over before the Berlin radio proclaimed: "On the subject of the members of the French forces who have just been captured in the fighting at Bir Hakeim, no misunderstanding is possible. General de Gaulle's soldiers will be treated as soldiers." And so indeed they were.

While the 1st Light Division was regrouping at Sidi Barrâni and Catroux was busy bringing it immediately up to strength again, our Alsace air group continued to take part in the redoubled activity of the British fighters, and our Lorraine group, together with the Royal Air Force bombers, made a great many attacks on enemy communications. At the same time our parachutists carried out several brilliant raids. So it was that, in the night of June 12 to 13, their teams destroyed twelve aircraft on the enemy airdromes in Libya, and that Captain Bergé, who was dropped in Crete with a few men, set fire to twenty-one bombers, fifteen lorries, and a petrol dump at the Candia airfield before being captured.

Meanwhile the VIIIth Army, overcome by sudden moral fatigue, abandoned Cyrenaica, leaving behind a considerable amount of war matériel. General Auchinleck hoped at least to keep Tobruk, a position that was solidly organized and supplied by sea. But on June 24 the garrison, numbering 33,000 men, surrendered to the Germans. It was with great difficulty that the British managed to recover when they reached El Alamein. One sector of the position was held by General Cazaud and his 2nd Light Division, placed at last in the line, in their turn. Among the reserves there figured Colonel Rémy's armoured group, hastily provided with matériel. The situation was grave. The whole Middle East, shaken by disquieting tremors, was expecting to see the Germans and Italians enter Cairo and Alexandria.

This depression on the part of our allies was to be no more than temporary. A day would come when, thanks to the mastery of the sea, to fresh reinforcements, to great air superiority, and, lastly, to the qualities of General Montgomery, they would in the end win the upper hand. Rommel indeed, with his supplies strained, was suspending his advance. Nonetheless events as a whole made the importance of our action stand out. General Auchinleck recognized this nobly. On June 12 he published a magnificent communiqué in honour of the 1st Light Division: "The United Nations," he declared, "owe it to themselves to be full of admiration and gratitude towards these French troops and their valiant general."

In London, six days later, ten thousand French people, military and civilian, met to celebrate the second anniversary of the appeal of June 18. The four tiers of the Albert Hall were as packed as the safety regulations allowed. A great Tricolour screen with the Cross of Lorraine superimposed was stretched behind the rostrum and drew the gaze of all. The "Marseillaise" and the "Marche Lorraine" rang out; all hearts echoed them. As I took my place, surrounded by the members of the National Committee and the volunteers most recently arrived from France, I heard every mouth in that enthusiastic crowd crying out faith to me.

But on that day, besides hope, I could feel the soaring of joy. I spoke. It was necessary. Action employs men's fervour. But words arouse it.

Quoting Chamfort's saying, "Men of reason have endured. Men of passion have lived," I recalled the two years which Free France had just gone through. "We have lived much, for we are men of passion. But we have also endured. Ah! what men of reason we are! . . . What we said, from the first day—that France has never left the war, that the authority established under the shelter of abdication is no legitimate authority, that our alliances continue—we are proving by deeds, which are the battles. . . . To be sure, we had to trust that Great Britain would hold out, that Russia and America would be brought into the war, that the French people would not accept defeat. Well, we were not wrong. . . ." Then I paid homage to our fighters all over the world and to our resistance movements in France. I paid homage also to the Empire, the loyal Empire, basis of the country's recovery. Certainly its structure would have to be transformed after the war. But France unanimously intended to maintain its unity and integrity. "Even the heart-rending courage displayed in the defence of one part or another of the Empire against Fighting France and against her allies by troops still misled by the lies of Vichy is proof, distorted yet unquestionable, of this determination on the part of the French. . . ." I drew the conclusion that, in spite of everything, Fighting France was rising from the ocean. "When a ray of her reborn glory touched the bloodstained brows of her soldiers at Bir Hakeim, the world recognized France. . . ."

The tempest of cheers, then the national anthem sung with indescribable fervour, were the response that came from those present. It would be heard also by those who, at home, behind closed doors, shutters and curtains, were listening in to the wave lengths that would bring it to them.

The acclamations fall silent. The meeting is over. Each person returns to his task. There I am, alone, face to face with myself. For that confrontation it will not do to take up an attitude, or to cherish illusions. I draw up the balance sheet of the past. It is favourable, but cruel. "Man by man, bit by bit," Fighting France as assuredly grown solid and coherent. But how many losses, sorrows, agonies, have been required to pay for this result! We are starting on the new phase with appreciable resources: 70,000 men under arms, leaders of high quality, territories working at full stretch, growing resistance at home, a government that commands obedience, an authority known, if not recognized, in the world at large. And without question the course of events is bound to raise up more sources of strength. Yet I am not deluding myself as to the obstacles in the path: the power of the enemy; ill will from the Allied states; and among the French, hostility from the officials and the privileged, intrigues from some people, inertia in a great many, and, finally, danger of general subversion. And I, poor man, shall I have the clear-sightedness, firmness, and skill to master these trials right to the end? Even if, indeed, I contrive to lead to victory a people at last united, what will be its future then? How many ruins will in the meantime have been added to its ruins, and divisions to its divisions? At that moment, with the danger passed and the illuminations extinguished, what waves of mud will break over France?

A truce to doubts! Poring over the gulf into which the country has fallen, I am her son, calling her, holding the light for her, showing her the way of rescue. Many have joined me already. Others will come, I am sure! I can hear France now, answering me. In the depths of the abyss she is rising up again, she is on the march, she is climbing the slope. Ah! mother, such as we are, we are here to serve you.

VOLUME II
UNITY

1942-1944

Translated from the French by
RICHARD HOWARD

CHAPTER 1

INTERLUDE

DURING the third spring of the war, destiny came to a climax. The die was cast; the scales began to tip the other way. The huge resources of the United States were transformed into means of battle; Russia had made a recovery, as we were to see at Stalingrad; the British managed to re-establish themselves in Egypt; Fighting France was growing, both at home and overseas; the resistance of the oppressed peoples, in particular the Poles, the Yugoslavs and the Greeks, assumed military significance. While the German war effort had touched its limit, while Italy grew demoralized and the Hungarians, Rumanians, Bulgarians and Finns lost their last illusions, while Spain and Turkey reaffirmed their neutrality, while the Japanese advance in the Pacific had been checked and the defense of China reinforced, everything inclined the Allies to strike rather than to endure. An operation of major scope was under way in the west.

I saw this enterprise take shape. Quite alone among my well-buttressed associates, quite poor among the rich, I was comforted by hope but racked with anxiety too, for France would be at the center of this undertaking, whatever its outcome. At stake was not only the enemy's expulsion from her territory, but also her future as a nation and a state. Should she remain prostrate until the war's end, her faith in herself would be destroyed, and with that faith her independence as well. From the "silence of the sea" she would pass into a permanent coma, from a servitude imposed by her enemies she would decline to a subordinate position in relation to her allies. On the other hand, nothing was lost if she returned to the ranks with her unity restored. Once again the future could be safeguarded on condition that France, at the end of the drama, was a belligerent reunited by its commitment to a single central authority.

But to which? Certainly not to Vichy; that regime personified, to the French as to the world, the acceptance of disaster. Whatever the circumstances that might account for the error of Vichy's princes, it was of such extent that the demon of despair now compelled them to persist in it. Of course, one or another of them might disavow it and play an episodic part; but who would see anything more than a recognition of expedience in such belated repentance? Had a great military leader summoned the Army to honorable battle, he could probably have rallied around him the professionals who secretly were hoping for nothing better. But such initiative would have no effect on a people whose allegiances were already determined. Furthermore, it was inconceivable that in France's agony the faith and hope of the masses would re-embrace the political system which the disaster had recently swept away. The most representative men of the French people were firmly decided on this point. Some joined Vichy; many came over to De Gaulle; some had not yet declared themselves; but not one dreamed of taking the helm of the former ship of state.

But the Communist Party was there. Since Hitler had invaded Russia, it had made itself the champion of war. Committed to a resistance in which no losses were spared, invoking the nation's misery and the people's woes in order to merge in a single rebellion the national insurrection and the social revolution, it coveted for itself the halo of public welfare. Provided with an organization which no scruple embarrassed and no divergence restrained, a past master at setting up its cells in other organisms, in speaking every tongue, the Communist Party wished to seem the element capable of assuring order of a kind on the day when anarchy would be unleashed upon the state. Furthermore, did it not offer despised France the active support of Russia, the greatest European power? Thus the Communist Party counted on Vichy's collapse to furnish the occasion for establishing its dictatorship in France. Yet this calculation was vain if the state could be differently reconstituted, if the place of supremacy in the French way of thinking were taken by a national government, if its leader, in the light of victory, were suddenly to appear in Paris.

Such was my task! To reinstate France as a belligerent, to prevent her subversion, to restore a destiny that depended on herself alone. Yesterday it was enough to throw a handful of Frenchmen into action on the fields of battle, to take a stand in the face of events. Tomorrow, everything would depend on the question of which central power the nation hailed and obeyed. For me, in this critical phase, it was no longer to be a question of sending a few troops into battle, rousing the allegiance of an occasional strip of territory, singing to France the ballad of her greatness. It was the entire French people, as it stood, that I would have to rally around me. Against the enemy, despite the Allies, regardless of terrible dissensions, I would have to constitute around myself the unity of lacerated France.

It is understandable how eagerly I desired to penetrate the mystery in which, during the interlude, Americans and British alike wrapped their plans. As a matter of fact, the decision was up to the United States, since the principal effort henceforth devolved upon her. In Washington the President, the Secretaries, the great leaders sensed that they had become the directors of the coalition. In England the advance guard of the American Army, Air Force and Navy could be seen establishing themselves in British bases and camps. The streets, the stores, the cinemas, the London pubs were filled with good-natured, bad-mannered Yankee soldiers. The commander in chief, General Eisenhower, and General Clark, Admiral Stark and General Spaatz, respectively in command of the American land, naval and air forces in Europe, were deploying the brand-new apparatus of their general staffs in the midst of the traditional machinery of the War Office, the Admiralty, the Royal Air Force. The British, whatever their self-control, did not conceal their gloom at no longer being masters in their own country and at finding themselves dispossessed of the leading role they had played—and so deservingly!—for the last two years.

It was not without concern that I watched them being taken in tow by the newcomers. Certainly one could discern in public opinion as well as in official circles many elements which were finding this kind of subjection hard to tolerate. This was particularly so in the case of the Foreign Office. But the supplying of lend-lease overwhelmingly repressed all independent impulses. Mr. Churchill himself, whether by craft or by conviction, affected to be no more than "Roosevelt's lieutenant." Should France be unable to play her traditional leading role on the Continent, this obliteration of England, who had been hitherto so directly involved with that leadership despite her insularity, was a distinctly evil omen of the way in which the affairs of Europe were ultimately to be settled.

For the moment, the Americans were hesitating as to their strategy. Two different conceptions attracted Roosevelt and his advisers. From time to time, yielding to the impetus of the national war machine which a magnificent effort of armament and organization had brought to its peak, Washington toyed with the notion of a swift invasion. The Russians, moreover, suffering agony and death in the grip of the German armies, loudly demanded the opening of the "second front." Their insistence impressed the British, who were privately worried about an eventual about-face on Moscow's part. However secret the American leaders were about their plans, we were not unaware of the fact that they were preparing an operation that toward the year's end would establish at least a bridgehead in France.

But even while toying with audacity, America heeded the counsels of prudence. The plan of a landing in North Africa was also considered, postponing until later the great shocks of a war on European soil. At the moment of engaging their country's armed might on the other side of the Atlantic, the American leaders were actually prey to many misgivings. This was the first time in history that the Americans found themselves constrained to take the lead in operations of a major scope. Even during World War I they had not appeared in force on the field of battle until the last engagements, and even then it was as a contributory factor and, so to speak, in the capacity of a subordinate. Since 1939, however, the United States had felt obliged to become a first-rate military power. But though the American Navy, already the world's strongest, easily absorbed as many ships and planes as could be turned out, the land and air armies, still embryonic yesterday, required time to adapt themselves to such colossal dimensions. Hence, while many divisions were mass-produced in camps at General Marshall's instigation, the anxious question in the barely finished Pentagon was what would be the effect against the Wehrmacht of so many hastily organized units, summarily instructed officers, and general staffs newly formed from top to bottom. On the eve of battle, America's inclination was to commit herself by stages and installments.

All the more so since the British were little disposed to hasten matters on their side. Having had to renounce leadership, they felt that a victory which would no longer be essentially their own need not cost them too dearly. Postponing the major battles would mean there would be time to increase the American armies and to husband the British forces. Moreover, observing the mounting stockpile of American armaments, London calculated that the material superiority the Allies already possessed would become considerable by 1943 and overwhelming by 1944. Besides, what good would it do to precipitate danger and perhaps run the risk of another Dunkirk, when every passing day contributed to the enemy's exhaustion on the Russian front? Especially as the bombing of German cities by the Royal Air Force and the flying squadrons of the United States was beginning to do severe damage to the Reich's industry, whereas the Luftwaffe now attacked England only rarely. Finally, the deployment of American convoys and escorts decided the question of transporting supplies. It must be added that England's strategy, in line with her usual policy, was directed chiefly toward the Mediterranean, where she was defending positions acquired in Egypt, in the Arab countries, in Cyprus, in Malta, in Gibraltar— and she had every intention of obtaining still others in Libya, in Syria, in Greece, in Yugoslavia. It was therefore toward this theater that the British were attempting to orient the Anglo-American offensive.

But according to whether Washington favored landing in France or seizing Morocco, Algeria and Tunisia, its intention and attitude toward Fighting France were completely different. In the first case the co-operation of the French resistance movement would be needed at once. Of course everyone knew, though there was some pretense at doubting the fact, what action General de Gaulle would be in a position to take. A place would therefore have to be made for him. The second hypothesis, however, would involve a return to the plan the State Department had followed since 1940: securing North Africa by obtaining the co-operation of local authorities and excluding De Gaulle from the operation altogether. We were, in fact, to see our American allies practice each of these policies toward us in alternation.

Toward the end of May 1942, they tended toward reconciliation. On May 21 John Winant, their splendid ambassador in London, consulted me formally as to the prospects a cross-Channel offensive would offer, the direct role we could play in it, and the relations which would consequently be established between the French National Committee and the Allied governments. On June 1 the ambassador requested a second interview. This time Mr. Eden was present; in fact, the British insisted on taking part in our conversations. On June 29 Mr. Eden discussed the question of recognition alone with me, submitting—like a good broker—a formula proposed by Washington. The next day, accompanied by Pleven, I had still another conversation with Winant. During this time Churchill, who was in Washington discussing questions of strategy, was urging the President to adopt toward me some appearance of compromise.

All of which culminated, on July 9, in a memorandum addressed to me by the State Department after I had approved its terms. The document, which, according to its preamble, General de Gaulle had "read with pleasure," declared that the Government of the United States and the French National Committee were already practicing a close co-operation in certain zones; that in order to make this co-operation still more effective, Admiral Stark was appointed as Washington's representative in order that concerted plans might be made with the National Committee on all questions dealing with the conduct of the war; that the United States recognized General de Gaulle's contribution and the efforts of the National Committee to keep alive the traditional spirit of France and its institutions; and that our common goals would be more easily achieved by America's lending total military aid and every possible support to the National Committee, symbol of French resistance against the Axis powers.

Four days later the British in their turn enlarged the basis of their relations with us by public proclamation, agreeing that the Free French movement would be known henceforth by the name of "Fighting France"; that Fighting France consisted of all French nationals, wherever they might be, and French territories which joined forces to co-operate with the allied nations in the war against their common enemies; and that in the United Kingdom, the French National Committee represented the interests of those nationals and those territories. If the words had any meaning, this declaration implied at the very least the guarantee on England's part that she would not prevent me from exercising my authority over the parts of France and her Empire which returned to combat.

Other signs, other actions indicated that, among the Allies, intentions had become more favorable to us. On July 14, as I was reviewing the French troops in London, I noticed the presence of General Eisenhower and Admiral Stark. That same day Mr. Eden, broadcasting greetings to the French people on the occasion of their national holiday, declared, "I speak to you not as to friends but as to allies. . . . Thanks to General de Gaulle's decision, France has never been absent from the fields of battle. . . . England has hopefully and admiringly watched the French people's resistance grow. . . . In our eyes, the re-establishment of France in its greatness and independence is not only a promise but a necessity as well, for it would otherwise be futile to attempt the reconstruction of Europe."

On July 23 General Marshall and Admiral King, both in London again, asked to meet me. I saw them, along with Arnold, Eisenhower and Stark. During our meeting I informed the American leaders of our position relative to the opening of the second front, of the co-operation which France could provide from within the nation as well as extraterritorially, and finally of the conditions to which the Allies must subscribe in order for the co-operation among us to be satisfactory.

Naturally I was in favor of a direct offensive in Europe, to be launched from England. No other operation would bring matters to a head. Moreover, the best solution for France was the one that would shorten the trials of the invasion and hasten national unification—that is, battle waged on the soil of metropolitan France. Doubtless Vichy would continue to co-operate with the Germans; but it would thereby lose whatever credit it still retained. Doubtless the invader would occupy the free zone; but in that case, all misunderstandings dispelled, the African army and perhaps the fleet would return to battle, while in France herself many would come over to the side of the resistance. It would become possible to reunite in a single authority the various French commands, thereby preventing subversion within the nation and assuring a worthy representation of France abroad.

It was still essential to keep the Allies from being thrown back into the sea. In my exchange of opinions with Churchill, Eden, Winant, Marshall, *et al.*, I estimated the forces necessary to the invasion. I said and wrote:

The Germans have in France, according to the information provided by our intelligence networks, twenty-five, twenty-six or twenty-seven divisions, depending on the time of reckoning. They could obtain some fifteen more from Germany. Therefore it is some forty divisions that the Allies must face at the outset. Considering the inexperience of a large portion of the Anglo-American troops and the advantage to the enemy of a prior organization of the terrain, the Allies must start out with at least fifty divisions at their disposal, of which six or seven will be armored. Furthermore, there must be a crushing superiority of Allied air power. If the offensive takes place during the coming autumn, the Germans, who will then be heavily engaged in Russia, will be unable to remove their troops from the eastern front without great difficulty. Besides, the combined action of the Allied air power and the French resistance on enemy communications, following the Green Plan established by Fighting France, will seriously hamper the transport of German reserves and matériel on French territory.

I pointed out to the Allied leaders that the Free French would be in a position to engage, in the first wave, one division from the Middle East, one mixed brigade from French Equatorial Africa, detachments of commandos and parachutists, four Air Force groups and all the warships and cargo vessels at our disposal. As of the beginning of July, I had given the instructions necessary to keep these various elements alerted for the transportation they would eventually require. I anticipated, moreover, that once a bridgehead had been established in France, our forces there would be replenished from the resources of the liberated territory. I considered it likely that eight divisions and fifteen Air Force groups, to be constituted in North and West Africa, as well as many of our ships temporarily immobilized at Toulon, Alexandria, Bizerte, Casablanca, Dakar and Fort-de-France, would and could, after several weeks' reconditioning, take part in a second landing, this one to be effected on our Mediterranean coast and in Italy. Finally, as the Allies made headway on French soil, a third echelon of French forces, having as its core the elements of the underground army, would be set up. On July 21 I had addressed to Mr. Churchill and to General Marshall and communicated to Moscow a note concerning the military co-operation which France was capable of providing in the successive phases of the war and specifying what armaments and equipment I would request from the Allies.

Nevertheless it soon appeared that the Anglo-American forces would not risk a landing in France in 1942. They would therefore aim for North Africa, excluding us from participation. We realized from many specific acts that the Americans did not want the Free French to concern themselves with Morocco, Algeria and Tunisia. Although we had been able to maintain our intelligence systems there until the spring of 1941, we had been cut off subsequently from all direct communication with these territories; our emissaries never reached their destinations; messages addressed to us never arrived, especially those from Colonel Breuillac in Tunisia, from Luizet in Algeria, and from Colonel Lelong and Franck Brentano in Morocco. Washington's intervention was evident. But by making use of roundabout methods, we were nonetheless kept informed as to the efforts the United States was making, both in Vichy and on the spot, to obtain co-operation in its own behalf.

We knew that Mr. Robert Murphy, American consul general in Algiers, was the source of the "special" activities conducted in France by the embassy, the consulates and the American secret services. Mr. Murphy, skillful and determined, long familiar with the best society and apparently rather inclined to believe that France consisted of the people he dined with in town, was organizing an underground movement in North Africa to aid the Allied landing. He was also trying to produce a "palace revolution" in Vichy itself. It was in this regard that Mr. Murphy had first supported General de La Laurentie, who, upon his return from Paris, professed to take the resistance into his own hands in order to put pressure on Marshal Pétain and gain access to the government. "And De Gaulle?" he was asked. "All right, we'll grant him an amnesty!" Murphy had also urged certain officers in Weygand's entourage to persuade the latter to make a pronunciamento of a sort and take Laval's place. Finally, since La Laurentie rallied no one and Weygand refused to rebel against Pétain, Mr. Murphy made contact with General Giraud, who had escaped from captivity, was burning to return to combat, and seemed to him capable of rousing the African army as soon as he should present himself before it.

As for me, I had attempted to consolidate my contacts with General Giraud. Since May 1942, when I referred to him during a press conference, I had spoken of him in the most favorable terms. In June and July several of my correspondents had seen him on a number of occasions in order to express our hopes that we should ultimately join forces. This great leader of whom I thought so highly had not been able, in 1940, to win success at the head of the Seventh Army. Later, unexpectedly named to the command of the Ninth Army, which was in full retreat, he had been overpowered and seized by the enemy before he could act. But it was quite likely that if he were empowered to act in other circumstances, he would take his revenge on his misfortunes. And now his remarkable escape from a German fortress was offering him his chance. His going over to the resistance, in my opinion, would be an event of the greatest importance. Considering it essential that North Africa should re-enter the war, I felt that Giraud could play a major part in that conversion, and I was ready to help him do so to the limit of my powers, provided that he acted without equivocation in reference to Vichy or to any foreign power. After which it was to be expected that in the battle of liberation he should assume command of the reunited French Army. Such were the perspectives that, from my point of view, opened before him. I hoped that he would respond to them in one way or another and that he would secretly express some tribute to those who for two years had sustained our flag before the enemy. No such thing happened. My advances to General Giraud met with nothing but silence. But since he was as prolix elsewhere as he was reserved with me, I lost no time in discovering his state of mind.

For him the problem was of a purely military order. Once an

important French force reappeared on the fields of battle, all other questions could be relegated to an accessory status. The moral and political aspects of our country's drama seemed secondary matters to him. He believed that the single fact of being in command of the most numerous forces immediately guaranteed him power. He did not doubt that his rank and his prestige would ensure him the obedience of all the mobilized and mobilizable elements and the deferential co-operation of the Allied general staffs. And from the moment he found himself at the head of an army, and thereby of the nation, Giraud would deal with the Marshal as with an extremely venerable old man whom he would liberate if he must, but who would be entitled only to a pedestal. As for General de Gaulle, he could do nothing but submit himself to the orders of his superior. Thus national unity would be re-established by the very fact that it would be identified with the military hierarchy.

General Giraud's train of thought was a constant source of concern to me. Aside from the fact that it resulted from a somewhat oversimplified notion of the respective domains of military and political activity, that it obviously proceeded from an illusion as to the natural authority which the interested party attributed to his own person, I saw in it the probable source of national divisions and foreign interventions. For the majority of the French resistance would certainly not accept a central authority founded solely on a career general's success. On the other hand, Pétain would not fail to condemn him. Finally, with an unsupported government like Giraud's at their mercy, the Allies would be tempted to take every advantage of it, to France's detriment.

Certainly General Giraud was convinced he was in a position to bring one capital advantage to the coalition. The reports that reached me from London indicated that he had a plan of his own devising. According to Giraud, the bridgehead was already in existence—in the so-called free zone. It was simply a matter of the Anglo-American forces landing there on a specified day; he himself would go so far as to ensure protection for their landing, thanks to the armistice army, of which he would take command and which

would reinforce the resistance contingents. But to my way of thinking, this project had no chance of success. If it was imaginable at
best that scattered units of the "free" zone might follow Giraud
despite the injunctions and curses the Marshal would pour upon
them, it was more than doubtful, in view of the ultra-reduction of
their armaments, that these dispersed fractions would be in a position to resist the Wehrmacht's onslaught and the Luftwaffe's raids.
Furthermore, the Allies would not adopt a plan which involved the
greatest possible risk for themselves. The success of the landing
and the subsequent operations implied, in fact, the engagement of
a very considerable air force and fleet, and consequently the utilization of airfields and ports that were both numerous and near at
hand. Yet if the Allies set foot in the south of France without being
assured of North Africa beforehand, they would have only Gibraltar and Malta as bases, both of them terribly confined, without resources, and vulnerable. And finally, what, in this hypothesis,
would be the attitude of the fleet at Toulon? The latter would at the
outset obey only Pétain and Darlan; and if, on their orders, the
fleet should oppose the Allies, Giraud's plan would become more
problematical still.

By the end of July I foresaw what would happen. Although their
intentions were carefully concealed from us, it seemed extremely
likely to me that the Americans would limit their year's effort to
seizing North Africa, that the British would willingly comply with
this plan, that the Allies would employ General Giraud in its accomplishment, that they would exclude me from the operation
altogether, and that thereby these preliminary steps to our liberation, auspicious though they were from many points of view, would
nevertheless confront us as Frenchmen with inner torments that
would raise fresh obstacles to national unity.

Under these conditions I decided I had only the French hand to
play, since the rest were also playing for themselves and only themselves. I decided that, above all, the cohesion of Fighting France
must be reinforced in order for her to present herself, through
all vicissitudes, as a solid breakwater to the general consent. I

deliberately adopted the tough, rigid attitude such concentration required. To encourage it during the interlude I decided to visit the territories of the Levant and Free French Africa and review our troops serving in the Middle East and the Chad. The Allies, who in May were flatly opposed to this action and had dissuaded me from it by alleging the imminent opening of the second front, did not on this occasion attempt to prevent my trip; I therefore assumed they were preparing operations in which I was not to be included. On the other hand, while tightening the inner links of that fragment of empire and that fraction of army which still remained to us, I intended to hasten the unification of the resistance in France. Since André Philip had just arrived from France, I appointed him, on July 27, National Commissioner of the Interior, with the task of supporting, with all the matériel, personnel and propaganda at our disposal, the mission entrusted to Jean Moulin.* At the same time I appointed Jacques Soustelle Commissioner of Information. I invited to London Frenay, D'Astier and Jean-Pierre Lévy, respectively heads of Combat, Libération and Francs-Tireurs, in order to bring them to a decisive common action. To hasten the fusion of the paramilitary elements, I selected General Delestraint to command the future secret army. Finally, intending to give greater weight to our organization, I asked certain men of quality to join us, men like Viénot, Massigli, General d'Astier de La Vigerie, General Coghet. It was Passy's job to establish the liaisons and to regulate the communications between France and England in such a way that I could determine each man's role on my return from Africa and the Near East.

I left on August 5, having first seen Mr. Churchill and Mr. Eden, whose somewhat embarrassed remarks confirmed my feeling that they were going to be party to an enterprise incompatible with the agreement which had bound us since June 1940. Mr. Averell Harriman, whom Roosevelt was sending to Moscow as ambassador, was in the plane taking me to Cairo; this ordinarily frank and fluent diplomat seemed on this occasion to be nursing some weighty se-

* Unifying the resistance in metropolitan France.—TR.

cret. As we passed through Gibraltar I saw the tremendous projects being completed there and noticed the sibylline behavior of the governor, General MacFarlane, so expansive on other occasions. All these symptoms assured me that a major operation would soon be under way without us in the Mediterranean. I reached Cairo on August 7.

Here the atmosphere was as heavy as the heat. The recent reversals suffered by the Eighth Army still weighed on everyone's mind. Although Rommel had halted his advance six weeks before, he was at El Alamein, from which point the next attack could carry his armored units to Alexandria. At the Ministry of State, at the embassy, at the British general headquarters, the enigmatic attitude of King Farouk and of many Egyptian leaders was being anxiously scrutinized, for they seemed ready to adapt themselves to an ultimate Axis victory. It is true that Nahas Pasha, a former adversary of the British lately reconciled with them to both parties' advantage, had been appointed by the King to head the government on the warm recommendation of the British ambassador, Sir Miles Lampson, who had arrived at the palace for an audience escorted by a squadron of tanks. The year before, Nahas Pasha had said to me, "You and I have one characteristic in common. In our countries we have the majority, not the power." Now he had the power too, but where would his majority be if the Italo-German forces reached the capital?

As for the British military men, I found General Auchinleck as calm and direct as ever and Air Marshal Tedder in full possession of himself and his skill. But many beneath them seemed bitter and anxious, expecting great changes in the high command, harassed by the criticisms of Parliament and the London press, exasperated by the disagreeable conduct and comments of the Egyptians, who, for instance, pointedly applauded only the Free French troops in the streets or the cinemas and, when I arrived in Cairo, spread the rumor that General de Gaulle would assume command in the Middle East. On the other hand, of course, leaders and general staffs alike were receiving the splendid troops, aviation squadrons and high-quality matériel which the British government unstintingly poured into Egypt in preparation for the forthcoming engagement.

If the British appeared divided between hope and depression, our men were in a state of euphoria. Bir Hakeim had consecrated them in their own eyes. I went to see them. On August 8 and 11, Larminat presented me to the troops. During a magnificent review of the First Light Division, I bestowed the Cross of the Liberation on General Koenig and several others, including Colonel Amilakvari. I also inspected the Second Light Division, commanded by Cazaud, and Rémy's command, all well-equipped units eager to see battle. Our flyers and parachutists received my visit in their turn. Together they constituted a force tempered by the ordeals of battle which I was certain nothing could alienate from my command. The sight of the battalions, the batteries, the armored units, the services, completely motorized, mingling in their ranks good soldiers of every race, led by officers who in advance had sacrificed everything to glory and to victory, marching past in dazzling formation beneath the blistering August sun, filled me with confidence and pride. A contact was established between us, a spiritual accord that released a mutual current of joy, making the very sand beneath our feet resilient to our stride. But when the last ranks of our troops had passed, I felt this exaltation fade, and my mind reverted to the thought of the other French soldiers, sailors and flyers who because of senseless orders were fated to fight against the "Gaullists" and the Allies.

At our delegation in Cairo I made contact with the important French colony in Egypt. Here Baron de Benoist worthily represented France. Thanks to him, and also to Baron de Vaux, René Filliol and Georges Gorse, who seconded him, our cultural, religious and economic interests found effective support, pending the time when the Egyptian government should recognize the French National Committee. The Egyptian press and radio received every possible assistance from our delegate, and most of the French in Egypt considered themselves morally pledged to him. At the same time M. de Benoist, whom we supported strongly and unceasingly from London, managed to maintain the French character of the Suez Canal services, although the British Admiralty would gladly have taken them into its own hands. In fact, it was the French who assured the operation of the canal for the entire duration of the war—an important and meritorious contribution to the Allied war effort, since the communications of the fleets and the armies in the East, as well as the supplies bound for Syria, Lebanon, Palestine and Transjordan, passed through Port Saïd, while the Germans were continually bombing the convoys and the locks. Consequently I went to Ismailia to greet the canal's personnel and to visit the tiny room from which De Lesseps had directed the execution of this glorious work, so vital now to the war in progress.

At the same time that I was giving the Free French there the encouragement they deserved, I approached our allies on the questions that were dividing us. Mr. Churchill was in Cairo; we lunched together on August 7.

"I am here," he told me, "to reorganize the command. At the same time, I shall see where we are in our disagreements over Syria. Then I shall go to Moscow. Which means that my trip is of great importance and gives me great concern."

"It is certainly true," I replied, "that these are three serious matters. The first is entirely your affair. As for the second, which involves me, and the third, concerning Stalin—whom you will doubtless inform that the second front will not be opened this year —I can understand your apprehensions. But you will easily surmount them the moment your conscience has nothing to reproach you for."

"You should know," Mr. Churchill growled, "that my conscience is a good girl I can always come to terms with."

I was to discover, in fact, that England continued to deal with the Syrian question without any scruples whatever. On August 8 I saw Mr. Casey, who although Australian was Minister of State in the London government and in charge of co-ordinating British affairs in the Middle East. He immediately spoke to me about the elections in the Levant States, which he considered an urgent matter.

I felt I must make things clear to this sympathetic interlocutor. "The French National Committee," I told him, "has decided there will be no elections this year in Syria and in Lebanon, because the mandatory power does not intend to have the people vote while Rommel is at the gates of Alexandria. Are there elections in Egypt, or Iraq, or Transjordan?"

Then, taking the offensive, I enumerated our grievances arising from the policies that England was pursuing in violation of her agreements with us. It was Casey's turn to hear me draw the same conclusion I had often expressed before. "Of course," I told him, "you are now much stronger in this part of the world than we are. Because of our weakness and in consideration of the successive crises in Madagascar, in North Africa, and ultimately in metropolitan France that will be added to those we are now at grips with, you are in a position to force us to leave the Levant altogether. But you will achieve this objective only by arousing the xenophobia of the Arabs and by abusing your power in relation to your allies. The result for you will be, in the Middle East, a position more unstable every day, and, among the French people, an ineffaceable grievance against you."

Annoyed, Mr. Casey protested his good intentions, alluding at the same time to the "higher responsibilities that weighed upon Great Britain in this zone." Nevertheless, at that meeting and on August 11 when I saw him next, he did not again refer to the elections.

Marshal Smuts, Prime Minister of the Union of South Africa, was also in Cairo, and we had a long discussion. This man, eminent and engaging but with something odd about him, this hero of Transvaal independence who had become the leader of one of His Majesty's dominions, this Boer dressed up as a British general, was a worthy contender against all the problems of this war. Although his capital, Pretoria, was as out of the way as it could possibly be, although his country, where black and white lived together and quite apart, was gripped by extreme racial tensions, although he himself was fighting a powerful opposition, Smuts wielded a genuine influence over the London chiefs. He owed this privilege not only to the fact that in English eyes he embodied the success of their conquest, but still more to the friendship of Churchill, whom he had held captive for several months during the Boer War and who in turn had seized the occasion to captivate Smuts for good.

Prime Minister Smuts clearly expressed his esteem for Fighting France. "If you, De Gaulle," he told me, "had not rallied Equatorial Africa, I should never have been able to hold South Africa together. Once the spirit of capitulation had triumphed at Brazzaville, the Belgian Congo would have succumbed in its turn, and from then on those elements in my country which oppose our military alliance with England would certainly have taken the upper hand and contrived a collaboration with the Axis powers. German hegemony would have been established from Algiers to the Cape. Had you done nothing but what you did in the Chad and on the Congo, you would have rendered a great service to our common cause. It is essential for us all that your authority should now extend throughout the French Empire and, I hope, soon to France herself."

I thanked Marshal Smuts for this friendly appreciation but indicated that other allies still did not appear to share it. As evidence I told him first of the British action in Syria and Lebanon, then of what was happening in Madagascar, and finally of the forthcoming Anglo-American action in North Africa, where the invading forces would attempt to set up an authority that was not mine.

Smuts agreed that I had reason to fear for the cause of Free France. "But," he declared, "these annoyances can only be incidental. The Americans always make mistakes at the start. As soon as they discover their error, they will draw the obvious conclusions. As for the English, two different points of view influence the conduct of their affairs: that of routine, supported by offices, committees and general staffs, and that of long-range views, embodied from time to time by a statesman—Churchill today—and supported by the feeling of the people as a whole. But believe me, the second is favorable to you, and in the long run it is always the second that prevails."

When we turned our attention to the practical problems raised by the situation in Madagascar, Smuts told me that the British were still pursuing the chimera of an entente with a governor loyal to Vichy, and that once they were disabused of this illusion they would resume the operations halted after the taking of Diégo-Suarez; he added that they would try to establish an administration functioning under their direct authority on the island, and that they would ultimately hand it over to the French National Committee, a solution which Smuts himself had been recommending from the start. He led me to understand that, so far as I was concerned, British consent that the Cross of Lorraine be raised over Madagascar was regard as a valuable trump card by London, with which it would have the means of compensating whatever annoyance Allied policy might elsewhere inflict upon Fighting France. To conclude, Marshal Smuts promised me that the Union of South Africa would countenance no dispossession of France in Madagascar, but on the contrary would urge London to permit General de Gaulle to establish his authority there. I must add that in Pretoria the acts which followed this assurance in no way contradicted it.

On August 12 I left for Beirut. I wanted to spend a month in Syria and Lebanon, to take men and affairs in hand once again, to cement relations with governments and leading circles alike, to reawaken popular sentiment, to demonstrate the predominance of France in both fact and spirit. In this connection, the country's reception of me furnished as striking a demonstration as possible. When I entered Beirut, accompanied by M. Alfred Naccache, President of the Lebanese Republic, I was greeted by an extraordinary wave of public feeling. The same thing happened in El Bika, in southern Lebanon, particularly at Saïda, and among the Maronite mountain people who had come en masse to Bekerbe to surround their patriarch, whom I was visiting. Accompanied by General

Catroux, I crossed the Hauran, now peaceful and loyal to our cause; I then reached Jebel Druze, a territory volcanic in every respect. At Es Suweida, after the review of the Druse squadrons, I received authorities and notables at the Maison de France and then, at the Seraglio, the eager and picturesque crowd of delegates from every canton. There, amidst a storm of acclamations, the speakers assured me of the devotion of a population by whom, on occasion, the French had been less well treated.

With Sheik El Tageddine, President of the Syrian Republic, beside me, I made my entrance into Damascus, which vibrated with an enthusiasm it showed but rarely. The official reception by the head of the state and by the government, the visits I was paid by the *corps constitué,* the authorities of various religions, the representatives of every minority and every activity, permitted me to realize how much, since the preceding year, the young republic had consolidated itself in its stately capital. I then went to Palmyra, where the homage of the Bedouin tribes awaited me, and passed on to the ancient yet new territory of the Euphrates. At Deir-ez-Zor, as elsewhere, the political, administrative and economic situation did not suffer from comparison with what I had found there on the morrow of the pathetic battles of 1941. Aleppo, the great northern city where the ethnic, religious and commercial currrents that cross Asia Minor have been mingling for centuries, surrounded me with enthusiastic demonstrations. Then the Territory of the Alawis was lavish in my honor with tokens of its traditional friendship for France. But it was in the cities of Homs and Hama, generally regarded as citadels of Islamic and Syrian hostility, that the fervor of the reception, of which former President Hachem Bey el Atassi graciously set the example, appeared most spectacular. On the way back, Tripoli and Batrun offered me the evidences of a moving loyalty.

Nevertheless, beneath the waves of popular demonstrations appeared the responsibilities which were incumbent upon the French mandate. There could be no question that France was still carrying the burden of that mandate over territories which did not belong to her and which treaties forbade her to arrogate to herself. On the other hand, it was apparent that the Syrian and Lebanese elite, whatever their divisions, were unanimous in their desire to institute in their own countries an independence to which France had always promised to lead them and which I myself had solemnly pledged. Conviction in this matter was so strong in both countries that it would have been absurd to oppose it. Beyond doubt the economic, diplomatic and cultural interests that had fallen to France's share in the Levant for many generations must be preserved, but that seemed reconcilable with the states' independence.

Nevertheless we did not intend to abolish the principle of our authority in Damascus and Beirut at once. Had we done so, the British would merely have taken our place, invoking strategic needs. Furthermore, I did not feel I had the right to tear up our mandate. Aside from the fact that here as elsewhere I was accountable to the nation, the international responsibility assumed by the French mandate could not, without being abdicated, be surrendered except by agreement with the mandators, and present circumstances kept such an agreement from being reached. That was why, while transferring to the Damascus and Beirut governments the powers which we could reasonably strip ourselves of during a state of war, while deciding to restore a normal basis to the public powers by means of elections as soon as Rommel had been repulsed, while committing ourselves to the accomplishment of the international acts that would make the independent regimes juridically valid as soon as possible, I was not willing to renounce the supreme right of France in Syria and Lebanon for the moment. Whatever impatience this delay might arouse among professional politicians, we were certain of making the necessary transitions without serious obstacles if England did not intervene and spoil our chances.

But she did spoil them altogether. Thus M. Naccache was subjected to attacks by Spears, who openly excited Naccache's adversaries and went so far as to threaten the President because some of his ministers were not satisfactory to the British or because he did not take it upon himself to proceed with immediate elections in Lebanon. Then again, under pressure from the British, who threatened to cut off all communication with other countries, Catroux had agreed to introduce them into the Franco-Syrian-Lebanese wheat board. They availed themselves of this to obstruct the board's operation and to provoke the opposition of the Damascus government. Overriding our right of option, they had assumed responsibility for the construction and ownership of the Haifa-Tripoli railroad. When, near Tripoli, at the terminus of the Iraq Petroleum Pipeline, the French authority put in operation a refinery that permitted them to furnish the Levant with gasoline deducted from France's petroleum allotment, the British tried in every way possible to close down our establishment so that we and the Levant States would be completely dependent on them for this vital resource. Finally, arguing from the financial agreement which I had made with them on March 19, 1941, and by virtue of which their treasury furnished us with a part of our public funds in the form of advances, they claimed jurisdiction over the use made of those funds in Syria and Lebanon and, by extension, over the budgets of the Damascus and Beirut governments. In every domain, every day, everywhere, there were interferences on the part of our allies, multiplied by an army of uniformed agents.

I was determined to oppose this suffocation, and, if it turned out that we were succumbing to it nevertheless, to act so that these abuses were exposed publicly. Having verified the state of affairs on the spot, I began my campaign by addressing a formal protest to Mr. Churchill on August 14.

> Since the beginning of my stay in the Levant States under French mandate [I wrote him], I have regretfully remarked that the agreements concluded between the British government and the French National Committee concerning Syria and Lebanon are being undermined. . . . The constant interventions of the representatives of the British government . . . are not compatible with the political disinterestedness of Great Britain in Lebanon and Syria or with respect for the

position of France, or with the mandate regime. . . . Furthermore, these interventions and the reactions they produce are encouraging the people of the entire Arab East to believe that serious divergences are compromising the understanding between Great Britain and Fighting France, though these latter are allies. . . . I find myself compelled to ask you to re-establish in these countries the application of our agreements . . .

The Prime Minister received my message while he was in Moscow. He replied on August 23, from Cairo en route to London. The British, he wrote, were in no way seeking to destroy France's position in the Levant; they agreed thoroughly that in the political realm the initiative must remain in the hands of the French authorities and that the mandate, from a technical point of view, could not be surrendered at this time. But although he made his bow to our agreements, Mr. Churchill, as usual, overrode them by invoking the unilateral claims on which Great Britain prided herself. Syria and Lebanon, he said, comprised part of a vital theater of operations; the events occurring in that zone affected British military interests directly or indirectly; London was eager that its guarantee of the Catroux proclamation declaring the independence of the Levant States be put into effect. Repeating what he had said in his speech of September 9, 1941, in the House of Commons, he added that the position of the Free French in Syria could not be the same as that heretofore enjoyed by Vichy. Mr. Churchill concluded, in an intentionally banal and lenitive fashion, by saying that he fully realized the importance of a close collaboration between our respective representatives in the Levant. "Our supreme objective is the defeat of the enemy . . ."

I was expecting from the British this dissimulated refusal to change their policies, but I had decided to force them out of the equivocations by which they were attempting to conceal their hand. Furthermore, in consideration of the probable results, I concluded it was wise to adopt a general attitude that would exclude all compromise. I immediately wired Mr. Churchill:

It is impossible for me to accept your notion according to
which the political interference of the British representatives
in the Levant would be compatible with the commitments
made by the British government in respect to the position of
France and her mandate. . . . Furthermore, the kind of
Franco-British rivalry created in Syria-Lebanon by the interference and the pressure of your representatives is harmful to the war effort of the allied nations . . . I urge you
to reconsider this pressing and essential matter at once.

By using such language I was relying less on the present, which
offered me few means of continuing the argument, than on the
future, when France perhaps would have the wherewithal to resume
it, provided that those who spoke in her name steadfastly refused
to give way. All the more as other abuses of the same order were
now being perpetrated in Madagascar, would be inaugurated tomorrow in North Africa, and threatened to be practiced, one day,
in Paris itself. We would resist those that loomed in the future only
if we opposed those that were upon us now. Besides, there was no
reason why we should let ourselves be despoiled in silence. I therefore considered it necessary to advise America and Russia as to
what was happening. Even if their governments, duly informed, did
nothing to induce the British to change their ways, at least the dispute would obtain world-wide attention.

On August 16, I had received a visit from the United States consul general, the excellent Mr. Gwynn, who had just heard the news
and was considerably disturbed by it. I did nothing to reassure him.
On August 24 I invited him to see me and gave him a note for his
government. This document set forth what was involved in the situation and what results it might have. The next day Mr. Gwynn
returned. He told me of the text of a cable sent by Mr. Cordell
Hull to Mr. John Winant, American ambassador in London, stressing the seriousness of this situation and instructing him to question
the British closely on the matter. This was precisely what I had hoped
for. The Secretary of State told his ambassador that Spears seemed
at the very least to have conceived of his task in a larger sense than

was customary for a foreign diplomatic representative. The United States government, he said, could not remain indifferent to a controversy which might affect the common war effort.

Mr. Hull also instructed Mr. Gwynn "to thank General de Gaulle for having informed him so completely." But, since he needed to conclude with a little venom, he urged him to make clear to me with an equal frankness the serious importance that the United States, as a nation engaged in the common struggle, attached to the pledges made to Syria and Lebanon, which must be scrupulously respected.

Meanwhile Dejean, in London, had revealed our disagreement to M. Bogomolov and had forewarned our Moscow delegation. On September 11 the Soviet ambassador came to tell him that his government was "disposed to assist us within its means."

I felt all the less inclined to compromise now that I had definite knowledge of the decisions taken by the Anglo-American leaders in regard to North Africa. Not, of course, that the Allies had let me know anything of their plans. On the contrary, everyone concerned with these preparations continued to observe absolute secrecy. But if this conspiracy of silence seemed ungracious to us, it was also futile. For information flowed in from America, from England, from France. A kind of rumor slipped across the face of the world, while in the Middle East everything in sight indicated that there would soon be an African campaign under way. Passing through Cairo, Mr. Churchill had appointed General Alexander Commander in Chief and had put Montgomery at the head of the Eighth Army. Many reinforcements, especially of armored units, continued to arrive from Great Britain. Tedder, the Air Force chief, received many planes. Everything heralded major operations that were not aimed at Europe.

On August 27 I was in a position to announce to our London delegation:

> The United States has now decided to land troops in French North Africa. The operation will be launched in conjunction with a forthcoming British offensive in Egypt. . . . The

Americans have arranged for local co-operation by making use of the good will of our partisans and giving the impression that they are acting in agreement with us. . . . Should the occasion arise, Marshal Pétain will beyond any doubt give orders to fight against the Allies in North Africa . . . The Germans will make the affair a pretext to rush in . . . The Americans thought at first that they would be able to open a second front in France this year. That is why, having need of us, they took the position indicated by their memorandum of July 9. Now their plans have changed . . .

From then on everything was clear. The Allies' strategy was apparent, determined by events. As for their political behavior, it had as its basis a kind of consecrated egoism. Therefore I was less than ever inclined to put faith in the ideological formulas they employed to conceal it. How could I take seriously the scruples paraded by Washington, scruples which affected to keep General de Gaulle at a distance under pretext of leaving the French free to choose their eventual government and which at the same time maintained official relations with the Vichy dictatorship and was preparing to deal with whoever would open the gates of North Africa to the American troops? How could I believe in the sincerity of declarations from London which, in order to justify British intervention in the Levantine territories where France had a mandate, invoked the Arab right to independence, when at the same moment the British were imprisoning Gandhi and Nehru in India, were severely punishing the followers of Rashid Ali in Iraq, and were dictating to King Farouk in Egypt the choice of his own government? No, today as yesterday, there was only the interest of France to attend to.

Mr. Casey, meanwhile, thought that he should show his hand. But however good his intentions, he did so in a fashion that could not make matters easier. On August 29 he proposed that we have a "frank discussion" to establish more satisfactory relations in the interest of both countries, for, he wrote, these relations, in Syria and Lebanon, had reached a critical point. Unfortunately the British Minister of State felt obliged to stipulate that we meet in Cairo and to add that failing this meeting he would be obliged to submit the situation as he saw it to the Prime Minister.

The terms of his message forced me to reply that I had been ready to discuss these serious matters with him, but at Beirut, "since during the two visits I had the pleasure of making to you in Cairo we were unable to reach an agreement."

Then Mr. Churchill entered the lists again. On August 31 he telegraphed me from London that he too considered the situation a serious one, that according to his way of thinking it was essential for him to talk it over with me with as little delay as possible, and that he urged me to hasten my return to London and to let him know on what date he could expect me. I could only thank the British Prime Minister "for the invitation you were so kind as to extend" and tell him that I would certainly undertake such a trip as soon as possible, but that the situation did not permit me to leave the Levant, repeating that in any case, "I was ready even today to meet with Mr. Casey at Beirut." Finally, on September 7, carrying the tension to its peak, I sent Ambassador Helleu, who had just reached me from Teheran, to Casey with a memorandum specifying our grievances.

And at the same time that I was stirring up this controversy, I applied myself to clarifying the mandate's internal affairs. It was a matter of convincing the two local governments to play their role firmly, particularly in the realms of finance and provisioning, where matters were making scarcely any progress. Further, it was essential to clarify our intentions with reference to the elections. Alfred Naccache and Sheik Tageddine came to see me on the second and the fourth of September, respectively. I received them with great ceremony. Both lavished upon me assurances of their good will. As a matter of fact, they felt encouraged in their own tasks by the solidity of the French authority and no longer hesitated to entertain measures capable of balancing the budgets, of operating the wheat board, of limiting speculation. In agreement with them and with General Catroux, I kept to the decision made by the National Committee not to proceed with election plans until the following summer. But the elections would take place then, unless strategic necessity forced their postponement.

During the time I spent in Beirut I made numerous contacts, according to the custom of the Middle East, where it is deemed both reckless and unbecoming to make judgments and take measures without having sampled opinion and paid respects. At the Résidence des Pins, where I was installed, I received many visitors; a number assured me of their desire to see the state fully acquit itself of its obligations in their country, but each appointed himself the apostle of one or another of the special interests that since the dawn of history have prevented such situations from becoming a reality; all confirmed me in my conviction that Syria and Lebanon, upon their accession to independence, had everything to gain, nothing to lose from the presence of France.

The advantages which this presence ensured to both countries were incontestable and, what is more, uncontested. Whether in the matter of public services, public works, construction, universal education, or law and order, the thousands of professional, intellectual and familial relations established by our people with the Syrians and the Lebanese were responsible for interest and feeling on both sides. As for the many offices, ship and building yards, schools, societies and hospitals I visited, everyone agreed that they must be maintained whatever regime was set up to deal with future political relationships between Paris, Damascus and Beirut.

Naturally I also attempted to give the strongest possible encouragement to the military organization. The majority of the elements of the French Army, properly speaking, were then in Egypt. We had left only a few detachments in the Levant. This extreme scantiness of French strength proved again that the authority of France had other foundations than that of force alone. It was therefore incumbent on the "special" troops—that is, the Syrian and Lebanese forces—to guarantee the immediate security of the two states. Yet this security was likely to be questioned at any moment. By the end of the summer of 1942, the Wehrmacht was actually penetrating into the heart of the Caucasus, while the Italo-German desert army threatened the Nile delta. If the enemy should win a victory in either of these theaters, Asia Minor would be laid open. That is why we did not cease our efforts to increase the value of the autochthonous Levantine forces.

Thus embryonic armies were formed; Syria furnished nine infantry battalions, one cavalry regiment, three groups of partially motorized squadrons; Lebanon provided three rifle battalions; while two artillery groups, one tank battalion, and some engineering, transport, and transmission units remained common to both countries. From the École Militaire at Homs came a splendid graduating class each year. Several French officers co-operated in the formation of the special troops, but it was apparent that among the troops valuable new officers were developing, whether Syrian like Colonels Znaïm and Chichakli, or Lebanese like Colonels Chehab and Naufal. The matériel recovered from Dentz allowed us to provide these troops with creditable armament and equipment, the maintenance of which was assured by the well-stocked artillery depot at Beirut.

I myself had the honor of inspecting the French, Syrian and Lebanese elements remaining on guard in the Levant under the command of General Humblot, Commander Kolb-Bernard and Lieutenant Colonel Gence for the land, sea and air forces respectively. Twenty-five thousand dedicated men protected the two states from any enemy attack; these sufficed, with the local police forces, to preserve order in a land that for thousands of years had comprised irreconcilable groups, a land one third the size of France, having 2,500 kilometers of frontier and bordering on Iraq, Transjordan and Palestine, where chronic agitation prevailed. The fact that the part of the Levant under French mandate was so calm and was held by troops so reliable considerably assisted the strategy of the Allies at this period of the war, removing from their armies embattled in Egypt, Libya and Ethiopia all serious concern as to their rear, confirming the Turks in their refusal to permit the Germans passage through their country, and deflecting the entire Arab world, disturbed by the events of the war, from hostile action.

Nevertheless, active though my stay was, the fundamental problems remained unsolved. I had been able to change the atmosphere and put the helm hard over, permitting us to gain time. How could I do more when I had brought no reinforcements of men or money? A policy is worth as much as its means. In the Middle East more than anywhere else, affairs would be settled by the appearance of fresh forces, not arguments.

A distinguished visitor came from America to confirm this point for me. This was Wendell Willkie, whom the Republican Party had opposed to Roosevelt in the Presidential election of 1940. Now the President, anxious to show that war made unity sacred, authorized his recent adversary to travel round the world and learn the facts from its leaders on the spot. Wendell Willkie had asked to pass through the Levant on his way to see Stalin and Chiang Kai-shek. He arrived on September 10 and stayed twenty-four hours, during which time he was my guest.

At his request I explained the circumstances of the French position in the Levant. But Wendell Willkie, who had never before been in the Middle East, apparently had already made up his mind on every issue. When he returned to Washington he affected to be convinced, in the summary manner of American public opinion, that the friction in Beirut was merely an episode in the rivalry between two equally detestable colonial systems. In reference to me, he employed the standard malevolent banter in the book that appeared in his name upon his return. Because we had conferred together in the High Commissioner's office, which M. de Martel had recently provided with a suite of Empire furniture, Willkie represented me as aping the Napoleonic style; because I was wearing the standard officer's summer uniform of white linen, he saw an ostentatious parody of Louis XIV; and because one of my men spoke of "General de Gaulle's mission," Mr. Willkie hinted that I took myself for Joan of Arc. In this matter, Roosevelt's rival was also his imitator.

Nevertheless, the very day I was conferring with the President's envoy a new item concerning France appeared on the bulletin of current events. At dawn on September 10, the British had again taken action on Madagascar. Realizing after five months of negotiations that they could obtain no valid guarantee from Governor General Annet, that Vichy was capable of letting the Japanese take over the island at any moment, and that the Laval ministry had given orders to let the latter do as they liked in that event, our allies had decided to occupy Madagascar for themselves.

Once more they were going into action without the co-operation of the Free French forces. But at least, and by contrast with what had happened at the time of the attack on Diégo-Suarez, they informed us before the act was already accomplished. On September 7 Mr. Eden, expressing to Pleven and Dejean his government's irritation at my attitude on the Levant, let them know beforehand that a forthcoming event on Madagascar would require their agreement. On September 9, requesting the presence of our two national commissioners, he informed them that the British troops would land at Majunga the next day, that his government had every intention of recognizing the authority of the French National Committee over Madagascar as soon as the military campaign was over, and that he would be eager to open negotiations with me for an agreement on this matter as soon as possible. On September 10, London announced that British forces had established a bridgehead at Majunga and that "a friendly administration, eager to collaborate wholeheartedly with the United Nations and to contribute to the liberation of France, would be established on the island." On the eleventh Mr. Strang declared to Maurice Dejean: "The British government intends the French National Committee to be the 'friendly administration' mentioned in the communiqué. It depends on you alone to see that this is the case. As for us, we are convinced that we can reach an understanding."

I decided to return to London. Unquestionably I would find the atmosphere there a disagreeable one. Unquestionably it would be to my advantage in some respects to establish residence in a territory under French sovereignty when the American operation in North Africa got under way. Unquestionably the settlement of the Madagascar affair would not be reached without delays and without suffering. But the stakes were such that I could not hesitate. I therefore addressed a message of good will to Mr. Eden, telling him that I had received reports from Pleven and Dejean, and that my intention was to accept his and the Prime Minister's friendly invitation soon. Eden immediately replied that he would be happy to discuss with me our relations in the Levant and the future civil administration of Madagascar, in accordance with what had been envisaged in his conversation of September 9 with Pleven and Dejean.

Before reaching England I decided to spend some ten days in Free French Africa. There, as in the Middle East, I intended to reaffirm the cohesion of Fighting France on the eve of events that threatened to shake it, and to determine the mission of our military forces in the forthcoming operation in North Africa. For the first time I was able to reach the Congo from Syria without having recourse to British planes. The fact is that under the direction of Colonel de Marmier, seconded by Colonel Vachet, several French airlines were beginning to operate again, from Aleppo and Deir-ez-Zor to Damascus and Beirut, from Damascus to Brazzaville, and between Fort-Lamy, Bangui, Brazzaville, Pointe-Noire and Douala, thanks partly to several private planes salvaged in the Levant, but above all to eight Lockheeds obtained from the United States in exchange for our authorization to use the base at Pointe-Noire, and to the Air France personnel, long marooned in Argentina and Brazil, that had now rejoined us.

On September 13, I made the three-thousand-kilometer flight nonstop from Damascus to Fort-Lamy; it was possible to travel between the Taurus and the Atlantic without landing anywhere save in Free French territory.

Leclerc was waiting for me at Fort-Lamy. Expecting the resumption of the Libyan offensive, he was completing the conditioning of his desert forces. Once again I was to see the motorized columns, squadrons formed of combat and transport vehicles, armed and equipped for the wide-open spaces, manned by crews eager for distant adventures, ready, under the orders of Ingold, Delange, Massu and Dio, to leave forever the ports of Faya, Zuara and Fada in order to navigate and join battle on the ocean of stones and sand. I visited the small motorized corps which was preparing to leave from the shores of Lake Chad and seize Zinder. At Douala, Libreville, Pointe-Noire, Bangui and Brazzaville I made contact with the various sections of the two brigades, one headed for Tananarive, another for Cotonou, Abidjan or Dakar as the opportunity arose. Colonel Carretier commanded the better part of the air groups we had left below the equator. Commander Charrier, with four small ships, a few planes and some guard posts, was keeping the long coast of the Cameroons, the Gabon, and the lower Congo under surveillance. The artillery, the commissariat and the health service worked wonders to furnish everyone with the necessary supplies despite distance and climate. Each man looked forward impatiently to the operations that would soon be under way between the Atlantic and the Nile and which even the enemy, as the bombing of Fort-Lamy indicated, seemed to be expecting.

On September 22 I entrusted Leclerc with his mission in the form of a "personal and secret instruction." He was to seize the oases of Fezzan, to organize the administration of the region in the name of France, then debouch to capture Tripoli, making sure of Gat and Gadàmes on the way. The operation was to begin as soon as the British Eighth Army had retaken Cyrenaica and penetrated into Tripolitania. Leclerc would be subordinate to Alexander and Montgomery only after the junction of their forces. Then he would participate, under their strategic command, in the eventual battle of Tunisia. On the other hand, in case the Vichy leaders were opposed to the landing and, aided by the Germans, gave battle to the Allies, we were to seize from them the French territories within our grasp. Moreover, our missions of Ponton in the Gold Coast and Adam in Nigeria provided us with valuable information as to the Ivory Coast, Upper Volta, Togo, Dahomey, and Niger. My instructions therefore stipulated that Leclerc was to take his troops, should the occasion arise, into French West Africa, starting at Niger. Finally, he must prepare the Madagascar-bound units to serve as a nucleus for future military regrouping. This was a great deal to do at one time, but we had no misgivings. The Free French in Africa constituted a working force that no ordeal could daunt.

As for the native Africans, their loyalty left nothing to be desired. Whether it was the sovereigns and traditional chieftains, like the sultans of Wadai, Kanem, Fort-Lamy, the influential Orahola at Fort Archambault, Ahmed Bey at Maho, who had recently been forced out of Fezzan by the Italians, Chief Mamadou M'baiki at Bangui, the Queen of the Batekes in the Congo, the King of the Vili at Pointe-Noire, Prince Felix of Gabon, High Chief Paraiso at Douala, the King of the Abrons, who escaped from the Ivory Coast with his men to rejoin General de Gaulle, and others; or the officials attached to the administration, to the Army, to commerce, to public instruction; or the mass of men themselves, farmers, soldiers, workers, servants—all made the cause of Fighting France their own and willingly assumed a large part of its sacrifices. But at the same time, a thrill of hope and liberation made these Africans tremble. The drama shaking the world to its foundations, the almost miraculous crusade the "Gaullists" had undertaken on their own continent, the spectacle of the efforts that the war had aroused and that were changing the conditions of their existence led thousands of black men in cabins and camps, savannas and forests, in the deserts and along the great rivers of their continent, men hitherto oppressed by ages of servitude, to raise their heads and question their destiny.

Governor General Éboué concentrated his energies on controlling this profoundly inspired movement; as a convinced humanist he regarded such a tendency as salutary, since it aimed at raising the people above what they had been, but as a great administrator he felt that the French authority should turn it to account as well.

He did not shrink at all before the material, moral and political transformation that was soon to penetrate the "impenetrable" continent. But he hoped that this revolution would bear the stamp of Africa herself and that the changes made in the life, the customs and the laws of her people, far from abolishing the ancestral rules, would instead be carried out so as to respect traditional institutions and forms. It was thus, according to Éboué, that Africa's progress, France's power and glory, and interracial co-operation would best be served. He oriented in this direction the administration of which he was the head and, in consequence, provided it with instructions as to the leadership of territories and societies, the working conditions of the natives, the police, the dispensation of justice, and the collection of taxes. At Brazzaville I congratulated him on his achievements; his views corresponded to my own, and in this domain as in others the unity of Fighting France seemed solidly cemented.

September 25! Suddenly, upon my arrival at London, everything was changed. How distant were the loyal territories, the eager troops, the enthusiastic crowds which even yesterday surrounded me with the assurance of their devotion. Here, once again, was what is known as power, stripped of the contacts and the recognition that occasionally manage to sweeten it. Here there was nothing but hard problems, harsh negotiations, painful choices among men and disadvantages. Again I would have to bear our burden in the heart of a country that was friendly, of course, but alien, where everyone pursued a goal and spoke a language not our own, and where everything made me feel that our prize was out of all proportion to our poor means of achieving it.

The resumption of contact with the British government was inevitably something of a shock. On September 28, accompanied by Pleven, I called at 10 Downing Street, where Churchill and Eden were expecting us. It was to be expected that the British ministers should express their irritation over affairs in the Levant; we were quite ready to manifest our own to them; after which one could suppose that the conversation would take a more practical turn. Perhaps, in particular, the settlement of the Madagascar question would be at least sketched out. But on this occasion and as a consequence of the Prime Minister's behavior, the bitterness of the discussion did not subside.

Mr. Churchill began, true enough, by thanking me for having come to London in response to his invitation. I received this compliment with a humor that was a match for that which had inspired it. Then the Prime Minister proceeded to the usual airing of our respective grievances in the Middle East. The British government, he said, insisted that elections be held this very year in Syria and in Lebanon; I replied that this would not be the case; he concluded our exchange on this subject by declaring that no agreement was possible with me in the realm of Franco-British collaboration in the Levant. "We are taking note of that," he said; to which I made no objection.

Then he broached the subject of Madagascar. But this was only to declare: "In consideration of the state of affairs at Damascus and Beirut, we are not at all eager to open a new theater of operations with you at Tananarive. I do not see why we should install a Gaullist command there."

I reacted strongly to this declaration, which seemed to me to comprise both the negation of England's commitment and a piece of bargaining at our expense. Pleven too did not conceal his feeling on this matter.

Mr. Churchill then attacked me in a bitter and highly emotional tone. When I pointed out that the establishment of a British-controlled administration in Madagascar would constitute an interference with the rights of France, he exclaimed furiously: "You claim to be France! You are not France! I do not recognize you as France!" Then, still as vehemently: "France! Where is France now? Of course I don't deny that General de Gaulle and his followers are an important and honorable part of the French people, but certainly another authority besides his could be found which would also have its value."

I interrupted him. "If, in your eyes, I am not the representative of France, why and with what right are you dealing with me concerning her world-wide interests?" Mr. Churchill did not reply.

Mr. Eden then intervened and brought the discussion back to the subject of the Levant. He repeated the justifications the British claimed to have for interfering with our affairs there. Then, losing his temper in his turn, he complained bitterly of my behavior. Mr. Churchill outdid him, shouting that in my Anglophobia a desire for prestige and personal aggrandisement through the instrumentality of the French people was dictating my behavior. These imputations of the British ministers seemed inspired by their eagerness to create grievances that would somehow justify the fact that Fighting France was to be kept out of French North Africa. I told them as much without softening my terms. By the time the discussion had reached this point it was futile to continue it. We agreed on this and separated.

The weeks that followed were extremely tense. We were surrounded by ill will. The British went so far as to cut off delivery, for eleven days, of telegrams addressed from London by the National Committee to the French authorities in Africa, the Levant and the Pacific. The Foreign Office, concentrating on Maurice Dejean the full force of all its departments and brandishing before his eyes the specter of a complete breakdown of relations—a diplomat's worst fear—affected him sufficiently for him to envisage what concessions we could make to re-establish good relations. Concessions? I would not hear of them! Dejean therefore handed in his resignation, with great dignity, and several weeks later became our representative to the governments in exile in Great Britain. Pleven, handing over the Ministry of Finance to Diethelm, took over the Foreign Affairs post during the interim, while waiting for the arrival of Massigli, whom I had invited from France.

Nevertheless, as was customary, the tempest soon subsided. The London telegraph offices were again willing to dispatch our wires. On October 23 Mr. Churchill sent Mr. Morton, his chief private secretary, to congratulate me on the exploit of the French

submarine *Juno*, which had just sunk two large enemy ships off
the coast of Norway, to express the thanks of the British government for the important and costly contribution our troops had
made the day before in the Allied offensive at El Alamein, and,
finally, to inform me of the good will Mr. Churchill himself had
never ceased to feel toward me. On October 30 Marshal Smuts,
again in London, asked to see me and declared that the British
had decided to recognize the authority of Fighting France at Tananarive. He added that this would also be the case, sooner or later,
in North Africa. Some days before, the Foreign Office had in fact
resolved to open negotiations with us in order to reach an agreement about Madagascar.

The first proposal was that once our administration was installed the British command should exercise a controlling influence
over it, and that in addition the English should have at their disposal all bases, lines of communication and transmission facilities
existing on the island. We rejected these claims. As we saw it,
French authority on Madagascar must be sovereign in the political
and administrative realms. As for the island's eventual defense,
we proposed that the strategic command, in case of operations
against the common enemy, be entrusted to a British general officer as long as the British had more forces on the spot than we.
If the balance of forces happened to change, a French officer
would assume command. Then again, it would be up to the French
authority to lend our allies, according to their needs, the co-operation of our installations and of our public services. I had already appointed General Legentilhomme High Commissioner for
the Indian Ocean with maximum civil and military powers. At
the same time Pierre de Saint-Mart, governor of Ubangi-Shari,
was appointed governor general of Madagascar. Both left to assume
command as soon as operations on the island were completed and
the conclusion of our own negotiations with the British permitted
them to exercise their functions effectively.

The British government soon came to an agreement with us on
the essential points involved. It must be said that in Madagascar

itself, in proportion as Vichy's power waned, the British discovered among the French as among the natives the virtually unanimous desire to join the cause of General de Gaulle. If the London cabinet still postponed the solution, it was obviously with the intention of offering it to us as an appeasement when, as could be expected, the Allied landings at Algiers and Casablanca provoked discords in our relations. Therefore when on November 6, the day after the Madagascar armistice had been concluded, Mr. Eden, all sugar and honey, proposed that we issue a joint communiqué, on the part of the British government and the French National Committee, announcing General Legentilhomme's immediate departure, I realized that events in North Africa were coming to a head.

Others who suspected as much were eager to give us proofs of their preference for our cause. On August 6, when I was flying to the Middle East, President Beneš had solemnly declared to Maurice Dejean, as the latter reported to me, that he "considered the National Committee under the direction of General de Gaulle as the real government of France." He had requested the Commissioner of Foreign Affairs to ask me in his behalf if we did not consider that the moment had come to repudiate, in the name of France, the Munich agreements and the amputations which had resulted from them in regard to Czechoslovakia. I had answered affirmatively. On my return I saw Beneš and we easily reached an agreement, which resulted, on September 29, in an exchange of letters between myself and Monsignor Shramek, President of the Czechoslovak Council. In my letter I declared:

> The French National Committee, . . . rejecting the Munich agreements, proclaims that it considers those agreements as null and void . . . and that it commits itself to do all in its power in order that the Czechoslovak Republic, within its pre-1938 frontiers, may obtain every guarantee concerning its military and economic security, its territorial integrity, and its political unity.

In Monsignor Shramek's reply the Czech government committed itself, on its part, to every effort in order that France might be restored to "its strength, its independence and the integrity of its metropolitan and overseas territories." The next day, speaking on the radio, I made public these reciprocal promises and emphasized their moral and political significance.

From Moscow came signs that were equally encouraging. The Soviet government, aware of what the British intended to do in North Africa, remarking the United States' attitude toward Fighting France and discerning in Litvinov's reports from Washington Roosevelt's intention of becoming the arbiter among the French minorities, was seriously concerned by this American tendency toward hegemony. In behalf of his government M. Bogomolov let me understand that Russia, engaged in a death struggle against the invader, was unable at the present time to intervene directly, but that she nonetheless disapproved of the Anglo-American policy and would know how to oppose it should the circumstances warrant her intervention. On September 28, in a widely publicized communiqué, Moscow announced that the Soviet Union recognized in Fighting France "all French citizens and territories . . . which, by every means in their power, are contributing to the liberation of France, wherever they may be," and in the National Committee "the executive body of Fighting France, alone qualified to organize the participation of French citizens and territories in the war." In Russian eyes, there could be neither a third force nor a third power between Vichy and Fighting France.

It must be said that if America, the new star of world history, believed herself in a position to direct the French nation, the European states, after centuries of experience, had no such illusion. Now France had made her own choice. The information that reached us every day showed that the resistance was unceasingly expanding, which was the same as saying that all those who took part in it were morally pledged to General de Gaulle and that any government established without him would be rejected by the people as soon as liberation had been effected.

Moreover, the way in which the Germans and their collaborators were behaving in metropolitan France was promoting this development. On June 22 Laval declared, to the general indignation, "I hope for a German victory." In July a "legion" of young Frenchmen was engaged in Russia under German orders and in German uniforms. In August the Marshal issued a law putting an end to the "activity" of both Chambers, which had previously gone through the motions of survival. Suddenly the parliamentarians cursed the regime they themselves had instituted. A public letter of protest was addressed to the Marshal by M. Jeanneney, President of the Senate, and M. Herriot, President of the Chamber of Deputies. The latter, having returned his Legion of Honor cross to indicate his reprobation of the awarding of decorations to the "volunteers" fighting the Russians, was arrested shortly afterward, while Messrs. Paul Reynaud, Daladier, Blum, Mandel, General Gamelin and others remained in the prisons into which Vichy had thrown them the day of its accession, without their having been condemned by law or even formally indicted. During the summer the persecution of the Jews grew worse, conducted by a special "commissariat" in collaboration with the invader. In September, because the Reich required increasingly numerous French manpower and because voluntary workers no longer sufficed to meet its quota, an obligatory workers' levy was instituted. The total sum of the occupation expenses reached two hundred billion francs at the beginning of this month, double what it had been for September the preceding year. Finally, German reprisals redoubled in violence and severity. During these same four weeks a thousand men were shot, 116 on Mont Valérien; more than six thousand went to prison or to concentration camps.

Upon my return from the Levant and Africa, I found unimpugnable witnesses waiting for me in London—Frénay, the head of Combat, and D'Astier, the head of Libération—who gave me their reports on action in the unoccupied zone. Their accounts emphasized the will toward organization and the pressure from the rank and file toward unity, but also the extreme individualism of the leaders, from which their rivalries resulted. Nevertheless, by finding out about the obstacles which our allies set in our path and which were scarcely suspected in France, by learning, in particular, what was to happen in Algeria and Morocco, these responsible men could estimate to what extent unity in metropolitan France was necessary.

I instructed them to hasten the formation, around Jean Moulin, of the National Council of the Resistance, which would include the representatives of every movement, syndicate and party. I also urged them to unite their combat groups into the secret army which was to be set up. These groups would then depend, in each region, on a single authority, the military delegate I would appoint. For the occupied zone, I instructed Rémy to take the same directives to our movements there, the Civil and Military Organization, Men of the Liberation, Men of the Resistance, Liberation North, the Voice of the North, and even the Communist-led Francs-Tireurs et Partisans organization, which asked to be affiliated with us.

Of course we did not fail to let Washington and London know what we had heard from France. Frénay and D'Astier saw the British ministers and services as well as the American diplomats and intelligence. André Philip left for Washington, armed with documentary proof and instructed to give Roosevelt a letter from General de Gaulle explaining the realities of the French situation. Mendès-France, having escaped from metropolitan France, carried out a mission to the United States to inform those who were not aware of what was happening in France of the circumstances there. Félix Gouin, who had arrived in August and who represented the Socialists, informed the workers' parties that the former French left was now ranged beneath the Cross of Lorraine. Shortly after, Brossolette, returning from the occupied zone, brought with him Charles Vallin, one of the hopes of the former right and of the Croix de Feu league. Vallin, hitherto a disciple of the Vichy regime, now renounced his errors; this ardent patriot, an apostle of tradition, joined my cause with all his heart. He publicly detailed his reasons for doing so, then left to take command of a combat company.

General d'Astier de La Vigerie and General Cochet, both important Air Force chiefs, joined us in their turn. The Communists did not lag behind; from France they prepared to send us Fernand Grenier, while in Moscow André Marty came several times to inform our delegate Garreau that he considered himself at my disposal. Finally, men as diversely oriented as Mandel, Jouhaux and Léon Blum, then imprisoned by Vichy, as well as Jeanneney, Louis Marin, Jacquinot, Dautry and Louis Gillet, sent me their advice as well as assurances of their support.

Thus whatever the immense difficulties of action in France, despite danger and loss, despite rivalry among leaders and the separate enterprises of certain groups employed by foreign powers, the cohesion of the resistance continually grew, became ever more pronounced. Having been able to assure it the inspiration and the direction which saved it from anarchy, I found in it at the crucial moment a valuable instrument in the struggle against the enemy and, in relation to the Allies, an essential prop for my policy of independence and unity.

We were now in the early days of November 1942. At any moment America was to begin its western crusade and direct its ships, troops and air squadrons toward Africa. Since October 18 the British, aided by French forces, had been striving to drive the Germans and the Italians out of Libya in order to join the United States' army in Tunisia later on, with perhaps a French army as well. On the eastern front, along the Volga and deep in the Caucasus, the enemy was being exhausted by the Russian might.

What an opportunity still offered itself to France! For her sons in misfortune how clear and simple everything would be now, were it not for the inner demons that strove to divide them and the evil genius that inspired foreign powers to make use of their dissensions. It was not without anxiety that I waited for the curtain to go up on the drama's next act. But I felt sure of my people. I believed they were sure of me. I knew to whom France was looking. On with the play, let the three knocks be heard!

CHAPTER 2

TRAGEDY

ALL day long on November 7 the American and British stations kept repeating, "Robert arriving! Robert arriving!" Hearing this, I had no doubt that "Robert"—Murphy's first name—was the term agreed upon to designate the American forces to the French in North Africa whose co-operation had been arranged for. Which meant that the landing had begun. The next morning's news confirmed the fact.

At noon I went to Downing Street on Mr. Churchill's invitation. Mr. Eden was also there. During the conversation the Prime Minister lavished upon me every sign of his friendship without, at the same time, concealing the fact that he felt some little embarrassment. He told me that though the British fleet and air force were playing an essential role in the operation now under way, British troops were serving in a purely accessory capacity. For the moment, Great Britain had had to leave all the responsibilities in the hands of the United States; Eisenhower was in command. Now the Americans were demanding that the Free French be left out.

"We have been obliged to go along with them in this," Mr. Churchill declared. "Rest assured, however, that we are not revoking any of our agreements with you. Ever since June 1940, we have promised you our support. Despite whatever incidents have occurred, we intend to keep that promise. Besides, as the North African engagement increases in scope, the British must come on the scene; we shall then have our word to say. And that word will be in your behalf." And Mr. Churchill, showing signs of emotion, added, "You have been with us during the war's worst moments. We shall not abandon you now that the horizon shows signs of brightening."

The British ministers then informed me that the Americans were in the process of landing at several points in Morocco, as well as at Oran and Algiers. The operation was being carried out with considerable difficulty, especially at Casablanca, where French forces were putting up a vigorous resistance. General Giraud had been taken onto a British submarine off the Côte d'Azur and brought to Gibraltar. The Americans were counting on him to take command of the French troops in North Africa and to reverse the situation. But already his success seemed dubious.

"Did you know," Churchill asked me, "that Darlan is in Algiers?"

To my interlocutors' explanations I replied, in substance, "The fact that the Americans have landed in Africa, where both English and Free French forces have been struggling for over two years, is in itself a highly satisfactory development. I can see in it, for France, the possibility of recovering an army and perhaps a fleet which would join the struggle for her liberation. General Giraud is a great soldier. My hopes accompany him in his endeavor. It is too bad that the Allies have prevented him from coming to an agreement with me, for I would have been able to procure other help for him besides hopes. But sooner or later we shall see eye to eye, and all the more readily if the Allies keep out of our way. As for the operation now in progress, I am not surprised that it is a difficult one. In both Algeria and Morocco there are military elements that opposed us in Syria last year and which you permitted to go free despite my warnings. Furthermore, the Americans wanted to play off Vichy against De Gaulle in North Africa. I have never doubted that, should the occasion arise, they would have to pay for such an attitude. Now the fact is that they are paying for it, and of course we

French must pay for it as well. All the same, given the feelings in our soldiers' hearts, I believe that the battle will not be a long one. But however short, the Germans will rush in."

I then expressed to Messrs. Churchill and Eden my astonishment at discovering that the Allied plan did not first of all aim at Bizerte. For the Germans and the Italians were obviously going to land in Tunisia at that point. If it were not for the American reluctance to risk a direct landing there, and if I had been consulted, we could have brought in the Koenig Division. The British ministers admitted this, while repeating that the operation was under American control. "I cannot understand," I told them, "how you British could stand aside so completely in an operation that is of primary concern to Europe."

Mr. Churchill asked me how I felt concerning future relations between Fighting France and the North African authorities. I replied that, as far as I was concerned, achieving unity was all that mattered. This implied that relations should be established as soon as possible, and also that the Vichy regime and its supporters be expelled from Algiers, for the resistance movement as a whole would not tolerate their maintenance in power. If, for example, Darlan was to control North Africa, no agreement was possible. "Whatever the case," I said in conclusion, "nothing matters more today than to reach a cease-fire. As for the rest, we shall see afterward."

That evening, speaking by radio "to the leaders, soldiers, sailors, airmen, officials and French *colons* of North Africa," I urged them: "Rise up, help our allies, join them without reservations. Don't worry about names or formulas—rise up! Now is the great moment. Now is the hour of common sense and of courage. Frenchmen of North Africa, let us re-enter the lists from one end of the Mediterranean to the other, and the war will be won thanks to France."

Actually the information arriving at Carlton Gardens indicated that the Americans were still fighting against heavy resistance everywhere. Certainly their advance intelligence had functioned effectively; certainly General Mast, in command of the Algiers Division, and General Monsabert, in command of the Blida subdivision, as well as Colonels Jousse, Baril, Chrétien, Commander Barjot and others had been able to facilitate matters for them for a few hours, while at Casablanca General Béthouart vainly tried to do the same; certainly groups of "Gaullists," acting under the orders of Paufilet, Vanhecke, Achiary, Esquerre, Aboulker, Calvet, Pillafort and Dreyfus, the last two of whom were to be killed in the operation, had temporarily managed to take possession of certain administrative buildings in Algiers and even to hold Admiral Darlan overnight in forced captivity in the villa of Les Oliviers; certainly some prominent men, such as Messrs. Rigault, Lemaigre-Dubreuil and De Saint-Hardouin, who had negotiated with the Americans, were playing their expected role as to local information and liaison work; certainly, too, Giraud's proclamation—which made no mention whatever of Fighting France—had been widely publicized by radio and American leaflets, while loyal officers and resistance elements of every kind organized a command post for him at Dar Mahidine. Nevertheless, on the whole it was clear that the plan prepared by Leahy, Murphy and Clark to permit the Allies to land without firing a shot, and the messages sent by Roosevelt to Pétain, Noguès and Estéva, had not had the desired effect.

On November 9 the situation was not at all promising. The Vichy authorities had everywhere retained or resumed the upper hand. The Marshal had given formal orders to fight off the "assailant." At Gibraltar, General Giraud, realizing that the Allies were not at all interested in putting themselves under his command, had not yet left for North Africa, where, furthermore, his proclamation had produced no effect at all. At Algiers, Darlan had just ordered the garrison to cease fire, but he permitted the "defense plan" to be carried out everywhere else and continued to defer to Pétain and Laval. At Oran, a full-fledged battle was under way. But the fighting was especially bitter in Morocco; Casablanca, Port Lyautey and Fedala were the scenes of particularly fierce battles. And lastly Admiral Platon had reached Tunis, sent by Vichy to instruct Admiral Estéva, the resident-general, and Admiral Derrien, the port admiral at Bizerte, that the Germans be permitted to land. The latter, in fact, during the course of the day landed their parachute troops near El Alaouina without firing a shot.

That same evening there were long faces in the Allied headquarters in London. Many wondered if the operation would not turn into a prolonged struggle between the French troops and Eisenhower's forces, with the subsequent irruption, throughout the region, of enemy forces to which Spanish troops would be joined willy-nilly.

But on the spot good sense carried the day. General Juin, who had been commander in chief until Darlan's arrival and second in command since the latter had been in North Africa, realized how absurd it was to join battle with the Allies and what disastrous consequences the Italo-German breakthrough would involve. He knew that this was the profound feeling of his subordinates and urged Darlan to order a general cease-fire, to which the latter agreed on November 10. Juin then made contact with Giraud, who had finally reached Dar Mahidine. Receiving him at Les Oliviers, Darlan informed Giraud that he was prepared to resign his own position to him. He ordered General Barré, in command of the troops in Tunisia, to group his forces near Medjez-el-Bab and to be in a position to open fire on the Germans. On the morning of November 11, hostilities between the French and the Allies came to a general halt.

It had cost dearly. On the French side, three thousand men had been killed or wounded. As for ships, the following were sunk or irremediably damaged: the cruiser *Primauguet,* the destroyers *Albatros, Épervier* and *Milan,* seven torpedo boats, ten submarines, a considerable number of smaller craft—dispatch boats, patrol and escort vessels—and several cargo ships. In addition, the battleship *Jean-Bart* was heavily damaged and two submarines had made for Toulon, where they were soon to be scuttled. Lastly, out of the 168 planes based in Morocco and Algeria, 135 were destroyed on the ground or in combat. On the Allied side, losses reached three thousand killed, wounded or missing. The Royal Navy lost the destroyers *Broke* and *Malcolm,* the escort vessels *Walney* and *Hartland,* and several transport ships. In the American fleet, the battleship *Massachusetts,* the cruisers *Wichita* and *Brooklyn* and the destroyers *Murphy* and *Ludlow* were seriously damaged; one hundred smaller craft used in the landing were destroyed offshore or on the beaches; seventy planes were shot down.

While these senseless battles were dying out, I took care to establish contact with French North Africa. As early as the afternoon of November 9 I asked Admiral Stark to meet with me. He arrived with tears in his eyes, profoundly moved, he said, by my radio appeal to the French on the preceding day, but also deeply upset by the Franco-American struggle, which he had not believed possible. "Eisenhower is also surprised and grieved to hear of it," he added.

"I should like to send a mission to Algiers," I told him. "I am asking the United States government to take the measures necessary for this mission to reach its destination."

Stark promised that this would be done. The next day I wrote Churchill, asking him to intervene in my behalf with Roosevelt, and alerted Pleven, Billotte, D'Astier and Frénay to leave at a moment's notice.

On November 11 a great rally which the "French of Great Britain" had long been awaiting took place. Never had Albert Hall been so packed. Obviously the thought of North Africa stirred the crowd; seeing and hearing this, I sensed that beneath the surge of enthusiasm minds were torn between joy and anxiety. If it was clear that union was hoped for, it was equally to be feared that De Gaulle and Fighting France might be forced into some unworthy compromise. When, from the top of one of the balconies, a retired general who had taken refuge in England raised his voice to adjure me to subordinate myself to Giraud, the poor man was immediately dragged from his seat by outraged groups and expelled from the hall, pursued by the shouts of the crowd.

In my speech, I reaffirmed our goal amidst the events now taking place or looming on the horizon. I did so quite moderately, in order to keep the door open to men of good will everywhere, but also distinctly enough to make clear that what was said was indeed what would be done. To begin with, I hailed the new phase of the war, in which, after so many reversals, the balance of forces was at last inclining toward liberty. I stated that, as always, France was at the heart of the drama. Then, appealing for unity, I cried, "France! That is, a single nation, a single territory, a single law!" Then I proceeded to explain how our people, dispersed by the disaster, had rallied to the resistance, and that Fighting France and only Fighting France was guiding this national movement and providing its leaders.

"The cement of French unity," I said, "is the blood of the Frenchmen who have never recognized the armistice, of those who since Rethondes have died for France all the same. The nucleus of our unity is ourselves, the France that fights. To the nation cast into a dungeon, we have offered since the first day of her captivity the means of combat, the light of day, and that is why the nation now endows Fighting France with her authority. Therefore we aspire to reunite all our peoples and all our territories. Therefore we suffer no one to come and divide our country's war effort by any of those so-called parallel enterprises—that is, divided enterprises—to which the secret but powerful expression of the national will, moreover, will soon do justice. Therefore it is in the name of France that the French National Committee speaks when it calls for the help of all to wrest our country from the enemy and from Vichy, to re-establish French liberties, and to cause the laws of the Republic to be observed." I concluded by crying, "A united battle for a united country!"

The audience clearly understood that in the difficult situation in which we stood I was ready to join with whoever deserved our alliance, but that I would abandon none of my fundamental commitments. A tremendous ovation indicated the approval of this throng of Frenchmen. Afterward I was to discover that the effect of my

words on the Allies was quite different. Their leaders and spokesmen, sighing and nodding their heads, were to censure our intransigence.

They themselves were less squeamish than we. Of course the
Americans, with whom the British aligned themselves, had been
astonished and annoyed by Giraud's failure. But since Eisenhower
had found no other way of quelling French opposition than to come
to an agreement with Darlan, well, then, it was with the latter that
America would open negotiations. On November 10 General Clark,
receiving word of the cease-fire which the Admiral had just declared, announced in the tones of a conqueror who holds the vanquished at his mercy that, under these conditions, "all civil and
military authorities will be maintained in their present functions."
On November 13 Noguès, Chatel and Bergeret met with Darlan. It
was understood among them that the Admiral would become High
Commissioner for North Africa. Boisson would soon put himself
under his command. Giraud, isolated from Vichyists and "Gaullists" alike, had done so immediately, in consideration of which he
was named commander in chief of the troops. On November 15
Darlan announced these measures and proclaimed that they had
been taken "in the name of Marshal Pétain."

In view of the impurity of their sources, an appearance of legality had to be found for these measures. Thus it was declared that
Noguès, having been delegated powers by the Marshal during Darlan's temporary confinement, had transmitted them to the Admiral,
who was now, therefore, reinvested with that authority. But this
casuistry did not long suffice, even to those who scrupled least. In
fact Pétain himself, after hysterical sessions during which, according
to our intelligence, Weygand and Auphan had urged him to approve
the North African cease-fire and Laval had demanded that he condemn it, took the latter course. By means of both radio and the
press, he made public his great indignation at his proconsuls'
"felony." He declared that "Darlan had betrayed his mission"; he
published a letter Giraud had written him on May 4, promising on
his honor as a soldier never to do anything that would contradict

his or Laval's policies; he let it be known that he himself would take command of the French armies; he reiterated his order to oppose the Anglo-American forces and to leave the way open to the Axis armies. On December 1, Admiral Platon, the minister sent by the Marshal "to co-ordinate the military affairs of the three branches," appealing to the African troops by radio, declared, "It is in France that, after so many ordeals, the Marshal and his government will reconstitute the national army. . . . France will reconquer Africa. Then you will see the traitors flee in foreign baggage trains."

Hence another subterfuge to "legitimize" Darlan's authority had to be found. It would be alleged that a telegram had been sent, by a subordinate, of which neither the text nor the signer's name was ever published but of which the mere mention permitted the tribe of augurs to insinuate to the gallery that Pétain secretly gave his approval to the Admiral. Finally, the supreme argument of those whom Vichy called "the perjurers" would be that, because of the occupation of the southern zone of France, the Marshal was henceforth at the mercy of the Germans and could no longer give valid orders, and that consequently authority belonged to those upon whom he had conferred it when he was free.

It required no more than this for President Roosevelt to surmount, in regard to Darlan, the democratic and juridical scruples which, for over two years, he had opposed to General de Gaulle. On Roosevelt's orders, Clark recognized the "High Commissioner" and entered upon negotiations that led, on November 22, to an agreement by virtue of which Darlan governed and commanded, provided that he gave satisfaction to his Anglo-American conquerors. True, the President issued a statement declaring that the political arrangements made by Eisenhower and Darlan were only "a temporary expedient." But on the twenty-third, when he received André Philip and Tixier and grew annoyed at their protests, he shouted at them, "Of course I'm dealing with Darlan, since Darlan's giving me Algiers! Tomorrow I'd deal with Laval, if Laval were to offer me Paris!" He added, however, "I should very much like to see General de Gaulle to discuss these matters, and I want you to tell him how desirable his visit to Washington would be." Finally on December 7 Darlan, having obtained the Allies' consent, decreed himself head of the French state in North Africa and commander in chief of land, naval and air forces, with the assistance of an "Imperial Council" consisting of Noguès, Giraud, Chatel, Boisson and Bergeret.

While in Algiers, Casablanca and Dakar the officials made an about-face to keep their positions, in France itself the enemy reaction was unleashed; the German forces overflowed the "free" zone, and Vichy forbade any opposition to them. The "armistice army" was to lay down its arms pending demobilization. General de Lattre, laboring under an illusion, tried valiantly to apply the defense plan and occupy a position in the Montagne Noire with the troops around Montpellier. He was immediately repudiated, forsaken by all and imprisoned. It was at this time that he made contact with Fighting France, which was later to aid in his escape and send him to London; there he was to join me for good. General Weygand, who had attempted to take cover at Guéret, was arrested by the Gestapo and deported to Germany. Thus, without Vichy's firing or permitting the firing of a single shot, was dissipated the lying pretense of independence which this regime had claimed in order to justify its capitulation and to deceive so many well-intentioned Frenchmen. Of the traces of its sovereignty, there remained only the fleet at Toulon. It was not to remain there for long.

This fleet—of which the permanently unattached portion was commanded by Admiral de Laborde and the rest, more or less disarmed, was assigned directly to Admiral Marquis, the port admiral—remained under Pétain's orders, refused to sail for Africa despite Darlan's urging, and saw the Germans appear within striking distance of the harbor. The "neutrality" agreement Vichy had made with the enemy helped to keep our sailors from effecting some last-minute revolt. It was a stage on the road to annihilation. For my part, I was all the more convinced of this since, having recently written in secret to Admiral de Laborde to attempt to enlighten

him as to the course both honor and duty commanded, I knew that
he had given vent to a series of outrageous remarks about me and
had threatened my emissary, Colonel Fourcault, though nevertheless keeping my letter. On November 26 the Germans rushed on
Toulon to seize our ships.

Since they had previously occupied the hilltops dominating the
arsenal, installed trench mortars in the harbor's immediate proximity and sown the roadstead with mines, the French fleet was at
their mercy. And the Marshal, his ministers, the port admiral and
the fleet commander in chief, paralyzed by the consequences of
their own surrender, found nothing to command these powerful
warships to do save to send themselves to the bottom. Three battleships, *Dunkerque, Strasbourg, Provence;* eight cruisers, *Colbert,
Dupleix, Foch, Algérie, Jean-de-Vienne, La Galissonnière, Marseillaise, Mogador,* seventeen destroyers, sixteen torpedo boats, sixteen submarines, seven dispatch vessels, three patrol boats, some
sixty transport ships, tankers, mine sweepers and tugs thus committed, on orders, the most pitiful and sterile suicide imaginable. One
destroyer, one torpedo boat and five tankers were not scuttled in
time and were seized by the Germans. Only five submarines, on the
initiative of their valiant commanders, went over to the "dissidents"
and attempted to leave the harbor. *Casabianca,* under Lherminier,
Glorieux, under Meynier, and *Marsouin,* under Mine, succeeded in
reaching Algiers. *Iris,* under Degé, was forced by lack of fuel to take
refuge in a Spanish port. *Vénus,* under Crescent, foundered in the
roadstead. As for myself, submerged in seas of anger and disappointment, I was reduced to watching what had been one of
France's major hopes sink out of sight, to hailing by radio the few
courageous episodes that accompanied the disaster, and to receiving by telephone the British Prime Minister's nobly expressed but
secretly complacent condolences.

Meanwhile, however, the turn events had taken generally
strengthened the cohesion of the French who were already pledged
to De Gaulle and inclined favorably toward him many of those who
had not yet been won over. The last surrenders on the part of

Vichy and the total occupation of metropolitan France produced final evidence, in fact, that the country's only salvation lay in resistance. Further, the advent of Darlan in North Africa with the support of the Americans provoked general indignation. Never before had I encountered among our people, on any subject whatever, such unanimity as there was on that score.

Of course some people—as was our case—who saw their allies deal with their adversaries felt frustrated and offended. But in their reprobation there was also the revolt of idealism. For example, it was with rage that we heard the American radio commentators, rebroadcast by the BBC, twang out the motto of the Free France radio, *"Honneur et patrie,"* to introduce their reports of Admiral Darlan's words, deeds and empty gestures. Finally, noting the reactions of the people who, in the depths of their suffering, condemned both the regime of defeat and that of collaboration, we were certain that if De Gaulle were to stand aside or, worse still, compromise, it would be the Communist ideology which would win the allegiance of the disgusted masses. The National Committee was convinced of this. Our comrades, wherever they were, no longer doubted the fact. For this reason, as for many others, I counted on the support of an undivided coalition when I informed the Washington and London governments that there was not the slightest chance of an agreement between Fighting France and the North African "High Commissioner."

On November 12 I requested that Admiral Stark inform his government of this decision in my behalf. In Washington, Philip and Tixier employed identical terms in conversations with Sumner Welles on the thirteenth and Cordell Hull on the fourteenth. On the twentieth, Colonel de Chevigné repeated our message to McCloy. On the twenty-third, Philip and Tixier very strongly confirmed their views to Roosevelt. On November 16 I had been to see Messrs. Churchill and Eden, who had invited me to participate in a discussion as soon as Darlan's proclamation that he was retaining power in the Marshal's name and with the agreement of the Allies had reached London. It must be said that this news had caused pro-

found discontent in many circles in England and even in the heart
of the British cabinet, and that the echoes of a shocked public
opinion were noticeable in London. The atmosphere that day was
therefore more strained than ever, and the Prime Minister, without
going so far as to repudiate Roosevelt, insisted on indicating some
reservation as to the policy the President was pursuing.

He declared to me at once that he understood and shared my
sentiments, but that what was most important was to drive the Germans and the Italians out of Africa. He guaranteed that the measures Eisenhower had taken at Algiers were essentially provisional
and let me read the telegrams he and Roosevelt had exchanged on
this subject.

"England gave her consent to this move," he declared, "only on
condition that it be merely an expedient."

"I am taking note of the British position," I told the British ministers. "My own is quite different. You invoke strategic reasons, but
it is a strategic error to place oneself in a situation contradictory to
the moral character of this war. We are no longer in the eighteenth
century when Frederick the Great paid the courtiers of Vienna in
order to be able to take Silesia, nor in the Italian Renaissance when
one hired the myrmidons of Milan or the mercenaries of Florence.
At least, we do not put them at the head of a liberated people afterward. Today we make war with our own blood and souls and the
suffering of nations." I then showed Churchill and Eden telegrams from France that revealed the stupefaction of public opinion.
"Think," I told them, "of the consequences you risk incurring. If
France one day discovers that because of the British and the Americans her liberation consists of Darlan, you can perhaps win the war
from a military point of view but you will lose it morally, and ultimately there will be only one victor: Stalin."

We then spoke of a communiqué the French National Committee was circulating to make known that it had nothing in common
with the Allied commitments in Algiers. In order to obtain wide
publicity, it was essential that we have the BBC antennas at our disposal. I asked the Prime Minister not to oppose us in this matter,

although the London radio, as far as the North African question was concerned, was subject to American approval.

"Of course," Churchill said. "Moreover, I shall telegraph Roosevelt that General de Gaulle must have the means to make his position public."

As we were about to separate, Eden, moved to the point of tears, took me aside to tell me how deeply disturbed he was personally. I replied that, knowing him, I was not at all surprised, for, "speaking man to man, we must agree that this is a dirty business." His attitude confirmed me in my feeling that Churchill's readiness to follow the American policy was distasteful to Eden and no doubt to part of the British cabinet.

After lunch in Downing Street, during which all of Mrs. Churchill's grace and charm was hard put to enliven conversation among the preoccupied guests, the Prime Minister and I resumed our discussion privately. "For you," Churchill declared, "if the present is painful, the prospect is magnificent. At present Giraud is politically liquidated. In any event Darlan would be impossible. You will remain the only choice." And the Prime Minister added, "Don't confront the Americans head on. Be patient! They will come to you, for there is no other alternative."

"Perhaps," I said. "But how much crockery will be broken in the meantime! And I fail to understand your own position. You have been fighting this war since the first day. In a manner of speaking you personally *are* this war. Your army is advancing in Libya. There would be no Americans in Africa if, on your side, you were not in the process of defeating Rommel. Up to this very moment, not a single one of Roosevelt's soldiers has met a single one of Hitler's soldiers, while for three years your men have been fighting in every latitude of the globe. Besides, in this African campaign it is Europe that is at stake, and England belongs to Europe. Yet you let America take charge of the conflict, though it is up to you to control it, at least in the moral realm. Do so! All of European public opinion will follow you."

This sally struck Churchill; I watched him waver. We parted

after having agreed that we must not permit the present crisis to crack Franco-British solidarity, which was more than ever in accord with the natural order of things when the United States intervened in the affairs of the Old World.

That evening the London radio announced, as I had requested, that "General de Gaulle and the National Committee took no share and assumed no responsibility in the negotiations in progress in Algiers," and that "if these negotiations were to lead to arrangements preserving the Vichy regime in North Africa, they would obviously be unacceptable to Fighting France." Our communiqué concluded: "The union of all the overseas territories in the battle for liberation is possible only under conditions in accord with the will and the dignity of the French people."

But the good impulse of the British could not resist American pressure for long. Three days later the British cabinet refused us permission to use the BBC facilities to broadcast a declaration made in support of our own by the organizations of the French resistance. This was contained in a note from France addressed to the Allied governments and signed by representatives of the three movements of the southern zone, Combat, Libération and Francs-Tireurs; of the French workers' movement, including the C.G.T. and the Christian syndicates; and of the four political parties, the Socialist Action Committee, the Republican Federation, the Popular Democrats and the Radicals. The note stated:

> General de Gaulle is the uncontested leader of the resistance movement, which now more than ever before unites the entire country behind him. . . . In no case will we agree to consider the about-face of those responsible for our political and military betrayal an excuse for their past crimes. . . . We urgently request that the destiny of liberated French North Africa be put into General de Gaulle's hands as soon as possible.

The censors from Washington had vetoed the publication of this document.

On November 21 I myself encountered their opposition. In an address to the French nation which had already been recorded by the BBC, I asked "whether the national liberation is to be dishonored" and of course replied, "No!" A few minutes before broadcast time, Mr. Charles Peake came to tell me that under the terms of the agreements made between the Allies and for military reasons, the London radio could not proceed with broadcasts concerning North Africa without the consent of the United States, that this consent had been requested for my address but that the reply required a postponement, for which the British government profoundly apologized. It was therefore the broadcasting facilities of Fighting France at Brazzaville, Douala and Beirut, free of all foreign interference, that carried my message and that of the resistance.

On November 24, during one of our discussions, Mr. Churchill felt that he must mention, though he did so with considerable embarrassment, the BBC's delay in broadcasting my address. "Since the problems you were dealing with concerned the lives of American and British soldiers," he told me, "I thought it politic to telegraph President Roosevelt for his approval. He has not yet given it."

"I did not know," I answered, "that on British territory the radio was not at my disposal." But Churchill's behavior made me realize that it was not at his either.

Thus, among so many upsets, I was attempting to remain steadfast and unwavering—as much by will and reason as by temperament, moreover, for the system established at Algiers seemed to me too artificial to resist the battering ram of events for long, whatever external support it might receive. The men who were in control obviously found themselves in a false position with regard to every section of public opinion. Opposed as they were to De Gaulle, repudiated by Pétain, alarming the procrastinators, they were supported by no popular current, strengthened by no mystique, and their successive attitudes, it was only too obvious, derived from mere speculation. Why then concede anything to an oligarchy without future and without hope? All the less since, at the very moment it came to power in Algiers, careful preparations were swelling our own strength. Immediately after the American landings in Morocco and Algeria, Fighting France extended its authority to all the French possessions in the Indian Ocean.

Of these, it was Réunion that first came over to our side. Isolated in the South Seas, out of the convoy route that doubled the Cape, poor in resources and inhabited by an extremely varied but ardently pro-French population, the island did not enter directly into the Allied plans. But it was exposed to a combined German-Japanese raid, especially now that the enemy was cut off from possible access to Madagascar. Then again, we were quite aware that the majority of Réunion's inhabitants wanted their country to take part in the war effort. I had long been looking for an opportunity to unite the island with Fighting France, but the British, while they themselves were preparing their Madagascar campaign and while the Americans were making ready to invade Africa, put off my intervention in order not to alert Vichy and the enemy. Therefore it was not until November 11 that I decided to effect the coalition with Réunion.

For several months the destroyer *Léopard,* under Commander Richard-Evenou, had been taking part in escort and patrol action off South Africa with just this intention. I gave orders that it make for Réunion and do what was necessary there, taking along Administrator in Chief Capagorry, whom I named governor in advance. On November 28 the ship reached St.-Denis. At the sight of the Cross of Lorraine, the populace rushed to the harbor en masse to welcome our sailors, while many officials and military men showed their sympathy. Only the Galets peninsula battery gave signs of hostility. The *Léopard* answered by a broadside of cannon shots and landed a detachment which, with the co-operation of Director of Public Works Decugis and a zealous local group, made short work of the incident. Unfortunately Decugis was killed, as well as several spectators. Since Governor Aubert had retired to his residence in the mountains, Commander Richard-Evenou made contact with him there. It was agreed "for reasons of public safety" that all resistance would cease and that Governor Capagorry would assume responsibility for the island. Amidst the liveliest enthusiasm, General de Gaulle's representative assumed his new functions.

The same thing happened a month later in Madagascar. In fact, since Governor General Annet's surrender to the British, the huge island's destiny was theoretically determined. But practically everything remained in suspense. True, on November 11, at Mr. Eden's reiterated request, I had agreed to the publication of a joint communiqué announcing that the French National Committee and the British government were holding conferences on the subject of Madagascar and that the National Committee had appointed General Legentilhomme High Commissioner. But I did not intend to take the control of Madagascar into my own hands if those hands were not free. It was essential, therefore, that the British agree to stand aside in political and administrative matters.

Yet it was on just these points that negotiations lagged; their conclusion was delayed by the behavior of the British colonials. After having attempted to bring the Vichy administration under their influence by using the British military command as a go-between, these colonials had tried to seize authority for themselves and had appointed Lord Rennell to direct their affairs, taking advantage of the co-operation of well-intentioned French officials. Lord Rennel and his group now abandoned their attempt and admitted the necessity of permitting Fighting France to take control. But they would have preferred retaining at the very least a controlling influence, with which, of course, we did not concur. The agreement that was finally signed, on December 14, by Mr. Eden and by me guaranteed all that was necessary. That evening, speaking on the radio, I announced the happy event, declaring, "By this act our great and beautiful colony will . . . be able to play an important military and economic role in the war effort," and emphasizing "the complete loyalty which our splendid and traditional ally England" had manifested once again.

The agreement specified that the arrangements made had as their goal "the re-establishment of the exercise of French sovereignty in Madagascar and its dependencies," the Comoro Islands, Crozet,

Kerguelen, St. Paul and Amsterdam; that the High Commissioner assumed all the powers delegated to the governor general by French law, as well as the powers of command over the French forces; and that the defense of Madagascar, its dependencies and Réunion would be ensured jointly. The High Commissioner was to proceed with the reorganization of the French forces as soon as possible. Until he could have the necessary means at his disposal, a British general would be in charge of the defense of the territory. At Diégo-Suarez a British naval officer would be in command.

Once this agreement was signed, General Legentilhomme left for Tananarive, where he was to join a mixed detachment sent by Free French Africa. Legentilhomme, seconded by Governor General de Saint-Mart and by the military commander, Colonel Bureau, was to reactivate the administration, the economy and the public services, re-establish trade and foreign exchange, and reorganize the troops. At the same time, he would do everything in his power to restore morale. In this way, then, several weeks after his arrival, half of his officers, two thirds of his noncommissioned officers and all of the soldiers from the units that had just been fighting against the Allies on Vichy's orders had resumed service under the authority of Fighting France. The remainder, transferred to England, would return to North Africa as soon as unity could be effected there.

In sending General Legentilhomme to Tananarive, I had the satisfaction of being able to order him to pass through Djibouti. On December 28, in fact, Fighting France had taken possession of Djibouti. This was, of course, a consequence of the recent events in Madagascar, for since the beginning of the British intervention there the Vichy authorities of the Somaliland coast had been prevented from getting necessary supplies from the huge island. But it was also the result of the efforts made for two years by our mission to East Africa. Turn and turn about, Palewski and Chancel, maintaining every possible relation with the colony, spreading our propaganda there, actively representing our cause to the Negus at Addis Ababa and to the British command at Nairobi, had arranged this change of allegiance. Then too, Colonel Appert and his detachment, posted in immediate contact with the garrison there, had urged it to join us and, setting the example of a leader and a corps of the best quality, they had gradually influenced the state of mind of a great many of the men. Despite everything, however, our forces had had to enter the colony.

Indeed General Dupont, governor of Djibouti (where he had replaced Noailhetas), did not decide to transfer allegiance, though his feelings inclined him in that direction and though I had written urging him to do so. Realizing this, a portion of the garrison, led by Lieutenant Colonel Raynal, had crossed the frontier and joined Colonel Appert's detachment at the beginning of November. Other elements indicated that they would be willing to take similar action. Thereupon the Washington government, in order to keep the colony from going over to De Gaulle, had sent its Aden consul to Djibouti. But the latter could find no solution in accord with American policy—that is, excluding both Vichy and De Gaulle. On the other hand, his intervention had resulted in irritating the "Gaullists" and had impelled them to act. On December 26, Fighting French troops under Appert's and Raynal's orders, and with the agreement of the British, entered French Somaliland and reached the outskirts of the city without a shot being fired. The question was decided. On December 28 General Dupont signed an agreement with Chancel, my delegate, and General Fowkes, representative of the British government, transferring the colony to the French National Committee. Chancel immediately took control. On December 30 Bayardelle, appointed governor of Djibouti, assumed his functions there.

The recovery of Somaliland was of considerable importance. All the French territories in the Indian Ocean had thereby re-entered the war, bringing to the Western powers strategic positions that would cover Africa and the East in case of the reappearance of the Japanese menace. The city of Djibouti was to resume its role of transit port at the entrance to the Red Sea and outlet for Ethiopia. Besides, Fighting France found in the three hundred officers, the eight thousand men and the matériel that equipped the base of operations a precious reinforcement for our troops in Libya and for those we were preparing to regroup in Madagascar. Finally, on the political level, it was significant that during these same weeks when the Algiers system was betraying its confusion, the National Committee should have succeeded in restoring to unity and to the war effort territories so distant and so coveted.

But above all, the fact that in Africa both pieces of the French Army were henceforth struggling against the same enemy was to encourage them toward union. No quibbling, in fact, could conceal from the officers and soldiers taking up positions along Tunisia's "dorsal" coast that they were now doing precisely the same thing as their comrades engaged in Libya and Fezzan. The same "government" that yesterday had condemned the latter today was repudiating the former under the same pretext, that all were "adding to the country's woes." In France the same resistance movement that was linked with the men who had not ceased fighting was also about to join forces with those who were turning their scanty arms against the invader in Tunisia. The same French people who put their hopes in De Gaulle and his followers included in those same hopes all French soldiers fighting the same battle. I was therefore sure that the desire for unity would swell each day from Rabat to Gabès. Thus although I still could not answer for the troops of French North Africa, I followed their operations with the same eager attention I accorded the others.

After several days of confusion which the enemy took advantage of to gain a foothold in the Regency, the Tunisian troops under Barré's orders were regrouped, one section toward Beja and Medjez-el-Bab, the other toward Tebessa, in order to block the roads to Algeria. Then the Constantine Division, under General Welwert, reached Tebessa in its turn, constituting with Barré's units a sector of army corps entrusted to General Koeltz, while, farther south, General Delay entered the campaign with his Sahara troops. On November 16 Juin took command of this "army detachment" which, on the nineteenth, opened fire on the Germans at Medjez-el-Bab and, on the twenty-second, reoccupied Gafsa and Sbeïtla. By the end of November, something of a front extending from northern to southern Tunisia, weak and discontinuous but held by determined men, assured a primary cover to the emplacement of the Allied battle corps.

The month of December saw both camps reinforced: the Germans and the Italians, under General Nehring's orders, receiving troops and matériel transported from one shore of the Straits of Sicily to the other or else brought from Tripolitania along the Gabès road; the British First Army under General Anderson sending its advance-guard corps into line along the coastal region west of Tunis and Bizerte; General Giraud completing Juin's forces first by the Algiers Division under Deligne, then by a division from Morocco under Mathenet; the Americans adding, on the one hand, an armored division to the British support, and on the other parachute troops and tanks to relieve the French.

All in all, two months after landing, General Eisenhower still had not been able to put in contact with the enemy anything more than a small number of Anglo-American units, delayed as he was in his deployment by the fear of seeing the Spanish take the offensive in Morocco, the desire not to engage his inexperienced troops hastily, and lastly by the difficulties he was having in obtaining bases for his planes, transporting his supplies and organizing his communications in territory as extensive as French North Africa, while at sea enemy ships and planes ceaselessly attacked his convoys. The first months of 1943 were to see, in fact, the greatest tonnage losses of the whole war. During this critical period the fate of the campaign as a whole rested essentially on the effort of the French troops—a role all the more meritorious for them considering that they played it with obsolete armaments and virtually without planes, armored units, heavy artillery, antiaircraft guns, antitank weapons and trucks—all matériel that had been recently returned to the armistice commissions or else destroyed during the fighting against the Americans. There remained only a few pieces kept in the units or camouflaged in *bled* shelters.

Meanwhile Bizerte had been the theater of a final surrender. Admiral Derrien, following orders brought from Vichy by Platon, had permitted the German troops to infiltrate freely into the area. On December 7 Nehring ordered the wretched man to disarm the garrison and hand over ships, harbor, arsenal and defenses, which was immediately done. An important base of operations thus passed into the hands of the enemy, who also seized one destroyer, three torpedo boats, two dispatch boats and nine submarines handed over intact in the roadstead or in the harbor basin. This deplorable episode marked the end of a shameful series. From now on, with the exception of the "African Phalanx" that fought against the Allies side by side with the enemy, Vichy no longer controlled any of our arms in Africa. The few that remained were in the hands of soldiers who would know how to wield them in the service of France, some in Tunisia, the rest in Libya.

It was in fact with the co-operation of the Larminat Group that the British had opened their offensive against Rommel. In the brilliantly handled breakthrough effected on October 23 by Montgomery near El Alamein, the First Light Division, under Koenig, had been placed on the front's southern wing along the steep slopes of Himeimat. Fighting over difficult terrain and on a very wide front against a solidly entrenched enemy, this division endured serious losses, especially that of the valiant Amilakvari, killed at the head of the Legion. Several days later the Second Light Division, under Colonel Alessandri's command, and the armored column of Colonels Rémy and Kersauson participated briskly in the start of the pursuit undertaken by the Eighth Army. I had previously approved the use which was being made of our forces, but meanwhile the Anglo-American landing in Morocco and Algeria and the opening of the Tunisian front convinced me that it would be a mistake to let the Larminat Group exhaust itself at the present time. It would be wiser to enable it to take part in full force in the later phase of operations, the one that would see the juncture of the Allied armies from east and west, the reunion on French territory of our troops under the Cross of Lorraine with those of North

372   U N I T Y

Africa, and the destruction of the enemy on the shores of *mare nostrum.*

Therefore I had ratified the decision of the British command which, on November 10, had retired the Free French from the front in order to place them in reserve in the Tobruk region. Shortly afterward I accepted Larminat's proposal to form a line division by combining both light divisions. We soon had the possibility of swelling this magnificent unit to the striking power of three brigades —Brosset, Alessandri, Lelong—and to equip it with a complete artillery, thanks to the elements of arms of all kinds recovered at Djibouti. Thus the Free French First Division was constituted. Larminat and his troops, controlling their impatience, waited for the moment to re-enter the line, this time decisively, in the great Battle of Africa which had lasted for two years and in which our troops had never ceased to participate.

During this period we took the long-hoped-for occasion to conquer Fezzan and to bring to the fighting on the Mediterranean coast a French corps that had crossed the Sahara from Chad. The execution of this project, which I had determined on the very day that Éboué and Marchand joined us at Fort-Lamy, had been in preparation by Leclerc since 1940 by a series of tours de force: the formation of desert columns, the establishment of supply lines, the taking of Cufra, the advance of reconnaissance units into the heart of the Italian positions. The moment had come to risk everything in order to gain everything. On November 14, confirming my instructions of the preceding September 22, I ordered General Leclerc to open the offensive having "the French occupation of Fezzan as the first objective, with possible reconnoitering either toward Tripoli or toward Gabès in conjunction with the Allied operations in Tripolitania." I added, "For this offensive, you will be subordinate only to me. But you must act in agreement with General Alexander, British commander in chief for the Middle East, so that from the moment you reach Fezzan you can receive an increasingly extensive air support. . . . At the latest, I count on your launching the drive by the time the Allies have reached the Gulf of Sidra.

As a matter of fact, at the time of the Anglo-American landing in Algeria and Morocco, I had thought of effecting a breakthrough of our troops in southern Libya to coincide with their entry into the Niger and had given orders to push the column prepared for this mission as far as Zinder. But the conclusion of the struggle between the French and the Allies inclined me to suspend this secondary operation; only the main one would take place.

The latter was to include arduous preliminary action: the launching of the columns from the Chad bases, the long approach of about a thousand kilometers until we made contact with the enemy's fortified bases, the transportation to the site of fuel, munitions, supplies and matériel reserves on which the attack proper would depend. Since by the end of November Montgomery's offensive was progressing under good conditions and since the Allied front in Tunisia was well on the way to being established, I gave Leclerc orders to proceed on November 28, specifying that he was to launch his attack after the second of December on his own initiative and taking into consideration General Alexander's suggestions. But whatever the eagerness to cross swords with the enemy that animated Leclerc and his troops, their offensive did not begin until December 12 because of a halt in the Eighth Army advance level with El Agheila.

Meanwhile we had had to parry the British intention to extend their authority over Fezzan once we had conquered it. General Alexander had written Leclerc on November 28 to inform him that he was sending officers appointed to administer the occupied territory. These officers, the British commander in chief specified, "are delegated to accompany the forces under your command. They will be responsible for the territories occupied by you until the definitive co-ordination of all Tripolitania under British military authority can be established." Further, Alexander advised Leclerc that London's economic policy prohibited the use of francs as currency in Fezzan. On December 1 Mr. Charles Peake, upon whom, either in spite or because of his merit, fell the frequent burden of ungrateful tasks, came without illusions to bring me Mr. Eden's note to the same effect. I replied to Mr. Peake by as friendly a refusal as possible and telegraphed to General Leclerc: "Fezzan must be France's share in the battle of Africa. It is the geographical link between southern Tunisia and Chad. You must purely and simply decline all forms of British interference in this region, whether political, administrative, monetary, etc."

On December 22 the approach was finished, and the attack began. In two weeks of bitter fighting, the Ingold and Delange commands, making respectively toward Oum-el-Araneb and Gatrún and supported by the "Bretagne" air group, seized enemy positions after having knocked out their mobile columns. Dio, Massu, Geoffroy, Sarazac, D'Abzac and others covered themselves with glory and trophies. On January 12 the taking of Sebha opened the road to Tripoli. On the thirteenth the Murzuq base fell into our troops' hands. We had taken approximately a thousand prisoners, including forty officers, twenty big guns, a number of armored pieces and hundreds of mortars, machine guns and automatic arms. While Leclerc's troops were preparing to drive northward, Colonel Delange assumed the functions of military commander of Fezzan.

Thus by sheer audacity and ingenuity, this savory fruit of the desert was plucked at last. On January 13, 1943, I announced our success to the nation. "Perhaps," I said in my broadcast, "the effort of these splendid soldiers is some consolation for the misery of France. Yes—the long, hard ordeals of a rigorous preparation beneath the equatorial sun, the mortal fatigue of the columns launched across deserts of sand and stone, the exhausting flights of the air squadrons, the bloody engagements against enemy bases, highly trained troops and planes, all the fine, strong men who bore the brunt of this battle, from their young and glorious general to the most obscure soldier among them, have made it a humble gift fervently offered to the pain and the pride of France."

But if on a military level the outlook seemed to be brightening, politically it was darker than ever. At Carlton Gardens we were kept well informed, for among the military men, officials and journalists who came and went between Africa and England, many made it their duty to bring us messages and information. Further, certain Algerian and Moroccan "Gaullists," profiting by the general confusion, managed to join us.

We therefore knew that the fact that Darlan was being maintained in command was producing virulent local criticism. The Vichyists were shaken by the Marshal's formal repudiation; the "Gaullists" had rebelled against the "temporary expedient"; the prominent men who had negotiated with Murphy for Giraud's abortive accession found their hopes frustrated. Among the latter, several military men and officials received severe punitive sanction; General Béthouart, Colonel Magnan and Controller Gromand, arrested in Morocco on Noguès's orders, narrowly escaped the firing squad; with great difficulty Eisenhower had them transferred to Gibraltar. General Mast and Colonel Baril had been obliged to seek refuge in the Levant. In the Navy, the Air Force and the Army there was indignation at seeing Darlan profit by his about-face while the wrecks of ships and planes and the corpses of soldiers, for all of which losses he was responsible, were still being counted. Lastly, the fact that the Toulon fleet had just been scuttled rather than obey him caused many to feel that Darlan's presence at the head of things could henceforth offer nothing but disadvantages.

This state of affairs increased my eagerness to make contact with Algiers. The mission which I had originally asked Roosevelt's and Churchill's permission to send to Africa had not, of course, been permitted to depart, Washington and London invoking a thousand pretexts to prevent it. At the beginning of December I addressed myself to General Eisenhower, asking him to receive at Algiers General d'Astier de La Vigerie, appointed by me to assume all useful liaisons with the French leaders there. On this occasion as on several others afterward, I discovered on the American commander in chief's part a comprehension which the political pressures of his country refused me. He acceded to my request. It is true that Eisenhower, struck by the resistance he had encountered during the landing, distressed by the cabals of which too many Frenchmen made a spectacle before him, disturbed by the unrest he perceived among the people, was haunted by the fear of seeing this agitation turn into general disorder, compromising the security of his communications in the middle of the battle of Tunisia. Therefore my intention of finding common ground in North Africa with those worthy of consideration seemed to him to correspond to the common interest of the Allies.

General d'Astier reached Algiers on December 20. What he saw and heard there gave him the impression of a bitter conflict, smothered for better or worse by the police machinery with which the authority had surrounded itself, but straining against its restrictions.

He found General Giraud annoyed at not having been able to persuade the Army to follow him at the moment of the landing, embittered by the Americans' refusal of his request that the Allied command be entrusted to him, humiliated at having duties only by virtue of Darlan's decisions. His discontent made him accessible to our suggestions. When my envoy invited him to come to an agreement with Fighting France, notably in connection with the co-ordination of military operations and the recruiting of troops, Giraud indicated his willingness to co-operate.

The Count of Paris, arriving from Morocco, informed General d'Astier how serious and harmful to the interests of France the situation seemed to him. Nothing, he declared, was more necessary, more urgent, than to dismiss the Admiral and then to unite all Frenchmen of good will. He himself was in Algiers to gather his followers together, to use them for the union's advantages, and to offer himself for any arbitration that might be asked of him. Moreover, this prince showed himself to be as disinterested as possible in what, should the occasion arise, would be most to his own interest.

As for Monsieur Lemaigre-Dubreuil, he did not conceal the fact that he, like his friends, was embittered by not being appointed to the command posts which, he claimed, his political capacities and the services he had rendered to the Americans deserved. Under the aegis of General Giraud, who was to have become head of the state following Monsieur Lemaigre-Dubreuil, he declared himself ready to assume the presidency of the Council in a coalition government and to entrust to General de Gaulle the portfolio of National Defense.

Further, D'Astier was informed that the local political circles, long silent and resigned, were being reawakened by the tornado. On November 24 Messrs. Saurin, Froger and Deyron, presidents respectively of the general councils of Oran, Algiers and Constantine, joined by an Algerian deputy, Monsieur Sarda, had written to Darlan:

> By placing yourself under the authority of the Marshal, whom you nevertheless recognized as not free to act, and by assuming the functions of a delegate of his government in North Africa, you are fulfilling none of the conditions that would confer upon you the powers of a legal and independent government.

Finally, among the Americans, my representative noted that even while collaborating with Admiral Darlan, Eisenhower and his General Staff affirmed that the High Commission must be only a transitional phase and stressed their desire to enter into direct relations with General de Gaulle.

As for the crowd of those who, for various motives, had joined the resistance under Vichy, some of whom had given assistance to the Allied intervention and now found themselves persecuted as much as ever, General d'Astier pointed out that they were secretly a prey to the most violent disturbance. His brother Henri, who occupied an important post on the High Commission, as well as Professor Capitant, leader of the Combat movement in North Africa, and many other informed visitors described the atmosphere of conspiracy in which these resistance elements were steeped and which at any moment might precipitate some bloody incident.

Strongly affected by this total picture and encouraged by Mr. Murphy, General d'Astier agreed to an interview with Darlan. He had expected that their meeting would be a private one, but found the Admiral surrounded by an Areopagus among which, in particular, were Generals Giraud and Bergeret. Every man looked gloomy, strained, full of suspicion and complaints. Darlan, visibly exhausted but eager, probably, to encourage his entourage, felt that he must attitudinize before my envoy. He declared that he had matters well in hand, that the necessity of forcing the French to unity was foremost in his mind, that in order to facilitate it he himself was agreeing to amnesty those who, since the armistice, had assisted the Allies and to make public his intention to retire as soon as the war was over, but that in the meantime he represented the only possible rallying point. This simulacrum of assurance contrasted too cruelly with the realities of the situation, the nervousness the Admiral himself betrayed and the atmosphere that surrounded him, for anyone to be deceived by it.

D'Astier said as much to Darlan, not without giving an account of public opinion in France, where he had just been. Then the Admiral, carried away, reproached him for being at Algiers and for stirring up trouble.

"Is that your opinion," D'Astier asked Giraud, "when I am expecting your answer to General de Gaulle's proposal to co-ordinate the operation of the troops under your orders with that of the forces of Fighting France?"

Giraud having remarked that he was ready to settle the question, Darlan interrupted dryly, "No, General. This is my affair."

There followed a profound silence. Ending this painful scene, General d'Astier told the Admiral quite bluntly that it was his presence which was the chief obstacle to unity and that he could do nothing better than stand aside at once.

Following this meeting, the Americans informed D'Astier that Darlan was insisting that he leave Algiers and that they agreed. D'Astier returned to London on December 24. From his sojourn at Algiers he was convinced that Darlan, feeling the ground give way beneath him, would shortly abandon his position.

On the afternoon of the same day, leaving a Christmas-tree-lighting ceremony for our sailors, I learned of Admiral Darlan's death. The man who had killed him, Fernand Bonnier de la Chapelle, had made himself the instrument of the aggravated passions that had fired the souls around him to the boiling point but behind which, perhaps, moved a policy determined to liquidate a "temporary expedient" after having made use of him. This young man, this child overwhelmed by the spectacle of odious events, thought his action would be a service to his lacerated country, would remove from the road to French reconciliation an obstacle shameful in his eyes. He believed, moreover, as he repeatedly said until the moment of his execution, that an intervention would be made in his behalf by some outside source so high and powerful that the North African authorities could not refuse to obey it. Of course no individual has the right to kill save on the field of battle. Moreover, Darlan's behavior, as a governor and as a leader, was answerable to national justice, not, certainly, to that of a group or an individual. Yet how could we fail to recognize the nature of the intentions that inspired this juvenile fury? That is why the strange, brutal and summary way the investigation was conducted in Algiers, the hasty and abbreviated trial before a military tribunal convened at night and in private session, the immediate and secret execution of Fernand Bonnier de la Chapelle, the orders given to the censors that not even his name should be known—all these led to the suspicion that someone wanted to conceal at any price the origin of his decision and constituted a kind of defiance of those circumstances which, without justifying the drama, explained and, to a certain degree, excused it.

Nevertheless, if the tragic character of Darlan's disappearance from the scene could not fail to be condemned by many, the very fact that he was forced from the stage seemed in accord with the harsh logic of events. For history, in its great moments, tolerates in positions of authority only those men capable of directing their own course. Yet at the point that matters had reached, Darlan could neither contribute to nor diminish, could no longer affect what was about to happen in any case. Everyone—and the Admiral first of all—realized that for him the page had now been turned.

He had missed his chance. In 1940 the Navy had found itself, in effect, in a position to play the leading national role, whereas for centuries the continental destiny of France had maintained it as a secondary power. Amid the military collapse of metropolitan France, it was, by chance, intact. At that moment the oceans, the distances and the speed that were the elements of its destiny became all-important. It had at its disposal the Empire, also unimpaired. The Allies, threatened by sea, would not have haggled for its co-operation. Combining its force with theirs, it could obstruct and hamper the enemy, cover and command Africa, transport there the means necessary to the liberating army, and, one day, return the latter to our own shores. But for such a task it would have required of its leader, beyond the taste for risk, a national passion that desired to serve only France whatever might happen to the fleet. This Darlan did not possess.

His ambitions, his efforts had been dedicated to the Navy, but to the Navy alone. In the atony of the nation, the state's lack of firmness during which almost the whole of his professional life had been led, it was this great force which exclusively absorbed his interest, his inclination and his skill. He had been able, in peacetime, to convince public authority by his ardor and expertise to build a well-equipped navy, but as a fief that existed only through him and on his account alone.

When France was defeated, what seemed of prime importance to Darlan was that the Navy should not be defeated. When the surrender was concluded, it was enough for him, to accept it, to believe that the Navy would remain beyond the reach of the disaster. When the conflict, now world-wide, multiplied the fleet's occasions to be the nation's unlooked-for recourse, his goal was not to engage but rather to preserve it. It was in the fleet's name that he wanted to become chief of the Vichy government; it was in hopes of assuring it a field of action and a *raison d'être* that despite the subjection exacted by the enemy he repeatedly gave orders to fight the "Gaullists" and the Allies; it was because he wanted to continue what he felt to be an essentially naval dispute that he persisted in collaboration with the German invader against England. In his ultimate decision to call off the battle waged by his orders on the shores of Africa against the Anglo-American forces, what carried the most weight in his soul? Was it the belated passion to overcome his country's invader, or rather the hope of recovering the scattered fragments of the fleet by changing camps? But when at Toulon, at Fort-de-France and at Alexandria the sailors refused to listen to him, and when at Casablanca, at Oran and at Bizerte the ships were nothing more than wrecks, Admiral Darlan knew that if France was going to win the war, he himself had lost his own battle.

France, without a great navy, could not remain France. But this Navy had to be hers. It depends on the governing powers to form it, to inspire it, to employ it as an instrument of the national interest. Unfortunately this was just what the regime which for so many, many years had floated upon the nation's surface without directing its vital forces did not know how to do. In my eyes, the outrage at Algiers illuminated in its turn the principal cause of our afflictions. Like other notorious misfortunes that had rained down upon France, Admiral Darlan's faults, the sad fate of our fleet and the fathomless wound inflicted upon the spirit of our sailors were the consequences of a long disease of the state.

CHAPTER 3

COMEDY

D ARLAN's disappearance from the scene was of great consequence to French unity. I would have to turn it to my advantage. On December 25 I telegraphed General Giraud that the outrage in Algiers was "a symbol and a warning," and that now more
than ever it was necessary to establish a national authority. Then I
wrote:

> I propose, General, that we meet as soon as possible
> on French territory, either in Algeria or in Chad. We will
> study ways that might enable us to concentrate under a pro-
> visional central power all the forces of both metropolitan
> France and her overseas territories that are capable of join-
> ing the struggle for the liberation and the welfare of France.

I was in haste to send this message because I wanted to point up
the fact that we had no right to delay once a possibility of agreement presented itself; I addressed it to General Giraud because I
believed he would be Darlan's successor. The way was now clear
for the Americans to establish at Algiers the very man they had
chosen at the outset and whose accession the Admiral's presence
had delayed. As for the necessary formalities, they depended only
on the "Imperial Council," that is, on Noguès, Boisson, Chatel and

Bergeret, all apparently ready to do Eisenhower's and Murphy's bidding. On December 26, in fact, General Giraud was invested with the powers and the rather astonishing title of "Civil and Military Commander in Chief." If he accepted my proposition, if we met unhampered by the intrigues and the foreign influences that surrounded us, if we offered an example of co-operation to those who wanted to drive the enemy from our country, then the foundation of a wartime government capable of asserting itself might be laid at once and long months of disorganization might be avoided. But, aside from the grudges and the pretensions of certain Frenchmen who happened to be on the spot, the Allied desire to keep the authority in North Africa under their control and to prevent France from reappearing as a sovereign power before the end of the war was to delay the triumph of national common sense.

The reply General Giraud sent me on December 29 was dilatory indeed. After expressing his agreement as to the need for French unity, he resorted, in order to postpone it, to the same motive I had invoked to hasten it. He wrote that as a result "of the disturbance the recent assassination has caused in both civil and military circles in North Africa . . . the atmosphere is at present unfavorable to a meeting between us." In regard to the military situation, however, he offered as his own, though not without somewhat modifying it, the suggestion I had originally made to him through General d'Astier to organize a reciprocal liaison: "I think that so far as you are concerned, it would be preferable to send me a qualified representative to help co-ordinate the French forces engaged in the struggle against the common enemy."

Obviously I could not put up with this evasive attitude. No sooner had I received General Giraud's answer than I telegraphed my reply, on January 1. In this second message I expressed satisfaction "that a first exchange of views has taken place between us." But I declared that "the unification of the Empire as a whole and of all French forces in contact with the resistance must not be postponed. . . . My conviction," I wrote, "is that only a provisional central power, based on national unity in the war effort, can ensure the leadership of the French forces, the complete maintenance of French sovereignty and the equitable representation of France abroad." I then renewed my offer of a meeting and added: "I am quite aware of the complexity of the situation in Algiers. But we can meet without hindrance either in Fort-Lamy, in Brazzaville or in Beirut, as you prefer. I confidently await your reply."

Even as I was drafting these appeals for unity, I strongly doubted the result such telegrams could have. It was not to be hoped that secret documents, minutely examined in Algiers under the surveillance of Anglo-American agents, would suffice to raise the great wind capable of sweeping away controversies and oppositions. Therefore I wanted to speak directly to French public opinion, hoping as a last resort that its pressure would be irresistible. On January 2 I made a public statement, calling upon the nation as my witness.

It happened that a serious incident which had occurred in Algiers two days before reinforced my arguments. Giraud had had several dozen people arrested, of whom all had aided the Americans during the landing and several held positions in the police or the administration. The "Civil and Military Commander in Chief" explained to the Allied newspapermen who flocked to his press conference that he was heading off a conspiracy aiming at new murders, particularly, he said, "that of Mr. Robert Murphy." It seemed, in fact, that certain disillusioned individuals who had hitherto been connected with the activities of the American diplomat now wanted to settle accounts. I therefore had a splendid opportunity to emphasize in my statement the confusion reigning in French North Africa. I accounted for it chiefly by the exclusion of Fighting France and detailed the consequences: "A difficult situation . . . for military operations; the fact that France is now deprived, at the crucial moment, of the trump card which the unity of her vast Empire would constitute . . . ; the stupefaction of the French people, overwhelmed in its misery . . ." I indicated the remedy: "the establishment . . . of an extensive provisional central power, having for its foundation national unity, for its inspiration the spirit of

combat and of liberation, and for its laws the laws of the Republic."
I also formally made known my offer to meet with Giraud and my
conviction that "France's situation and that of the war in general"
permitted no delay.

This declaration and the comment it aroused touched Washington at a sensitive point. It was disagreeable for the American government to have the distance separating its doctrines from its practices so publicly measured. As soon as it was known that I was
proposing an agreement with Giraud and that he was putting off
accepting it, everyone realized that his attitude was a direct reflection of Murphy's suggestions. How, therefore, avoid the conclusion
that the Americans, while preaching unity, were doing everything
they could to oppose it?

As a matter of fact, President Roosevelt, under cover of proclamations to the contrary, intended that French affairs should fall
within his own sphere of influence, that the leading strings of our
divisions should end up in his hands, and that the public powers
eventually emerging from this disorder should derive from his arbitration. That is why he had bet on both De Gaulle and Pétain at
the start, then launched Giraud onto the track when a rupture with
the Marshal was inevitable, then lowered the barrier in front of
Darlan as soon as Giraud's failure was apparent, and finally put
Giraud back on the track after the Admiral's assassination. Now
the President found it convenient to keep Fighting France and the
system at Algiers separate until the moment when he himself would
impose on both parties the solution of his choice, which, furthermore, would certainly not be the formation of a true French government.

Of course I was not unaware of Roosevelt's intentions, and I was
therefore not surprised to learn that my declaration had been taken
in bad part by Washington. On January 4 Undersecretary of State
Sumner Welles, receiving our delegate Tixier, informed him that
his government disapproved of my invitations to Giraud and the
publicity they had received, because in them I had given primacy
to political problems. When Tixier asked why this should seem

troublesome, the American diplomat alleged once again the exigencies of the military situation, as if the agreement proposed by De Gaulle threatened Eisenhower's communications in North Africa!

I had had implicit proof that the President had decided to intervene on the spot when, the day after Darlan's death, the Americans requested me to postpone my forthcoming trip to Washington. Yet Roosevelt himself, after the landing of his troops in Africa, had had me asked to visit him. Apparently everything was arranged for this visit: I was to leave on December 27, reaching Accra by plane and there boarding an American cruiser that would take me to the United States. Admiral Stark preceded me, having left London on December 20 to clear the routes. General Catroux, appointed to accompany me, had reached Accra from Beirut on the twenty-fourth. But that day Darlan was assassinated, and at the same time the President's new policy of intervention became evident. I immediately recognized the switch, for on the twenty-sixth Mr. Churchill, obviously acting in Mr. Roosevelt's behalf, asked me whether, in view of the circumstances, I did not think it advisable to postpone my departure. The next day the American government sent me a note to the same effect.

I was therefore convinced of the reasons influencing Giraud to ask for delays. His answer to my second message, which reached me on January 6, completed my enlightenment. He agreed with me in principle as to a meeting in Algiers and no longer spoke, on this occasion, of the unfavorable atmosphere created by Darlan's death. But invoking "previous commitments," he said he could see no possibility of a meeting before the end of January. I then replied, this time somewhat bluntly:

> I regret that your previous engagements should force you to postpone until the end of January the meeting I suggested to you on December 25. I must tell you frankly that the National Committee and I myself have an altogether different sense of the urgency which the unification of the Empire and the union of its efforts with those of the national resistance demand.

But while I was expecting a reaction from Mr. Roosevelt, it was Mr. Churchill who suddenly made a move. On January 17 Mr. Eden sent me a telegram which the Prime Minister had addressed to me from Morocco. Mr. Churchill asked me to join him there, writing that he might be able to arrange for a meeting between Giraud and me in conditions of complete privacy and under the most favorable auspices.

My reaction was unfavorable. Doubtless Mr. Eden intended me to understand that Mr. Roosevelt was also in Morocco, where the Allied leaders were holding a conference in order to determine their joint plans. But why, then, had Churchill neglected to tell me so? Why did he not assign any other goal to the invitation than a meeting with Giraud? Why was this invitation sent to me in his name alone? If I must go to the Anfa conference to enter a race wearing the British colors while the Americans backed their own entry against me, the resulting comedy would be indecent, not to mention dangerous. My reply to Churchill was negative. It was dispatched to him at the same time as a message I addressed to Giraud: "Remember that I am still prepared to meet you on French territory, as one Frenchman to another, when and where you choose."

Two days later Eden sent me another telegram from Churchill, who, pained by my refusal—all the more so since he had had to endure it under American eyes—urged me to reconsider the question. If I did not do so, he declared, public opinion would be very severe toward me, and he himself would do nothing more to aid Fighting France vis-à-vis the United States as long as I remained at the head of the "movement." But this time he declared he was authorized to inform me that the invitation to the conference had been addressed to me by the President of the United States as well as by himself, that questions concerning North Africa would be those primarily under discussion, and that the President, like himself, would be happy to have me participate in the talks on these subjects.

Without paying much attention to the threats in this message—

which, after many such experiences, no longer affected me very strongly—I decided that the circumstances of the war and France's immediate situation did not permit me to refuse to meet the President of the United States and His Britannic Majesty's Prime Minister. It was in such terms that I finally drafted my acceptance, calling attention to the fact that the questions which were to be discussed were the result of an enterprise in which Fighting France was not taking part and which, it seemed, had "led to a situation scarcely satisfactory for the Allies and . . . not at all so for France."

Before dispatching my reply, I formally convoked the National Committee, which after an exhaustive study of the question agreed that I should go to Anfa, if only to see Roosevelt there in person. We purposely took some time over our deliberations, and afterward I made no particular haste to begin my trip with my designated colleagues: Catroux, D'Argenlieu, Palewski (now chief of my personal staff) and Hettier de Boislambert (recently arrived from France after escaping from the Gannat prison, where Vichy had incarcerated him because of his role in the Dakar affair). At the last moment, bad weather conditions delayed our departure still further. We did not arrive at Fedala until January 22.

We were received in great secrecy by the American General Wilbur, whom I had previously known at the École Supérieure de Guerre and who greeted me in behalf of President Roosevelt, by Mr. Codrington, who brought me Mr. Churchill's compliments, and by Colonel de Linarès, sent by General Giraud to invite us to lunch. No troops presented honors, although American sentries maintained a wide periphery around us. Some American cars drove up next to the plane. I stepped into the first one. Wilbur, before getting in with me, dipped a rag in the mud and smeared all the windows. These precautions were taken in order to conceal the presence of General de Gaulle and his colleagues in Morocco.

At Anfa the Allies had requisitioned a group of villas, all of whose inhabitants had been billeted elsewhere; even the houses surrounding those we were to occupy had been emptied. A barbed-wire fence encircled the conference area. American sentries were posted both inside and outside this circle, and no one was permitted to enter or to leave. American soldiers were assigned to household tasks in everyone's lodgings. In short, it was captivity. I had no objection to the Anglo-American leaders' imposing it on themselves, but the fact that they were applying it to me, and furthermore on territory under French sovereignty, seemed to me a flagrant insult.

My first words to General Giraud were therefore something less than cordial. "What's this?" I said to him. "I ask you for an interview four times over and we have to meet in a barbed-wire encampment among foreign powers? Don't you realize how odious this is from purely a national point of view?"

Giraud, embarrassed, replied that he had not been free to act otherwise. I had, in fact, suspected as much, given the circumstances in which he had put himself in regard to the Americans.

Nevertheless, the meal was a cordial one. We discussed experiences we had shared, and at my request our host recounted his extraordinary escape from Koenigstein. But once we had left the table, General Giraud spoke of other matters. He repeated with insistence that he gave his attention solely to military matters, that he did not wish to concern himself with political questions, that he never listened to anyone who tried to interest him in a theory or a program, that he never read a newspaper or turned on the radio. Whether it was as a result of his convictions or in consequence of prior commitments, he declared himself on the side of the "proconsuls"—Noguès, "indispensable to Morocco"; Boisson, "who was able to defend his colony against every foreign attack, even that of Germany"; Peyrouton, recently arrived to replace Chatel in the Algerian government-general and "a man with a fist"; Bergeret, "the one strategic mind of the lot." He did not conceal the fact that apart from his determination—unquestionably resolute—to join battle with the Germans, he had nothing against the Vichy regime. He indicated, lastly, that the elementary, popular, revolutionary character of the resistance in France was incomprehensible if not reprehensible to him. After this first conversation, I left Giraud's villa for my own.

Later in the afternoon, while I kept to my quarters with calculated reserve, I received a visit from Mr. Macmillan, the British
Secretary of State assigned to Algiers to co-ordinate British affairs in the western Mediterranean. Macmillan indicated that, in
co-operation with Murphy, he was doing his best to find a formula
for unity acceptable to both Giraud and myself which could be
proposed to us by Roosevelt and Churchill. Here indeed was the
expected intervention. I explained to Macmillan that a Giraud-de
Gaulle entente could be realized only between Frenchmen. Nevertheless, at the British minister's urgent request, I went to Churchill's
quarters.

On first meeting the Prime Minister, I told him in no uncertain
terms that I would never have come had I known I was to be surrounded, on French territory, by American bayonets.

"This is an occupied country!" he cried.

Both of us having relieved our feelings somewhat, we began to
discuss fundamental questions. The Prime Minister informed me
that he had come to an agreement with the President on a projected solution of the problem of the French Empire. Generals
Giraud and De Gaulle would be established as joint presidents of a
governing committee on which they themselves, as well as all the
other members, would enjoy equal status in every respect. But
Giraud would exercise supreme military command, especially since
the United States, having to provide the reunified French Army with
matériel, did not intend to deal with anyone else. "Undoubtedly,"
Mr. Churchill remarked, "my friend General Georges could make
your group complete in the capacity of a third president." As for
Noguès, Boisson, Peyrouton and Bergeret, they would retain their
positions and sit on the committee. "The Americans, in fact, have
now accepted them and want them to be trusted."

I replied to Mr. Churchill that this solution might appear adequate at the quite respectable level of an American sergeant, but
that I did not dream he himself could take it seriously. As for
me, I was obliged to take into account what remained of France's
sovereignty. I had, as he must know, the highest consideration for

him and for Roosevelt, without, however, recognizing in any respect their authority to deal with questions of sovereignty within the French Empire. The Allies had, without me, against me, instituted the system now in operation in Algiers. Apparently finding it of only middling satisfaction, they were now planning to swamp Fighting France in it too. But Fighting France would not play their game; if it must disappear, it preferred to do so honorably.

Mr. Churchill did not seem to grasp the moral aspect of the problem. "Look here," he said. "Consider my own government. When I recently formed it, appointed as I was for having fought so long against the spirit of Munich, I constituted within it all our most notorious Munich partisans. Well, they followed along so well that today you can't tell them from the rest."

"To speak that way," I replied, "you must have lost sight of what has happened to France. As for me, I am not a politician trying to make up a cabinet and find a majority in Parliament."

The Prime Minister urged me nevertheless to reconsider the project he had just explained to me. "Tonight," he added, "you will confer with the President of the United States, and you will see that we are both firmly resolved on this matter."

He accompanied me as far as the garden gate, where a British sentry presented arms. "Please observe," he remarked, "that if there are American sentries here, there are also British soldiers side by side and co-operating with them."

A little later, Mr. Roosevelt sent someone to arrange our meeting, to which I went late that evening. We spent an hour together sitting on the same couch, in a large room of the villa where he was quartered. Although my interlocutor affected to be alone in my company, I noticed shadows at the rear of a balcony and saw curtains moving in the corners. I learned later that Mr. Harry Hopkins and several secretaries were listening without revealing themselves and that armed police were guarding the President. Because of these indistinct presences, the atmosphere of our first discussion was a strange one. That evening, as on every occasion when I saw him afterward, Roosevelt showed himself eager to reach a meeting of minds, using charm rather than reason to convince me, but attached once and for all to the decisions he had made.

Franklin Roosevelt was governed by the loftiest ambitions. His intelligence, his knowledge and his audacity gave him the ability, the powerful state of which he was the leader afforded him the means, and the war offered him the occasion to realize them. If the great nation he directed had long been inclined to isolate itself from distant enterprises and to mistrust a Europe ceaselessly lacerated by wars and revolutions, a kind of messianic impulse now swelled the American spirit and oriented it toward vast undertakings. The United States, delighting in her resources, feeling that she no longer had within herself sufficient scope for her energies, wishing to help those who were in misery or bondage the world over, yielded in her turn to that taste for intervention in which the instinct for domination cloaked itself. It was precisely this tendency that President Roosevelt espoused. He had therefore done everything to enable his country to take part in the world conflict. He was now fulfilling his destiny, impelled as he was by the secret admonition of death.

But from the moment America entered the war, Roosevelt meant the peace to be an American peace, convinced that he must be the one to dictate its structure, that the states which had been overrun should be subject to his judgment, and that France in particular should recognize him as its savior and its arbiter. Therefore the fact that France was reviving in the heat of battle, not in terms of a fragmentary and hence convenient resistance but as a sovereign and independent nation, thwarted his intentions. Politically he felt no inclination toward me—all the less since he found himself ceaselessly criticized by public opinion in his own country. It was America that conferred his power upon him, but she could also deprive him of that same power; during the course of the war Roosevelt twice had to submit to elections, and during the intervals the press, the radio and every sort of special interest harassed the President. Diligent at charming others, but hampered deep within himself by the painful infirmity against which he struggled so valiantly, Roosevelt was sensitive to partisan reproaches and gibes. Yet it was precisely his policy in regard to General de Gaulle that aroused the fiercest controversies in America. It must be added that like any star performer he was touchy as to the roles that fell to other actors. In short, beneath his patrician mask of courtesy, Roosevelt regarded me without benevolence.

That evening we set to with a will, but by mutual agreement we maintained a certain vagueness on the question of France: he sketching lightly the same figure Churchill had outlined so heavily and gently permitting me to understand that such a solution would ultimately be adopted because he himself had decided upon it; I as delicately indicating that the national will had already made its choice and that, sooner or later, the authority established in the Empire and ultimately in metropolitan France would be the one France chose for herself. Nevertheless, we took care not to meet head on, realizing that the clash would lead to nothing and that, for the sake of the future, we each had much to gain by getting along together.

The following day I received General Giraud. We spoke together quite openly, quite alone. "What do you intend to do?" I asked him.

He explained his plan, which was, on the whole, that of Messrs. Roosevelt and Churchill. There would be three of us at the top: he first of all, I second, and General Georges, whom the British would send for from France, third. So that we might enjoy equal status, I would be named General of the Army! But Giraud would keep military control entirely for himself; he would be commander in chief of the French forces, including those of Free France and the armed elements of the resistance, and in this capacity he would be subordinate only to Eisenhower. The "proconsuls" would remain at their posts; only Bergeret might be discarded. An "Imperial Council," including Noguès, Boisson and Peyrouton, to whom Catroux and perhaps Éboué might be added, as well as several "secretaries," would co-ordinate the administration of the Empire's territories, but without exercising any political action.

I regarded Giraud's conception as unacceptable. "What you suggest," I told him, "boils down to appropriating the real power to yourself under Roosevelt's protection while establishing beside you a more or less impressive collection of supernumeraries. Actually, it's the Consulate at the mercy of foreign powers. But Bonaparte, as First Consul, during the war and the subsequent period of independence obtained virtually unanimous approval from the people. What kind of plebiscite do you envisage? If you hold one, will it be in your favor? Besides, Bonaparte presented himself as a leader who had showered France with great victories and conquered vast provinces. I hope with all my heart that you will do as much. But for the moment, what are your triumphs? I might add that the First Consul excelled in legislative and administrative affairs. Are these really your aptitudes? Furthermore, you are not unaware that in France public opinion will henceforth condemn Vichy. Yet it is from Darlan first of all, then from Noguès, Boisson, Chatel and Bergeret that you derive your powers. It is in the Marshal's name that you have assumed them. Everyone knows of your letter to Pétain in which you gave your word you would never act against his policies. Do you think that under these conditions you will obtain that elementary adherence of the French people without which a government is nothing but a fiction unless it becomes, in fact, the target of a revolution? Lastly, considering the dependent position in which the artificial nature of your authority keeps you in relation to the Anglo-American powers, how will you safeguard French interests?"

General Giraud declared once more that these were political matters; that he had no desire to concern himself with such things; that for him the question was simply to re-create the French Army; that he had full confidence in our American allies. "I have just signed an agreement with President Roosevelt," he said, "by virtue of which the United States is committed to equip as many units as I can constitute. I intend to have a dozen divisions at my disposal within six months. As for you, will you have even half as many in the same period of time? And who will give you weapons for them?"

"The question is not one of a rivalry between us in the area of fighting strength," I replied. "The troops in North Africa at the present time belong to France. They are not your possession. You will soon find this out for yourself if we fail to reach an agreement. The problem is one of French unity within the Empire and within metropolitan France, calling for the institution of a central authority that answers these needs. Once this is done, the various forces will be unified and utilized without difficulty. Events have brought it to pass that Fighting France symbolizes resistance against the enemy, the upholding of the Republic, the rivival of the nation. It is to Fighting France that popular feeling naturally turns at the moment when the illusion that was Vichy is on the point of dissolution. Further, many esteem you highly as a military leader. I myself consider you, in this regard, as a French asset that I should be extremely unwilling to lose. The common-sense solution therefore consists of the following: that De Gaulle should form at Algiers a wartime government which, at the appropriate moment, will become that of the Republic; that Giraud should receive from this government the command of the army of liberation. If necessary, should a transition seem mandatory, we constitute the central authority jointly. But from the very first this central authority must condemn Vichy, proclaim that the armistice was always null and void, and identify itself with the Republic and, in the eyes of the world, with the independence of France."

General Giraud held to his point of view. Nevertheless, realizing that he was stubborn rather than actually convinced, I continued to hope that the pressure of events would ultimately lead him to change his mind. Meanwhile problems of national interest required concerted solutions. This was the case in regard to military action, finances, exchange, currency, the fate of Tunisia and of Indochina, the allegiance of the Antilles and French Guiana and of the Alexandria fleet. We therefore agreed to establish a reciprocal liaison.

I announced my intention to send a mission to North Africa with General Catroux at its head; to this Giraud immediately agreed, after which he and his staff took lunch at our table. Catroux, D'Argenlieu, Palewski and Boislambert, as well as Linarès, Beaufre and Poniatowski, already informed by their contacts, learned without surprise though not without disappointment that no agreement had been reached. The luncheon was a gloomy one.

Mr. Robert Murphy later paid me a visit. He seemed convinced that everything would turn out according to the plans he himself had formulated. When I indicated my doubts and asked him what he thought the public reaction would be in Morocco and Algeria when it was learned that no agreement had been reached at Anfa, he answered that many would be satisfied and even relieved. "North Africa," he added, "is not ten per cent Gaullist." He confirmed the fact that President Roosevelt and Mr. Churchill had just signed an agreement with General Giraud providing for certain deliveries of weapons and supplies to North Africa—which I approved unreservedly—but, on the other hand, according the "Civil and Military Commander in Chief" a recognition that, until now, had been neither formulated by the United States nor accepted by Great Britain. The agreement specified:

> In the interest of the French people, and in order to safeguard the past, the present, and the future of France, the President of the United States and the Prime Minister of Great Britain recognize that the French commander in chief, whose headquarters are at Algiers, has the right and the duty to act as director of the French military, economic and financial interests which are or will be associated with the liberation movement now established in North Africa and in French West Africa. They pledge themselves to aid him in this task by every means in their power.

Thus America and England, appointing themselves arbiters of the interests of the French people, were dealing with General Giraud only, and he, under pretext of not playing politics, accepted their authority. I learned that Mr. Churchill had of his own accord, while talking with Giraud the day before, written on a corner of the table that the pound sterling would be worth 250 French francs in North Africa. According to the agreements we had made with London, it was worth only 176 francs. I also learned that President Roosevelt had entertained the Sultan of Morocco at dinner and had spoken to him in terms that did not tally well with the French protectorate, without Giraud's finding anything in this to criticize.

In the evening came Mr. Harold Macmillan to confront me with a tirade of concern as to the future of Fighting France. Lastly, General Wilbur informed me that the conference would be over within twenty-four hours and delivered messages which the French officers on duty in Casablanca had asked him to transmit to me. I requested that he inform his superiors how strange it seemed to me that during the height of the Battle of North Africa, in which the French Army—including Free French forces—was participating heavily, none of the Allied military authorities assembled for the Anfa conference had considered it pertinent to say the least word to me about either plans or operations.

Early the next day, Macmillan and Murphy sent me a communiqué drawn up during the night by Messrs. Roosevelt and Churchill which the latter asked Generals de Gaulle and Giraud to authorize and make public. Giraud had already agreed to do so. According to this Anglo-American text, which was now to become French, the two generals would proclaim themselves in agreement "with the principles of the Allied Nations" and announce their intention of forming a joint committee to administer the French Empire during the war. Certainly the formula was too vague to commit us to much, but it had the triple disadvantage of being dictated by the Allies, of implying that I renounced whatever was not merely the administration of the Empire, and lastly of giving the impression that an agreement had been reached when in reality no such thing had occurred. After having ascertained the opinion—unanimously negative—of all four of my colleagues, I informed the messengers that enlargement of the French national authority could not come as a result of the intervention of a foreign power, no matter how high and how friendly. Nevertheless, I agreed to see the President and the Prime Minister before the conference was concluded the next afternoon.

My meeting with Mr. Churchill was characterized, on his part, by extreme acrimony. Of all our encounters during the war, this was the most ungracious. In the course of a furious scene the Prime Minister showered me with bitter reproaches in which I could see nothing but an alibi for his own embarrassment. He declared that on his return to London he would publicly accuse me of having obstructed the agreement, would rouse public opinion in his country against me personally and would appeal to the people of France. I confined myself to replying that my friendship for him and my attachment to our alliance with Britain caused me to deplore such an attitude on his part. In order to satisfy America at any cost, he was espousing a cause unacceptable to France, disquieting to Europe, regrettable for England.

I then went to see Roosevelt. My reception at his hands was a skillful one—that is, kind and sorrowful. The President expressed his disappointment that French support should remain uncertain and that he himself had not been able to prevail upon me to accept even the text of a communiqué. "In human affairs," he said, "the public must be offered a drama. The news of your meeting with General Giraud in the midst of a conference in which both Churchill and I were taking part, if this news were to be accompanied by a joint declaration of the French leaders—even if it concerned only a theoretical agreement—would produce the dramatic effect we need."

"Let me handle it," I replied. "There will be a communiqué, even though it cannot be yours."

Thereupon I presented my colleagues to the President; he introduced me to his. Then Mr. Churchill, General Giraud and their suites came in, followed by a crowd of military leaders and Allied officials. While they were all gathering around the President, Churchill loudly reiterated his diatribe against me with the evident intention of flattering Roosevelt's somewhat disappointed vanity. The latter affected to pay no attention, adopting instead the kindest manner in order to make me a last request on which he had his heart set.

"Will you at least agree," he said, "to being photographed beside me and the British Prime Minister, along with General Giraud?"

"Of course," I answered, "for I have the highest regard for this great soldier."

"Will you go so far as to shake General Giraud's hand before the camera?" the President cried.

My answer, in English, was, "I shall do that for you."

Then Mr. Roosevelt, delighted, had himself carried into the garden, where four chairs had been prepared beforehand, with innumerable cameras trained on them and several rows of reporters lined up with their pencils poised. The four actors put on their smiles. The agreed-upon gestures were made. Everything went off perfectly! America would be satisfied, on such evidence, that the French question had found its *deus ex machina* in the person of the President.

Before leaving Anfa, I drafted a short communiqué which I submitted to Giraud without, of course, having let the Allies get wind of it. It began, "We have seen each other. We have spoken together," and went on to affirm our faith in the victory of France and in the triumph of human liberties, and to announce the establishment of a permanent liaison between us. Giraud signed. On his request I substituted "human liberties" for the expression "democratic principles" which I had written originally.

The weeks that followed were painful ones. I had thought that after Anfa I would go to Libya, where our troops were fighting. But the Allies opposed this intention. Alleging technical difficulties, they permitted us no other means of leaving the Anfa enclosure than a British plane flying directly to London. We returned on January 26. During a press conference on February 9, I made clear that what had actually happened at Anfa bore little resemblance to what the Anglo-American sources had publicized. I emphasized strongly the real motives of the American officials and opinion-mongers who reproached Fighting France for "playing politics" and thereby hoped to keep France from having any of her own. Subsequently, when I again voiced my intention of going to the Middle East, the British government informed me on March 3, this time in writing, that it was refusing me the means to do so.

The contest of ill will in which London and Washington were engaged found its widespread echo in the press and on the radio. With a few noble exceptions, the newspapers and commentators in America and even in Great Britain seemed to entertain no doubt that French unity must be constituted around Giraud. Almost everything that one could find to read or to hear spread the severest possible judgments about me. "Deplorable pride," said some, or else "frustrated ambition." But most were of the opinion that I was a candidate for a dictatorship; that my entourage, riddled with fascists and felons, was encouraging me to establish an absolute personal power in France after the liberation, whereas General Giraud, a soldier with no political pretensions or, for that matter, intentions, was the bulwark of democracy; that the French people could rely on Roosevelt and Churchill to prevent me from enslaving them.

Of course those elements among the French emigrants who had not joined me and who, by that very fact, depended on foreign powers, espoused and inspired this point of view. In America the newspaper *Pour la Victoire,* in England the daily *France,* the *Agence Française Indépendante,* the magazine *La France Libre* and even the majority of the staff of "Les Français Parlent aux Français" at the BBC openly declared themselves for Giraud. On the other hand, the "Gaullist" organs of expression, such as Henry Torrès' *La Voix de la France* in New York, François Quillici's *La Marseillaise* in London, the voice of Maurice Schumann on the British radio and the chief station of Fighting France at Brazzaville hailed our decision.

It must be said that if the Allies pelted us with abuse, in French Africa the evidences of approval kept multiplying. The Combat movement in which the "Gaullists" gathered was swelled with new members; René Capitant came to London to report this to me. Those of Leclerc's units that made contact with the Sahara troops near Gadàmes received an enthusiastic welcome and numerous requests to be allowed to join them. In Niger, in Dahomey, in Togo, in Guinea, in the Ivory Coast, in Upper Volta, our emissaries now found the easiest access. But it was among the sailors in particular that the popular choice made itself felt. Most of the crews from warships and merchant vessels who reached American or British ports from Morocco, West Africa or Algeria took advantage of the opportunity to sign up at the recruiting offices of Fighting France. Thus the *Richelieu,* sailing from Dakar to New York to be reconditioned, saw three hundred sailors abandon her in order to serve on ships of the Free French Navy. The destroyer *Fantasque,* the tanker *Wyoming,* the cargo ship *Lot,* also docking in America, were emptied in the same manner. In the Scottish port of Greenock the crews of the transport vessels *Eridan, Ville d'Oran, Champollion, Groix, Meonia* and *Jamaïque* rallied to General de Gaulle and obliged their vessels to fly the Cross of Lorraine.

Such incidents as these exasperated Washington—all the more since there were many indications that once the Italo-German army still separating Giraud's troops from Leclerc's and Larminat's men in Tunisia was cut down, an irresistible current would sweep many military units of North Africa into the Free French forces. Therefore the Americans, fearing that the end of the North African campaign would provoke a "Gaullist" tidal wave, made a great effort to bring us to some compromise.

They did so with a heavy hand. In the United States some of the sailors who had left their ships to join Fighting France were arrested and jailed. Our delegate, Adrien Tixier, and Admiral Gayral, chief of our naval mission, were assailed by comminatory proceedings from the State Department and the Navy. In Great Britain, while the English were content to assume a regretful attitude, the Americans threatened the French crews from Africa who asked for my orders. The ship *Jamaïque,* docked at Greenock, was actually occupied by a detachment of American Marines. At Carlton Gardens, Admiral Stark, distressed at having to oppose a cause to which his mind and his heart were both attached, but bound by his instructions, made importunate complaints to D'Auboyneau, our Naval Commissioner, to Diethelm, whose responsibilities included the merchant marine, and, on occasion, to me. The United States press and radio publicized official and semiofficial declarations accusing General de Gaulle of sabotaging the war effort by preventing French ships from carrying out their missions.

I had, indeed, given orders to incorporate the volunteers, considering their choice a desirable one as long as the Algiers organization functioned without us, believing that it was in accord with the interest of the service to use these men where they preferred to be rather than to press them into a framework where they would exist in a state of clandestine revolt, and lastly judging that their demonstration would enlighten world-wide public opinion. But at the same time I invited Algiers, through Admiral Fénard, the chief of its naval mission in America, to man the emptied warships with its own men in place of those who were changing command. As a matter of fact, available men were numerous in North Africa, since many ships had been scuttled during the Allied landing. As for merchant vessels, I myself intended to order them to return, under the Cross of Lorraine, to their Algerian or Moroccan bases, provided that their adherence to the Free French was accepted as fact. Receiving Admiral Stark on March 11, I notified him of these arrangements, which in fact had already been carried out.

The United States, incidentally, offered us honey along with its vinegar. On February 22 Sumner Welles wrote Tixier that Roosevelt once again hoped to receive me in Washington. Once again I replied that I was ready to leave. Once more the invitation was not to be made specific. This project, vanishing as soon as it showed itself, seemed to play a sort of fantastic sea-serpent role in White House policy.

But the uproar abroad did not deter us from seeking to learn the sentiments of the French nation. On this point there had not been the shadow of a doubt since the day when the enemy, occupying the whole of the country, completely enslaved Vichy. On November 17 Laval, in order to be able to operate without hindrance, forced Pétain to give him, on his return from the Fuehrer's headquarters, the right to promulgate all laws and decrees over his own signature alone. During the course of the winter the persecution of the Jews redoubled, despite public indignation, the protests of bishops—such as Monsignor Saliège in Toulouse and Cardinal Gerlier in Lyon—and the condemnation of Pastor Boegner, president of the French Protestant Federation. On January 30, 1943, the militia was created, with Darnand, already a member of the German police, as its secretary general, and was put into active service hunting down patriots. On February 16 the compulsory labor service was instituted to provide the "government" with means of furnishing the enemy the unlimited manpower he required. On April 29 Hitler, receiving Laval again, drew up supplementary collaboration measures with him. If a part of the population remained, either out of distress or out of pity, indulgent to the Marshal, the mind of every Frenchman—with the exception of a few energumens—condemned the policies pursued in his name. The nation's leading school of thought was now the resistance, and the resistance was identified with Fighting France.

Hence there was no diminution of goings and comings between metropolitan France and London. The offices in Carlton Gardens, the house in Duke Street where the B.C.R.A.* was working, and various private houses in the city and the suburbs witnessed the camouflaged visits of those whom planes, vedette boats and trawlers had fetched from France and those who were beginning to be taken there. During the first four months of 1943, while the African crisis was reaching its peak, our "air and naval operations service" transported in one direction or the other hundreds of emissaries and delegates. Our central office was expanded by many notables, among them René Massigli, whom I appointed National

* Bureau Central de Renseignements et d'Action—Central Intelligence and Operations Office.—TR.

Commissioner of Foreign Affairs on February 5; General of the Army Beynet, who was to direct our military mission in Washington; General de Lavalade, soon appointed commander of the troops in the Levant; General Vautrin, who was sent to Libya as chief of staff of the Larminat Group and who was to be killed in action at this post; Jules Moch, who immediately took up his service in the Navy in a military capacity; Fernand Grenier, who was brought over by Rémy on the Communists' request and who, under Soustelle, worked on propaganda with every indication of the most rigorous "Gaullism"; Pierre Viénot, an intelligent, sensitive idealist whom I planned to make the French ambassador to England when the National Committee was established in Algiers, and who was to die at his post; André Maroselli, placed in charge of our prisoner-of-war relief organization which managed to send more than a million packages every month; Georges Buisson and Marcel Poimboeuf, delegated respectively by the C.G.T. and the Christian Workers group and forming, with Albert Guigui, who had preceded them, and Henri Hauck, my colleague from the earliest hour, an active syndicalist representation. The well-known Members of Parliament Gouin, Queuille, Farjon, Hymans and, shortly thereafter, Jacquinot, Auriol, Le Troquer and Louis Marin hastened as soon as they arrived to declare on the radio and in the press, as well as to repeat to the Allied politicians, diplomats and journalists, what elsewhere Messrs. Jeanneney, Herriot, Blum, Mandel, Paul-Boncour and others were affirming—namely, that no government except General de Gaulle's would be conceivable after liberation.

In France itself the resistance, in proportion as its activities and its sufferings increased, cemented its unity. Moreover, the occupation of the so-called "free" zone effaced certain differences and encouraged concentration. At the end of 1942 I had been able to make the acquaintance of the leaders of several movements. Now I saw others, who came between one full moon and the next, emerging suddenly from the haze of feverishness, guile and anguish in which they concealed their weapons, their raids, their printing presses, their letter boxes, and returning just as suddenly. Among those who crossed over during this period were, notably, Cavaillès, a philosopher whose nature inclined him toward prudence but whose hatred of oppression impelled him to the greatest feats of audacity, until he suffered torture and death for France; Daniel Mayer, the methodical artisan of the Socialist Action movement; the modest and intrepid Jean-Pierre Lévy; and Saillant, a splendid syndicalist sent by Léon Jouhaux. Several, such as Pineau and Sermoy-Simon, visited us for the second time. During the same period, our own delegates went everywhere in France: Rémy, a magnificent practical organizer, animating and directing underground activity as if it were a huge, calculated sport, operated chiefly in Paris and in the west; Bingen focused his activity on the Midi; Manuel inspected our local intelligence networks and communications. In January Brossolette, and a month later Passy-Dewavrin, reached France. A young British officer, Yeo Thomas, accompanied the chief of the B.C.R.A. on our invitation in order to furnish the London cabinet with direct information. Passy and Brossolette, acting together, were to make contact with the various organizations, to persuade those of the north to set up a genuine co-ordination among themselves as an example to those of the south, and to prepare the union of both by means of a common council and a single military system.

In February Jean Moulin, my delegate in metropolitan France, and General Delestraint, commander of the secret army, arrived. Again I met with the former, impressive now in conviction and authority alike, conscious that his days were numbered but determined to accomplish his task of unification before their end. I instructed the latter, who found himself invested with a mission for which, in many respects, his career had not prepared him but which he nevertheless undertook with the steadfastness of a soldier who is surprised by nothing in the line of duty.

I directed Moulin, who had prepared the way for some time, to form without further delay the National Council of the Resistance, which would include representatives of all the movements in both zones, of all the political parties, and of the two syndicalist movements. The order of mission I gave him regulated this arrangement, defined the council's role and specified the nature of the relations linking it to the National Committee. Jean Moulin himself was to head the new body. I appointed him a member of the French National Committee and awarded him the Cross of the Liberation during a most moving ceremony in my house at Hampstead. Delestraint, during his stay, was able to work usefully with the Allied leaders, particularly General Brooke, General Ismay and Admiral Stark, who recognized him as one of their peers. Thereby the operations of the secret army during the landing in France would be linked as closely as possible to the plans of the Allied command. The instructions which General Delestraint received from me established his authority, that of an inspector general before the great battle began, and ultimately that of an army commander as soon it was necessary to co-ordinate operations within the nation with those from without. But a few months after his return to France this man of honor was to be arrested by the enemy, deported and, at the end, hypocritically struck down at the gates of a concentration camp, offering his country the life which he had long since dedicated to it. Moulin and Delestraint left on March 24 for battle and for death.

All these indications of the progress French unity was making at home were to aid that of the Empire. The National Committee immediately took the initiative in the negotiations with Algiers. Eight days after our return from Anfa, General Catroux returned to North Africa, where he saw many people. Later, having made it clear that our goal was mutual understanding and that the undesirables whose elimination we sought could be counted on the fingers of both hands, he returned temporarily to Beirut, while Marchal, Charbonnières, Pechkoff, Pélabon and others installed our liaison mission at Algiers. Shortly afterward General Bouscat arrived in London as General Giraud's delegate to me. The exchanges of outlook were beginning.

On February 23 the National Committee drew up the terms of a memorandum addressed to the "Civil and Military Commander in

Chief" specifying the conditions indispensable to unity. These conditions were: to regard the 1940 armistices as having always been null and void; to admit the political and moral impossibility of retaining certain men in the positions of command they now occupied; to re-establish republican law in North Africa; then, once these principles were accepted by the Giraud organization, to form a central power having all the prerogatives of a government, in order that France would have at its disposal in the war a single responsible authority and a single representation; to create, further, a consultative assembly of the resistance, which would furnish as large an expression as possible of the public opinion of the "suffering and militant" nation. Thus our position was formulated once again. The memorandum was sent to Giraud on February 26 and published on March 12.

It was henceforth impossible for the Algiers system to adopt publicly a different attitude. For, independently of what was happening in France, in Africa itself things were going our way to an accelerated rhythm. Among the people as a whole the fundamental feeling prevailed that De Gaulle had won since Vichy had lost. In influential circles the artificial character of the "Civil and Military Commander in Chief's" powers and his dependence on the Americans inspired a growing uneasiness. Furthermore, under the pressure of the Anglo-American missions, themselves scrutinized by the journalists and legislators of their own countries, political censure of our action and attitude was falling off. The scales fell from many eyes. The news from France, the statements made by those whom the occupation of the former "free" zone or the desire to fight now brought to North Africa, the battle raging in Tunisia—all gave the final lie to the anti-Gaullist nonsense which the authorities had professed for so long.

Some of the men around General Giraud had enough political sense to try to channel this current. M. Jean Monnet was the inspirer of this development. In February he had left Washington for Algiers in order to give Giraud the benefit of his economic and administrative abilities and his American connections. The Na-

tional Committee's memorandum made him realize that he must
rapidly transform the features of the "Civil and Military High
Command." On this point M. Monnet soon found himself in
harmony with the adroitness of Mr. Murphy and the shrewdness of
Mr. Macmillan. The month of March was therefore filled with
democratic manifestations from Giraud.

On the fourth a new statute of the "Légion des Combattants"
was decreed in Algiers. On the fifth Giraud declared on the radio,
"France has no racial prejudices." On the eighth he confiscated the
Journal Officiel d'Afrique du Nord of the day before, which, like
the numbers preceding it, promulgated Marshal Pétain's decrees
picked up by radio. On the fourteenth, during an assembly of
Alsatians and Lorrainers, Giraud read out a speech condemning
Vichy and paying homage to the Republic. On the fifteenth he
wrote to General Catroux, "I insisted on explaining yesterday the
principles guiding my conduct. There remains therefore no equivocation between us. . . . I am ready to receive General de Gaulle
in order to give a concrete form to this union. I ask you to invite
him." On March 18 Giraud signed a series of ordinances abolishing Vichy legislation in many areas.

The following day we heard Messrs. Churchill and Cordell Hull,
who had not seemed to notice the French National Committee's
memorandum when it appeared, declare that their respective governments gave their complete support to the principles General
Giraud had enunciated. On the nineteenth General Noguès, on the
twenty-first Governor General Boisson made public their full agreement with "the republican actions and words of the Civil and
Military Commander in Chief." Then General Bergeret, Monsieur
Rigault and Monsieur Lemaigre-Dubreuil resigned from their posts.
As these actions occurred, most American and English newspapers
and commentators raised a chorus of eulogies and urged Fighting
France to join with Giraud, to whom, they declared, the "Gaullists"
could no longer raise any valid objection.

Meanwhile taking advantage of Giraud's speech of March 14
and of the message he had asked Catroux to send me, the National

Committee announced that "the declarations made in Algiers indicate, in many respects, a great progress toward the doctrine of
Fighting France as it has been sustained since June 1940 and
again expressed by the memorandum of February 23." I myself
let General Giraud know that I had received his message with
pleasure and that I expected to be able to go to North Africa in the
near future. I announced this news on the radio, invoking national
union in such a way and in such a tone that those listening knew
that French unity had not changed its champion, nor the latter his
principles. I telegraphed General Eisenhower that I would be
pleased to see him upon my arrival in Algiers, to which he replied
that he would be delighted to have me do so. I requested that when
the time came the British government put a plane at my disposal.
But at the same time I declared quite openly that I was adhering
strictly to my well-known position and that before leaving I would
wait until the National Committee had received a satisfactory reply
from Algiers to the February 23 memorandum. It was then that
the supreme effort to cut us down was launched.

Mr. Macmillan opened fire. On March 17 in Algiers he summoned Guy de Charbonnières, in the absence of General Catroux.

"Now that the Civil and Military Commander in Chief has publicly allied himself with the principles Fighting France insists on,"
he said, "there is nothing to prevent the union from being constituted around General Giraud." When Charbonnières indicated
reservations, the British Secretary of State gave vent to a violent
outburst of irritation. "If General de Gaulle refuses the hand held
out to him today," he exclaimed, "be assured that America and
Great Britain will abandon him altogether, and then he will be
nothing." Although Mr. Macmillan showed more moderation later
in the discussion, his behavior could not be considered as anything
but a first assault wave.

The next was conducted by Archbishop Spellman of New York.
He arrived from Algiers and asked to see me on an explicit mission
from the President of the United States. I met with the archbishop-
ambassador on March 23. This eminently pious prelate approached

the problems of this world with an evident concern to serve God's cause only. But even the greatest piety could not keep *les affaires* from being *les affaires*. Therefore it was with the utmost urgency that the Archbishop of New York gave me counsel out of his wisdom.

"Liberty, equality, charity"—this, according to him, was the motto that should most suitably inspire my conduct. "Liberty" meant that I should refrain from stipulating conditions for Fighting France's union with General Giraud; "equality" that I must join the triumvirate mentioned to me at Anfa; "charity" that pardon was called for in the case of the men in office in Algiers, Rabat and Dakar. "Think," Monsignor Spellman reminded me, "what a misfortune it would be for you if someone were to refuse you the benefit of a formula you will have refused others! Can you see yourself condemned to remain in England and officially kept out of action while France is liberated without you?"

I replied to the archbishop that in that case there would be no such thing as the liberation of France, since victory would consist in the imposition upon my country of an authority chosen by the Anglo-American powers in place of the one that had ruled it by favor of the Germans. One could be sure beforehand that the French people would then turn to a third kind of liberator with whom the Western Allies would have no reason to be pleased. It would be much better not to interfere with the national will— which, I told the archbishop in conclusion, was in the process of revealing itself despite every obstacle. I cited as examples the shift of thinking in North Africa, the attitude of the sailors and, above all, the news from France. All things considered, Monsignor Spellman did not seem annoyed by this. I must even say that later I had evidence that I had won his sympathy during our conversation.

Mr. Churchill next intervened. At his request, I went to see him on April 2, accompanied by Massigli. The Prime Minister, assisted by Sir Alexander Cadogan, explained that my arrival in Algiers would present serious inconveniences if the entente between Giraud and myself were not achieved beforehand. For Mr. Churchill, the entente signified, of course, the acceptance of the conditions that I had been informed of at Anfa. He conjured up the disagreeable consequences that, unless agreement could be reached on this basis, my presence in North Africa would have from the point of view of public order and the military situation. The plane I had requested was ready, the Prime Minister affirmed. But would it not be better to wait until Mr. Eden, then on a trip to the United States, had time to return and until General Catroux, who had been in Algiers only a week, could exercise his influence? Wanting Mr. Churchill to expose himself, I made public upon leaving him that I was still planning to fly to Algiers without accepting any conditions beforehand. The Prime Minister then announced that General Eisenhower requested me to postpone my trip. But I readily established the fact that Eisenhower had requested nothing of the kind, which forced Churchill to acknowledge publicly that the initiative for such behavior had been entirely his own and that it was indeed he who opposed my departure.

On April 6 I saw first Mr. Eden and then Mr. Winant, both of whom were just back from Washington. They painted a lurid picture, evidently prepared beforehand, of the anger my obstinacy had aroused in America, and of all that France would fail to gain by it. They then described, in contrast, the advantages which the good will of the Allies would assure her if I consented to subordinate Fighting France to General Giraud.

"I should have done so with all my heart," I told them, "had Giraud been in command of North Africa on June 18, 1940, and had he continued the war by repudiating Pétain's and Weygand's injunctions. But today the facts are there. The French nation has taken cognizance of them."

At the very moment I was resisting the Allies' pressure, I had to endure that of several of my colleagues as well. Some, in fact, under the influence of the anxiety the London and Washington *parti pris* inspired in them, of the insinuating accusations they themselves were subjected to, and lastly of their tremendous desire to see the union effected at whatever cost, ended by yielding. In the bosom of the National Committee, those who felt this way did not conceal it. Even General Catroux, who in Algiers was inevitably plunged into the milieu of the men in office and of the Murphy and Macmillan parties, proposed in his dispatches that we let Giraud have political preponderance and the military command. Without mistaking these intentions, I did not follow such advice. For behind the trees which these immediate difficulties constituted for us was the forest—that is, the French nation.

And indeed it was the nation's future that was at stake. The entire National Committee recognized the fact when, on April 10, it received Giraud's answer to the February 23 memorandum, brought by Catroux from Algiers. This document did make an outward show of attachment to high principles. But its suggested application consisted, in reality, of keeping France from having a government until the war's end and in enabling the authority of the commander in chief—that is, the power of the Allies—to be exercised without limits.

In effect, the proposal was made to us once again that we establish at Algiers only a "Council of Overseas Territories" which would include Giraud, De Gaulle, the residents-general and governors general and a number of "commissioners" having certain special tasks. The said council would be denied any political power whatever. It would play a role of administrative co-ordination but not of national leadership. As for the commander in chief, General Giraud, he would be subordinate to the inter-Allied command and, in his military functions, would be answerable to no French authority. Further, it would depend on him, as the liberation permitted and under cover of the state of siege, to assure public order and to appoint officials throughout the entire territory of metropolitan France. Thus, without a genuine central French authority, the essentials of power would be at the discretion of a military chief dependent on a foreign general. This strange apparatus was to operate as long as the war lasted. After that, far from proceeding at once to a national plebiscite, there were plans to invoke a law dating back to 1872, the so-called Tréveneuc Law, which provided that in the absence of a National Assembly it devolved upon the general councils to provide an administration and appoint a government. All in all, according to the memorandum signed by General Giraud, everything would transpire as if France no longer existed as a state, at least until the victory. Such was indeed Roosevelt's intention.

The effect of this document was to restore the unanimity of our London committee. Every member saw clearly where the national course lay. At the session of April 15 only a single motion was required to determine the text of the note General Catroux was to take to Algiers. The note was simple and firm. Acknowledging what was satisfactory in General Giraud's declaration of principles, the committee reiterated the conditions necessary for their application: the formation of an effective power exercising its authority over all territories that were or would be liberated, particularly that of metropolitan France, and having under its command all French forces without exception; the subordination to this power of all residents-general and governors general, and, above all, of the commander in chief; the removal of the men who had taken a personal responsibility in the capitulation and in the collaboration with the enemy. In order to constitute the governmental organ, it was, we repeated, indispensable that the president and several members of the National Committee be able to go to North Africa without any conditions being imposed upon them. Further, in order to cut short the rumors that the press was spreading on the subject of our divergences, all the members of the committee issued a formal statement that they were more than ever of one mind with General de Gaulle.

Since Fighting France remained unshakable, the obstinacy with which the Algiers system had attempted to subordinate us now approached its end. In Africa itself the situation no longer allowed of delay. What dominated men's minds, what was written on walls, what echoed in the streets was, "Let De Gaulle come!" On March 14, when Giraud left the hall where he had announced his new orientation, the crowd that had gathered outside received him with cries of *"Vive De Gaulle!"* No one doubted that the attitude recently adopted by the local authorities, the changes made in the Vichy legislation, the dissolution of the Légion, the release of political prisoners and the dismissal of prominent persons were so many successes for the National Committee. The Cross of Lorraine appeared everywhere. The Combat movement moved to the first rank. On April 19 the general councils of Algiers, Oran and Constantine sent me their respects at the opening of their sessions. On the twenty-sixth M. Peyrouton, paying a visit to General Catroux, informed him that as soon as I arrived and in order to facilitate union, he would resign his position as governor general of Algeria and would request to serve in a purely military capacity. On May 1 the parades organized for the May Day labor holiday marched to the rhythm of "We want De Gaulle!" The day before, Mr. Churchill and I had had a satisfying conversation. Having read me Mr. Macmillan's latest reports, the Prime Minister admitted that, in his opinion, I had won the first hand.

How, moreover, justify the distance at which I had been kept, when African troops and Free French forces were engaged on Tunisian soil in the same battle, with the same ardor, toward the same objectives? And the Tunisian struggle was a fierce one. By the end of February Rommel had come on stage. Delaying Montgomery's victorious march by rear-guard action, then covering himself by the fortified Mareth line to the south, he drove from Sfax toward Tebessa to open an Algerian corridor. An American Army corps and the French Welwert Division—whose valiant general was to be killed shortly afterward—had kept him in check with the greatest difficulty. At the same time, General von Arnim, Nehring's successor, attacked both along the northern coast in the region of Tabarca, which was defended by General Monsabert's Volunteer Corps and the Moroccan *tabors,* and toward Medjez-el-Bab, defended by the British. Serious reversals were to be feared. But the whole of the Allied position held, despite everything, thanks particularly to the energy of the French troops, badly armed and equipped though they were, and to the leadership of General Juin, who, out of the bits and pieces that he had to deal with, found the means of making an effective combat instrument. In the middle of March the Eighth Army's entry into the line, and with it the units of Fighting France, was to be the decisive factor.

Montgomery, with Leclerc constituting his left wing and Larminat one of his reserves, attacked, turned the Mareth line and reached Gabès. This breakthrough permitted Patton to retake Gafsa. On April 11 Sfax, on the twelfth, Sousse and Kairouan were liberated in their turn. Then the Allied general offensive was launched. On May 7 Bradley and Magnan took Bizerte, Anderson entered Tunis, Koeltz carried Pont-du-Fahs. On May 11, the Larminat Division seized Takrouna. The next day General von Arnim, trapped on Cape Bon, surrendered with 250,000 men.

But in proportion as our soldiers from Chad and the Middle East made contact in the heat of battle with their brave comrades in Tunisia, Algeria and Morocco and with the populations of those regions, popular enthusiasm mounted around them. On March 26 Larminat telegraphed me that the centers of southern Tunisia, Medenine, Djerba, Zarzis and others, were multiplying their requests to be joined again to Fighting France. On April 6 Leclerc informed me that upon seeing him with his men Gabès had presented the spectacle of an explosion of joy. On April 14 the American press reported that during the entry of the British and the Free French into Sfax, everyone shouted, *"Vive De Gaulle!"* The New York *Herald Tribune,* under the headline "Where Our Strength Resides," wrote:

> The wildest enthusiasm came as some bit of dusty tricolor, fluttering from a lorry, announced the Fighting French. The correspondents who report these scenes seem themselves to have been a little staggered. . . . Before the enthusiasm with which men of all former parties have responded to De Gaulle's simple demand, before the tears, the cheers, the flowers in the liberated Tunisian towns, is it possible any longer to doubt where the real strength and glory of our cause is to be found?

On April 30 Colonel Vanecke, former commissioner of Vichy's Chantiers de Jeunesse,* now commander of the Seventh African Chasseurs, asked to come under my command with his entire regiment. On May 3 at Sfax, the Fourth Spahis, with the exception of a few officers, addressed themselves in a body to General Leclerc to obtain the same favor. As soon as the battle was over, many soldiers in African units went so far as to leave the ranks in hopes of being incorporated in the forces under the Cross of Lorraine. On May 20 the Free French detachment received its fair share of cheers during the Allied military parade at Tunis in honor of victory.

Thus it was popular judgment that finally meted out justice to all tergiversations. On April 27 General Giraud wrote me that he renounced preponderance. Nevertheless, he still maintained his conception of the "council" without real powers on which, with himself and me, would be seated the residents-general and governors general. Further, doubtless fearing mob reaction, he proposed that our first meeting take place in a remote place, either at Biskra or at Marrakech. On May 6 I replied by declaring once again the firm intention of the National Committee as to the character, the composition and the authority of the governmental organ that was to be formed, rejecting the notion that this could be done in a remote oasis and stressing that I must go to Algiers. Two days before, in a public address, I had quite bluntly declared that the matter must be settled.

Now, on the night of May 15, Philip and Soustelle triumphantly brought me a telegram just received from Paris. Jean Moulin informed me that the National Council of the Resistance had been formed and in its name addressed the following message to me:

> Every movement, every party of the resistance, from both northern and southern zones, on the eve of General de Gaulle's departure for Algeria, pledges anew its total adherence to the principles he and the National Committee embody and uncompromisingly uphold.

* Youth camps.—TR.

Every movement, every party formally declares that the designated meeting must take place at the seat of the government-general in Algeria, openly and among Frenchmen.

They further declare: (1) that political problems cannot be excluded from these talks; (2) that the French people will never tolerate the subordination of General de Gaulle to General Giraud and demands the immediate installation at Algiers of a provisional government under the presidency of General de Gaulle, General Giraud being made the military chief; (3) that General de Gaulle will remain sole leader of the French resistance whatever the result of the negotiations.

On May 27 the National Council of the Resistance, assembling in full and with Jean Moulin presiding, held its first meeting at 48 Rue du Four, Paris, and confirmed its message to me.

Thus on every hand, and especially on the aching soil of France herself, a well-prepared harvest was ripening against the crucial moment. The telegram from Paris, sent to Algiers and made public by the American, British and Free French broadcasting stations, produced a decisive effect not only because of what it declared, but also and especially because it proved that the French resistance had been able to achieve unity. The voice of this crushed yet rumbling and reassured France suddenly drowned out the whispers of intrigue and the palavers of compromise. I was at once the stronger for it, while Washington and London measured without pleasure, but not without lucidity, the significance of the event. On May 17 General Giraud asked me to come to Algiers at once to form the central French power with him. On May 25 I replied, "I plan to reach Algiers by the end of this week, and I shall be delighted to work directly with you in the service of France."

Before leaving England, I wrote King George VI to tell him how grateful I was to him, to his government and to his people for the reception they had given me during the tragic days of 1940 and for the hospitality they had subsequently accorded Free France and its leader. Intending to pay a visit to Mr. Churchill, I learned that he had just left for an "unknown destination." It was therefore Mr. Eden to whom I made my adieux. The meeting was a friendly one.

"What do you think of us?" the British minister asked me.

"Nothing could be more agreeable than the British people," I observed. "As for your politics, I cannot always say the same."

When we were discussing the many occasions on which I had had dealings with the British government, Mr. Eden good-humoredly asked, "Do you know that you have caused us more difficulties than all our other European allies put together?"

"I don't doubt it," I replied, smiling in my turn. "France is a great power."

CHAPTER 4

ALGIERS

O<small>N</small> midnight of May 30 a Fighting French plane with Marmier as chief officer landed me at Bufarik. Massigli, Philip, Palewski, Billotte, Teyssot and Charles-Roux accompanied me. General Giraud was there to meet us and General Catroux as well, and behind them the representatives of the American and British missions. The *garde mobile* presented arms; a band played the "Marseillaise"; the automobiles were French. Such indications as these, compared with those marking our reception at Anfa, showed me that Fighting France, and thereby France herself, had been making progress in North Africa.

The public did not know of our arrival. All the censors of Algiers, London and New York had forbidden announcement of the news. Hence the localities our entourage passed through did not, on the whole, give any particular demonstration. Only certain vigilant "Gaullists" applauded when we happened to encounter them. At Bir Kadeim the people, alerted on the spur of the moment, rushed out to meet us, shouting, *"Vive De Gaulle!"* But the local authorities had made sure that our entrance into Algiers would occur without a public gathering. From Bufarik, whose remote and isolated airfield had been chosen intentionally in preference to that of Maison-Blanche, we reached the Summer Palace without crossing the city itself.

A great banquet was served. This splendid French habit asserts itself whatever terms the guests are on, and whatever their troubles. Giraud and I were seated opposite each other. On my right I was not surprised to find General Georges, who told me how the English had just brought him from France. On my left was Monsieur Jean Monnet, who immediately began to talk to me on economic subjects. Catroux and Massigli sat on either side of Giraud. André Philip and René Mayer, Palewski and Couve de Murville, Linarès and Billotte entered into conversation, as did thirty other guests. Here then were all these Frenchmen reunited, so diverse and yet so much alike, whom the tides of events had swept toward such different shores and who now found themselves just as active and as self-confident as they had been before the drama began! Glancing down the table, one might have thought that nothing tragic had occurred during the past three years. All the same, two parties were there.

It was easy to establish the apparent relationship of forces between them. On one side, everything; on the other, nothing. In Algiers the Army, the police, the administration, the treasury, the radio, the press and communications were under the sole domination of the "Civil and Military Commander in Chief." The Allied might, thanks to which he had been put in power, was oriented in his favor alone. For myself, I had no troops in this country, no police, no officials, no funds, no fitting means of making my voice heard. Yet the attitudes, the remarks, the looks of those I had met during the last two hours already revealed where the ascendancy lay. Each man knew in his heart how the contest would end.

The crowd shouted it at the top of its lungs in the Place de la Poste, where at four o'clock I placed a Cross of Lorraine at the foot of the monument to the dead. Although this ceremony was quite extemporaneous, unmentioned by any newspaper, unattended by any troops, thousands of patriots alerted by the Combat movement had gathered swiftly and welcomed me with great acclamation. After my tribute to all the Algerians who had given their lives for France, I struck up the "Marseillaise," in which innumerable voices joined me. Then, surrounded by overwhelming enthusiasm, I reached the villa Les Glycines, where I was to establish my residence.

Already messages had begun to flow in. The first letter I read was from General Vuillemin, former Chief of the General Staff of the Air Force, who after the misfortunes of 1940 had retired to his home with his grief and his hopes. In the noblest terms this great leader asked me to give him the command of a Fighting French air squadron, with corresponding rank. After the cheers of the crowd, Vuillemin's gesture made the essence of the situation clear to me. Here, as elsewhere, national feeling had made its choice. In the game about to be played, the trump card was in my hand. Among the Frenchmen of Africa my only obstacles would be the narrow-mindedness of people in office and the mistrust of certain prominent individuals. On the other hand, I would have to reckon on the determined opposition of the Allies, who would back the rival clan.

A painful duel! It began the very next morning. At the Lycée Fromentin, where the future government would hold its sessions and install certain of its services, I met with General Giraud. He was accompanied by Monnet and Georges, I by Catroux, Philip and Massigli. We were all in agreement as to the procedure to be followed. The seven men present would constitute themselves a government committee and would be joined subsequently by other members to complete the administration. But I intended to take the initiative before anything had been concluded.

"In order to form ourselves into a single team working in co-operation," I said, "certain essential points must be established. Until our country is in a position to express its own wishes, the authority we establish here must assume every national responsibility. The military command, even though the man who wields it may be a minister or a president, will therefore be appointed by the government and will remain subordinate to it. If it is thought that this army chief should be placed, during operations, under the strategic command of a foreign general, this can be done only by order of the French authority. I cannot, for my part, consent to replace the French National Committee by any other if it is not understood from the start that the responsibility and the authority of the new organism will be supreme in every area, especially the last named. Further, in order to indicate clearly that France has never left the war and that she repudiates Vichy entirely, it is necessary that we relieve General Noguès, Governor General Boisson and Governor General Peyrouton of their duties."

Giraud lost his temper. He did not agree that the military command should be subordinated to the government. As for the "proconsuls," he declared with extreme vehemence that he would not give them up. I insisted on my conditions. We agreed to adjourn the session and resume the debate later on the basis of written proposals. During the discussion only General Georges had agreed with Giraud; Monnet sought compromise; Catroux, Philip and Massigli all approved, though in different ways, the position I had taken. After this unpromising start, the government could scarcely be said to be launched. But I saw myself as a navigator enveloped by a heavy squall, certain that if he keeps his course the horizon will clear.

In the interim the storm redoubled. A crisis broke that seemed likely to jeopardize everything, had we not felt that the crux of the matter was already decided. On the first of June I assembled at Les Glycines all of the newspapermen then in Algiers. This numerous band arrived burning with curiosity, at their head the Allied reporters, who did not conceal their satisfaction at breathing henceforth this keen air which produced big headlines and explosive articles, the French somewhat withdrawn, divided between sympathy toward me and fear of the censorship wielded by the Director of Information of the "Civil and Military High Command." In a short statement, I indicated that I had come to North Africa with my colleagues in order to create here an effective French power, an authority directing the national war effort, insisting on the sovereignty of France, established in accord with the resistance and excluding a few individuals who symbolized something else. This language and this tone, hitherto unknown in these parts, were immediately reported everywhere.

The evening of the same day, Colonel Jousse brought me a letter from M. Peyrouton. The governor general of Algeria, "realizing that unconditional union among Frenchmen is the only means of obtaining a victory that can restore our greatness, and in hopes of facilitating its achievement," sent in his resignation and asked me to intervene on his behalf with the military authority so that he might have a chance to serve in the Army. Nothing in the letter indicated that a similar message had been sent to Giraud. I replied to M. Peyrouton that I accepted his resignation and that, "in the terrible ordeal our country is undergoing, I am sure that the French people will appreciate as I do the disinterested courage of your action." I sent copies of the governor general's letter and my reply to General Giraud without delay and issued a statement to the representatives of the press. The next day the news appeared in newspapers throughout the world.

M. Peyrouton's retirement, effected under such circumstances, immediately produced a considerable stir. It was learned that he had subsequently written to General Giraud in the same terms, but this fact did not change the situation. That the former Vichy ambassador to Brazil, who had come to Algeria to assume the governor-generalship at Roosevelt's request, should hand over his office to me and publicly comply with my demands was a repudiation the Algiers system had inflicted upon itself. As a result, the confusion among the men of this system and their Allied advisers reached its peak—all the more so since the city was bubbling over with excitement, and from every quarter came signs of the massive exodus of volunteers loading into trucks and pouring down the roads to attempt to join Larminat's and Leclerc's troops. Some days earlier Giraud, with Eisenhower's agreement, had forced the Cross of Lorraine units out of the territory. These were now bivouacked around Tripoli, but their distant encampments attracted thousands of young soldiers. Giraud, yielding to anxiety, went so far as to appoint a new prefect of police to maintain order in the city and its environs: Admiral Muselier, who had been brought over by the British and who intended now to make up for his former misfortunes.

I was therefore not surprised to receive, on June 2, a letter signed by the "Civil and Military Commander in Chief" but written in a style that betrayed its inspiration. In the customary tone of the London emigrants who had not joined Free France, it accused me of attempting to drive from their posts men worthy of every confidence, to damage our alliances and to establish a dictatorship composed of myself and the criminals who formed my entourage. While I was digesting the contents of this communication, I was informed that the garrison had been confined to quarters, that armored units were concentrated in the gardens of the Summer Palace, that all meetings and parades had been forbidden in Algiers, and that the military and the police were holding the exits from the city as well as the adjacent airfields. But at Les Glycines, under the sole guard of ten spahis Larminat had sent me, I learned that this to-do was not affecting the eagerness with which those I wished to consult responded to my call. Later that night I informed Giraud that this *Putsch* atmosphere, created under the eyes of foreign powers, was deplorable to me, that we must either break off relations or reach an agreement, and that a new explanation was called for on the following day.

On June 3 at ten o'clock in the morning, the "Seven" met again. This time General Giraud's obstinacy gave way. I had brought drafts of a decree and a declaration instituting the new committee; both were adopted without change. The declaration announced the creation of the French Committee of National Liberation, with both of us as its presidents and with Catroux, Georges, Massigli, Monnet and Philip as members; others were to be appointed soon. We proclaimed:

> The committee . . . is the central French power. . . . [It] directs the French war effort in all its forms and in all places. . . . It exercises French sovereignty . . . It assures the management and the defense of French interests the world

over. . . . It assumes authority over the territories and the
military forces hitherto under the French National Committee
and the Civil and Military Commander in Chief.

We added that the committee would turn over its powers to the
future provisional government of the Republic when liberation was
achieved, and that until such time it pledged itself "to re-establish
all French liberties, the laws of the Republic, and the republican
regime, while destroying entirely the arbitrary regime of personal
power today imposed upon the nation."

At the same time the question of the "proconsuls" was settled.
We decided that since M. Peyrouton's resignation was a *fait accompli,* General Catroux would become governor general of
Algeria while still remaining a member of the committee, that
General Noguès was to leave Morocco and that M. Boisson would
be recalled from Dakar as soon as the Ministry of the Colonies had
received a titular. Further, General Bergeret was to be retired.

Despite obvious defects, the organism thus created constituted,
in my eyes, a workable starting point. True, temporarily we would
have to put up with the absurd duality that existed at its head;
and it could be expected that Allied politics, intervening in the
inner working of the committee through individuals they had introduced there, would give rise to acrimonious incidents before the
commander in chief was subordinated to the central power in
reality, as he was now on paper. But the French Committee of
National Liberation answered well to the principles which Fighting
France had not ceased to champion. As for the application which
would be made of it, that was up to me. In confronting the committee with its responsibilities, I intended that its internal evolution,
under the pressure of public opinion, should concentrate it around
me and assist me to obviate whatever was erratic and centrifugal
in it. In the immediate future, the sort of close association initially
adopted put me in a position, despite all its disadvantages, to act
on the military and administrative elements of North Africa that
hitherto had been outside my authority. As for all those who, in

France and elsewhere, had given me their confidence, I was sure that they would continue to follow no one but myself with any willingness. When the session was adjourned, I had the feeling that a great step had been taken on the road to unity. Overlooking, for such a stake, many painful vicissitudes, I embraced General Giraud with all my heart.

But if my satisfaction was considerable, that of the Allies was greatly mitigated. The establishment in North Africa of a central French authority arrogating to itself the powers of a government, laying claim to French sovereignty and excluding the "proconsuls" was in flagrant contradiction to the position flaunted by Roosevelt and his ministers. Therefore the declaration, released at noon on June 3 by the French Committee of National Liberation and announcing its own birth, was suppressed by the American censors until nine that night. For my part, I hastened to inform the representatives of the press of what had been done, knowing that this would sooner or later cause the barrier to fall. The next day, speaking on the radio—where already "Gaullists" were officially moving in—I announced to the people of France that their government was now functioning at Algiers pending its return to Paris. On June 6 a Fighting France rally attended by an audience of thousands gave me, and Philip and Capitant as well, the occasion to make heard publicly the words and the tune that would henceforth be official. It goes without saying that the British and American missions showed little eagerness to permit our speeches to be spread round the world.

The Allies' ill-humor did not, moreover, limit itself to the sphere of propaganda. Thus, when I telegraphed London to request that several of my colleagues immediately be brought to take part in the new government, none of them arrived for ten days; the British, under various pretexts, were delaying their departure. And in Algiers itself the British government, whether solely on its own account or not, followed the development of our affairs without a sign of good will.

No sooner had I landed at Bufarik on May 30 than I learned

that Mr. Churchill himself, later joined by Mr. Eden, had arrived in great secrecy. Since then he had stayed in his secluded villa, not without keeping himself informed, through General Georges, of the progress of our discussions. Once the French Committee of National Liberation was established, the Prime Minister showed himself. On June 6 he invited Giraud and me, as well as several committee members, to a so-called "country dinner," an invitation which my sense of the respect due him as a personage prevented me from refusing.

When I indicated how strange his presence at this time and under these conditions appeared to us, he protested that he was in no way attempting to meddle in French affairs. "All the same," he added, "the military situation compels His Majesty's Government to keep track of what is happening within this essential zone of communications. We should have had to take steps if too brutal a shock had occurred—if, for example, you had devoured Giraud in one mouthful."

This was not at all my intention. Resolved as I was that as a result of my efforts the French government should be a united one, I intended to proceed by stages, considering not foreign apprehensions but the national advantage. I hoped to influence General Giraud to range himself, of his own accord, on the side of public opinion. Although he had already delayed too long, I was still disposed to have him play the leading role in military affairs, provided that he confined himself to them and that he held his post by virtue of French authority.

As a matter of fact, his role as a military leader could not be in the capacity of a real commander in chief. More than anyone else I regretted this fact, but what could be done about it? The strategy of the Allied powers included only two conceivable theaters of war in the west, that of the north and that of the Mediterranean. Unfortunately, it would be impossible for us to raise enough land, naval and air forces to require a French general to exercise anything like a high command, properly speaking. To be sure, there were more than enough men; we could, if need be, recruit them from the brave and loyal populations of the Empire. But the officer strength and the specialists at our disposal narrowly limited the number of our units. Again, it was out of the question for us to provide them with arms and equipment ourselves. In comparison to the resources which the Americans and the British were to muster in the battles of Italy and France, the strength we could offer there would not constitute a major force. On land especially, it would not for some time exceed the strength of an army detachment—at the most, an army. There was therefore little likelihood that, either in the north or in the south, Americans and British would agree to entrust the direction of the common battle to a French leader.

The situation would, of course, have been a different one if in June 1940 the government of the Republic, invested with the appurtenances of legitimacy, accompanied by the core of the central administration, making use of diplomatic means, had had itself transported to Africa and with it the five hundred thousand men crowding the depots, whatever campaign units could still be shipped, the entire war fleet, the merchant fleet, all the personnel of the pursuit planes and the entire bombing force—which, moreover, did go to North Africa and which was forced to return to yield its planes into the invader's hands. What France possessed at that time in the way of money and credit would have permitted the nation to buy an abundant supply of American matériel while waiting for lend-lease. With all these resources added to those of Algeria, Morocco, Tunisia, the Levant and French West Africa, there would have been means of rebuilding a formidable military force protected by the wide sea and by the French and British naval squadrons, particularly by one hundred submarines. Given this situation, the Allies, coming to take up positions at our side in the French North African bases, by our own request and, doubtless, a year earlier, would quite naturally have recognized the supreme authority of a French general or admiral in this theater.

But the terrible panic, and then the disastrous surrender, which had kept the still available resources from being transported to the Empire, which surrendered or demobilized most of those that were there, which put the public powers and the military command at the enemy's mercy, which decreed the reception of the Allies by cannon fire, had already deprived France of this opportunity as of many others. Never in all my life had I felt such disappointment and grief as in these bitter circumstances.

Meanwhile, if General Giraud's experience and capacity could not be deployed at the head of operations, they were none the less capable of rendering great services. Renouncing the direction of the government, he could either exercise the responsibilities of Minister of the Armies or, if little inclined to play this administrative role, he could become Inspector General of our forces and at the same time military adviser to the committee and its representative to the inter-Allied command. I must say that although I was not opposed to the first solution, it was the second that I regarded as the more appropriate. On many occasions I proposed both to General Giraud's choice, but he never agreed to espouse either one. His illusions, the appeal of certain circles and certain interests, and the influence of the Allies made him determined to keep for himself the entire disposition of the Army and at the same time, as cosignatory of statutes and decrees, be able to prevent the administration from making a move without his own consent.

It was therefore inevitable that Giraud should find himself gradually isolated and rejected, until the day when, walled within limitations he did not accept and, moreover, deprived of the external supports which were the source of his dizzying ambitions, he determined to resign. As for myself, it was not without sorrow that I found myself forced to deal with this painful affair, wounding to the quick a soldier of high quality for whom I had always felt deference and attachment. Along the road that led to the nation's unity, I encountered many times such personal questions, in which the duties of my trust transcended but nevertheless afflicted my own feelings. I may say that in no case did it cost me more to impose the iron law of national interest.

This was to happen only by degrees, however. On June 5 the "Committee of the Seven" reconvened. This time it was a question

of selecting further members and assigning their functions. General
Georges was named Commissioner of State while Catroux retained
the title he held. Massigli and Philip kept respectively Foreign
Affairs and the Interior, with which they had already been entrusted. Monnet received the responsibility for Armament and
Supply. At General Giraud's request the following became members of the committee: Couve de Murville for Finance, René Mayer
for Transportation and Public Works, Abadie for Justice, Education and Health. I myself appointed Pleven for the Colonies,
Diethelm for Economy, Tixier for Labor, Bonnet for Information. Further, Ambassadors Puaux and Helleu were appointed to
Morocco and the Levant respectively, while General Mast was
confirmed in his functions in Tunisia.

These choices were subsequently to make my position secure.
At Algiers, Rabat and Tunis, as was already the case at Beirut,
Brazzaville, Douala, Tananarive and Nouméa, authority would be
wielded by men who were convinced as to the necessity of the war
effort and upon whom I could rely. At Dakar, Boisson would be
replaced fifteen days later by Cournarie, transferred from Came-
roun. At Fort-de-France there was every indication that we would
soon be in a position to set our affairs in order. As for the government itself, it was composed of men of reason and quality the
majority of whom had always been connected with me while the
remainder, with a few exceptions, asked only to be so in their turn.
Certain that this group was prepared to support me, I began the
next play. But before throwing the dice I shook them hard.

On June 8 the committee, which still consisted of only seven
members—pending the arrival of those still in London—approached the crucial problem of the military command. We found
ourselves with three proposals before us. One, presented by General Georges, provided for the unification of all French forces under
the authority of General Giraud, who would act as both minister
and commander in chief, also keeping his post as president but
remaining independent of the French government in the military
domain. The second plan, proposed by Catroux, aimed at directly

entrusting De Gaulle with the Department of National Defense and Giraud with the command of the troops. The third program, my own, gave the commander in chief the mission of training all the French forces and of co-operating with the Allied military leaders on joint plans of operations. As soon as possible, he would take an active field command, thereby ceasing to play a part in the government. According to my plan, the organization and distribution of forces would be controlled by a military committee including De Gaulle and Giraud, the ministers concerned and the chiefs of staff, subject, should the occasion arise, to the government's arbitration. The majority of the committee voted against the first proposal. Giraud, backed by General Georges, would accept neither of the other two. Since most of the members had not yet reached the point of being willing to make the "commander in chief" yield or resign, the impossibility of reaching a settlement was obvious.

But then what was the committee for? That was the question I asked, in writing, of its members. Pointing out that in the space of eight days "we have not even managed to decide the problem of the respective powers of the government and the military command, of which the logical and national solution stares us in the face," and that "the slightest question, which should be settled in a few moments, involves us in interminable and disagreeable discussions," I declared that I could no longer associate myself with the committee under the conditions in which it was operating. Then I shut myself up at Les Glycines, shrouded in sorrow, letting it be known to the ministers, officials and generals who came to see me that I was preparing to leave for Brazzaville.

The impression produced by this calculated outburst actually precipitated the march of events. When General Giraud, without regard for the consequences, convened the committee for a session at which I was not present, every member pointed out to him that under such conditions no valid decision could be made. On the other hand, the deficiency of the bicephalic system, evident to the well-informed and provoking abroad an avalanche of gibes, aroused both anxiety and exasperation in all French circles. The Army did not escape it; General Juin came to Algiers to tell me as much and to urge Giraud to reduce his claims. General Bouscat, Chief of the General Staff of the Air Force, spoke in the same vein. The governor general's office, the university, the editorial offices all seethed with alarming rumors.

After six days of confusion, I decided that the affair had ripened. Besides, the commissioners whom London had detained had just reached Algiers. The government was thereby in a position to hold a plenary session, and I counted on finding in the full group a less reserved support than that which the "Seven" had given me. I therefore took the initiative and called a meeting of the "Committee of the Fourteen" so that it could attempt, in its turn, to settle the question choking the central power. The meeting took place, but Giraud, in front of his colleagues, flatly refused to have the question brought up, denying the committee the very jurisdiction defined in a decree signed by his own hand. Thus, even during the last act of this distressing vaudeville show, while the after-effects of Vichy and the interference of foreign powers dragged out the humiliation of France for seven months, Giraud persisted in playing the role of a council president who did not want a government.

Of course the Allies did not want one any more than he. Seeing where events were leading, they made a new effort to prevent France from achieving its government. But their very intervention was to end by further unsettling General Giraud's position.

On June 16 Messrs. Murphy and Macmillan handed to Massigli for submission to the French Committee of National Liberation a request from General Eisenhower, inviting Generals de Gaulle and Giraud to confer with him on the subject of problems relative to the command and the organization of the French armed forces. The conference took place June 19. The three of us were the interlocutors, with one silent witness, General Bedell Smith. But Messrs. Murphy and Macmillan, as well as several British and American officials and military men, stayed in the neighborhood, attentive and audible.

I purposely arrived last and spoke first. "I am here," I told Eisenhower, "in my capacity as President of the French Government. For it is customary that during operations the chiefs of state and of the government should come in person to the headquarters of the officer in command of the armies they have entrusted to him. If you wish to address a request to me concerning your province, be assured that I am disposed beforehand to give you satisfaction, on condition, of course, that it is compatible with the interests in my charge."

The inter-Allied commander in chief, making an effort to be pleasant, then declared, in substance, "I'm preparing, as you know, a very important operation which will soon be launched against Italy and which directly concerns the liberation of Europe and of France. For the security of our rear during this operation, I need an assurance which I ask you to give me. It is essential that the present organization of the French command in North Africa undergo no change. In particular, General Giraud must remain in office with all his present powers and keep complete control of the disposition of troops, communications, ports and airfields. He must be the only one to deal with me on all military subjects in North Africa. Although your interior organization is not my concern, these matters are essential for us. I tell you so in behalf of the British and American governments, which are furnishing arms to the French forces and which cannot continue shipments if the conditions I indicate are not fulfilled."

"I am taking note of your course of action," I replied. "You are asking a promise of me which I will not give you, for the organization of the French command is the province of the French government, not yours. But having heard what you have to say, I should like to ask you several questions.

"All states waging war—America, for example—entrust to generals the command of their troops in the field and to ministers the responsibility of outfitting them. Do you claim to forbid the French government from doing as much?"

General Eisenhower confined himself simply to repeating that his request aimed at the integral maintenance of Giraud's powers.

"You have referred," I said, "to your responsibilities as commander in chief in relation to the British and American governments. Are you aware that I have responsibilities toward France, and that by virtue of those responsibilities I cannot admit the interference of any foreign power in the exercise of French authority?" Eisenhower kept silence.

I continued. "You who are a soldier, do you think that a leader's authority can subsist if it rests on the favor of a foreign power?"

After a new and heavy silence, the American commander in chief said, "I quite understand, General, that you have long-standing preoccupations as to the fate of your nation. Please understand that I for my part have immediate military preoccupations."

"So have I," I answered, "for my government must immediately effect a merger of the various kinds of French forces—those of Fighting France, those of North Africa and those forming in metropolitan France, which the present system obliges us to keep separate. It must also arm them, thanks to the resources which you are furnishing them in the interest of our alliance and in exchange for the many services we also provide you. Here too I have a question to ask you.

"Do you recall that during the last war, France played a role analogous to that which the United States is playing today with regard to furnishing arms to several Allied countries? At that time it was France who armed the Belgians and the Serbs, procured many resources for the Russians and the Rumanians, and lastly outfitted your own army with a large share of its matériel. Yes, during World War I, you Americans fired only our cannon, drove only our trucks, flew only our planes. Did we, in return, demand of Belgium, Serbia, Russia, Rumania, did we demand of the United States, that they appoint this or that leader or institute this or that political system?" Once again the silence weighed upon us.

General Giraud, who had not yet opened his mouth, now declared, "I too have my responsibilities, in particular as regards the Army, which is small and cannot exist save in the Allied framework. This is as true for its command and its organization as it is for its operations."

At this I stood up, left the room and returned to Les Glycines.

The next day, as I had requested, Allied headquarters sent me, as well as Giraud, a note specifying the Anglo-American requirements as far as the functions of the French Army were concerned. I wanted a written record of these requirements. The note, after having formulated the demands concerning Giraud's powers, concluded with this sentence: "The Allied commander in chief wishes to emphasize the assurances given by the British and American governments guaranteeing that French sovereignty will be respected and maintained in the French territories in North and West Africa."

Although this last touch, serving as an ironic conclusion to the demands that contradicted it, was signed by the Allied commander in chief, I recognized in it the procedure frequently employed by Washington and London—paying lip-service to rights even while infringing them. But I knew that such a course of action, if it corresponded to the policies pursued in regard to France by the British and American governments, proceeded from neither the initiative nor the character of General Eisenhower.

He was a soldier. To him, by nature and by profession, action seemed natural, immediate and simple. To put into play, according to time-honored rules, specific means of a familiar nature—this was how he envisaged warfare and consequently his task. Eisenhower approached the test trained for thirty-five years by a technique and a philosophy beyond which he was in no way inclined to go. Yet now he found himself abruptly invested with an extraordinarily complex role. Removed from the hitherto rigid framework of the American Army, he had become commander in chief of a colossal coalition. Because he had to lead the forces of several peoples in battles on which the fate of their states depended, he was to see national susceptibilities and ambitions irrupt into the tried and tested system of the units under his orders.

It was a piece of luck for the Allies that Dwight Eisenhower discovered in himself not only the necessary prudence to deal with

these thorny problems, but also an attraction toward the wider
horizons that history opened before his career. He knew how to be
adroit and flexible. But if he used skill, he was also capable of
audacity. The latter quality was indeed a prerequisite for hurling
upon the beaches of Africa an army transported from one side of
the ocean to the other; for invading Italy in the face of an enemy
still intact; for landing heavy units on a strip of Normandy coast in
the teeth of an adversary well entrenched and skilled in maneuvering; for launching through the Avranches gap Patton's mechanized
army and pushing it as far as Metz. Yet it was chiefly by method
and perseverance that he dominated the situation. By choosing reasonable plans, by sticking firmly to them, by respecting logistics,
General Eisenhower led to victory the complicated and prejudicial
machinery of the armies of the free world.

It will never be forgotten that in this capacity he had the distinction of leading them in the liberation of France. But since a great
people's needs are on the scale of its misfortunes, it will doubtless
also be thought that the commander in chief might have been able
to serve our country still better. Had he linked his strategy to
France's great struggle as he bound it to the schemes of the Anglo-
American powers, had he provided our troops, including those of
the secret army, with heavy arms, had he in his disposition of forces
still entrusted a first-class mission to the reviving French Army,
our military recovery might have been more brilliant, the future
more profoundly marked.

In my own relations with him, I often had the feeling that this
generous-hearted man inclined toward these points of view. But I
was soon to see him turn away from them, as if regretfully. Actually,
politics dictated his behavior from Washington and necessitated his
reserve. He complied, yielding to Roosevelt's authority, influenced
by the advisers the latter sent to him, spied on by his peers—his
rivals—and not yet having acquired, in the face of power, that
assurance which the military leader derives in time from having
rendered great services.

Nevertheless, if occasionally he went so far as to support the pretexts which tended to keep us in obscurity, I can affirm that he did so without conviction. I even saw him submit to my intervention in his own strategy whenever national interest led me to do so. At heart this great soldier felt, in his turn, that mysterious sympathy which for almost two centuries has brought his country and mine together in the world's great dramas. It was not of his doing that this time the United States was less affected by our distress than by the appeal of domination.

In any case, the course of action that politics had forced upon Eisenhower on June 19 produced an effect contrary to the one that Washington had reckoned on. The Committee of National Liberation, learning of the Anglo-American demands on the twenty-first, decided, as I urged it to do, to ignore them and make no reply. But, displeased and humiliated, it notified Giraud that he must either accept subordination to the French government or else cease to be a member of it and resign his command.

Besides, since Giraud was alleging the disadvantage, from the point of view of secrecy, of examining military questions by an Areopagus of fourteen ministers, it was decided, as I suggested, to institute a Military Committee comprising, under my chairmanship, the commander in chief and the chiefs of staff, and having authority from the government to determine measures relative to organization, to recruiting and to the merging of our forces as well as to their distribution among the various theaters and territories. As for operations, two military commands provisionally subsisted, Giraud remaining responsible for the North African forces and De Gaulle for the rest, including the secret army. However, the principal decisions were still reserved to the Committee of National Liberation meeting in plenary session.

This compromise gave me no satisfaction whatever. I should have preferred that we go further along the road of common sense, that the unity of the government's leadership had been established once and for all, that General Giraud's powers had been clearly defined, that one or several ministers had undertaken the administration of the armies as well as the direct exercise of military authority outside the zone of operations, and that within this framework the merging of the French forces of North Africa with those of Fighting France might at last be realized. But the committee, if it saw the goal to be reached, was still too unsure of itself to reach it swiftly. Besides, General Giraud announced meanwhile that he had received an invitation from President Roosevelt to go to Washington to discuss the question of arms shipments. The commander in chief urgently requested that we await his return before discussing the structure of the committee and of the command. The majority of the ministers chose to temporize. As for me, I agreed to these provisional arrangements with the firm intention of soon putting each piece of the service in the place it should have.

Giraud left on July 2. His trip had been organized by agreement between the American government and himself without consulting the Committee of National Liberation. Independently of his practical goal, the arming of our troops, his visit was conceived by the United States government as the occasion to manifest its policy in regard to France, to affirm, by discussing only military matters with one of our leaders, its refusal to admit that we had a government, to publicize the support it continued to accord to the French general it had chosen for North Africa, and lastly to build up the latter in American public opinion. Mr. Churchill had decided he must lend President Roosevelt a hand in this matter by addressing to the British representatives abroad and to the editors of the British newspapers a memorandum in which the Prime Minister's grievances against General de Gaulle were set forth. Of course this memorandum, ungracious as it was, was also published by the American newspapers.

Yet despite the efforts expended, results did not come up to expectations. For since the President and his ministers insisted on receiving Giraud in his military capacity alone, and since the latter laid claim to no other, American public opinion took only a moderate interest in his visit. The crowds were not stirred by the technicality of the operation, which consisted in arming a few French divisions, and their feelings in no way recognized as the champion of France the docile visitor whom many American newspapers eulogized. As for informed circles, they were repelled by the subservient attitude Giraud saw fit to adopt and by the White House's insistence on exploiting his presence to advertise a policy of which many did not approve.

The same was true of Giraud's statement to the Washington press, which it was known he had agreed to submit beforehand to the United States government and had even modified a few moments before the press conference; and of the remarks made on July 10 by Roosevelt apropos of Giraud's visit, which, the President said, was merely that of a French soldier fighting for the Allied cause, since at that time France no longer existed; and of the White House dinner attended only by military personnel, to which not even Ambassador Henri Hoppenot, the accredited representative of the Committee of National Liberation, had been invited; and of the speeches the President and Giraud exchanged that evening, making not the slightest allusion to the Algiers government nor to the unity, the integrity or the independence of France; and of what occurred on July 14, the national holiday, when Giraud received neither tribute nor message from the government that was his host and addressed none to it, confining himself, in the morning, to boarding the *Richelieu,* and in the afternoon to attending a reception given by the French colony in a New York hotel.

On the way back, the stop he made in Canada and his journey through England did not modify the effect the General produced in the United States. To the Ottawa newspapermen Giraud declared that his only purpose was to reconstitute a French Army, for nothing else mattered. To the London press, which for three years had watched the Free French effort to sustain the national cause, he declared, "No one has the right to speak in the name of France!" On the whole, those among the Allies who, whether in responsible positions or not, had seen and heard General Giraud received the impression that if his person and his career merited respect, he was not made to lead his country in wartime. Many concluded that his role in France's recovery could be only secondary.

Meanwhile in Algiers the government, extricated from its bicephalism, began to take shape. The reuniting of the Empire, the moral and material necessities of the war effort, foreign relations, the connections with the resistance of metropolitan France and the obligation to prepare what must be done there at the time of the liberation confronted our committee with many problems. We held two sessions each week. The subjects we discussed bristled with thorns, each minister setting forth on the one hand his difficulties and on the other the inadequacy of his means. At least we attempted to have the discussions well prepared and to reach positive conclusions. Furthermore, if opinions differed my arbitration was delivered without difficulties, for there was no profound divergence on any question within the government itself. It must be added that without Parliament, elections and parties, no politics were played among the members of the committee. My task of leadership was thereby facilitated.

All the more since, technically speaking, I was ably assisted. On June 10 we had provided the government with a Secretariat-General and had placed Louis Joxe at its head with Raymond Offroy and Edgar Faure as his associates. Joxe provided connections among the ministers and between them and myself, set up the dossiers upon which, according to the order of the day, the committee deliberated, took note of the decisions, assured the publication of the statutes and decrees, and saw that they were put into effect. A model of conscientiousness and a tomb of discretion, he was to attend, as a silent and active witness, all the committee's sessions for over three years. The Secretariat-General inaugurated at Algiers was to remain thereafter the instrument of the government's collective work.

In July the Juridical Committee was born. With René Cassin as director and with the help of François Marion, Chairman Tebahar and others, this committee played the role which devolved normally upon the Council of State in regard to opinions to be given and texts to be formulated. Since the Algiers government had to adapt the application of the laws to the circumstances of war and to prepare the legislative, judicial and administrative measures to be taken in France at the time of liberation, the importance of the Juridical Committee can readily be seen. Further, the Committee on Disputes, presided over by Pierre Tissier and also functioning in the absence of the Council of State, handed down provisional judgments of sanction or of reparation which the abuses committed by Vichy made necessary within the public services. Lastly, the Military Committee was provided with a secretary, Colonel Billotte, who assisted me directly.

During the course of the month of July, administrative personnel, military staffs and public alike realized that the men appointed to the different departments into which governmental authority was traditionally distributed had become ministers, endowed with the authority and the responsibility inherent in their functions; that the chronic improvisation practiced by the Algiers system since the end of the Vichy regime in North Africa had been replaced by the operation of a competent and controlled body; that a central administration was now functioning instead of the spurious federation of Algeria, Morocco, Tunisia and West Africa, which had been instituted for personal reasons and in default of an authority of a national character; in short, that the central power had a head, followed a line, acted in an orderly fashion. The effect produced was such that, in influential circles, the unity around me, which hitherto had been hoped for only by individuals, was now admitted by everyone, as was the case with the mass of Frenchmen.

All in all, it was the state that we saw reappearing in fact and in influence, all the more prominently since it was not anonymous. As soon as Vichy could no longer deceive anyone, enthusiasm and assent, not to mention ambition, automatically inclined toward De Gaulle. In North Africa the ethnic and political structure of the populations, the attitude of the authorities and the pressure of the Allies had delayed this evolution, but henceforth it was irresistible. A tide of will and feeling consecrated that profound legitimacy which derives from the public welfare and which France has always recognized during her worst ordeals, whatever the so-called "legal" formulas of the moment. Here was an elemental requirement of which, for being its symbol, I felt myself no less the instrument and the servant. It was especially during public ceremonies, of course, that this was demonstrated to everyone: the passionate acclamation of the crowds, the tribute of the constituted authorities, the official gestures that centered upon me, served as an expression of the popular instinct. The national resolve, more powerful than any formal decree, openly appointed me to incarnate and lead the state.

On June 26 I went to Tunisia; I found the Regency suffering under the shocks which the invasion had inflicted upon it, the Vichy prejudice in favor of the Axis forces and the collusion of certain local nationalist elements with Germany and Italy. The material damage was serious, and so were the political contretemps. Before my arrival in Algiers, the "Civil and Military High Command" had dismissed Moncef Bey, whose attitude during the occupation had shown itself to be troublesome with regard to the obligations that linked him to France. A number of members of the two nationalist Destour parties were in prison. In the countryside, it had been necessary to mete out punishment for outrages committed with the invader's tolerance and, on occasion, his complicity against the persons and property of many French *colons* by looters or fanatics.

Resident-General Mast was working to repair the situation. He was doing his job with intelligence, limiting the lot of those punished, making as many conciliatory contacts as possible and moderating those who thirsted for vengeance. I gave him my support. To the authorities, the delegations and the French and Tunisian notables presented to me, I pointed out that there were only too many extenuating circumstances in what had occurred. To judge the faults committed by the native people, I said, one must first take into account the example of surrender set for them by Vichy, for instance the shocking "African Phalanx" established by its orders to fight at the side of the enemy. I declared that nothing was of greater importance now than to strengthen the union of

France and Tunisia, first by restoring the country's normal activity. After this period, it must be said, my government never met with serious difficulties in Tunisia. On the contrary, this noble kingdom once more associated itself with France by its co-operation in the war effort and the valor of its soldiers who were incorporated in our Army.

I went to see Sidi Lamine Bey, who had ascended the throne, in the order of succession, after Moncef had been deposed. He received me at Carthage, surrounded by his ministers, notably M. Baccouche. Despite the eddies of public opinion which the departure of his popular predecessor had aroused, the new sovereign assumed his task with a worthy simplicity. I was struck at seeing in his person, beneath the wisdom of age and character, a greater devotion to the service of his country. He himself, I have reason to believe, considered me as personifying a confident and thereby generous France, a France Tunisia had often imagined and occasionally encountered. Since then I have felt for Sidi Lamine an esteem and a friendship that have not altered.

On Sunday, June 27, amid popular acclamation after reviewing the troops and attending the services at the cathedral, I proceeded to the Esplanade Gambetta. Here, addressing the crowd of French with whom many Tunisians were mingled, I spoke of France, warning the enemy that she would strike with every means in her power until she overcame him, saluting her great allies and assuring them of her loyal understanding provided that this was reciprocal. After which I declared that if, until the ordeal of war was over, I solicited everyone's co-operation, I renounced in advance any subsequent claims on them; that the termination of the task I had undertaken for liberation and victory would be indicated by victory and liberation; and that once this was accomplished De Gaulle would not be a candidate for any office.

"To France," I cried, "to our lady France we have only one thing to say, that nothing matters to us except to serve her. We must liberate her, conquer her enemy, punish the traitors, preserve her friends, tear the gag from her mouth and the chains from her limbs so that she can make her voice heard and resume her march toward her destiny. We have nothing to ask of her except, perhaps, that on the day of liberty she will open her motherly arms to us so that we may weep for joy within them, and that on the day when death comes to take us she will bury us gently in her good and sacred soil."

On July 14 it was Algiers, capital of the Empire and of Fighting France, that provided a demonstration of the revival of the state and the recovery of national unity. The traditional military parade assumed the character of a kind of resurrection. In saluting the troops that marched past, I saw rising toward me like a wall of flame their tremendous desire to take part in the coming battles. The air of lighthearted confidence emanating from the army and the people revealed that spiritual accord which past disappointments had shaken and recent misfortunes destroyed but which today's hope resuscitated. I received the same impression from the huge crowd which I addressed in the Forum.

"So, then," I declared, "after three years of unspeakable torments, the French people reappear. They reappear en masse, gathered together, enthusiastic, beneath the folds of their flag. But this time they reappear united. And the union which the capital of the Empire demonstrates so emphatically today is the same union which tomorrow all our cities and all our villages will demonstrate as soon as they have been torn from the enemy and his henchmen." Taking this as my point of departure, I stressed for the benefit of the Allies, who I knew were all ears, the absurdity of plans that intended to make use of the French war effort while leaving France out of account. "Elsewhere in the world," I said, "some individuals have thought it possible to consider the operations of our armies independently of the feelings and the will of the great body of our people. They have imagined that our soldiers, our sailors and our flyers, differing in this from all the soldiers, sailors and flyers in the world, would go into battle without concerning themselves with the reasons for which they were braving death. In short, these supposedly realistic theoreticians have concluded that for the

French and for the French alone the national war effort could exist apart from national policy and national morale. We assure these 'realists' that they do not know what reality is. The French citizens who have been fighting the enemy on every front, whether for four years or for eight months, are doing so in the name of France, to attain the goals of France, in agreement with what France desires. Any system established on other foundations than these would lead to jeopardy or impotence. But France, who is staking her life, her greatness and her independence, admits in a matter as grave as this neither impotence nor jeopardy."

The nation that would be victorious tomorrow must have a goal after its liberation, a goal capable of inspiring and maintaining it in its effort. Therefore, after having lauded the activities and the sacrifices of the resistance, I invoked the flame of regeneration that was inspiring it in its fight. "France is not the sleeping beauty whom the prince of liberation will waken gently. France is a tortured captive, who, beneath the blows that afflict her in the cell where she lies, has once and for all measured the causes of her misfortunes as well as the infamy of her tyrants. France has already chosen a new road." And I indicated what objectives the resistance aimed at both at home and abroad once the victory was achieved. I concluded by summoning the people to a sense of pride. "Frenchmen, for fifteen hundred years our country has remained alive in its griefs and in its glories. The present ordeal is not over. But already the end of the worst drama in all our history is in sight. Let us lift our heads. Let us close ranks fraternally and march together, in the struggle, beyond victory to our new destinies."

The flood of emotion with which the crowd replied to these words revealed on the spot the definitive failure of the intrigues which certain individuals had long opposed to me. It was quite obvious that the artificial systems successively set up in Algiers to protect incompetence and satisfy foreign powers were crumbling relentlessly and that even if certain formalities still remained, De Gaulle had won the game.

Mr. Murphy, apparently impressed, came over to me on the

platform to pay me his compliments. "What an enormous crowd!" he told me.

"Those," I answered him, "are the ten per cent Gaullists that you reckoned on in Algiers."

Morocco in its turn furnished a similar spectacle. On August 6 I reached Rabat. Here those who revealed their sympathy for Free France had long been harshly punished and vilified, while many kept silence in the shadows. Now, beneath the brilliant sun, the population, the authorities and the prominent citizens acclaimed me without reserve. Ambassador Puaux, the resident-general, gave me his report. His immediate concern was to keep alive a country cut off from all supplies and threatened by famine. As for the future, he saw looming there the problems posed by the political development of the protectorate. Nevertheless, the resident-general was certain that Morocco would remain attached to France and assume its great share of the effort put forth by the Empire to liberate her.

Beneath the official pomp I made more intimate contact with Sultan Mohammed ben Youssef. This young, proud, personable sovereign did not conceal his ambition to be at the head of his country on its march toward progress and, one day, toward independence. Watching and listening to him as he spoke, sometimes ardent, sometimes prudent, always skillful, one felt that he was ready to come to an agreement with whoever would help him play this role, but that he was capable of bringing a great deal of obstinacy to bear against those who wished to oppose him in this design. Furthermore, he admired France, believed in her recovery and did not dream that Morocco could advance without her. If he had on occasion lent an ear to certain intimations which Germany in her triumphs had whispered to him, and if during the Anfa conference he had listened to Roosevelt's insinuations, he had nevertheless shown himself loyal to our country. It must be admitted that Noguès' influence had been happily exercised, in this regard, on the sovereign's mind.

I believed I should take the Sultan Mohammed ben Youssef for precisely what he was, a man resolved to become great, and that I should show myself to him for what I was, the leader of a France that was his suzerain but disposed to do much for those who stood by her. Making use of the credit which the success and the inspiration of Fighting France had stored up for me in his mind, I created bonds of a personal friendship with him. But we also concluded an alliance on the grounds of understanding and common action which neither of us ever broke as long as I could speak to him in the name of France.

On Sunday, August 8, I made my entry into Casablanca. The walls had disappeared beneath flags and banners. Six months before I had had to reside in the city's outskirts, constrained to secrecy and surrounded with barbed wire and American sentry posts. Today my presence served as a symbol and a center of French authority. Once the brilliant review of the troops was over, I addressed the human tide that covered the Place Lyautey. I spoke in tones of calm assurance. France's share in the victory was henceforth certain thanks to her unity and that of the Empire, I said, citing as an example Morocco, "who cries out her fervor, her confidence and her hope with the great voice of Casablanca." That afternoon I visited Meknès. August 9 was spent at Fez. The Arab city, which I rode through in all directions in a tumult of trumpets and beneath a forest of banners, exploded in acclamations quite exceptional for this traditionally withdrawn city. Finally on the tenth, in the region of Ifrane, I received a magnificent welcome from the Berbers and their leaders.

At the very moment when the last clouds of misunderstanding were disappearing in Tunisia, Algeria and Morocco, the French Antilles joined us with great enthusiasm. They did so of their own accord, without the Allies having directly intervened.

Since 1940 Admiral Robert, the High Commissioner, had kept these colonies under oath to the Marshal. Having at his disposal the cruisers *Émile-Bertin* and *Jeanne d'Arc,* the aircraft carrier *Béarn,* the auxiliary cruisers *Barfleur, Quercy* and *Esterel* and the tankers *Var* and *Mékong,* as well as an important garrison, he applied austerity measures and, by guaranteeing his neutrality, obtained essential supplies from the Americans. But as events changed, the population and many military units indicated their desire to join those who were fighting the enemy.

In the spring of 1941 I had sent Jean Massip, alias Colonel Perrel, to the Martinique and Guadeloupe area; his mission was to spread the influence of Free France and to send on to our fighting forces those volunteers who succeeded in escaping from the islands. Massip, despite many obstacles, had done everything possible. Operating from a base in the British colonies of St. Lucia, Dominica and Trinidad and assisted locally by several loyal Frenchmen such as Joseph Salvatori and Adigard des Gautries, he had managed to establish contact with the resistance units of Fort-de-France and Basse-Terre and to send into the active theaters more than two thousand volunteers. At the beginning of 1943 there was every indication that a great movement would soon sweep the French territories in the New World and the troops serving there into the camp of liberation.

In the month of March, Guiana rid itself of Vichy's authority, as it had aspired to do for some time. As early as October 1940 I had seen a detachment of two hundred men from the banks of the Maroni landing in Free French Africa, under Major Chandon's command. Later, a "Rally Committee" had been formed, headed by M. Sophia, the mayor of Cayenne. On March 16, 1943, the population gathered in the Place du Palmiste, loudly demanding the removal of the governor, and paraded through the city beneath Cross of Lorraine banners, cheering General de Gaulle. Faced with this outbreak, the governor had retired. M. Sophia had then telegraphed to inform me of his people's rallying to our cause and to ask that a new governor be sent to Cayenne. But on the urgent advice of the United States consul he had sent a similar telegram to General Giraud. At this period union had not been effected between the London committee and the Algiers organization. Therefore the Americans, who controlled Guiana's means of communication with the outside world, had arranged that Governor Rapenne, delegated by Giraud, should arrive in Cayenne as soon as possible, while Governor Bertaut, sent by me, could not reach the colony. After which, taking advantage of the fact that the colony's supplies depended entirely on their good offices, our allies had forced Guiana to accept an administrator who, though very creditable, was not the one they had requested. It is true that two months later the formation of the Committee of Liberation at Algiers was to permit the regularization of what strongly resembled a hoax.

In June Martinique took decisive action. For several months Admiral Robert had been receiving innumerable petitions urging him to permit this ardently French territory to do its duty toward France. I myself had found occasion to send Surgeon General Le Dantec to Fort-de-France in April 1943 to offer Robert a satisfactory way out of his predicament, and in May proposed to Giraud to send the High Commissioner a letter signed by both of us, inviting him to re-enter the war at our side. These steps had been taken in the Admiral's behalf, but they remained without a reply. On the contrary, threats and sanctions against the local resistance redoubled on the island.

Meanwhile the island's Liberation Committee, having at its head Victor Sévère, the deputy mayor of Fort-de-France, as well as Emmanuel Rimbaud, Léontel Calvert and others, appeared openly. On June 18, the anniversary of my 1940 appeal, this committee placed a Cross of Lorraine before the monument to the dead. Then it called upon the population to stage a mass meeting, which took place on June 24. Five days later Major Tourtet and his battalion joined the movement. The excitement spread to the Navy. Admiral Robert was obliged to yield to it. On June 30 he made public that he had asked the government of the United States to send a plenipotentiary to establish the means of effecting a change of the French authority, and that he would then retire. This announcement restored calm, although there was no evidence whatsoever that the Americans were needed to settle this national affair. Two days later a delegation from Martinique arrived in Dominica, informed Jean Massip of the colony's rallying to the cause of Free

France and asked that General de Gaulle send a delegate armed with full powers.

At Guadeloupe events had followed an analogous course. For a long time the population's hopes and desires had been inclined toward Free France. M. Valentino, president of the executive commission of the general council, with M. Meloir, M. Gérard and other prominent citizens, had formed a Committee of the Resistance. Valentino, arrested and then transferred to Guiana, managed after that colony's liberation to return to Guadeloupe in secret. On May 2, 1943, a demonstration in favor of Fighting France took place at Basse-Terre and was ended by a bloody fusillade directed on the crowd by soldiers acting under orders. On June 4 Valentino and his cohorts vainly tried to seize power, but subsequently managed to reach Jean Massip. At the end of the same month, Robert's retirement at Martinique finally decided the matter at Guadeloupe.

On July 3 the Committee of National Liberation, informed of these events, sent as delegate extraordinary to the Antilles its representative in Washington, Ambassador Henri Hoppenot. The latter, accompanied by high Army, Navy and Air Force officers, reached Fort-de-France on July 14. Beneath a sea of Cross of Lorraine flags, in a storm of *"Vive De Gaulles!"* he was received by Sévère, his committee and an immense throng. Hoppenot and his mission took affairs in hand immediately. With tact and firmness they put everything and everyone in order. Admiral Robert went to Puerto Rico and from there to Vichy. Governor Ponton, sent from Equatorial Africa, was appointed Governor of Martinique. Secretary General Poirier and later Governor Bertaut received the responsibility for Guadeloupe. The Bank of France's gold stored at Fort-de-France passed into the control of the Algiers committee. The naval squadron was ordered to the United States, and after being reconditioned it reached North Africa. The troops were incorporated into the army of liberation. In particular, the Antilles Battalion, under the orders of Lieutenant Colonel Tourtet, was to take a brilliant part in the battle of Royan, where its leader was killed by the enemy.

The rallying of the Antilles completed the fulfillment of a great national plan which had been glimpsed during the disaster by the last government of the Third Republic, adopted by Free France immediately after the "armistice" and subsequently pursued at all costs, but to which the Vichy governors, obeying, conscientiously or not, the enemy's intentions, had been unremittingly opposed. Except for Indochina, which Japan held at her mercy, all the territories of the Empire had now re-entered the war for the liberation of France.

As for the French overseas forces, they too had all joined us. The Alexandria squadron, stranded in neutrality since 1940, had in June 1943 placed itself under the government's orders, by its commander's decision. In August Admiral Godfroy brought to the ports of North Africa by way of the Red Sea, the Cape and Dakar the battleship *Lorraine,* the cruisers *Duguay-Trouin, Duquesne, Suffren* and *Tourville,* the destroyers *Basque, Forbin* and *Fortuné,* and the submarine *Protée.* These splendid units, like those from the Antilles, re-entered the struggle in their turn. Such reinforcements, along with the ships remaining to the fleet in the African ports and those flying the Cross of Lorraine, were to permit the reappearance on the seas of an important French naval force by which Europe would see victory approach.

The obscure harmony by which events arrange themselves made the renewal of French power coincide with the weakening of the enemy's. Italy, once again, in Byron's phrase, "the sad mother of a dead empire" and about to be invaded, was heading toward a breach with the German Reich. For the French Committee of National Liberation, the problems posed by Italy's change of face were to lead it to consolidate itself as a government. At the same time, the Allies would be compelled to realize that there could be no valid settlement of the Italian question without French participation. Then too, the rigorous campaign they were beginning in the peninsula would soon lead them to ask for the co-operation of our troops and our ships. They would therefore be inclined to accord us a larger share in the diplomatic realm as on the field of battle. Having need of France, they would willy-nilly have to address themselves to the central French power.

On July 10 a British army and an American army under the command of General Alexander landed in Sicily. We had not been asked to take part in this operation, the reason given being the insufficient armament of our units, which in fact had as yet received only a small amount of American matériel. In reality, Washington and London, counting on the imminent collapse of Italy, preferred us not to be involved in the decisive battle, nor in the armistice that would follow.

In Sicily our allies ran into stiff resistance from the Germans, who had rushed to defend the island. Nevertheless, after six weeks of hard-fought battles, the Anglo-American forces ended by taking Sicily. But meanwhile it was learned that the Fascist Grand Council had repudiated Mussolini, that the King of Italy had had the Duce arrested, that Marshal Badoglio had been appointed Prime Minister. To be sure, the latter proclaimed his resolve to continue the war on the Axis side, but it was obvious that this attitude masked contrary intentions. The Fuehrer was no more deceived than anyone else. In the speech he made on the radio the next day, the anxiety of the betrayed ally could be discerned beneath the screams of threatening assurance. Also noticeable was a human note rare for the dictator. Hitler hailed in Mussolini the fallen comrade; he did so in the tone of a man who was soon to fall himself but who intended to measure himself against destiny until the end.

The Roman *coup de théâtre* occurred on July 25. On the twenty-seventh I took my stand publicly. Speaking on the radio, I declared that Mussolini's fall, the sign of the certain defeat of the Axis and a proof of the failure of the Fascist system, was for France the first of justice's revenges. "Mussolini's example," I said, "is now added to the history of all those who outraged the majesty of France and whom destiny has punished." Having stressed the fact that we must redouble our efforts to achieve victory, I stated, "The collapse of Italian Fascism may very soon lead to a new settlement of accounts. And it is quite obvious that despite the terrible situation in which our country still finds herself, such a settlement can be neither valid nor lasting without France." I let it be understood, moreover, that in this participation we would be animated by a desire for reconciliation rather than by the spirit of revenge, "since the close proximity and, to a certain degree, the interdependence of the two great Latin peoples are still, despite present grievances, the elements on which the reason and the hope of Europe do not despair of establishing themselves." Lastly, I reaffirmed "the duties imposed and the rights conferred in this matter on the Committee of National Liberation by the ardent confidence of the overwhelming French majority and its own character as a body responsible for the sacred interests of the nation."

But how sustain such a policy if we ourselves remained plunged in confusion? On July 31, Giraud having returned from his trip abroad, I took up the question with the committee in a hand-to-hand struggle. This time the government adopted measures that brought us nearer our goal.

Leadership of the committee and the chairmanship of the sessions henceforth devolved upon De Gaulle alone. Although Giraud retained, along with the title of president, the privilege of signing, like myself, all ordinances and decrees, this was no longer anything but a mere formality, since their texts were previously determined in council and under my sole arbitration. In the military domain, a coalition of all forces was decided on; the Military High Committee became, under my chairmanship, the Committee for National Defense; General Giraud was decreed commander in chief of the French forces, it being understood that he would cease to be a member of the government if occasion should eventually arise for him to assume command in a definite theater of war. General Legentilhomme, recalled from Madagascar, assumed the functions of Vice-Commissioner and, shortly afterward, of Commissioner of National Defense. General Leyer, Admiral Lemonnier and General Bouscat became the chiefs of staff respectively of the Army, the Navy and the Air Force, with General Koenig, Admiral Auboyneau and General Valin to second them as deputy chiefs. As for Juin, he was confirmed in his mission of preparing and, shortly, of commanding the expeditionary corps destined for Italy.

These arrangements settled the essential problems in principle; they would still have to be applied. Despite previous experiences, I wanted to believe this would be possible; that General Giraud, having received the highest title and the most extensive powers the committee could give to a military leader without relinquishing its own, would renounce his claims to governmental authority; that he would operate only in his own domain, apart from the man who bore the burden of directing the government. At the very beginning it appeared possible to believe this.

Throughout the month of August and the first days of September, the Committee of National Liberation, continuing to function as it had in July, played its governmental role. Thus, for matters concerning mobilization, finance, supply, transportation, housing, the merchant marine, outfitting of ports and airfields, public health, etc., many problems could be settled. These were often rendered very difficult by the extreme penury of those territories dependent in peacetime on goods from abroad now no longer available, deprived of important military matériel, subject to multiple taxation and overpopulated because of the presence of Allied troops and large numbers of refugees from metropolitan France.

At the same time the committee defined its position in regard to the resistance as well as to Vichy. It convoked the Consultative Assembly for November, while on September 3, without objection from a single one of its members, it passed the following resolution which was immediately made public:

> *Resolved,* To assure, as soon as circumstances permit, the operation of justice in regard to Marshal Pétain and to those who have taken or are taking part in the pseudogovernments formed by him, who have capitulated, violated the constitution, collaborated with the enemy, handed over French workers to the Germans and compelled French forces to fight against the Allies or against those of the French who were continuing the struggle.

Abroad the committee's action was affirmed in the same way. The diplomatic, economic and military missions which Fighting France and the Algiers system had respectively and separately maintained in England and the United States were now unified. Viénot in London and Hoppenot in Washington were now our sole representatives, each having under his authority all officials and military men present in the country to which he was accredited. In August we appointed Jean Monnet, Commissioner of Armament and Supply, to engage in negotiations with the American, British and Canadian governments that would result in reciprocal lend-lease agreements including matériel, foodstuffs and services to be furnished by one party or the other, and to prepare what must be done at the time of liberation to assure France's basic necessities. During this time Couve de Murville, Commissioner of Finance, and the Chancellor of the Exchequer terminated the financial agreement made in March 1941 between Free France and England. On September 7 we addressed to Washington and London a draft of an agreement specifying the "methods of co-operation to be established, from the day when the Allied forces land in France, between these forces on the one hand and the authorities and the population on the other," and requesting the immediate discussion of this matter by three governments. We suspected, in fact, that our allies were cherishing the plan of assuming, under cover of their military command, the governmental control of our country as they penetrated it, and we were of course resolved to keep them from doing so.

Finally, realizing that the Italian capitulation was imminent and that our allies would associate us with the advantages and honors of the triumph only to the least possible degree, we informed them officially that the French Committee of National Liberation intended to take part "first in the armistice negotiations, then in the deliberations and decisions of those bodies whose task it will be to assure the execution of the conditions imposed upon Italy." This was how we expressed ourselves in a note René Massigli took to Messrs. Macmillan and Murphy on August 2. The same note specified the points directly concerning France which we felt should be inserted in the future convention.

In the military domain, the collaboration of the head of the government and the commander in chief seemed, at present, satisfactory. General Giraud, delighted to see himself confirmed in a capacity dear to him and to take the Free French forces under his command, flaunted his loyalism. The Committee for National Defense had no difficulty adopting the measures concerning the merging of our forces. Leclerc and his column reached Morocco. The Larminat Group took up positions in Tunisia. Various ships and several air groups originating in North Africa were sent to Great Britain to operate from English bases side by side with Cross of Lorraine units. At the same time the Committee for National Defense determined the plan for reorganizing the Army, the Navy and the Air Force on the basis of the officers and fighting strength at our disposal and according to the armament coming from the United States. As for the use of these forces within the coalition, our intentions were established in the form of a De Gaulle-Giraud memorandum addressed on September 18 to Roosevelt, Churchill and Stalin.

Having reckoned the units we could put into the field, we indicated that, without prejudice to what could be done beforehand in Italy with the co-operation of our troops, the principal French effort on land, on sea and in the air would be dedicated directly to the liberation of France and would be engaged in the south of metropolitan France, leaving from North Africa. All the same, we wrote, it was necessary that certain forces furnished by us take part in the northern operations. At least one French armored division must be transported to England in time to assure the liberation of Paris. Also, a regiment of parachute troops, some commandos, several ships and five or six air groups would be engaged from the beginning of the landing. Lastly, we made known our willingness to send to the Far East, once the battle of Europe was won, an expeditionary corps and the bulk of our naval forces in order to co-operate in the struggle against Japan and to liberate Indochina.

All of this was in fact to be accomplished in that order, point by point.

During the month of August I inspected the troops in Algeria, the warships outfitted in the ports of Algiers and Oran, and the air bases. Everywhere I conferred with the officers. Ever since the disaster of 1940, the defection of the Vichy leaders, the weakening of discipline and chance circumstances had led many of these men of honor and duty into other paths than those they were now following. But none, in his heart of hearts, had ever lost hope of reentering the battle against the enemies of France. Beneath their attitude of attention and respect they were profoundly impressed by the presence of this De Gaulle whom a certain political group had often commanded them to disapprove and occasionally ordered them to oppose, but whom the national instinct and the logic of events now endowed with the supreme power and whose authority not one of them dreamed of questioning. I watched them straining to hear and understand me while I spoke to them with the dignity but also with the frankness due to us both. The speech delivered, the salutes exchanged, the handshakes given, I left their company and went on to some other task, resolved more than ever that the French Army should exact its share of the victory and thereby reopen the future to the nation.

The consolidation of French authority obliged the Allies to depart somewhat from the attitude of doubt and distrust they had hitherto adopted in its regard. Official recognition was granted the Committee of Liberation by the United States, Great Britain and Soviet Russia on August 26. Mexico, Cuba, Norway, Greece, Poland, Chile and Belgium had already taken the necessary steps.

As a matter of fact, the formulas chosen by the three other great powers revealed profound differences. Washington employed the most restricted, announcing that the committee was recognized as administering the overseas territories which recognized its authority. London used the same terms, but added that in the eyes of Great Britain the committee was the body qualified to pursue the conduct of the French war effort. Moscow revealed itself as the most generous. For Soviet Russia, the committee represented "the interests of State of the French Republic"; it was "the only executive body and the only qualified representative of all French patriots struggling against Hitlerism." The example of the Big Three was rapidly followed by others. On September 3, speaking on the radio on the occasion of the war's fourth anniversary, I was able to say, "The recognition of the French Committee of National Liberation by twenty-six states furnishes striking proof of our solidarity for victory and for peace."

However, the organization of the central power as it had been determined on July 31 could subsist only if the subordination of the military command to the government were confirmed without equivocation within the committee and abroad. The Italian affair was to demonstrate that this was not the case.

On September 3 Badoglio, who for several weeks had been making secret contact with Anglo-American agents, surrendered to them through the intermediary of a delegation sent to Syracuse. At the same time the Allied forces landed in Calabria. An American army under the command of General Clark prepared to land in the vicinity of Naples to join and, if need be, protect the King of Italy and his government as well as the troops loyal to them which they had concentrated at Rome. On August 29 Macmillan and Murphy had sent Massigli a memorandum in anticipation of the Italians' surrender, asking the French Committee of Liberation to agree that in its name, as in the name of all the Allied Nations, General Eisenhower was empowered to sign with Marshal Badoglio an armistice convention covering all Allied needs, notably those of France. The memorandum indicated the broad outlines of the instrument envisaged and ended with an assurance that the governments of the United Kingdom and the United States would do what they could to make it possible for the French Committee of National Liberation to send a representative to the signing if it should so desire.

We had answered on September 1 by a note agreeing that Eisenhower should conclude the armistice in our name, as in the name of all the Allies, asking that the text of the document be sent to us immediately, and declaring ourselves ready at a moment's notice to send a representative of the French command to wherever the armistice convention was to be signed.

Now came the moment for Washington and London to show whether or not they intended that France should be their full partner in the successive settlements that were to terminate hostilities. This occasion seemed all the more propitious since it concerned, first of all, Italy, whom French forces had never ceased to fight, whose territory, it was already known, would not be wrested from the Germans without the co-operation of our army, and who had no other neighbor among the Western countries but France and would not be able to have her territorial, political, economic and colonial future decided without France. Nevertheless, we were to discover that in this crucial affair Americans and British alike would proceed quite without scruple in regard to our committee only a few days after having formally recognized it.

In fact, on the afternoon of September 8 Macmillan and Murphy came to tell Massigli that the Italian surrender was a *fait accompli* and that General Eisenhower would announce it in half an hour. They also sent to the Commissioner of Foreign Affairs—ridiculous formality!—the text of the declaration in which the Allied commander in chief made public at virtually that very moment that he had granted the Italian government a military armistice the terms of which had been approved by the British, American and Soviet governments.

When Massigli pointed out that there was no mention of France, contrary to what England and the United States had, in writing, given us to believe on August 29, his interlocutors replied that Eisenhower's declaration was above all a maneuver hastily employed to impress the Italian Army and population while the Allies were carrying out a new and difficult operation in the peninsula.

"Maneuver or not," Massigli returned, "you tell me that an armistice has been signed. When was it signed? What were its terms?"

Macmillan and Murphy confined themselves to saying that General Giraud, president of the French Committee, had been kept *au courant* by Supreme Headquarters and that he had had nothing to add in France's behalf. That night again, Massigli saw Macmillan and questioned him; the British Secretary of State admitted that the negotiations of the London and Washington governments with the Italian government had been in progress since August 20. But he repeated that Giraud had been informed of everything.

On September 9 I convened the Committee of Liberation. The report of the Commissioner of Foreign Affairs naturally aroused emotion and displeasure as to the procedure and the probable intentions of the Anglo-American powers. We issued a communiqué expressing France's satisfaction at Italy's defeat, recalling the contribution of the French armies and the resistance, and acknowledging General Eisenhower's declaration, but stating that "the vital interests of metropolitan France and the French Empire involve the participation of France in any convention concerning Italy."

During the session I asked General Giraud his reasons for not informing the government and, in particular, its head of the vital news which had been communicated to him by the Allies and which, had we known about it in time, would have permitted us to make the most of what was due to France. Giraud assured us that he had received no information relative to the armistice. When, on the evening of that same day, Massigli reported this denial to Macmillan and to Murphy, they maintained their assertions, at the same time suggesting with some embarrassment that the ignorance of French in Eisenhower's headquarters and of English among Giraud's General Staff might be the cause of the misunderstanding. The next day they came to apologize, saying that after an investigation they had discovered it was only that morning that General Eisenhower had informed General Giraud of the terms of the armistice.

There could be no doubt: our allies were in agreement to keep us at as great a distance as they could from decisions concerning Italy. We could expect that tomorrow they would make still greater efforts to determine the destiny of Europe without France. But they must be made to realize that France would not tolerate this exclusion, and that they could not count on her in the future if they disregarded her now.

On September 12, on the occasion of my official visit to Oran, I dotted my i's and crossed my t's. Speaking to an enormous crowd before the City Hall, I declared, "The country wishes to redouble its efforts in order to hasten the enemy's defeat. It also wishes to take part, in its proper rank, in the settlement of the conflict and in the reconstruction of the world." On this point I appealed to the "solidarity of the nations of good will," adding, "There exists among them an interdependence which is such that each has an obligation to consider the vital interests and the dignity of the others." Referring to the suffering French people and the French soldiers of the Empire and of metropolitan France who were taking and would take part in the great battles, I warned, "The only true realism is the realism that does not deceive them.

"In the fifth year of the war," I acknowledged, "France unfortunately is not in a position to put into the line many of those divisions, ships and air squadrons by which the contribution of states may be reckoned summarily. As a result of a disaster endured when France, almost alone, confronted Hitler and Mussolini, the spirit of surrender that possessed certain individuals partially sabotaged the national war effort. We staggered, it is true. But was this not, first of all, a result of all the blood we had shed some twenty years before in others' defense as much as in our own?" I concluded by declaring, "France claims, in the interest of all, the place she deserves in the resolution of the drama whose denouement is now beginning." All the eloquence in the world was in the popular acclamation that greeted this speech.

It was evident, from the behavior of Messrs. Macmillan and Murphy, that our allies had invoked if not employed the ridiculous dualism of our government as an alibi for breaking their word. Now, almost immediately afterward, the same dualism was to betray its inadequacy in regard to an important national and military operation: the liberation of Corsica.

In 1941 Free France had sent Captain Scamaroni to the island with a mission to prepare action there. For two years Scamaroni had done excellent work, managing to unite all resistance groups so that no party, no clan, could monopolize the general effort for its own advantage. The "National Front," with Giovoni as its political leader and Vittori as its military chief, both of them Communists, had accepted the delegate of Free France, as had the patriots morally committed to Raimondi and the Giaccobbi brothers, and even the bands led by former soldiers, such as that of Lieutenant Alphonse de Peretti. Unfortunately, our valiant delegate had fallen into the hands of the Italians, who had occupied the island the day after the Allies landed in North Africa. Tortured horribly, Scamaroni had died to keep his secrets.

At this period—March 1943—the Battle of Tunisia was drawing to its close. There was every indication that Corsica would be next among the operations directed toward Italy and the south of France. In this island of maquis,* fiercely attached to France, where the invader's presence and pretensions provoked the most intense patriotism, a great tide of rebellion was secretly rising. Thousands of resolute men, supported by the population's active sympathy, awaited impatiently the occasion to open fire.

The Algiers system, in turn, made contact with Corsica. The "Civil and Military Commander in Chief" first sent a few agents, then, in April 1943, Major Colonna d'Istria. In itself, this was entirely praiseworthy. What was less so was the fact that once our Algiers committee was constituted in June, General Giraud did not breathe a word to me of the action he was taking in Corsica. Colonna described himself on the island, no doubt in good faith, as the representative of the entire government. In this capacity he dealt exclusively with the Communist leaders Giovoni and Vittori, either because he did not realize the disadvantage of this preference, or because he wished to simplify his task, or because he had received orders to do so. It must be added that the Communist Party had sent on a mission to Giraud from France Deputy Pourtalet of

* The scrubby brushland of Corsica, which is often used as a place of hiding by local outlaws and which gave its name to the French underground fighters resisting the occupation forces during World War II.—Tr.

the Alpes-Maritimes, who had been in contact with Giovoni for some time from Nice. Pourtalet had not failed to provide Giraud with information concerning the situation in Corsica and suggestions that were advantageous to his party. During the months of July and August, General Giraud's secret services were extremely active, without my knowledge, in their efforts to arm the Corsican resistance. British intelligence, which ordinarily did not go out of its way to be generous without ulterior motives, procured ten thousand machine guns. These were shipped from Algiers, some by the submarine *Casabianca,* which made several perilous crossings, others by British planes which parachuted them into areas indicated by Colonna. All these weapons, received and distributed by the leaders of the "National Front," decisively conferred on Giovoni and Vittori the monopoly of authority. The Communist leaders seized control of the whole resistance movement, in which, however, the members of their party comprised only a minority. All communication between Algiers and the island's "Gaullists" being cut off, the latter, lacking any other recourse, compromised with this organization to the point where my own cousin, Henri Maillot, agreed to become a member of the National Front committee in the belief that he was fulfilling my intentions.

On September 4, the day after Badoglio signed the armistice which I was not to hear about until the eighth, Giovoni was brought to Algiers by the *Casabianca.* I did not know he was there. He came to confer with the commander in chief concerning an operation which the Syracuse surrender was to permit by rendering neutral or favorable the eighty thousand Italians occupying Corsica. Giraud told me nothing of this visit; Giovoni made no contact with me and left Algiers on September 6. On the evening of the ninth we learned that the resistance party had taken control of Ajaccio, that the prefect himself had proclaimed the department's support of the Committee of National Liberation, and that the Italian garrison had offered no opposition. It was then that General Giraud came to tell me for the first time what he had been doing in Corsica.

When he had told his story I replied, "Amid all the good news now reaching us, General, I am offended and disturbed by your manner of proceeding in regard to me and to the government, by your concealing your activities from us. I do not approve of the monopoly you have given to the Communist leaders. I consider it unacceptable that you have let it be thought that this was done in my name as well as in yours. Lastly, having heard what you have to say concerning Giovoni's recent visit, the operation you worked out with him, the conditions under which it was launched, I cannot understand how you could say this morning to our council of ministers that you did not know of the imminence of the Italian armistice. From all this I shall draw the obvious conclusions once we have extricated ourselves from the difficulties which now engage us. For the moment, we must deal with the military situation. Corsica must be given aid at once. The government will then do what it must to stop up, once and for all, the source of our disagreements." At least Giraud and I were in accord that troops should be sent to Corsica immediately. As for the execution of this operation, it was in his sphere of activity. From that point of view I had no doubt he would decide for the best.

The Committee of Liberation convened the next day and adopted a similar attitude toward the commander in chief. At the same time that they entrusted him with powers to settle the military situation, they reproached him for having taken action deliberately and alone in a sphere which did not properly pertain to him. During the same session Charles Luizet was appointed prefect of Corsica. He was to leave without delay with a trustworthy team. General Mollard would accompany him as military governor of the island.

The military action in Corsica was carried out with great ardor. Nevertheless, the intervention of the regular troops and of the ships carrying them was quite improvised. Actually a complete plan had been drawn up several weeks before by General Juin at the commander in chief's request. On the supposition that the Italians would remain neutral, Juin advised simultaneous landings on the east and the west coasts with the aim of cutting the Germans off from the two coastal roads. He anticipated the engagement of two divisions, one of them mountain troops, a *tabor* group, a hundred armored units and some commandos. In this way the German forces already stationed on the island and those that would come from Sardinia could be liquidated or captured. On September 9 the elements of such an expedition were available and eager to get into action, but their transportation required a considerable tonnage, as well as heavy naval and air protection. Since the necessary warships, merchant ships and planes had not been assembled in advance, the commander in chief was in no position to execute so extensive an operation with our own means. Turning to the Allies for aid, he met with a refusal, for at that moment they were fully engaged in their attempt to land at Salerno.

However, matters were at a point where some immediate action had to be taken. Giraud decided, and I approved his decision, to effect the operation on a reduced scale. The troops he could manage to infiltrate into Corsica in the space of three weeks would, with the help of the resistance, be able to protect the greater part of the island against German points of attack, to harass the German columns during their retreat and to inflict important losses on German personnel and matériel. It was true that despite the vigor of their action they could not prevent the enemy from putting to sea; nevertheless, the liberation of Corsica by French forces and only French forces would make a profound impression on the French and on the Allies.

On the night of September 12, the valiant *Casabianca* landed our first units at Ajaccio. Day after day the troops arrived: the "Shock Battalion," the Moroccan First Rifle Regiment, the Second *Tabor* Group, a mechanized squadron of the First Spahi Regiment, units of artillery, engineers and services; as well as the indispensable matériel: munitions, gasoline; the whole transported by the cruisers *Jeanne d'Arc* and *Montcalm,* the destroyers *Fantasque* and *Terrible,* the torpedo boats *Alcyon* and *Tempête,* the submarines *Aréthuse* and *Casabianca.* An air pursuit squadron took the Campo del Oro base. As for the Germans, their goal was to evacuate the

S.S. brigade they had on the island, and also the Ninetieth Panzer Division, which they hastily withdrew from Sardinia. Their maneuver was executed on the east on the Bonifacio-Bastia road under protection of heavy air cover and strong reconnaissance forces which they launched toward the island's interior. Many motorized barges took them on at Bastia and headed for the island of Elba and for Leghorn.

General Henry Martin was at the head of the French troops. He handled the operation with perfect competence: first assuring himself a bridgehead at Ajaccio; then sending commandos to support the resistance, which was grappling fiercely with the enemy at Bastia, Bonifacio, Quenza, Levie, Inzecca and other points, and holding the passes along the island's "spine"; then mopping up Porto Vecchio, Bonifacio, Favone, Ghisonaccia; and lastly approaching Bastia, driving back the Germans over the wooded, mountainous terrain of St. Florent and Cape Corse. General Martin had also come to a useful agreement with General Magli, commander of the Italian forces. The latter, despite the confusion of the odd situation in which he found himself, was to furnish our men with trucks and mule teams and to support them at certain points with his batteries. General Louchet headed the advance in the north, Major Gambiez the shock troops, Colonel de Latour the Algerian contingents, Colonel de Butler the rifles, Colonel de Lambilly the armored units; all led their troops brilliantly. General Giraud himself reached Corsica a few days after the first landings, examining the terrain, communicating to everyone the resoluteness that animated him. On October 4 our men entered Bastia, from which the enemy had been able to pull out his rear guard, but not without leaving a great deal of matériel.

The evening of the same day, I went to the commander in chief to congratulate him in the name of the government on the splendid results of his military operation. He had prepared and launched it, he had assumed the risk. The credit for it was his. Although the means at his disposal were on a rather small scale, the difficulties were great since without preparation he had to take elements from the Army, the Navy and the Air Force, hurl them nine hundred kilometers from our bases into the unknown, and combine them in a single action. On September 24 I said over the radio from Algiers, "The nation and the Empire hail the French fighters of Corsica, where the commander in chief of the French Army has just gone into the field himself to give his instructions for tomorrow's engagements. To these fighters and to their leaders, to those who have risen from the Corsican soil to liberate themselves and those whom the reviving French Army, Navy and Air Force have so boldly sent to them, the Committee of National Liberation addresses heartfelt testimony of France's love and pride."

But, justice having been done to General Giraud's military capacities, the fact remained that he had proceeded in an inadmissible fashion vis-à-vis the government. I repeated this to him that evening after having complimented him.

"You're talking politics," he said.

"Yes," I answered. "Because we are fighting a war. And war is one kind of politics." He heard but did not heed my words.

Fundamentally, Giraud could not resign himself to any form of subordination whatever. What he appeared to accept was never actually established. By nature and habit, but also by virtue of a kind of tactic, his mind shut itself within the purely military sphere, refused to consider human or national realities and made him blind to the prerogatives of the government. With such a psychology, he could not, in relation to me, disregard the old hierarchy. Not that he too did not feel the exceptional character of the mission that had devolved upon me. Moreover, he could give generous and moving evidence of his recognition, in public as in private. But he did not perceive its practical consequences. It must be added that the circumstances that had lately brought him to supreme power in North Africa, the support which American policy accorded him, the bitterness and the ill will nursed in my regard by certain French elements were not without influence on his ideas and his manner of behavior.

It was essential to put an end to this unsound situation. From that time on I was determined to induce General Giraud to leave the government, while continuing to make use of his services. Furthermore, the members of the Committee of Liberation also understood that we could no longer delay. Two new members whom I had invited to join us during September reinforced the trend toward categorical solutions. François de Menthon, arriving from France, had been appointed National Commissioner of Justice. Pierre Mendès-France, resigning from the "Lorraine" Air Force group on my orders, assumed the Finance post, replacing Couve de Murville, who had requested to be appointed France's representative to the Commission on Italian Affairs. Indeed, what seemed to be happening now in Corsica in the political sphere was making an impression on the ministers. André Philip, having visited the island to see how matters stood, had ascertained that the Communists, making use of the resistance, were installing town councils of their own choosing and were seizing control of all mass media. At no price did the ministers wish to see this precedent followed tomorrow in metropolitan France. They therefore urged me to make the changes in the government's structure which would protect it from such surprises.

Their concern was my own. But I intended to proceed to the last with circumspection in regard to the great soldier who, throughout his career, had rendered so many brilliant services and whose family the enemy had seized and was treating in a disgraceful manner at that very moment.

As for Corsica, everything was to fall into place there. I arrived on the island on October 8 and spent three magnificent days. My visit dispelled the shadows that remained. At Ajaccio I addressed the people in the town hall square. In response to the welcome I was given, my first words were to acknowledge "the tide of national enthusiasm which today bears us all onward." I paid tribute in the same breath to both the Corsican patriots and the African army. I indicated the complete collapse of the Vichy regime. "Where then," I said, "is the famous National Revolution today? How has it happened that so many portraits and insignia have given way in the wink of an eye to the heroic Cross of Lorraine? It was enough that the first tremor of liberation should cross the Corsican earth for this part of France to turn with a single impulse toward the government which is fighting the war, the government of unity, the government of the Republic."

Then, remarking that I was speaking "in the center of the Latin sea," I spoke of Italy. I emphasized how ridiculous had been the ambitions of our Latin neighbor, "impelled only yesterday to a monstrous alliance with German greed and alleging our decadence as a pretext to attempt to seize Corsica." But I also declared, "Once justice has been done, the France of tomorrow will not congeal in an attitude of bitterness toward a nation which is closely related to us and which nothing fundamental should divide from us.

"Victory is approaching," I said in conclusion. "It will be the victory of liberty. How could such a victory not be the victory of France as well?"

At Ajaccio I was in a position to see that Luizet, the prefect, Mollard, the military governor, and Eugène Macchini, the mayor, had affairs well in hand. Corte was vibrant with acclamation, though losing nothing of its rugged dignity. I went to Sartène and then visited Bastia, its streets filled with rubble, where the enemy had burned or exploded great stocks of matériel and munitions before fleeing, and where the miserable cemetery, torn apart by detonations, revealed the saddest spectacle of all. Surrounded by the first inhabitants to return to their homes, General Martin presented me to the victorious troops. Everywhere the paramilitary groups showed themselves justly proud of having upheld Corsica's glory by fighting for France. Every village in which I stopped lavished the most moving demonstrations upon us, while the Italian soldiers billeted there did not conceal their sympathy. Both upon arriving and upon my departure, my face stung by the rice my hosts flung according to the old Corsican custom, I heard the crackling of the liberation's machine guns.

Four weeks later the transformation of the Algiers committee became a *fait accompli*. In any case, the convening of the Consultative Assembly at the beginning of November made its overhauling necessary. After perilous journeys the resistance delegates arrived among us, bringing to North Africa the spirit of their constituents. Suddenly a fierce and salubrious spirit swept through the meetings, the offices and the newspapers of Algiers. The delegates made public the messages of trust in De Gaulle with which they had been charged. They could not speak enough of the underground, of its heroes, of its needs. They were brimming with ideas for the nation's future. In the task of extricating the government from its bicephalic state I wanted to associate myself with certain of these men coming to us from France.

During October the Committee of Liberation adopted, at my instance, a measure by virtue of which it would have only one president. Giraud himself set his signature to this. Furthermore, as the outlook for sending a French expeditionary corps into Italy grew brighter, he began again to hope that the Allies would call upon him to assume the high command in the peninsula. On November 6, in the presence of General Giraud and with his explicit agreement, the committee requested that "General de Gaulle proceed with those changes he considers it necessary to make in its composition."

This was done on November 9. A year after the bloody landing of the Anglo-American forces in Algeria and Morocco, five months after my own uncertain arrival in Algiers, the national will, oppressed and muffled as it was, had ended by carrying the day. So obvious was the current that the malevolence of its opponents could subsist only in obscurity. As for the Allies, they had to resign themselves to seeing France at war led by a French government. No longer invoking "military necessities" and "security of communications," their policy came to terms with what it could not prevent. The common effort was to gain much thereby. For myself, I felt strong enough in my cause to be certain that tomorrow the battle and the victory of the others would also be the battle and the victory of France.

CHAPTER 5

POLITICS

THERE was every indication that the approaching winter of 1943–44 would be the last before arms decided the fate of the war. But what government was to be established in Paris tomorrow? And what would such a government do? These were questions that assumed a pressing and prejudicial importance in every mind. They concerned a matter that was no longer a remote prospect but an imminent day of reckoning; this was why calculations and estimates were stimulated and brought to light. Political debate could be muffled a little while longer by blood and tears, veiled by the constraints imposed upon public opinion; but in spite of everything it was opened not only in the chancelleries and by men in office but in the thoughts of a tremendous mass of French people and in the discussions of great numbers of men abroad. Everyone knew France would reappear. Everyone wondered what France she would be.

This was what I had in mind when, at the beginning of November 1943, I changed the form of the Committee of Liberation. The country's only hope, during the decisive period now opening before it, was national unity; I intended that the government should bear its seal. Each of the principal parties, or, more accurately, each of the spiritual families among which the French people have traditionally distributed themselves, would have its representation assured by men whose affiliations were well known. But today it was the resistance that furnished the war effort and bore within it France's hope of regeneration. It was therefore essential that some of its leaders who as yet had no label should also sit beside me in the government. Lastly, several eminent authorities must be invited to serve on the committee in order to illuminate its activities and reinforce its credit.

Henri Queuille, Commissioner of State, and Pierre Mendès-France, Commissioner of Finance, were Radical members of Parliament. André Philip, in charge of the committee's relations with the Consultative Assembly, André Le Troquer, Commissioner of War and the Air Force—both deputies—and Adrien Tixier, Commissioner of Labor and Social Security, belonged to the Socialist Party. Louis Jacquinot, Commissioner of the Navy, was a Moderate deputy. François de Menthon, Keeper of the Seals, sat on the executive committee of the Christian Democratic Party. Such was our share of politicians. René Pleven, Commissioner for the Colonies, Emmanuel d'Astier of the Interior, René Capitant of National Education, André Diethelm of Production and Supply, Henri Frénay of Prisoners, Deportees and Refugees were all resistance members who had previously given no evidence of a specific political leaning. General Catroux, Commissioner of State in charge of Moslem affairs, Henri Bonnet, Commissioner of Information, René Massigli of Foreign Affairs, René Mayer of Communications and the Merchant Marine, Jean Monnet, Commissioner on special mission to the United States for provisions and armament, compelled recognition for their skill and their repute. Lacking the explicit assent of the religious hierarchy, I could not ask Monsignor Hincky to join the government as I should have liked.

Hence the recasting was not an overturning. Of the sixteen members now comprising the Committee of Liberation, only four had just joined it. It is true that four were also leaving it—General Giraud, whose military functions were henceforth recognized by everyone, including himself, as incompatible with the exercise of governmental power; General Georges, who withdrew with dignity; Dr. Abadie, who wished to return to his scientific work; and General Legentilhomme, who had requested a post in Great Britain.

And the Communists? The part they were playing in the resistance, as well as my own intention that their forces be incorporated with those of the nation at least for the duration of the war, led me to the decision to include two in the government. Since the end of August, the party, foreseeing this, had willingly promised the co-operation of several members. But, at the moment of complying, all kinds of setbacks managed to keep those whom I invited to join the Committee of Liberation from giving me a positive answer. On one occasion the party's delegation proposed other possible members, on another it demanded the details of my program, on still others it insisted that its members receive certain specific portfolios. Eventually, antagonized by this prolonged haggling, I broke off the negotiations.

In reality, two viewpoints divided the delegation. The extremists, following André Marty, wanted the party to make no alliances and to prepare, in the midst of the struggle against the enemy, to seize power by direct revolutionary action. The tacticians wanted to infiltrate the state by collaborating with others, first of all with me; the originator of this strategy was Maurice Thorez, still in Moscow and demanding to be permitted to return. Finally in March 1944 the Communists were to make their decision: They would permit Fernand Grenier and François Billoux to accept the posts I offered them—the Air Ministry to the first and a position as Commissioner of State to the second. On this occasion a further change of assignments took place within the government: Le Troquer was appointed national commissioner assigned to the liberated territories and Diethelm replaced him as Commissioner of War, while Mendès-France combined under his direction both Economy and Finance.

The committee, thus composed, devoted itself to its consecrated task of raising and organizing the means of making war, and also to preparing what must be done in order that the country could be fed, administered and set on its feet after liberation. For a long time a whisper from across the sea had prompted metropolitan France to struggle and to hope. Now it was the nation's call that impelled to action those outside of France who wanted to come to her aid. Harmony was established among the active elements at home and abroad. In order to turn this to the best account, I made the reshaping of the Algiers government coincide with the meeting of the Consultative Assembly of the resistance during the first days of November.

In accordance with the statute of September 17, some fifty of the delegates from France represented resistance organizations, some twenty the political parties, the latter chosen from those members of Parliament who had not voted to give full powers to Pétain in July 1940. The designation of both groups was made by committees necessarily limited and clandestine. Nevertheless, all arrived with the sense of being there in the name of the great mass of those who were struggling in the shadows. To these two categories were added a dozen Communists, in particular the deputies from the Seine department, arrested in 1939, interned since then at Algiers and released by General Giraud; twenty representatives of resistance groups in the Empire; and ten general advisers from Algeria. Whatever their origin, the delegates had common features that gave the "Consultative" its character.

What they had in common, what kept them in harmony, was on the one hand a passionate concern about the assistance to be furnished to the comrades of the resistance in the way of arms, money and propaganda, which, of course, they considered still insufficient, and on the other the rather confused but impassioned ideology that filled the minds of the members of the underground, exposed as they were to betrayals, ignored or denied by the cowardice of many, engaged not only against the German invader but also against the police and judicial apparatus of what, in metropolitan France, still passed for the French state. The burning solidarity of all those who "belonged," their distrust of and even their aversion for the administrator, the policeman, the official, and lastly a stubborn desire for purification—this was what obsessed them and, when the opportunity presented itself, united them in fervent demonstrations.

There was also the attachment they felt for Charles de Gaulle because he had protested against conformism, because he had been condemned to death, because throughout the nation his words, however remote and blurred, defied discretion and aroused nostalgia. Nevertheless, the effort he was leading for the restoration of national unity, the preservation of French sovereignty, the recovery of the state was less accessible to the majority of the delegates. Not that they were unconcerned about the nation's future. On the contrary, ideas and plans abounded in their councils. But if they were enthusiasts of formulas for reconstructing the universe, they showed themselves more reserved in relation to that authority without which a government can accomplish nothing. If they dreamed of seeing France once again among the first rank of nations, they hesitated to take the arduous action that might put her there and preferred to cherish the illusion of a Roosevelt and a Churchill eager to make room for her beside them. If they did not conceive of any other Frenchman but me at the country's head after liberation, if they had some idea that I could remain there while they, having become the elect of the people, were advancing toward some vague and marvelous rebirth, they remained reticent as to the powers I must have to direct such an operation. Even while fervently acclaiming De Gaulle, they were already whispering against "personal power."

In agreement among themselves in the sphere of feelings, the delegates were distributed into several families of minds. Some were simple fighters, absorbed by the struggle itself. Others, poets of action, were inspired by the heroism and brotherhood that the resistance manifested. The Communists, comprising a solid bloc, dealt harshly with affairs, eagerly outbid the others, and applied themselves above all to propaganda. Lastly, the "politicians," convinced that our cause was the cause of France and serving it to their best ability, did not, for all that, refrain from thinking of their careers, from maneuvering to push themselves forward according to the rules of their profession, and from considering the future from the point of view of elections, offices and the power it might one day offer them.

Among the last-named, the *"anciens,"* proud of having done their duty by refusing the late abdication but knowing what an ocean of unpopularity the regime had foundered under, walked on tiptoe, spoke softly and renounced all ambition. Yet deep in their hearts they looked forward to a return to the old ways, on condition that a few reforms be made. The *"nouveaux"* were very severe in regard to the old system. They wanted many changes made in it. Even so, beneath these reservations they exposed themselves in advance to the attractions of political life. On the whole, seeing around me these courageous colleagues of such good will, I felt myself full of esteem for all and of friendship for many. But also, probing their souls, I reached a point where I asked myself if among all those who spoke of revolution I was not, in truth, the only revolutionary.

The inaugural session of the Consultative Assembly took place on November 3, 1943. It was a profoundly moving ceremony; those who took part had the sense of being there in the name of an army of sufferers and soldiers, of representing a great French force. After greeting the assembly, "gathered despite extraordinary obstacles," in the name of the Committee of Liberation, I indicated the reasons that had long since decided me to convoke it as soon as possible and showed why and how I asked for its co-operation. What qualified it, I said, was that it proceeded from the resistance, "the fundamental reaction of the French people and the elementary expression of the national will."

To support the government in a war effort "requiring moral cohesion as much as material means"; to uphold its overseas activity "enabling France to resume, to the advantage of all, her great international role"; to help guide her in choosing the measures "to be imposed after liberation by the need to live when the termination of the struggle has left our soil covered with ruins and barren of all reserves of foodstuff and raw material, by the obligation to re-establish everywhere, in order and in dignity, the authority of the Republic, by the duty to assure the justice of the state, which is the only valid and admissible kind, by the changes to be made in the civil service, by the return of our imprisoned and deported youth"; lastly, to study "the great reforms that must be accomplished when the war is over"—such, I said, was what the Committee of Liberation expected of the assembly. I declared myself "certain of the result, for twenty centuries can attest that there has always been justification for having faith in France."

The assembly, having elected Félix Gouin as its president and having divided into groups—metropolitan resistance presided over by Ferrière, overseas resistance under Bissagnet, independent resistance groups under Hauriou, members of Parliament under Auriol, Communists under Marty—did not, in fact, fail to discuss the principal questions which I proposed for its examination. Between the date of its first session and that of its disbanding, it met more than fifty times and its committees worked mightily. All the ministers worked with it. Philip, in charge of the committee's relations with the assembly, Commissioner of the Interior d'Astier, Commissioner of Justice Menthon, Commissioner of Foreign Affairs Massigli and Commissioner of Finance Mendès-France were those who most often made themselves heard.

For my own part, I attended some twenty sessions. I took part on these occasions either to give reports of the general situation or during the course of the discussion. I was extremely interested in the ideas and the feelings which this exchange of views brought to the surface, for what I wanted was the real convictions of the French people. Therefore I did my best to animate the discussions, to cause the delegates to reveal themselves, to make them say what they thought. And indeed the assembly gave evidence of a conscience and a conviction that impressed both the French public and the foreign informants. Nevertheless, the subjects that absorbed it longest were, of course, those which concerned it most deeply: national purification, aid to the resistance, and the establishment of law and order in France during the liberation.

There were, in fact, many bitter and prolonged arguments on the action to be taken against the Vichy leaders, the punishments to be inflicted on the officials accused of having added to the severity of their orders, the compensations to be awarded to those who had suffered. On these points the delegates urged the committee to act vigorously, even to change, as much as possible, the normal rules and procedures. So great was the emotion roused by the problem that several national commissioners were harshly taken to task for their supposed weakness. While understanding only too well that this question of justice should preoccupy the resistance assembly to the highest degree, I did not abandon the line of conduct I had determined for myself: to limit the retributions to the persons who had played prominent roles in Vichy politics and to the men who had made themselves the enemy's direct accomplices. In the overseas territories this meant very few people. But the state of mind revealed by the debates of the Consultative permitted me to foresee the difficulties I would have in restraining the spirit of vengeance in metropolitan France and allowing justice alone to pass sentence.

The assembly brought as much concern and passion to the formulation of its opinion on the assistance sent to the resistance elements in France, the liaisons established with them and the advantage our propaganda derived from their actions and their suggestions. It was only natural that the secret army, so badly equipped and so constantly threatened, should often have the impression that London and Algiers were not doing all they could in its behalf. Hence in the beginning many delegates began with remarks of reproach and recrimination in regard to the "services." But after verification they realized the extent of the work already accomplished and the obstacles encountered. They also had to take into account the disadvantages presented by the activities of the Allied services in France, which produced all kinds of local discord and deprived the French authority of a share of the hearing which the French war effort was assuring it abroad. Nevertheless, the fear of offending the Anglo-American powers, which for the "politicians" was second nature, kept the assembly from adopting on this point the categorical motion I should have preferred.

The assembly's deliberations on the manner in which the powers of the Republic were to be reconstituted in France were calmer, but no less searching. No one, of course, imagined that the Marshal and his "government" could do anything but disappear. On the other hand, everyone felt that the French people must be consulted immediately and that a national assembly would have to take care of the constitutional question. But the delegates were not in total agreement as to what kind of assembly this should be.

The Communists, in discreet terms, revealed their scheme of elections to be carried out in the public squares, preferably by acclamation, under the control of the organizations and the troops of the resistance. Obviously they calculated that their own *savoir-faire* would reap results advantageous to their cause from such a procedure. Members of Parliament of long service such as Senators Marcel Astier, Marc Rucart and Paul Giacobbi suggested that the National Assembly of July 1940 be reconvened. That body, under the inflence of the liberation, would not fail to abolish the powers it had given Pétain, to receive President Albert Lebrun's resignation as a matter of form, to elect a new President of the Republic and to give my government a vote of confidence. It would then dissolve to make way for a Chamber of Deputies and a Senate elected according to the past method, after which the alterations to be made in the constitution of 1875 would be accomplished according to the rules which the latter had established. Such was the plan of those who desired a return pure and simple to the institutions of the Third Republic.

They were not many. According to the voice of the great majority, the *ancien régime* was doomed. But it is important to realize that in the minds of many delegates what had been faulty about the old system was not so much an excess as a lack of demagogy. The confusion of powers and responsibilities that had deprived it of a strong government, that had denied it any firm and continuous policy and set it adrift at the mercy of events, was not, in the majority's eyes, what must be reformed. Or rather, the reform was supposedly to be made by going still further in the direction of making the chief executive nothing more than a figurehead.

To attribute to a single Assembly all powers without exception, to give it the capacity to invest and provide ministers, to abolish the Senate that might constitute a useful counterbalance, to suppress the chief of the state or, at least, reduce him to a still more ridiculous condition than the one in which the past system had imprisoned him—such was the conception of a great number of the delegates. They dreamed aloud of a "single and sovereign" Assembly like the Convention of the Revolution, which though it spared itself the guillotine would nevertheless find no obstacle to its energies, and in which most of the politicians who emerged from the resistance intended to sit some day.

I did not share this inclination. On the contrary, what seemed to me essential for the nation's future recovery was a regime of action and responsibility. As I saw it, it was essential that the powers be separated so that there would be, respectively and effectively, a government, a Parliament and a judiciary. It was essential that the chief of state, by the method of his election, by his rank, his powers, be in a position to fulfill the function of national arbiter. It was essential that the people be able to associate themselves directly, by means of a referendum, with the crucial decisions that would determine its destiny. I was deeply concerned when I realized the state of mind of those who would control the state tomorrow and who were striving to reconstruct the regime for the sport of politicians rather than for the service of the nation. Were we to learn no other lesson from this confusion, this inconsistency which had brought France to disaster and the Republic to abdication, than to go on to further confusion, more serious inconsistency still?

But this was not the moment to organize a public discussion of this subject. Letting the flood of theories sweep past and taking advantage of the prudence of some individuals—Dumesnil de Gramont, Vincent Auriol, René Cassin, Louis Vallon and others— I led the assembly to a cautious conclusion. It was agreed that during the liberation the Consultative Assembly, transferred to metropolitan France and suitably enlarged, would continue to function in the government's behalf; that once the territory was liberated and the prisoners and the deported men were returned, the country would successively elect municipal councils, general councils and a National Assembly, but that the composition and the functions of the latter would not be determined until later on. Further, the right to vote and to hold office was extended to women. The decree of April 21, 1944, making this tremendous reform official, put an end to controversies that had lasted for fifty years.

Although the Consultative Assembly had no other right than that of expressing its opinion and although the responsibility for what was done or not done continued to devolve upon me until the day the people could speak for themselves, the Allies followed carefully what was being said on the rostrum and in the antechambers. The members of their missions as well as their journalists were assiduous in their attendance at the sessions and in the corridors. The American and British newspapers gave a large amount of space to the Algiers discussions. Doubtless they regretted that this parliamentary representation was not empowered to overturn the government, that the lion tamer could not be eaten. At the very least they were trying to discover and expose divergences.

All these observers were there the day the assembly broached the subject of France's situation in relation to the rest of the world. On this occasion, by the voices of the "resistants" such as Bissagnet, Father Carrière and Mayoux, by those of the "politicians" like Auriol, Hauriou and Rucart, by those of the Communists, including Bonte, Grenier, and Mercier, the delegates approved strongly the position of principle I had adopted toward the Allies in the face of the enemy. The assembly stated explosively that as far as it was concerned General de Gaulle represented France at war and his government was that of the Republic; it was in this capacity that the Committee of Liberation was to co-operate with the Allied Nations and that the latter must recognize it. The order of the day formulating this unanimous opinion, which was to be spread by information sources the world over, brought a very appreciable support to my policy. For my part, I did not fail to see to it that the news of the decision resounded far and wide.

But the assembly was content to stop there. It preferred not to confront directly such burning problems as Italy, the Middle East and Africa, with which the committee's foreign-affairs operations were grappling, nor others such as Germany, Eastern Europe and Indochina, which were to beset France and the world in the near future. The same circumspection kept it from making an issue of the political and administrative power which the Allies planned to wield in France under cover of their military command. As for the conduct of the war and the share which the French government and General Staff would take in it, the Consultative listened to me with scrupulous attention while I explained this crucial question, the policies which I had followed since 1940, and the difficulties which were unceasingly put in our way. It approved statements of principle in regard to France's place in world-wide strategy and the contribution which French forces could make. But it did not move to formulate demands in relation to our allies.

All in all, on the major subjects the assembly instinctively kept to generalities expressed from the rostrum in terms broad enough to be approved by all. General de Gaulle was applauded when he came to explain what action had been undertaken or when he lifted spirits by pulling a debate together in order to get at the conclusion. In compensation, everyone made a point of treating coldly and critically one or another national commissioner who specified the measures employed. But almost no one ventured any concrete opinion, any fixed plan of action.

The fact that the assembly was merely consultative, that it did not react to the incentive of an electoral constituency and that its attitudes and its votes could not stimulate a ministerial crisis contributed, of course, to its reserve in regard to such questions. Also to be taken into account were its intention to leave my hands free, its desire to deal tactfully with the Allies and its concern for unanimity. But above all, its reticence was something of a confession of ineptitude. The assembly felt itself capable of expressing inclinations, not of resolving problems, fit to suggest a policy, not to adopt one. Its consequent dejection was to recur later on in intensified form in the representative assemblies possessing plenary powers and incapable of wielding them. As for me, seeing in the remarks of the various groups the parties' future pretensions and, at the same time, their impotence, I discerned the coming French constitutional drama. "Deliberation is the work of many men. Action, of one alone." For this very reason, they desired only to deliberate.

Nevertheless, the unity of the Algiers government, together with the meeting of the Consultative Assembly, and lastly the choice made by French public opinion settled the political question in principle for the period of liberation. But if to a great majority the facts seemed determined in advance, the speculations inspired by malevolence did not entirely cease, either in France or elsewhere. On the contrary, the various opposition circles which persisted in regarding my success as abhorrent multiplied many cunning stratagems against it in proportion as the force of events prepared its inevitability. Without exception these men regarded the collapse of the Vichy regime as a certainty, but there was not one among them who did not strive to replace that regime without an accompanying De Gaulle triumph.

Meanwhile the enemy's behavior in regard to Vichy hastened the latter's downfall. The Germans, convinced by what had occurred in North Africa that the Marshal and his government did not possess the necessary authority to keep the French from turning against them at the first occasion, realizing the imminence of the Allied landing, anxious as to what, in that event, the national insurrection would do in their rear and requiring French resources for their own war-torn economy, ascribed only a trifling importance to the so-called French state and squeezed all the tighter the iron shackles of oppression. Thereby the fiction of internal autonomy to which Vichy had clung disappeared altogether.

In any case, Pétain, having transmitted all his powers to Laval, could no longer pretend to the role of protector on which he had hitherto prided himself. He now stepped aside, renouncing any intervention in the "government's" work, which, moreover, consisted of scarcely anything but adopting measures of constraint or repression. In November Pétain found himself literally forbidden to speak on the radio. In December Laval, returning from a visit to the Fuehrer and re-forming his ministry with a view to a more complete collaboration with the invader, invited Brinon and Darnand to join it pending the time when Déat could do the same, without the Marshal's taking any firm stand against him. The man who still called himself "chief of state" permitted at his side the presence of a German overseer in the person of Herr Renthe-Fink and actually came to the point of writing to Hitler on December 18: "The modifications of French laws will henceforth be submitted to the occupation authorities." Although subsequently he was still to find an opportunity to show himself publicly in Paris, Rouen, Nancy and St.-Étienne, where until the end testimonials of pity and sympathy were to be addressed to him as an unfortunate old man, he did so without once saying a word in which one might perceive the sob of violated independence.

Thereafter certain appearances might still surround Vichy's absurd power, braggarts or madmen claim ministerial posts, propagandists—Philippe Henriot and Hérold Paquis—employ the resources of a misled talent to deceive the multitude, the public prints overflow with scurrilous attacks on those who were fighting, but the fact was that the whole people now condemned the regime and wished only to see it collapse when the Germans fled.

The French people had, of course, no doubt as to the kind of government which would then be installed in Paris, for which they were preparing a fervent welcome. But among the politicians who had established Pétain and who feared that their careers would thereby be compromised, many did not resign themselves to such a prospect. Since the end of 1943 many intrigues had been afoot to bring about a solution that would limit General de Gaulle's powers when the time came and, if possible, keep him at a distance. The Marshal himself made secret arrangements providing that his powers, if he himself were barred from wielding them, should be assumed by a college of prominent persons who had taken extremely diverse attitudes in the face of events. A "constitutional act" installing this directory of neutrality if the occasion should arise was put into safe hands. A little later, by another "constitutional act" in apparent contradiction to the preceding one and destined, in this case, to be made public, the Marshal specified that if he himself should die before having promulgated the constitution he was supposed to be preparing, the powers which the National Assemby of 1940 had conferred upon him would revert to this same assembly. The Germans, of course, opposed the publication of this document, although to the public at large Pétain's codicil was virtually of no interest.

At the same time, those members of Parliament who had not joined me in either fact or spirit did not leave off their agitation. They invoked their constituencies—as if they had not betrayed them. They declared that the National Assembly of July 1940 was still legitimate—although it had formally abdicated. They demanded that this Assembly be convened in order to settle officially all questions of state. Anatole de Monzie, champion of this plan, received the assent of several hundred of his colleagues and, to the Marshal's intensifying distress, ordered him to comply with it. But Hitler, annoyed by this to-do, had Ribbentrop write Pétain a threatening letter forbidding him ever to consider a disqualified Parliament when the German Wehrmacht was the "only guarantee of law and order in France." The impatient legislators relapsed into silence, hoping to resume their project later on.

The Allies, on their side, no longer able to rely on Giraud to counterpoise De Gaulle, were looking for some new expedient. Intelligence from France informed me that they had hoped to find it in the person of President Lebrun. The latter, since the vote of the Vichy Assembly which had stripped him of his functions and which he had not contested, had retired to Vizille. Would there not be some means, asked those in Washington and in London who aimed at controlling the political destiny of France, of bringing the President to North Africa? Since he had not formally resigned and since his attitude in regard to the enemy left nothing to be desired, could he not lay claim to an untainted legitimacy upon arriving at Algiers? Recognized at once as the President of the French Republic by the Allied powers and also—at least so it was hoped—by a great number of French citizens, how could he be challenged by De Gaulle and his followers? From then on it would be up to Lebrun to appoint the ministers, to preside over their councils, to sign the laws and the decrees. In comparison with the anxiety which De Gaulle's intransigent primacy caused the White House and Downing Street, what a change, what a relief! I was informed that during the last days of August the American and British conspirators were on the point of seizing their opportunity.

This occurred at the moment when Badoglio, hard pressed, had entered into clandestine negotiations with the Anglo-American powers with a view to arranging Italy's surrender. The negotiations were taking place at Lisbon in the profoundest secrecy. The conquerors were in a position to make semiofficial suggestions to the conquered which the latter would be grateful to receive. Now it happened that Vizille, where Lebrun was living, was in the Italian occupation zone. One evening officers from Rome presented themselves to the President. Stressing the critical situation into which the imminent course of the war might throw the region and his own person, they proposed to Albert Lebrun in behalf of their government that he come to Italy, where he would find security and a suitable residence. He would be guaranteed all escorts and safe-conducts in advance. It is known that at the same time that this contact was made, the Allied command, in agreement with Badoglio, was preparing an operation which, as soon as the Italian armistice was announced, was to bring the Anglo-American forces to Naples and, if possible, to Rome and in any case to protect King

Victor Emmanuel, his ministers and other well-known individuals. It was the intention of those who were pulling the strings that once Lebrun was in Italy, he could also be transferred wherever it was convenient to have him.

According to my informants, the President categorically refused this proposition, either because he did not see its true purpose or because, having discerned it, he did not wish to play any part in it. He replied to the Italians, "Your country is in a state of war with mine. From my point of view, you are the enemy. You can take me by force. I shall not follow you of my own free will." The mission retired. But shortly afterward Hitler, alerted and infuriated by the "French obstructions," sent the Gestapo to arrest President Lebrun. The latter, transferred to Germany, was forced to remain there a year.

I must say that these manipulations, devised by various hands to avoid the inevitable, impressed me as little more than a Chinese shadow play. I marveled at how lively and tenacious the spirit of intrigue still managed to be in the midst of the terrible realities besetting the world, but actually I paid little attention to it. What disturbed me more was the fate of the resistance in metropolitan France. For during this same period tragedy, striking at its heart, compromised both its framework and its orientation.

On June 9, a few days after my arrival in Algiers, General Delestraint had been arrested in Paris. The loss of the commander of the secret army threatened the disorganization of the paramilitary elements at the very moment when their leader was beginning to unify them. Therefore Jean Moulin decided to convoke the delegates of the various movements at Caluire on June 21, in order to work out the necessary measures with them. Yet on that very day, during a Gestapo raid that was, to say the least, strangely apt as to the particulars of time, place and persons involved, my delegate fell into the enemy's hands along with those with him. He was tortured to death some weeks later.

The disappearance of Jean Moulin had grave consequences, for he was one of those men who incarnate their jobs and who therefore cannot be replaced. The mere fact that he was no longer there caused serious difficulties in the functioning of those services—liaison, transportation, distribution, intelligence—which he directed personally. Yet it was just these services which made a coherent whole of the resistance operation. But, above all, this loss was to have political consequences and throw serious obstacles in the way of unity.

Not, of course, that the feelings of the combatants were influenced by it. To the majority of these the various groups concerned with inspiring them were almost unknown and the men who belonged to them generally anonymous. Morally it was to De Gaulle that they pledged themselves in the underground struggle, while practically, in regard to the conditions of life in the maquis, the raids, the sabotage, the smuggling of arms, the transmitting of information—all operations necessarily carried out on a small scale—they merely followed their group leaders. But on the level of committees, influences and countersigns, matters were not so simple. Although the political elements consented to set aside their ambitions to a certain degree in the heat of the battle, they did not renounce them altogether, especially at the moment when they glimpsed, with the end of the ordeal, the chance of gaining power. The personal character of Moulin, who had been delegated and supported directly by me, had been able to unite and control these factions. Now that he was dead, certain individuals would be inclined to play their own hands more actively.

This was to be the case with the Communists first of all. They were to do so particularly within the National Council of the Resistance, aiming to acquire preponderance there and also to make it a sovereign body theoretically pledged to my government but qualified to act of its own accord and for its own advantage. It would then be possible to make use of the council to carry on those activities, to put in office those authorities, to formulate those programs and, perhaps, to seize those powers thanks to which, in the shakeup of the liberation, the future would be theirs.

If I had been in a position to appoint Jean Moulin's successor without delay and if my new agent had also been able to assert himself personally among all the elements representing the resistance, he would have assumed the leadership of my delegation and the presidency of the National Council; thus the duality which some individuals were trying to create would not have resulted. But circumstances kept me from finding immediately the man I needed.

Not that we lacked men of ability and courage at the head of the various movements, despite the continual decimation to which the resistance was subject. But each of these men, belonging to a faction, could not impose his authority upon the rest, so rigorous was the particularism of the leaders and their groups. Moreover, the day was approaching when France, suddenly emerging from oppression, would find that the life of the nation, her law and order, and the judgment of the world would depend heavily on the French administrative structure. To represent me in France and to lead our services there, but also to prepare everywhere the confirmation or the substitution of authorities, I needed someone of the "great administrator" type, someone who had taken part in our battle and knew its prejudicial and tangled fundamentals but was not committed in his own right to any particular tendency and, furthermore, was capable of rallying at the crucial moment the kind of administration which the government would soon require. Months were to pass before I could choose and establish the man who would answer to these manifold qualifications.

In the interim Claude Bouchinet-Serreulles and Jacques Bingen, whom I had sent from London to work with Jean Moulin, were to vouch for the delegation. The former, in Paris, found means of maintaining all contacts despite the terrible ravages that devastated the executive committees of the various groups during this period. The latter, in the southern zone, devoted himself chiefly to organizing the assistance to be given to the rebels whose forces were growing in the southwest, the Massif Central and the Alps, until, captured by the enemy, he took his own life. In September I appointed Émile Bollaert as the representative of General de Gaulle and the delegate of the Committee of National Liberation. This great leader had refused ever since 1940 to give his allegiance to the Marshal and had gone into retirement. His feelings and his capacities qualified him for the post to which I now called him. But shortly after his appointment Bollaert was arrested by the Germans on the Breton coast while preparing to embark for Algiers, where he was to receive the government's instructions. He was subsequently deported to Buchenwald. As the climax of our misfortunes, Pierre Brossolette fell into the enemy's hands at the same time as Bollaert; he was later killed trying to escape from a window of the Gestapo building. This valiant colleague was also endowed by nature to fulfill such a post, by virtue of his courage, his ardent willingness, the prestige he enjoyed among the various elements of the resistance, and lastly because he was independent of all political parties, like Jean Moulin, and expected nothing to be effective, today in wartime or tomorrow in peace, except "Gaullism" established as a social, moral and national doctrine. In March 1944 Alexandre Parodi, a member of the Council of State and director general of the Ministry of Labor, who had also refused to serve under Vichy and whose brother René had been one of the first to die for France in the resistance, received the trust in his turn.

The avatars of my delegation favored the Communists' intentions in regard to the National Council of the Resistance. They managed to bring it about that of its fifteen members five were openly or secretly party members. The council, on its own authority, decided to give itself a president and elected Georges Bidault. The latter, an eminent resistance leader having in the highest degree the taste and the gift for political life, well known before the war for his talent as a journalist and his influence among the Christian Democrats, and ambitious to see this little group become a great party with himself at its head, willingly accepted the position he was offered and assumed its risks. One of these, and not the least, was to find himself overpowered at the very heart of this Areopagus by a disciplined group experienced in revolutionary action and excelling in the use of conflict as well as of camaraderie. I soon received indications of this group's encroachments, of the asperities its pressure involved for Georges Bidault, of the obstacles of its making which I was soon to find in my path. The council made known, in fact, that since its plenary sessions were necessarily exceptional it was delegating its powers to a board of four members, of whom two were Communists, and instituting an "Action Committee," dominated by party members, to deal with military questions.

What was happening to our movement in metropolitan France at the end of 1943 and the beginning of 1944 was of particular concern to me because, being in Algiers, I had the sense of being even less in a position to make myself heard or understood than when I had been in London. The personal contact which the radio had permitted me to make with the French people had more or less slackened. Indeed, the Algiers frequencies were less well known in France than those of the BBC. It is true that the efforts of Henri Bonnet, Commissioner of Information, of Jacques Lassaigne, director of Radio France, of Jean Amrouche, Henri Bénazet, Jean Castet, Georges Gorse, Jean Roire and others succeeded in giving our broadcasts from Algiers, Tunis and Rabat a certain interest and character. Furthermore, the major station at Brazzaville, now in full-time operation under the direction of Géraud Jouve, was finding an increasingly large audience around the world. Yet despite everything, I realized that my voice was reaching the French people in a muffled manner. And at the same time that I was finding it more difficult to speak to the nation, our secret liaisons with France were also becoming more complicated.

It was from the London base that these had been organized. It was from there that our instructions and our missions had been sent. It was there that reports, agents, visitors and refugees arrived. In the use of planes, motorboats, telegrams, radio messages and couriers, a kind of gymnastics set to a rhythm from the English capital had become habitual to the valiant army of informants, transporters and purveyors. It was unthinkable to tear this web apart. As for weaving another which would operate from North

Africa, we could do so only in the most summary fashion, for want of specialized means and because of the distances involved. For example, a light single-engine plane leaving from an English base landed after two hours' flight on a makeshift field in the center of France and returned immediately. But we would require a two-engine plane, a lengthy flight, an orthodox landing strip and the means of refueling in order to connect metropolitan France with Algiers, Oran or even Ajaccio. We had therefore left the principal machinery of our communications setup in Great Britain. But as a consequence there were many retransmissions, delays and mis-understandings.

All the more so since outside the specialized networks of Fighting France there existed another, the former Intelligence Service of the Army General Staff. This service, which remained in Vichy until November 1942 and which, under the direction of Colonels Ronin and Rivet, had opposed the Germans to the limit of its ability, had reached North Africa during the enemy's occupation of the southern zone. The "Civil and Military Commander in Chief" had made it his instrument of contact with metropolitan France. As long as the bicephalism of the Committee of Liberation lasted, this state of affairs went on, with all the disadvantages involved in having one intelligence service attached to me and another working for Giraud. As soon as the latter had left the government for a purely military job nothing, it seemed, need prevent the unification of the specialized services.

But several months were to pass before this was accomplished, even though on November 27, 1943, the Committee of Liberation ordered the merger, appointed Jacques Soustelle director general of Special Services and attached the whole unit directly to the head of the government. This organization did not at all intend to eliminate the officers of the former Intelligence Service; on the contrary, their abilities were to be widely employed in their own sphere. But the kind of warfare we had to wage required that our system be constituted as a whole, that it transcend the framework and the formulas of the past, and that by the complex means of

the networks, the maquis, the independent groups, the large movements, the tracts and underground newspapers, the raids and the
administrative sabotage it include all forms of the resistance and
penetrate into every branch of national activity. Unfortunately,
General Giraud obstinately opposed the decisions which the government had taken in this matter.

Arguing from his position as commander in chief, he claimed
the right to keep entirely at his own disposal the service that had
hitherto been his. In the course of many interviews I wore myself
out explaining to him that unity was necessary and that he himself
had every latitude to employ the combined service directly. Nothing
would do: General Giraud continued to bear down with all his
authority on the officers involved in order to keep them outside the
prescribed jurisdiction.

It was obviously not for reasons of strategy that he behaved in
this way; for, whatever title had been left to him, he was not to
exercise actual command of operations, which our well-provided
allies kept jealously to themselves. But a certain group, espousing a
certain policy, had not given up hope of making use of General
Giraud. In France, in Africa, and among the prominent French
émigrés in the United States, various circles still offered him an
opportunity in the hope that it would be theirs as well. Further, the
Allied missions and general staffs remained secretly faithful to their
former schemes and did not discourage Giraud from cherishing,
despite everything, ambitions to play the supreme role. This was
why, despite my warnings, he persisted in maintaining separate
contacts with one or another element in metropolitan France,
sending there, thanks to American aid, agents who were his alone
and who created much confusion.

The vessel overflowed at last. In April 1944, following an incident more serious than the rest, I was forced to call upon General
Giraud to cease his activities. Since he persisted in a dilatory
attitude, the government stripped him, by decree, of his theoretical
function as commander in chief and appointed him inspector
general, which definitively rid his status of all ambiguity and

which, furthermore, corresponded to the services he could perform usefully. In order to soften the blow, I wrote him an official letter expressing the government's recognition of his services and another, personal letter urging him, in our country's present tragic circumstances, to set an example of self-abnegation. Simultaneously the Committee of National Liberation decided to award him the Médaille Militaire with an extremely fine citation.

General Giraud preferred to retire. He declined the post to which he was appointed, refused the medal and went to live near Mazagran. "I want to be commander in chief or nothing," he said.

His departure provoked no reaction on the part of the troops, nor among the people. It must be added that at this same period those former advocates of Vichy who had been attached to him censured his behavior during the Pucheu trial. Called to bear witness before the court, he had not, they reproached him, categorically taken the defense of the accused, although the latter had come to North Africa solely because of the "Civil and Military Commander in Chief's" formal guarantee. As for myself, seeing General Giraud abandon all activity when the war was far from its conclusion, I deplored his stubbornness. But what could regret matter when the order of the state was jeopardized?

Then, especially, was a time when France suffered. We were kept informed by the intelligence reaching us by successive couriers, particularly that which our "cell organization in public administration" service provided from Paris, by the information received from the delegates to the Consultative Assembly or else from refugees who had managed to cross the Pyrenees, and by the reports from our *chargés de mission* who came and went between Algiers and metropolitan France—Guillain de Bénouville, Bourgès-Maunoury, François Closon, Louis Mangin, General Brisac, Colonel Zeller, Gaston Defferre, François Mitterand, my nephew Michel Cailliau and others.

Never had the material conditions under which the French people lived been worse. For almost everyone, marketing was a daily tragedy. From the spring of 1943 to that of 1944, the official ration did not exceed one thousand calories a day. Without fertilizer, labor force, fuel or means of transport, agricultural production reached scarcely two thirds of what it had been before. Furthermore, the invader took a large share of whatever was produced, including half of all meat supplies. Further, by means of the black market the enemy reduced what remained, which should have been turned over to the public. What the German ate in this manner he paid for with money drawn from the French Treasury—more than 300 billion francs by August 1943, more than 400 billion by March 1944. There were still 1,500,000 French prisoners of war in enemy camps which, it is true, had sent back a spectacular 100,000; but in return a total of one million civilians would be handed over to the Germans by the "Labor Service." Further, the Reich employed directly for its own benefit a third of our factories, burned half of our coal, took over 65 per cent of our locomotives, 50 per cent of our railroad cars, 60 per cent of our trucks, made use of our contractors, our tools, our materials to construct the Atlantic Wall. To secure food, clothing, heat and light, not to mention moving from one place to another, became exhausting, often insoluble problems in the miserable existence which the great majority of Frenchmen were leading.

And now once more war was wreaking its endless destruction, its irreparable losses upon our soil. The respite which had followed the "armistices" and which the authors of the capitulation had boasted of so loudly now gave way to bloody alarms. At Dieppe, then at St.-Nazaire, British forces, aided by French groups, made a number of raids in the midst of the residents. The bombardment of our cities redoubled. In particular, Paris, Nantes, Rouen, Lyon, St.-Étienne and their environs suffered serious damage, a prelude to what was to be inflicted upon us during the coming great battle. Before the Allied landing in France thirty thousand persons were killed by air raids. In many places, particularly the Ain, the Massif Central, the Alps, Limousin and the Dordogne, the local maquis joined battle with the Germans, who took revenge with firing squads, arsons, arrests of hostages, and reparations. Here the enemy was aided by the militia, whose courts-martial summarily judged and condemned to death a host of patriots.

Furthermore, German repression had become a veritable military operation, carried out with a method as precise as it was frightful. The enemy wanted to "settle" his arrears before the battle which he sensed ahead of him. This was why the action of the Gestapo and the German police, combined with that of the local police and the militia, now under Darnand's control—Darnand, lately made "secretary general for the maintenance of order"—was turned in all its strength against our underground networks and our organizations. Every form of intimidation, torture and persuasion was employed to tear from the wretched people whom they had been able to capture the confessions that would deliver still others into their hands. The period preceding the landing was marked by the death of a great number of leaders, among them Cavaillès, Marchal, Médéric, Péri, Politzer, Ripoche and Touny, the execution of twenty thousand members of the resistance and the deportation of fifty thousand others. During the same period the shameful horrors of the persecution of Jews were unleashed. Lastly, this was the period when the Reich made Vichy turn over its political prisoners, notably Herriot, Reynaud, Daladier, Blum, Mandel, Gamelin and Jacomet, arrested others, including Albert Sarraut, François-Poncet and Colonel de La Roque, seized many high officials, prominent businessmen and general officers and transferred them to Germany so that they could serve as hostages or eventual mediums of exchange.

Yet the resistance continued to spread. While it was striking by raids, assassinations and derailings, in all of which many Germans died, and by the execution of an increasing number of traitors and informers, it was at the same time being put into written words, published and disseminated everywhere. A great human and national movement, it aroused ideas and feelings, delineated doctrines, inspired art and literature. By miracles of ingenuity the secret newspapers were regularly furnished with paper, composed, printed and circulated. *Franc-Tireur, Combat, Résistance, Défense de la France* reached a total of 600,000 numbers a day. Magazines such as *Les Lettres Françaises, Les Cahiers de la Libération, Les Cahiers du Témoignage Chrétien, L'Université Libre, L'Art Libre* passed secretly through many doors. The Éditions de Minuit distributed books secretly, among them Vercors' *The Silence of the Sea,* of which innumerable copies were printed and circulated. By the efforts of the Algiers government, the work of those fighting by thought and pen was constantly disseminated by radio. In the name of the free as well as of those imprisoned in silence, I addressed solemn testimonial to them on the occasion of a great meeting on October 30 organized by the Alliance Française and broadcast from Algiers.

The flowering of French thought confirmed our policy. The incessant intrigues, the disguised ambitions, the subversion that certain individuals were contemplating—how could such things prevail against this gushing spring of courage and regeneration? Perhaps this was to be merely an episode, after which, tomorrow, the sluggishness and the abasement would resume. But "tomorrow is another day." As long as the war lasted I had the means, morally speaking, to muster the French people.

All the more since the national instinct seized upon me, more clearly than ever, as the core of its unity. It was indeed in relation to me that the politicians maneuvered in seeking guarantees for the near future. It was toward me that the so-called "ruling class" turned—that is, those established as to situation, fortune, repute. In this category, a fraction—generally that group whom money concerned the least—had long followed me; as for the others, whose troubled consciences hoped I would spare them fearful reversals, they now yielded with great deference and postponed their criticism and their insults until later on. The masses, for whom the drama included no speculation, hoped for nothing more than my arrival, which would be their liberation. Lastly, by those who were fighting I found myself regarded as the symbol of what they wished to obtain at the price of their sacrifice. How describe what I felt when one evening Sermoy-Simon, arriving from France—

where he himself was soon to die—brought me the supreme testimonials from a group of young men condemned to death: photographs of the walls of their prison cells, where they had scratched my name during their last hours, last letters written to their families, invoking me as their leader; accounts of witnesses who, before the execution squad could fire the last bullet, heard their cry, *"Vive la France! Vive De Gaulle!"*

It was these men who showed me my duty at the very moment when my need for guidance was greatest. For I felt only too heavily the wear and tear to which exhaustion and the moral ordeal of my task exposed me. At the beginning of 1944 I fell seriously ill; but the enlightened care of Doctors Lichtwitz and Lacroix permitted me to overcome the crisis just when the rumor of "the General's" possible disappearance from the scene was at its height. Of course the two years through which Free France had endured had also been filled with reversals and disappointments, but then we had had to stake everything to win everything; we had felt ourselves surrounded by a heroic atmosphere, sustained by the necessity of gaining our ends at any price. Between myself and those—all volunteers—who placed themselves under my direction there existed a profound accord that had been of powerful help to me. Now the goal was within sight, but in proportion as we neared it I had the sense of crossing a terrain less firm, of breathing an air less pure. Around me interests imposed their claims, rivalries clashed, men were every day more human.

In my office at Les Glycines I kneaded a heavy dough: papers to read, although my immediate co-workers, Palewski, Billotte and Soustelle, brought me, on my orders, only the most essential; decisions to make, even if it was a question only of determining principles; people to receive, despite the system which I put into effect in order to limit the audiences to national commissioners, foreign diplomats, top Allied and French military leaders, a few high civil administrators, messengers from France or those who were to be sent there, and certain visitors of note. On principle, I used the telephone only on rare occasions, and no one was ever permitted to call me. The confrontation of points of view and the choice of measures to be taken I reserved purposely for the government councils. My nature warned me, my experience had taught me, that at the summit one can preserve one's time and one's person only by remaining habitually on the remotest heights.

It was therefore all the more necessary to make contact at crucial moments with people and affairs; I did so, as much as possible, by going to see them on the spot. During the fifteen months my post was at Algiers, I spent, independently of the meetings and the ceremonies which took place in the capital, one hundred days traveling. In Algeria, visits to the cities and the countryside, inspections of troops, ships, air squadrons. Four visits to Morocco, three to Tunisia, one to Libya. In Equatorial Africa, a long tour that took me through the entire area. I crossed Corsica three times, made three trips to Italy to spend some time among the troops in action. During the Allied landing in Normandy I went to England and from there to Bayeux in France; shortly afterward occurred my first trip to the United States and to Canada. Such journeys comforted me. Men, so exhausting to regard in the maneuvers of ambition, are so engaging when acting for a great cause!

By taste and expediency, my private life was very simple. I had established my residence at the villa of Les Oliviers, where my wife had joined me, as well as my daughter Anne, whose health still worried us as much as ever, and later Elisabeth, who returned from Oxford to work in the office that analyzed the foreign press. As for Philippe, he continued to navigate and to fight in the Channel and on the Atlantic. During the evenings at Les Oliviers I tried to keep my time to myself in order to work on the speeches which were my constant chore. But often we received. Many foreign and French guests did us the honor of sitting at our table; the dinners, however, were extremely simple, for rationing necessarily applied to everyone. Frequently we spent our Sundays in a cottage in Kabylia.

At intervals, some news of our family reached us. My brother Xavier had been able to take shelter at Nyon, whence he sent useful information to Algiers; his daughter Geneviève, falling into the enemy's hands with the editors of *Défense de la France,* had been deported to Ravensbrueck; his elder son was fighting in Italy. My sister, Madame Alfred Cailliau, arrested by the Gestapo, had spent a year in prison at Fresnes and from there had been transferred to Germany, while her husband, at the age of sixty-seven, had been sent to Buchenwald; one of their sons, Charles, a young infantry officer, had been killed by the enemy during the Battle of France; three others had crossed the Mediterranean to join our forces. My brother Jacques' three sons had done the same; Jacques himself, a paralytic, had been shielded from the German police by Abbé Pierre and his group, who carried him over the Swiss frontier. My brother Pierre had been continually under close surveillance; in 1943 he was arrested by the Germans and deported to Eisenberg. His wife and their five children, as well as an adopted girl, the daughter of a resistance fighter who had been executed, crossed the Pyrenees on foot and reached Morocco by way of Spain. In the Vendroux family, my wife's brothers and sister had chosen to serve our cause. In France and in Africa, all our relatives and connections were risking their lives. With so many other encouragements, I evoked those that came to me from my own family when the burden grew overly heavy.

True, my ministers carried their share of this burden. If, in the past, the reduced dimensions of our organization concentrated everything in my hands, today, in order to encompass a domain that was about to be enlarged, authority had to be distributed. Among the national commissioners, of course, various rivalries and centrifugal distractions broke out. But on the whole my ministers formed a disciplined team around me. Meanwhile each of them had his own authority and his own responsibility.

Each also had his own way of fulfilling it. Henri Queuille brought to the chairmanship of the interministerial commissions all the good sense and prudence he possessed by nature, as well as all the experience he had acquired under the Third Republic as a member of twelve governments. René Massigli, a brilliant man of many resources, wise in the ways of diplomacy, worked to establish the network of foreign relations that had been damaged by events. Pierre Mendès-France, a clear mind and a strong will, solved the apparently insoluble problems overwhelming our finances at Algiers. René Mayer, a man of varied abilities, restored the railroads, the ports, the roads of North Africa to maximum efficiency. André Le Troquer, truculent and generous, made himself the first servant of the Army which he administered. André Philip grappled with the flood of ideas that gushed from his own brain and with the assembly's successive "malaises." Jean Monnet, with a tremendous range of expedients at his fingertips, applied himself to convincing our American allies to organize in time the aid they were willing to lend us. Henri Bonnet played his role of conciliator among the groups already disputing the means of information. François de Menthon, Emmanuel d'Astier, René Capitant and Henri Frénay, whose ministerial departments were respectively Justice, the Interior, National Education and Prisoners and who were above all engaged in preparing what was to be done in France tomorrow, vied with each other in their innovative zeal. Fernand Grenier and François Billoux, the one blunt, the other cunning, both gifted, divided their close attention between on the one hand their respective posts, the Air Ministry and the State Commission, and on the other their party, which observed them from outside. As for those ministers who had surrounded me since the time of Free France—Georges Catroux, experienced in the practice of affairs of state, René Pleven, André Diethelm and Adrien Tixier, all of whom had been hard at work for four years and under what conditions!—each brought to his task (Moslem Affairs, Colonies, Production and Labor) a competence which nothing could discourage or surprise.

All these ministers, whatever their origin, their inclinations or their personality, proudly associated themselves with Charles de Gaulle and assumed responsibility with him. Theirs was all the more meritorious a role since their administrations were made up of bits and pieces. Yet in spite of all lacunae these administrations, like their leaders, devoted themselves to their tasks with a com-

mendably constant intelligence and fervor if not without that proliferation of projects inspired by the consideration of national rebirth. If, in the offices of Algiers as in the assembly or in the committee meetings, every possible scheme was entertained that might
serve to reconstruct France and the world, nonetheless everyone
did his job conscientiously and reasonably. Officials such as Hubert
Guérin, Chauvel, Alphand, Paris, in Foreign Affairs; Chevreux,
in the Interior; Gregh, Guindey, Leroy-Beaulieu, in Finance;
Laurentie, for the Colonies; Anduze-Frais, in Transportation; Pos-
tel-Vinay, at the central funds; chiefs of executive committees such
as Leyer at the War Ministry, Lemonnier for the Navy, Bouscat
for the Air Force, were the pillars and the models of our services.
Ultimately, however, it was at my feet that everything came to rest,
and I could not be ignorant of how narrow our limits were. But
what is the energy that animates political life if not the art of
possibilities?

The government now met in the Summer Palace; its sessions
took place twice a week. With the assistance of Louis Joxe, I had
determined the order of the day. On each question, the committee
heard the report of the ministers concerned. The debate followed.
Each member gave his opinion. If necessary, I called on him to do
so. I then offered my own, generally at the discussion's conclusion.
Then I formulated the council's resolution and, if necessary, settled
the disputes. The decisions were subsequently reported to the ministerial departments. Often they were handed down in the form of
decrees. In that case, the texts were edited beforehand by René
Cassin and his Juridical Committee, deliberated in council and
finally published in the *Journal officiel de la République française,*
which was published in Algiers in its traditional format.

It was thus that the decrees of January 10, March 14, April 21
and May 19, 1944, settled the organization of powers and the
exercise of authority during the course of the liberation. Seventeen
"Regional Commissioners of the Republic," provided with exceptional powers and posted at Lille, Nancy, Strasbourg, Châlons,
Dijon, Clermont-Ferrand, Lyon, Marseille, Montpellier, Limoges,

Toulouse, Bordeaux, Poitiers, Rennes, Angers, Rouen, Orléans and in the Prefecture of the Seine, were appointed "to take all measures necessary to insure the security of the French and Allied armies, to provide for the administration of the territory, to re-establish republican legality and to satisfy the population's needs." Further, in each ministry, a high official, previously appointed secretary general, was to insure the continuance of services until the minister's arrival. The municipal councils of 1939, which Vichy had often replaced by delegations of its own composition, would be re-established in the communes. In order to grant a share in the reconstruction program to local resistance groups, along with a means of expression and a writ of execution for the inevitable outbursts, the creation of a "Committee of Liberation" was provided for in each department. This committee, composed of local delegates from the movements and parties represented on the National Council of the Resistance, would give its advice to the prefect, as the general council had done previously, pending the time when the latter was re-established by election. Lastly, a "National Commissioner Delegated to Liberated Territory" would take those immediate measures which seemed necessary locally.

In April, André Le Troquer was appointed to this function. As for the Commissioners of the Republic and the Prefects of the Liberation proposed to the government's choice by Alexandre Parodi assisted by Michel Debré, they were appointed in secret, received the authentic text of the decree instituting them in office and were ready at a moment's notice to rise out of the smoke of battle. Two of them, Verdier and Fourcade, were to be killed by the enemy; two, Bouhey and Cassou, seriously wounded; in all, nine prefects were to die for France. But among the French people, in the face of the Allies as of the defeated invader, the authority of the state would appear: integral, responsible and independent.

Its justice must appear at the same time. In consideration of the ordeals endured, the liberation would doubtless unleash an elementary impulse of punishment, retribution and revenge. When men and women defending their country have been shot by the tens of thousands, deported by the hundreds of thousands to camps of hideous wretchedness whence few were to return; when thousands of fighters in the resistance networks, in the maquis, in the action groups, considered by the enemy as exempt from the laws of war, have been killed on the spot; when innumerable murders, arsons, lootings and brutalities have been committed besides, all accompanied by tortures and betrayals and with the direct co-operation of the "ministers," officials, police, militia and French traitors; when for years on end many newspapers, magazines, books and speeches have lavished insults upon those fighting for France and tributes upon the invader; when, in the "government," the administration, in business, industry and the world of society, certain individuals have paraded, amid national humiliation and want, their collaboration with the enemy, then certainly the German retreat was to be the signal for summary and bloody revenge. Yet in spite of everything, no individual had the right to punish the guilty; it was the state's concern. Therefore the state must provide, and with no delay, that its justice investigate cases and render verdicts, or else be swamped by the fury of groups or individuals.

The Committee of Liberation was therefore, by the decree of June 26, 1944, completed by that of August 26, empowered to establish the conditions under which the crimes and misdemeanors of collaboration were to be punished. The juridical basis of indictments existed in our codes under the rubric "dealings with the enemy." But on this occasion the circumstances would be exceptional, in certain cases attenuating, because of the attitude and the orders of the Vichy "government." To take account of this unprecedented political situation and to place the judges in a position where they need not apply automatically the punishments habitually invoked for faults that were not habitual, we established a new classification of punishment, "National Disgrace," which included the loss of political rights, exclusion from public employment and, at the maximum, exile. Thus, enlightened as to the nature of the misdemeanors and crimes they were to reprimand and with a sufficiently elastic scale of punishment at their disposal, the tribunals would pass sentence as they saw fit.

What tribunals? It followed of itself that the ordinary criminal and correctional jurisdictions were not made to apply in such cases, either by their nature or their composition, for many magistrates had been forced to lend their allegiance to the Marshal and to pronounce judgment in accordance with Vichy's orders. We should therefore have to introduce changes. This the Committee of Liberation did by prescribing, in advance, the creation of "Courts of Justice" to sit beside the Courts of Appeal. The president of the court and the public prosecutor would be magistrates chosen by the Chancellery. The four jurors would be chosen by lot from a list drawn up by the president of the Court of Appeal assisted by two representatives of the resistance designated by the Commissioner of the Republic. In every respect, it was important to associate the resistance with the official work of justice. As for those who had assumed, either in the "government" or in key positions elsewhere, an important responsibility for the capitulation or the collaboration, they would be answerable to the High Court.

Nevertheless, the fate of one of these was to be determined at Algiers. This was Pierre Pucheu, who as Minister of the Interior in the Vichy "government" had distinguished himself by his severity in regard to the resistance fighters, to the point of appearing in their eyes as a champion of repression. Having resigned his "ministry" in 1942, Pucheu went to Spain. On his request, General Giraud, then "Civil and Military Commander in Chief," authorized him to come to Morocco in order to serve in the Army, on condition that he did so in secret. But since the former minister ostentatiously showed himself everywhere, Giraud had had him put under surveillance. Subsequently, the Committee of Liberation having decided to insure the action of justice in regard to the members of the Vichy "government," Pierre Pucheu was imprisoned. Now the question was asked: should he be judged at once?

The government, on the unanimous decision of its members,

decided to open his trial. From the point of view of principles, there was no reason for postponement. Above all, the state itself required a swift example. This was the moment when the resistance was to become, in the imminent battle, an essential element of national defense. This was the moment when the Laval ministry, in which Darnand held a post "to maintain order," put forth its greatest effort to crush the resistance with the co-operation of the Germans. It was essential that our combatants, and equally essential that their adversaries, have immediate proof that the guilty would have to answer for their actions. I confirmed this on the rostrum of the Consultative Assembly, quoting Georges Clemenceau: "War and only war! Justice defers: the nation will know it is defended!"

In order to judge Pucheu, the Committee of Liberation, since it could not convene the High Court, had the accused brought before the "Army Tribunal." The president was Monsieur Vérin, first president of the Algiers Court of Appeal; the judges were Counselor Fischer and Generals Chadebec de Lavalade, Cochet and Schmidt; the public prosecutor was General Weiss. The accused defended himself skillfully and energetically, but two facts, among others, led the tribunal to pronounce its severest sentence: Pucheu, as minister, had sent his prefects imperative memorandums ordering that the workers the Reich demanded be handed over; furthermore, there was every indication that at the moment the Germans were preparing to execute a certain number of prisoners at Châteaubriant in reprisal for attacks against their soldiers. Pucheu had voluntarily supplied them with a list of names of men whose execution he requested according to his preference. The enemy gave him this disgraceful satisfaction. Formal proof of this was discovered after the liberation.

During the trial, General Giraud, called as a witness, spoke of the accused only with great reticence. After Pucheu's condemnation Giraud asked me to suspend the sentence. I could only refuse. To his last hour Pierre Pucheu declared that he had acted only in the public interest. In his final statement to his judges, referring to De Gaulle, he cried: "If my life can serve him in the mission on which he bears the supreme hope of France, then let him take my life! I give it to him." He died bravely, he himself giving the order to fire.

During the fearful cataclysm through which France was staggering, men divided into two camps had claimed to lead the nation and the state toward different goals, by contradictory paths. From that moment, the responsibility of both groups was measured on earth not by their intentions but by their acts, for the country's salvation was directly at stake. Whatever they might have thought, whatever they might have wished, judgment on all of them could only be pronounced according to their works. But afterward? Afterward? Let God judge their souls; France would bury their bodies!

But the nation must live. The Committee of Liberation made every effort to permit it to do so when its chains were torn away. Convinced as I was that, once confronted with the ocean of financial, economic and social problems that would be our immediate concern, we could do nothing in the practical sphere which had not been planned and worked out beforehand, I concentrated a great part of the present share of the government's effort on its future object. Here three mortal perils lay in wait for us: inflation, the intolerably low level of wages and the price of services, and the lack of supplies.

As a matter of fact, the fiduciary circulation, as a result of the payments the invader had required, was three times higher in the spring of 1944 than the 1940 total, while the quantity of merchandise was on the average lower by half. The result was an enormous rise in actual prices, a wild black market and, for the majority of the population, unspeakable privation. At the same time, as a result of enemy pressure to entice French workers to Germany, workers' salaries and employees' wages were kept very low. On the other hand, certain businessmen, financiers and intermediaries made scandalous profits. The country, at the liberation, taking into account the psychological slackening which the latter would involve, risked simultaneously monetary collapse, the explosion of social claims for recovery, and famine.

For the government to adopt a policy of *laisser faire et laisser passer* would be to hand the nation over to irremediable disturbances, for under the shock of the liberation, inflation would be unleashed and all dikes flooded. Yet an anti-inflation policy implied crushing constraints, and it was difficult to see how the nation would endure them, having scarcely emerged from years of oppression. Such a policy would also provoke social upheavals incompatible with the necessity of revitalizing production; it would empty the markets without the public powers having the means to provide foodstuffs in any other way, since all reserves had disappeared, since the treasury had no means to pay for the tremendous purchases required from foreign powers, and since the Allied merchant fleet would then be in use transporting supplies into battle. Between the two extremes, the Committee of Liberation adopted a middle solution which nevertheless was to be easy for no one.

By exchanging promissory notes, taxing profits, confiscating illicit gains; by permitting holders of bank accounts the use of a sum corresponding only to their immediate needs; by taking advantage of the optimism victory would inspire throughout the nation to float a huge loan and absorb the liquid assets, the fiduciary circulation would thus be limited. By readjusting the prices paid to producers and at the same time subsidizing the essential produce in order to keep the price scale down, it would be possible to keep the markets supplied. By according a "substantial" increase in salaries and wages—on the order of 30 per cent—the social crisis would be avoided. But also it would henceforth be necessary to assure an extra reinforcement of supplies from abroad. Which is why in the spring of 1944 the government constituted in the overseas territories stocks of goods worth ten billion francs at the time and arranged a "six months' plan" with Washington to provide for the first American aid.

These measures would stave off the worst, but nothing would keep the nation, once liberated, from undergoing a long period of penury and rationing. No magic formula and no technical skill would change its ruins into riches. Whatever ingenuity and organization could accomplish, it would take time, order, work and sacrifice to reconstruct what had been destroyed and to renew demolished or dated equipment. Co-operation in this effort was still to be sought from the laboring classes, without which everything would collapse in disorder and demagogy. For the nation to acquire ownership of its principal sources of energy—coal, electricity and gas (which, moreover, it was alone in a position to develop as they required); to assure it the control of credit in order to keep its activities from being at the mercy of financial monopolies; to make accessible to the working class, by labor commissions, the way to association and union; to free our men and women from anxiety in their lives, as in their labor, by officially insuring them against sickness, unemployment and old age; and lastly, thanks to a system of generous government allowances, to raise the French birth rate and thereby increase the vital source of the nation's power: these were the reforms I proclaimed on March 15, 1944, reforms which my government aimed to accomplish and which, in fact, it did accomplish.

In this area of our policy, we could count on public opinion. For there is a concordance between men's misery and their impulse toward progress. Many sensed that the ordeals of war would lead toward a vast transformation of the human condition. If nothing was done in this direction, the slow movement of the masses toward Communist totalitarianism would be rendered inevitable. On the other hand, by acting immediately, the soul of France could be saved. Furthermore, the opposition of the privileged class would scarcely make itself felt, so severely had this social category been compromised by the error of Vichy and frightened by the specter of revolution. As for the resistance, it was entirely favorable to this development: combatants who had run the same risks were inclined toward fraternity.

But the same profound reasons that required great and immediate reforms in metropolitan France also demanded the transformation of the status of the overseas territories and the rights of their inhabitants. I was as convinced of this as anyone while I was fighting the war with the co-operation of the Empire's men and resources. How could I doubt, moreover, that on the morrow of the conflict that now enflamed the world, the passion for freedom would rise and swell universally? What was happening or heralded in Asia, in Africa, in Australasia, would have its repercussions everywhere. Now if in our overseas territories our misfortunes had not destroyed the loyalty of the people, the latter had nevertheless witnessed events that were cruelly prejudicial to our prestige: the collapse of 1940, the abasement of Vichy beneath the enemy's heel, the arrival of the Americans speaking as masters following the ridiculous battles of November 1942. On the other hand, throughout all of French Africa the native populations had been aware of the example of Fighting France; they recognized, on their own soil, the beginning of the French recovery; they participated in it with high hopes. Indeed this was the point where everything must begin again, but on the formal condition of not maintaining these states and these territories at their former level. And since, in such matters, it is never too soon to begin, I intended that my government take the initiative without delay.

In December 1943 I therefore approved General Catroux, National Commissioner for Moslem Affairs, when he proposed to the Committee of Liberation an important reform concerning Algeria. Heretofore, the inhabitants in this country were divided into two electoral colleges. The first, consisting exclusively of Frenchmen, whether by origin or naturalization, wielded in relation to the second, which comprised the bulk of the Moslem population, an overwhelming majority in the municipal councils and the general councils; it alone was represented in the French Parliament. We decreed that some tens of thousands of Moslems, among those "qualified," should comprise part of the first college without regard to their "personal status." Further, all the rest would have the right to vote within the second college. Lastly, the proportion of those elected by the second college in the assemblies, including the French Parliament, would be increased to parity. This was a considerable step in the direction of the civic and political equality of all Algerians.

Of course this reform raised muffled protests, as much among the French *colons* as among certain Moslem clans. But many Arabs and Kabyles felt a spurt of hope and gratitude toward France, who, without waiting until she herself had emerged from her miseries, thus raised their own condition and associated their destiny all the more closely with her own. Furthermore, in every milieu, the authority and rapidity with which the government had adopted all its measures was striking in comparison with the past regime which had temporized for so many, many years. On December 12, 1943, accompanied by General Catroux and several ministers, I went to Constantine. There, in the Place de la Brèche, among an enormous crowd, I made public our decisions. Before me, near the platform, I saw Dr. Bendjelloul and many Moslems weeping with emotion.

We created another occasion to confirm the new policy that was leading to the French Union: the African Conference at Brazzaville. René Pleven, National Commissioner for the Colonies, had proposed and organized it; around him would be convened twenty governors general and governors, among the foremost Félix Éboué; also present would be Félix Gouin, the president, as well as some ten members of the Consultative Assembly, in addition to various unofficial authorities. The goal of the conference was to bring together ideas and experiences "in order to determine on what practical foundations a French community comprising the territories of Equatorial Africa could progressively be constructed" to replace the system of direct administration.

With deliberate solemnity, I left for Brazzaville. From Morocco I reached Dakar, where the authorities, the Army, the fleet, the *colons* and the population as a whole displayed an indescribable enthusiasm. Yet only three years ago it was here that I had been forbidden access to Senegal by cannon shots! Konakry, Abidjan, Lomé, Cotonou, Douala and Libreville received my visit in their turn and burst into demonstrations that revealed the vibrant certainty of victory. Brazzaville gave me a moving welcome that marked its pride at having served as a refuge for French sovereignty in its worst years. I took up quarters in the "Case De Gaulle," the official residence which the territory, in its generous devotion, had built for my use on the magnificent bank of the Congo.

On January 30, I opened the conference. After Pleven's speech to me, I indicated why the government had decided to convene it: "Without wishing," I said, "to exaggerate the urgency of the reasons impelling us to broach these African questions all at once, we believe that the events now sweeping the world oblige us not to delay." Having hailed France's effort in Africa, I noted that even before the war "had appeared the necessity of establishing here on new foundations the conditions of Africa's development, those of the progress of its inhabitants and those of the exercise of its sovereignty." How much more urgent this was today, "since the war, which will have been, in a large share, an African war, is being fought to determine the nature of man's condition and since, beneath the action of the psychic forces it has everywhere unleashed, every population looks ahead and questions itself as to its destiny!" Yes, France, I declared, had chosen to lead down the road to the future "the sixty million men associated with her own forty-two million sons." Why? "First of all, because she is France. . . . Second, because it is in her overseas territories and in their loyalty that she has found her refuge and the starting point for her liberation. . . . And lastly, because, today, France is animated . . . with an ardent will for renewal."

The conference then began its work which was to result in propositions of an administrative, social and cultural nature. For a meeting of governors obviously could not decide the constitutional questions posed by the Empire's transformation into the French Union. But the route was traced and needed only to be followed. The spirit had blown which had the possibility of making this reform a national undertaking on a universal scale. No one was deceived about this in the rest of the world, where attention was suddenly fixed on Brazzaville. This conference had taken place by France's own choice at the moment when her reviving power and her reanimated confidence put her in a position to bestow what no one would yet dare claim to tear from her. Having accoladed Éboué, who, exhausted by too many efforts, was to die three months later without having seen the liberation, I left the capital of Equatorial Africa by way of Bangui, Fort-Lamy, Zinder, Niamey, Gao, returning to Algiers, where the legitimacy of the banner floating over my roof was no longer questioned by anyone.

But what is accomplished in action must be recorded in words. It was time that the government assume the name that fell to it by right. Despite terrible divisions, procrastinating until the last possible moment, I had preserved the hope that this proclamation could ultimately be made in national unanimity, permitting a reorganization of the state before events settled matters once and for all. In behalf of certain men who had considered themselves invested with the public authority when they assumed responsibility for the national capitulation, I had for four long and terrible years safeguarded the possibility of their one day saying, "We were wrong. We now see the way of honor, duty and combat. Here we are, with those appearances of qualification that the forms of legality still leave us, accompanied by those who, without having done anything unworthy, still follow us out of discipline and loyalty. Whatever the enemy makes us pay for it, we order them to combat him by every means wherever he may be. Later on, if you wish, the verdict of politics, of justice and of history! For the supreme effort, make room for us beside you, in the name of the unity and the salvation of France!"

But this cry was not to be heard. "There are more regrets than avowals in this world." Now, from one day to the next, the armies of the liberation were to land on our country's soil. For the nation and for the world, it was urgently necessary that our power, such as it was, be confirmed in its capacity to hold all the rights which the choice of the people confers.

On May 7, in Tunis, I declared: "As for those who suppose that at the time of the liberation France can return to her feudal past and divide herself up among several governments, we ask them to meet us soon at Marseille on the Canebière, at Lyon in the Place Bellecour, at Lille in the Grand-Place, at Bordeaux in Les Quinconces, at Strasbourg in the Cours de Broglie, in Paris somewhere between the Arc de Triomphe and Notre-Dame!" On May 15, I received a motion unanimously passed by the Consultative Assembly on Albert Gazier's proposal and which was to be translated into a decree on June 3, 1944. At the very moment I left for England, where the liberating invasion was to set forth three days later, the Committee of National Liberation became the Provisional Government of the French Republic.

CHAPTER 6

DIPLOMACY

B ENEATH its formal conventions, diplomacy recognizes only realities: destitute, Fighting France could move men to sympathy, but seldom to assistance. Today, the dawning French unity began to be of material consequence. Proportionately, France reappeared in the world's diplomatic perspectives. The Allies did not contest the fact that soon they must accord her a place there any more than Frenchmen henceforth doubted their country's salvation. In anticipation of this occasion, their foreign policy now paid us particular attention.

Furthermore, our co-operation was more appreciable every day. Without our troops, the Battle of Tunisia would have been marked by an initial failure. Soon, French action in the decisive sector would determine the Italian victory. As for the coming struggle in France, the Allied governments and general staffs counted on the share which our resistance forces, the Empire's army and the remains of our fleet would take in it. And how valuable to the Allies were our African and Corsican bases, as well as the effective aid they found there. Further, our presence beside them constituted a considerable moral triumph. This is why France—her interests, her reactions—assumed an ever-increasing importance in their manner of envisaging their relations with the world.

Nevertheless, if they concerned themselves on our account, Washington, London and Moscow limited their official relations to what was indispensable. The United States, fearing European involvements and planning to determine the peace settlement by direct arrangement with Soviet Russia, felt that France's admission to the combine of "big" powers would thwart her intentions. Already, the presence of the British frequently seemed inopportune, despite London's constant concern never to stand in America's way. But how many more difficulties there would be if France also appeared among the victors, with her principles and her ruins. And what was more, she would take her place there as the spokesman of the small and medium-sized nations. How, henceforth, obtain that Soviet co-operation the White House planned on and whose price would necessarily be the independence of the Vistula, Danube and Balkan states? As for Asia and her frontiers, it was the American intention that the European empires there be brought to an end. As for Australasia, the question was virtually settled: it was unlikely that Holland would be able to hold out in Indonesia; but how deal with Indochina if the French now were to resume their place among the Great Powers? Thus, while willingly acknowledging our recovery, while coming to terms with us when it was advantageous to do so, Washington would affect, as long as possible, to consider France as a fallow field and De Gaulle's government as an inconvenient accident scarcely requiring the attentions one paid to a state.

England did not proceed in quite so summary a fashion, knowing that the presence, the power, the influence of France would be as necessary tomorrow to Europe's equilibrium as they had been yesterday. England had never assumed responsibility for Vichy's renunciations, which had cost her dear. British instinct and policy alike hoped France would reappear in her avatar as yesterday's partner, tractable and familiar. But what was the good of hurrying matters? Victory was henceforth certain, and it was certain too that the French forces would aid the Allies with all the means in their power. As to the successive settlements, perhaps it would be for the best that France participate in them, but on condition that she do so as a subordinate, an auxiliary, and that she give way before the American stratagem to which Great Britain had already acceded. But would General de Gaulle submit to such plasticity? Nothing was less certain. Everything considered, it was advisable that France's sovereignty remain somewhat nebulous. All the more so since this vagueness could be put to good advantage to abolish what remained of the old French competition in the Middle East.

Soviet Russia observed, calculated and remained on her guard. Certainly everything led the Kremlin to favor the rebirth of a France capable of assisting it to subdue the German menace and to remain independent in regard to the United States. But there was no hurry. For the moment, it was victory that mattered, the opening of the second front from the Channel to the Adriatic, and not the assumption of a political position too different from that of the Anglo-American powers. Furthermore, if General de Gaulle's France was to be associated directly with the European settlements, would she agree to the disappearance of the sovereignty of Poland, of Hungary, of the Balkan states, of—who knows?—Austria, of Czechoslovakia? Lastly, what was the France of tomorrow to be? Her domestic status would heavily influence her foreign policy, especially in regard to the Soviets. Who could be sure she would not turn against them under the action of the same elements that had created Vichy? On the other hand, wasn't it conceivable that the Communists might accede to power in Paris? In the one case as in the other, it would be better not to have made too many advances to the Algiers government. In short, while giving every evidence of attentive sympathy to our cause, Russia, in all essential matters, chose to wait and see.

On the whole, if in Washington, London and Moscow diplomatic policy differed as to basic motives, it was in agreement that our place should be reserved without any need for haste in returning it to us. As for De Gaulle, everyone acknowledged him as the guide and symbol of France's recovery. But it was regarded as essential that his action be checked. Already, the fact that he was on the way to uniting a people as divided as the French and that he had been able to constitute a solid and coherent governmental power seemed abnormal to the foreign experts—virtually scandalous. Everyone was quite willing that France, with such a leader, should climb out of the abyss; but there must be no question of her scaling the summit. Officially, therefore, De Gaulle was treated with consideration, not enthusiasm. Less officially, whatever was said, written or plotted against De Gaulle was encouraged. Later, every possible effort would be made to unearth again that "political" France, so malleable in Europe's chancelleries, which everyone was used to.

As for myself, I must confess it was of little concern whether the diplomatic situation of the Algiers government was regularized or remained indefinite. Looking back, I sensed that the worst was over and that, if we persevered, the formalities still remaining would also be solemnized sooner or later. Besides, it was not fitting that what we were or were to become should depend on the decisions of others. Henceforth we were sufficiently well established to make ourselves heard where and when we chose. As for the future of France, it would develop of itself, not according to the Allies' convenience. Once the Reich was overthrown, taking into account the difficulties which would confront even the greatest states, nothing would prevent France from playing the role she chose, on condition that it was France that made the choice. This conviction of mine permitted me to consider the gray faces of the Allies with detachment. Not concealing my regret that they should have adopted, so detrimentally to our common action, the reservations characterizing their co-operation, the position I took was never that of the plaintiff.

Doubtless Massigli, who was in permanent contact with the diplomatic corps in Algiers and who, by his own admission, suffered cruelly from such ill-defined foreign policies; doubtless Viénot, who throughout his career had been an apostle of the alliance with Britain and who was disappointed at encountering London's present reticence; doubtless Monnet, whose negotiations with Washington for "aid and recovery" could not be brought to a conclusion because the question of Franco-American relations was still in suspense, or Hoppenot, whose intelligence and sensibility deplored the negative prejudice of the United States; doubtless Garreau, who compared the fervor of Moscow's declarations in France's behalf with the circumspection of the people's commissars—doubtless they were less serene than I. I permitted them to express their feelings when the opportunity arose. I sympathized with the impatience of our representatives to the other allies: Dejean, delegated to the governments in exile in Great Britain; Baelen, in charge of our relations with the Greek and Yugoslav governments in Cairo; Coiffard in Chungking; Bonneau in Ottawa; Pechkoff, and later Grandin de L'Éprevier, in Pretoria; Clarac, later Monmayou, in Canberra; Garreau-Dombasle, Ledoux, Lancial, Arvengas, Raux, Casteran and Lechenet in Latin America; Grousset in Havana; Milon de Peillon in Port-au-Prince. I realized how trying the situation was for our delegates to the neutral countries: Truelle in Spain; Du Chayla in Portugal; De Saint-Hardouin in Turkey; De Benoist in Egypt; De Vaux Saint-Cyr in Sweden; De Leusse in Switzerland; De Laforcade in Ireland. All the same, I myself deliberately persisted in the attitude of a chief of state ready to come to an agreement with the others if they would ask him to do so, but who would solicit nothing of what anyone might offer him today since he was sure of having it tomorrow.

Such were the *données* of the game. They were revealed in the Italian question, where, by virtue of the principle of a makeshift compromise, the Allies kept us at a distance without, all the same, excluding us altogether. On September 27, 1943, the representatives of England and the United States brought Massigli the complete text of the armistice, which was to be returned the same day in order for Marshal Badoglio to sign it. The Anglo-American diplomats pointed out—quite rightly—that this text took into account what we had previously requested. But they found nothing to answer to the French minister's question: "Why did you not associate France with you in the armistice?" Some days later,

Badoglio was to declare war on the Reich with the joint approval of Great Britain, America and Russia but with no mention of ours. At the same time, we learned that a conference to settle the Italian question among the British, American and Soviet foreign ministers was to take place in Moscow; we were not invited.

When Mr. Cordell Hull passed through Algiers on his way to the conference, I restrained myself from expressing the slightest recrimination, but made it clear that no one would make use of what we were and what we had for nothing. "We are delighted," I told him, "to see you making direct contact, in America's behalf, with Soviet Russia; I intend to go to Moscow myself one of these days in behalf of France." When the Secretary of State inquired as to our position on the subject of the Italian question, I replied: "We shall not fail to express our own point of view when we are in a position to know that of the other states concerned."

Mr. Cordell Hull then indicated that the Moscow conference would probably result in the creation of an inter-Allied commission for Italian affairs. "Perhaps," he added, "you will take part in it." "We shall see," I told him. "In any case, to determine the fate of the peninsula, it is first of all essential to recover its territory from the Germans, which implies the co-operation of French forces and bases. I know that Eisenhower is planning to request this co-operation, and we are prepared to accede to his request. But to do so, it is obviously necessary that we determine with you, and in the same capacity as you, what will become of Italy. We can engage our soldiers only in behalf of a goal in which we too have a share." Mr. Cordell Hull understood that he was facing a firmly held position, as did Mr. Eden after I spoke to him on October 10. As for M. Bogomolov, he had outstripped the others by explaining that the Mediterranean commission had been a Soviet notion and that his government would insist we be invited to participate in it.

Indeed, on November 16, Massigli received Messrs. Macmillan, Murphy and Bogomolov. The latter informed him that their three governments intended to institute an "Advisory Commission for

Italian Affairs." This commission would represent the Allies on the spot, would propose to their governments the measures to be taken in common, and would establish policy for the military command in all matters relating to politics and administration. We were asked to sit on this commission. The Committee of Liberation accepted the proposition. On November 29, I received M. Vishinsky, who came to assure me of his government's eagerness to co-operate closely with us on this commission. The latter, composed of Macmillan, Massigli, Murphy and Vishinsky, then began its work. Soon Couve de Murville was to replace Massigli, since the latter was kept too occupied by his ministry. Thus we were directly informed as to what was happening on the peninsula; we would take part in the measures destined either to punish Italy for her crimes or to permit her to recover from her misfortunes; we would be in a position to pursue our policy on the peninsula, a position essential to her destiny, to ours and to that of the West.

I had explained this policy to Count Sforza, who slipped into my office at Les Oliviers one October evening. The old statesman was returning to Italy after twenty years of exile. On the ruins of the Fascist system he had unceasingly opposed, he was preparing to assume the direction of his unfortunate country's foreign affairs. I was struck with the nobility and the courage with which Sforza envisaged his coming task. "That I am here before you," he told me, "is proof of my desire to do everything possible to establish that Franco-Italian co-operation for whose lack you and I are paying dearly and which our Europe is going to need more than ever." I indicated to Count Sforza how closely I saw eye to eye with him on this crucial point, but that after what had happened a reconciliation with Italy could not be made altogether gratuitously, although it was our intention to prepare it as sparingly as possible.

To liquidate the privileges which Italian nationals enjoyed in Tunisia; to award France the cantons of Tende and La Brigue which, although French, had been granted to Italy after the plebiscite of 1860; to rectify the frontier along the passes of Larche, Mont Genèvre, Mont Cenis and Little Saint Bernard in order to abolish several awkward encroachments on our territory; to accord Val d'Aosta the right to be what it was—that is, a region spiritually French; to demand certain reparations, particularly in regard to warships and commercial vessels: these were the limited but precise advantages which I had determined to assure France.

Given the fact, furthermore, that Yugoslavia had joined the Allied camp and considering the effort which the troops of General Mikhailovitch and those of Tito had unceasingly furnished, it was evident that Italy could not keep her prewar possessions on the eastern coast of the Adriatic. Nevertheless, we were ready to support her claim to Trieste. Having informed Count Sforza on all these points concerning the Italian frontiers, I added: "As for your colonies, if Cyrenaica, where the English wish to remain, is lost to you, and if we ourselves intend to remain in Fezzan, on the other hand, we hope to see you remain not only in Somalia but also in Eritrea and in Tripolitania. For the latter, you will doubtless have to find a means of association with the local populations; for the former, in exchange for the rights you will retain, you must recognize the Negus' sovereignty. But we consider it justifiable that you should be an African power. If you yourselves claim that power, we shall support you firmly."

In December, on General Eisenhower's request, the Committee of Liberation sent to Italy the first elements of the French Expeditionary Corps. The latter was subsequently to be reinforced to the point where it furnished the decisive Allied action during the Battle of Rome. In proportion as this military participation increased, we spoke louder in the political sphere. Such amplification was necessary, moreover, for the Anglo-American forces, applying a system of expedient devices and maintaining King Victor Emmanuel and Marshal Badoglio in office, were setting obstacles in the way of Franco-Italian reconciliation and accumulating motives for revolution in the peninsula.

The King, in 1940, had permitted war to be declared on France at the moment she was succumbing to the German onslaught, though it was France whose costly effort of 1859 had liberated

Italy and assured its unity and whose Army in 1917 had helped bring the disaster of Caporetto to a halt at the Piave. He had accepted and submitted to Mussolini until the moment when the Duce succumbed to events. Badoglio, merely by virtue of the German victory, had had an "armistice" signed with the plenipotentiaries of Pétain and Weygand according to the terms of which the Italians were to occupy a part of French territory and control our Empire's forces. Further, it was from the Fascist regime that the Marshal–Prime Minister held his honors and his command. How could this sovereign and this chief of government organize the co-operation of their country with ours and lead Italy along a new road? This was the substance of the Committee of Liberation's communication, on January 22, 1944, to Washington, London and Moscow, declaring that the throne and the government must be swept clean.

During the months of March, May and June, I was in Italy inspecting our troops; I observed many disturbing signs, particularly in Naples. The most obvious spectacle was that of extreme poverty and of the deplorable effects which contact with well-supplied troops produced on public morals. As a Christian, a Latin, a European, I was cruelly sensitive to the misery of this great nation that had been misled but to whom the world owed so much. Perhaps the Italian people instinctively sensed my feelings; perhaps, in their ordeal, the thought of France was closer to them, as to all nations in agony. In any case, I was always surprised to find enthusiastic groups following after me whenever I appeared in public. Couve de Murville, our extremely well-informed and self-possessed representative, itemized the state of Italy's politics, torn by contrary currents in which it was already apparent that the future would be played out between the Papacy and the Party. During these trips, I was forced to refuse to meet both Umberto and Badoglio, although with some regret; I was not, however, prepared to admit that the Prince's father should continue to wear the crown and that the Marshal should remain at the head of the government.

But while we were beginning to pluck the fruits of long effort in the western Mediterranean, in the Near East we had to endure many disappointments. In the Levant States, the agitation of the local politicians, as a result of British provocation, organized a spectacular crisis in order to take advantage of France's diminished status while there was still time to do so.

Lebanon, on this occasion, served as the field of operations. The elections had taken place in July 1943. After a period characterized by so many events disastrous to French prestige, it was understandable that the new parliament should manifest an unrestrained nationalism. The English, having strongly contributed to the electoral result, now wished to take advantage of it. With M. Béchara Khoury, the newly elected President of the Republic, and with the government of M. Riad Solh, Spears assumed the attitude of France's adversary, encouraged his faction to outbid our own and promised the protection of his government no matter what the result.

It must be said that Spears's action in Syria and Lebanon corresponded to the general policy Great Britain tended to pursue in the Middle East during the war's final phase. The victorious conclusion of the operations in North Africa had put a great number of British forces at their disposal. While a portion of the latter were sent into combat in Italy, the rest took up positions on both banks of the Red Sea. Seven hundred thousand British soldiers occupied Egypt, the Sudan, Cyrenaica, Palestine, Transjordan, Iraq and the Levant States. Besides, London had created at Cairo an "Economic Center" which, thanks to the manipulation of credits, the shipping monopolies and the imperatives of the blockade, controlled the entire foreign exchange of the Arab nations and thereby, in fact, the life of their people, the opinion of their leaders and the attitude of their governments. Lastly, the presence of an army of specialists provided with vast financial means and, in the world of society, the action of a perfectly organized diplomacy and propaganda completed the elements of power, thanks to which England, rid of her enemies' threats in the Near East, intended to affirm her status as sole suzerain.

We were not in a position to counterbalance such pressure. Three Senegalese battalions, some cannon, some tanks, two dispatch boats and about fifteen planes comprised all the forces the French had in the Levant. True, there were also the Syrian and Lebanese troops, some 18,000 good soldiers under our command. But what would be their decision should the Damascus and Beirut governments take a hostile position openly to us? Besides, our extreme poverty did not permit us to offer anything to anyone. As for struggling against the flood of tendentious propaganda which all Anglo-American scurces, whenever the occasion arose, unfailingly poured out the world over, it was beyond our means to do so. Above all, now that the liberation of France was on the horizon, I would have no chance of urging the French, even my ministers, to think of any other undertaking. All in all, we were too ill provided and too occupied elsewhere to be able to counteract any interferences with our position on the spot.

The facts crystallized during the month of November. The Beirut government found itself, for reasons of domestic policy, in a difficult parliamentary situation. To create a distraction, M. Riad Solh, President of the Council, and M. Camille Chamoun, Minister of Foreign Affairs, noisily raised the Lebanese claims against the mandate power. Our delegate-general to the Levant, Ambassador Jean Helleu, who saw the crisis rising, had come to Algiers to consult the government. On November 5, he presented his report to me in the presence of Catroux and Massigli and received our instructions; we urged him to take decisive steps to open negotiations at Beirut and Damascus with a view to transferring to the local governments certain services concerning the economy and the police which the French authority had hitherto maintained.

But at the same time, we reconfirmed Helleu concerning our theoretical position on the mandate which, entrusted to France by the League of Nations, could not be deposed except as a result of future international solicitations and by French powers which would no longer be provisional. This was the position we had always presented to the Allies, notably to Great Britain, without ever having received any objection to it in principle. Juridically, if Syria's and Lebanon's independence had any international value, it was because we ourselves had accorded it to them by virtue of our mandate. But for the same reasons, we found ourselves obliged to preserve certain responsibilities in the Levant as a result of the state of war. Given the world-wide scope of the conflict, we decided the Damascus and Beirut governments could wait until it was decided before settling the last formalities that still limited the sovereignty of their states. There was no doubt that they would have waited, in fact, had London not encouraged their demands and offered the support of the British forces in order to impose them.

While Helleu was in Algiers, the Lebanese parliament revised the constitution by removing from it all matters mentioning the mandate, as if the mandate had been abolished. From Cairo, which he passed through on his way back to his post, the ambassador had telegraphed the Beirut government, informing it that he was carrying his government's instructions for the opening of negotiations and requesting that the promulgation of the new constitutional law be postponed. But the Lebanese ignored his message. Then Helleu, back in Beirut and outraged by this provocation, opposed the constitution by a formal veto on November 12, suspended the parliament and had the Lebanese chief of state, the President of the Council and several other ministers arrested, while M. Émile Eddé became provisional President of the Republic.

While regarding our delegate's actions as perfectly justifiable, and in particular the sentiments that had dictated them, the Committee of Liberation was immediately convinced that they exceeded the measures which the general situation might permit him to sustain. All the more so since without renouncing the principle of the mandate, we did not intend to question the independence we had already conceded. This is why, on the morning of the thirteenth, informed of what had occurred at Beirut the day before, we decided to send General Catroux there to re-establish a normal constitutional situation without, at the same time, disavowing

Helleu. This meant that Catroux, after consultations on the spot, would have Khoury, Riad Solh and their ministers released and would re-establish the President in his functions. After which the Lebanese government would be re-formed, including, last of all, the Chamber of Deputies. As for our delegate, his presence in the Levant would not be justified as soon as Catroux was there with full powers; we therefore summoned Helleu to Algiers "on conference" after a few days' delay.

In order that there should be no misunderstandings as to Catroux' mission, I myself, on November 16, made a placating declaration to the Consultative Assembly: "What has occurred in Beirut," I declared, "alters neither France's policy in Lebanon, nor the commitments we have made, nor our desire to fulfill them. Our intention consists of seeing a normal constitutional situation established in Lebanon, in order that we can deal with its government, on questions of common interest, both parties in complete independence." I concluded by saying: "The passing cloud will not darken the horizon." The next day, Catroux, passing through Cairo, saw Mr. Casey, the British Minister of State, and indicated to him that he would have Messrs. Khoury and Riad Solh released without delay. On November 19, having arrived at Beirut, he had a discussion with M. Béchara Khoury, received the President's many assurances of loyal friendship and informed the latter that he was to be released and restored to office. No one henceforth could doubt our desire to "link up" as soon as possible and to adopt a conciliating policy.

But the British could not reconcile themselves to conciliation. Subsequent events made it appear as if London were determined to throw oil on the fire in order to make the arrangement we were seeking in Lebanon appear to have been imposed upon us by British intervention, and perhaps, too, in order to take revenge on De Gaulle for the recent alteration of the Committee of Liberation. Already on November 13, Mr. Makins, replacing Mr. Macmillan, had sent Massigli a "verbal" but comminatory note demanding an immediate Anglo-Franco-Lebanese conference to settle the incident and insisting on behalf of the British government that we recall Helleu. But on the nineteenth, when it had been proved for several days that the path we had taken led to complete agreement, England hurled her thunderbolts. This could only be for the gallery's benefit, of course, and to create the impression of a French loss of face.

On that day, in fact, Mr. Casey came to Beirut and, flanked by General Spears, delivered an ultimatum to General Catroux: Great Britain, ignoring the alliance that united us, her promises of political disinterestedness in the Levant States, the agreements with me Mr. Oliver Lyttelton had signed in her name, ordered the French representative to agree to the tripartite conference and to release the President and the Lebanese ministers within thirty-six hours. Unless this was done, the British, with the excuse of maintaining order—which it was not their responsibility to do—would proclaim what they called "martial law," seize power by force and send their troops to liberate the prisoners under our soldiers' guard.

"Here we are back in the Fashoda days," General Catroux remarked to Messrs. Casey and Spears. With this difference nevertheless: that France, at the time of the Fashoda incident, was in a position to offer England resistance, but that in the present instance the latter ran no risk whatever. The Committee of Liberation ordered General Catroux to refuse to attend the tripartite conference, to release, as had been agreed, M. Khoury and his ministers and, if England carried out her threat of seizing power in Lebanon, to collect our officials and our troops at some port and bring them back to Africa. I would then take it upon myself to explain to France and to the world the reasons for this departure.

Ultimately, a kind of *modus vivendi* was re-established in the Levant: the British muted their threats; General Catroux negotiated the transference to the states of the "common interest" services; those in office continued to wobble and war with each other amid the agitation created by those who desired their place; the "leaders" of the neighboring Arab countries, for the same reasons, came forward with many protests against France, proceeding at Cairo from Nahas Pasha, the president of Farouk's council imposed by the English ambassador; at Baghdad from Noury Pasha Saïd, who had only returned to power thanks to the action of the British troops; at Amman from the Emir Abdullah, whose budget was settled in London and whose army was led by General Peake and Colonel Glubb, known as "Peake Pasha" and "Glubb Pasha."

In February, Catroux having returned to Algiers, the Committee of Liberation appointed General Beynet as delegate-general and minister plenipotentiary of France to the Levant. Helleu was not to return. Casey had left Cairo and Chamoun Beirut, where Spears was to remain to foment the next crisis. With much skill and steadfastness, the new French representative took the situation in hand. Meanwhile, it was clear that a constantly renewed *tour de force* could not be repeated in every case. All the less since our poor means, the anguished passion of French public opinion and the whole world's attention would henceforth be absorbed by the military events that were to decide the destiny of Europe.

In this regard, politics preceded events themselves, oriented everywhere to the situations likely to follow victory. In the Allied camp, this was particularly the case in regard to the small and middle-size states. At Algiers, we could scarcely hear even the echo of the discussions centering on these states, since their sovereigns and ministers were in London, their diplomacy operating chiefly in Washington and their propaganda directed primarily toward the Anglo-Saxon countries. Nevertheless, we knew enough to understand their anxieties. Nothing, moreover, demonstrated more clearly and more sadly how the fall of France yesterday and the pressure of the three other great powers to keep her at a distance today seriously mortgaged the peace in preparation for tomorrow.

As a matter of fact, Belgium and Luxembourg, completely surrounded by Western powers, did not doubt that their frontiers and their independence would be restored to them by the liberation. The problems then confronting them would be of an economic order: ruined France and an exhausted England could help them to solve their difficulties only after prolonged delays; in the immediate future, it was to be America on whom they counted. Hence we saw Messrs. Spaak, Gutt and Bech haunt the conferences at Atlantic City, Hot Springs and Dumbarton Oaks, where the United States was laying its plans for the revictualing, the reconstruction and the development of Europe, while Monsieur de Romrée, Belgian ambassador to the French Committee of Liberation, was chiefly interested in schemes for a confederation of western Europe. The Dutch, who had scarcely any political anxiety as to metropolitan Holland, were, however, hugely concerned as to the future of their Australasian possessions. Henceforth, their government was to be subject to American pressure which would eventually constrain them to renounce their sovereignty over Java, Sumatra and Borneo. The remarks of the Dutch minister plenipotentiary, M. van Wijk, as well as the reports Dejean was sending us from London, indicated that M. van Kleffens foresaw with some bitterness that the Allied victory in the Pacific would involve the liquidation of the Netherlands Empire. The Norwegians felt already, through neutral Sweden and a virtually conquered Finland, the crushing weight of all the Russias. Hence M. Trygve Lie was already working out plans for an Atlantic alliance which M. De Hougen, Norwegian minister at Algiers, came to discuss with us. But above all it was the refugee governments of Central and Balkan Europe which betrayed their anxiety. For, realizing that the Soviets would follow the Germans over their territories, they were devoured by their fears for tomorrow.

The Teheran conference, held in the month of December 1943, merely fanned their fears. Of course the participants—Roosevelt, Stalin and Churchill—had launched a number of lenitive statements declaring that their meeting was of a purely strategic nature. But what leaked out was not at all reassuring for the governments in exile. Despite official secrecy, it was not difficult to discern the essentials of what had happened at Teheran. Stalin had spoken there as the man to whom an accounting must be made. Without revealing the Russian intentions to the other two, he had obliged them to explain theirs to him and even alter them according to his requirements. Roosevelt had agreed with him in rejecting Churchill's plan for a vast Western offensive in Italy, Yugoslavia and Greece, sweeping toward Vienna, Prague and Budapest. Further, the Americans had followed the Soviet lead in refusing, despite the British suggestions, to examine all political questions concerning Central Europe, in particular Poland, which the Russian armies were meanwhile on the verge of entering. We ourselves had been excluded from the proceedings to the point where Roosevelt and Churchill—the former flying over North Africa, the latter sailing along its coast to reach Cairo and Teheran—had taken care not to make contact with us.

Suddenly the prospects so alarming to the sovereigns and ministers of the Balkans and the Vistula and Danube States began to crystallize. This was why, in Greece, a notable part of the resistance elements, developed and directed by Communists, allied itself with the E.A.M. organization, which was fighting against the invader and at the same time breaking ground for the revolution. The military instrument of this movement, the "E.L.A.S.," incorporated a number of maquis groups operating in the Greek mountains and profoundly influenced the army and fleet units stationed in the Middle East. In order to keep contact with the soldiers and sailors and to communicate more readily with the country's interior, the President of the Council, M. Tsouderos, and the majority of the ministers had established their residence in Cairo. Soon King George II joined them there, arriving just in time for a violent ministerial crisis. In April 1944, M. Tsouderos was forced to retire. His replacement, M. Venizelos, left office in his turn, and it was only with great difficulty that M. Papandreou formed a ministry. At the same time, serious rebellions broke out among the troops and on board the ships. To quell them, nothing less than the bloody intervention of British forces was required. Although the representatives of all the political tendencies, meeting later at Beirut, were to proclaim national union, dissension soon broke out again. There was every indication that in Greece the German retreat would be the signal for civil war.

In fact, the United States had prudently withdrawn its finger from this pie long beforehand. But the Soviets were exerting pressure on the Greeks, while the British, aiming at hegemony in the eastern Mediterranean, did not conceal the fact that, in their eyes, Greek questions belonged to their sphere of influence. For this reason the French government had never involved itself in them. Nevertheless it would have been to the interest of a united Europe had the influence and force of France joined those of England in Greece, as had frequently been the case in the past. No one was more convinced of this than M. Argyropoulo, Greek representative to the National Committee; this patriot, deeply disturbed by the threats hanging over his country, this politician, convinced that a Europe without France had every chance of miscarrying, deplored that a barrier should be established by foreign powers between his government and that of the French Republic.

In regard to Yugoslavia, our allies proceeded in the same fashion. The Serbo-Croatian-Slovene kingdom, even before the war a prey to impassioned dissensions among its ethnic groups, now found itself in a state of total upheaval. The Italians had set up a Croat State and annexed Dalmatia and the Slovene province of Ljubljana. Colonel Mikhailovitch had valiantly conducted a guerrilla war against the Germans in the mountains of Serbia, and later on Joseph Broz, known as Tito, had begun the struggle on his own account under Communist encouragement. The invaders had reacted to these facts by massacres and destructions of an unheard-of brutality, while Mikhailovitch and Tito had become adversaries. In London, the very young King Peter II and his unstable government were victims not only of severe national difficulties, but of British political pressure as well.

The British, in effect, considered Yugoslavia as one of the principal fields of action for their Mediterranean policy. Further, Mr. Churchill had made it his personal concern. Cherishing the scheme of a tremendous Balkan operation, he wanted Yugoslavia for its bridgehead. Hence a British military mission had been sent first to Mikhailovitch, whom London was furnishing with arms and advice, and subsequently to Tito, to whom the Prime Minister delegated his son Randolph. Finally, according Tito preference, the British government sent him what was necessary to equip his troops. As for Mikhailovitch, he found himself without any aid whatsoever, vilified by the London radio, even accused of treason before the Commons by the Foreign Office representative. Then, in June 1944, the hapless Peter II was ordered by Mr. Churchill to dismiss M. Pouritch's government, in which Mikhailovitch was serving as Minister of War, and to entrust its control to M. Soubachitch, who had previously received Tito's investiture. This reversal received, of course, Moscow's approval, while M. Fotich, the Yugoslav ambassador to Washington, did not succeed in obtaining America's support for his sovereign.

The French Committee of National Liberation was systematically excluded from these events and their development. I had been able to make episodic contact with General Mikhailovitch, who on his side indicated an ardent desire to communicate with me. Various messages had been exchanged. In February 1944, I awarded him the Croix de Guerre and made public announcement of the fact in order to encourage him at the moment when the ground seemed to be giving way beneath his feet. But the officers I tried to send him from Tunis or Italy never succeeded in reaching him. As for Tito, we never received the slightest sign of recognition from him. I had been on cordial terms with King Peter II and his ministers during my stay in Great Britain; Maurice Dejean, our representative to them there, and M. Jodjvanovitch, their delegate to us at Algiers, served as intermediaries for exchanges of opinion and information; but on no occasion did the Yugoslav government —doubtless not being permitted the latitude to do so—turn to us to request our good offices. England herself did not once decide to consult us in even an advisory capacity. I was therefore confirmed in my resolution to devote what resources we had directly to the liberation of France and not to engage them in Balkan operations. Why should we offer our military co-operation in a political undertaking from which we found ourselves deliberately excluded?

If the Soviet advance and the action of their agents tortured some refugee governments with anxiety, President Beneš and his ministers, on the other hand, affected to be relatively undisturbed by it in regard to Czechoslovakia. Not that they were any more confident in their heart of hearts; but they decided that instead of trying to defer the inevitable, it would be better to turn it to account. Their representative, M. Cerny, kept us informed, moreover, of the progress of this viewpoint. In December 1943, Beneš had gone to Moscow to sign a "friendly alliance" with Stalin, stipulating "mutual co-operation and assistance." Returning to London, he stopped in Algiers on January 2. We respectfully received this head of state who, through the most terrible vicissitudes, had always remained a friend to France.

Beneš informed me of the subjects of his conversations in Moscow; he described Stalin as reserved in his remarks but steadfast in his intentions, his ideas both well concealed and well determined on every European question. Then he explained his own policy. "Look at the map," he said. "The Russians have reached the Carpathians. But the Western powers are not yet ready to land in France. Hence it is the Red Army that will liberate my country from the Germans. Afterward, in order for me to be able to establish my administration, it is with Stalin that I must come to an agreement. I have just done so and on conditions that will not mortgage Czechoslovakia's future. For according to what he and I have agreed upon, the Russian command will not involve itself in our political affairs."

Turning to the European question as a whole, President Beneš undertook to prove to me, as he had already done on other occasions, that the Czech state could revive only on condition of an alliance with Russia. He moved his finger over the map, exclaiming, "Here is the Sudetenland, which must be recovered from the Germans. Here is Teschen, which the Poles are demanding. Here is Slovakia, which the Hungarians plan to recover and where Monsignor Tiso has formed a separatist government. Tomorrow, eastern Germany, Poland and Hungary will be in Soviet hands. If

Russia should espouse their various claims and dissensions, dismemberment is certain. You can see why the Russian alliance is a categorical imperative for us."

When I referred to the possibility of a Western counterbalance, Beneš expressed his doubts. "Roosevelt," he said, "is anxious to come to an agreement with Stalin and withdraw his troops as soon as he can after the victory. Churchill is little concerned with us; for him, the British line of defense is along the Rhine and the Alps. Once this is assured, nothing will rouse his interest save the Mediterranean. As for us, he will follow Roosevelt's lead in exchange for a few advantages in the Middle East. By mutual agreement, Czechoslovakia was not mentioned at Teheran. It is true that there remains General de Gaulle, artisan of that steadfast, strong France which is so indispensable to European equilibrium. Had you not appeared after the fall of your country to urge it on to recovery, there would no longer be any hope for the freedom of Europe. No one, therefore, has more zealous hopes for your entire success than I. But I must point out that Washington and London are hardly of my opinion. Where and what will you be tomorrow? And I must also remind you of Clemenceau's dismissal by the French Parliament just after World War I; I was working with the great Masaryk when the news reached Prague; we both had the same thought: 'This is France's renunciation!' "

What Beneš told me of Washington's and London's attitude toward Soviet ambitions was already being verified by the situation in Poland. The nearer the Red Army approached Warsaw, the more clearly appeared Moscow's intention to dominate Poland and alter its frontiers. It was apparent that Stalin wanted, on the one hand, to add the territories of Lithuania, White Russia and Eastern Galicia to Russia, and on the other to extend Poland as far as the Oder and the Neisse to the German detriment. But it was no less clear that the master of the Kremlin intended to establish a regime answerable to himself on the Vistula and one which the Anglo-American powers would not oppose.

The Polish government in exile in London was thus at grips with terrifying problems, materially impotent to oppose Moscow's decisions but morally armed with that somber assurance which a patriotism tempered by centuries of oppression confers on the Polish spirit. Actually, General Sikorski, President of the Council and commander in chief, had first tried to reach an agreement with the Soviets. When the Wehrmacht was at the gates of Moscow, such an agreement had seemed possible; a number of Polish soldiers imprisoned by the Russians in 1939 had been authorized to reach the Middle East with their leader, General Anders, while Stalin had adopted a moderate tone in speaking of frontiers and future relations. Now the picture had become quite different, as had the map of war. Suddenly the Poles gave way again to the hatred and the panic which the Russians have traditionally inspired in them. In the spring of 1943, they had officially accused the Soviets—not without an appearance of reason—of having massacred 10,000 of their captured officers in the Katyn Forest some three years before. Stalin, irritated, had suspended diplomatic relations. Then, in July, General Sikorski, returning from Egypt, where he had gone to inspect Anders' troops, was killed in an airplane accident in Gibraltar. This eminent man, who enjoyed enough prestige to dominate the passions of his compatriots and enough international attention to be treated with respect, was irreplaceable. From the moment of his loss, the Russo-Polish crisis assumed the quality of a bitter conflict.

Nevertheless, the new Polish government, on the authority of its leader, M. Mikolajczyk, had promised that after the liberation the public powers in Warsaw would be oriented so as to afford Moscow every guarantee of neighborly relations. As to the frontiers, Mikolajczyk did not reject any plans a priori and merely declared that the question could be settled only by the peace treaty. He gave orders to the resistance forces on national territory to co-operate with the Soviet armies. Lastly, he turned to the United States and to Great Britain "to resolve differences and bring to a solution all problems as yet undecided." But these conciliatory moves were not echoed in the Kremlin. Quite the contrary, the Russian grievances increased in proportion to their own advance. In January, on the occasion of the entry of their troops into Polish territory, the Soviets published a declaration according to which the so-called "Curzon line" was to be adopted as the eastern frontier and the government in exile in London completely re-formed. Simultaneously appeared a Polish army corps formed under Russian inspiration and whose leader, Berling, rejected the legal government's authority, while a "Polish Committee of National Liberation," prepared in Moscow and directed by M. Osuska-Morawski, entered Galicia on the heels of the Soviet troops.

It was obvious that Poland's independence would find only a precarious support from the Anglo-American powers. In January 1944, Mr. Cordell Hull made an evasive reply to M. Mikolajczyk's request for mediation. And although Roosevelt, facing an electoral campaign that year, cultivated ambiguity in consideration of the voters of Polish origin, it could be foreseen that once this cape was rounded he would leave Stalin's hands free. The British showed less resignation, but it was likely that their concern to toe the American line would ultimately lead them to yield as to the essentials of the matter, so long as there was some formal arrangement to conceal it.

Actually, Messrs. Churchill and Eden, while pronouncing words favorable to Poland's independence, urged M. Mikolajczyk to go to Moscow. His visit took place in August, at the very moment the Soviet Army had reached Warsaw and the Polish secret army, under General Komorowski, known as "Bor," was taking action against the Germans within the city. After a heroic struggle, the Poles were overwhelmed, accusing the Russians of having done nothing in their aid, and even of having kept British planes from landing on Soviet bases whence they might have taken action to the defenders' advantage. In Moscow, the Polish ministers had obtained only discouraging replies from Stalin and Molotov, while receiving word of an agreement signed by the Soviet Union and the "Polish Committee of National Liberation," assigning the administration of the liberated territories to this committee.

Our government was in no position to prevent this gradual

subjugation of Poland. Since it was not really associated with its great allies on a diplomatic level and did not participate as an equal in the elaboration of the common strategy, how could it have convinced the Western powers to adopt the political attitude and the military decisions that doubtless would have saved Polish independence even while according Russia the frontier she demanded? As for myself, Stalin's idea of according the Poles new acquisitions in Prussia and Silesia in compensation for the amputations they would suffer in the East was quite acceptable, provided he proceeded with humanity in the necessary population shifts. But I felt that his intention of establishing the dictatorship of his followers in Warsaw must be opposed. I considered that America, England and France, by jointly declaring these matters to the world, by acting in co-operation with regard to the Soviet and Polish governments, by stipulating future access to the Baltic ports for the combined Western fleets in return for opening the North Sea ports to Russian ships, would be able to effect a restoration of liberty to the noble and valiant nation of Poland.

But confronted by Soviet Russia's demands, America decided to keep silence. Great Britain looked for a formula. France did not have a say in the matter. To M. Morawski, the active and able ambassador from Poland to the French Committee of Liberation, with whom I continued to confer on many occasions; to General Sosnkowski, who had succeeded Sikorski as commander in chief and whom I received at Algiers in December; to General Anders, whom I saw in March 1944, with his troops before Monte Cassino; to M. Raczkiewicz, President of the Polish Republic, with whom I exchanged visits during my visit to London in June 1944; and to M. de Romer, his Minister of Foreign Affairs, who was at his side, I could indicate only what our own position was and promise to make its weight felt when we had the means to do so.

Meanwhile we found an occasion to bring some assistance to the Polish government in the matter of the ultimate destination of an important stock of gold which the State Bank of Poland had entrusted to the Bank of France in September 1939 and which the latter, in June 1940, had stored at Bamako. In March 1944 the Committee of Liberation, having received the urgent requests of M. Mikolajczyk, decided to put the Poles in possession of their gold again. M. Bogomolov did not fail to make a number of urgent demands that the measure be revoked; having requested an audience with me as a last resort, he said, "The Soviet government formally protests against the transfer of the Polish gold to the government in exile in London. For the latter will not be the government of Poland tomorrow." I replied that it was such today, that it was so recognized by all our allies, including Russia, that on its orders the Polish forces were now fighting beside our own in Italy, and that lastly I did not see in what capacity the Soviet Union was interfering in a matter that concerned only Poland and France. M. Bogomolov retired without concealing his displeasure.

Thus despite the counsels of abstention from Washington, London and Moscow, the small and medium-sized European states sought contact with us. Others, geographically remote, also tended to align themselves with us on a moral basis. General Vanier, the Canadian delegate, brought us the encouragement of his country that was proving so exemplary in the war effort and negotiated the economic aid which Canada was already lending us, as well as that which it would provide after the liberation. Our Latin American allies, by their plenipotentiaries' remarks, indicated that France's return to her position in world politics profoundly affected their own feelings and interests; such, for example, were the assurances that came from M. Vasco da Cunha, for Brazil; from M. de Aramburu, for Peru; from M. Freila Larrea, for Ecuador; and from M. Suarez Solar, for Cuba. Lastly, M. de Sangroniz, the extremely distinguished and adroit Spanish delegate, although the only neutral among the belligerents and somewhat hampered by a rather vague status, showed great concern in all questions affecting Morocco, the fate of Tangier (the destination of all the Frenchmen crossing the Pyrenees) and trade between French Africa and the Iberian Peninsula. We had, in fact, insisted on establishing the indispensable relations with the Spanish, who desired as much themselves. All the same, I hoped that it would soon be possible to restore normal relations between Paris and Madrid under conditions worthy of the two great neighboring peoples.

But at Algiers, it was naturally our relations with the three great Allied delegations that accounted for our principal diplomatic activity. Without my having to intervene in this domain as directly as at the time when we had no ministers, properly speaking, I nevertheless had to follow affairs closely. I was therefore in constant touch with the representatives of the United States, of Great Britain and of Soviet Russia. For if their governments were supposed to be in doubt as to who or what was really France, they nonetheless did not fail to send us their ambassadors, who in no way concealed from us that they intended, before long, to accompany us to Paris.

After the Committee of Liberation was altered so that it was under my Presidency alone, Washington and London, making the best of a bad bargain, had taken suitable steps in my regard. Mr. Robert Murphy, in the vague capacity of "President Roosevelt's delegate," was transferred to Italy and replaced by Mr. Edwin Wilson, whose title as his government's representative to our committee was quite official. Mr. Murphy's departure and his successor's attitude produced an agreeable relaxation in our relations with the American embassy. For if the first incumbent scarcely appreciated the "Gaullists' " success, the second, on the other hand, appeared to be greatly pleased by it. Mr. Wilson's visits were as agreeable and numerous as my interviews with Mr. Murphy had been infrequent and uncomfortable. A gifted diplomat, Wilson was also a man of feeling. Though his loyalty did not permit him to disavow the attitude of the White House and the State Department, he evidently found them painful. By his personal action, he was frequently able to make comprehensible if not acceptable to either party the other's point of view, and on occasion to forestall the explosions that were imminent, either on the American side or on ours.

Mr. Duff Cooper did as much on the British account. Until December 1943, it was Mr. Macmillan who had represented Great Britain at Algiers while assuming other responsibilities as well; now he was leaving for Italy, where his post as Minister of State had been transferred. Originally directed by Churchill to associate himself, although with some reservations, with the political actions of the Americans in North Africa, Macmillan had gradually come to understand that he had better things to do. His independent spirit and lucid intelligence had found themselves in sympathy with the French group that desired a France without fetters. As our relations developed I sensed that the prejudices he had nursed toward us were dissolving. In return, he had all my esteem. But as soon as he left, London determined to give him the best possible successor and, at the same time, normalize the British representation. Mr. Duff Cooper was appointed ambassador to Algiers, pending his occupying that position in Paris. This was one of the most friendly and far-seeing gestures which His Majesty's Government had made in regard to France.

Duff Cooper was a superior man upon whom had been showered many gifts. There was little he did not understand, nothing that failed to interest him in the realms of politics, history, letters, art or science. But he brought to everything a kind of moderation, perhaps of modesty as well, which in conferring its charm upon him kept him from forcing himself upon others. His convictions, nevertheless, were strong ones; his principles, unshakable; his entire career bore witness to them. In his country and at a period when events demanded the service of the best, he might well have been the Prime Minister. It was conceivable that he had been kept from this office by one trait in his nature—scrupulosity—and by one circumstance in fact: the presence of Winston Churchill. But if he was not Prime Minister in London, he was to be ambassador to Paris. As a humanist, he loved France; as a politician, he dealt with affairs with noble serenity; as an Englishman, he served his King unwaveringly. Placed between Churchill and myself, he made it his duty to absorb the shocks. Occasionally he succeeded; had it been possible for a man to do so in every instance, Duff Cooper would have been that man.

In regard to the Russians, we dealt, as before, with M. Bogomolov, concerned to grasp all the facts and careful not to give in— eager, in fact, to take the firmest possible stand at the first instance in order to formulate what his government had to say in the most categorical way possible. In certain cases, M. Vishinsky, temporarily in charge of Italian affairs but familiar with the broadest domain of world politics, came to discuss various problems. He revealed in this task a great breadth of mind but also—and somewhat surprisingly in the former Soviet prosecutor—an amiable playfulness. Nevertheless, there were flashes that revealed how implacable were the orders to which he was bound. When I said to him, in the hearing of the others: "It was a fault on our part not to have negotiated an open alliance with you against Hitler before 1939. But how wrong it was of Soviet Russia to have come to an agreement with him and to permit us to be defeated!" M. Vishinsky, suddenly pale, drew himself up. His hand seemed to brush away some mysterious threat. "No! No!" he murmured. "Never—that must never be spoken of!"

On the whole, France's relations with her allies were developing on the practical level despite the precautions introduced in the formulas. January 1, 1944, was the occasion of an indicative spectacle: on that day the diplomatic corps came with great ceremony to Les Oliviers to offer me its wishes for the new year, as it is customary to offer them to the chief of state. There was even a heated controversy, in the waiting room, between the Russian and English ambassadors as to which of the two was the dean of the corps and should deliver the traditional address. Mr. Duff Cooper emerged victorious. But this formal visit and this rivalry were the signs of our ascension.

The fact nevertheless remained that the intentions of the Allied leaders, in regard to France, maintained their diplomats in a state of chronic tension. Roosevelt persisted in denying us the capacity to exercise French authority during the liberation. While permitting it to be said that she regarded this attitude of America's as excessive, England nevertheless followed suit. If it were merely a question of terminology, the matter would have concerned us only slightly. But the refusal to recognize us as the French national authority masked, in reality, the American President's *idée fixe* of establishing his arbitration in France. I felt in a position to render this claim on our independence vain in practice; should the occasion arise, Roosevelt would be forced to recognize the fact. All the same, the delay resulting from his stubbornness would keep the military command from knowing in advance with whom it was dealing in its relations with the French. Further, there would result from it, until the last minute, many incidents between us and our allies which might otherwise be avoided.

The Committee of Liberation had, nonetheless, in September 1943, addressed to Washington and London a memorandum specifying the conditions under which the co-operation of the French administration with the Allied forces should function during the battle of France. The memorandum stipulated that in the combat zone the military command would address itself to the local authorities for the use of communications, transportation facilities and all public services. Subsequently the French government would do what was necessary according to General Eisenhower's requests. In order to insure contacts, it had been arranged that each major unit would be accompanied by French officers "for administrative liaison," that we would assign a general provided with the necessary personnel and powers to Eisenhower, and that pending the arrival of the government in metropolitan France, one of its members would be sent there as its delegate to make all necessary arrangements. In fact, the administrative liaison corps, created in September 1943, under the direction of Hettier de Boislambert, had already been recruited, instructed and sent to England. In March 1944, I had appointed General Koenig and General Cochet to assist the Allied commanders in chief in the northern and Mediterranean theaters respectively. On the same date, André Le

Troquer was appointed National Commissioner Delegated to the Liberated Territory. These measures were found satisfactory by the Allied general staffs. But in order that they could be put into effect, we required the agreement of the Washington and London governments. Yet the latter were not replying to our memorandum.

The President, in fact, kept the document on his desk from month to month. During this time, in the United States, an Allied Military Government (A.M.G.O.T.) was being prepared in order to take the administration of France in hand. Into this organization flowed all kinds of theoreticians, technicians, lawyers, propagandists, and also former Frenchmen, recently naturalized Americans. The steps which Monnet and Hoppenot felt they must take in Washington, the observations which the British government addressed to the United States, the urgent requests which Eisenhower sent to the White House produced no change in plan. Since, however, some sort of documentary arrangement had to be made, Roosevelt determined, in April, to give Eisenhower instructions by virtue of which the supreme power in France would belong to the commander in chief, who was, in this capacity, to choose the French authorities who would work with him. We soon learned that Eisenhower urged the President not to burden him with this political responsibility and that the British disapproved of so arbitrary a procedure. But Roosevelt, somewhat revising his letter of instructions, retained its essence.

Actually the President's intentions seemed to me on the same order as Alice's adventures in Wonderland. In North Africa, Roosevelt had already ventured, in conditions much more favorable to his plans, on a political enterprise analogous to the one he was now contemplating for France. Yet of that attempt nothing remained. My own government, in Algeria, in Corsica, in Morocco, in Equatorial Africa, wielded an uncontested authority. The individuals Washington had counted on to throw obstacles in our path had disappeared from the scene. No one paid any attention to the Darlan-Clark agreement, considered as null and void by the Committee of National Liberation and concerning which I had openly declared on the rostrum of the Consultative Assembly that in the eyes of France it did not exist. That the failure of his policy in Africa had not been able to dispel Roosevelt's illusions was a situation I regretted for him and for our relations. But I was certain that his intentions, venturing this time into metropolitan France, would not even begin to be applied in fact. The Allies would encounter no other ministers and officials in France than those I had established there. They would find no other French troops than those of which I was the leader. Without any presumptuousness, I could defy General Eisenhower to deal lawfully with anyone I had not designated.

He himself, moreover, did not dream of doing so. He had come to tell me as much on December 30, before going to Washington and from there to London, where he was to prepare for the landing in France. "You were originally described to me," he said, "in an unfavorable sense. Today, I realize that that judgment was in error. For the coming battle, I shall need not only the co-operation of your forces, but still more the assistance of your officials and the moral support of the French people. I must have your assistance, and I have come to ask you for it." "Splendid!" I replied. "You are a man! For you know how to say, 'I was wrong.'"

We spoke of the vagueness that still remained in regard to the co-operation to be established in France between our authorities and the military command. Eisenhower did not conceal how much he was worried by it. "But," he added, "beyond principles, there are the facts. Now I can assure you that as far as I am concerned and whatever apparent attitudes are imposed upon me, I will recognize no French power in France other than your own in the practical sphere." I then pointed out that we should probably have the occasion to manifest our mutual understanding in regard to the way Paris would be liberated. "It must be French troops," I told him, "that take possession of the capital. In view of this operation, a French division must soon be sent to England, as the French have requested." Eisenhower acquiesced.

As the May–June period which the general staffs had chosen

for the Allied landing approached, the British increasingly manifested their desire to free the political situation from the impasse in
which it still was wedged. Mr. Churchill himself assumed the
courtier's role, plying between President Roosevelt's claims and
General de Gaulle's refusals. But since the greatest weight of
strength and the greatest volume of publicity were on the American
side, the Prime Minister's efforts primarily consisted in applying
pressure on me to yield to Roosevelt's requirements.

At the beginning of January, Mr. Duff Cooper came to tell me,
"Churchill, as you know, has fallen ill in Tunis on his way back
from Teheran. He has subsequently been taken to Marrakech.
He would very much like to see you, but his state of health makes
it impossible for him to move about. Would you consent to visit
him there?" On French territory, the British Prime Minister's visit
was normally due to the President of the French government;
nevertheless, in consideration of the person and the circumstances
involved, I went to take lunch with Mr. Churchill on January 12. I
found him well on the road to recovery. We had a long conversation, our first in six months. Also present were Mr. Duff Cooper
and Lord Beaverbrook, as well as Gaston Palewski.

The Prime Minister applied himself in the warmest and most
picturesque terms to describing the advantages I would garner for
myself by coming around to the President's point of view. It was a
matter, in sum, of my recognizing Roosevelt's supremacy in French
affairs under the pretext that the latter had adopted a public position he could not abandon and that he had made promises to certain French personalities compromised by Vichy which he must
keep. Concretely, Mr. Churchill suggested that I immediately put a
stop to the proceedings opened against Messrs. Flandin, Peyrouton
and Boisson. "I have studied the Flandin dossier," the Prime
Minister told me. "There is nothing serious against him. The fact
that he was in North Africa proves that he had left Vichy. And if
Peyrouton came to Algeria to be its governor, it was because he
was appointed to that post by the President of the United States.
As for Boisson, the President had guaranteed him his post and I

myself told him, 'Go in and fight and don't worry about the rest.'"
Mr. Churchill qualified as regrettable the fact that Generals Giraud
and Georges had had to leave the French government. "Even
though," he said, "Roosevelt had chosen the first, and I had
brought over the second." According to Mr. Churchill, I must
realize, if I had not done so already, that for the President of the
United States and the British Prime Minister, France was a sphere
where their choices compelled recognition and that their principal
grievance against General de Gaulle was that he did not admit this
fact.

Quite good-humoredly I replied to Mr. Churchill that his and
Roosevelt's interest in our internal affairs was, in my eyes, the
proof of France's recovery. Therefore, I insisted on not disappointing them by permitting the occurrence, tomorrow, of those revolutionary convulsions which would fatally be the case if justice were
not rendered. I wished no evil to Messrs. Flandin and Peyrouton.
With regard to the former, I was not unaware of his ability and his
intentions; nor was I forgetting the service the latter had done our
unity by putting his post at my disposal when I arrived in Algiers.
But I believed it was in agreement with the national interest that
they should both give an account of their actions as ministers of
Vichy before the High Court. The post assigned to Governor General Boisson concerned only his chiefs. The presence or absence of
Generals Giraud and Georges in my government was my affair. I
would therefore continue on my way, that of independence, convinced that it was best not only for the state and the nation whose
trust I bore, but also for our alliance, which I dearly prized.

In order to lighten the atmosphere, I invited Mr. Churchill to
join me in reviewing the garrison the next day, and he gladly accepted. The ceremony took place amid the liveliest popular enthusiasm. For the crowd of Marrakech, as for those everywhere
else who would see the newsreels without knowing what went on
behind the scenes, the appearance of Churchill and De Gaulle side
by side signified that the Allied armies would soon march together
to victory, and that was all that mattered. I said as much to the

Prime Minister, and we agreed that it was the crowd which was right after all.

Unfortunately the Anglo-American powers employed, in order to penetrate my defenses, certain procedures not always of the same quality as a conversation with Winston Churchill. During the winter, a sordid affair that was destined to spatter me with filth was trumped up by certain British interests in evident collusion with the corresponding American services. It had begun by an American-launched press campaign to the effect that Fighting France and its leader intended to establish a dictatorship in France and were already employing totalitarian practices. The entirely spurious text of a ridiculous oath was published, purporting to be the enlistment form for Free French volunteers. Our services, above all the Bureau Central de Renseignements et d'Action, were accused of maltreating and torturing their men in order to break them in to our fierce discipline. After this softening-up process suddenly emerged the "Affaire Dufour."

Under this name an "intelligence" agent recruited in France without our knowledge had been brought to Great Britain by the British during 1942, had presented himself to Fighting France and asked to enlist in our forces. He gave himself out as a lieutenant and a Chevalier de la Légion d'Honneur. His chiefs soon realized that he was neither the one nor the other, but instead a member of the British intelligence service. Punished with imprisonment for having usurped a rank and a title he did not possess, Dufour had begun a new enlistment in his real capacity, that of a man of the ranks. But one day, as he was working out his sentence in the camp at Camberley, he escaped with the help of the "Intelligence" and rejoined his employers. From the French point of view, he was therefore merely a deserter, improperly employed and protected by a foreign service. Not being able to seize the man on British territory, the French command in England had ceased to concern itself with him for over a year, when in September 1943 Pierre Viénot, summoned to the Foreign Office, received an astonishing communication concerning him.

"Dufour," the British government said by this official means, had "put into the hands of the British magistracy a complaint for maltreatment against several French officers and against their leader, General de Gaulle. Because of the separation of powers, which in England is absolute, the British government cannot prevent justice from taking its course. Furthermore, General de Gaulle does not have diplomatic immunity in our country. Perhaps the General could settle the matter by a friendly arrangement with Dufour? Otherwise, he will be implicated in the trial. We must urge General de Gaulle to attach a serious importance to this matter, for a conviction is likely, and would constitute an occasion for disagreeable publicity, particularly in the United States press, with regard to the methods and procedures of Fighting France." In fact, malevolent allusions appeared at this time in those American newspapers that habitually made a point of attacking us.

I could not mistake the origin or the motives of this basely inspired action. Obviously Dufour, a British agent and a French deserter, was entering an action against me before the British courts only because he had been urged to do so by his masters. As for the London government, if it ignored the agreements it had signed with Free France by virtue of which Free French military men in Great Britain were justifiable only to French military tribunals; if it denied to General de Gaulle the immunity it accorded to the least secretary in fifty foreign legations; if it attempted to intimidate me by the prospect of scandalous calumnies, it did so because it was involved in a political enterprise intended to extricate the Anglo-American leaders from an untenable position. To the demands of public opinion, which urged them to adopt toward General de Gaulle, his government and toward France an attitude worthy of their alliance, the White House and Downing Street were pleased to reply: "We must refrain from any action until this question is settled."

I determined to deal with the affair without the slightest compromise. Since several officers serving in England had permitted themselves to be impressed by the Foreign Office's advice and had of their own accord entrusted our case to solicitors, I gave orders that these officers be immediately disseized. I forbade my subordinates to answer any interrogations and any summons of the British magistracy. I charged Viénot to inform the Foreign Office that I perceived the operation's goal; that the latter was intended to besmirch me in order to justify a political error committed by the Allies; that I took the affair for what it was—that is, an infamy —and that the absurd consequences of this "New York Mystery" or this "Washington Mystery" would not affect me, of course, but only those who had devised it. Four months passed before London manifested itself otherwise than by episodic warnings to which we did not reply.

But in March the plot came up for discussion again. It must be added that the decree relative to the re-establishment of public powers in France had been adopted on March 21. The world's newspapers had carried the story stating—and it was only true— that General de Gaulle and his committee regarded themselves as the government of France and claimed to be empowered as such without having obtained the consent of the Allies. Roosevelt, hard pressed by the reporters, said bitterly, "No one, not even the French Committee of National Liberation, can know what the French people really think. For the United States, the question still exists." Meanwhile, a week after our decree was signed, the final attack in the "Affaire Dufour" was launched against us. On March 28, Mr. Duff Cooper, apparently not daring to approach me on a subject which was nevertheless supposed to concern me, asked Massigli for an audience. He requested the latter to tell me that the British magistracy could wait no longer, that the British government must allow it to act and that the trial was about to be opened.

But it happened that we had the means to make a suitable reply to this communication. In the beginning of 1943, a Free Frenchman, Stéphane Manier, assigned by us to make broadcasts on the British radio at Accra, had returned to England on our orders, after honorable service. By error or by intention, the "Intelligence" had seized him the moment he arrived and confined him for questioning in the premises of the "Patriotic School." But here, either as a result of his dazed state or, more likely, of a malaria attack, the unfortunate man happened to die in confinement. His son, serving in the North African navy, had just written me on this subject; the young sailor asked that the circumstances—at the very least, suspect—of his father's death be made clear. He announced his intention of lodging a complaint with the French magistracy against the officers of the Intelligence Service present in French territory and against the members of the British government, including Mr. Winston Churchill, whenever they happened to be there. I ordered Massigli to send the British ambassador the text of the plaintiff's letter and to add, in my behalf, that the French government saw no means of preventing the magistracy from doing its duty and that one of the unfortunate consequences of the trial, it was to be feared, was a disagreeable press campaign as to the methods and the procedures of the British Intelligence Service, itself responsible to its government. I never knew why the British magistracy renounced its intention to let justice take its course, or how the London cabinet arranged to keep it from doing so, despite the separation of powers. It was not, moreover, my responsibility. But from that day on, I never heard of the "Affaire Dufour" again.

A warm bath followed the cold shower. On April 17, Mr. Duff Cooper brought me a communication from the Prime Minister. The latter, according to the ambassador, had been profoundly distressed by the state of my relations with Roosevelt. But he was convinced that if I would deal with the President as man to man, the situation would vastly improve. In particular, the question of the Committee's recognition by the Allies would surely find a solution. Mr. Churchill was quite prepared to send Mr. Roosevelt a request that I go to Washington, and assured me a favorable reply.

I informed Duff Cooper that this so-called invitation, following several others equally nonexistent, had little attraction for me. If the President of the United States wished to receive the President of the French government, he had only to ask me himself. But why should I have to solicit the President, even with Mr. Churchill as my intermediary, to consent to my visit? What interpretation would be made of my behavior, when Mr. Roosevelt openly professed that all authority in France must proceed from his own investiture? As for me, I had nothing to ask of the President. Formal recognition no longer interested the French government; what mattered to that government was to be recognized by the French nation. And that fact was now established. The Allies might have helped us to gain countenance when such accessions were useful; they had not done so. At present, the matter was of no importance.

As for the relations between our administration and the military command, I informed the ambassador that they would readily be established as soon as the command agreed not to usurp any powers not its own. In the contrary instance, there would be chaos in France, which would be disastrous for both the operations and the policies of the Allies. I concluded that I would doubtless go to Washington some day, but only when facts had settled the discussion; when, on the first strip of liberated territory in metropolitan France, my government's authority would be uncontestably established; when the Americans would have furnished proof that they had abandoned their intervention in France on any level but that of military operations; when it was definitively admitted that France was one and indivisible. Meanwhile, I could only express the hope that this condition would be a matter of fact as soon as possible and the desire that it would permit me to go to the United States under satisfactory conditions. I was, in any case, grateful to Mr. Churchill for his trouble in my behalf and for concerning himself with my trip, and I thanked him in advance for what he might still be willing to do in matters relating to this subject.

Having avoided giving any satisfaction to the Allies' advances, I must now expect, according to the law of the pendulum, some retaliation on their part. And in fact, we were notified on April 21 that the code telegrams sent between us and our diplomatic and military delegations in London would no longer be transmitted. The necessity of safeguarding the secrecy of the preparations for the landing was advanced in explanation of this move. But this precaution, taken unilaterally by the Anglo-American powers in regard to the French, whose forces, like their own, were to play an essential role in the operations and whose territory would be the theater of the battle, affected us as an outrage and an insult. The Committee of Liberation then forbade its ambassador, Viénot, and its military delegate, Koenig, to settle any question as long as the Allies demanded to know the orders that we gave and the reports addressed to us. This abstention greatly embarrassed Eisenhower and his general staff, while the diplomatic strain was intensified by it. Of course, our code dispatches continued to reach us, thanks to the French officials and military men who came and went between London and Algiers.

The crisis having reached its paroxysm, and the occasion for the landing being imminent besides, the Allies could no longer postpone the issue. I was therefore not surprised when, on May 23, Duff Cooper urgently requested me to receive him. Since, theoretically, we could no longer communicate by code with London, I had, to my great regret, abstained from receiving the British ambassador. On this occasion my door was open to him because he had announced "a new orientation." He informed me that the British government was inviting me to London to settle the question of recognition and that of administrative co-operation in France. But the ambassador also informed me that his government hoped I would be in Great Britain at the time of the landing.

I replied to Duff Cooper that I was very grateful for this attention. I was in fact very anxious to be at the embarkation point when the armies of the liberation were launched, and I intended thereafter to set foot on the first acres of liberated territory in metropolitan France. I therefore gladly agreed to go to London. But as for signing an agreement with political implications, I would have to make many reservations. I repeated to the ambassador that we were not interested in formal recognition; I informed him, moreover, that the Committee of Liberation would at once assume the title of the Government of the Republic, whatever the opinion of the Allies on this matter might be. As for the conditions of our co-operation with the military command, we had long since specified them in a memorandum to which we had received no answer. At present the British government was perhaps disposed to agree to them. But the American government was not. What good would it do for the French and the English to agree subsequently on measures which could not be applied without Roosevelt's consent? We were, of course, prepared to negotiate the practical means of co-operation, but it must be among all three powers, not between two. Lastly, I informed Mr. Duff Cooper that I would go to London only if I had his assurance that I could communicate in code with my government.

On May 26, the Committee of Liberation adopted the position which I had indicated to the British ambassador. It was agreed that no minister would accompany me on my trip, in order to make clear that I was to observe the beginning of operations and to visit the French population in the combat zone, should the occasion arise, but not to negotiate in any way. Then the committee passed a measure by virtue of which it became, by title, the "Provisional Government of the French Republic." The next day I received Mr. Duff Cooper again and confirmed my earlier remarks to him. He gave me the desired written assurance in the matter of the code.

Now Roosevelt, in his turn, decided it was time to indicate the beginning of a policy of resipiscence. But since he insisted that this evolution be a discreet one, he had chosen a rather circuitous path by which to apprise me of it. First of all, then, Admiral Fénard, head of our naval mission in the United States, who maintained good personal relations with the White House, arrived in great haste from the United States and presented himself to me on May 27 with the following speech: "The President has formally asked me to transmit to you his invitation to come to Washington. In consideration of the position which he has hitherto adopted in this regard, he cannot, without losing face, come to the point of doing so officially. He must therefore proceed unofficially. If, under the same conditions, you accept his invitation, the normal procedures of the embassies will arrange your trip without its being necessary to make public that either Roosevelt or you has taken the initiative." However strange the President's procedure may have been, I could not despise the desire which he himself formally expressed, nor disregard the interest that our meeting would doubtless entail. I therefore agreed that the time for me to go to Washington was near at hand. But effusion was not called for: I charged Admiral Fénard to make an anticipatory answer, acknowledging Roosevelt's invitation, observing that no decisive project could be envisaged at present since I was about to leave for London, and concluding that it was advisable to resume our contact later on.

The President's behavior completed my enlightenment. It was apparent that the struggle we had waged so long against the Allies for French independence was to conclude in the desired way. Doubtless there would be some ultimate crisis to surmount; but the issue was no longer in doubt. On June 2, a message from Mr. Churchill asked me to come to England at once. He had graciously sent me his personal plane. I left the next day, accompanied by Palewski, Béthouart, Billotte, Geoffroy de Courcel and Teyssot. After stopping at Casablanca and Gibraltar, we landed near London on the morning of June 4, to be immediately caught up in the mesh of events.

A letter from Mr. Churchill, presented to me on my arrival, asked me to join him in the quarters where—an original idea!—he had established himself somewhere near Portsmouth, pending the day and the hour of the landing. We went there with Pierre Viénot. The Prime Minister received us; with him were several ministers, particularly Eden and Bevin, and some generals, notably Ismay. Marshal Smuts was also there, somewhat embarrassed by the character he was playing: as a matter of fact, some months earlier, he had said in a meeting that France, now that she was no longer a great power, should join the Commonwealth, and the Anglo-

American press had given his remarks great publicity. We sat down to luncheon, and Churchill immediately showed his steel.

First he described with great vividness the enormous military enterprise that was to be deployed from the British ports and indicated with satisfaction that the initial phase would be conducted largely by British means. "In particular," he said, "the Royal Navy is to play the crucial role in the landing's transport and protection." In all sincerity, I expressed my admiration to the Prime Minister for this result of his endeavors: that Great Britain, after so many ordeals so valiantly endured and thanks to which she had saved Europe, should today be the base of attack for the landing on the Continent and should engage in that operation such tremendous forces was the striking justification of the courageous policy which he himself had personified since the war's darkest days. Whatever coming events were still to cost France, she was proud to be in the line of attack, in spite of everything, at the side of the Allies for the liberation of Europe.

At this moment, a similar flood of esteem and friendship carried away everyone present, Frenchmen and Englishmen alike. But afterward we got down to business. "Let us make an arrangement," Churchill said, "as to our co-operation in France. You will subsequently go to America to propose it to the President. It is possible that he will accept it, and then we can put it into effect. In any case, you will talk with him. And he will grow less adamant and will recognize your administration in one form or another." I replied: "Why do you seem to think that I need to submit my candidacy for the authority in France to Roosevelt? The French government exists. I have nothing to ask, in this sphere, of the United States of America nor of Great Britain. Once this is recognized, it is still essential for all the Allies that we organize the relations between the French administration and the military command. Nine months ago we proposed as much. Since the armies are about to land in France, I understand your haste to see the question settled. We ourselves are ready to do so. But where is the American representative? Without him, as you well know, we can conclude nothing in this matter. Furthermore, I notice that the Washington and London governments have made arrangements to do without such an agreement. I have just learned, for example, that despite our warnings, the troops and the services being prepared for the landing are provided with a so-called French currency, issued by foreign powers, which the Government of the Republic refuses to recognize and which, according to the orders of the inter-Allied command, will have compulsory circulation on French territory. I expect that tomorrow General Eisenhower, acting on the instructions of the President of the United States and in agreement with you, will proclaim that he is taking France under his own authority. How do you expect us to come to terms on this basis?"

"And you!" Churchill cried. "How do you expect that the British should take a position separate from that of the United States?" Then, with a passion which I sensed was destined more for his British colleagues than for myself: "We are going to liberate Europe, but it is because the Americans are in agreement with us to do so. This is something you ought to know: each time we must choose between Europe and the open sea, we shall always choose the open sea. Each time I must choose between you and Roosevelt, I shall always choose Roosevelt." After this outburst, Eden, shaking his head, seemed to me quite unconvinced. As for Bevin, the Laborite Minister of Labor, he came up to me and declared loudly enough for everyone to hear him: "The Prime Minister has told you that in every case he would side with the President of the United States. I want you to know that he is speaking on his own initiative and not at all in the name of the British Cabinet."

After this, Churchill and I left together for Eisenhower's headquarters, which were nearby. In the middle of a woods, in a hut whose walls were covered with maps, Eisenhower explained to us, with great clarity and self-command, his plan for the landing and the state of preparations to date. The ships were ready to leave port at any moment. The planes could take off at the first signal. The troops had been entrained for several days. The great machinery of the embarkation, the crossing and the landing of eight divisions and the matériel which formed the first echelon was prepared down to the minutest detail. The protection of the operation by the navy, the air forces and the parachute troops left nothing to chance. I realized that in this extremely hazardous and complex question, the Anglo-American gift for "planning" was deployed to the maximum degree. All the same, the commander in chief still had to fix the day and the hour and, in this matter, was subject to the severest perplexity. Everything had been calculated, in fact, for the landing to take place between the third and the seventh of June. Once this date was passed, the tide and the moon would require the operation to be postponed for about a month. The weather was extremely bad at this time. For the barges, the landing stages and the landing craft, the state of the sea made navigation and boarding problematical. Nevertheless, the order for launching or postponement had to be given by the following day at the latest. Eisenhower asked me, "What do you think I should do?"

I replied to him that the decision at stake was of course entirely his responsibility, that my opinion committed him to nothing, and that I approved in advance and without reservation whatever decision he determined to make. "I will only tell you," I added, "that in your place I should not delay. The atmospheric dangers seem to me less than the disadvantages of a delay of several weeks, which would prolong the moral tension of the executants and compromise secrecy."

When I prepared to leave, Eisenhower handed me a typewritten document with evident embarrassment. "Here," he said, "is the proclamation which I am preparing to make to the peoples of Western Europe, particularly the French people." I read through the text and declared to Eisenhower that I did not find it satisfactory.

"It's only a draft," he assured me. "I am ready to alter it according to your suggestions." It was agreed that the next day I would inform him in detail of the changes that seemed to me explicitly necessary. Mr. Churchill escorted me to his quarters where we would find our own. I did not conceal my concern from him, for over the clear prospect of battle had fallen once again the shadow of a cunning policy.

In fact, the proclamation drawn up in Washington for Eisenhower's use was unacceptable. According to this text, Eisenhower spoke first to the people of Norway, Holland, Belgium and Luxembourg in his capacity as a soldier in charge of a military operation having nothing to do with their political destiny. But subsequently, in quite another tone, he addressed himself to the French nation. He urged that nation to "carry out his orders." He declared that "in the administration, everyone will continue to fulfill his functions unless contrary instructions are received"; that once France was liberated, "the French themselves would choose their representatives and their government." In short, he appeared to be taking control of our country even though he was merely an Allied general entitled to command troops but not in the least qualified to intervene in the country's government and, moreover, quite incapable of doing so. In this factum, not a word of the French authority which for years had aroused and directed the war effort of our people and which had done Eisenhower the honor of placing under his command a great part of the French Army. At all events, I sent back to his headquarters, on the morning of June 5, a text which we considered acceptable. As I expected, I was told that it was too late, for the proclamation was already printed (it had been ready for eight days) and was to be rained down on France momentarily. The landing, in fact, would begin the following night.

In London, as on a previous occasion, I established my office at Carlton Gardens and my residence at the Hotel Connaught. With great pleasure for myself, with some commiseration for him, I learned that the Foreign Office had again assigned Mr. Charles Peake to us for liaison work. And precisely at five in the afternoon, this diplomat, who was a great friend to our cause, came to give an account of the scenario that was to be presented on the radio the following morning. First the chiefs of state of Western Europe would speak to their peoples: the King of Norway, the

Queen of Holland, the Grand Duchess of Luxembourg, the Prime Minister of Belgium. Then Eisenhower would make his proclamation. Lastly, it was planned that I should address France. I informed Mr. Charles Peake that as for my part in it, the script would not "play." By speaking immediately after Eisenhower, I should appear to sanction what he said—of which I disapproved—and assume a place in the succession unsuitable to the dignity of France. If I were to make a speech, it could only be at a different hour and disjunct from the series.

At two o'clock in the morning, Pierre Viénot came to see me. He had just left Mr. Churchill, who had summoned him to shout out his fury in regard to me. Mr. Peake arrived in his turn. I assured him that the oratorical chain would be played out, later that morning, without my participation. On the other hand, I hoped to be able to use the B.B.C. facilities during the evening. After several harsh confrontations in the wings, the London radio was in fact put at my disposal under the conditions I had requested. I spoke individually at six o'clock in the evening, a prey to intense emotion, declaring to my countrymen: "The supreme battle has been joined. . . . It is, of course, the Battle of France, and the battle for France! For the sons of France, wherever they are, whatever they are, the simple and sacred duty is to fight the enemy by every means in their power. . . . The orders given by the French government and by the leaders which it has recognized must be followed precisely. . . . From behind the cloud so heavy with our blood and our tears, the sun of our greatness is now reappearing!"

During the several days I spent in England, the news of the battle was good. The landing had succeeded. A bridgehead was established in the vicinity of Bayeux. The artificial ports were installed as planned. As for the French forces taking part in the operations—ships, air squadrons, commandos, parachute troops— the reports which D'Argenlieu, Valin and Legentilhomme gave of them were excellent. Leclerc and his division were waiting in good order, although with impatience, for the moment to set foot in Normandy. Our services, especially that of the Commissariat, which since the distant days of Free France had been directed by Senior Commissariat Officer Manguy, were busy supplying by far the highest level of French forces yet seen in England and preparing aid for the liberated territories. Lastly, Koenig gave me accounts of the action of our resistance forces, engaged in many regions either on missions he had given them or on their own initiative. Several large German units were already delayed at the rear of the front by this action. Everywhere, moreover, the demolition foreseen by our plans was being put into effect. It is true that for the first time the Germans launched their V-1s over London. But these bombardments, painful as they were, could not alter the course of the battle.

Meanwhile, if the strategic horizon seemed bright, the diplomatic firmament cleared only very slowly. Mr. Eden did his best to make the clouds vanish. He accepted personal responsibility, obviously with the agreement of the British Cabinet, for the problem of administrative co-operation in France, hitherto dealt with by Mr. Churchill alone. Eden came to dine and discuss the matter with me on June 8, in company with Duff Cooper and Viénot; he insisted that the French government reconsider its decision, send Massigli to London and sign a Franco-British agreement. "If you come to an agreement with us," he told me, "the Americans cannot keep to an isolated position. When you go to Washington, I shall go too, and Roosevelt will have to assent to what we have determined on." Eden confirmed his request by a letter which he addressed to Viénot. But we French remained steadfast. I repeated to the British that I was not in London to make deals. The government, consulted at Algiers, substantiated my statement. Massigli remained where he was. Viénot replied to Eden that if the British Cabinet desired to enter into negotiations on the subject of our 1943 memorandum, he himself, in his capacity as ambassador, was in England to make or receive the necessary communications.

At the same time, we did not miss the opportunity to emphasize publicly the absurdity of the situation in which the Allied armies would find themselves, lacking an organized liaison service with the French authority and officials, and openly denied all value to the currency being circulated in France by foreign powers. On June 10, in a brief interview with a news agency, I made the matter quite clear. Further, I had decided that the administrative liaison officers, with the exception of a few informants, would not accompany the American and British general staffs, for we did not intend to contribute to the usurpation. It followed of itself that a hue and cry was raised against me in the habitually hostile section of the American press. But in other quarters, and in the majority of the British newspapers, Roosevelt's stubbornness was condemned. This was the moment when, with a single voice, those who had never ceased to support us with all their talent, whether in the press or on the radio, spoke out most emphatically: in the United States, Walter Lippmann, Edgar Mowrer, Dorothy Thompson, Jeff Parsons, Eric Hawkins, Helen Kirkpatrick, Mac Wane, Charles Collingwood, Sonia Tomara, etc.; in Great Britain, Harold Nicolson, Harold King, Bourdin, Glarner, Darcy Cillie and still others—all made it clear that the joke had lasted long enough.

This was also the opinion of the governments in exile in Great Britain. The liberation now appearing imminent, almost everyone shed the psychology of exile. All were disturbed by the offhand manner with which the great powers were inclined to settle the destiny of Europe in the absence of the interested parties. Speaking with the King of Norway, the Queen of Holland, the Grand Duchess of Luxembourg and their ministers, dining with Messrs. Pierlot, Spaak, Gutt and their colleagues of the Belgian government, exchanging visits with Presidents Beneš and Raczkiewicz, I found that they were delighted by France's rejection of the Anglo-American encroachments. Between June 8 and June 20, the governments of Czechoslovakia, Poland, Belgium, Luxembourg, Yugoslavia and Norway officially recognized the Provisional Government of the French Republic despite the immediate American and British appeals that they abstain. Only the Dutch still recognized us as the Committee of Liberation, hoping that by deferring in this matter to Washington's desires they would obtain greater American sympathy in regard to Indonesia. This quasi-unanimous attitude of the European states did not fail to impress America and Great Britain; but it was the recognition of the tiny piece of France which the battle had just liberated that definitively dissipated all shadows.

On June 13, in fact, I left to visit the bridgehead. For several days I had been prepared to make this trip; but the Allies showed no eagerness to make it possible for me to do so. Even the day before, while I was dining at the Foreign Office with all the British ministers except Mr. Churchill, at the very moment I was being congratulated on being able to set foot on the soil of metropolitan France, a letter from Mr. Churchill, sent to Mr. Eden during the meal, raised last-minute objections to my plan. But Eden, having consulted his colleagues around the table, in particular Clement Attlee, informed me that the majority of the Cabinet decided to stand by the arrangements the British had made. Therefore the courageous destroyer *La Combattante,* under the command of Corvette Captain Patou, which had just distinguished itself in the course of operations, was able to stop at Portsmouth and take me on board as planned, accompanied by Viénot, D'Argenlieu, Béthouart, Palewski, Billotte, Coulet, Chevigné, Courcel, Boislambert and Teyssot. On the morning of June 14, we cast anchor as near as possible to the French coast and landed together with a Canadian regiment on the beach between the communes of Courseulles and Sainte-Mère-Église.

General Montgomery, commander of the Allied forces in the bridgehead, notified of our arrival an hour beforehand, had graciously put cars and guides at our disposal. Major Chandon, French liaison officer, hurried to join us with his troops. I immediately sent François Coulet, whom then and there I appointed Commissioner of the Republic for the liberated Norman territory, to Bayeux, and put Colonel de Chevigné in charge of the military subdivisions. Then I returned to headquarters. Montgomery received me in his trailer where he worked in front of the portrait of Rommel, whom he had beaten at El Alamein but for whom he felt all the more consideration because of that fact. In this great

British leader, prudence and rigor went hand in hand with zeal and humor. His operations were proceeding as planned. To the south, the first objective was achieved. It was now a matter, the General said, of the Americans taking Cherbourg to the west and the British taking Caen to the east, which operations involved the engagement of new units and matériel reinforcements. Hearing him, I was certain that under his orders matters would proceed vigorously, but with neither haste nor temerity. Having expressed my confidence in him, I left Montgomery to his affairs and went to mine, in Bayeux.

Here Coulet had taken over his post. In fact, Bourdeau de Fontenay, Commissioner of the Republic for Normandy, had not been able to leave Rouen or abandon his clandestine status. Pending the time when he could appear, I was eager to indicate without delay that everywhere the enemy had retreated, the authority now proceeded from my government. When I reached the gates of the city, Coulet was there with Mayor Dodeman and his municipal council. We proceeded on foot, from street to street. At the sight of General de Gaulle, the inhabitants stood in a kind of daze, then burst into bravos or else into tears. Rushing out of their houses, they followed after me, all in the grip of an extraordinary emotion. The children surrounded me. The women smiled and sobbed. The men shook my hands. We walked on together, all overwhelmed by comradeship, feeling national joy, pride and hope rise again from the depths of the abyss. At the subprefecture, in the waiting room where the Marshal's portrait was still hanging an hour before, Rochat, the subprefect, put himself under my orders pending his relief by Raymond Triboulet. All those who held any office, wielded any power or fulfilled any function rushed up to greet me. The first visit I received was from Monsignor Picaud, Bishop of Bayeux and Lisieux. Since the population was gathered in the Place du Château, I went there to address them. Maurice Schumann announced my address by the usual words: *"Honneur et Patrie! Voici Général de Gaulle!"* Then, for the first time in four terrible years, a French crowd heard a French leader say that the enemy was the enemy, that their duty was to fight him, that France would be victorious. And in truth, was that not the "national revolution"?

Isigny, cruelly destroyed, where the corpses were still being carried out of the debris, paid me the honors of its ruins. Before the war-torn monument to the war dead, I addressed the inhabitants. With a single heart, we raised our faith and our hope above the smoking debris. My last visit was the fishing village of Grandcamp, also ravaged by bombs. On the road, I greeted the detachments of Allied troops reaching the front or returning from it and several squads of our resistance forces. Some among these had effectively aided the landing. At nightfall we returned to Courseulles, then put out to sea and boarded our ship. Several hours passed before we headed back, for the German planes and torpedo boats attacked one after the other the ships anchored offshore which had been ordered to remain where they were. On the morning of June 15, having returned to Portsmouth, I disembarked from *La Combattante*. The day before, at the moment we approached France, I had awarded the Croix de Guerre to this valiant ship, which was soon afterward to be sunk.

The proof was given. In metropolitan France as well as in the Empire, the French people had shown to whom they entrusted the duty of leading them. On the afternoon of June 15, Mr. Eden came to see me at Carlton Gardens. He was quite aware of what had happened at Bayeux, news of which was being broadcast and published around the world. According to Eden, Roosevelt expected no better occasion than my visit to Washington to revise his position. While regretting that the French government had not adopted the procedure suggested by London, Eden now proposed to establish a plan with Viénot which he himself would communicate to Washington and which, he was certain, would be signed simultaneously by France, England and America. This was a procedure that seemed acceptable; I said as much to Anthony Eden; then I wrote to Mr. Churchill to salve the wounds he had inflicted on himself. He immediately replied, deploring that we had not been able to establish Franco-British co-operation on better bases, since he had so often proved, in good days and bad, that he was a sincere friend to France; he had hoped that my trip to London might provide the chance for an arrangement: now he could only hope that it was not the last chance. Nevertheless, the Prime Minister ended his letter confident that my imminent meeting with President Roosevelt would permit France to establish with the United States "those good relations which are a share of her heritage." He himself would aid me in this regard, he declared.

On the evening of June 16, I took a plane for Algiers, where I arrived the next day. Here I learned in detail the fortunate events that had occurred in Italy. At the very moment I was leaving for London, the Allied offensive in the Peninsula had achieved a great victory. In particular our expeditionary corps, having broken the enemy's fortified lines on the Garigliano, opened the road to Rome. Frenchmen, Americans and British drove toward the city on June 5. The military success producing its effects, King Victor Emmanuel had abdicated his powers to his son, Badoglio had resigned and Bonomi formed the new government at Salerno. Eager to see our victorious troops and to appreciate on the spot the significance of these changes, I went to Italy on June 27.

First of all, I made a brief visit to Naples, where Couve de Murville presented M. Prunas, Secretary General of the Italian Ministry of Foreign Affairs. This high official brought me his government's greetings from Salerno, where it was still established. I asked him to indicate to M. Bonomi my desire to establish direct contact with him by the intermediary of Couve de Murville, to which the President of the Council replied in writing that he accepted such an arrangement with much satisfaction. Then came the inspection of the front and meetings with Juin, Wilson, Alexander and Clark. Lastly I went to Rome and by staying at the Farnese Palace signified that France was returning to a lodging that was hers.

On June 30, I was granted an audience with the Pope. The Holy Office, in accord with its eternal prudence, had hitherto maintained an absolute reserve in regard to Fighting France, later to the Algiers government. Monsignor Valerio Valeri, who occupied the nunciature in Paris in 1940, had retained his functions in Vichy as nuncio to the Marshal, whom M. Léon Bérard represented at the Vatican. Nevertheless, we had not ceased using whatever means were available to inform the Apostolic See of our goals and our sentiments, not without finding there, moreover, active sympathies in our behalf, notably those of the eminent Cardinal Tisserant. We knew that the defeat of Hitler and his system was prayed for by the Holy Father and we wanted to establish relations with him as soon as possible. On June 4, while fighting was still going on in Rome, Major Panafieu and Lieutenant Voizart had brought Monsignor Tisserant a letter from General de Gaulle addressed to Pius XII. The Pope had answered me on the 15th. Today, I went to the audience he had been so good as to grant me.

At the Vatican I first made contact with Cardinal Maglione, Secretary of State, who though ill and near death insisted on getting up to converse with me. Even as Rome, from the height of her serenity, watches from one century to the next while the tides of men and events flow by beneath her walls, ceaselessly attentive to all, so the Church, impavid but compassionate and well informed besides, observed the war's ebb and flow. Monsignor Maglione, convinced of the Allied victory, was especially concerned as to its consequences. In the case of France, he counted on Vichy's disappearance and declared that he saw in my person, in fact, the head of the French government. He hoped that the change of regime could be effected without serious shocks, particularly with regard to the French Church. I indicated to the Cardinal that the Government of the Republic intended this should be the case, although certain French ecclesiastical circles had adopted an attitude that would not make things easier for the Republic tomorrow. As for the future of Europe after the Reich's defeat and Russia's ascendancy, I declared that France's recovery, at home and abroad, would be the condition of a new equilibrium. I asked the Vatican to aid in this task by its immense influence.

The Holy Father received me. I was struck, beneath the kindness of his reception and the apparent simplicity of his remarks, by the sensitivity and power of his thought. Pius XII judged everything from a point of view that transcended men, their enterprises and their factions. But he knew how much the latter cost them, and took compassion on all. The supernatural charge with which he alone was invested evidently weighed heavily on his soul, but it was equally evident that he bore it indefatigably, certain of his goal, confident of his path. His reflections and his information services left him in no ignorance of the drama inflaming the world. His lucid mind was fixed on the consequences: the unleashing of the mingled ideologies of communism and nationalism over a great part of the earth. His inspiration revealed to him that only Christian faith, hope and charity could surmount them, at the very moment when the latter were everywhere and long since overwhelmed, submerged. For him, therefore, everything depended on the Church's policy, its action, its language, the manner in which it was led. This is why the Shepherd had fashioned that policy into a domain reserved for his personal attention, displaying there the gifts of authority, effulgence and eloquence which God had showered upon him. Pious, pitying, politic, in the highest sense these words can have, was how this pontiff and this sovereign affected me, beyond the respect which he inspired.

We spoke of the Catholic peoples whose fate was in the balance. As for France, he felt that she would be threatened, at the start, only by herself. He discerned the occasion she would find, despite her ordeals, to play a great role in a world where so many human values were reduced to the last extremity, but also the danger she ran of falling back into the dissensions which all too often had paralyzed her genius. It was toward Germany, which in many respects was particularly dear to him, that his chief solicitude tended at this time. "Those wretched people!" he said several times. "How they will suffer!" He foresaw a long confusion in Italy without its moving him, however, to an extreme of distress. Perhaps he thought that after the collapse of Fascism and the fall of the monarchy, the Church, morally very powerful in this country, would remain the only force for order and unity—a prospect he seemed quite willing to entertain. While he was speaking to me, I thought of what various witnesses had recently reported: scarcely was the battle over yesterday when an enormous crowd rushed to Saint Peter's with a single impulse to acclaim the Pope, just as if he had been the liberated sovereign of Rome and the salvation of Italy. But it was the action of the Soviets, today on Polish territory, tomorrow in all of Central Europe, which filled the Holy Father with anxiety. In our conversation, he described what was already taking place in Galicia, where, behind the Red Army, was beginning the persecution of the faithful and their priests. He believed that, in this direction, Christianity was to endure the cruelest ordeals and that only the close union of those European states inspired by Catholicism—Germany, France, Italy, Spain, Belgium, Portugal—could build a dam against the danger. I realized that this was Pope Pius XII's grand design. He blessed me and I withdrew.

On my departure as at my arrival, a great throng of the Roman people had gathered near the Vatican to greet me with shouts of sympathy and reassurance. After a visit to the church of Saint-Louis-des-Français, where Monsignor Bouquin received me, and to the Villa Medici, where the hopes of French art would soon blossom again, I received the French colony of Rome. The latter, since 1940, included scarcely anyone—and with reason!—but members of various religious orders. All had come. Cardinal Tisserant presented them to me. Whatever the eddies and currents of the past had been, all floated, today, on the same tide of joy and hope. The pride of victory united souls whom the disaster and its afflictions had been able to disperse.

The indications of French unity were now too clear for anyone to ignore such a sun in broad daylight. The President of the United States at last acknowledged as much. In order that this reversal manifest itself on the occasion of a new event, appropriate to a change of heart, he redoubled his insistences that I visit him in

Washington. Admiral Fénard had reappeared while I was in London. Roosevelt had instructed him to indicate those dates that were most convenient for him. Then on June 10, General Bedell Smith, chief of Eisenhower's general staff, paid me a visit at Carlton Gardens, sent by his chief, who was then in the Normandy bridgehead, and by General Marshall, who happened to be in London. Bedell Smith literally beseeched me to agree to a meeting with the President, so eager was the military command to know where to turn for administrative co-operation in France. In Algiers, Mr. Seldon Chapin, who was acting as interim ambassador in place of Wilson, appeared equally urgent. Lastly, I knew that the Allied offensive in French territory was to be launched in August. If it was possible to reach some practical agreement, there was no more time to lose.

After a searching deliberation with my government, I decided to go to Washington, but indicated that I was doing so at the same time as my visit to London, that I had no favors to ask, and that I would undertake no negotiations. The conversations between General de Gaulle and President Roosevelt would have no other object besides their reciprocal inquiries into the world-wide problems of interest to both countries. Further, my presence in the United States at this decisive period of the war would symbolize the homage rendered by France to the American war effort and a proof of the active friendship that linked the two peoples. If, following the White House conversations, the American government resolved to open negotiations with the French government relative to the relations between the Allied armies and our administration, it would do so, like the British government, by the normal diplomatic channels. It was on this basis that the State Department and our ambassador, Hoppenot, drew up the program of my visit. It was understood that in Washington I should be the guest of the President and of the government of the United States in every respect; this should suffice to give the lie to those communiqués and articles already suggesting that I was coming to America not as a guest but as a suppliant. Further, Canada also requested my visit, and it was with eagerness that I instructed Gabriel Bonneau, our delegate in Ottawa, to settle with Mr. Mackenzie King's government the details of my stay in his beloved and courageous country.

Taking the plane which the President of the United States had kindly sent me, and accompanied by Mr. Chapin, I landed in Washington on the afternoon of July 6. Béthouart, Palewski, Rancourt, Paris, Baubé and Teyssot were with me. Franklin Roosevelt greeted me at the door of the White House, all smiles and cordiality. Cordell Hull was beside him. After tea, the President and I conferred alone with each other for a long time. The same was to be the case the next day and the day after that. I was staying in Blair House, an old and odd residence which the American government customarily puts at its guests' disposal. A formal but extremely cordial luncheon at the White House, two dinners given respectively by the Secretary of State and by the Secretary of War, a reception I gave at our embassy, the latter in temporary quarters since the premises of the former and future French embassy were still closed to us, offered a number of occasions for my conversations with the political leaders and the military chiefs advising the President.

These were: Mr. Cordell Hull, who acquitted himself of his crushing task with great conscientiousness and distinction of spirit, somewhat hampered as well he might have been by his summary understanding of what was not American and by Roosevelt's interference in his domain; Messrs. Patterson and Forrestal, adopting, in their capacity as ministers, the psychology of big business, for in three years their departments—War and Air for the former, the Navy for the latter—had assumed dizzying dimensions and absorbed the greater share of American resources, capacities and self-esteem; Mr. Morgenthau, a great friend to our cause, in charge of a treasury which, for being inexhaustible, was no less subject to his scrupulous ordering; General Marshall, a bold organizer but a reserved interlocutor, the animating spirit of a war effort and a military strategy of global dimensions; Admiral King, zealous and imaginative, not

concealing his pride that the scepter of the seas should pass into
the hands of the American Navy; General Arnold, who by sheer
method had been able to weld a mass of planes hastily designed,
constructed and tested, and a personnel quickly recruited, instructed and thrown into battle, into the great military corps which
the American Air Force had become; Admiral Leahy, astonished
by the events that had defied his counsels of conformity, surprised
to see me there, but persisting in his prejudices; Messrs. Connally
and Sol Bloom, respectively chairmen of the Senate and House
committees on foreign affairs, eager to be informed of everything.
This general staff formed a coherent ensemble which, because of
the character of each of its members and of Roosevelt's own glittering personality, permitted itself only a restricted brilliance but
which was, without any doubt, equal to its tasks.

Meanwhile, I did not fail to salute the Tomb of the Unknown
Soldier in the solemn cemetery at Arlington. I visited General
Pershing, who was ending his days in serene simplicity at the mil-
itary hospital there. To pay homage to the memory of George
Washington, I made a pilgrimage to Mount Vernon. At Blair
House I received many prominent personalities, first among them
Mr. Henry Wallace, Vice President of the United States, who in
his dream of social justice wished to gain victory "for the sake of
the common man," and M. Padilla, Mexican Minister of Foreign
Affairs, who was in Washington at the time. At the offices of our
missions, I made contact with the French diplomatic personnel
serving with Henri Hoppenot; then General de Saint-Didier, Admiral Fénard and Colonel Luguet presented our officers to me.
Before leaving Washington, I held a press conference and talked
with the greatest possible number of the journalists who had come
to hear and to question me. During five days in the capital, I observed with admiration the flood of confidence that sustained the
American elite and discovered how becoming optimism is to those
who can afford it.

President Roosevelt, of course, did not doubt for a moment that
he could. During our meetings, he avoided any reference to imme-

diate issues, but permitted me to glimpse the political objectives he wished to achieve through victory. His conception seemed to me an imposing one although disquieting for Europe and for France. It was true that the isolationism of the United States was, according to the President, a great error now ended. But passing from one extreme to the other, it was a permanent system of intervention that he intended to institute by international law. In his mind, a four-power directory—America, Soviet Russia, China and Great Britain—would settle the world's problems. A parliament of the allied nations would give a democratic appearance to the authority of the "big four." But, short of handing over the quasi-totality of the earth's surface to the other three, such an organization, according to him, would have to involve the installation of American forces on bases distributed throughout the world and of which certain ones would be located in French territory.

Roosevelt thus intended to lure the Soviets into a group that would contain their ambitions and in which America could unite its dependents. Among the "four," he knew, in fact, that Chiang Kai-shek's China needed his co-operation and that the British, in danger of losing their dominions, would yield to his policy. As for the horde of small and middle-size states, he would be in a position to act upon them by the aid he could provide. Lastly, the right of peoples to decide for themselves, the support offered by Washington, the existence of American bases would give rise to new sovereignties in Africa, Asia and Australasia, which would increase the number of states under obligation to the United States. In such a prospect, the questions relative to Europe, notably the fate of Germany, the destiny of the states along the Vistula and the Danube, as well as of the Balkans, and Italy's destiny, seemed to him quite subordinate. In order to find a satisfactory solution for them, he would certainly not go to the lengths of sacrificing the monumental conception that he dreamed of turning into a reality.

I listened to Roosevelt describe his plans to me. As was only human, his will to power cloaked itself in idealism. The President, moreover, did not explain matters as a professor setting down principles, nor as a politician who flatters passions and interests. It was by light touches that he sketched in his notions, and so skillfully that it was difficult to contradict this artist, this seducer, in any categorical way. I answered him, nevertheless, that in my opinion his plan risked endangering the Western world. By considering Western Europe as a secondary matter, was he not going to weaken the very cause he meant to serve—that of civilization? In order to obtain Soviet approval, would he not have to yield them, to the detriment of Poland and the Baltic, Danubian and Balkan states, certain advantages that threatened the general equilibrium? How could he be assured that China, emerging from the ordeals in which its nationalism was being forged, would remain what she was now? If it was true, as I was the first to think and say, that the colonial powers must renounce the direct administration of the peoples they ruled and practice with them a regime of association, it was also true that this enfranchisement could not be effected against those powers themselves, at the risk of unleashing, among the unorganized masses, a xenophobia and an anarchy dangerous for the entire world.

"It is the West," I told President Roosevelt, "that must be restored. If it regains its balance, the rest of the world, whether it wishes to or not, will take it for an example. If it declines, barbarism will ultimately sweep everything away. Now, Western Europe, despite its dissensions and its distress, is essential to the West. Nothing can replace the value, the power, the shining examples of these ancient peoples. This is true of France above all, which of all the great nations of Europe is the only one which was, is and always will be your ally. I know that you are preparing to aid France materially, and that aid will be invaluable to her. But it is in the political realm that she must recover her vigor, her self-reliance and, consequently, her role. How can she do this if she is excluded from the organization of the great world powers and their decisions, if she loses her African and Asian territories— in short, if the settlement of the war definitively imposes upon her the psychology of the vanquished?"

Roosevelt's powerful mind was open to these considerations. Furthermore, he felt a genuine affection for France, or at least for the notion of it he had once been able to conceive. But it was precisely because of this inclination of his that he was at heart disappointed and irritated by yesterday's disaster among us and by the mediocre reactions the latter had aroused among so many Frenchmen, particularly those whom he knew personally. He told me so quite plainly. As for the future, he was anything but convinced of the rebirth and renewal of our regime. With bitterness he described what his feelings were when before the war he watched the spectacle of our political impotence unfold before his eyes. "Even I, the President of the United States," he told me, "would sometimes find myself incapable of remembering the name of the current head of the French government. For the moment, you are there, and you see with what kind attentions my country welcomes you. But will you still be there at the tragedy's end?"

It would have been easy but pointless to remind Roosevelt how much America's voluntary isolation had counted in our discouragement after the First World War, and again in our collapse at the beginning of the Second. It would have been equally futile to point out to him to what degree his own attitude toward General de Gaulle and Fighting France, having aided a great part of our elite to play a waiting game, encouraged in advance the French nation's return to that political inconsistency he had so justly condemned. The American President's remarks ultimately proved to me that, in foreign affairs, logic and sentiment do not weigh heavily in comparison with the realities of power; that what matters is what one takes and what one can hold on to; that to regain her place, France must count only on herself. I told him this. He smiled and concluded: "We shall do what we can. But it is true that to serve France no one can replace the French people."

Our conversations ended. They had taken place in Roosevelt's office, near his desk cluttered with an enormous number of astonishing objects: souvenirs, insignia, good-luck charms. When I was leaving, the President, who was being rolled along in his wheelchair, accompanied me along the gallery where a door was open. "Here's my pool. That's where I swim," he declared, as if in defiance of his infirmity. Before leaving Washington I sent him a toy submarine, a mechanical marvel made by the workers in the Bizerte arsenal. He thanked me with a charming note and sent me his photograph: "To General de Gaulle, who is my friend!"

Later, however, an anonymous source sent me a photostatic copy of a letter Roosevelt had written, eight days after my departure, to Congressman Joseph Clark Baldwin. In it the President alluded to some shady American deal with the French *"Compagnie Générale Transatlantique"* and warned his correspondent to be careful I did not get wind of it, for once I was informed I would not fail to liquidate the company's director. In his letter, Roosevelt further formulated his estimate of myself and our meetings: "De Gaulle and I," he wrote, "have examined in outline the subjects of the day. But we talked more deeply about the future of France, its colonies, world peace, etc. In relation to future problems he seems quite 'tractable,' from the moment France is dealt with as a world power. He is very touchy in matters concerning the honor of France. But I suspect that he is essentially an egoist." I was never to know if Franklin Roosevelt thought that in affairs concerning France Charles de Gaulle was an egoist for France or for himself.

On July 10, I paid a rapid visit to New York. In order not to furnish occasions for popular manifestations which, three months away from the Presidential election, might seem to be directed against what had hitherto been the President's policy, it had been agreed that my public appearances would be very restricted. All the more so since Dewey, the candidate opposing Roosevelt, was the governor of New York State. Nevertheless, Mayor Fiorello La Guardia, bubbling over with friendship, received me with great ceremony at the City Hall, where a great crowd had gathered. Afterward, he took me on a tour of the city. I placed a Cross of Lorraine on LaFayette's statue; I visited our consulate-general, headed by Guérin de Beaumont, in Rockefeller Center; I went to the offices of "France Forever," an association uniting many

Frenchmen and Americans who had supported our cause, where Henry Torrès spoke for the feelings of all. The French colony of New York, joined by various delegations from other regions, had gathered at the Waldorf Astoria, and I greeted them all. Among the Frenchmen present, many had hitherto remained on their reserve in regard to General de Gaulle. Some had even lavished their criticism, not to mention their insults, upon him. But the extreme warmth of the welcome I was given that evening betrayed no such divergences now. It was proof that, in the great dissension of which she had been the object, France was now to bear off the victory.

Such was indeed the opinion in Canada, where everything had been arranged to furnish moving testimony to the fact. First of all, visiting the city of Quebec, I felt as if I were being inundated by a tide of French pride mingled with an inconsolable affliction, both sentiments flowing from history's backwaters. We next reached Ottawa in company of the ambassador, General Vanier. Mr. Mackenzie King, the Prime Minister, was at the airport. It was with pleasure that I again saw this worthy man, so strong in his simplicity, this head of the government who had from the first engaged all his authority and experience in the service of liberty. Canada had followed him with all the more merit in consideration of the fact that the country included two coexisting peoples not at all united, that the conflict was a remote one and that none of the national interests was directly in question.

Under its government's urgings, Canada was now engaging in a powerful war effort. By way of large units, crews incorporated into His Majesty's Navy and squadrons furnished to the Royal Air Force, Canada had put considerable forces into the line, all of a high military value. Her armament factories were producing a significant proportion of the Allies' matériel. Even her laboratories and mills were participating in the country's research and operations, which were soon to produce the first atom bombs. I was secretly informed of the imminent results by Pierre Auger, Jules Guéron and Bertrand Goldschmidt, French scientists who with my

authorization had joined the Allied teams consecrated to this apoca-
lyptic work. But in comparison with what had happened during the
First World War, Canada's effort now assumed a national character.
The result, for the state and the people, was a sort of preferment
which filled the ministers, the parliamentarians, the officials and the
citizens with satisfaction. Mr. Mackenzie King explained this to
me, and M. Louis Saint-Laurent, his principal colleague, repeated
it, insisting meanwhile on Canada's intention to aid France's reconstruction to the limit of its powers.

During my stay I was the guest of the Earl of Athlone, governor general of Canada, and his wife, Princess Alice, the aunt of
George VI. They received me with unforgettable kindness and invited a number of prominent Canadian guests to be introduced to
me. The hours scarcely sufficed for the official discussions, the
audiences I had to grant, the official ceremony at the monument
to the Ottawa war dead, the inspection of the French aviators
training in the vicinity, the dinner given by the Canadian government, a press conference, the speech—was there not always at least
one?—which I made in answer to M. Saint-Laurent's address before Parliament, in the presence of the governor general, his ministers, the high officials and the diplomatic corps. Speaking of
international co-operation for tomorrow's peace, particularly in
the West, emphasizing the role my country wished to take in it,
I concluded: "France is sure of finding at her side and in agreement with her the people who know her well. That is to say, she
is sure of finding Canada there first of all."

On July 12, I reached Montreal, which gave the most moving
demonstration of its enthusiasm. After the reception at the City
Hall and the ceremonies at the two monuments to the memory,
respectively, of the Canadian and the French war dead, I spoke
to an enormous crowd gathered in Dominion Square and the adjoining avenues. Adhémar Raynault, the mayor, shouted to his
fellow citizens: "You must show General de Gaulle that Montreal
is the second French city in the world!" Nothing can begin to
suggest the thunder of bravos which rose from every heart and

passed through all those mouths. That evening, our plane took off and on July 13 we were in Algiers.

Here I was to find the text of a declaration published the day before by the American government. "The United States," it said, "recognizes that the French Committee of National Liberation is qualified to exercise the administration of France." The State Department immediately opened negotiations with Hoppenot and Alphand for an agreement on administrative co-operation in liberated territory. Already, Eden and Viénot, for their part, had arrived at a satisfactory text. By the beginning of August, Washington, Algiers and London had agreed on common terms. What was concluded was astonishingly similar to what we had proposed a year before. The Provisional Government of the French Republic was designated by name. It was admitted without reservation that it alone wielded the public powers; that it alone should delegate the liaison organizations to the Allied forces; that it alone could put the required services at the disposal of the military command; that it alone could issue currency in France and furnish what was necessary, in return for pounds and dollars, to the American and British troops on its territory.

And now the great battle for France was to begin! The Allied armies, side by side with our own and aided by our resistance forces, drove from Normandy toward Paris and up the Rhone Valley. Between the North Sea and the Mediterranean, from the Atlantic to the Rhine, the nation was to be liberated from the enemy, the nation that for fifteen hundred years no holocaust, not even this last, had been able to strip of her sovereignty nor strike down as she raised her last weapons. We returned to France bearing independence, Empire and a sword.

CHAPTER 7

BATTLE

B UT how short France found her sword to be, at the moment the
Allies launched their attack upon Europe! Never had our
country, on so crucial an occasion, been reduced to forces relatively so limited. Those who struggled for her liberation were
often embittered to recall the might of her great past. But never
before had her army been of better quality—a recovery all the
more remarkable in that it had taken its start in an abyss of submission.

For fourteen centuries, military power had been second nature
to France. If our country had on many occasions neglected her
defense, misprized her soldiers, lost her battles, she had nonetheless
appeared at all times eminently capable of the greatest military
actions. The vicissitudes of the contemporary period had not proved
an exception to this rule. Whatever our weakness after the Napoleonic conquests, however cruel the defeat of 1870, we retained
the psychology and the means of a strong people. Principal artisans
of the victory in 1918, we had led the others toward it. That our
army should outstrip every other army in the world, our fleet be
one of the best, our air force of the first order, our generals the
most able—that, for us, was only natural.

Hence the collapse of 1940 and the capitulation that followed

seemed to many monstrous and irremediable. The image of themselves the French had always had, the world's opinion of them,
the testimony of history itself, had suddenly been abolished, annihilated. There was no opportunity for France to recover her
dignity in her own eyes and in others' unless she took up arms
again. But nothing was to help her re-create her unity and recover
her prestige as much as this astonishing fact: that she could find
in her scarcely mustered Empire, in her persecuted nation, enough
conviction and military valor to reconstitute an army—and an
army that would fight extremely well. After Sedan and Dunkirk,
the capitulation of Rethondes and Turin, Vichy's acceptance of
military defeat and the subjection of the state, it was to be an
amazing reversal that would bring our forces to take an important
and brilliant share in the victory, though the enemy was occupying the whole of our territory, when two million Frenchmen were
prisoners in their hands, when the "legal" government persisted in
punishing the combatants.

There were enough men in Africa who could be mobilized to
reach the strength of a campaign army. The restrictions, however,
were many; for if it was possible to draw on the native populations
of Algeria, Morocco, Tunisia, Equatorial Africa and Madagascar
for as many soldiers as we wished, the number of active military
men and of reserves prepared to serve as officers and specialists
was, on the contrary, very low. Generally, only those of French
origin supplied these categories, so indispensable to the formation
of large-scale modern units. Yet the population of French origin
totaled no more than 1,200,000 persons in these territories. Of
course, by calling up all classifications as far back as those of 1918,
we would have a total of 116,000 men, a figure all the higher in
consideration of the fact that the administration, economic life
and law and order absorbed an important proportion of qualified
elements and that many of those mobilized had been in German
captivity since 1940. It was true that Free France contributed
15,000 young Frenchmen, that Corsica furnished 13,000 soldiers,
that 12,000 boys escaped from France through Spain, that 6,000

women and girls entered the service; it was true that the recruits were eager to be incorporated into our forces. But in spite of everything, we could not muster enough officers and specialists to reach an important military strength.

It must be added that the Americans, who provided us with arms and equipment, did so on condition that we adopt their own rules of organization. Now their system furnished, in relation to the active forces, an extremely high proportion of supply services as well as many reserves to compensate for losses. The life and action of the American combat units must rely on a well-supplied rear. They were willing to arm the French divisions only after having verified that the corresponding logistic formations were composed of a numerous and qualified personnel. On the other hand, our African troops, accustomed to live under the most improvised conditions, regarded the accumulation of so many men and supplies in depots, supply centers, convoys and workshops as a waste. This divergence of viewpoints produced frequent and, on occasion, vehement disputes between the Allied general staff and our own; furthermore, among the French, it gave rise to keen disappointment at having to disband crack regiments to make them into auxiliary fractions.

First and foremost, General Giraud had difficulty resigning himself to this necessity. Having understood Roosevelt to promise, during the Anfa conference, that the United States would assure the supply of as many troops as we could muster, Giraud had hoped to equip fourteen French divisions and to form only a few maintenance and replacement groups. He was therefore distressed and indignant at his foreign masters' requirement that he establish complete supporting units and, in consequence, reduce his active troops before they would distribute the expected matériel. Besides, we also had to maintain on our African territories the minimum forces to guarantee sovereignty. Lastly, we were reserving two brigades to take to Indochina as soon as the opportunity arose. These minimum forces and these brigades, being supplied with French arms, did not figure on the American scales. But they absorbed officers from our other groups, which further diminished the possibilities of our campaign army.

For myself, while sensitive to what was painful in the American insistence that the adoption of their military procedures be a condition of their loans of matériel, I was of the opinion that the imminent European campaign would, in fact, require extremely well-supplied and reinforced services. Furthermore, in the matter of the delivery of arms, I was eager to bring to an end the sudden stoppages that were delaying our appearance at the front. Having become sole head of the government, I therefore settled the question; the decree I issued on January 7, 1944, concerning the active troops, the irreducible *données* of the organization, the conditions on which the Allies were furnishing us arms and equipment, established as follows the ensemble of the land forces destined for the Battle of France: one army command, three army corps commands, six infantry divisions, four armored divisions, all with the necessary services and replacements. Even so, one of the infantry divisions and one of the armored divisions called for in this program could not be completely established in the desired time. On the other hand, three units of *tabors,* two regiments of parachute troops and commandos would be added to our large-scale units. It is difficult to do justice to the effort exerted by the Army's general staff, under the direction of General Leyer, to create, despite the deficiencies and the delays, the exemplary military instrument that France was able to engage in Italy, then to bring into the field in the nation itself, and finally to launch in Germany and Austria.

Our Navy was no less zealous. Absorbed by the technique which is its life and its passion and which kept its recent ordeals from deterring it, it reconstituted itself while taking an active share in operations. Admiral Lemonnier, appointed in July 1943 as the chief of the Navy's general staff, brought to this feat of reorganization a remarkable ability and a tenacious will, disguised beneath manners of an artful modesty. On October 14, 1943, the armament plan proposed by Lemonnier was adopted by the Committee for National Defense. It provided that in the course of the following spring our fleet put into combat: two battleships, the *Richelieu* and the *Lorraine;* nine cruisers, the *Gloire,* the *Georges-Leygues,* the *Montcalm,* the *Émile-Bertin,* the *Jeanne d'Arc,* the *Duguay-Trouin,* the *Duquesne,* the *Suffren* and the *Tourville;* four light cruisers, the *Fantasque,* the *Malin,* the *Terrible* and the *Triomphant;* three auxiliary cruisers, the *Cap des Palmes,* the *Quercy* and the *Barfleur;* two aircraft carriers, the *Béarn* and the *Dixmude;* fourteen torpedo boats; eighteen submarines; and eighty smaller craft—escort vessels, tankers, pursuit craft, scout boats and minesweepers.

This plan specified for the majority of the ships a modernization of their armament and a reconditioning, which the half-destroyed arsenal at Bizerte, the limited means of the one at Casablanca, and the embryonic one at Dakar were not in a position to furnish by themselves but which the Allied shipyards in Brooklyn and Bermuda had generously undertaken to provide. The program would therefore be actively put into effect. In addition to the ships provided for were to be added: the torpedo boats *Tigre* and *Trombe* previously seized by the Italians and now recovered; an Italian submarine, the *Bronzo,* which had become the new *Narval;* four frigates transferred to us by the English; six torpedo-escort boats given by the Americans and of which the first, the *Sénégalais,* had been formally presented to our Navy by President Roosevelt; and six flotillas of flying boats, rearmed with Sunderlands and Wellingtons, caused the reappearance of the French naval air force in the Atlantic skies. Lastly, two armored regiments of naval riflemen, one group of heavy artillery and several commando groups would participate in the Navy's name in the battle of Europe, while twenty-two shore batteries and seven antiaircraft batteries, manned by the Navy, would contribute to the defense of the African and Corsican ports.

Our air forces had to constitute thirty aviation groups by the spring of 1944, according to the plan proposed by General Bouscat and adopted on December 22, 1943, by the Committee of National Defense; seven units, four for pursuit and three for bombardment, to be based in Great Britain; twenty-one groups, eight for pursuit, four for bombardment, six for defense of coasts and airfields, one for reconnaissance; two for transport, operating in the Mediterranean theater; two pursuit groups operating in Russia. Since there were practically no French planes left in Algeria, Morocco and Tunisia after the landing of the American forces, it was these former adversaries who generously undertook to furnish the planes for our squadrons in North Africa, the English and the Russians supplying those groups assigned to their territory. With method and authority Bouscat commanded the French air forces, hastily furnished with new planes suddenly integrated in an Allied ensemble whose conventions and procedures had to be immediately assimilated, but more than ever eager to get into battle.

All in all, we would put into the field: a campaign army of 230,000 men, sovereignty forces amounting to 150,000 soldiers, a fleet of 320,000 tons manned by 50,000 sailors, 1,200,000 tons of cargo vessels and steamships of which two thirds were manned by French crews, an air force of 500 fighting planes manned by 30,000 men. A great part of the matériel would be provided by our allies in accordance with the lend-lease agreements in return for the services we provided them by way of ports, transports, communications, transmissions, installations, labor, etc. From the moral point of view, our armies found themselves joyously reestablished in their *raison d'être* and rid of the oaths and incantations which had largely paralyzed or misled them. It was wonderful to see the fervor with which troops and crews greeted the modern matériel, the enthusiasm roused by the order of departure in the units called into combat. During this period, I inspected each regiment, each ship, each air squadron. In every gaze as it met my own, I read the pride of arms. There was our perennial French military establishment!

The maquis forces gave every indication of the same regenerative powers. Until the end of 1942, they were occasional and weak in striking force. But subsequently their hopes rose and with them the number of men who were willing to fight. Besides, the forced labor service, which mobilized 500,000 young men in a few months, particularly workers to be used in Germany, as well as the dissolution of the "armistice army," drove many rebels into the secret army. By more or less important groups, the maquis multiplied and began the guerrilla warfare that was to play a role of the first importance in the attrition of the enemy and, later, in the evolution of the Battle of France.

The conditions under which these autonomous factions were formed, lived and fought were evidently very diverse, according to the nature of the terrain over which they were operating and the weapons at their disposal. On this occasion the natural barriers of France assumed the same importance they had had when the Celts, then the Gauls and then the Franks defended the country's independence against the invaders—Germans, Romans, Saracens. The Massif Central, the Alps, the Pyrenees, the Jura, the Vosges, the Forest of Ardennes, the interior of Brittany were particularly strong maquis centers. There too the Allied planes found the best emplacements to land or parachute in their agents and "containers." Remote from the coasts, big cities, the principal communication centers, here the enemy occupation was not so dense, the police surveillance not so close. The old pitted and heavily wooded mountains of the Auvergne, Limousin, the Cévennes, Lannemezan; the high plateaus of the Alpine massifs of Savoy and the Dauphiné; the wooded and precipitous hideouts of the Vosgian-Jurassian-Langrois-Morvandiau group; the steep slopes of the French and Belgian Ardennes region; the moors, thickets, hollows and pools of the Ar-goat served as refuges for the partisans during the long waits, as bases for attacks, as hiding places after skirmishes. Who, now, spoke of *"la douce France"*?

The resistance gathered in bands of about ten comrades each. This was ordinarily the maximum number that could be grouped at a single point, given the extent of the hiding places and the difficulties of supply. The men came together by means of some network, often from far away and with many precautions. Once you were incorporated into the network, it was without thought of return. You were quartered in dugouts, huts, caves, sometimes in a hunting blind, a ruined farm house, a woodsman's hut. You had to endure difficult living conditions, cold, rain and, above all, anxiety. The maquisards were ceaselessly on the alert, ready to make off somewhere else, informed as well as possible by the spider web of complicities that started on the spot, spread to police department posts and even administrative offices, warning in case of danger or indicating opportunities for action. The neighboring farms and villages furnished supplies to the little band. Children, girls, old men served as carriers, messengers or orderlies not likely to raise suspicion. Fiercely, silently, the French peasantry aided these courageous men. The enemy took vengeance by shooting those of the civilian population they suspected to be accomplices, by deporting prominent citizens, by setting fire to whole towns.

The ambush of the roads used by the German supply convoy, the derailing of the train transporting enemy personnel or matériel, the attack on the careless patrol or the badly guarded post, the destruction of vehicles in depots, of gasoline in tanks, of munitions in storage—these were the objectives upon which the maquis expended their efforts until the day when the landing of the Allied armies offered them a larger field of action. When an operation was determined upon, it was essential to prepare it scrupulously, for there were few men and fewer weapons, and to execute it briskly, for success depended on surprise. The objective accomplished, those involved had to make their getaway as rapidly as possible because the enemy immediately brought in troops, blocked the roads, combed the surrounding country. Once in hiding, the panting maquisards drew up their balance sheet. And with what triumph they saw the soldiers of the Wehrmacht fall beneath their bullets, the trucks burn, the railway cars leap from the tracks, the routed German troops leave their weapons behind! But how many times too the enemy engaged the maquis! Then the battle was merciless; if it turned against them, those French survivors who could not escape were shot on the spot or else, after a mockery of a trial, executed against a wall. Whether they died standing, heads high, or lying on the ground because of their wounds, they shouted *"Vive la France!"* into the faces of the Germans who fired at them. Later, a stele erected on the spot would testify that they had fallen there. The Cross of Lorraine, engraved on the stone, would say why and how.

But in a great proportion of the country, the terrain did not lend itself to the existence of the maquis. Here the resistance was divided into extremely small teams which functioned each man for himself. Provided with false papers procured by the centers who made use of certain ministries, prefectures, mayors' offices and commissariats, they made contact with woodcutters, quarriers, road-menders, slept in remote farms or lost themselves in the big cities. Often factories, building yards or offices gave them cover while waiting for the raid, after which they disappeared. These scattered partisans conducted operations on a very small scale, but nevertheless they increased their objectives every day. Isolated Germans were struck down, grenades exploded under the invader's feet, vehicles sabotaged. In the Paris basin, the North, the Lyonnais, etc., the small-scale sabotages were continual, reaching the point where we had to create a protection service to safeguard certain installations which the Allied armies would eventually need.

It was impossible, of course, to know precisely the striking power of all these groups which furnished neither statements nor lists to anyone. During the creation of the secret army, in the early part of 1943, we had estimated the total at about 40,000 men, independent of some 30,000 men and women who belonged to our sixty intelligence networks. A year later, at least 100,000 maquisards were in the countrysides. At the beginning of the Battle of France, their number exceeded 200,000. But the striking force of the resistance soldiers depended directly on the armament they received. When, by chance, a group received what it needed, volunteers flowed into it. On the other hand, the leader of a troop without supplies had to refuse recruits. Naturally the question of arms to be furnished to the resistance was one of the government's primary concerns.

In France herself, resources were weak. Doubtless certain military authorities had concealed matériel in 1940. But almost all the hiding places had been discovered by the enemy or betrayed by Vichy; the combatants had only a few French weapons at their disposal. It was true that we managed to send them some from North Africa, but not many, since there were few to be had and the bases from which our planes took off were too far from France. As for the weapons seized from the Germans, the quantity was not appreciable until the major engagements of the summer of 1944.

It was therefore our allies who possessed the desired means. Yet however frequent and urgent our mediation, they did not intend to send their specialized planes over France to drop rifles, machine guns, pistols, grenades, submachine guns and mortars unless they were assured a thorough knowledge of the facts. Besides, despite every precaution, half the parachuted matériel fell into the enemy's hands. Furthermore, if the American and particularly the British secret services had gradually come to realize what they could expect of the French resistance, the Allied command was behindhand in measuring the effectiveness of this form of warfare, quite new, for its general staffs prepared only for battles conducted according to the rules. Until the last minute, there were to be cruel differences between what the maquis asked for, sometimes desperately, and what was sent to them. Nevertheless, more than a half million individual arms and 4,000 collective pieces were furnished to our clandestine forces, four fifths of them by our allies, before the end of the fighting.

The maquis, the intelligence networks, the movements that supported them, the propaganda that inspired them, all required a considerable amount of money. The government did its best to procure this in terms of usable currency that would not betray them. All the Bank of France notes stored in England, Africa and the Antilles was used for this purpose first of all; then the "liberation bonds" issued by the Algiers government and with its guarantee were sent to our Paris delegation and secretly exchanged against specie by credit houses or by individuals. At the moment of

the supreme crisis, some local leaders, pressed by necessity, proceeded to requisitions of funds for which responsibility would
ultimately be assumed and made good by the state. All in all,
more than fifteen billion francs—100 billion today—were officially
distributed to the resistance. Although certain abuses inevitably
followed, more than three quarters of the expenses could be regularly accounted for in the reports of the Court of Accounts.

Who were the leaders of the resistance troops? Almost always
those who established themselves as such on their own initiative
and whom the men recognized in that capacity because of their
influence and ability. The majority among them proved worthy of
this elemental confidence. Some—exceptions—were to commit
blameworthy actions. If the conditions under which they were
recruited are taken into consideration (how else obtain leaders,
unless the army officers had immediately renounced Vichy *en masse*
and taken command of the combat groups?), it must be recognized that these isolated, improvised leaders, in the face of terrible
tasks, served their country well. Furthermore, once the former
"free" zone was occupied, the "armistice army" dissolved and the
sentimental and legalistic scruples which the Marshal still inspired
were swept away, a number of regular officers and noncommissioned officers joined the maquis under the stimulus of the Army
Organization of Resistance and its leader, General Revers.

As long as the clandestine forces had to act spontaneously, as
opportunities permitted and in separate groups, there could be no
question of imposing a regular hierarchy on them or of assigning
them, from Algiers or London, specified missions as to time or
place. But there would be serious disadvantages in leaving them to
themselves without some connection to the central authority. For
we would then risk seeing them slip into the anarchy of the "great
companies" or hand them over to the Communist ascendancy. The
latter, in fact, predominated and frequently presided in the "Francs-
Tireurs et Partisans" group which comprised almost a third of the
maquis. If De Gaulle did not maintain everyone's allegiance,
this faction would become a separate force at the disposal not of the

government but of the enterprise intending to seize it. Furthermore, other elements, not knowing where to turn, would yield to the attraction of this organization and pass into its orbit. This was the time, moreover, when the Communists made every effort to seize control of the National Council of the Resistance, to turn it into a kind of interior government opposed to that in Algiers, and to monopolize all clandestine forces by an "Action Committee" on which they themselves played the dominant role.

We had therefore created a system which without thwarting the initiative and the separatism of the maquis attached all groups to the French command by links that could express its central action. In each of the administrative regions and in certain departments, the government placed a "military delegate" appointed by me. The latter maintained contact with the armed groups of his region, integrated their activities, connected them with our center by the radio means at his disposal, transmitted our instructions to them and sent us their requests, instructed the air operations of our services that parachuted in their arms. The maquis had inspectors: Michel Brault for the territory as a whole, Georges Rebattet for the southern zone, André Brozen-Favereau for the northern. After the enemy arrested General Delestraint, his second, General Desmazes, and his adjutant, Colonal Gastaldo, the secret army was sent a general chief of staff, Colonel Dejussieu. I also appointed a "national military delegate"—that is, a general staff officer representing the command with regard to all combat elements, maquis, intelligence networks, sabotage teams, and to the National Council of the Resistance. Louis Mangin, Colonel Ély, Maurice Bourgès-Maunoury and Jacques Chaban-Delmas successively assumed this mission which demanded, and to which they brought, great flexibility combined with great firmness.

In proportion as the interior forces multiplied in the zones favorable to their activity, as the signs of collapse appeared among the enemy, as collective resistance action became possible, we saw one or another leader, whether a regular officer or not, take command of all or part of the maquis of the sector: Major Valette d'Ozia in Haute-Savoie; Colonel Romans-Petit in Ain; General Audibert in Brittany; Colonels Gaillaudot in Ille-et-Vilaine; Morice in Morbihan; Garcie, Guédin and Guingouin in the Auvergne and Limousin; André Malraux in Corrèze, Lot and the Dordogne; Ravanel in Haute-Garonne; Pommiès in the Pyrenees; Adeline in the Gironde; Grandval in Lorraine; Chevance-Bertin in Provence; Rol and De Marguerittes in Paris; Chomel in Touraine; General Bertrand in Berri; etc.

But at the moment of the landing, it was essential for the military command to permit these scattered elements to assist the Allied operations, to assign them, in consequence, determined objectives, to procure them the means of carrying out what was expected of them. As for the demolitions that were to paralyze the enemy movements, general plans were laid beforehand, in liaison with competent specialists in each sphere: the "Green Plan" applied to the railroads and had been proposed by the leaders of "Resistance-*fer*," Hardy, Armand, etc.; the "Violet Plan" was established with the co-operation of the P.T.T. workers, such as Debeaumarché, and aimed at the telegraphic and telephonic communications, notably the undersea cables; the "Tortoise Plan" provided for road blocks at strategic points, under Rondenay's leadership; the "Blue Plan" would neutralize the electric power stations. Yet it was just as important that the local actions of the clandestine groups assume, at the desired moment, the character of a national effort; that they function with enough consistency to become an element of the Allied strategy; that they ultimately lead the army of shadows to merge with the regular troops into a single French Army.

Therefore in March 1944 I created the "French Forces of the Interior," obligatorily including all clandestine troops; ordered that they be organized as nearly as possible into military units according to regulations—sections, companies, battalions, regiments; decreed that the commanding officers would provisionally assume the ranks corresponding to the number of fighting forces under their orders. It was certainly likely that these arrangements would involve, in regard to stripes sewn on berets and sleeves, many exaggerations which the reclassification commissions would have to deal with later on. But I held that by referring these troops to the traditional norms, to which, moreover, they aspired, French unity would ultimately be well served. In April, I appointed General Koenig Commander of the French Forces of the Interior and sent him to serve in Great Britain at Eisenhower's side. Once there, he could further the resistance action by integrating it with the Allied strategy, communicate with the groups by every available means and furnish the necessary arms and supplies. Koenig would also take under his orders the heterogeneous elements which, under the rubrics "Alliance," "Buckmaster," "War Office," etc., the Allies had hitherto directly employed in France.

How would the forces that France managed to reconstitute be used? In this regard, the dualism at the summit of the French authority had for some time frustrated any real decision. Nevertheless, this had been the case only after the Tunisian campaign and before the Italian one—that is, during a period of relative inaction. It was furthermore true that on the whole Giraud's conceptions were analogous with my own. But the autumn of 1943 offered the prospect of a Continental offensive. At the same time, the sole presidency of the committee was made over to me. Therefore, at the moment when it was essential to act, I had the possibility to do so, though within narrow limits, and, admittedly, painful restrictions imposed by a coalition in which the forces of France were not the principal elements.

My notion of how to conduct the war was the same that I had settled upon as long ago as 1940: our army, reconstituted in Africa, should re-enter metropolitan France, contribute with our clandestine forces to the country's liberation, take part in the invasion of the Reich, and obtain on the way the desired pledges so that a final settlement could not be reached without us. This implied that the Allied effort was to be directed toward our territory, that it would call for not only a landing in the north but another in the south, and that we would participate heavily in this second operation. I agreed, in the interim, that the Western powers should continue their Italian campaign, as much to exhaust the German forces as to clear the maritime routes, and that it was essential for our troops, our fleet and our air forces to be engaged in this enterprise.

Meanwhile the Allies' strategy remained vague. In September 1943 they had been in agreement to invade Italy. But they were not so unified as to what was to be done next. The United States, for their part, now felt able to begin the Battle of Europe in the shortest possible way—i.e., through France. To establish a foothold in Normandy and from there drive on to Paris; to land in Provence and drive up the Rhone Valley; to integrate these two operations and then, with the Allied armies united from Switzerland to the North Sea, cross the Rhine: in such a strategy the Italian campaign was a diversion not intended to reduce the importance of the main objective.

The British, and Churchill first of all, saw matters otherwise. In their eyes, the American plan tended to attack the enemy where he was strongest, to take the bull by the horns. It would be better to aim for the weak points, to strike at the creature's belly. Instead of fixing Germany as the direct objective and reaching it through France, the attack should aim toward Danubian Europe, according to the English, through Italy and the Balkans. The coalition's great offensive would thus consist of driving up the Italian peninsula, landing in Greece and Yugoslavia, obtaining the intervention of the Turks, and then taking Austria, Czechoslovakia and Hungary.

Naturally this strategy corresponded with London's foreign policy, which aimed at establishing British supremacy in the Mediterranean and particularly feared seeing the Russians debouch there in place of the Germans. During the Teheran and Cairo conferences, in the messages which the Prime Minister addressed to the President, in the course of the work done in Washington by the Anglo-American body called the "Combined Chiefs of Staff Committee," it was this plan, we knew, which the English were attempting to impose.

But whatever care our Allies took to exclude us from their deliberations, we now had forces important enough so that they could not ignore our own resolutions. Now, without disregarding the attractive aspects of Churchill's strategy, I did not agree with it. From the military point of view, an operation conducted from the Mediterranean toward central Europe seemed to me to involve too many risks. Admitting that we might manage to crush the enemy forces occupying Italy with some dispatch—though nothing indicated that a swift decision was to be anticipated—we would then have to cross the enormous barrier of the Alps. If we could conceivably land in Dalmatia, how could we get over the mountains of Yugoslavia? Greece, doubtless, was accessible, but further north what obstacles the complex Balkan massifs held in store! Yet the American and British armies were equipped to function chiefly in level country, were heavily reinforced by machinery and accustomed to live without too many privations, thanks to regular supply convoys. It was difficult to imagine them making their way over the difficult terrain of the Balkan peninsula, without convenient ports to serve them as bases, with mediocre roads for communications, with scarce and slow railways, and before them the Germans, masters in the art of using the natural advantages of the territory. No, it was in France that the decision must be sought —in France, that is, on a terrain favorable to rapid operations, in immediate proximity to air and naval bases, and where the resistance, acting on the enemy's rear, could put a trump card of the first order in the Allied hand.

It was also in the name of French interests that I felt I must reject the British project as far as we were concerned. While the invader held France enslaved, should we permit the West to engage its armies in a direction that was, to say the least, excentric? Was our country to be liberated at a distance and indirectly, without having seen her soldiers and her allies achieve their victory and her rescue on her own soil? Would her army march ultimately on Prague, while Paris, Lyon and Strasbourg still remained in the enemy's hands? By not permitting our forces constituted overseas to fight and conquer in metropolitan France, would we lose our chance to cement French union, after so many divisions and discontinuities? Lastly, amid the confusion that would follow the German retreat and Vichy's collapse, what regime would emerge from the chaos if our army happened to be in Austria or Hungary and could not amalgamate itself with the interior forces? For England and the United States, the choice of strategy engaged their foreign policy. But for France, this choice engaged her entire destiny.

It happened that the American schemes carried the day soon enough in regard to the landing in the north of France. In December 1943, our Anglo-American allies, in response to keen urgings from the Russians, decided to execute before the spring's end that imposing strategy which they called "Operation Overlord." We could only approve this choice. But the landing in the south of France, although planned in theory and baptized "Operation Anvil" in advance, remained in the discussion stage. Mr. Churchill did not abandon his notion of focusing on Italy and the Balkans the entire Allied war effort in southern Europe: he obtained for General Maitland Wilson the high command in the Mediterranean, Alexander already being at the head of the armies in Italy; he made every effort to keep the largest possible number of American and French divisions and landing craft at their disposal; unless there were some reaction on our part, the Prime Minister's insistence would lead to the application of the British plan in the southern theater.

But how intervene? Given the game's stakes and the means we could put into the field during this phase of the conflict, it was to be expected that the French be associated with the principal decisions of the coalition; that the head of the French government participate in the conferences in which the President of the United States and the British Prime Minister decided on the strategy for the conduct of the war; that the French command—in the person of General Giraud, for example—be one of the elements of the "combined general staff" where the plans for military action were worked out. We would thereby have been in a position to make our point of view bear weight and to influence the conclusions reached. Then the Allied strategy would become as much our own as it was that of the two states who had adopted it. The fact that, in execution, an American general commanded the northern theater and a British general the southern would certainly have inspired in us a certain nostalgia for the past, but no anxiety as to the present and the future. Yet the Anglo-American powers never consented to deal with us as genuine allies. They never consulted us, as from government to government, on any of their intentions. By policy or expediency, they sought to make use of the French forces for goals they themselves had determined on, as if these forces belonged to them, and in justification citing the fact that they had contributed to their armament and supply.

Such was not my philosophy. I considered that France brought to the Allies, in a variety of forms, co-operation worth much more than the matériel they furnished her. Since she was excluded from their discussions, I felt myself justified, whenever it was necessary, to act in her own behalf and independently of the others. Such actions were not taken without disagreeable incidents, but they succeeded in forcing our allies to compromise with us and to come to the ultimate conclusion that what was to the advantage of France was to the advantage of all.

In December, the opportunity arose to indicate that in our present situation we set great store by our autonomy. This was the period when our troops were beginning to participate in the Italian campaign. Three French divisions were there already. Actually, the Fourth Moroccan Division, sent the last of the three, had not been received with much eagerness on the part of the Allies. The latter would have preferred that we content ourselves with reinforcing General Juin's troops with a few battalions. I found myself obliged to intervene to keep the Fourth Moroccan Division from being used piecemeal, for we intended it to go into battle as a whole. Once this was done, the results on the field of battle were such that everyone was pleased. Meanwhile, and elsewhere, the

Allied command had changed its attitude and invited General Giraud to send a fourth large-scale unit to Italy. The Committee for National Defense agreed to this request and selected the First Free French Division. Now we suddenly learned that the latter was not to enter the line and that the Ninth Colonial Division was designated in its place on Eisenhower's orders. I immediately notified Eisenhower that the Ninth Division was not at his disposal and would remain in North Africa. Eisenhower then referred, on the one hand, to the arrangements he had made with General Giraud without consulting us, and on the other to the agreements signed by Giraud and Roosevelt at Anfa and according to which French troops armed by the Americans would be entirely at the disposal of the American command. These arguments could only confirm me in my position. I maintained the decision I had taken, and proposed to Messrs. Edwin Wilson and Harold Macmillan that all three governments settle the conditions under which the French forces could be employed by the Allied command in the same capacity as the American and British forces.

Something of an uproar resulted. The Allied general staff protested that our behavior compromised operations. The ambassadors declared that the matter did not concern the Washington and London governments and must be settled between General Eisenhower and the Committee of Liberation. But since our troops did not leave Africa and were urgently needed in Italy, an agreement had to be reached. On December 27, as we had proposed from the first, a conference was assembled under my chairmanship, in which participated Messrs. Wilson, Macmillan and General Bedell Smith replacing Eisenhower, who was away; René Massigli and General Giraud were beside me.

I let it be known that the First Division—and no other—having been put at the disposal of the Allied commander in chief, would rejoin those already in Italy, as soon as its departure was requested according to regulation procedure. Of course, no French force could be used in any theater of operations without the orders of the French government. Then I indicated that the incident forced us to specify how the French government intended its forces to co-operate with those of her allies.

"We are," I said, "naturally disposed to provide this co-operation. But we must do so with full knowledge of the circumstances. Yet we are not included in your conference. With a view to correcting this awkward state of affairs and in order to organize the co-operation of all three governments in the conduct of the war and of all three commands in the strategy, we have prepared a draft of an agreement. If this agreement is found satisfactory, well and good. If not, the French government will not place its forces under the Allied command except on conditions to be established by itself and with the reservation of rescinding them, entirely or in part, when the national interest appears to require it."

I added: "At present, the Allied command is receiving the co-operation of the French Army, fleet and air force in the Italian campaign, without our knowing to what point or to what date that campaign is to be conducted. Now, for us, the future landings in France are of prime importance. The moment has come to say that we cannot reinforce our troops in Italy, or even leave them there much longer, unless the American and British governments give us their guarantee that Operation Anvil will take place, that all the French forces in Italy can be engaged in it as well as all of those in North Africa, that a French division will be transported to Great Britain in time to participate in Operation Overlord and to liberate Paris. Should it happen that these guarantees, once given, are questioned, the French government will *ipso facto* resume the disposition of its forces."

The next day, Massigli notified Messrs. Wilson and Macmillan of our propositions and our conditions by letter. He received a reply stating that our agreement was being studied by their governments and provisionally granting the guarantees we had requested on the subject of the campaign in France. Hence the transports of French troops to Italy resumed.

From this moment on, the Allied command no longer failed to keep us informed of its plans, to consult our opinion, to address its request for French reinforcements by regular channels. A satisfactory co-operation between the general staffs was established at Algiers. For my part, I had many meetings with the principal American and British leaders, including General Eisenhower, Air Marshal Tedder and General Bedell Smith before their departure for Great Britain, where they would prepare and launch Operation Overlord; General Maitland Wilson when he assumed his command and on several further occasions; Admiral Sir Andrew Cunningham; Admiral Hewitt, in charge of the transport, escort, protection and landing operations that Anvil would require; General Doolittle, commander of the Strategic Air Force in the Mediterranean theater; Generals Devers, Gammel and Rooks; Air Marshal Slessor; etc. At the time of my inspections of our troops in Italy, General Alexander, commanding the Allied forces, General Clark, commanding the Fifth American Army to which the French Expeditionary Corps was attached, General Leese, commanding the Eighth British Army, General Eaker, commanding the air forces, informed me with confidence of their plans and inquired as to the French national point of view.

Such an attitude on the part of these leaders corresponded, doubtless, to the needs of the moment; it was no less meritorious. These men had to overcome an astonishment that was, in fact, quite comprehensible: this chief of state without a constitution, without electors, without a capital, who spoke in the name of France; this officer wearing so few stars, whose country's ministers, generals, admirals, governors and ambassadors considered his orders as indisputable; this Frenchman condemned to death by the "legal" government, vilified by many prominent men, opposed in battle by a part of his own troops and before whom the flags dipped—he could not fail to amaze the conventional spirit of the British and American military men. I must add that they were capable of overlooking these matters and seeing France in the place she truly occupied. In return, my deep and friendly regards were won by these eminent servants of their countries and our cause, these honorable men, these good soldiers.

Furthermore, the organization with which they were dealing in their contacts with us facilitated cohesion. The French government, since it no longer had more than one head, took care not to divide the right to take decisions and the duty of answering for them. The framework given to the command was as clear and simple as possible. Founding my authority upon the organization of the nation in time of war, I bore, in my capacity as chief of state, the title of Chief of the Armies and, as president of the government, the duty of directing national defense. What concerned the use of our forces and thereby the strategic co-operation with the Allies necessarily devolved upon me. In the armature by which I bound everything together, the Ministers of War, the Navy and the Air Forces had to establish, administer and supply the armies and deal with the American and British services for their provisions and armaments. Lastly, the leaders appointed by me exercised the command of our forces within the Allied system. These were precisely the powers which, for their part and for the same reasons, Roosevelt, Churchill and Stalin exercised, in proportion, of course, to the relative importance of their means and ours.

To assist me in my task, I had created the General Staff of National Defense and put General Béthouart at its head, with Naval Captain Barjot and Air Force Colonel De Rancourt as his adjutants. It was Béthouart who gathered the elements of the decisions together, notified those concerned of the results and verified their execution. He also assured the military liaisons with the Allies on the highest level, keeping in touch with the local commander in chief (Eisenhower, later Wilson), and having at his disposal, outside of France, our military terrestrial, naval and air missions. Aside from the asperities of my own making, these functions were difficult as much as a result of their own complexity as from the fact that they touched the susceptibilities of the Allied governments and general staffs, those of the French ministers and upper echelons, and those of individuals everywhere. Béthouart acquitted himself brilliantly at his task.

In the kind of preferment we were trying to obtain within the coalition, the quality of the generals commanding our large-scale units was to count for a great deal. They were, as it happened, remarkable men. To judge the enemy, the terrain and the means on the spot, to combine the different weapons, to maneuver the troops is the job of division commanders; Generals Dody, De Monsabert, Sevez, Leclerc de Hauteclocque, Du Vigier, De Verne-joul, Guillaume, Brosset and Magnan all distinguished themselves in this regard, each in his own way. Generals Poydenot and Chail-let excelled in using artillery of every type. Commanding the engineers, General Dromard faultlessly assured our forces pas-sage over all obstacles, including, ultimately, the Rhine itself. In commanding an army corps, a wide and far-reaching view is es-sential, in order to adjust within a single effort the various and successive actions of several large-scale units. Generals Henry Martin and De Larminat, who first had this duty, gave every proof of such capacities. Events themselves, moreover, were to carry them forward; their means were destined not to fail: fortunate the leaders who feel themselves borne on toward victory!

At sea, since the enemy was not in a position to engage its fleet, the naval battle consisted in the contending over immense areas with the pursuit of submarines, the destruction of raiding vessels, protection against aircraft, the escort of convoys and the defense of bases. Our navy was therefore to act in units distributed among the Allied system. The French admirals, at the side of their Brit-ish and American peers, knew how to contribute what was nec-essary to this struggle on the high seas where they were forever being caught short, as in a game in which some pieces are always missing. Commanding the whole group—Lemonnier; for the sectors or the divisions—D'Argenlieu, Collinet, Nomy, Auboyneau, Ronar'h, Sol, Barthe, Longaud, Missoffe, Battet, etc.: these men did honor to the French Navy.

As for our Air Force, obliged by the force of events to distribute its squadrons among the great pursuit, direct support or bombard-ment groups into which the West's air power was articulated, its

Generals—Bouscat in command; Valin, Gérardot, Montrelay, Lechères, etc., in charge of the fractional groups—showed themselves worthy of an air army burning to regain its rank. Leaders of a new force still seeking its doctrines, they knew how to function in both moral and technical spheres in order to make the most of men and matériel.

In the first rank of the leaders who, at the time of this resurgence, were in command of our forces, two had the privilege of commanding in alternation the only army which France could engage in the battle. Generals Juin and De Lattre de Tassigny had many characteristics in common. Of the same age and education, having scaled their careers at the same rapid tempo, both emerging unscathed from the traps which the disaster of 1940 and after it the "armistice" regime had laid for their honor, they now offered themselves to wield the high command for which they had been made and of which they had always dreamed. Furthermore, they were generous enough, despite their rivalry, to do each other justice. Yet how different they were!

Juin, reserved and self-confident, isolating himself deep within his duties, deriving his authority less from apparent brilliance than from a profound and secret ability, not disdaining guile to clear his path on occasions but avoiding complications wherever possible. De Lattre, emotional, flexible, farsighted and widely curious, influencing the minds around him by the ardor of his spirit and winning loyalty by the exertions of his soul, heading toward his goal by sudden and unexpected leaps, although often well-calculated ones.

All the same, both were masters of their craft. For each operation, Juin drew up the plan of maneuvers beforehand with a firm line. He based his strategy on the material he received from intelligence or from his own intuition; in every case, the facts confirmed his procedure. He chose as a strategic axis a single idea, but an idea clear enough to enlighten his men, complex enough to survive the pressures of action, strong enough to be imposed, ultimately, on the enemy. His successes, even if they were dearly won, did not seem costly and, meritorious as they were, appeared quite natural.

De Lattre, at each conjuncture, courted opportunity above all. Until the moment he found it, he endured the ordeal of his tentative efforts, devoured by an impatience that provoked many shocks in his contacts with others. Suddenly discerning where, when and how the issue could be determined, he then deployed, to create and exploit it, all the resources of a rich talent and an extreme energy, demanding a limitless effort of those he engaged in it, but certain that he was preparing for them the fanfares of success.

Like Larminat, Leclerc and Koenig during the night's darkest hours and with the poorest means, Juin and De Lattre, when the dawn broke, leading the action on a larger although unfortunately a still limited scale, restored the French military command to honor in the eyes of the nation, the Allies and the enemy.

It was in December 1943 that our Expeditionary Corps was engaged in Italy. If room was made for it, it was to be given a difficult task. For at this moment the Allies, under Alexander's command, were between Naples and Rome, in contact with the Tenth and Fourteenth German armies under Marshal Kesselring, from the mouth of the Garigliano on the Mediterranean to that of the Rapido on the Adriatic, passing through Monte Cassino. The Germans, under their skillful and energetic commander, occupied a solid position all along the front, behind which they had organized two others: the "Gustav Line" and the "Hitler Line," the whole supplied with good troops, weapons in casemate, protected artillery and mines. At the beginning of winter, the French zone of action, on the southern slopes of the Abruzzi around Acquafundata, comprised a mountainous, snowy, desolate region with rocky peaks and hillsides of mud and clay masked in fog and swept by rain. Here our troops, attached to the Fifth American Army, connected the latter's right wing to the Eighth British Army.

Rome was the Allied objective. To reach it, General Clark, commanding the Fifth Army, wanted to debouch into the plain of the Liri, where his armored formations would function to good advantage. But access to the plain was blocked by the natural barrier of Monte Cassino. Yet it was straight toward the mountain, where the enemy was most strongly entrenched, that Clark wanted to drive the front. It was true that he counted on his powerful artillery and, still more, on his air force, which he expected to be able to crush everything. The French Expeditionary Corps' mission was to drive a wedge into the enemy defenses north of the famous monastery, enabling the Allies to take it directly.

The second fortnight of December was marked by arduous advance of the Second Moroccan Division, which, of our major units, was the first engaged. Across mountains rising about 2,400 meters, in snow or driving rain, at grips with an enemy that fought with desperation, this division, commanded by Dody, took the massifs of Castelnuovo, Pantano and the Mainarde, advancing foot by foot. Further south, our allies had approached Monte Cassino, but still could not take it. In the north, the British Army remained in its position. In January, a group effort was decided on by General Clark. The attack resumed along the entire line. At the same time, an Allied corps landed at Anzio in order to turn the adversary. Fierce battles were to be prolonged until the middle of March without providing a solution.

This was not for lack of effort and even success on the part of the French Expeditionary Corps. At the beginning of January, General Juin had taken command. The Third North African Division, under General de Monsabert, and General Guillaume's group of *tabors* were put into the line next to Dody's division. Later the Fourth Moroccan Division under Sevez came to join them. In addition, General Utile's Italian division was assigned to the French sector. The attacks began on January 12. Three weeks later, the French had overrun a zone twenty kilometers deep, knocked out the first German position, penetrated the second, and taken 1,200 prisoners, all over extremely difficult terrain in which the enemy engaged against our men more than a third of the forces he was opposing to the entire Fifth Army. This success was crowned, one might say, by the investment of the Belvedere, an organized massif which was the key of the "Gustav Line." On this position, several times taken, lost and taken again, the Fourth Regiment of Tunisian rifles accomplished one of the most brilliant military exploits of the war at the cost of enormous losses. Here were killed, in particular, its chief, Colonel Roux, and nine of its twenty-four captains. But on the left, Monte Cassino remained in the enemy's hands despite terrible bombings and the valiantly re-peated assaults of American, Hindu and New Zealand troops. On the right, the Eighth Army did not noticeably advance. Under these conditions, Juin had to suspend his advance.

The latter, however, had left the French with the sense of a vic-tory: the enemy had not ceased to retreat before them; they had responded to a command both lucid and firm whose strategy had been realized point by point; the co-operation of the various large units and the liaison between the armies left nothing to be desired; lastly, our men had discovered that for fighting in moun-tainous country, which demands maximum effort and maneuver-ability, they had proved themselves without peer in the Allied camp. The Allies, moreover, said so quite openly. Nothing was more noble and more generous than the acknowledgment made by King George VI and Generals Eisenhower, Wilson, Alexander and Clark to General Juin and his troops.

When, on a tour of inspection in early March, I examined the natural fortresses our troops had taken, I felt, as did everyone present, a great pride and a solid confidence in our men. But it seemed obvious to me that a new effort could be asked of them only in the framework of a larger strategy. Juin was convinced of this from the start. He had already, with this intention, made urgent recommendations to the Allied command; soon he was to suggest to that command a new strategy altogether.

According to Juin, it was essential, in order to take Rome, that the Allied action involve a general maneuver and, above all, a principal effort to which everything would be subordinated. This effort was to be made over the terrain that led to the objective—

that is, south of the Abruzzi. It would therefore be necessary to concentrate the Fifth Army's front in order for it to operate power-fully from the Garigliano, while the Eighth Army, extending its line southward, would operate on its left toward Cassino and the Liri. Thenceforth, General Clark's zone would be reduced to two sectors: to the north, the Aurunci Mountains; to the south, the plain bordering the sea. The commander of the French Expedition-ary Corps proposed to take the Aurunci Mountains himself, while the Americans would advance on his left over less uneven ground.

Having visited our men, I made contact with Alexander at the general headquarters in Caserta. This great leader, of lucid mind and firm character, seemed to me extremely well qualified to com-mand the Allied forces. It was a complex role, for he had to use side by side a British army, an American army, a French army de-tachment, a Polish corps, Italian contingents and a Brazilian divi-sion; to direct and integrate the easily offended subordinates; to negotiate with various navies and several air forces; to submit to advice and requests for explanations from Washington and London: all in order to join a frontal battle between two seas, which nar-rowly limited the possibility of maneuvering. General Alexander picked his way among these difficulties without ever ceasing to be clearheaded, courteous and optimistic. He described his plans to me. I heard him out, taking care not to intervene in his plan of operations, believing that governments must respect both freedom of mind and the responsibility of the command in battle. But when Alexander informed me that he was inclined to change his strategy in the direction Juin recommended, I indicated my satisfaction on this point.

Clark, too, was disposed to accept this modification. I went to see him in the trailer where he lived and worked. He made an extremely good impression on me, not only because he said what he had to say so clearly, but because, too, he remained simple and direct in the exercise of his command. There was all the more merit in this because among the American generals he was the first to command an army in the Western theater and his country's self-esteem was therefore eager for his success. Like Alexander, Clark gave evidence of the highest respect for Juin and praised the French troops with an ardor that was certainly not simulated. General Anders, in his turn, expressed the same judgment. In a sector adjoining our own, he was in command of the Polish corps that was lavishing its bravery in the service of its hopes. The Italian General Utile and his division lent a very considerable support to our soldiers with the best of hearts. In Algiers, General Mascanheras, arriving from Brazil with his division soon to be engaged in Italy, declared his intention to take the French leaders as his models. These were words to salve many wounds!

Shortly afterward, Wilson informed me that Alexander's decision had been made. The offensive was to resume, in May, on the basis of Juin's recommendations. We immediately reinforced the Expeditionary Corps. The First Free French Division, a second group of *tabors,* several artillery and engineers groups, and an armored detachment were sent to Italy. Further, the services which were hitherto those of an army corps received the necessary complements to become those of an army. After which, the Second Armored Division having left for England, there remained in North Africa, of our large units, only the First and Fifth Armored Divisions and the Ninth Colonial Division which were finishing their training. We therefore were engaging in the peninsula more than half of all our means, which was quite enough! To General Wilson, who vaunted the advantages of a more extended effort along both shores of the Adriatic and expressed his hope of engaging there not only the French troops already on the spot but even those being held in reserve, I repeated that this was not their final destination and that the French government intended to devote both its troops and its reserves to Operation Anvil. "Meanwhile," I told Wilson, "our army, which includes 120,000 men in Italy, or more than a quarter of the combatants, will assume a share in the coming offensive which I trust will be decisive."

This was to be the case. The battle began on the night of May 11, when the French Expeditionary Corps attacked the Aurunci

Mountains. It might have seemed that this tangle of massifs forbade a swift advance. But it was for just this reason that the French command had chosen it as its terrain of action. The enemy, in fact, had every reason to think that he must protect himself not in the mountains themselves, but to the north and the south where the slopes were gentle, the site of the two main roads to Rome. The Germans were therefore surprised by our attack in force in the most difficult sector. Furthermore, in this same sector, General Juin's maneuver was to catch the enemy napping, for it was by the highest, least likely peak, where the Germans did not at all expect our breakthrough, that the French undertook an accelerated advance, continually overrunning the German positions to the right and the left and everywhere penetrating his three successive lines before the enemy found time to re-establish his positions on any one of the three. Again, to take full advantage of the surprise, though having to run all the more risks as well, the commander of the Expeditionary Corps had decided to capture—without warning, in the middle of the night and without artillery preparation—the slopes of Mount Majo, a tremendous mountain mass covering the entire system of the German defenses.

It was true that the Expeditionary Corps included first-class troops particularly skillful at mountain warfare. In particular, the Fourth Division and the Moroccan *tabors* were capable of advancing over any terrain, and General Juin knew this better than anyone. He therefore confided to this division and to these *tabors,* united under Sevez's orders, the mission of driving as quickly as possible along the upper part of the terrain, flanking the German positions on the south, and taking as their final objective the Petrella massif, near Pico, in the enemy's rear. An admirable regiment of the Second Moroccan Division, the Eighth Rifles, under Colonel Molle, would open the front by seizing Mount Majo in one thrust. Then the First Free French Division would flank the group of massifs to the north and assist the Eighth Army's left to debouch on the Liri. Lastly, the difficult task of taking the German defenses in the interior of the Aurunci Mountains would fall to the Third North African Division and the Second Moroccan Division.

Like a living machine whose gears were set in motion by men with a single goal, the French Army in Italy achieved precisely what its leader had planned. On May 17, I was in the peninsula once more, accompanied by André Diethelm, Minister of War, and Generals De Lattre and Béthouart. On this occasion, I recognized the fact on the spot: after years of humiliation and dissension, what a magnificent spectacle the troops of De Monsabert and Dody offered us, driving toward Esperia and San Oliva, those of Brosset engaged around San Giorgio, those of Sevez and Guillaume reaching the region around Pico, Poydenot's batteries following close behind the infantry clinging to the slopes, Dromard's sappers having effected the *tour de force,* on the eve of the attack, of secretly constructing bridges across the Garigliano and now using every hour of every day and every night to render usable the mined and blockaded roads. Our convoys circulated in an exemplary order; our depots and workshops supplied the units without slip-ups and without delays. In our ambulances, amid the stream of French and German wounded, the capacity of our hospital services, as well as the devotion of the nurses and drivers under Mesdames Catroux and Du Luart, was at the level of their task. Each man in each echelon in each emplacement, despite losses and fatigue, showed that brisk and eager attitude so characteristic of the French when matters are going as they wish.

On May 20, all the German positions for some thirty kilometers had been pierced by the French, who were already overrunning Pico. On the left, the Second American Army Corps had seized Fondi and was driving toward the Pontine Marshes. To the right, meanwhile, the British and the Poles had taken, respectively, San Angelo and Monte Cassino, but, since this was the sector where the enemy had accumulated his greatest strength, had stopped before the Aquino-Pontecorvo line. The French Expeditionary Corps, before plucking its laurels, counting its 5,000 prisoners and gathering the cannons and matériel left in its hands, was to par-

ticipate in a new battle and attack on the Pontecorvo-Pico front
in order to aid General Leese's left wing to reach the open terrain
toward Rome. On June 4, our first groups penetrated the front.
On the 5th, Americans, British and French marched into the capital.

With Marshal Kesselring's approval, the German writer Rudolf
Böhmler, himself a combatant in Italy, wrote the history of the
German Tenth Army in his book *Monte Cassino*. Describing the
brilliant share taken in the winter campaign by the French Expeditionary Corps, notably on the "Belvedere," the author refers
to the confusion of the German high command when it realized
that the French had left this sector for an unknown objective elsewhere. A new Allied effort to reach Rome was certainly to be looked
for; "but," writes Böhmler, "only the adversary's offensive would
reveal in which region the chief danger would arise. In this regard,
it was the position of the French Expeditionary Corps that would
give us a precise indication. . . . Where, then, would it be? When
Juin appeared anywhere, it meant that Alexander was planning
some essential operation there. No one knew this better than Kesselring. 'My greatest concern,' the Field Marshal declared, 'came
from my uncertainty as to the direction of the French Expeditionary
Corps' attack, its components and its location. . . . It was only
after I knew this that I could make definitive plans.' " Böhmler
adds: "These apprehensions were well founded. For it was Juin
who destroyed the right wing of the Tenth Army and opened the
road to Rome to the Allies. After months of battle, his Expeditionary Corps broke down the door that led to the Eternal City."

Military valor, virtue of arms, service and suffering of the soldiers—without these no country can stand upright or struggle to
its feet. Our race has always been able to furnish such riches in
abundance. But there must be a national soul, a will, an action,
which is to say, a policy. Had France, between the wars, possessed
a capable chief of state, had she found herself, before Hitler's ambition, inspired by a genuine government, had her army, facing
the enemy, been equipped and commanded, what a destiny might
have been ours! Even after the disaster of May 1940, our Africa,

our fleet, the remains of our army still offered us a great role, if only the regime and later the leaders had aspired to it. But since, after so many capitulations, the nation must start upon its own recovery from the bottom of the abyss, nothing could be done save by the effort of the combatants. After Keren, Bir Hakeim, Fezzan and Tunisia, the glory of our troops' Italian victories restored France her opportunity. Receiving the accounts of their operations on my arrival in London the day before the great landing in Normandy, I telegraphed their commander: "The French Army has won its generous share in the great victory of Rome. Naturally! You have made it so! General Juin, you and the troops under your orders are worthy of our country!"

While the Second and Fourth Divisions and the Moroccan *tabors* were regrouping near Rome, Juin launched an army corps commanded by General de Larminat in pursuit of the enemy in his sector. This corps, formed of the Brosset and De Monsabert divisions and reinforced by armored units and artillery, headed toward the Lake of Bolsena, Radicofani, the Orcia pass and Siena. Each of these points was to be the scene of bitter fighting where, in particular, along with many good soldiers, we lost Colonel Laurent-Champrosay and Major Amyot d'Inville, respectively in command of the artillery and the regiment of naval riflemen of the First Free French Division. Meanwhile De Larminat, maneuvering and attacking, settled his accounts among the German rear guard. It must be added that the Allied air forces completely dominated the skies and crushed the enemy columns. Nothing gave our troops the measure of the German defeat better than the mountains of scrap metal that lined the roads.

Meanwhile, the French had seized the island of Elba with the support of the special ships furnished by the British and several American pursuit and bombardment squadrons. The operation had been proposed by General Giraud the day after the liberation of Corsica. But the Allies, then involved with the Anzio landing, had not permitted themselves to be convinced. Now they asked us to effect the island's capture. I gave them my agreement: under the command of General Henry Martin, the attack would be led by the Ninth Colonial Division, the Shock Battalion and the commando groups, all being units posted in North Africa and assigned to De Lattre's army for the imminent offensive in the south of France.

During the night of June 16, General Martin landed Commander Gambiez' "shock" troops in small groups which quickly seized the seven German shore batteries. Next the Magnan Division landed in Campo Bay. On June 18, after bitter fighting at Marino di Campo, Porto Longone and Porto Ferrajo, our troops occupied the entire island, having destroyed the German garrison under General Gall, taken 2,300 prisoners and seized sixty cannons and a great deal of matériel. General de Lattre, who had gone to the island, telegraphed me that evening from the Maison Napoléon, reporting the results and reminding me of the fact that they had been achieved on the anniversary of my call to honor in 1940.

Elba's capture appeared as a good omen for the great undertaking I had dreamed of when I sounded that call, covering as it did the coast of Provence. But everything still depended on the Allies' final decisions. Impressed by the extent of the victory in Italy, would they not, *in extremis,* renounce Operation Anvil to adopt a different scheme of exploitation in the peninsula? During the last trip I made there, at the end of June following my return from London and Bayeux, I found the command extremely eager, in fact, to pursue the campaign with the means now at its disposal and even to extend it by means of new reinforcements. This was quite natural, but nevertheless, for reasons involving my responsibilities to the French nation, I did not assent to this point of view.

In any case, the Americans, bitterly engaged in Normandy, demanded that a landing be made in Provence. Marshall and Eisenhower urgently requested it for August. In order to make assurance doubly sure, I informed Generals Wilson and Alexander, for my part, that the French government requested them in an express manner to regroup all the forces which it had put at their disposal in time for them to be transported to France during the month of August at the latest. I agreed that our groups pursuing the enemy should continue their operations for several weeks more. But they must in no case be engaged after July 25, nor drive beyond the Arno Valley. To our army in Italy as well as to our forces being prepared in Africa, I gave direct orders informing them of their imminent destination. As for General Juin, despite his regret at leaving his command and the distress I myself felt at removing him from it, I named him General Chief of Staff of National Defense, an essential post in the period of active operations, profound re-organization and inevitable friction with the Allies which the libera-tion would inaugurate. Until the day I left power, Juin would be beside me as one of the best seconds and surest military advisers any French leader ever had.

Finally, the date of the landing in the south of France was fixed for August 15. As we had stipulated, all French land, sea and air forces available in the Mediterranean would participate in it. Mean-while, some of our troops would be at grips with the enemy until the last minute in the Italian peninsula. Continuing his advance with the De Monsabert and Dody divisions and a group of *tabors,* General de Larminat seized Siena on July 13, taking every precau-tion that nothing be destroyed in that city of marvels. On July 22, our troops, under Juin's direct orders (Juin himself insisted on leading the last battles in Italy), took Castelfiorentino in sight of Florence and the Arno Valley, where the enemy was to re-establish his positions for long months. Then, transferring their sector to Allied groups, our men hastened to the ships that would land them in France.

Their transport was to be effected across a sea dominated by the Western navies. In September 1943, the Syracuse armistice had withdrawn from the Axis hand almost the entire Italian fleet, al-ready damaged by Andrew Cunningham's attacks. Further, in the spring of 1944, the *Scharnhorst* and the *Tirpitz,* the last fast battle-ships of the German Navy, were destroyed by the British. Never-theless, the enemy still possessed a great number of submarines, raiding vessels and scouting craft, which in co-operation with the German Air Force continued to cause heavy losses to the convoys.

We therefore had to continue clearing the seas before risking our landing armadas.

This was why, in the Atlantic, the North Sea and the Arctic Ocean, French cruisers, torpedo boats, submarines, frigates, corvettes, pursuit boats, scouting craft and escort vessels, operating out of British ports under Admiral D'Argenlieu's orders, took part in the vast system of attack and defense organized by the Allies. For Operation Overlord all our ships in English ports—that is, forty small warships and some fifty steamships and cargo vessels—were employed in the bombardment, escort and transport operations which the landing of Eisenhower's forces required. To this action were joined those of a division of two cruisers, the *Georges-Leygues* and the *Montcalm,* commanded by Admiral Jaujard and playing, off Port-en-Bessin, an extremely effective role in the bombardment of the beaches and later in the support of the landed troops. The old battleship *Courbet,* which for four years had served as a floating landing stage in Portsmouth harbor, received, on this supreme occasion, a reduced crew and a good commander, Wietzel, and was scuttled near the French coast under enemy fire in order to serve as a breakwater for the artificial port of Arromanches. Lastly Naval Lieutenant Kieffer's *Commando-Marine* leaped onto the beach at Ouistreham with the first Allied groups.

In the South Atlantic, the French Navy, waiting for Operation Anvil, vigorously contributed to the Western action. Seven of our cruisers distributed into two divisions, commanded respectively by Admirals Longaud and Barthe, and soon reinforced by the two cruisers under Admiral Jaujard, made up part of the barrage between Dakar and Natal to intercept the German "blockade forces." One of the latter, the *Portland,* was sunk by the *Georges-Leygues.* Up and down the entire west coast of Africa, the naval and air forces of Admiral Collinet took up operations against the German submarines, raiders and airplanes.

In the Mediterranean, a division of French light cruisers under the order of Naval Captain Sala, succeeded by Lancelot, with many British and American formations, supported the Italian armies.

Hence in September 1943 the *Fantasque* and the *Terrible* were engaged off Salerno during the landing of the troops. In January 1944 the *Fantasque* and the *Malin* assisted the Anzio landing by shelling the German reinforcements at close range along the Appian Way. Then, reaching the Adriatic, this division assumed responsibility for attacking the supply ships the enemy sent down the Italian coast at night, since Allied aviation prevented his matériel from traveling overland. On March 1, in the vicinity of Pola, our light cruisers sent five ships to the bottom, including one torpedo boat. On March 19, they sank five vessels off the coast of the Morea. In June, in the northern Adriatic, they destroyed four more. During the same period, all the Allied convoys navigating off England and Normandy or else toward Italy, Corsica and North Africa included French vessels in their escort. We lost the torpedo boat *La Combattante,* the submarine *Protée,* the dispatch boat *Ardent,* the minesweeper *Marie-Mad,* the tanker *Nivôse,* a pursuit boat and several freighters.

Last of all, in the Pacific, the splendid *Richelieu,* under Commandant Merveilleux du Vigneaux, joined the fleets of the line. In April off Sabang, in May off Surabaya, it powerfully supported the action of the Allied aircraft carriers. Everywhere, in fact, the French Navy took full advantage of the means it had reconstituted.

If the mastery of the sea permitted the landing on the Continent, it was because it was integrated with the domination of the air. In the latter as in the former, the French played an active and effective role, if it could not be a decisive one. Seventeen groups of our air forces accompanied our armies in Italy. Seven groups supported the Battle of France, of which two participated in the long-distance bombardments that crushed German industry. Two pursuit groups figured with honor in the implacable struggle from which Russia was emerging the victor. On the North African coast, several groups were helping to cover the land bases and the convoys at sea. The records of a Clostermann, a Maridor, a Marin la Meslée, the deliberate sacrifice of a Saint-Exupéry, as well as still other valorous actions, were like sparks flying out of the overwhelming machinery of the "big top."

The battle for France formed a whole. The military energy that increased the role of our regular armies was the same that swelled our interior forces. The latter, well before the landings, no longer risked only skirmishes, but ventured into engagements properly so-called. To the reports concerning the operations of the troops, the ships and the air squadrons were now added daily accounts of the activity of the maquis and the intelligence networks. Quite naturally the fire broke out first in the Massif Central, Limousin and the Alps.

On September 10, 1943, at Dourch in Aveyron, a regular combat was joined which seemed to be a sort of signal. A German company was put to flight by our own men and left its captain and ten soldiers dead behind it. At La Borie, in return, the victorious maquis was to be decimated and its chief, Lieutenant De Roque-maurel, killed by the enemy; but in other points of Aveyron and Cantal occurred new outbreaks in which our men had the advantage. Corrèze was filled with maquisards. At Saint-Ferréol, at Terrasson, brisk engagements in which the invader lost several hundred men were the prelude to the action of the entire region which would be made to coincide with the landing. In the Puy-de-Dôme, after several well-led raids, Colonel Garcie gathered 3,000 men on the tactical position of Le Mouchet and began there, on June 2, a series of battles in which the Germans were to be worsted. In Limousin, in Quercy, in Périgord, the many engagements caused the enemy serious losses.

In Haute-Savoie, increasingly intense battles were the rule. Already as far back as June 1943, at the Dents de Lanfon, and in the month following at Cluses, the Italians occupying the department had been sorely harassed. The Germans who relieved them during the winter had been attacked at many points. In February 1944, five hundred Frenchmen, along with some sixty Spaniards, took up a position on the Plateau des Glières, under Lieutenant Morel. The Germans, after thirteen days of battle, succeeded in taking it; six hundred of their men had fallen, but even at this cost they had not destroyed the troops of the defenders, of whom two thirds had escaped.

The Ain department was the theater of continual engagements. The forces of the interior, well commanded and organized, dominated the situation. They proved this on November 11 by occupying Oyonnax during the whole day of this glorious anniversary. Here, Colonel Romans-Petit reviewed his men before the monument to the war dead and had them parade through the city amid popular acclaim. Early in 1944, in order to reduce the Ain maquis, the Germans began a large engagement which cost them several hundred dead. In April, they made a new effort which cost them still more dearly. In June, it was our men who took the offensive everywhere, taking four hundred prisoners.

In the Drôme, through which the great Lyon-Marseille network passed, as well as those from Grenoble and Briançon, the maquis of Colonel Drouot took action against the railroads in particular. In December, a train of German soldiers on leave was blown up at Portes-les-Valence; the wagons stopped or overturned were machine-gunned by our men, who killed or wounded two hundred soldiers. Several days later, at Vercheny, a troop train was derailed and thrown into the Drôme. In March, in the Donzère Pass, the maquisards opened fire on an obstructed military convoy from which three hundred dead and wounded were removed. Shortly afterward, a French group, attacked near Séderon, fought to the last man. Meanwhile, the department was prepared to cut off the enemy's communication lines when the great battle began.

What happened in the Isère also made it possible to foresee some vast operation of our interior forces at the moment this battle was joined. The preliminaries were costly for the enemy. For instance, at Grenoble, on November 14, the resistance blew up the artillery depot where the Germans had stored munitions, gasoline and vehicles. The latter arrested three hundred hostages. Ordered to release them, they refused to do so; in retaliation, the barracks at Bonne where several Wehrmacht batteries were quartered were destroyed by an explosion which killed two hundred and twenty

Germans and wounded five hundred more. Further, according to the instructions left by General Delestraint and the orders of Colonel Descour, chief of our forces in the Isère, resolute combatants seized the Massif du Vercors under Major Le Ray, in order to make it a drill ground. Access to the Vercors was forbidden to the enemy reconnaissance.

It was here, during this period, that perhaps the most striking of all the resistance actions mentioned in our reports occurred. But many others, smaller in scale or concealed, were accomplished at the same time. Through the messages, where places were indicated by numbers, orders and reports formulated by code phrases, combatants designated by strange pseudonyms, we could discern to what degree the resistance had become an effective instrument of war. The enemy confirmed it by cruel reprisals. Before the Allied armies set foot on our land, the German lost thousands of men in France. He was everywhere surrounded by an atmosphere of insecurity that affected the morale of the troops and confused the officers. All the more so since the local authorities and the French police, whether in voluntary complicity with the resistance or fearing the punishments in store for "collaborators," opposed the repression much more than they helped it.

It must be added that the Germans, even when they were not the targets for the bullets and grenades of our secret army, were the continual victims of espionage. Nothing in regard to the invader escaped our intelligence networks. General Bedell Smith wrote to the Bureau Central de Renseignements et d'Action: "During the month of May, 700 telegraph reports and 3,000 documentary reports reached London from France." In fact, the day the battle began, all the German troop emplacements, bases, depots, landing fields and command posts were precisely known, the striking force and matériel reckoned, the defense works photographed, the mine fields spotted. The exchanges of questions and information between Koenig's staff and the intelligence networks were immediately transmitted by a well-established radio system. Thanks to the ensemble of the information furnished by the French resistance, the Allies were in a position to see into the enemy hand and to strike with telling effect.

The news of the landing gave the maquis its cue for a concerted action. I had ordered it in advance by notifying the interior forces, on May 16, by means of the "Cayman Plan," the goals they must attempt to achieve. However, the Allied command regarded the extension of guerrilla warfare with a certain mistrust. Furthermore, it foresaw a prolonged battle. Therefore it hoped that the resistance would not precipitate matters except in the region of the bridgehead. The proclamation General Eisenhower read on the radio on June 6 warned the French patriots to stay on their guard. On the same day, however, I urged them to fight with all the means in their power according to the orders given by the French command. But the delivery of arms depended on Allied headquarters and remained, at the start, limited. It was especially with regard to demolitions of railroads, roads and transmissions of essential importance that the "Combined General Staff" was concerned.

As for the railroads, the objectives were distributed between the air forces and the resistance. The latter accounted for the more remote regions—Lyon, Dijon, Doubs, the East, the Center, the Southwest, where during June and July six hundred derailings took place. Our men also took responsibility on all lines for the sabotage that immobilized 1,800 locomotives and more than 6,000 cars. As for the underground telegraph cables which the enemy reserved for its own use, skillful demolitions on June 6 and the days following put out of commission those serving Normandy and the region around Paris. As to the wires above ground, they were cut in countless numbers. It can be imagined what difficulty the German camp was thrown into by such a chaos in transports and transmissions. All the more so since at the same moment a military insurrection was launched in a number of departments, producing noticeable influence on the course of operations. At last the Allied high command recognized the advantage of this kind of warfare and furnished the maquis with assistance which was no less effective for remaining circumspect.

As for Brittany, we were to wait no longer. General Eisenhower insisted on seeing the Armorican Peninsula cleared of German troops before pushing his armies toward the Seine. Now Brittany was swarming with maquisards, especially in the Côtes-du-Nord and Morbihan, where the terrain was favorable to their work. It was therefore decided to furnish arms to the Bretons and to send our First Regiment of parachute troops, trained in England under Colonel Bourgoin. The day before the landing and during the days following, our interior forces received a great number of "containers" and parachute troops. At once the resistance burst out. Thirty thousand men entered the campaign, some organized in regular units, others conducting a sort of individual *Chouannerie*. But the Germans, having spotted at Saint-Marcel, near Malestroit, one of the bases where our men received arms from England, attacked it on June 18. The position was defended by a battalion from Morbihan and several teams of parachute troops under the orders of Major Le Garrec. Retired General de La Morlaye commanded a company which he himself had formed at Guingamp. After a struggle of several hours, the enemy managed to seize a terrain now covered with his own corpses. But the defenders had been able to escape.

The news of the battle of Saint-Marcel managed to rouse all of Brittany. The invader found himself blockaded in the larger cities and the ports. Nevertheless, he fought furiously and gave no quarter. But the British combatants assailed him everywhere and without respite. Among them, Colonel Bourgoin and his men acted as yeast in the dough. The First Parachute Regiment lost twenty-three of its forty-five officers. When Patton's armored units, having crossed the Avranches gap, debouched into Brittany at the beginning of August, they found the country entirely occupied by our men, who had already buried 1,800 German corpses and taken 3,000 prisoners. In order to help reduce the garrisons, the maquisards served in the American tanks as perfectly informed guides and as escort infantry. The enemy gave battle only in the ports—Saint-Malo, Brest, Lorient—which he had organized beforehand.

The campaign in Brittany cost him, all in all, several thousand dead, almost 50,000 prisoners, and much matériel. Four German divisions were destroyed.

At the other end of the territory, the battles of the Vercors Massif furnished similar proof of the military effectiveness of the French resistance. During the first days of June, 3,000 men had taken up their positions within the massif. Since the extremely choppy terrain lent itself to the defense conducted by the autonomous groups, as elsewhere the Alpine groups appeared particularly well established, a larger effort could be obtained from the Allied command to assure their armament; fifteen hundred "containers" were parachuted in to them. A mission including British, American and French officers was sent from England and installed itself in the Vercors Massif to connect the garrison with Allied general headquarters. Several instructors and specialists from Algiers joined the maquisards. In agreement with the Allied air forces, a landing strip was constructed in the massif's center to permit the landing of a detachment of regular troops, supplies for the combatants and the evacuation of the wounded.

On July 14, the enemy assumed the offensive. For ten days he continued his effort with considerable forces. His planes machine-gunned the defenders and bombarded the few localities. Since the German pursuit forces were in the sky every day, the Allied air force refused to take action, alleging that the distance from its bases kept it from protecting its transport and bombardment planes by its own pursuit planes. The enemy even made use of the landing strip on which the defenders hoped to see reinforcements land, and brought in several companies of their elite troops on gliders. Despite everything, the garrison, struggling in its bases of operations with exemplary stubbornness, held the assailant in check until July 24. On this date, the Germans managed to occupy the Vercors Massif. They had engaged in the task the equivalent of a division and had lost several thousand men. In their fury, they killed all the wounded and a good number of the villagers. At Vassieux, the population of the town was entirely massacred. Of the Vercors Alpine Rifles, half gave their lives for France; the others managed to withdraw.

Such military exploits had a vast repercussion in every other region. Of course the Algiers, London and New York radios did not fail to give them wide publicity. By the middle of July, forty departments were in open revolt. Those of the Massif Central, Limousin, the Alps, as well as Haute-Garonne, the Dordogne, the Drôme, the Jura, like the Breton departments, belonged to the maquisards whether the latter were a part of the "secret army," the "Francs-Tireurs et Partisans," the "Army Organization of Resistance," or the "Corps francs." Willy-nilly, the prefects made contact with the resistance and the "prefects of the liberation"—whether or not these were the same—appeared as such openly. The municipalities of 1940 resumed their functions where they had been revoked. The Cross of Lorraine appeared on lapels, on walls, on the flags of public monuments. As for the German garrisons, attacked, overworked, cut off from each other, they lived in incessant anxiety. Their isolated men were killed or taken prisoners. Their columns could not be moved without running into skirmishes at every step. They reacted by massacre and arson, as at Oradour-sur-Glane, Tulle, Asq, Cerdon, etc. But while the battle in Normandy grew harder for them every day, their situation in a great part of France tended to become desperate.

By the end of July, the French forces of the interior engaged eight enemy divisions, of which none could reinforce those fighting at the front. The First Infantry Division and the Fifth Parachute Division in Brittany, the 175th Division in Anjou and in Touraine, the 116th Panzer Division in the vicinity of Paris, the "Ostlegion" Division in the Massif Central, the 181st Division at Toulouse, the 172nd Division at Bordeaux and the equivalent of a division drawn from the army defending the Rhone Valley found themselves nailed to the spot. Besides, three Panzer divisions which the German command had called to emergency service in Normandy—which meant that they were supposed to be engaged within forty-eight hours—were subjected to enormous delays. The 17th Panzer, at grips with our men between Bordeaux and Poitiers, lost ten days before its columns managed to clear a road for itself. The 2nd Panzer S.S. Division, known as *"Das Reich,"* left Montauban on June 6 and could not utilize the railroads—all out of commission—and found its groups delayed in Tarn, Lot, Corrèze and Haute-Vienne; only on June 18 did it arrive at Alençon, exhausted and decimated. The 11th Panzer, taking eight days to come from the Russian front by railroad to the French border, took twenty-four days to cross France from Strasbourg to Caen. And how estimate the effect produced on the material and moral condition of all German units by the failures of supply and liaison?

For the same reasons, it was foreseeable that the rear of the enemy forces charged with the defense of the Mediterranean coast would be unable to hold out as soon as the French and Americans landed in Provence. During the first days of August, the military delegate to the Southeast, Colonel Henri Zeller, came from France to tell me as much. He declared that once Toulon and Marseille were taken, our troops could quickly overcome the successive resistance that would block the Rhone Valley, for the region of the Alps and the Massif Central was already in the possession of our interior forces. Zeller repeated his remarks to Generals Patch and De Lattre, to whom I immediately sent him. The latter consequently modified the rhythm they had prepared for their advance. Events proved Zeller correct. Lyon, which the command did not count on taking before two months of battle, was to be in our hands seventeen days after the landing.

The same movement which in France and in Africa drove the French into battle did not fail to have its repercussions in Indochina. In Saigon and Hanoi, while living under the threat of a sudden show of force by the invader, no one doubted, any more than elsewhere, the ultimate victory of the Allies. Aside from the prodromes of the German collapse, Japan's recession was also acknowledged. Not only had the offensive of the Nipponese fleets and armies been checked, on the whole, since the summer of 1943, but it was the Allies who were now taking the initiative: Admiral

Nimitz advancing from island to island in the central Pacific, General MacArthur moving toward the Philippines, Lord Mountbatten gaining ground in Burma with the co-operation of Chiang Kai-shek's forces.

This is why certain French authorities in Indochina gradually turned toward the Algiers government. Monsieur François, a bank director, came from Saigon to tell us so; M. de Boisanger, head of the Political Office of the Government General, extended discreet antennae toward General Pechkoff, our ambassador to Chungking; General Mordant, high commander of the troops, secretly made contact with Colonel Tutenges, chief of the information service we had installed in Yunnan.

In my eyes, the immediate goal to be achieved in the Far East was the participation of our forces in the military operations. The notion that by maintaining to the end an attitude of complacent passivity toward the Japanese we might eventually safeguard France's position seemed to me unworthy and ridiculous. I had no doubt that in a strategic position, taking Indochina as its center, the Japanese, hard pressed and thrown back on all sides, would necessarily be reduced to suppressing any risk of opposition in the peninsula. How, in case of a reverse on the nearby field of battle, could they tolerate amid their own groups the presence of a French army of 50,000 men, when furthermore the fiction of France's neutrality would crumble with Vichy? There was every indication that the Japanese would eventually want to liquidate the French troops and administration. And if, in return for new and dishonorable guarantees, they permitted some vestiges of our garrisons to subsist along with some scraps of our authority, it was inconceivable that on the one hand the states and the peoples of the Federation and on the other the Allies would countenance the restoration of French power on territories where we had taken no part in the world-wide struggle. It was therefore a question of preparing a military resistance on the peninsula, in order that the enemy not be able to seize our posts, sweep away our representatives and make us lose face altogether, without firing a shot. We must also send to the

Far East a force destined to re-enter the territories of Indochina as soon as the opportunity arose. On February 29, 1944, I wrote General Mordant to confirm him in the good intentions I knew were his and to stipulate what the government expected of him and his troops in the extraordinarily difficult situation in which he found himself. Shortly afterward, I appointed General Blaizot to command the forces assigned to the Far East. But since these forces could only act from bases in the Indies, Burma or China, the Allies must approve their departure. Yet Washington, London and Chungking appeared very reticent to do so. Nevertheless we persuaded the British government and Lord Mountbatten, British commander in chief in the Indian Ocean, to grant to General Blaizot permission to establish himself at New Delhi in order to prepare what was to follow. An advance echelon of our troops left with the General. This was a first step toward the goal. But fundamentally, we knew that the problem of Indochina, like the entire future of France, would be settled only in Paris.

Now, on August 15, the first elements of the French First Army and the American Sixth Corps landed on the coast of Provence. General Patch initially commanded the whole operation. De Lattre was at the head of our troops. I had approved the plan of their operation: as soon as the troops landed, the Americans were to march toward Grenoble along the axis of the "Route Napoléon"; the French were to take Toulon and Marseille, then drive up the Rhone Valley. That evening, under the protection of a gigantic naval and air bombardment, the landing of the first American groups took place between Cavalaire and Le Trayas; that of the parachute troops at Carnoules, Le Luc, Le Muy; that of our African commandos at Le Rayol and Le Lavandou took place at night as planned; and, during the course of the day, three American divisions began their landing. The 16th saw the beginning of the action of the Brosset, De Monsabert and Du Vigier divisions, which landed at Le Rayol, Cavalaire, Saint-Tropez and Sainte-Maxime in order to attack Toulon, while the Americans reached Draguignan.

In human undertakings, it happens that by virtue of long and exacting labor a sudden and single *élan* is constituted from many various and dispersed elements. On August 18 the news, arriving in great waves, illuminated all the areas of combat at once, revealed in each of them what part the French were taking, showed that the actions of our men formed a coherent whole.

In Provence, De Lattre, realizing the confusion of the German XIX Army, drove his advantage home. Under his orders, De Larminat's and De Monsabert's army corps succeeded in investing Toulon, and certain of our groups were already rushing toward Marseille. The Magnan Division, Guillaume's *tabor* divisions and the services were on the sea to join them. The Dody, Sevez and De Vernejoul divisions were prepared to embark. Our air force began to cross the sea. Our fleet, with all its cannons, rushed to the support of the troops. It was on the same day that the German front in Normandy collapsed altogether. Leclerc's division, engaged since August 11, distinguished itself in the operation. The road to Paris was opened. In the capital, the police and the partisans fired on the invader. From every region messages flowed in announcing that the resistance was at grips with the enemy. As we had intended it to be, the Allied battle of France was also the battle of Frenchmen *for* France. The French were fighting "a united battle for a united country."

Politics, diplomacy and arms had together prepared unity. Now the nation must be rallied and unified as soon as it emerged from the abyss. I left Algiers for Paris.

CHAPTER 8

PARIS

F OR over four years, Paris had been the remorse of the free
world. Suddenly it became the loadstone as well. So long as the
great city seemed to be asleep, captive and stupefied, everyone
settled for her formidable absence. But scarcely had the German
front been penetrated in Normandy than the French capital suddenly found itself the center of strategy and the stake of politics.
The campaigns of the military leaders, the calculations of governments, the intrigues of the ambitious, the emotions of the crowd
immediately turned toward the City. Paris was to reappear among
us. How many things could change!

First of all, Paris, left to her own decision, would settle the question of authority in France. No one doubted that if De Gaulle
reached the capital without being met by some *fait accompli* there,
he would be sanctioned by popular acclaim. Hence those who, in
the city and elsewhere, in whatever camp, nursed hopes of frustrat-
ing this outcome, or at least of rendering it incomplete and dis-
putable, attempted at the last moment to exploit the liberation in
order to produce a situation by which I would be hampered and, if
possible, paralyzed. But since the nation had made its choice, public feeling was to sweep their endeavors into oblivion.

One such attempt was led by Pierre Laval. During the very days of August when I was receiving reports of the progressive and decisive victories of the Normandy campaign, the landing in Provence, the battles of our interior forces and the advance symptoms of the Parisian insurrection, I was informed of the conspiracy hatched by this creature of the collaboration. He intended, in fact, to convene in Paris the "National" Assembly of 1940 and form a so-called "union" government which, invoking legality, would receive the Allies and De Gaulle in the capital. Hence the rug would be pulled from under the General's feet. Of course, room would have to be made for him within the executive body and, if need be, at its head, but after having morally uncrowned him and stripped his position of popular support, it would be easy to get rid of him by means suitable to the regime: the attribution of sterile honors, the increasing obstruction of political parties and, finally, general opposition under the double imputation of impotence to govern and aspirations to dictatorship. As for Laval, having engineered the return of the parliamentarians, for which they would be suitably grateful even if they had to inflict a theoretical condemnation upon him, he would step aside and wait until the people forgot and circumstances changed.

But to consummate such a plan, the co-operation of various mutually antagonistic elements was necessary. In the first place, Laval required the participation of a celebrated and eminent person, sufficiently representative of the Parliament, sufficiently outspoken in his opposition to Pétain's policy, sufficiently esteemed abroad, in order that the operation assume the appearance of a republican restoration. Monsieur Herriot appeared to fulfill all these conditions; all that remained was to convince him of the fact. Another essential condition was that the Allies, on their entrance into Paris, be likely to recognize the new power. The Germans, too, must be willing to do so, since their troops were still in possession of the capital. And lastly, the Marshal's consent must be obtained, for without it the invaders would refuse their authorization, the Allies their recognition, the parliamentarians their co-operation, while in any case the indignant refusal of the resistance was certain.

Laval might have thought, at the beginning of August, that he would obtain the indispensable support and co-operation he sought. Through M. Enfière, a friend of Herriot's used by the Americans for their liaisons with the President of the Chamber and who was in touch with Mr. Allen Dulles' services in Berne, he learned that Washington would favor a scheme that inclined to silence or set aside De Gaulle. Having consulted the Germans, the head of the "government" found them equally sympathetic; as a matter of fact, Abetz, Ribbentrop and others considered thàt once France was liberated, it would be of considerable advantage to have an executive in Paris who would prolong the aftereffects of Vichy rather than a government *sans peur et sans reproche*. With the blessing of the Germans, Laval went to Maréville, where Herriot was interned, and persuaded the latter to accompany him to Paris in order to convene the 1940 Parliament. As for Pétain, he let it be understood that he too would be ready to accede to the strategy.

I must add that despite the apparent complicity granted Pierre Laval, his desperate plot seemed to me to lead nowhere. Its success, in the last resort, required my own adherence, and nothing, not even the pressure of the Allies, could have brought me to consider the 1940 Assembly as qualified to speak in the name of France. Furthermore, given the whirlwind the resistance was raising everywhere and which it was about to unleash in Paris itself, I had no doubt the enterprise would be nipped in the bud. Already, on July 14, significant manifestations had occurred in the outskirts. In various places the tricolor had been displayed, the "Marseillaise" sung, and parades held to the chant of *"Vive De Gaulle!"* At the prison of La Santé, that very day, the political prisoners, sending the word from cell to cell and defying the worst reprisals, had decked all the windows with flags, driven away their jailers and made the neighborhood ring with their patriotic songs. On August 10, the railwaymen stopped working. On the 15th, the police went on strike. On the 18th, it was the post-office employees' turn. I expected to hear from one moment to the next of the start of the street fighting that would obviously dispel whatever illusions the parliamentarians had left.

Far more likely to succeed than Laval's plan was one by which certain political elements of the resistance had determined to seize power. The latter, I knew, hoped to take advantage of the exaltation and perhaps of the anarchy the struggle would arouse in the capital to manipulate the levers of command before I myself could grasp them. Such was, quite naturally, the intention of the Communists. If they managed to establish themselves as directors of the uprising and to control the authority in Paris, they could easily establish a *de facto* government there in which they would be preponderant.

Benefiting by the confusion of battle; overpowering the National Council of the Resistance, many of whose members, aside from those already committed to the party, might be accessible to the temptation of power; taking advantage of the sympathy which the persecutions they had suffered, the losses they had endured and the courage they had displayed gained them in many circles; exploiting the anxiety aroused in the people by the absence of all law and order; employing, finally, an equivocation by publicizing their adherence to General de Gaulle, they intended to appear at the insurrection's head as a kind of Commune which would proclaim the Republic, answer for public order, mete out justice and furthermore be sure to sing only the "Marseillaise," run up no flag but the tricolor. On my arrival, I would find this "popular" government installed; it would bind my brows with laurel, invite me to assume the place it would show me to, and henceforth pull all the strings itself. The rest, for those in control, would be nothing more than the alternation of audacity and prudence, penetration of the state machinery under cover of purges, inhibition of public opinion by means of an effectively used propaganda and militia, gradual elimination of their early associates until the day when the dictatorship of what was called the proletariat would be established.

That these political schemes should be mingled with the energies and efforts of battle seemed to me quite inevitable. That the insurrection in the great city must, for some, lead to the establishment of an authority dominated by the Third International, I had known for a long time. But I nevertheless considered it essential that the arms of France act in Paris before those of the Allies, that the people contribute to the invader's defeat, that the liberation of the capital bear the impress of a military and national operation. Hence I ran the risks of encouraging the revolt without rejecting any of the influences that were capable of provoking it. It must be added that I felt myself in a position to direct the operation so that it would turn out for the best. Having taken the appropriate local measures beforehand, prepared to bring a great French unit into the city in good time, I was planning to appear there myself in order to crystallize around my own person the enthusiasm of liberated Paris.

The government had done what was necessary in order that the command of the regular forces should be in the hands of the leaders consecrated to it. In July, Charles Luizet, Prefect of Corsica, had been appointed Prefect of Police. After two fruitless attempts, he was able to enter Paris on August 17, just in time to assume his functions when the police captured the prefecture from the Germans. Further, General Hary was to put himself, at the suitable moment, in command of the Garde Républicaine—which Vichy had called the Garde de Paris—of the regiment of firemen, the *garde mobile* and the *gendarmerie,* all being units delighted to receive a chief appointed by De Gaulle.

But events dealt otherwise with the groups of partisans banded together in the various parts of the city. These factions naturally followed the leaders they themselves had chosen and whom the Communists, either directly or under cover of the "National Front," made every effort to provide from their own ranks. As for the upper echelons, the party tried to furnish them by relying on the National Council of the Resistance. The Council had referred itself, in military matters, to "Comac," the Committee of Action, composed of three members, including Kriegel-Valrimont and Villon. The title of Chief of the General Staff of the Interior Forces had been given in the same way to Malleret-Joinville after the Germans had arrested Colonel Dejussieu. Rol-Tanguy had been appointed chief of the Ile-de-France forces. Judging by these nominations, one could suppose that the direction of the combat elements would be in the Communists' hands.

But these were still only titles, not official attributions. As a matter of fact, those who bore them did not exercise command in the hierarchical sense of the term. Rather than by orders given and followed according to the military norms, they proceeded by proclamations or by personal action limited to certain districts. The partisans, in effect, numbering at the most 25,000 armed men, formed autonomous groups each of which functioned less according to orders from above than to local opportunities and scarcely left the neighborhood where concealment and combat were a matter of experience. Furthermore, Colonel de Marguerittes, an extremely loyal officer, was chief of the interior forces of Paris and the suburbs. General Revers and General Bloch-Dassault advised, respectively, "Comac" and the "National Front." Lastly, Chaban-Delmas, the government's military delegate, returning to Paris on August 16 after a visit to London to receive Koenig's instructions, was at the center of everything. Perspicacious and skillful, alone having the means to communicate with the exterior, he supervised the proposals and, by means of long and, often, extremely outspoken palavers, checked the tendencies of the Council and the committees. At the summit, General de Gaulle and his government had their local representative.

This function was fulfilled by Alexandre Parodi. On August 14, reinforcing his authority, I had appointed him minister delegate to the territories not yet liberated. Since he spoke in my name, what he said weighed heavily. Because his conscience was clear, his disinterestedness complete, his dignity absolute, he had assumed a conclusive moral ascendancy above all passions and factions. Familiar with government service, he prevailed amid the confusion by the prestige of his experience. He had, moreover, his own policy, in accord with his character, which willingly conceded in matters of detail but held to what was essential with gentle firmness. Doing justice to the demands of ideology and the claims of individuals, he applied himself to ordering the consequences so that I might arrive in Paris to confront a situation without problematical commitments. It must be added that Georges Bidault, President of the National Council of the Resistance, was in agreement with Parodi and did everything in his power to avoid excesses by using, on his part, the compromise tactics of audacity in words, prudence in actions. As for the administrations, no one questioned the authority of my delegate and of those I had appointed to direct the services. It was without the trace of a difficulty that Parodi, at the right moment, would be established in the Hôtel de Matignon; that the secretaries general would install themselves in the ministries; that Luizet, the Prefect of Police, would assume Bussière's functions; that Flouret, Prefect of the Seine Department, would replace Bouffet. The official armature which the Algiers government had established beforehand would immediately establish the administration in Paris as in the provinces.

On the afternoon of August 18, I flew from Algiers in my usual plane under Marmier's command. General Juin and a group of my colleagues followed in a "Flying Fortress" which the Americans had insisted on lending us, alleging that its crew knew the route and the landing field perfectly. First stop: Casablanca. My intention was to take off again that same night in order to land the next day at Maupertuis near Saint-Lô. But the "Fortress" had had some mechanical difficulties on the way which required repairs. Furthermore, the Allied missions, insisting on the authority of the air lanes, stipulated a landing at Gibraltar before proceeding up the coast of Spain and that of France. We were therefore a day late.

On the 19th, I left Casablanca. A considerable crowd lined the roads on the way to the airport. The tension in every face revealed that the goal of my journey had been guessed, though we had kept it secret. Few cheers, but every hat off, arms raised, eyes fixed. This ardent yet silent greeting affected me as the people's acknowledgment of a decisive moment. I was moved by it, as was the president-general beside me. "What a destiny you have!" said Gabriel Puaux.

At Gibraltar, while we were dining with the governor, some Allied officers came in to tell us that the "Fortress" was not in condition to leave, that since my own Lockheed had no armament it might be imprudent to approach the sky over Normandy without an escort and that it would be advisable, all things considered, for me to postpone my departure. Without doubting the sincerity of the motives that inspired this advice, I decided not to follow it. Boarding my plane, I took off at the scheduled hour. A little later the "Fortress" found means of following us. On Sunday, August 20, toward eight o'clock, I landed in Maupertuis.

Koenig was waiting for me there, as well as Coulet, Commissioner of the Republic in Normandy, and an officer sent by Eisenhower. I went first to the headquarters of the Allied commander in chief. On the way, Koenig explained the situation in Paris to me as described in messages from Parodi, Chaban-Delmas, Luizet and the information brought by emissaries. I learned that the police, who had been on strike for three days, had occupied the Prefecture at dawn on the 19th and opened fire on the Germans; that teams of the partisans were doing the same thing throughout the city; that the ministries were in the hands of detachments designated by the delegation; that the resistance was being installed in the mayors' offices of the *arrondissements* and in the suburbs, not without an occasional struggle, as in Montreuil and later in Neuilly; that the enemy, busy evacuating his services, had not hitherto reacted very savagely, but that several of his columns were in the process of crossing Paris, which might lead to reprisals at any minute. As for the political situation, it appeared that Laval had been unsuccessful, while in Vichy the forced departure of the Marshal was expected from one day to the next.

Eisenhower, having received my compliments as to the overwhelming speed of the Allied forces, explained the strategic situation. The Third Army, under Patton, leading the pursuit at the head of Bradley's army group, was prepared to cross the Seine in two columns. The one, north of Paris, was to reach Mantes. The other, to the south, was driving toward Melun. Behind Patton, General Hodges, commanding the First American Army, regrouped the forces that had just finished mopping-up operations in Orne. To Bradley's left, the Montgomery army group, pushing back stiff German resistance, was advancing slowly toward Rouen. But to the right was a gap through which Eisenhower intended Patton to drive toward Lorraine as far as fuel and supply lines would permit. Subsequently, the De Lattre and Patch armies would come from the south to join the Allied position. The commander in chief's stratagem seemed quite logical to me, save for one point that concerned me deeply: no one was marching on Paris.

I indicated to Eisenhower my surprise and my concern. "From the strategic point of view," I said, "I don't see why you cross the Seine at Melun, at Mantes, at Rouen—in short, everywhere—and yet at Paris and Paris alone you do not. All the more so since Paris is a communications center which will later be essential and which it will be to your advantage to re-establish as soon as possible. If any location except the capital of France were in question, my advice would not commit you to any action, for normally, of course, the conduct of operations must proceed from you. But the fate of Paris is of fundamental concern to the French government. Which is why I find myself obliged to intervene and to ask you to send French troops there. The French Second Armored Division, of course, is the obvious choice."

Eisenhower did not conceal his embarrassment from me; I had the sense that fundamentally he shared my point of view, that he was eager to send Leclerc to Paris, but that for reasons not entirely of a strategic nature he could not yet do so. As a matter of fact, he explained the delay in making this decision by the fact that a battle in the capital risked vast destruction and heavy loss of life among the civilian population. Nevertheless, Eisenhower did not contradict me when I pointed out that this point of view could be justified if nothing were happening in Paris, but that it was not acceptable from the moment the patriots were at grips with the enemy there and every sort of upheaval likely. He declared, all the same, that the resistance had started fighting too soon. "Why too soon," I asked, "since at this very moment your forces are on the Seine?" Ultimately he assured me that without yet being able to establish a precise date, he would shortly give orders to march on Paris and that it would be the Leclerc division that he would assign to the operation. I acknowledged this promise, adding nevertheless that the matter was of such national importance in my eyes that I was ready to take action on my own responsibility and, if the Allied command delayed too long, would launch the Second Armored Division toward Paris myself.

Eisenhower's uncertainty suggested to me that the military command found itself somewhat hampered by the political project pursued by Laval, favored by Roosevelt and requiring that Paris be protected from all upheavals. The resistance had doubtless put an end to this scheme by engaging in battle, but it took some time for Washington to admit as much. This impression was confirmed when I learned that the Leclerc division, hitherto quite logically assigned to Patton's army, had been reattached to Hodges' army for the last three days, placed under the close supervision of General Gerow and kept in the area of Argentan, as if someone feared it might make off toward the Eiffel Tower. Furthermore, I remarked that the celebrated agreement as to relations between the Allied armies and the French administration, although it had been concluded several weeks ago between Algiers, Washington and London, had not yet been signed by Koenig and Eisenhower because the latter was still waiting for authorization to do so. How account for this delay if not by a summit-level intrigue which was keeping back the White House's surrender? Juin, visiting Allied headquarters in his turn, came to the same conclusions as I had drawn from his contacts with the general staff.

At the moment of the Allied armies' most striking success, and while the American troops were giving evidence of bravery deserving every praise, I found this apparent stubbornness of Washington's policy quite depressing. But consolation was not far

to seek. A great tide of popular enthusiasm and emotion seized
me on my entry into Cherbourg and bore me onward as far as
Rennes, passing through Coutances, Avranches and Fougères. In
the ruins of demolished cities and burned-out villages, the population gathered along the roads and burst out in jubilant demonstrations. All the windows that survived were hung with flags and
banners. The last bells were all set ringing. The streets, pitted
with shell holes, were festive with flowers. The mayors delivered
martial speeches that ended with sobs. I spoke a few words, not
of pity, which no one wanted, but of hope and pride, concluding
with the "Marseillaise," which the crowd sang with me. The
contrast was remarkable between the ardor of their spirit and the
ravages endured by their persons and property. Certainly France
would live, for she was equal to her suffering.

That evening, accompanied by André Le Troquer, minister-
delegate to the liberated territories, Generals Juin and Koenig and
Gaston Palewski, I arrived at the prefecture of Rennes. Victor
Le Gorgeu, Commissioner of the Republic for Brittany, Bernard
Cornut-Gentille, prefect of Ille-et-Vilaine, and General Allard,
in command of the military area, presented their personnel to me.
Here the administrative life was invincibly recovering, as was
tradition itself. I went to the town hall, where the mayor, Yves
Millon, surrounded by his council, colleagues of the resistance
and prominent citizens requested me to reopen the golden book
of the Breton capital, adding another link to the chain of time.
Then, beneath the rain, at nightfall, I addressed the crowd that had
gathered in front of the building.

The next day, the 24th, news flowed in from Paris. I learned, in
particular, of the end of Laval's attempt. Édouard Herriot, having
received the warning that the resistance sent him, realizing the
nature of the storm that was about to break, acknowledging the
confusion of the Vichy ministers, the high Parisian officials and
the German ambassador, did not let himself be persuaded to convene the "National" Assembly. Furthermore, his contacts with the
parliamentarians, particularly with Anatole de Monzie, had in-

dicated to him that the latter, impressed by the tragic events that touched them closely (the assassination of Georges Mandel, Jean Zay and Maurice Sarraut by Darnand's militia, the execution of Philippe Henriot by a group of resistance fighters), were no longer interested in convening in the threatening atmosphere of Paris. The Marshal, on his part, estimating that, all things considered, such a path was no way out and now following another plan, had not agreed to come to the capital. Hitler, finally, infuriated by an intrigue predicated on his defeat, had called it to a halt, ordered Laval to be transferred to Nancy with his "government" and had Pétain taken to join them there, either by choice or by force. As for the President of the Chamber, he was returned to Maréville. On August 18, Laval, Herriot and Abetz made their farewells at a lunch at the Hôtel de Matignon. On August 20, the Marshal was taken away from Vichy by the Germans.

Thus Laval's last scheme came to nothing. Until the end he had sustained a faction which no casuistry could clear from guilt. Inclined by nature and accustomed by the regime to approach matters from the underside, Laval held that no matter what occurred it was essential to be in power, that a certain degree of cunning would always dominate circumstances, that there was no event that could not be turned to his advantage, no man inaccessible to manipulation. He had, in the cataclysm, sensed the nation's misery but had also seized the opportunity to take the reins and to apply on a tremendous scale his infinite capacity for compromise. But the victorious Reich was a partner that did not intend to compromise in return. To keep the field open despite everything, Pierre Laval had had to espouse the disaster of France. He accepted this condition; he decided it was possible to take advantage of the worst, to utilize servitude, to associate himself with the invader, to make even the severest repression a trump card in his own hand. In order to effect his policy, he renounced the country's honor, the state's independence, the nation's pride. Now these elements were reappearing, energetic and exigent in proportion as the enemy retreated before them.

Laval had played. He had lost. He had the courage to admit that he must answer for the consequences. Doubtless, in his government, deploying the limitless resources of guile and the last resorts of obstinacy in order to support the insupportable, he sought, somehow, to serve his country. Let that be left to his credit! It was a fact that in the worst of their agony, those few Frenchmen who chose the muddy road did not renounce their country even as they advanced along it—the tribute rendered to France from those of her sons "who had so lost themselves." A door half open to Pardon.

Vichy's liquidation coincided with the development of the battle in the capital. What had been reported to me of it during my brief stay at Rennes intensified my eagerness to see the crisis past. It was true that the German command, for reasons that were still vague, did not seem to wish to bring matters to a head. But this passive attitude might give way at any moment to a sudden and furious repression. Furthermore, I found it intolerable that the enemy should occupy Paris even a day longer than was necessary from the moment we had the means to drive him out of it. Lastly, I did not wish the capital to fall victim to anarchy because of the upheavals it would be subject to. A report from Pierre Miné, director of provisions and supply in Paris, described the situation as critical. Cut off from all communication with the country for several weeks, the capital was virtually reduced to famine. Miné indicated that the pilfering of the last stocks of supplies and of the shops was beginning in certain places and, should the absence of all police action be prolonged, that serious excesses must be expected. Nevertheless, the day drew to its close without the Allied command having given Leclerc orders to move forward.

I had written General Eisenhower from Rennes, passing on the information I received from Paris, urging him to hasten the movement of French and Allied troops, emphasizing the unfortunate consequences, even from a military point of view, of the nascent disorder in the capital. On August 22, Koenig took him my letter with further recommendations of his own, then returned to his post in London, where his liaisons with the resistance were more easily effected than in our field camp. Juin, for his part, went to make contact with General Patton, who was conducting the pursuit in masterly fashion. I myself left Rennes, after ascertaining that by requisition of trucks and mobilization of drivers the Commissioner of the Republic was already setting up supply convoys heading for Paris. I traveled by way of Alençon, astir with enthusiasm and covered with flags, stopping first in Laval.

The moment I reached the Laval Prefecture, where I was greeted by Michel Debré, Commissioner of the Republic, I received an officer with a letter from General Leclerc. The latter described the incertitude under which he still labored as to his next mission and informed me of the initiative he had taken in sending an advance-guard group under Major de Guillebon to make contact with Paris. I immediately gave him my approval of this action, indicating in my reply that Eisenhower had promised to establish Paris as his direction, that Koenig had been to see Eisenhower for this very reason, that Juin had also done so, and lastly that I myself intended to see Leclerc himself the next day in order to assign him his mission. I soon learned that at the very moment I was writing Leclerc, General Gerow was censuring him for having sent a detachment toward Paris and ordered him to recall Major de Guillebon at once.

Finally, a few hours after having read the letter I had sent him, General Eisenhower gave orders to launch the Second Armored Division toward Paris. It must be added that the information coming at almost every moment from the capital, especially the news Cocteau and Dr. Monod brought to General Bradley, were all in support of my intervention. Furthermore, general headquarters was no longer ignorant of the failure of Laval's attempt. While Leclerc spent the night organizing his advance, the messages I received from the Prefecture of Le Mans informed me that the events in Paris were moving at break-neck speed.

Thus I learned that on the morning of the 20th, the Hôtel de Ville had been occupied by a Parisian police detachment led by

Roland-Pré and Léo Hamon. The Prefect of the Seine Department, Flouret, went there to assume his functions. But I was also informed that Parodi and Chaban-Delmas on the one hand, and the majority of the Council of the Resistance on the other—warned by the American and British agents that it would be a long time still—weeks, they were told—before Allied troops entered the capital, knowing the weakness of the arms at the partisans' disposal in comparison to the 20,000 men, eighty tanks, sixty cannons and sixty planes of the German garrison, eager to avoid the destruction of the bridges over the Seine which Hitler had ordered and to save the political and military prisoners—had decided to yield to the suggestions of M. Nordling, the Swedish consul general, and by his mediation conclude a cease-fire with General von Choltitz, in command of the enemy forces in Paris and the suburbs.

This news affected me very disagreeably. All the more so since at the moment I learned of the signing of the cease-fire, the latter no longer corresponded to the military situation, now that Leclerc was preparing to advance. But on the morning of the 23rd, at the moment I was leaving Le Mans, I was informed that the cease-fire, opposed by the majority of the combatants, had only been partially observed, although it had permitted Parodi and Roland-Pré, previously arrested by the Germans on the Boulevard Saint-Germain, to be released after an interview with Choltitz himself. I learned, furthermore, that hostilities had resumed on the evening of the 21st, that the prefectures, the ministries and the mayors' offices in the *arrondissements* were still in our hands, that the Parisians were throwing up barricades and that the German general, while reinforcing his strongholds, was not engaging in any repressive action. Were these tactics inspired by fear of the future, a desire to spare Paris or by an agreement made with the Allies, whose agents had contacted his general staff ever since Oberg and the Gestapo had left the capital? I could not determine which was the principal motive, but I was inclined to believe that in any case help would arrive in time.

There were no doubts about it along the road I took on August 23. Passing between two lines of snapping flags and cheering crowds, I felt swept on by a veritable flood of joy. At La Ferté-Bernard, at Nogent-le-Rotrou, at Chartres, as well as in all the towns and villages we passed through on the way, I had to stop to receive the homage of the people and to speak in the name of a reviving France. In the afternoon, overtaking the columns of the Second Armored Division, I installed myself in the Château de Rambouillet. Leclerc had written me that he would be in the town. I immediately summoned him.

His plan of attack was ready. If the bulk of his division, which was advancing from Argentan, would not be in place before nightfall, the advance groups, on the front from Athis-Mons to Palaiseau, Toussus-le-Noble and Trappes, were in contact with an entrenched and resolute enemy. This position must be penetrated. The chief effort would be led by the Billotte group, taking the road from Orléans to Paris through Antony as its axis. The Langlade group would act through Toussus-le-Noble and Clamart, while a detachment commanded by Morel-Deville would cover it toward Versailles. As for the Dio group, temporarily held in reserve, it would follow Billotte's. The action would begin at dawn the next day. I approved these arrangements and ordered Leclerc to establish his command post at the Gare Montparnasse when he had entered Paris. I would join him there in order to settle what to do next. Then, observing this young leader already at grips with the demands of battle, and whose valor was confronted with an extraordinary series of well-prepared circumstances, I murmured, "How lucky you are!" And I also thought how in war the luck of generals is the honor of governments.

Dr. Favreau, having left Paris that morning, reached Rambouillet during the afternoon, bringing me a report from Luizet. According to the Prefect of Police, the resistance had gained supremacy of the streets. The Germans were now cornered in their strongholds, venturing out only on occasional raids in armored vehicles. In fact, the London radio announced that evening that the interior forces had liberated Paris. The next morning King George VI sent me a telegram of congratulations which was made public at once. The information and the telegram were, of course, premature, but doubtless they were intended to force the Americans to renounce their ulterior motives which the English did not approve. The contrast I noticed between the warm satisfaction indicated by the BBC with regard to the events in Paris and the reserved, even bitter, tone of the Voice of America led me to realize that this time London and Washington were not entirely in agreement about France.

I sent the valiant Favreau back to Paris with my answer to Luizet. I specified my intention of going not to the Hôtel de Ville, where the Council of the Resistance and the Parisian Committee of Liberation were in session, but "to the center." In my mind, this meant the Ministry of War, the obvious center for the government and the French command. Not that I was not eager to make contact with the leaders of the Parisian insurrection, but I wished to establish that the state, after ordeals which had been unable either to destroy or enslave it, was returning, first of all, quite simply, to where it belonged. Reading the newspapers—*Combat, Défense de la France, Franc-Tireur, Front national, L'Humanité, Libération, Le Populaire* —which the political elements of the resistance had been publishing in Paris for the last two days in the place of the collaboration sheets, I felt both pleased by the spirit of struggle that was expressed in them and confirmed in my intention of accepting no investiture for my authority save that which the voice of the people would give me directly.

This is what I declared, furthermore, to Alexandre de Saint-Phalle, associated with my delegation and whose influence in legal and commercial circles was well known. He came accompanied by Jean Laurent, Director of the Bank of Indochina; M. Rolf Nordling, the Swedish consul-general's brother; and the Austrian Baron Poch-Pastor, an officer of the German Army, who was also Choltitz's aide-de-camp and an Allied agent. All four had left Paris on the night of August 22 in order to obtain the swift intervention of regular troops from the American command. Having learned from Eisenhower that Leclerc was already on the way, they came to present themselves to me. Saint-Phalle suggested that I convene the "national" assembly on my entry into Paris in order that a parliamentary vote of confidence might give my government the character of legality. I answered negatively. Nevertheless the composition and destinations of this delegation offered a strange perspective as to the state of mind of the local German command. The four "missionaries" were provided with two safe-conducts, the one from Parodi, the other from General von Choltitz. In crossing the enemy sentry posts, they had heard the soldiers grumble, "Treason!"

On the evening of the 24th, the bulk of the Second Armored Division, after fierce engagements, arrived in the immediate proximity of Paris, Billotte and Dio having taken Fresnes and La Croix de Berny, and Langlade holding the bridge at Sèvres. A detachment commanded by Captain Dronne had reached the Hôtel de Ville. The next day would be spent forcing the enemy's last outer resistance, then incapacitating the German strongholds within the city, and lastly assuring protection in the direction of Le Bourget. Leclerc would push the Billotte group toward the Porte de Gentilly, the Luxembourg, the Hôtel de Ville and the Louvre, as far as the Hôtel Meurice, General von Choltitz's command post. The Dio group would enter by the Porte d'Orléans and would march through the organized blocks of the École Militaire and the Palais-Bourbon in two columns—Noiret's following the outer boulevards to the Auteuil viaduct and along the Seine, Rouvillois' passing by way of Montparnasse and Les Invalides. As for the Étoile and the Majestic, this would fall to the Langlade group. Everyone would make connections at the Place de la Concorde. At Leclerc's right, the Americans were to send a fraction of their Fourth Division to the Place d'Italie and the Gare d'Austerlitz.

On August 25, everything was to follow these plans. I myself had already determined what I must do in the liberated capital: I would mold all minds into a single national impulse, but also cause the figure and the authority of the state to appear at once. Walking up and down the terrace at Rambouillet, I was kept informed from hour to hour of the Second Armored Division's advance, and I thought of the difficulties which a mechanized army composed of seven such units might have spared us in the past. Then, considering the causes of the impotence which had deprived us of them—that is, the insolvency of governmental power—I resolved all the more firmly not to let my own be infringed. The mission with which I was invested seemed as clear as it could be. Getting into the car to drive to Paris, I felt myself simultaneously gripped by emotion and filled with serenity.

How many people, on the way, watched for our passage! How many flags floated before the houses! After Longjumeau, the crowds grew thicker; toward Cour-la-Reine they were jammed still more closely; at the Porte d'Orléans, near which shooting was still to be heard, the mob formed a jubilant tide; the Avenue d'Orléans was black with people. It was apparently believed I would go to the Hôtel de Ville. But by forking off at the Avenue de Maine, almost deserted by comparison, I reached the Gare Montparnasse toward four in the afternoon.

General Leclerc had just arrived. He informed me of General von Choltitz's surrender. The latter, after a last negotiation arranged through Nordling, had personally come to Major de La Horie, chief of Billotte's general staff. Then, brought by the latter to the Prefecture of Police, he had signed an agreement with Leclerc according to the terms of which the German strongholds in Paris must cease fire. Moreover, several had been captured during the day. Then the German general had ordered the defenders to lay down their arms and give themselves up as prisoners. Officers of Von Choltitz's general staff, accompanied by French officers, went to notify the German troops of the order. I saw my son, an ensign in the Second Armored Regiment of Naval Rifles, leave for the Palais-Bourbon accompanying a German major to receive the garrison's surrender. The result of the battles of Paris was highly satisfactory. Our troops brought off a complete victory without the city's suffering the demolitions or the population the losses that had been feared.

I congratulated Leclerc on this. What a stage on his road to glory! I also congratulated Rol-Tanguy, whom I saw beside him. It was, in fact, the action of the interior forces which, during the preceding days, had driven the enemy from our streets, decimated and demoralized his troops and blockaded his units in their fortified strongholds. Furthermore, since morning, groups of partisans with only the most meager weapons had bravely assisted the regular troops in mopping up the nests of German resistance. By their action, in fact, they had just reduced the block of the Clignancourt barracks. Nevertheless, reading the copy of the German surrender which Leclerc gave me, I disapproved the mention made after the event, on Rol-Tanguy's insistence, according to which it was to Rol as well as to Leclerc that the German command had surrendered. "First of all," I told Leclerc, "that is not exactly true. Secondly, you were the highest-ranking officer in the matter, therefore the only person responsible. But above all, the insistence which has led you to admit this formulation proceeds from an unacceptable tendency." I read to Leclerc the proclamation published the same morning by the National Council of the Resistance in behalf of the "French nation" and making no reference to the government or to General de Gaulle. Leclerc understood at once. With all my heart I embraced this noble colleague.

Leaving the Gare Montparnasse, I headed for the Ministry of War, where a small advance-guard detachment under Colonel de Chevigné had preceded me. The cortege was a modest one. Four cars: mine, Le Troquer's, Juin's and a machine-gun car. We wanted to take the Boulevard des Invalides to the Rue Saint-Dominique, but at Saint-François-Xavier a burst of fire from the nearby houses forced us to take the Rue Vaneau and the Rue de Bourgogne. We reached our destination at five o'clock.

I was immediately struck by the impression that nothing had changed inside these venerable halls. Gigantic events had overturned the world. Our army was annihilated. France had virtually collapsed. But at the Ministry of War, the look of things remained immutable. In the courtyard, a unit of the Garde Républicaine presented arms, as in the past. The vestibule, the staircase, the arms hanging on the walls—all were just as they had been. Here, in person, were the same stewards and ushers. I entered the "minister's office," which M. Paul Reynaud and I had left together on the night of June 10, 1940. Not a piece of furniture, not a rug, not a curtain had been disturbed. On the desk, the telephone was in the same place, and on the call buttons exactly the same names. Soon I would learn that this was the case in all the other buildings in which the Republic housed itself. Nothing was missing except the state. It was my duty to restore it: I installed my staff at once and got down to work.

Luizet came to present his report. Then it was Parodi's turn. Both were beaming, anxious, exhausted by the week without respite or sleep which they had just lived through. For them, in the immediate future, two problems dominated all others: public order and public supply. They described the irritation expressed by the Council of the Resistance and the Parisian Committee of Liberation when they learned I was not proceeding directly to them when I entered Paris. I repeated my reasons to the minister-delegate and to the Prefect of Police. But soon, on leaving my office, I would go to the Hôtel de Ville after stopping, first, at the Prefecture to greet the Parisian police force. We set up the plan for these visits. Then I arranged for the next day's parade, concerning which Parodi and Luizet showed themselves both enthusiastic and preoccupied. After their departure, I received a message from General Koenig. He would not be able to accompany us on this great day. That very morning, Eisenhower had asked him to sign the agreement settling the relations of our administration and the Allied command. Done at last, and better late than never!

At seven in the evening, inspection of the Paris police force in the courtyard of the Prefecture: at the sight of this corps, whose service had kept it on the spot under the occupation, now trembling with joy and pride, it was evident that by giving the signal and the example of battle the men had revenged themselves for a long humiliation. They had also, and rightly, taken the opportunity to increase their prestige and their popularity, as I informed them while cheers rose from the ranks. Then, on foot, accompanied by Parodi, Le Troquer, Juin and Luizet, proceeding with difficulty through the crowd that surrounded me with deafening acclamations, I reached the Hôtel de Ville. Before the building a detachment of interior forces, under the orders of Major Le Percq, presented arms impeccably.

At the foot of the staircase, Georges Bidault, André Tollet and Marcel Flouret received General de Gaulle. On the steps, the combatants, tears in their eyes, presented arms. Beneath a salvo of cheers, I was led to the center of the salon on the first floor. Here were grouped the members of the National Council of the Resistance and the Parisian Committee of Liberation. Around me were many colleagues; a number wore the insignia of the interior forces on their sleeves, as prescribed by a governmental decree. All wore the Cross of Lorraine. Glancing around the group vibrant with enthusiasm, affection and curiosity, I felt that we had immediately recognized one another, that there was among us, combatants of the same battle, an incomparable link, and that if there were divergences of policy and ambition among us, the fact that the majority and I found ourselves together would carry the rest along with us. Furthermore, despite the fatigue evident in every face, the excitement of the dangers risked and the cataclysms survived, I did not see a single gesture or hear a single word which was not of perfect dignity. How admirable the success of a meeting long dreamed of and paid for with so many efforts, disappointments, deaths!

Feeling had spoken. Now it was politics' turn. This, too, was a noble voice. Georges Marrane, substituting for André Follet, greeted me in splendid terms in the name of the new Parisian municipality. Then Georges Bidault delivered a discourse of the highest possible level. In my improvised reply, I expressed "the sacred emotion that grips all of us, men and women alike, in these moments that transcend each of our poor private lives." I acknowledged that "Paris has been liberated by her people, with the help of the army and the support of all of France." I did not fail to associate in our success "the French troops which at this moment are driving up the Rhone Valley" and the forces of our allies. Lastly, I called the nation to its duties at war and, in order that it fulfill them, to national unity.

I entered the office of the Prefect of the Seine. Marcel Flouret presented me to the principal officials of his administration. As I was preparing to leave, Georges Bidault cried out, "General! Here, around you, are the National Council of the Resistance and the Parisian Committee of Liberation. We ask you formally to proclaim the Republic before the people who have gathered here." I replied, "The Republic has never ceased. Free France, Fighting France, the French Committee of National Liberation have successively incorporated it. Vichy always was and still remains null and void. I myself am the President of the government of the Republic. Why should I proclaim it now?" Stepping to a window, I greeted the crowd that filled the square and proved by its cheers that it demanded nothing more. Then I returned to the Rue Saint-Dominique.

That evening, Leclerc drew up the accounts of the battles within Paris. The surrender of all the German strongholds was now accomplished. The so-called "Luxembourg" block which included the Palace, the School of Mines and the Lycée Montaigne, that of the Place de la République, organized in the Barracks of Prince Eugène and completed by the central telephone offices of the Rue des Archives, ceased fire last of all. During the day, our troops took 14,800 prisoners. Three thousand, two hundred Germans were dead, not counting those—at least a thousand—whom the partisans had killed on the preceding days. The losses of the Second Armored Division amounted to twenty-eight officers and six hundred soldiers. As for the interior forces, Professor Vallery-Radot, who had taken charge of the health service, estimated the cost of the battles which had been raging during the last six days at 2,500 men killed or wounded. Furthermore, more than 1,000 civilians had fallen.

Leclerc informed me that north of Paris the enemy's pressure continued to make itself felt. At Saint-Denis and at La Villette, some units refused to lay down their arms, alleging that they were not under Choltitz's orders. A part of the 47th German Division was entrenching itself at Le Bourget and Montmorency, doubtless to cover the columns in retreat farther north. The enemy was advancing small units as far as the entrances to the capital. General Gerow, commanding the Fifth American Army Corps, to which the Second Armored Division was still attached for operations, had given it the mission of making contact with the German positions with a view to attacking them.

However, I was—more than ever—resolved to follow the Étoile-Notre Dame itinerary the next day, keeping my rendezvous with the people, and I intended that the Second Armored Division should participate in the ceremony. Doubtless the manifestation would involve a certain amount of risk, but it would be well worth it. It seemed to me, moreover, highly unlikely that the German rear guard would suddenly transform itself into an advance guard and march toward the center of Paris, where the entire German garrison was now a prisoner. There were certain precautions to be taken, in any case.

I settled with Leclerc on a tactical group commanded by Roumaintzoff to be posted early in the morning as covering troops toward Le Bourget; we also regrouped the factions of the interior forces skirmishing in this direction. The rest of the division would be formed into three other units during the parade, and would be on guard respectively at the Arc de Triomphe, the Rond-Point des Champs-Élysées, and in front of the cathedral; should the occasion arise, they would move toward the desired points. Leclerc himself, marching behind me, would remain in constant communication with his various elements. Since the Allied command had not resolved to make the slightest liaison with me, I ordered Leclerc to inform it of the arrangements I had decided on. This command, moreover, had all the means necessary to supply the temporary reserve of a part of the French division if need be. To the contrary orders which the Allies might send, Leclerc was to reply that he was maintaining his positions according to General de Gaulle's orders.

The morning of Saturday, August 26, brought nothing of a nature to modify my plans. Of course I was informed that Gerow had ordered Leclerc and his troops to remain aloof from any manifestation. The American general even sent me an officer to let me know his orders directly. Naturally I ignored this advice, not without observing that on such a day and in such a place, this attitude, which of course was not adopted without instructions from above, testified to the most remarkable incomprehension. I must say that apart from this incident, as futile as it was disagreeable, our allies did not attempt to meddle with affairs in the capital. General Koenig, who had been appointed military governor on August 21, Fleuret, the Prefect of the Seine Department, and Luizet, the Prefect of Police, did not have to reject the slightest effort at encroachment. No American troops were stationed in Paris, and the units that had passed by the Place d'Italie and the Gare de Lyon the day before had immediately withdrawn. Except for the presence of reporters and photographers, the Allies would take no part in the next day's parade. For the entire distance it was to cover there would be only Frenchmen.

But there would be many of these. Since the night before, the radio, which Jean Guignebert, Pierre Crenesse and their crews had made every effort to restore to its normal functions, had announced the ceremony. During the morning, I was informed that throughout the entire city and its suburbs, in this Paris that had no *Métro,* no buses and no cars, innumerable pedestrians were on the march. At three in the afternoon I reached the Arc de Triomphe. Parodi and Le Troquer, as members of the government; Bidault and the National Council of the Resistance; Tollet and the Parisian Committee of Liberation; Generals Juin, Koenig, Leclerc, D'Argenlieu, Valin and Bloch-Dassault; Prefects Flouret and Luizet; the military delegate Chaban-Delmas; many leaders and combatants of the interior forces were ranged around the tomb of the unknown soldiers. I greeted the Chad Regiment, drawn up in battle formation before the arch and whose officers and soldiers, standing on their cars, watched me pass before them to the Étoile as though I were the materialization of a dream. I relit the flame. Since June 1940 no one had been able to do so save in the invader's presence. Then I left the vault and the platform. The observers made way for me. Ahead stretched the Champs-Élysées!

Rather the sea! A tremendous crowd was jammed together on both sides of the roadway. Perhaps two million people. The roofs too were black with many more. At every window were crowded other groups waving flags. Human clusters were clinging to ladders, flagpoles, lampposts. As far as the eye could see, there was nothing but this living tide of humanity in the sunshine, beneath the tricolor.

I went on foot. This was not the day for passing in review with arms glittering and trumpets sounding. Today we were to revive, by the spectacle of its joy and the evidence of its liberty, the self-awareness of a people who yesterday were crushed by defeat and scattered in servitude. Since each of all those here had chosen Charles de Gaulle in his heart as the refuge against his agony and the symbol of his hopes, we must permit the man to be seen, familiar and fraternal, in order that at this sight the national unity should shine forth. It was true that the general staffs feared that an outburst of the enemy armored cars or a machine-gunning pursuit plane would decimate this mob and unleash panic upon it. But that afternoon, I believed in the fortune of France. It was true that the services of public order feared they would not be able to restrain the pressure of the crowd. But I was convinced, on the contrary, that the people would discipline themselves. It was true that in the cortege of colleagues entitled to follow me a number of supernumeraries figured improperly. But it was not at them that the people were looking. It was true, finally, that I myself had neither the physique nor the taste for those attitudes and gestures that can charm the public. But I was sure they did not expect them of me.

I went on, then, touched and yet tranquil, amid the inexpressible exultation of the crowd, beneath the storm of voices echoing my name, trying, as I advanced, to look at every person in all that multitude in order that every eye might register my presence, raising and lowering my arms to reply to the acclamations: this was one of those miracles of national consciousness, one of those gestures which sometimes, in the course of centuries, illuminate the history of France. In this community, with only a single thought, a single enthusiasm, a single cry, all differences vanished, all individuals disappeared. Innumerable Frenchmen whom I approached first at the Étoile, then at the Rond-Point, then at the Place de la Concorde, before the Hôtel de Ville, on the steps of the cathedral —if you knew how much alike you were! The children—so pale, dancing and screaming for joy; the women—bearing so many griefs, now smiling and cheering; the men—flooded with a long-forgotten pride, shouting their gratitude; the old—doing me the honor of their tears: how closely they resembled one another! And I myself, at the center of this outburst, I felt I was fulfilling a function which far transcended my individuality, for I was serving as an instrument of destiny.

But there is no such thing as pure and perfect joy, even during a triumphal march. With the happy thoughts rushing through my mind were mingled many anxieties. I knew well that all of France was eager for nothing more than its liberation. The same ardor for rebirth which broke out yesterday in Rennes and Marseille and today transported Paris would reveal itself tomorrow at Lyon, Rouen, Lille, Dijon, Strasbourg, Bordeaux. One had only to look and listen in order to be certain of the nation's will to revive. But the war continued; it was still to be won. At what price, then, must the victory be won? What ruins would be added to our own? What new losses would decimate our soldiers? What moral and physical agonies would the French prisoners of war still have to endure? How many of our deported would return—the hardest fighters, the greatest sufferers, the most deserving of us all? Lastly, in what condition would our people find themselves, and in what kind of world?

It is true that around me rose extraordinary testimonials of unity. It might appear likely that the nation would surmount its dissensions until the conflict's end; that Frenchmen would choose to remain together with mutual recognition in order to re-create their powers; that having chosen their goal and found their guide, they would give themselves the institutions permitting them to be governed. But I could no longer ignore the obstinate purposes of the Communists, nor the bitterness of so many prominent individuals who would not forgive me for their own errors, nor the agitation festering again in the political parties. Even while marching at the head of the cortege, I sensed that at this very moment ambition as well as fervent devotion was following behind me. Beneath the waves of popular confidence, the reefs of politics would not be slow to surface.

At each step I took along the most illustrious avenue in the world, it seemed to me that the glories of the past were associated with today's. Beneath the Arc de Triomphe, the flame burned brightly in our honor. This avenue down which a triumphant army marched twenty-five years ago opened brilliantly before us. On his pedestal, Clemenceau, whom I hailed in passing, looked as if he were springing up to march beside us. The chestnut trees of the Champs-Élysées that L'Aiglon, in prison, dreamed about and which had seen for so many, many years the grace and prestige of France displayed beneath them offered themselves now as joyous grandstands to thousands of spectators. The Tuileries, which framed the majesty of the state under two emperors and two monarchs; the Place de la Concorde and the Place du Carrousel, which had observed the frenzies of revolutionary enthusiasm and the reviews of conquering regiments; the streets and the bridges named after battles won; on the other bank of the Seine, Les Invalides, its dome still sparkling with the splendor of Le Roi-Soleil, the tombs of Turenne, of Napoleon, of Foch; and the Institute, hon-

ored by so many illustrious minds—these were the benevolent witnesses of the human stream that flowed between them. Here, in its
turn, was the Louvre, where the succession of kings had also succeeded in building France; on their mounts, the statues of Joan of
Arc and of Henri IV; the Palace of Saint Louis, whose anniversary
had occurred the day before; Notre-Dame, the prayer of Paris, and
the Île de la Cité, her cradle—all shared in the event. History, gathered in these stones and in these places, seemed to be smiling
upon us.

And warning us as well. This same Cité was once Lutèce, sub-
jugated by Caesar's legions, then Paris, which only Geneviève's
prayer had been able to save from Attila's fire and sword. Saint
Louis, his crusade abandoned, died on the sands of Africa. At
the Porte Saint-Honoré, Joan of Arc was repulsed by the city
which she had just restored to France. Quite near me, Henri IV
fell a victim to fanatic hatred. The Revolt of the Barricades, Saint
Bartholomew's Massacre, the outrages of La Fronde and the furious torrent of August 10 all bloodied the walls of the Louvre.
At the Place de la Concorde the heads of the King and Queen of
France rolled on the ground. The Tuileries were to see the destruction of the old monarchy, the exile of Charles X and of Louis-
Philippe, the despair of the Empress, and were finally put to the
torch, like the old Hôtel de Ville. How often the Palais-Bourbon
was the scene of the most disastrous confusions! Four times within
two lifetimes the Champs-Élysées was to submit to the outrage of
invaders parading in time to their own odious fanfares. Paris, this
afternoon, if it gleamed with all the greatness of France, took lessons
from its terrible days.

Toward four-thirty, I went, as planned, to Notre-Dame. Just
before, in the Rue de Rivoli, I had got into a car and, after a short
stop on the steps of the Hôtel de Ville, reached the cathedral
square. The cardinal-archbishop was not to receive me at the door
of the basilica. Not that he had not desired to, but the new authority had requested him to abstain. For Monsignor Suhard had found

it necessary, four months ago, formally to receive Marshal Pétain on his way through the city when Paris was occupied by the Germans, and then, the month following, to conduct the funeral service which Vichy had had celebrated in honor of Philippe Henriot. Because of this fact, many resistance members were indignant at the idea that the prelate could, now, introduce General de Gaulle into the cathedral. For my part, realizing that the Church regarded itself as obliged to accept the "established order," not unaware of the fact that the cardinal's piety and charity were so eminent that they left little room in his soul for the appreciation of temporal matters, I should willingly have overlooked such things. But the state of tension of a great number of the combatants the day after the battle and my own desire to avoid any unpleasant manifestation against Monsignor Suhard had led me to approve my delegation's request that he remain in the archbishop's palace during the ceremony. What was soon to occur confirmed my conviction that this had been a wise measure.

The moment I stepped out of the car, shots crackled in the square, rapidly becoming a running fire. Everyone who had a weapon began to fire at random, aiming at the roofs. The men of the interior forces made their powder speak on all sides. Soon even the seasoned troops of the Second Armored Division, posted near the portals, began aiming their bullets at the towers of Notre-Dame. It was immediately apparent to me that this was one of those contagious shooting matches which high feeling sometimes sets off in overexcited troops on the occasion of some fortuitous or provoked incident. Nothing could be more important than for me not to yield to the panic of the crowd. I therefore entered the cathedral. Without electricity, the organs were silent, and the shots echoed inside the structure. As I advanced toward the choir, the more or less bowed congregation murmured its acclamations. I took my place, my two ministers, Le Troquer and Parodi, behind me. The canons were in their stalls. The archpriest, Monsignor Brot, came to bring me the greetings, regrets and protests of the cardinal.

I requested him to express to His Eminence my respect in all religious matters, my desire for reconciliation from the national point
of view and my intention to receive him shortly.

The *Magnificat* rose around us. Was it ever sung more ardently?
Meanwhile, the shooting was still going on. Several gamesters,
posted in the upper galleries, kept up the fusillade. No bullets
whistled by my ears, but the projectiles directed toward the arches
of the roof struck off splinters, ricocheted and fell. Several persons
were hurt. The policemen whom the Prefect sent to the highest
parts of the building found several armed men who claimed that
they had opened fire on antagonists they could not see very clearly.
Although the attitude of the clergy, the official personnel and the
congregation continued to be exemplary, I abbreviated the ceremony. Around the cathedral, the promiscuous firing had now
stopped. But as we left I was informed that at points as remote as
the Étoile, the Rond-Point and the Hôtel de Ville, the same thing
had happened at exactly the same time. There were several people
hurt, almost all as a result of stampeding crowds.

Who had fired the first shots? The investigation never discovered.
The hypothesis of snipers on the roofs, German soldiers or members of the Vichy militia, seemed highly unlikely. Despite all efforts
to find out who was responsible, no one was arrested. Furthermore,
why would the enemy have taken the chimneys for targets instead
of aiming at me, when I was passing by quite openly? It was
possible to suppose that coincidence of the firing in several parts
of Paris was purely fortuitous. I myself felt that we were concerned
with an affair inspired by a policy that wanted to justify the maintenance of a revolutionary power and an exceptional force because
of mob violence. By shooting a few bullets into the air at the
agreed-upon hour, without perhaps foreseeing the bursts of fire
that would be the consequence, an attempt had been made to
create the impression that certain threats were still lurking in the
shadows, that the resistance organizations must remain armed and
vigilant, that the "Comac," the Parisian Committee of Liberation
and the neighborhood committees were still to take the respon-

sibility for all operations concerning police action, justice and purging of collaborators in order to protect the people against dangerous conspiracies.

Naturally I intended to institute a regime of order. Moreover, the enemy made it his duty to remind us that war admits of no other law. At midnight his planes came to bombard the capital, destroying five hundred houses, setting fire to the wine market, killing or wounding a thousand persons. If Sunday, August 27, was a day of relative relaxation for the population, if I had the time to attend, amid several thousand men of the interior forces, a Mass officiated at by their chaplain, Father Bruckberger, if I could cross the city in a car, observe men's behavior and the aspect of the city itself without being too often recognized, the Second Armored Division was no less bitterly engaged from morning to night. At the cost of considerable losses, the Dio group seized the airfield at Le Bourget, and the Langlade group invested Stains, Pierrefitte and Montmagny.

As a searchlight suddenly reveals a monument, so the liberation of Paris, assured by the French themselves, and the proof given by the people of its confidence in De Gaulle dissipated the shadows that still concealed the reality of the national will. Consequently or coincidentally, there occurred a kind of upheaval in which various obstacles that still encumbered the road collapsed. The day of August 28 brought me quantities of satisfying news.

I learned, first of all, that in the northern suburbs, after our troops had taken Gonesse, the Germans were in full retreat, which put the finishing touches on the battle of Paris. Furthermore, Juin presented me the reports of the First Army, confirming the surrender of the enemy garrisons at Toulon on the 22nd, at Marseille on the 23rd, and announcing that our forces were rapidly advancing toward Lyon on both sides of the Rhone, while the Americans, following the Route Napoléon cleared by the maquisards, had already taken Grenoble. Further, the reports of our chief delegates south of the Loire—Bénouville for the Massif Central, General Pfister for the Southwest—indicated the German withdrawal, some troops trying to reach Burgundy in order to avoid being surrounded, the rest shutting themselves up in fortified pockets along the Atlantic coast, all in contact with the French forces of the interior attacking their columns and harrying their posts. Bourges-Maunoury, delegate for the Southeast, reported that the maquisards were masters of the terrain in the Alps, Ain, Drôme, Ardèche, Cantal and the Puy de Dôme, which could only accelerate the advance of Generals Patch and De Lattre. In the east and the north, lastly, our activity was increasing, while in the Ardennes, Hainaut and Brabant, the Belgian resistance was also conducting a fierce guerrilla warfare. It could be foreseen that the enemy, driven back from the Seine, pursued the length of the Rhône, assailed on every point of our soil, would not re-establish himself except in the immediate proximity of the Reich's frontier. Thus our country, whatever her wounds, was soon to find the possibility of national recovery.

On condition that it had a government which excluded any authority that paralleled my own. The iron was hot: I struck. The morning of August 28, I summoned the twenty principal leaders of the Parisian partisans, to meet them, to congratulate them, to inform them of my decision to combine the interior forces with the ranks of the regular army. Then came the secretaries general, who evidently were awaiting nothing better than their instructions from me and my ministers. Then I received the bureau of the National Council of the Resistance. In the minds of the colleagues who took their places before me, there existed two simultaneous tendencies which I received in quite distinct ways. Their pride in what they had accomplished I welcomed without reservations. But the secret intentions of certain individuals as to the direction of the state I could not admit. Now, if the popular demonstration of August 26 exposed General de Gaulle's primacy in full light of day, there were still some who clung to the project of constituting at his side and excluding him an autonomous authority, of turning the council into a permanent organism controlling the government, of entrusting to the "Comac" the military formations of the resistance, of deriving from the latter certain "patriotic" militias which would act in the "people's" behalf, though naturally in a certain direction. Furthermore, the council had adopted a "program of the C.N.R." consisting of a list of the measures to be taken in every sphere, which it proposed to brandish constantly under the executive's nose.

While acknowledging quite loftily the share my interlocutors had taken in battle, I left them in no doubt of my intentions in their regard. As soon as Paris was torn from the enemy, the National Council of the Resistance would be a part of the glorious history of the liberation, but would have no further *raison d'être* as an organ of action. The government would assume entire responsibility. Doubtless I would include within it this or that member of the council. But in that case, the latter would renounce all allegiances that were not ministerial. On the other hand, I intended to integrate the council with the Consultative Assembly, which would be arriving from Algiers and which was to be enlarged. As to the interior forces, they would make up a part of the French Army. Hence the Ministry of War would take direct charge of their personnel and their arms in proportion as they emerged from clandestinity. The "Comac" was to disappear. As for public order, it would be maintained by the police and the *gendarmerie* with, should the occasion arise, the assistance of the garrisons. The militias had no further object. The existing ones would be dissolved. I read my visitors a decree I had just signed ordering the regular incorporation of the resistance forces and appointing General Koenig, the military governor, to do what was immediately necessary in Paris.

After having made note of the accordant or protesting observations of the members of the bureau, I put an end to the audience. From it, I had drawn the conclusion that certain individuals would try to engage in various equivocations or misunderstandings in order to keep the greatest possible number of armed units in their control, that there would be formalities to complete, frictions to endure, orders to maintain, but that, in the end, the government's authority would be imposed. I was eager that the road be cleared in this quarter.

It was soon to be so with regard to the Americans. General Eisenhower paid me a visit. We congratulated each other on the happy outcome of events in Paris. I did not conceal from him, however, how dissatisfied I was with Gerow's attitude at the moment I was entering my own capital and grasping the boiling caldron in my hands. I informed the commander in chief that for reasons relating to popular morale and, ultimately, law and order I would keep the Second Armored Division at my immediate disposal for a few days. Eisenhower stated that he planned to install his headquarters at Versailles. I approved this move, believing it was advantageous to have the Allied commander in chief not lodged in Paris but useful that he be nearby. At the moment he took his leave, I expressed to this great and good leader the esteem, confidence and gratitude of the French government. Soon after, the Americans, without consulting us, published a communiqué according to which the military command, in accord with its agreements, transferred to the French administration the powers which it held in France. Of course, the Allies transferred nothing because they held nothing: they could hardly give away what they had never had. But President Roosevelt's self-esteem doubtless had its requirements, all the greater now that the United States elections were approaching and in six weeks Franklin Roosevelt would confront universal suffrage.

At nightfall, I learned of the last act of the Marshal and "chief of state." Juin brought me a communication which Admiral Auphan, former minister of Vichy, had delivered. It was a letter and a memorandum which the admiral addressed to me, informing me of the mission he had received from the Marshal and which the latter had formulated in two secret documents. The first was a so-called "constitutional" act dated September 27, 1943, appointing a college of seven members to fulfill his functions as "chief of state" if he himself were prevented from doing so. The second, dated August 11, 1944, was a delegation of power to Admiral

Auphan "to make eventual contact with General de Gaulle in his
behalf, in order to find, with regard to the French political problem at the moment of the liberation of French territory, a solution of
a nature to prevent civil war and to reconcile all Frenchmen of good
faith." The Marshal specified that in case Auphan could not refer
the matter back to himself, he trusted he would act for the nation's
best interests. But he added, "Provided that the principle of legitimacy which I incarnate be preserved."

Admiral Auphan wrote me that when he learned on August 20
that the Marshal had been taken away by the Germans, he attempted
to convene the "college." But two of the appointed members,
Weygand and Bouthillier, were being held in Germany; one, Léon
Noël, a French ambassador, who had belonged to the resistance for
four years, formally refused to enter the combination; two—
Porché, vice-president of the Council of State, and Gidel, rector
of the University of Paris—did not attend the meeting. Auphan,
finding himself alone with Caous, the procurer general of the High
Court of Appeal, decided that the "college" had given up the ghost
before being born and that he himself was henceforth the "principal depository of the Marshal's legal powers." He requested
me to receive him.

This procedure did not surprise me. I knew that since the beginning of August the Marshal, who expected to be ordered to leave
for Germany, had made contacts with various resistance leaders.
Henry Ingrand, Commissioner of the Republic at Clermont-
Ferrand, had informed me on August 14 of a visit from Captain
Oliol, the Marshal's envoy. The Marshal had proposed placing
himself under the protection of the French forces of the interior and
indicated, at the same time, that he was retiring from power.
Ingrand had replied that if the Marshal surrendered to him, the
French forces of the interior would answer for his security. But
Pétain had not pursued this plan, doubtless prevented from doing
so by the surveillance measures taken by the Germans before they
took him to Belfort and to Sigmaringen. Now his proxy presented
me with a formal request for negotiation.

What a conclusion! What a confession! Thus, in the annihilation of Vichy, Philippe Pétain turned to Charles de Gaulle. This, then, was the term of that dreadful series of capitulations in which, under pretext of "saving the furniture," servitude had been accepted. What unfathomable wretchedness brought it about that such a policy had been endorsed by the old age of a glorious military leader! Reading the text he had had referred to me, I felt simultaneously elevated in what had always been my certainty and gripped by an inexpressible sadness. *Monsieur le Maréchal!* You who had always done such great honor to your arms, you who were once my leader and my example, how had you come to this?

But what reply could I make to this communication? In such matters, sentiment could not stand in the face of the rights of state. The Marshal referred to civil war. If by that he meant the violent confrontation of two factions of the French people, the hypothesis was quite out of the question. For among those who had been his partisans, no one, now, rose up against my power. There was not, on liberated soil, one department, one city, one commune, one official, one soldier, not even one individual who professed to oppose De Gaulle out of loyalty to Pétain. As for reprisals, if certain factions of the resistance might commit retaliatory actions against the people who had persecuted them in collaboration with the enemy, it devolved upon the public authority to oppose itself to such actions, while insuring the action of justice. In this matter, no compromise was conceivable.

Above all, the condition which put Pétain in agreement with me was precisely the motive that made this agreement impossible. The legitimacy which he claimed to incarnate was denied absolutely by the Government of the Republic, not so much because he had once received the abdication of a hysterical Parliament as because he had accepted the enslavement of France, practiced an official collaboration with the invader and ordered armed opposition to the French and Allied soldiers of the liberation, while not for a single day did he permit his countrymen to fire on the Germans. Furthermore, in the mission Pétain gave to Auphan and in the adieu which the

Marshal had just addressed to the French, there was not one
sentence condemning the "armistice" or crying "Rise against the
enemy!" Yet no French government could be legitimate when it
had ceased to be independent. We, the French, had in the course
of time endured many disasters, lost provinces, paid indemnities,
but the state had never accepted the domination of a foreign power.
Even the King of Bourges, the Restoration of 1814 and that of
1815, the government and the Assembly of Versailles in 1871 had
not yielded themselves to this. When France acknowledged herself
as a power that submitted to the yoke, she was putting an end to
her own future.

A call to honor from the depths of history, as well as the instinct of the nation itself, had led me to bear responsibility for the
treasure in default of heirs: to assume French sovereignty. It was I
who held the legitimacy. It was in its name that I could call the
nation to war and to unity, impose order, law and justice, demand
from the world respect for the rights of France. In this realm, I
could not renounce, not even compromise in the slightest degree.
Without disregarding the supreme intention which inspired the
Marshal's message, without overlooking what significance there was
for the moral future of the nation in the fact that it was ultimately
toward De Gaulle that Pétain turned, the only reply I could give
him was my silence.

That night, moreover, after so much uproar, all was still around
me. It was the moment to acknowledge what had just been accomplished and to confront what was to come. Today, unity had won a
victory. Sheltered at Brazzaville, matured in Algiers, it had been
consecrated in Paris. This France, which had seemed condemned to
disaster, despair and dissension, had now the opportunities to
endure to the end of the present drama without breaking asunder,
to share the victory along with her allies, to recover her land, her
rank and her dignity. It was conceivable that the French might
remain regrouped as they were now long enough so that the categories among which they were normally distributed and which, by
reason of their objectives, always struggled to disjoin the national

cohesion might prove powerless to overcome that cohesion before the immediate goal was reached.

Having taken the measure of the task, I must gauge my own capacities. My role consisted in bending to the common interest the various elements of the nation in order to lead it to salvation; my duty, whatever capacities I might lack, was to fulfill that role as long as the crisis continued, and then, if the country willed it so, until the moment when institutions worthy of it, adapted to our times and inspired by their terrible lessons, would receive from my hands the trust of leadership.

Ahead of me, I knew, I would find along the way every group, every school, every party revived and hostile in proportion as the danger faded. There would not be a single habit or hostility, not one weakness or claim, not one attitude of surrender or self-interest that would not, first in secret, later openly, rise up against my enterprise of rallying the French in France and building a state that was just and strong. With regard to human relationships, my lot was therefore solitary. But in lifting the burden, what a lever I had in the loyalty and adherence of the people! This massive confidence, this elemental friendship which their acknowledgments lavished upon me—here was what would steel me to my task.

Gradually, the call was heard. Slowly, severely, unity was forged. Now the people and the leader, helping each other, were to begin the journey to salvation.

VOLUME III

SALVATION

1944-1946

Translated from the French by
RICHARD HOWARD

CHAPTER 1

LIBERATION

THE rhythm of the liberation was one of extreme rapidity. Six weeks after the Allies and the French had effected the breakthrough at Avranches and landed in the Midi, they reached Antwerp, were driving toward Lorraine and were penetrating the Vosges. By the end of September, except for Alsace, the Alpine passes and the pockets on the Atlantic coast, all of France was purged of the invaders. The German Army, broken by the mechanized might of the Allies, lacerated by the French resistance, was expelled from our territory in less time than it had taken, five years before, to appropriate it. Now that army took its stand only on the frontier of the Reich, where insurrection no longer paralyzed its rear. Thus, the tide, receding, suddenly revealed from one end to the other the convulsed body of France.

Consequently the innumerable and immediate problems raised by the guidance of a nation emerging from the abyss beset the government most insistently at the very moment when their solution was most arduous.

First of all, for the central authority to function normally, it must be in a position to be kept informed, to transmit its orders and to confirm their execution. Yet for many long weeks, the capital was

669

to remain without means of regular communication with the provinces. Telephone and telegraph lines had been subject to countless breaks. Radio stations had been destroyed. There were no French liaison planes on the fields pitted with shell holes. The railroads were virtually paralyzed. Of our 12,000 locomotives, 2,800 were left. No train from Paris could reach Lyons, Marseilles, Toulouse, Bordeaux, Nantes, Lille, Nancy. None could cross the Loire between Nevers and the Atlantic, or the Seine between Mantes and the Channel, or the Rhone between Lyons and the Mediterranean. As for our roads, 3,000 bridges had been blown up; scarcely 300,000 vehicles, out of the 3 million we once had, were in condition to travel; lastly, the gasoline shortage made an automobile trip something of an adventure. It would take at least two months to establish any regular exchange of orders and reports, without which the government could function only by fits and starts.

At the same time, the transportation holdup disorganized all supply services. Especially since the acknowledged stocks of food supplies, raw materials, fuels and manufactures had altogether vanished. And though a "six-month plan" based on a series of American imports had been agreed on by Algiers and Washington, how could it be put into effect when our ports were unusable? Dunkirk, Brest, Lorient, St.-Nazaire, La Rochelle, as well as the approach to Bordeaux, remained in enemy hands; and Calais, Boulogne, Dieppe, Rouen, Le Havre, Cherbourg, Nantes, Marseilles and Toulon —damaged by British and American bombings and then altogether destroyed by the German garrisons before they laid down their arms —offered nothing but ruined docks, flooded harbors, jammed floodgates and waterways choked with wrecks.

It is true that the Allies made every effort to furnish us equipment in order to re-establish roads and railroads along the strategic routes, Rouen–Lille–Brussels and Marseilles–Lyons–Nancy; that they immediately helped us restore our airports to the north, the east, and around Paris; that they quickly laid a pipeline from Cotentin to Lorraine; that, already holding the artificial ports of Arromanches and St.-Laurent-sur-Mer, they made haste to take Brest and to clear Cherbourg, Le Havre and Marseilles so that an adequate tonnage could be unloaded on our shores. But the trains and trucks in running order, the planes landing and the ships putting in were chiefly intended for the forces already in operation. Further, on the urgent request of the military command, we were obliged to furnish it a share of whatever coal was on hand at the mines, to permit it to use a certain number of our factories in working condition, and to place at its disposal an important fraction of our remaining manpower. As could have been foretold, the liberation was not going to bring any immediate material relief to a generally drained and dismembered nation.

But at least it would provide an immediate moral emancipation. This almost supernatural event, dreamed of so long and so fervently, had suddenly become a reality! At one blow, the people were released from that psychology of silence into which the constraints of four years' occupation had plunged them. Overnight, they could speak out, meet anyone they chose, come and go as they liked! With delighted astonishment, each man saw revealed perspectives he no longer had dared to hope for. But just as the convalescent forgets the crisis he has survived and imagines his health restored, so the French people, savoring the joy of their freedom, were inclined to believe that all their trials were at an end. In the immediate circumstances, the widespread sense of euphoria had its justifications. But at the same time, many permitted themselves illusions which were the cause of as many more misunderstandings.

Thus, many Frenchmen tended to identify the liberation with the end of the war. There was a temptation to regard the battles still to be waged, the losses to be sustained, the restrictions to be endured until the enemy's defeat, as empty—and therefore all the more burdensome—formalities. Misapprehending the extent of our debacle, the terrible penury we were confronting, and the servitudes the prosecution of the conflict imposed upon us, our citizens supposed that production would resume rapidly and on a large scale, that provisioning would be immediately improved, that all the elements of a quick renewal would soon be co-ordinated. The Allies were imagined, like story-book heroes, to possess inexhaustible resources and to be eager to lavish them upon a France they had fondly delivered and now desired to restore to all her former glory at their sides. As for De Gaulle, that almost legendary character who incarnated this prodigious liberation in all eyes, it was naturally assumed that he would be able to accomplish all these anticipated miracles by himself.

As for myself, having reached this poverty-stricken Paris at the end of a dramatic summer, I labored under no such illusion. I took account of the food-stocks at famine prices, remarked the threadbare clothes, the cold houses and dark windows; I passed by empty shops, shut-down factories, forsaken railroad stations; already I heard the complaints of the people, the demands of factions, the rivalries of demagogues. Certain that though we could rely on sympathy from the people, the iron-clad rule of states is to give nothing for nothing; convinced that we would regain our status only if we paid for it; evaluating the sacrifices to be made before we could seize our share of the victory and consummate even a partial recovery, I could not delude myself with fancies. Especially since I knew I was lacking any sort of talisman that would permit the nation to achieve its goal painlessly. On the other hand, I intended to apply the entire credit France had accorded me to lead her to salvation. To begin with, this meant establishing the government; it meant inspiring the support of every region, every cause; it meant uniting the troops from the Empire and the Forces of the Interior into a single army; it meant enabling the country to resume its life and its labor without yielding to the paroxysms which would only occasion further misfortunes.

Action would have to be taken at every level, to put the government in operation. Most of the Algiers "commissioners," whether they had been with me since the time of "Free France" or had joined me in North Africa, would remain ministers in Paris. But I was also determined to invite others to join the government—men, consecrated by the resistance, who had remained in Metropolitan France. Yet this alteration could not be an immediate one, for the ministers in office arrived from Algiers only turn and turn about. Four of them—Diethelm, Jacquinot, d'Astier, and Philip—had been visiting the troops of the First Army and the southern departments. Massigli had gone to London during the liberation of Paris to maintain our foreign relations more readily. Pleven had been able to join me. But the rest had been obliged to postpone their departure. As for those I selected in Metropolitan France, several had just emerged from their clandestine condition and could not come to Paris at once. It was only on September 9, two weeks after my arrival in the Rue St.-Dominique, that the government assumed its new composition.

It included two Ministers of State, President Jeanneney and General Catroux. The former, whom we had summoned from Haute-Saône where the enemy was still entrenched, was to elaborate successive measures which would direct the powers of the Republic toward its normal functioning; the latter would remain Co-ordinator of Moslem Affairs and Governor General of Algeria. François de Menthon remained Minister of Justice, André Diethelm Minister of War, Louis Jacquinot Minister of the Navy, René Pleven Minister of the Colonies, René Mayer Minister of Public Works and Transportation, René Capitant Minister of National Education, Paul Giacobbi Minister of Provisioning and Supply, Henri Frenay Minister of Prisoners, Deportees and Refugees. The Ministry of National Economy became the domain of Pierre Mendès-France, that of the Interior went to Adrien Tixier, that of Public Health to François Billoux. Eight portfolios were entrusted to men who had just emerged from the struggle: Foreign Affairs to Georges Bidault, Finance to André Lepercq, Air to Charles Tillon, Production to Robert Lacoste, Agriculture to François Tanguy-Prigent, Labor to Alexandre Parodi, Postal Services to Augustin Laurent, Information to Pierre-Henri Teitgen.

On the other hand, eight national commissioners from Algiers were no longer Council members: Henri Queuille asked to resign; René Massigli was to represent us in London, where Pierre Vienot had just died in July; Henri Bonnet would take charge of our embassy in Washington, which had finally been recognized as such by the United States; André Le Troquer became president of the Municipal Council of Paris; Emmanuel d'Astier, whom I should have preferred to divert from purely political affairs, had declined the diplomatic post that had been offered to him; André Philip, whose impetuous aptitudes were ill-adapted to the administrative framework, was not able to keep his portfolio; nor was Fernand Grenier, induced by a maneuver of his party during the battles of the Vercors Massif to adopt a public attitude contrary to the government's solidarity; and Jean Monnet, whose mission as economic negotiator with the United States became incompatible with a ministerial function once the Department of National Economy was created.

Around me, then, twenty-one ministers fell to their task with the presentiment that there would be no end to it. Hence there was an even greater necessity to specify its goal. Since June 1940, I had led France toward liberation, and the resistance had been her means. Now a new stage was at hand which involved the effort of the entire nation.

On September 12 a meeting at the Palais de Chaillot, attended by 8,000 people—National Council of the Resistance, executive committees of movements and networks, municipal council, state bodies, principal functionaries, University of Paris, representatives of management, trade unions, the press, the bar, etc.—gave me the occasion to set forth my policy. I did so all the more sharply since, in an atmosphere where the wings of chimeras were already beating, I felt obliged to call things by their names.

Having evoked "the tide of joy, pride and hope" which had swept the nation, having hailed the resistance, the Allies, and the French Army, I turned the spotlight on the obstacles still to be overcome, the efforts to be made. No complacency, no slackening could be tolerated! No latitude accorded to any organization which claimed to intervene in affairs of justice and administration independently of the state. And I turned to the burning question of the "militias." "We are at war!" I cried. "In today's battle as in those to come, we intend to participate to the fullest extent. The same will be true, to-morrow, in the case of the occupation of Germany. . . . For this, we require large units adapted to maneuver, to give battle and to triumph, in which will be incorporated the ardent youth that constitutes our Forces of the Interior. . . . All of France's soldiers are a part of the French Army, and the French Army, like France herself, must remain one and indivisible."

Taking up the question of our foreign relations, I did not fail to put the emphasis on the difficulties, whatever shock this occasioned in those among us who preferred illusion to lucidity. "We expect," I said, "that France's right to participate in the future settlement of the conflict will no longer be contested and that the official relegation inflicted upon her by her allies will give way to the same kind of relations which we have had the honor and the habit of maintaining with the other great nations for centuries. . . . We believe it is in the higher interests of mankind that the arrangements which will tomorrow settle Germany's fate should not be discussed and adopted without consulting France. . . . We believe any decision concerning Europe reached without consulting France to be a grave error. . . . We believe any determination of the political, economic and moral conditions of the earth's inhabitants after the conflict to be a foolhardy one if that determination is reached without France . . . for, after all, one hundred million loyal men live under our flag, and any large-scale human edifice will be arbitrary and ephemeral if the seal of France is not affixed to it."

To regain her status was not all. France must also be able to maintain it. This too, this especially, would not be accomplished without sacrifice, without severity. Having given an account of the ravages we had endured and the conditions hindering our recovery, I declared, "We find ourselves in an extremely difficult period, one in which liberation allows us no relief, but calls instead for the maintenance of severe restrictions, a period which demands great efforts of organization as well as those of discipline." I added that "the government intends, in this regard, to impose all necessary regulations." Then I specified the objectives the government had set itself: "To raise the workers' standard of living as the rate of production rises; to requisition or sequestrate certain public services and enterprises for the direct use of the state; to appropriate for the nation the illegal profits of those who collaborated with the enemy; to fix commodity prices and regulate commerce as long as what is produced and transportable is not equivalent to consumer demand. . . ."

Certainly these were circumstantial measures. But they were in harmony with the principles of recovery which it had been the aim of the resistance to realize—"To subordinate private interest to public advantage; to exploit the natural resources of the nation and administer them to the general advantage; to abolish coalitions of interest once and for all; finally, to permit each of France's sons and daughters to live, to work and to raise their children in security and dignity."

To conclude, I appealed "to the men and women of the resistance; and you, crusaders under the cross of Lorraine! You who are the yeast of the nation in her combat for honor and liberty, tomorrow it will be up to you to marshal France toward sacrifice and toward greatness. It is then, and only then, that the great victory of France will be won."

At this time I had spoken not of intentions formulated with an eye to the future, but of measures immediately engaging interests and individuals. Yesterday, in London or in Africa, it had been a question of what could be done. Now, in Paris, it was a matter of what we were doing. The energies of Free France had been inspired by a mystique which had necessarily dimmed in the schemes of the Algiers Committee. Now it was politics that dominated the government's actions. But were not the same imperious and contradictory realities which now confronted our leaders going to cleave ambition and interest into separate factions? Could that cohesion of feeling which the resistance had established be maintained once the national peril was past? The impressions I received from the Chaillot meeting led me to doubt it.

It is true that as I entered the hall, took my place and made my speech after Georges Bidault's eloquent introduction, I received ringing ovations. Listening only to the cheers, I might have imagined I was back in the unanimous assemblies of Albert Hall and Brazzaville or among the sympathetic audiences of Algiers, Tunis, and Ajaccio. Yet some varying tonality in the enthusiasm, a kind of self-consciousness in the applause, the signals and significant glances exchanged by the participants, the calculated and composed faces that acknowledged my remarks, reminded me that "politicians," old or new, had many nuances in their approbation. It was apparent that their dealings would be complicated, as they proceeded, by an ever greater number of reservations and conditions.

More than ever, then, I had to seek support from the French people rather than from the "elite" groups which tended to come between us. My popularity was a kind of capital with which I could pay off the disappointments that were inevitable among the ruins. To begin with, I would employ it to establish the state's authority in the provinces as I had done in Paris.

The news that reached us from a vast majority of the departments gave evidence of tremendous confusion there. Doubtless the commissioners of the Republic and the prefects appointed in advance were fulfilling their functions. But they had the greatest difficulty restoring matters and men to theirs. Too much outrage, accumulated over four years, was fermenting under the lid to avoid an explosion in the chaos following the enemy's flight and the collapse of his accomplices. Many resistance units were going to proceed with punishments and purges on their own. Armed groups, appearing out of the woods, yielded to the impulse to render justice against their persecutors without due process of law. In many places, public anger exploded in brutal reactions. Naturally, political calculation, professional rivalry and personal reprisals took advantage of the circumstances, so that irregular arrests, arbitrary fines and summary executions added their confusion to that resulting from the general destitution.

The local authorities had all the more difficulty mastering the situation since the forces at their command were desperately inadequate. Even had the *garde mobile* and the *gendarmerie* been at full force and sure of themselves, they could not have coped with the situation. And they were all the more insufficient, reduced as they were by the departure of a large number of their units into the maquis and morally inhibited by the use Vichy had made of them. Where the Army corps had passed—in Normandy, in Provence, in Paris, along the Rhone, the Saône, the Doubs—the mere presence of the troops prevented most untoward incidents. But in the regions where the regular units had not penetrated, commissioners and prefects alike found themselves without means of securing order. I could, of course, have provided those means by reassigning the forces from Africa to the interior of the territory. But that would have meant withholding the French Army from battle and thereby compromising our participation in the victory. To this disastrous renunciation I preferred the risk of more or less violent explosions.

The risk, actually, would have been a limited one if the Communist party had not made it a policy to exploit these disturbances in order to seize power in the provinces as it had tried to do in Paris. Though government orders prescribed the formation in each department of a single Committee of Liberation, composed of representatives of every movement, party and trade union, and designed to furnish the prefect provisional assistance, there had appeared in various localities, enterprises, public services and administrations a swarm of committees which claimed to set the pace, control the mayors, employers and directors, and to hunt down the guilty and the suspect. The Communists, skillful and united in aims, employing various labels, and utilizing the sympathies and loyalties which many of them had won from various milieus during the conflict, were careful to provoke and sustain these splinter groups strengthened by arms. The "Comac,"* playing on the uncertainty as to the respective powers of the government and the National Council of the Resistance, continued secretly to delegate emissaries, give orders and confer ranks. I decided to make immediate visits to the most sensitive points to give the national governmental machine a start in the right direction. A two-months' series of trips was to put me in contact with the provinces, while in the intervals I directed the government's work in Paris.

On September 14, accompanied by André Diethelm, Minister of War, I landed at the Bron airfield, still littered with the scrap of its demolished hangars. Ten days before, the city of Lyons had been liberated by the French First Army and the Americans. It was now making every effort toward recovery, though the problem was arduous. All the city's bridges over the Saône and the Rhone had been destroyed save the Homme de la Roche and that of the Guillotière, and they could be used only by pedestrians. The Vaise, Brotteaux and Perrache stations and all the railroads serving the city were out of commission. The industrial suburbs, particularly Villeurbanne, bared their gutted factories. But the enthusiasm of the populace made a vivid contrast to these ruins.

The Commissioner of the Republic, Yves Farge, a resistance leader in a region distinguished for its action against the enemy, had his hands full. Imaginative and ardent, he readily adapted himself to what was unprecedented in the situation, but avoided taking extreme action. I ordered him to enforce the same policy elsewhere. Accorded in the streets the acclamations of every group, receiving at the prefecture the functionaries and the *corps constitués* presented to me by Prefect Longchambon, making contact at the *hôtel de ville,* with the "temporary" mayor, Justin Godard—"until Édouard Herriot returns," he told me—the municipal council, Cardinal

* Communist Action Committee.—TR.

Gerlier, the representatives of industry, commerce, the trade unions, the liberal professions and the workers, I perceived that the Lyonnais as a whole had no intention of overthrowing the national order. Given certain changes, spectacular but ill-defined, and certain chastisements, exemplary but vague, they hoped, instead, for order.

The next day I reviewed the Forces of the Interior. Colonel Descour, who had distinguished himself in the maquis battles and, more recently, in the recapture of Lyons, and who now was in command of the military district, presented a body of troops that were as moved by the occasion as I was. It was touching to see them attempting to assume the aspect of regular units despite their disparities; the strongest military tradition impregnated this self-created force. I left Lyons convinced that the government, provided it truly governed, would here surmount all obstacles, and that order would prevail since the state was reappearing at the nation's head.

At Marseilles, however, the atmosphere was ominous. I arrived the morning of the fifteenth, accompanied by three ministers— Diethelm, Jacquinot, and Billoux. The destruction of the Old Harbor sector by the Germans in 1943, then the Allied bombings, and finally the battle of the preceding August, had completely demolished large areas of the city, the piers and the harbor. In addition, the channel was full of mines and every means of unloading onto the ruined quays had been blown up by the enemy. Of course the public services, aided by the Americans who wanted to use this base, were busy clearing the harbor. But the damages were such that it was doubtful that the port could be used for a long time to come. As for the populace, provisioned only at the cost of great effort, and extremely badly, it was combating destitution at every turn. Furthermore, an atmosphere of tension and almost of oppression floated over Marseilles, caused by a series of unwarranted actions. The Communists, taking advantage of old local dissensions and the persecutions inflicted by Vichy agents, had established an anonymous dictatorship in Marseilles which made arrests on its own account and even performed executions without the public authority's decisive opposition.

In this regard, the Commissioner of the Republic, Raymond Aubrac, who had distinguished himself in the resistance, found it difficult to adopt the psychology of high officialdom. To him, to the regional prefects and to their colleagues gathered at the prefecture, I indicated in the proper tone that the government expected them to do their job, that henceforth it was a matter of applying the laws and decrees, in a word, of administrating, and that they were the responsible parties, to the exclusion of all others. The Forces of the Interior had valiantly aided General Monsabert's troops in taking Marseilles. I congratulated them upon this while they passed in review. It was easy to see which units—the majority—desired to be sent into battle in Alsace and which, subject to a secret allegiance, wished to remain where they were. I ordered General Chadebec de Lavalade, recalled from the Levant to command the military district, to give satisfaction as soon as possible to the former and to dissolve the latter; I instructed the Minister of War to send a regiment from Algeria to Marseilles at once to facilitate matters.

Nowhere better than in this great city, chaotic and stricken as it was, did I feel that only the resistance movement could determine France's recovery, but that this supreme hope would certainly founder if liberation were confused with disorder. Besides, the very authorities which, in Marseilles, endorsed compromise showed themselves quite pleased with my own firmness. It must be said that the appearance of General de Gaulle speaking to the crowds gathered in the Place de Muy and the Rue St.-Ferréol, or crossing the Cannebière, or received at the *hôtel de ville* by Mayor Gaston Defferre, aroused a wave of popular enthusiasm which made every problem appear simpler. Most likely they were, in fact, as soon as they seemed so.

During the afternoon, a quick flight took me to Toulon. Nothing could surpass the spectacle of desolation offered here by the arsenal, the Quai Cronstadt, the entirely demolished neighboring districts and the hulls of ships scuttled in the roadstead. Yet nothing, by comparison, was more comforting than the aspect of the naval squadron stationed out to sea for the review. Three divisions were presented to me, under the commands of Admiral Auboyneau, Admiral Jaujard and Captain Lancelot respectively. They included: the battleship *Lorraine;* the cruisers *Georges Leygues, Duguay-Trouin, Émile Bertin, Jeanne d'Arc, Montcalm, Gloire;* the light cruisers *Fantasque, Malin, Terrible;* and some thirty torpedo boats, submarines, escort ships and minesweepers. Accompanied by Louis Jacquinot, Minister of the Navy, Admiral Lemonnier, Chief of the General Staff and Commander of the Naval Forces, and Admiral Lambert, the Maritime Prefect, I boarded the escort vessel *La Pique* and slowly passed down the line. Reviewing the forty vessels arranged in fighting trim, receiving the salutes their officers addressed me from the bridge of each, hearing the cheers of the crews lining the rails, I felt that our navy had swallowed its disappointments and recovered its hopes.

On September 16, I was in Toulouse, a city considerably disturbed. Dissensions had always been marked in our southwest departments. But Vichy's policies and the drama of the occupation had raised them to fever pitch. Besides, it happened that the maquis, numerous in the region, had waged a bitter battle. Hence there were grave disturbances and many accounts to settle. Especially since enemy troops operating in Aquitaine had been guilty of particularly cruel brutalities, not without odious complicity. Further, among the Forces of the Interior, the best units were already rushing for Burgundy to join the First Army. The most heterogeneous groups remained on the spot. Finally, the immediate proximity of Spain increased the tension still more. For many Spaniards, having sought refuge since the Civil War in the Gers, Ariège and Haute-Garonne departments, had recently joined the maquis. Now they were leaving it, proposing to return to their country in arms. Naturally the Communists, advantageously placed and well organized, stirred up these sparks in order to take matters in hand. They had partially succeeded.

I found the Commissioner of the Republic at grips with the encroachments of certain leaders of the Forces of the Interior. Pierre Bertaux, who directed an important resistance network, had been designated to occupy the position whose incumbent, Jean Cassou, had been seriously wounded during the riots that marked the German withdrawal. At present, Bertaux was trying to hold the reins of command; but Colonel Asher, alias Ravanel, leader of the Haute-Garonne maquis, had assumed command of the military district and exercised an authority as vast as it was vague.

Around Ravanel, leaders of the armed units constituted something like a soviet. The members of this council claimed to accomplish the necessary purges with their own men, while the *gendarmerie* and the *garde mobile* were confined to remote barracks. It was true that the Chief of the General Staff, Colonel Noetinger, an officer of wide experience, was attempting to divert these abuses into the administrative labyrinth. But he did not always succeed. Furthermore, a Spanish "division" was forming in the region with the loudly publicized purpose of marching on Barcelona. To top it all, an English general known as "Colonel Hilary" and introduced into the Gers maquis by the British services, held under his command several units which took orders only from London.

On the morning of the seventeenth, with calculated formality, I passed all military elements in review. By making direct contact with the maquisards, I hoped to rouse in each man the soldier he wished to be. As I approached the ranks, a certain quiver of expectation made it clear that I had been understood. Then Colonel Ravanel presented the entire corps. The parade was a picturesque one. At its head, bayonets crossed, marched a Russian battalion consisting of men from the "Vlassov Army" who had deserted from the German side in time to join our own resistance. Then came the Spanish troops, led by their own generals. After these passed the French Forces of the Interior. The sight of their improvised flags and banners, their concern to organize themselves into regulation sections, companies and battalions, the effort they had made to give their clothing a uniform appearance, and above all the attitudes, the glances, the tears of the men who passed before me, showed the high degree of virtue and effectiveness in military order. But there was also, with regard to me, the same kind of plebiscite which was manifested everywhere.

The day before, I had been given a similar testimonial at the prefecture and at the *hôtel de ville* where I received the officers and notables, first among them the valiant archbishop, Monsignor Saliège. As for the crowd that shouted out its joy in the Place du Capitole where it had gathered to hear me, or lined the streets in two hedges of acclamation, it had provided the same demonstration. I was, of course, not at all sure that this adherence would compensate for all we lacked to assure public order. At least I could hope it would enable us to prevent either the dictatorship of a few or general anarchy.

Before leaving Toulouse, I rescinded the order that kept the *gendarmerie* in barracks and restored these brave men to their normal service. I decided to appoint General Collet, recalled from Morocco, to the command of the military sector. I informed the Spanish leaders that the French government would not forget the services they and their men had rendered in our maquis, but that the access to the Pyrenees frontier was forbidden them. Moreover, following my instructions, the First Army had dispatched a good-sized unit to Tarbes and Perpignan in order to insure the patrolling of the Pyrenees passes. As for "Colonel Hilary," within two hours he was sent to Lyons, and from there immediately returned to England.

In Bordeaux, on September 17, I found an atmosphere of strain. The Germans had retreated but remained in the vicinity, entrenched at Royan and on the Graves peninsula, cutting off access to the port and threatening to return. Under the command of Colonel Adeline, the Bordeaux Forces of the Interior and those of the surrounding region were brought into contact with the enemy on both shores of the Gironde, while Colonel Druille, commander of the military sector, attempted to reinforce their supply service and officer force. Actually, the German Admiral Meyer, while evacuating the Bordeaux region and occupying the coastal batteries, had led us to believe he was about to surrender. He was still negotiating at the moment of my arrival. But it was soon apparent that this was only a ruse of the enemy's in order to withdraw without damage. Since the Germans had a considerable stock of material at their disposal and since our Forces of the Interior were neither well organized nor well enough armed to endure a pitched battle, Bordeaux tempered its joy at being free with its fear of ceasing to be so. Besides, many grievances which had accumulated during the occupation of a city whose Mayor, Marquet, was a notorious collaborator were brought to light. And in this troubled atmosphere operated various armed groups which refused to obey the official authorities.

Here as elsewhere, I applied myself to consecrating these authorities. Gaston Cusin, Commissioner of the Republic, a man full of good sense and presence of mind, presented to me the customary parade of functionaries, officers and delegations at the prefecture. The archbishop, Monsignor Feltin, was first among the visitors. From the same balcony where Gambetta had harangued the crowd in 1870, I addressed the Bordelais. Then I went to the *hôtel de ville* where the new mayor, Fernand Audeguil, was waiting for me, and drove through the various sectors of the city. Finally, on the Intendance Parade Grounds, I inspected those Forces of the Interior still under arms. Almost all expressed a co-operative attitude on which I complimented them. To some leaders who appeared recalcitrant, I offered the immediate choice of two alternatives: to submit to the orders of the Colonel in command of the sector, or to go to prison. All preferred the former. As I left Bordeaux, it seemed to me that the ground had grown firmer under our feet.

I headed for Saintes in order to make contact there with Colonel Adeline's troops. The department, beneath the flags of liberation which appeared at every window, was in a constant state of alarm. For the Germans were occupying, on the one hand, Royan and the Île d'Oléron, and on the other La Rochelle and Ré. They had established themselves there under heavy fortification, awaiting the intervention of the major Allied units. General Chevance-Bertin, appointed during the tumult of those first days to co-ordinate the actions of our southwestern Forces of the Interior, had impressed Admiral Schirlitz, commander of the La Rochelle pocket, to the point of determining him to evacuate Rochefort. But days passed without the Germans seeing before them anything but our partisans, completely without heavy arms, cannon, armored units, or planes. From one moment to the next, the enemy might resume the offensive. As for our own men, banded together as they had been in the maquis, they infiltrated from the Gironde, Vienne, Dordogne, and both Charente departments, eager to fight but without the equipment necessary to open a front. Besides, lacking services, supplies and transport, they were living on what was available on the spot. Hence a frequent confusion aggravated by the abuses of those leaders who considered that the hierarchy applied no higher than themselves. Finally, the interventions of the "Comac" and its agents made their effects felt. Jean Schuhler, Commissioner of the Republic for the Poitiers region, Prefect Vaudreuil and the mayors of the region were confronted by many problems.

Colonel Adeline applied himself to clearing up the confusion. In contact with the two German pockets of Royan and La Rochelle, he installed communications posts, constituted units that were as regular as possible, and tried to organize their supply service. When this grouping received arms and assumed its consistency, attack could be planned. In Saintes, I passed in review several thousand poorly equipped but eager men. The parade was impressive. I then summoned the heterogeneously trained officers, most wearing improvised insignia but all proud, and justifiably so, of being there voluntarily and thrilled to be gathered around De Gaulle who, beneath a composed serenity of countenance, felt no less moved than they. I told them what I had to say, and then I left this force-in-the-making, resolved to conclude the struggles of the Atlantic coast in French victory.

Orléans was the last stage of this journey. With a shudder at the sight of the ruins, I drove through the massacred city. The Commissioner of the Republic, André Mars, explained the problems he was patiently confronting. Yet tried as it was, this sector was not suffering many outbreaks. In contrast with the inhabitants of the Garonne, the people of the Loire seemed quite temperate. It must be said that Colonels Bertrand and Chomel, commanding the Forces of the Interior of La Beauce, Berri, and Touraine, had organized them into regular battalions, then led them in brilliant engagements against the German troops withdrawing south of the Loire. This time, the maquisards, disciplined and self-assured, served as a guarantee of order. When I saw the splendid detachment which presented arms on the Bricy parade grounds, I thought sadly of what the resistance forces could have been had Vichy not prevented the military cadres from taking their places at the head of these young troops everywhere. I returned to the capital on the evening of September 18.

On September 25, after spending two days with the First Army, I went to Nancy, which General Patton's troops had just liberated. In Lorraine, the invader had never been anything but the enemy. Hence there was no political problem in the region. Law and order ran no risk of infringement; civil duties and rights seemed quite natural. On that day, the cheers of the crowd in the Rues de Mirecourt, de Strasbourg, St.-Dizier, St.-Georges and des Dominicains, by which I crossed the departmental capital, and later in the Place Stanislas, where I spoke from the balcony of the *hôtel de ville,* the addresses of Commissioner of the Republic Chailley-Bert and Mayor Prouvé, the speeches of the delegations, the attitude of the 2,000 maquisards whom their leader, Colonel Grandval, presented to me, bore witness to this ravaged region's faith in France, though part of it was still in German hands.

Back in Paris, I left again on September 30, accompanied by Ministers Tixier, Mayer and Laurent, this time for Flanders. We passed through Soissons and St.-Quentin, where Pierre Pène, Commissioner of the Republic, guided us through the rubble of these demolished cities. In Lille, François Closon, his colleague for the Nord and Pas-de-Calais departments, was trying to furnish means of work to an entire populace which had lost them. No sooner on the scene, I was struck by the dramatic and urgent nature of the problem of the workers' subsistence in the region. During the occupation the working classes had been forced to accept wages which the enemy's orders kept fixed at the lowest possible rate. And now many workers found themselves out of work while the factories were without coal, the workshops without fuel. Further, provisioning had fallen beneath the vital minimum. Crossing the city of my birth, cheered by the Lillois, I saw too many faces whose smiles effaced neither their pallor nor their emaciation.

Sentiment and reflection had already convinced me that the liberation of the country must be accompanied by a profound social transformation. But in Lille I discerned its absolute necessity stamped on the faces of the people. Either there would be an official and rapid move to institute a marked change in the conditions of the working people, and profound limitations upon financial privilege, or the embittered and suffering mass of workers would founder upon those disturbances which risked depriving France of what remained of her substance.

On Sunday October 1, having attended the Mass celebrated by Cardinal Liénart in the Église St.-Michel, visited the *hôtel de ville,* where I was met by Mayor Cordonnier, having passed in review the Forces of the Interior in the Place de la République, and received the authorities, committees and notables, I informed the crowd gathered before the prefecture on what foundations the government was undertaking to establish the nation's economic recovery: "State control of the nation's economic resources; . . . security and dignity assured to each worker." The impassioned swell that swept through the multitude on hearing these promises assured me my words had touched them to the quick.

On the way back to Paris, I visited the Lens mines. The damage to the installations, the absence of half the miners, the disturbance of the personnel, maintained the yield at a level well below average. Counting coal alone, barely a third of the prewar yield was produced. To re-establish production, it was obvious that a far-reaching reform was needed to alter morale and, further, large-scale operations involving credit which the national collectivity alone was in a position to provide. The only solution was to make that collectivity the owner of the coal mines. I headed for the capital by way of Arras, my resolutions made.

A week later I was in Normandy, a province that surpassed all others in devastation. The ruins here seemed all the more tragic since this was a region famous for its wealth, ancient and modern. Accompanied by Mendès-France and Tanguy-Prigent, conducted by Bourdeau de Fontenay, Commissioner of the Republic, and General Legentilhomme, commander of the military sector, I visited Le Havre, Rouen, Évreux, Lisieux, and Caen, or more precisely their ruins. If, a few days before, my contacts with the inhabitants of the northern departments had confirmed my conviction that the national effort required great social changes, the extent of the damages endured by Normandy strengthened my intention to put the state back on its feet, a condition *sine qua non* of the country's recovery.

Besides, in contrast with the fallen cities, the countryside presented a heartening spectacle. In August, in the middle of battle, means had been found to bring in the harvests. Although the villages and farms had suffered heavily, and despite everything the farmers lacked in the way of equipment, there were cultivated fields and cared-for cattle everywhere. In Neubourg, the farmers I addressed seemed resolved to keep their shirt sleeves rolled up. This persistence of the French farmers cast a favorable light on the prospects of national provisioning and constituted an essential element of recovery for the future.

On October 23, I received the same impression crossing Brie and Champagne. Once I left Boissy-St.-Léger, the fields, stretching toward the horizon, appeared under their eternal productive aspect. As before, a wilderness of haystacks heralded Brie-Comte-Robert. Provins was still surrounded by tillage for wheat and sugar beets. There were as many regular furrows and no more fallow than before, in the plains of Romilly-sur-Seine. The rain falling on Troyes when I entered the city disappointed Marcel Grégoire, Commissioner of the Republic, and the townspeople who had gathered to express their joy by cheers, but as usual delighted the farmers. Sleek cattle still grazed in the pastures of Vendeuvre and Bar-sur-Aube. At Colombey-les-deux-Églises, I made a stop. The townspeople, gathered around Mayor Demarson, greeted me ecstatically. Thrilled by the liberation, they were preparing to take every advantage of it to increase the productivity of their fields. As I reached Chaumont, where the official reception party of the Haute-Marne department was awaiting me, it was with a sense of solace that I watched night fall over this faithful and familiar countryside.

Having paid another visit to the First Army from here, I returned to Paris by way of Dijon. The great city had suffered only relatively light damages, but was still excited at having witnessed the invader's downfall. While the streets and squares resounded with cheers, the *corps constitués* were presented to me in the Ducal Palace by Commissioner of the Republic Jean Mairey—replacing Jean Bouhey, seriously wounded during the liberation of the city—and Canon Kir, the popular and truculent mayor. General Giraud, who had returned to his family in the Burgundian capital, was first among the notables. "How things have changed!" he said to me. "True enough —for things," I thought. But as I looked at the noisy and excited crowd, I doubted if such was the case for the French.

On November 4, 5 and 6, I traveled through the Alpine departments. There had been fighting everywhere and there was fighting still at the approaches to the passes into Italy. Our mountains, with their passionately freedom-loving inhabitants, had furnished the resistance many strongholds and many fighters. At present, life was beginning to resume its normal course despite great difficulties of provisioning, the problems of action led by Moroccan troops and Alpine maquisards against the enemy, and incidents precipitated by clandestine fighters who wanted to render their own justice. Accompanied by Ministers Diethelm and de Menthon, Commissioner of the Republic Farge, and Generals Juin and de Lattre, I went first to Ambérieu. Next came Annecy and Albertville where I passed in review the Dody division and the Tabors. Chambéry, overflowing with enthusiasm, gave me the measure of Savoyard loyalty. Finally, I entered Grenoble.

The ardor that swept over the "Allobroges"* in the Place de la Bastille and along the Boulevard Gambetta, which I covered on foot, and in the Place Rivet, where the crowd gathered to hear the speeches, was indescribable. I presented Mayor LaFleur with the Cross of the Liberation on behalf of the city of Grenoble. Then the 27th Alpine Division passed in review. I saluted it with particular satisfaction, for, eager to assure France the mountain enclaves formerly in the possession of Italy and knowing that, as far as the Allies were concerned, we would obtain them only by taking them, I had plans for this growing force. On November 6 I was in Paris.

Thus, in several weeks, I had covered a great deal of the territory, been seen by ten million Frenchmen in the appanage of power and among demonstrations of national adherence, delivered on the spot the urgent measures of authority, shown to those in office that the state had a head, revealed to the scattered elements of our forces that their only future lay in unity, their only duty in discipline. But how harsh the reality of the French situation appeared! What I had seen, beneath the speeches, the cheers and the flags, left me with

* A people of Gaul, inhabitants of the region of Dauphiné and Savoy. —TR.

the impression of enormous material damage and of a profound rift in the nation's political, administrative, social and moral structure. It was clear that under these conditions, the people, delighted though they were by their liberation, would still have to endure long and arduous trials which party demagoguery and Communist ambition would not fail to exploit for their own purposes.

But I had also remarked, in the provinces as in Paris, the enthusiasm expressed in my regard. Instinctively the nation discerned that the confusion of the moment threatened it with anarchy and ultimate dictatorship if I were not there to serve as its focus and guide. Today it pledged itself to De Gaulle to escape subversion as yesterday it had counted on him to drive out the invader. By this token I considered myself reinvested by liberated Frenchmen with the same signal and unprecedented responsibility which I had assumed during the whole of their servitude. Such would be the case until the day when, all immediate danger averted, facility and faction would once again sunder the French people.

Hailed by the voice of the people, recognized without reservation if not without murmurs by every political group, the legitimacy of this public trust was never contested for a moment. Administration, magistracy and educational system showed no more reticence with regard to my authority than the armies. The Council of State, now headed by President Cassin, served as an example of this complete loyalty. The Audit Office followed suit. Wherever I made an appearance, the clergy promptly paid its official respects. On September 20 I had received Cardinal Suhard and been assured of the episcopate's moral support. Through M. Georges Duhamel, its permanent secretary, the Académie Française sought my support. Not even the representatives of previous regimes withheld the signs of their adherence. The Count of Paris, inspired by national concern, wrote that he was sending me an authorized emissary. Prince Napoleon, an exemplary maquisard and a captain in the Chasseurs Alpins, came to offer me his support. General Giraud, arriving from Algeria where he had escaped a fanatic's bullet, immediately offered his services. The former supporters of Vichy capitulated before the evidence. Pétain, in Germany, kept silence, and those functionaries, diplomats, military men and journalists who had assiduously served him now lavished their obeisances and justifications with respect to the government. Finally, M. Albert Lebrun added to the general approval that of the sad ghost of the Third Republic.

I received him on October 13. "I have always been, I am still," the President declared, "in full agreement with what you are doing. Without you, all was lost. Thanks to you, all can be saved. Personally, I could not express myself in any other way than by this visit, which I request you to make public. It is true that I have not formally resigned. But to whom would I have sent my resignation, since there no longer existed a National Assembly qualified to replace me? But I wish you to be certain that you can count on my total support."

We spoke of the events of 1940. Albert Lebrun referred with disappointment to that June 16 when he accepted M. Paul Reynaud's resignation and appointed the Marshal to form a new cabinet. With tears in his eyes, raising his arms to heaven, he admitted his mistake. "What put me on the wrong road," he said, "along with most of the other ministers, was Weygand's attitude. He was so categorical in his insistence on the armistice! He declared so peremptorily that there was nothing else to be done! And yet I believed—like Reynaud, Jeanneney, Herriot, Mandel, and you yourself—that we should go to Africa, that we could continue the war with our army there, the forces we still had means to send there, our undamaged fleet, our empire, our allies. But the Council yielded to Weygand's vehement arguments. What could we do? His reputation, his prestige were so immense! What a terrible thing it is when, in times of extreme danger, it is the generals who refuse to fight!"

President Lebrun took his leave. I shook his hand with compassion and cordiality. Essentially, as chief of state, he had lacked two things: He was not a chief, and there was no state.

While the nation's passions crystallized, Allied military action continued in the north and east. Eisenhower, applying his principal force on his left flank, intended to traverse Belgium quickly, then cross the Rhine near its mouth to seize the Ruhr and with it victory. This was the mission entrusted, at the end of August, to General Montgomery, who was given maximum aviation support. In the center, General Bradley was to reach the Rhine between Düsseldorf and Mainz, linking his movement with that of the armies in the north. As for the French First Army and the American Seventh, ordered to combine under General Devers' orders, they would drive north from the Mediterranean to occupy the right wing of the Allied position and approach the Rhine through Alsace. It was my wish, of course, that the advance take place as soon as possible, that the Allied armies push on to the heart of Germany, and that French forces play a major role in the operations. This is what I wrote Eisenhower on September 6, urging him to accelerate the movement of our First Army, putting the 2nd Armored Division at his disposal, and informing him of the French government's desire to see its troops penetrate the German territory at the same time as the Americans and the British. But the offensive, speedily conducted until the frontier was approached, was stopped before it reached enemy territory.

As a matter of fact, in the Low Countries, the Ardennes, Lorraine and the Vosges, the adversary found means of re-establishing his line of battle. Hitler himself, whose prestige as well as his health had suffered from the preceding July's assassination attempt, now resumed the upper hand. Discounting the effect of the "secret weapons"—robot planes, V-2 rockets, new tanks, perhaps even atom bombs—which the Reich was feverishly preparing, the Fuehrer planned to resume the offensive and obtained a supreme vote of confidence from the German people. Moreover, the Allies, reduced to increasingly precarious supply services the farther they advanced, found that the lack of fuel, shells and replacements greatly hampered their operations.

This was particularly true in the case of our First Army. As for the forces marching north from the Midi, the Allied command had foreseen a difficult progress. It was believed that the fortified German strongholds of Toulon and Marseilles could be taken only after several weeks' fighting, that afterward the necessity of covering themselves along the entire Italian frontier would force Patch and De Lattre to accept setbacks and delays, and lastly that the German Nineteenth and First Armies, totaling ten divisions, the former occupying Provence, the latter Aquitaine, Languedoc and Limousin, would be in a position to obstruct the French and American forces for a long time against the Alpine foothills, in many points along the Rhone valley, and in the Massif Central. This is why plans for transporting troops and matériel from Africa, Corsica and Italy, as well as for subsequent supply services from the Mediterranean coast to the major units, involved prolonged delays. As it turned out, however, the forces of Generals de Lattre and Patch advanced at a rate which invalidated all such plans. The other side of the coin, for our victorious troops, was a continual lack of gasoline and munitions.

The French First Army, which had landed its first units at St.-Tropez and its environs on August 15, was, by the twenty-eighth, in complete possession of Toulon and by the thirtieth held all of Marseilles. It had captured 40,000 prisoners and mountains of weapons and matériel. General Patch's initial intention, since it was his job to co-ordinate forces in the Midi, had consisted of moving the Americans directly north, while the French, once they held the two major Mediterranean ports, would assure a rear cover for their allies along the Alpine passes. But General de Lattre, still glowing with the victories won in Toulon and Marseilles, was not satisfied with the secondary mission anticipated for him. He intended to move up on the American army's right and left flanks and then advance with them. I had, of course, supported this view. Patch himself, now full of regard for the French First Army, adopted our suggestion with good grace.

Hence our IInd Corps, under Monsabert and consisting, at first, of Du Vigier's and Brosset's divisions, crossed the Rhone at Avig-

non, then, operating on the eastern bank, drove the enemy out of
Lyons on the second and third of September. Shortly afterward, in
the Autun region, the left wing of this corps engaged the rear guard
of the German First Army, which was retreating through the Massif Central in an attempt to clear itself a road to Burgundy. But the
trap was sprung by Du Vigier's division, so fast had the latter advanced. After four days of desperate fighting, the last enemy echelons, with our southwest Forces of the Interior on their heels as well
as those of Berri, could find no way out and finally capitulated.
However their leader, General Elster, his conscience horrified at
the notion of surrendering to the French, had contacted the American officers posted at Orléans. On September 11, he surrendered to
them the 22,000 men still under his orders. On the same day, Du
Vigier liberated Dijon. The next day, the Brosset division, having
become the left wing of De Lattre's army, joined up at Montbard
with Leclerc, who had arrived from Paris on Bradley's right wing.
On September 13, Langres was taken by troops of the IInd Corps
and the Haute-Marne maquis. After which, General de Monsabert's
advance guard approached the upper Saône from Jussey and Port-
sur-Saône.

During this time, the Americans had marched at the same speed
along the Grenoble–Bourg–Besançon route, forcing a crossing of
the Rhone between Lyons and Ambérieu. But this entire position
had to be covered along the Alps, since Marshal Kesselring's
troops, still entrenched in northern Italy, occupied the passes to
France and were moving into the Hautes-Alpes, Savoie and Haute-
Savoie departments, threatening our communications there. It was
true that the local Forces of the Interior were relentlessly attacking
the German detachments and the Italian Fascist units operating on
the French border. But this flanking action had to be completed. To
do so we employed one American division and Dody's 2nd Moroccan Division. The latter, aided by the Forces of the Interior and by
the Moroccan Tabors, had taken Briançon, Modane, and Bourg-
St.-Maurice.

On September 5, General Béthouart assumed command of the Ist Army Corps and deployed it on the Rhone between Ambérieu and the Swiss border, on the Americans' right wing. Initially having at his disposal Guillaume's 3rd North African Division and Magnan's 9th Colonial Division, he pushed across the Jura and, on September 12, reached the Doubs valley.

Thus ended the extraordinary pursuit in which the French and Americans had covered over 700 kilometers in three weeks. They would have moved more quickly still, if the lack of fuel had not constantly delayed them. Gasoline was laboriously unloaded in Marseilles, Nice and Toulon. Then it had to be delivered to the lines. Since the railways on both banks of the Rhone had been destroyed, only convoys of trucks assured provisioning—for the French First Army an average of 1,500 metric tons a day. Besides, the American services, having to divide supplies between Patch and De Lattre, were inclined, as was only human, to grant priority to our allies. It can be imagined what fits of impatience, following upon hours of enthusiasm, the French troops, general staffs, and commanding general suffered when they found themselves deprived of the success whose occasion they saw before them. The same lack of fuel caused three major units, the 9th Colonial Division, the 4th Moroccan Division, and the 5th Armored Division, as well as numerous reserve units, to lag behind the bulk of the First Army over long periods.

These setbacks must be taken into account in any fair reckoning of our progress from the Mediterranean to our entry into Alsace. On the other hand, our advance was greatly facilitated by the action of the maquisards. The hampering action the latter inflicted on the enemy, the fact that they had gradually made themselves masters of a large proportion of the routes to be covered, the support they furnished the regular units, had counted for a great deal in this overpowering result. On September 12, at the end of this great pursuit, 120,000 Germans were in French captivity, as many taken by the First Army as by the Forces of the Interior and by the 2nd Armored

Division. This was a third of all the prisoners captured by all the Allied armies.

On September 13, General John Lewis, assigned to me by Eisenhower, brought me a letter from the Supreme Commander. The latter informed me that the Allied position was now secure from Switzerland to the North Sea; the French First Army and the American Seventh constituting henceforth the Southern Army Group. Within this group, the Americans were to form the left wing and head for Saverne and later Strasbourg. As for the French, they were to regroup on the right wing around Vesoul, take Belfort and finally Colmar. Eisenhower asked my consent to this use of our forces. I gave it to him on September 21, considering it suitable that the French should have their own zone of action, just as the British and the Americans had theirs, and regarding it as proper that this zone be Alsace. However, I informed the Supreme Commander that I reserved one condition in the case of the 1st Free French Division—the privilege of recalling it to Paris in case of necessity. Further, I invited Eisenhower to send one of our divisions to Bordeaux as soon as possible in order to take Royan and Graves. The great port would thereby be cleared and we could use it for provisioning all of France. Lastly, I indicated to the Supreme Commander that there was every reason to send a major French unit toward Strasbourg.

This was to be the Leclerc division. After having kept it in Paris for several days, I had once again put it at the disposal of the Allied High Command on September 6. Now, I wanted to see it operating with the American Seventh Army. As a matter of fact, the Alsatian capital was Patch's objective. For obvious national reasons, I wished it to be liberated by French troops, and I had no doubt that Leclerc, once he was properly situated, would be able to find an opportunity to do so. The 2nd Armored Division therefore continued to operate in the American sector.

But there was every indication that the capture of Strasbourg would not occur in the immediate future. The German Nineteenth Army had solidly entrenched itself on the slopes of the Vosges. Its leader General Wiese, whose troops withdrawn from Provence were reinforced by units from the interior, was in control of the entire region. Fierce fighting was to succeed the triumphant rout without transition. And such was to be the case along the entire Allied front. At the mouth of the Meuse, the offensive began by Montgomery on September 20 ended in failure. In Lorraine and in Luxembourg, Bradley, too, had to call his offensive to a halt. It was clear that on the western front the breakthrough would be postponed for several months. There was no reason for thinking it would come any sooner in the east, for if the Russians had occupied Rumania and Bulgaria, thrown back the Germans from a large part of Poland and Yugoslavia, and established a foothold in Hungary and the Baltic States, they had still not penetrated the Reich itself at any point.

That the war was to continue was certainly tragic from the point of view of losses, damages and expenses which we French would still have to endure. But, from the viewpoint of France's higher interests—which is something quite different from the immediate advantage of the French—I did not regret it. For with the war dragging on, our aid would be necessary in the battle of the Rhine and of the Danube, as had been the case in Africa and in Italy. Our position in the world and, still more, the opinion that our own people would have of themselves for many generations to come depended on this fact. Furthermore, the delays to come before the cessation of hostilities would permit us to value what was our due at its true worth. Lastly, what an opportunity this supreme phase offered to national unity, for now every Frenchman would be subjected to the same trial, no longer divided, as they had been yesterday, into the free Empire and oppressed Metropolitan France, but henceforth placed in identical conditions and governed by a single power! To begin with, we were able to resolve in time the problem of our military organization, burdened with political commitments as it was—in short, to cast our forces into a whole, whatever their origins.

In the First Army, fragmentary attempts had been made in this direction. One way or another, a certain pairing-off had been established between the African divisions and the maquisard groups. By September 20, more than 50,000 men from the Forces of the Interior were already participating in General de Lattre's operations; 50,000 more were preparing to do the same. Hence, with the regular troops had been bracketed: thirteen Alpine battalions formed in the departments of Savoie, Isère, Ain, Drôme, and Ardèche; the "maquis" from Provence, Chambarrand, Haute-Marne, Morvan and Ardennes; the "groups" from Charolais, Lomont, Yonne, and Franche-Comté; "commandos" under various names; many minor groups; and a large number of individual men. Furthermore, considerable columns of maquisards from the central departments and from Aquitaine were also arriving.

At the end of August, I had received in Paris General Chevance-Bertin, military delegate in the southwest, and directed him to shift the greatest possible share of the Forces of the Interior in his region to the First Army. Chevance-Bertin had done this, entrusting to his subordinate Schneider the leadership of this huge and inchoate group. Schneider had managed to lead into Burgundy the "Toulouse Light Division," including, in particular, the "Corps Franc des Pyrénées," the "Brigade Alsace-Lorraine" and contingents from the Tarn, Tarn-et-Garonne and Aveyron departments. He also brought "brigades" from Languedoc, Lot-et-Garonne and Corrèze. Finally, he sent toward the same destination the "brigades du Massif Central" and the "Artillerie du Puy-de-Dôme," as well as the "Gardes Mobiles de Vichy," forming together the "Groupe d'Auvergne."

The afflux of these units, diverse as they were, obviously delighted the command of the First Army, the general staffs and the services, but plunged them, on the other hand, into great difficulties. It is true that questions of subordination were soon resolved. General Cochet, whom I had put in charge of the Forces of the Interior south of the Loire, put an end to those outbursts of separatism that certain leaders manifested and put all the units that reached his zone of action directly under General de Lattre's orders. But how organize these forces, how equip them, how employ them under normal military conditions? The decisions would have to be made and the means furnished by the government itself, following the plan it had adopted for this final phase of the war.

A certain demagoguery was noisily urging us to mobilize all men old enough to bear arms. This mass conscription, a practice revived from the Revolutionary period, would, of course, have secured considerable manpower, despite the fact that two and a half million men were in enemy hands as prisoners of war, deported or at forced labor, and that 300,000 more had been killed or seriously wounded since the beginning of the conflict. But this was no longer a period where numbers counted more than anything else. What would we have done with this host of conscripts, when we had neither arms nor officers nor equipment to give them, and when it would have been both criminal and cretinous to send them as they were into open country to face the German Army's cannons, tanks, machine guns and planes? Taking advantage of circumstances wherever possible, but taking facts as they came, I had determined what my intentions were to be.

To organize for battle the eager and valiant youth which had conducted the clandestine struggle and to add it to the troops from Africa—that was what seemed realizable from the military viewpoint and necessary from the national one. Given our state of extreme material impoverishment, this would be all we could do for the autumn and winter. If the war were going to last longer, we should know in plenty of time. In practice, I intended to incorporate as many maquisards into the First Army as it could absorb and with the remainder to constitute new major units.

As soon as we were able to determine the real situation of the paramilitary units with sufficient exactitude, that is, when I returned from my trip to the Rhone and the Midi, I explained the plan of this transformation to the Committee for National Defense. Four hundred thousand—this was the approximate number of men in our

Forces of the Interior. What an honor to France in this new wave of combatants! All voluntarily accepted the dangers of the maquis, despite the number of young men who were *hors de combat* and the fact that the official Vichy machine, until its last hour, had hunted down and condemned all who resisted the enemy. We first decreed, on September 23, that all men remaining under arms would be under contract in due form for the duration of the war. Thus the situation of the maquisards would be legally settled. Forty thousand were transferred into the Navy and the Air Force. To assist the Minister of the Interior to maintain public order, those *gendarmes* and *gardes mobiles* who had joined the maquis would return to their original groups; besides, sixty "Compagnies Républicaines de Sécurité" were formed, an innovation universally reproved at the time but still in existence today. Finally, certain specialists of whom the nation's economy stood in the greatest need—miners, railway men, etc.—were requested to return to their professions. Ultimately, the land army alone retained more than 300,000 soldiers who had spontaneously transferred to it from the Forces of the Interior.

From these latter, following my decision, De Lattre would at once take some hundred thousand under his command. The others would constitute seven new divisions. Already in formation were: in the Alpes department, the 27th Division under Valette d'Ozia, in Paris the 10th Division under Billotte, in Brittany the 19th Division under Borgnis-Desbordes. The maquisards in contact with the German pockets in St.-Nazaire, La Rochelle, Royan and the Graves peninsula were to form the 25th Division under Chomel and the 23rd under Anselme. At the beginning of spring, the 1st Division under Caillies and the 14th under Salan would be sent on foot into Berri and Alsace respectively. Aside from these major units, the Minister of War would reconstitute regiments of all arms in order to insure instruction in the interior regions and to replace losses at the front. In December, the class of 1943 was to be called to the colors. In April, it would be the turn of the classes of 1940, 1941 and 1942, insofar as the young men comprising them were not already conscripted. As for the military schools, they were immediately reopened.

This program was realized. But the problem was not so much to create bodies of troops as to arm and equip them. The miscellaneous rifles, the rare machine guns and mortars, the few pathetic automobiles which the maquisards possessed and had used in skirmishes and ambushes were no longer anything but absurd for participating in pitched battle. By regrouping these chance means, by sending to Africa for the few available French armaments still there, by collecting and repairing the matériel captured from the enemy in France and even what we had lately been able to collect in Tunisia and Italy, we could assure the new-formed units an elementary supply service. But this was not enough to measure against the forces of the Wehrmacht. They needed heavy armaments. Yet there no longer existed in France a single establishment capable of manufacturing them. The installations and equipment of our specialized factories had been dismantled and removed by the Germans; the remaining workshops had kept only what they required for the accessory work executed in the enemy's behalf. Unless we were to wait until production began again—a matter of many months—we were obliged to depend on the good will of the United States.

Their good will was scanty. It must be said that our allies were having incontestable difficulties transporting from America the enormous tonnage of matériel required in battle. They were therefore not at all eager to furnish additional and unexpected consignments to be handed over to the French. Especially since they would have been furnished to units comprised of our Forces of the Interior. In the eyes of the Anglo-American powers, these forces still appeared outrageous to the general staffs and disquieting to the politicians. Certainly, during the battles of the liberation, supplies had been furnished to the "troops of rebellion." But in Washington and London there was no queston, now, of providing them heavy armament which would have to come from America by additional convoys. And who could be certain that some day these irregular forces would not use the powers they acquired for subversive ends? Particularly since by furnishing General de Gaulle's government the means to equip eight or ten divisions, it was apparent that by the end of the winter the French Army would have doubled, that it would play a larger, perhaps decisive role in the battle, and that therefore France would have to be included in the armistice settlement, which Roosevelt wished to avoid. These motives brought the requests we made to the British and American governments to nothing. From the day of the landing in Normandy to that of the German capitulation, our allies would not furnish us supplies to equip a single additional major unit. During his October visit to Paris, General Marshall had left us under no illusions on this point.

Would the Allies at least agree to equip the 100,000 men which our First Army was trying to absorb into its divisions, its services, and its reserves? Certainly not. Referring to the provisioning plans drawn up in their offices, they still refused to take account of this increase. As for food supplies and clothing, our own commissariat furnished the First Army its necessary supplements. But in other respects, we had to fall back on makeshifts.

Since winter in the Vosges threatened the health of our Negro troops, we sent the 20,000 soldiers from Central and Western Africa serving in the 1st Free French Division and the 9th Colonial Division to the Midi. They were replaced by a similar number of maquisards who were immediately equipped. Several North African regiments, particularly exhausted by two years' fighting, would return to their original garrisons, while troops drawn from the Forces of the Interior would inherit their arms and their position in the the order of battle. De Lattre, skillfully employing the reserve matériel previously granted to his army, divided the contents among the new units. Finally, the ingenuity displayed by every echelon, either in wheedling a little new matériel from the American depots to replace weapons declared outdated, in repairing the latter and then using them alongside the replacements, or in adopting without concern for status all Allied armored weapons, cannons and vehicles lying within reach, afforded us certain resources. Unfortunately, our poverty compelled us to adopt any means of reviving our military strength which, down through the centuries, had often been superfluous, even squandered, and now was so terribly reduced. Finally the First Army was somehow furnished with the supplies necessary for its reinforcing manpower.

On September 23 I inspected this army. With Diethelm and Juin, I landed at Tavaux, near Dôle. We first visited general headquarters at Besançon and the next day examined the terrain. This was the moment when the First Army was making contact with the German positions. General de Lattre, still enthusiastic after his swift advance from the Mediterranean, believed he could drive his left wing across the Vosges into Alsace. In this sector—that of the IInd Corps—General de Monsabert was leading sharp action against the foothills around Servance and Ronchamp. Optimistic and high spirited, taking enormous risks, lavishing his unfailing enthusiasm, his sharp eye, his sense of combat on every sector, De Monsabert used every man to the limit of his ability. Yet he was devoted to his men and completely disinterested where his own person was concerned. At a time when it was my duty to bestow military honors, I often heard him speak of others' merits, never of his own.

The Ist Corps formed the right wing of the First Army from Lure to Lomont. I found it in the process of organizing its base in order to take the Belfort Gap. The undertaking would be an arduous one, given the narrowness of the terrain on which the enemy must be engaged and the power of the German opposition. But the general on whom this responsibility fell seemed made to lead the enterprise to a successful conclusion. General Béthouart left nothing to chance. His plans were methodically conceived and calmly executed, which earned him the trust of his subordinates and also, on occasion, the impatience of his superior.

Only a complete success could satisfy General de Lattre. Ardent to the point of effervescence, as sensitive as he was brilliant, De Lattre was extremely anxious that nothing should fail, regarding each vicissitude as a personal matter. Those who served under him received many rebuffs and pinpricks. But so forceful was his excellence that their resentment was always short-lived.

On the occasion of my inspection, I had many contacts with General de Lattre in the exercise of his command. Despite the faults for which he was reproached and which were rather the excesses of his virtues, I always regarded him as highly qualified to lead operations. Without yielding to the favorable prejudices of my friendship for him, and occasionally intervening in his domain when reasons of national interest required as much, I accorded him unceasing confidence in the task to which I had called him. Besides, he never failed to evince, in his relations with me and as long as I was in power, not only his loyalty, but also his conviction as to the pre-eminent character of the mission I was performing.

On that day, in his company, I visited the troops and services. Everything was a pleasure to see. Of course, after their victorious pursuit, the men had reason to be proud. Besides, they were literally beaming with good humor. And technically speaking, they were second to none. It was readily apparent that the French, all things being equal, had achieved victories at least comparable to those won by the British and American troops. The Germans, of course, were the last to be aware of this, for they sent a relatively high proportion of their forces against our men.

But I also observed that the amalgam of troops from Africa and Forces of the Interior could be brought to a high point of effectiveness. Not that the reciprocal prejudices among the units of various origin had altogether disappeared. The "Free French" maintained a somewhat exclusive pride toward all others. The men of the secret army, long persecuted, feverish and destitute, would readily have claimed to represent all of the resistance forces. The regiments from Algeria, Morocco and Tunisia, although they had recently been divided among varying tendencies, appeared unanimously touchy as to their *esprit de corps*. But whatever the complications to which fate had subjected every group, the satisfaction of finding themselves side by side and engaged in the same battle triumphed over all other considerations in the minds of soldiers, officers and generals alike. It must be said that in the cities and villages they passed through, the popular reception left no doubt as to public sentiment in their behalf. Indeed the French Army, for all the unfortunately reduced proportions its reconstruction had made necessary, revealed a quality which it had never exceeded.

This was particularly so in the case of the 2nd Armored Division. On September 25, leaving General de Lattre's zone, I visited its positions at Moyen, Vathiménil, and Gerbéviller. During its brief sojourn in Paris, this division had recruited several thousand young volunteers. In addition, it attracted matériel as naturally as a magnet attracts iron. In short, it had everything. On September 10, this division had crossed the Marne north of Chaumont and then, during the succeeding days, fought its way to Andelot and Vittel, threw back the counterattacks of many German tanks to Dompaire, and finally established a front along the Meurthe. Leclerc and his lieutenants were dissatisfied with this standstill. I appealed to their good sense. For, like genius, a brilliant feat of arms is a matter of patience. With Baccarat—still a captive city— before him, Leclerc now concentrated his ambitions upon it, in order to take it at the right moment.

A month later, paying a return visit to our troops, I found them ready for the general offensive which Eisenhower would shortly inaugurate. At the end of October, in the French sector, the restiveness of officers and men alike was evident. Especially since emissaries were continuously arriving either through Switzerland or across the lines from the Vosges—from Belfort and Alsace urging our men to push forward. I first visited our aviation group, under Gérardot, confirming its mission, in accord with the Allied command, to support the French Army. On the front lines which I examined next, the men displayed their optimism. "At the time of the disaster," De Lattre asked me, "could you have imagined something like this?"

"It is because I counted on something like this," I replied, "that we are both here today."

My movements throughout the country and my visits to the armies had produced their desired effect. But it would be an episodic one unless it was followed by practical arrangements. In this respect, our plans had been determined since Algiers. We could congratulate ourselves on that. For despite the troubled conditions during which the government was established in Paris, the Councils which I convened during an overcrowded autumn were not wasted in tergiversations. In the space of several weeks, the government adopted a group of measures which kept the nation from drifting from its course.

The greater the confusion, the greater the necessity to govern. After enormous disorder, our first task was to restore the country's labor force to its functions. But the first condition of this restoration was that the workers be able to live. On July 16, in Algiers, the government had decided "that upon the liberation there would be occasion to proceed with an immediate and substantial wage increase." On August 28, immediately following the liberation of Paris, a conference of the secretaries general of the ministries, presided over by Le Troquer, Minister Delegate to the Liberated Territories, proposed that the increase be one of 40 per cent. It was this average coefficient which the Council of Ministers adopted on September 13. On October 17, an additional decree provided for the reorganization of family allowances and increased them by 50 per cent. This increase in wages and allowances, substantial as it might appear, was nonetheless a modest one, since it raised the average level of remuneration to 225 in relation to the October 1938 reading of 100, whereas in the same period official prices had risen from 100 to 300, and some actual prices to 1,000.

But what was the use of better wages if the value of the money paid collapsed and the state went bankrupt? In this regard, we were walking along the brink of an abyss. It was true that the levies—520 billion francs!—made by the enemy upon the public funds had ceased. But on the other hand, the war effort had to be financed, as well as the reconstruction of railroads, the ports, canals, electric plants and buildings, without which no recovery was imaginable. On the other side of the ledger from these crushing expenditures stood the critically inadequate receipts. In the month of September, the nation's economic activity declined to about 40 per cent of the 1938 level. Further, fiduciary circulation and short-term liabilities reached 630 and 602 billion francs respectively—that is, three times higher than the prewar level. This immense total of means of payment, completely disproportionate to an extremely reduced production, threatened an inflation which could become ruinous from one day to the next. To obtain funds from the treasury and at the same time control the inflation would require a major public loan.

This was the "Liberation Loan." André Lepercq, Minister of Finance, set forth its methods of payment, which we adopted—a permanent rate of 3 per cent and at par. The issue, open on November 6, was closed the twentieth. The operation claimed one victim, in the person of its director. André Lepercq, a man of faith and hope, was killed in an accident during a tour he was making in the northern departments to solicit subscriptions. On November 19, thirty hours before the closing of the issue, I announced to the nation by radio that the figures reached already indicated a success, but I added: "I ask you for a triumph!"

When the totals were finally calculated, the liberation loan produced 165 billion francs, which would be worth 1,200 billion today. Of that, 127 billion were in "cold cash," the rest in treasury bonds. A third of the total was subscribed during the last day. If we take into account the enormous economic distress in which the country was plunged at the time, severely limiting the resources of almost every Frenchman, and if we recall that since World War I no credit operation had ever raised so much money and that none of those to follow even approached this result, we perceive that the liberation loan was a triumph of the confidence Frenchmen placed in France. The circulation of bank notes was immediately reduced from 630 to 560 billion, and the short-term liabilities from 601 to 555 billion. The catastrophe that would have been caused by an unchecked inflation was thereby avoided. Further, the funds furnished to the treasury by the loan, as well as by the confiscation of illicit profits, as decreed on October 18, provided us with what was needed to finance the exceptional expenses of the war effort and the reconditioning of our communications and sources of energy. By taking into account the payment of taxes, the state had the wherewithal to pay what must be paid.

It would also have to be master on its own grounds. Among the various currents that had roused passions to a pitch where the slightest concession would sweep away its authority, the state must discharge two imperative obligations: Justice must be rendered and public order assured. This must be done vigorously and without delay, or it would never be done at all. The necessary measures were taken.

By September 13 the government had constituted the special courts of justice provided for by the decree of June 24. In each region there would be a tribunal presided over by a magistrate and including a jury appointed by the president of the Court of Appeals. The list of citizens qualified to serve on this jury was drawn up by the Commissioner of the Republic. This tribunal was to judge cases of collaboration with the enemy under legal forms and guarantees—the right to a defense counsel, the possibility of taking a case to the Supreme Court of Appeals, recourse to the chief of state. As the courts of justice fulfilled their function, the local authorities were to dissolve the courts-martial set up during the conflict by the Forces of the Interior; arbitrary arrests became formally illegal; fines were to be regarded as pure extortion; summary executions, no better than indictable crimes. Immediately the reprisals by which the resistance risked being dishonored ceased. There were still some kidnaping, pillaging or assassinations, though those guilty of such action were to suffer the law's extreme rigor. But these last outbursts were quite exceptional.

Of those Frenchmen who, by murder or delation, had caused the death of the resistance fighters, 10,842 were killed without due process of law, 6,675 during the maquis struggles before the liberation, the rest afterward, during the course of reprisal action. Further, 779 men were to be executed as the result of sentences pronounced by the courts of justice and the military tribunals. A total painful in itself, though actually extremely limited in relation to the number of crimes committed and to their dreadful consequences, and far from the extravagant figures later advanced by the inconsolable lovers of defeat and collaboration; but it was saddening to realize that the behavior of those executed was not always inspired by the lowest motives. Among the militiamen, officials, police and propagandists were some who had answered the postulate of obedience blindly. Some had let themselves be lured by the mirage of adventure. Some believed they were defending a cause sufficiently lofty to justify any means. If they were guilty, many among them were not cowards. Once again, in the national drama, French blood had flowed on both sides. The nation saw its finest sons perish in its defense. With honor, with love, it embraced them in its bereavement. Others, alas, had fallen in the enemy camp—the nation approved their punishment, but quietly mourned these fallen children too. Now time had done its work. One day, the tears would dry, the transgressions dim, the tombs disappear. But France would remain.

Once justice was functioning, there remained no excuse for maintaining irregular armed forces. Yet, despite the government's instructions, several organizations, particularly the "National Front," insisted on keeping paramilitary elements at their disposal. These "patriotic militias" claimed to prevent "an offensive return of fascism." But they were also prepared, obviously, to apply a pressure which might constrain or even overthrow the government

as it stood. Of course, under this camouflage, it was the "Comac"
that held the reins. This final ambiguity had to be dispelled. Passing over the objections of several ministers and the representations
of various committees, I induced the government to decree the
formal dissolution of the militias. On October 28 this measure was
passed and published.

As I had expected, reactions were violent. On Sunday, the
twenty-ninth, the National Council of the Resistance requested an
audience. I received these comrades of yesterday's struggle at my
residence with respect and friendship. But to the objurgations they
unanimously raised, pressing me to reconsider the decision taken,
I could answer only by complete refusal. Was this the effect of the
intimidation wielded by the Communists or of the illusions common
among the reactionaries? The most ardent in their protest were
those who represented moderate factions. On the other hand, the
representatives of the "party" maintained a reserved attitude during the interview, either because they observed that the outcome
was already fixed or they were intending to manifest their irritation
in another manner. On the thirty-first, detailed measures were
adopted in the Council of Ministers. Any force which was not a
part of the Army or the police was to be dissolved at once—if need
be, by the authorities. It was forbidden, under penalty of severe
punishments, to be in possession of arms without the warranted
authorization of the prefects. Any armament in the possession of
private citizens was to be turned in within a week to the police
commissariats or the *gendarmerie* brigades. An invitation was issued to—though rarely answered by—"those citizens who desire
to contribute to the defense of republican institutions and liberties,"
in order that the authorities could call upon their aid in case of
need.

Whether coincidence or provocation, on the following day,
November 1, a munitions train was blown up in Vitry-sur-Seine.
Some thirty people were killed and over a hundred wounded. The
disaster occurred during the same morning that I was visiting

Mont Valérien, the Ivry cemetery, and the Château de Vincennes to pay All Saints' Day homage to the resistance dead. The Communists immediately declared the disaster "a crime of the fascist fifth column." On November 2, the "party's" political bureau issued a communiqué referring to the "Vitry outrage" and vehemently attacking General de Gaulle for wishing to dissolve the militias. "Once again," the bureau declared, "the President of the Government has assumed the responsibility of treating the French resistance as a negligible quantity." Two days afterward, at the Vélodrome d'Hiver, a public meeting was held, organized by the National Front. The speakers shouted their protests. On November 25, at the Château de la Timone, where a security company was billeted, a bomb exploded killing thirty-two men. The inquest did not succeed in discovering those responsible. But there was every evidence that this was the epilogue of the *affaire des milices*. The last illegally armed groups had disappeared. No further mysterious explosion was to occur.

However, it was in the nation's interest that the men who had led the struggle against the invader should participate equally in the work of recovery. Apart from the Communist leaders, who aimed at a definite goal, the resistance fighters as a whole were somewhat disoriented. As the enemy withdrew and Vichy disappeared, they had been tempted, like Goethe's Faust, to say to the moment, "Stay, you are so splendid!" The liberation, in fact, deprived their activity of its principal points of application. Nostalgia was upon them. Especially since these ardent and adventurous men had experienced, in the height of danger, the somber attractions of the clandestine struggle, which they would not renounce. Those among them who were pre-eminently combatants were absorbed into the ranks of the Army. But the majority of the "politicians," whether they had always been or recently become so, were eager to see the revival of public life. They aspired to an arena where they could make themselves heard and gain access to posts of command.

For my part, I desired to put as representative an Assembly as possible in contact with the Cabinet. The measures determining the establishment of powers in Metropolitan France provided, moreover, that the Algiers Assembly would convene in Paris after being enlarged. Not that I conceded such a body the capacity to act. I was well aware of the fact that Assemblies, beneath their fine speeches, are ruled by the fear of action. Besides, I knew the rivalries already dividing the men of the resistance; therefore I had no expectation that the representatives would effectively support a resolved policy. But at least I hoped they would support a mystique of recovery which would inspire the French people. In any case, I considered it wise to offer a writ of execution to their seething spirits. And besides, how could I neglect the suggestions which such an Assembly would furnish the government and the credit it would inspire abroad? On October 12, a decree determined the composition of the new Consultative Assembly.

The latter consisted of 248 members—173 representatives of resistance organizations, 60 members of parliament, 12 overseas councilors general. In particular, the 18 members of the National Council of the Resistance participated in the Assembly, which met on November 7. It convened at the Palais du Luxembourg, for, symbolically, I had insisted on reserving the Palais Bourbon for the future National Assembly. Félix Gouin was elected president, as in Algiers. On November 9 I inaugurated the first session.

From the tribune which I had mounted in order to address the government's greeting to the Assembly, I saw the amphitheater filled with comrades delegated by all the movements of the national resistance and belonging to every political tendency. From one end of the span to the other, all did me the honor of applauding. Those present were, like myself, imbued with the feeling that this gathering commemorated a great French victory following upon an inordinate disaster. Here, in fact, was the end of France's oppression, but also the denouement of the dramatic shock of her liberation. Our actions had reopened the seas to the ship of state, though she had narrowly missed being scuttled at the outset.

Ten weeks had passed since Paris had been retaken. How much would depend on what had been done in this short space of time! Contact had been made between the people and its guide, and thereby all dispute as to the national authority was silenced. The state was exercising its powers. The government was at work. The Army, reunified, enlarged, more eager than ever, was fighting at the gates of Alsace, in the Alps, on the Atlantic coast, shoulder to shoulder with our allies. The administration was functioning. Justice was fulfilling its function. Public order was established. Tremendous reforms were being instituted, averting the threat of chaos and upheaval that hung over the nation. Bankruptcy had been avoided; the treasury was adequately filled; the value of currency temporarily assured. Above all, France was recovering a sense of herself and looking toward the future.

The future? It was being forged in the trials which separated us from victory and eventual recovery. As long as the war lasted, I would answer for it. But afterward, everything would depend on the very men who, today, were gathered around me in the Palais du Luxembourg. For tomorrow the French people would transform them into its elected and legal representatives. If they remained united for recovery as they were even now for combat, all hopes were permissible. If they turned away from me and disputed the appearances of power among themselves, then decline would once again take its course.

But we were only in the present. France at war was again on her own territory. Now it was a matter of her appearing elsewhere.

CHAPTER 2

STATUS

E VERY state turned its eyes upon liberated France. This nation, which had figured among the first for so many centuries, which yesterday had collapsed in an incredible disaster but for whose sake some of its sons had not stopped fighting, which today declared itself a sovereign and belligerent nation—in what condition would it reappear, what road was it about to take?

Many certainly believed that General de Gaulle, now established in Paris, would remain at the head of some executive body for a time. But just over whom, and over what, would his authority be exercised? Would this leader whom no sovereign, no parliament, no referendum had installed in office, and who had at his disposal no political organization, properly speaking—would this leader be followed for long by the most mercurial and intractable nation in the world? On a ravaged territory, among a population exhausted by privation, confronting a profoundly divided public opinion, would he not encounter such difficulties that he would find himself helpless against them? Finally, who could tell if the Communists, grown stronger in the resistance, with only the dregs of parties and the debris of police, justice and administration to deal with, would not seize power? Before adopting a specific attitude toward the

716

Provisional Government, the chancelleries of the world waited to see which way France would turn.

They would have to admit she had turned the right way: no civil war, no social upheaval, no military disorder, no economic collapse, no governmental anarchy. Just the opposite! A nation recovering its equilibrium despite its poverty, eager to rebuild, developing its war effort under the leadership of a virtually uncontested government—here, despite the shadows, was the spectacle we offered to the world. The Allies and the neutral powers could no longer delay giving a normal form to their relations with us.

Had they done so sooner, of course, those of the great powers who were fighting beside us could have provided significant moral support during the critical period from which we had just emerged. But the susceptibilities of the President of the United States and the grievances of the British Prime Minister had kept the decision in abeyance until the last possible moment. Now there was no further means of postponement! Moreover, Franklin Roosevelt himself was obliged to settle the matter, in consideration of the American voters whose endorsement he was about to seek a fourth time and who were impatient with his unjustifiable attitude toward their ally France. The election was to be held November 7; it was on October 23 that Washington, London and Moscow officially recognized the Provisional Government of the French Republic. The White House and Downing Street averred, to save face, that Eisenhower now considered it possible to "transfer his authority on French territory to the De Gaulle government," as if the Supreme Commander had ever exercised this authority for even a moment over anyone but his soldiers. Seeing that the "great powers" yielded to the inevitable, all the other states who had lagged behind now fell in line in their turn. We naturally refrained from thanking any of them for this formality performed *in extremis*. During a press conference I held on October 25, when I was asked "my impressions as to the recognition of the government by the Allies," I confined myself to replying, "The French government is pleased that it is to be called by its name."

Paris then saw all the great embassy doors reopen which had been kept shut during the occupation and only ajar since. The same diplomats who had been delegated to us in Algiers appeared before me to offer their credentials, but this time in formulas that were no longer ambiguous. Mr. Jefferson Caffery, sent by Washington to replace Mr. Edwin Wilson, was the only ambassador among the Allies whom we did not already know. As for the neutral states, the diplomatic corps they had constituted in Vichy soon vanished, and the French Government good-naturedly welcomed their new representatives. The only difficulty was in the case of the Apostolic Nuncio. The Vatican, apparently, desired Monsignor Valerio Valeri to be accredited to General de Gaulle after his having been Nuncio to Marshal Pétain. This was, from our point of view, impossible. After a number of fluctuations, the Holy See asked our approval of Monsignor Roncalli.* We gave it at once, though I was careful to express to Monsignor Valerio Valeri, upon his departure, our profound esteem for his own person.

For our part we had to supplement and rearrange our representation in the capitals of the world. René Massigli was assigned to London, Henri Bonnet to Washington, Jacques Maritain to the Vatican, General Pechkoff to Chungking. Among the Allies, our representatives were henceforth addressed by the traditional titles, while in Madrid, Ankara, Berne, Stockholm, Lisbon, etc., our ambassadors officially assumed their functions. The Quai d'Orsay, long the Sleeping Beauty's castle, now awakened to activity. The Foreign Minister Georges Bidault, seconded by the Secretary General Raymond Brugère, dealt with a multiplicity of affairs suddenly confronting him all at once.

What would happen to Europe after the defeat of Germany, and what would be the latter's fate? These were the chief dilemmas

* Now Pope John XXIII.—Ed.

which events proposed from one day to the next and by which, of course, I was particularly concerned.

In one man's lifetime, France had survived three wars instigated by her neighbor across the Rhine. The first had terminated in the mutilation of the national territory and crushing humiliation. Victorious in the second, France had recovered Alsace and Lorraine, but at a cost of men and material that left her bloodless and ruined. Furthermore, the ill will of the Anglo-American powers, taking advantage of the inconsistency of our regime, led us, subsequently, to renounce the guarantees and reparations which had been granted us in exchange for control of the Reich and the Rhine frontier. The third war had seen our army fall to pieces at the first encounter, the government rush to capitulate, the nation endure occupation, organized pillage, forced labor and the detention of two million men. By virtue of a kind of miracle, independence and sovereignty had been maintained in the remotest parts of the Empire. Gradually an army had been reconstituted, while the resistance grew in Metropolitan France. France contributed to her own liberation with important military forces, a solid government, a united public opinion. She had, henceforth, the assurance of being present at the victory. But it was all too obvious she would then find herself reduced to such a weakened condition that her world situation, the adherence of her overseas territories, and the very sources of her life would be compromised for a long time. Unless by this very occasion—perhaps the last—she could reconstruct her power. This is what I wished to effect.

To make France's recovery possible, the German collectivity must lose its capacity for aggression. In the dangerous world already looming before us, existence under the threat of war from a neighboring state which had so often demonstrated its taste and its talent for conquest would be incompatible with France's economic recovery, her political stability, and the moral equilibrium without which all efforts would remain futile. It is true that the exhaustion of Germany, the Allied occupation, the annexation of her eastern territories, would prevent the worst for years to come. But afterward? What would become of the German people, what changes would they undergo after their imminent defeat? Perhaps they would choose wisdom and peace? Perhaps this transformation would prove to be a lasting one? Obviously the conditions of our security would vary accordingly. But as long as we did not know the answer, we had to proceed as if Germany might remain a threat. What guarantees, what pledges would reassure us, while granting the great German people an opportunity to live, advance and co-operate with us and the rest of the world?

The abolition of a centralized Reich! This, in my opinion, was the first condition necessary to prevent Germany from returning to its bad ways. Each time a dominating and ambitious state had seized the German polities, obliterating their diversity, imperialism had been the result. This had been only too evident under Wilhelm II and under Hitler. Conversely, if each of the states within the German federation could exist by itself, govern itself in its own way, handle its own interests, there would be every likelihood that the federation as a whole would not be led to subjugate its neighbors. This would be even more likely if the Ruhr, that arsenal of strategic matériel, were given a special status under international control. Further, the Rhineland would, of course, be occupied by French, British, Belgian and Dutch armies. But if its economy were moreover linked to a grouping of the Western powers—and with no opposition to other German units joining this alliance as well— and if the Rhine itself became an international freeway, then co-operation between complementary nations could be instituted forthwith. Lastly, there was every reason to suppose that the Saar, retaining its German character, would be transformed into a separate state and united to France by trade agreements which would settle the question of our reparations in terms of coal. Thus the German federation, recovering its diversity and turning its eyes toward the west, would lose the means of war but not those of its own development. In addition, none of its fragments would be annexed by the French, thus leaving the door to reconciliation open.

This conception of tomorrow's Germany was closely related to my image of Europe. After the terrible lacerations she had undergone in the last thirty years, and the vast changes which had occurred the world over, Europe could find equilibrium and peace only by an association among Slavs, Germans, Gauls and Latins. Doubtless she must take into account what was momentarily tyrannical and aggrandizing in the Russian regime. Utilizing the procedures of totalitarian oppression and, on the other hand, invoking the solidarity of the Central and Eastern European peoples against the German peril, Communism was apparently trying to gain control of the Vistula, the Danube and the Balkans. But once Germany ceased to be a threat, this subjection, for lack of a *raison d'être,* would sooner or later appear unacceptable to the vassal states, while the Russians themselves would lose all desire to exceed their own boundaries. If the Kremlin persisted in its enterprise of domination, it would be against the will of the nations subject to its government. Yet in the long run there is no regime that can hold out against the will of nations. I believed, moreover, that timely action by the western Allies with regard to the masters of the Kremlin, on condition that such action be concerted and categorical, would safeguard the independence of the Poles, the Czechs, the Hungarians and the Balkan peoples. After which the unity of Europe could be established in the form of an association including its peoples from Iceland to Istanbul, from Gibraltar to the Urals.

This was the plan I had conceived, knowing perfectly well that in such matters nothing turns out exactly as one has hoped. I sounded the weaknesses in our policy of credit abroad and support at home, yet I remained convinced that France could undertake great actions, assume great proportions, and greatly serve her own interest and that of the human race as well. But to begin with, we would have to insinuate ourselves into the dissimulated and discordant argument by which America, Russia and England were determining what was at issue without us.

To reach such a position, we were certainly starting off at a great disadvantage. The Dumbarton Oaks conference of the preceding September, intended to prepare the future "United Nations Organization" had convoked representatives of the United States, Great Britain, Russia and China, to the exclusion of France. Discussing the composition of the "Security Council," which would exercise control of the organization, the conference had determined that this Council would consist only of the same four "Great Powers." "It is a splendid arrangement" declared Mr. Connally, head of the Senate's Foreign Relations Committee, "since the United States, England, Russia and China are the four nations which have shed their blood for the rest of the world, while France has played the role of only a minor state in this war."

In London the "European Commission" had been sitting for over a year and delegates to it from the British, American, and Soviet governments were studying the questions concerning Europe and, in particular, Germany, while we were excluded again. In September, the President and the Prime Minister had met in Quebec to determine their position, though not inviting us to attend. In October, Churchill and Eden had gone to Moscow to reach an agreement with Stalin and Molotov without our being informed by either party as to the results. Everything occurred as if our Allies were intent on excluding France from the mere knowledge of their arrangements.

We could not bring this relegation to a halt immediately, but we could make it unendurable to those inflicting it upon us. For none of their decisions concerning Europe, particularly Germany, could be put into effect if France did not lend her voice. Soon we would be on the Rhine and the Danube with a strong army. Moreover, the war's end would leave us in force on the continent, while America would be back in her hemisphere and England on her island. Provided that we knew what we wanted, we would then have the means to break out of the circle of resigned acceptance and docile renunciation inside which our three partners intended to imprison us. Already the liberation of our territory, the reinstatement of the government, the restoration of order throughout the country put us in a position to deal with the situation. On October 30 we invited Messrs. Churchill and Eden to visit us in Paris. At the same time, for form's sake, and with no illusions as to its acceptance, we had sent Mr. Roosevelt and Mr. Cordell Hull a similar invitation, which was declined.

Churchill and Eden arrived on November 10. We gave them the best possible reception. Paris cheered them with all its heart. With Bidault and several other ministers, I had met them at Orly and driven the Prime Minister to the Quai d'Orsay where he was to stay. The next day was the celebration of victory. After the visit to the Tomb of the Unknown Soldier and the reviews of the troops, Churchill and I, in the same automobile, moved down the triumphal avenue beneath a storm of cheers. The Prime Minister laid a bouquet at the foot of Clemenceau's statue while, on my orders, the band played "Le Père la Victoire"—"For you!" I said to him in English. And it was only justice. Then too, I recalled how at Chequers, the evening of a black day, he had sung me our old song about Paulus without missing a word. We visited Les Invalides and bowed at the grave of Foch. After which, the illustrious Englishman leaned forward for a long moment over Napoleon's tomb. "In all the world," he said to me, "there is nothing greater!" The official luncheon at the Ministry of War, seat of the Presidency, ended with speeches in which friendship glowed on both sides.

After the meal, Winston Churchill told me he had been deeply touched by what he had just seen and heard. "Would you tell me," I asked, "what struck you the most?"

"Yes," he answered, "your unanimity! After so many events during which you and I have been so fiercely attacked and reviled in France by so many pens in so many pages, I remarked with astonishment that only enthusiasm met us as we passed. This means that deep in its heart the French people was with you, who have served it, and with me, who have helped you to do so." Churchill added that he was impressed by the orderliness of the ceremonies. He admitted that the British Cabinet had hesitated to approve his trip, so great had been its apprehensions of upheaval in Paris. And here he had seen everything in its normal order, the crowds respecting the barricades and quite capable of bursting into cheers or keeping silent according to the demands of the situation, and the splendid troops—yesterday's French Forces of the Interior—parading in perfect marching order. "I felt," he declared, "as if I were watching a resurrection."

During the course of the day, we had a meeting in my office in the Rue St.-Dominique, during which we examined the possibility of a Franco-British alliance for world-wide settlements. Churchill was seconded by Eden and Duff Cooper; with me were Bidault and Massigli. On this occasion we were no longer concerned with sentiment, but with business. Hence we found our interlocutors more reserved.

Regarding the armament of French forces, they granted us no appreciable assistance and did not appear disposed to support our requests for co-operation from the United States. As for Germany, they agreed that France too should have her zone of occupation there, but remained evasive as to what that zone would be. They were even less willing to consider anything specific as to Germany's future regime, the fate of the Ruhr, the Rhine frontier, the Saar Basin, etc. On the other hand, they made no effort to conceal the fact that in Moscow, a few days before, they had sanctioned Stalin's proposal for the future Russo-Polish frontier; had brought from London to the Soviet capital three Polish ministers, Messrs. Miko-lajczyk, de Romer and Grabski, urging them to come to an agreement with the "Lublin Committee" as the Russians asked; and lastly had reached an informal agreement with the Kremlin on the division of the Balkans into two spheres of influence. "In Rumania," Churchill said, "the Russians will have ninety per cent, the British ten per cent. In Bulgaria, they will have seventy-five per cent and we twenty-five per cent. But in Greece we will have ninety per cent, they ten per cent. And in Hungary and Yugoslavia, our influence will be equal." The British ministers avoided all our attempts to discuss the question of the Levant, and continued vague with regard to Indochina and the Far East in general.

For all the well-mannered discretion of Churchill's and Eden's remarks, it was evident that they considered themselves participants in a game to which we ourselves were not admitted and that they maintained toward us a reserve imposed by the other players. Nevertheless, they continued to express their faith in France and their confidence of seeing her resume her place among the great states. They proposed immediate negotiations relative to a Franco-British treaty of alliance. They even brought us the joint invitation of England, the United States and Soviet Russia to take part with them in the London "European Commission."

This first step was not a negligible one, though it in no way satisfied us. In any case, our remarks left Churchill no doubt that the only situation we found acceptable was that of full associate. As he continued his trip, he could also realize, as he had already noticed on the Champs-Élysées, that the French people deserved to settle its own affairs without outside intervention.

On November 12, he was received at the Hôtel de Ville of Paris and met there, by his own request, not only the Municipal Council, but also the Council of the Resistance, the Parisian Committee of Liberation, and many combatants of the preceding August. "I am going there," he had told me, "to see the men of the insurrection!" Perhaps, too, he cherished the hope of finding adversaries of De Gaulle among them. Upon his return, he described his astonishment. "I expected," he told me, "to find myself surrounded by noisy and undisciplined insurgents. I was received by a procession of members of parliament, or men who looked like members of parliament, saluted by the Garde Républicaine in full-dress uniforms, taken into a hall filled with an ardent but reasonable crowd, addressed by two orators who were certainly preparing their candidacy for the elections. Your revolutionaries look like Labour Members! This is fine for law and order, but a great loss for the picturesque." That evening, after we had had another conference, accompanied by Eden and Bidault, and a dinner at the British Embassy, I took Churchill on a visit to our First Army.

During the entire day of November 13, under ceaselessly falling snow, Mr. Churchill saw the renascent French Army, its major units in position, its services functioning, its general staffs at their work, its generals confident; all were prepared for the offensive which was, in fact, to be launched the next day. Churchill appeared deeply impressed, and declared that he felt more justified than ever in placing his confidence in France.

Churchill's confidence, however, was insufficient for him to adopt, in our regard, that policy of frank solidarity which might have re-established Europe and maintained Western prestige in the Middle East, in Asia and in Africa. The visit he paid us was perhaps the last possible occasion to bring him to a change of heart. I took every opportunity to do so during the conversations we had together.

I repeated to Churchill: "You see that France is making a recovery. But whatever my faith in her, I know that she will not regain her former power all at once. You English, of course, will emerge from this war covered with glory. Yet to what a degree—unfair though it may be—your relative situation risks being diminished, given your losses and expenditures, by the centrifugal forces at work within the Commonwealth, and, particularly, the rise of America and Russia, not to mention China! Confronting a new world, then, our two old nations find themselves simultaneously weakened. If they remain divided as well, how much influence will either of them wield? On the other hand, should England and France act in accord on tomorrow's peace settlements, they will weigh heavily enough in the world's scales so that nothing will be done which they themselves have not consented to or determined. It is this mutual resolve which should be the basis of the alliance you offer us. Otherwise what is the good of signing a document which would be, at best, ambiguous?

"The equilibrium of Europe," I added, "the guarantee of peace along the Rhine, the independence of the Vistula, Danube and Balkan states, the creation of some form of association with the peoples all over the world to whom we have opened the doors of Western civilization, an organization of nations which will be something more than an arena for disputes between America and Russia, and lastly the primacy accorded in world politics to a certain conception of man despite the progressive mechanization of society—these, surely, are our great interests in tomorrow's world. Let us come to an agreement in order to uphold these interests together. If you are willing to do so, I am ready. Our two nations will follow us. America and Russia, hobbled by their rivalry, will not be able to raise any objection. Moreover, we shall have the support of many states and of world-wide public opinion, which instinctively shies away from giants. Thus England and France will together create peace, as twice in thirty years they have together confronted war."

Winston Churchill answered: "Certainly I do not foresee a Franco-British schism. You are the witness and the proof of what I have done to prevent such a thing when it was most likely. Even today, I offer you an alliance in principle. But in politics as in strategy, it is better to persuade the stronger than to pit yourself against him. That is what I am trying to do. The Americans have immense resources. They do not always use them to the best advantage. I am trying to enlighten them, without forgetting, of course, to benefit my country. I have formed a close personal tie with Roosevelt. With him, I proceed by suggestion in order to influence matters in the right direction. At present, Russia is a great beast which has been starved for a long time. It is not possible to keep her from eating, especially since she now lies in the middle of the herd of her victims. The question is whether she can be kept from devouring all of them. I am trying to restrain Stalin, who, if he has an enormous appetite, also has a great deal of good sense. And after the meal comes the digestion period. When it is time to digest, the surfeited Russians will have their difficult moments. Then, perhaps, Saint Nicholas can bring back to life the poor children the ogre has put in the salting tub. Meanwhile, I attend every meeting, yield nothing for nothing, and manage to secure a few dividends.

"As for France," Churchill repeated, "thanks to you, she is reappearing in the eyes of the world. Don't be impatient! Already, the doors are ajar. Soon they will be open to you. It will be only natural for you to sit at the table of the Administration Council. Nothing, then, will keep us from working together. Until then, leave matters in my hands!"

The Prime Minister took his departure on November 14 to inspect the British sector of the front. Eden had already returned to London. From the statements both had made, it was apparent that England favored France's political reappearance, that she would continue to do so for reasons of equilibrium, tradition and security, that she desired a formal alliance with us, but would not consent to link her strategy with ours, believing herself in a position to function independently between Moscow and Washington, to limit their demands, but also to take advantage of them. The peace we French hoped to build in accord with what we regarded as logic and justice, the British found it expedient to approach with formulas of empiricism and compromise. Furthermore, they were pursuing certain precise goals which, in areas where the positions of states and the balance of power were not yet determined, offered British ambitions numerous possibilities of manipulation and aggrandizement.

This was especially the case in regard to the Mediterranean. Athens, Belgrade, Beirut, Damascus and Tripoli, under London's various labels, would tomorrow supplement a British preponderance previously dependent on Gibraltar, Malta, Cyprus, Cairo,

Amman and Baghdad. Thus the concessions which Great Britain
had not been able to avoid making to Russian voracity and American capitalist ideology found their counterpart. No ordeal changes
the nature of man; no crisis that of states.

In short, we found occupying the comfortable chairs in the club
of the great powers as many hallowed egotisms as there were
charter members. On my visit to Washington, Roosevelt had disclosed the American ambitions, draped in idealism but actually
quite practical. The London leaders had just demonstrated that
they aimed at achieving specifically British goals. And now, the
masters of the Kremlin were to show us that they served the interests of Soviet Russia alone.

Indeed M. Bogomolov, immediately after Mr. Churchill's and
Mr. Eden's visit to France, took every occasion to urge me to visit
Moscow. Since France was once again free and able to take an
active part in the conflict, and since her government was once
again established in Paris, it was my intention to make direct
contact with Stalin and his ministers. I therefore accepted their
invitation, as well as the schedule drawn up by M. Molotov and
our ambassador, Roger Garreau. It was agreed that I, accompanied
by Georges Bidault, would spend a week in the Soviet capital. In
this way we and the Russians could learn how each of us conceived the future peace settlement. Perhaps it would be possible to
renew the old Franco-Russian solidarity which, though repeatedly
betrayed and repudiated, remained no less a part of the natural
order of things, as much in relation to the German menace as to
the endeavors of Anglo-American hegemony. I even envisaged a
pact by virtue of which France and Russia would commit themselves to act in common if Germany should ever become a threat
again. This dangerous hypothesis would probably not be realized,
at least not in the foreseeable future. But the signing of a Franco-
Russian treaty could help us to participate at once in the elaboration of the European settlements.

Before setting out for the Kremlin, I wished to formulate publicly France's conditions for future settlements. The Consultative Assembly had opened a debate on foreign affairs. As usual, the speeches reveled in generalities or quivered with idealism, but the discussion remained vague as to its practical objectives. All condemned Hitlerism, but failed to specify what should be done with Germany. They lavished their warmest tokens of admiration upon our allies, but asked them for nothing but their friendship. They regarded it as essential that France recover her status, but dodged any indication as to the route and the means. In my declaration of November 22, I therefore took particular pains to make our conditions explicit.

I remarked, first of all, that "we are beginning to possess means of diplomatic action worthy of France. . . . Almost every foreign government," I said, "has now recognized the government of the Republic. As for Germany, our artillery, in Alsace and other places, is in the process of gaining recognition in the only suitable manner—that is, by victory. . . . Elsewhere, we are participating in the European Commission in London and in that on Italian Affairs. . . . We have just had a series of frank, extensive and friendly meetings with the British Prime Minister and Secretary of State for Foreign Affairs. We propose to have the same kind of meetings with the Soviet government during our imminent visit to Moscow. . . . We intend to confer eventually, under similar conditions, with the President of the United States of America." Thus I demonstrated that France was regaining the status she required to play her role again.

This role was to be that of one of the greatest states. I emphasized the fact by referring to the future organization of the United Nations and to our wish to sit on the Security Council. "We believe," I said, "that the powers which are in a position to act materially and morally in the various parts of the world should exercise in common the duty of encouragement and orientation. . . . In our eyes, France is, beyond all possible doubt, one of these powers." I added, "We are ready to bear, once again, our share of the burdens which preponderating powers imply. In return, we expect to be committed by no measure concerning Europe and by no major disposition concerning other parts of the world in which we have not deliberated under the same conditions as those who have adopted them."

This was particularly the case in regard to what was done in Germany. "As for the occupation of German territory, the administrative system decided on for the occupied German peoples, their own future regime, the ultimate eastern, western, southern or northern German frontiers, the measures of economic, moral and military control to be imposed, or the fate of the populations which can be separated from the German state, France will be a party to such arrangements only if she also will have been an adjudicator." I specified, "We can countenance a settlement only if it assures us the elemental security which nature has defined by the Rhine, for us as for Belgium, Holland and, to a large degree, England." But I declared that by imposing upon Germany a fate that was obligatorily pacific, France intended to lay the foundations for that valuable edifice which would be the unity of Europe. "We believe in this unity!" I proclaimed, "and we hope that it will be translated, to begin with, into specific acts binding its three poles, Moscow, London and Paris."

After indicating our intention of determining with Italy "the reparations for the injuries she had caused us," and our desire "to institute subsequently with the Italian government and people those relations which would establish a sincere reconciliation"; then, after mentioning the events in the Pacific, our decision "to play an increasingly important role in the common war effort there," and our desire "to recover all that the enemy has snatched from us," I concluded, "Perhaps France is now confronting one of those moments in history when a people is offered a destiny great in proportion to the gravity of its ordeal. But we cannot uphold our rights nor accomplish our duties if we forgo power itself. . . . Despite our losses and our woes, despite human weariness, we must reinstate the power of France! This, henceforth, is our great cause!"

The Assembly warmly applauded this speech. It unanimously passed an order of the day approving the government's action with regard to foreign policy. In this area, however, there were profound differences of attitude between the "politicians" and myself. Not that these parliamentarians of yesterday or tomorrow had reservations as to the concrete goals I had indicated. But they hailed them from afar and, in point of fact, committed themselves only vaguely. Rather than the problems confronting states—frontiers, security, the balance of forces—they were concerned with doctrinal attitudes affecting public opinion. Hence their expressions were as nebulous as they were affecting.

As long as we celebrated, for instance, "the coming victory of justice and liberty by the defeat of fascism," or "the revolutionary mission of France," or "the solidarity of the democracies," or "the building of peace on the co-operation of peoples," the delegates were in a receptive state of mind. But once explicit dealings with the Saar Basin, the Rhine, the Ruhr, Silesia, Galicia, the Levant or Indochina were suggested; once someone said "No!" ahead of time to what our allies would decide without us; once it was stated that if we were throwing in our lot with theirs it was not because England was a parliamentary nation, America democratic, and Russia a soviet state, but because all three were fighting against our invaders—then the members of the audience, while appearing attentive and even approving, indicated by various signs that it found the light too bright. On the present occasion, however, the notion that I should go to Moscow and even conclude a Franco-Russian pact received the Assembly's adherence. Its members were in favor of this action to the degree that they preferred to regard it solely as a friendly gesture toward an ally.

On November 24, I flew to Russia, accompanied by Georges Bidault. With us were General Juin, Messrs. Palewski, Dejean, etc.; M. Bogomolov was to serve as our guide. Stopping over in

Cairo, I visited King Farouk. Prudent, well informed, quick-minded, the young sovereign made no attempt to conceal his anxiety over the situation in Egypt. Although his country was taking no direct part in the world conflict, the King was delighted by the coming defeat of Hitler. But he was no less fearful that the Western victory would destroy an already precarious balance in the Middle Eastern Arab states. He feared that a Sudanese-Egyptian union would be checkmated by such a victory and, above all, that a Jewish state would be established in Palestine. The consequences of these events in the Arab world would be a wave of extremist nationalism, a serious crisis of foreign relations, and severe internal upheavals.

The sovereign, moreover, declared his and his people's sympathy for France. "We have every confidence in your future," he said, "for we have great need of you." When I pointed out that his government had nevertheless censured us harshly regarding the conditions under which Syria and Lebanon were achieving independence, he declared, smiling, "That's only politics!" I knew that personally he was not in favor of Nahas Pasha, whom the English had appointed as his Prime Minister. Finally, Farouk assured me of his esteem for the French colony which was vitally contributing to his country's progress.

Teheran was the next stop on our journey. The capital of Iran betrayed the strain of the triple occupation imposed on it. British, Russians and Americans jostled each other in the streets and observed each other among the poverty-stricken crowd, while the Persian elite sulkily withdrew. What a contrast to the favor with which cultivated circles regarded France! I received touching proofs of the latter when I received many distinguished personages whom Ambassador Pierre Lafond had invited to our legation.

During my visit to him, the Shah also showed himself to be extremely friendly. Sadly he explained the situation foisted upon his empire and himself by the presence and the demands of the three great powers whose rivalries threatened to dismember the state and the national territory. The sovereign, obviously discouraged, asked my advice. "You see," he said, "what we have come to. In your opinion, what should be my position? Having taken your country's destiny upon yourself at the most difficult moment, you are qualified to tell me."

I replied to Mohammed Riza Pahlavi that if there had ever been a moment for Iran to have an emperor symbolizing the country's sovereignty and unity, that moment was now. Therefore he himself must not leave the throne under any pretext. "As for the foreign powers," I declared, "in relation to them, Your Majesty must be independence personified. You may find yourself obliged to endure humiliation, yet you must always repudiate them. If one or another of the three occupying powers attempts to obtain your co-operation to his advantage, let him find you inaccessible, even when this attitude involves considerable discomfort for yourself! Sovereignty can be nothing more than a spark in a woodpile; once it has been struck, it will sooner or later catch fire." I assured the Shah that as France recovered her forces and her status, she would not fail to support Iran's efforts to effect the departure of the Allied troops, as soon as the German threat was averted from the country. The emperor thanked me, adding that he took comfort in the counsel I had given him.

On November 26 we landed in Baku. Following the welcome of the Soviet authorities, I received the military salute and watched while a splendid detachment of troops—bayonets down, chests out, steps thundering—marched by. Here indeed was the eternal Russian Army. Afterward we were driven into the town at great speed, to a house where our hosts, M. Bogomolov showing particular zeal among them, lavished attentions upon us. But while we should have preferred continuing our trip as soon as possible, the Soviets indicated that since our plane crew did not know either the route or the signals, it would have to be Russian planes that would carry us; furthermore, since bad weather made flight too hazardous at the beginning of winter, a special train had been reserved for us and was soon due in Baku to take us on to Moscow. In short, we had to spend two days visiting the half-deserted city, attending a performance at the municipal theater, reading the Tass news dispatches, and eating meals of an incredible luxury and abundance.

The special train was called the "Grand Duke" because Grand Duke Nicholas had used it during the First World War. In its well-furnished cars we made a trip that lasted for four days, due to the slow speed imposed by the state of the roadbeds. Stepping outside at the station stops, we were invariably surrounded by a silent but obviously cordial crowd.

I had requested a visit to Stalingrad, a gesture of respect to the Russian armies who had here won the war's decisive victory. We found the city completely demolished. Yet among the ruins, a numerous populace was working, while the authorities applied the watchword *reconstruction* in the most spectacular manner. After taking us on a tour of the battlefield, our guides drove us to a wrecked iron factory where, in a blast furnace only recently patched together, iron ore was again being smelted. But the great tank factory, which we visited next, had been completely rebuilt and re-equipped. As we entered the shops, the workers gathered around us to exchange friendly greetings. On our way back we met a column of men escorted by armed soldiers. These, it was explained, were Russian prisoners going to the yards. I must say that in relation to the "free" workers, these condemned men seemed neither more nor less passive, neither better nor worse dressed. Having delivered to the municipality the sword of honor I had brought from France for the city of Stalingrad and attended a banquet whose menu contrasted vividly with the poverty of the inhabitants, we returned to the "Grand Duke." We reached Moscow on Saturday, December 2.

M. Molotov met us at the station. He was surrounded by People's Commissars, officials and generals. The entire diplomatic corps was present. Patriotic songs resounded. A battalion of "cadets" paraded by in splendid array. As we came out of the station, I saw that a considerable crowd had gathered, from which rose a hum of sympathetic voices. I then went to the French embassy where I had decided to stay in order to remain apart from the comings and goings that negotiations inevitably provoked. Bidault, Juin and Dejean were installed in the house the Soviet government put at their disposal.

We stayed in Moscow eight days. During this time, many ideas, inquiries and suggestions were exchanged between the Russians and ourselves. Bidault and Dejean, accompanied by Garreau and Laloy—both of whom spoke Russian fluently—had various meetings with Molotov and his functionaries. Juin, accompanied by Petit, chief of our military mission, had a long conversation with the Russian general staff and its chief, General Antonov. But as was to be expected, it was Stalin and De Gaulle who said and did what was essential in these meetings. In Stalin's person, and on every subject we discussed, I had the impression of confronting the astute and implacable champion of a Russia exhausted by suffering and tyranny but afire with national ambition.

Stalin was possessed by the will to power. Accustomed by a life of machination to disguise his features as well as his inmost soul, to dispense with illusions, pity, sincerity, to see in each man an obstacle or a threat, he was all strategy, suspicion and stubbornness. The revolution, the party, the state and the war had offered him the occasions and the means of domination. He had seized them, using a thorough knowledge of the complexities of Marxist dialectic and totalitarian rigor, bringing to bear a superhuman boldness and guile, subjugating or liquidating all others.

Thenceforth, with all Russia in his hands alone, Stalin regarded his country as more mysterious, mightier and more durable than any theory, any regime. He loved it, in his way. Russia herself accepted him as a czar during a terrible epoch and tolerated Bolshevism to turn it to her own advantage, as a weapon. To unite the Slavs, to overcome the Germans, to expand in Asia, to gain access to open seas—these were the dreams of Mother Russia, these were the despot's goals. Two conditions were essential to their realization: to make Russia into a great modern, which is to say industrial, power, and at the right moment to bring her into a world conflict. The first had been fulfilled, at the price of an unprecedented expenditure of human suffering and human loss. Stalin, when I saw him, was accomplishing the second in the midst of graves and rubble. His fortune was to have found a people so vital and so patient that the worst servitudes did not paralyze them, a soil full of such resources that the most terrible destruction and waste could not exhaust it, and allies without whom he would not have conquered his adversary but who would not have triumphed without him.

During the fifteen or so hours which comprised the total of my interviews with Stalin, I discerned the outlines of his ambitious and cryptic policy. As a communist disguised as a Marshal, a dictator preferring the tactics of guile, a conqueror with an affable smile, he was a past master of deception. But so fierce was his passion that it often gleamed through this armor, not without a kind of sinister charm.

Our first conversation took place in the Kremlin on the evening of December 2. An elevator took us to the door of a long corridor punctuated by an imposing number of secret service men and off one end of which opened a large room furnished with a table and chairs. Molotov led us in and the "Marshal" appeared. After an exchange of the usual compliments, we sat down around the table. Whether talking or silent, Stalin kept his eyes lowered and doodled with his pencil.

We approached the matter of Germany straightway. None of those present doubted that the Reich must soon capitulate beneath the blows of the Allied armies; the Marshal emphasized the fact that the severest of these blows had been delivered by the Russians. We reached immediate agreement on the necessity of putting Germany in a position of harmlessness. But when I indicated to what degree the geographical separation of Russia and France had affected the outburst of German ambitions, the French capitulation, and consequently the invasion of Soviet territory, when I sketched the prospect of a direct entente between the Moscow and Paris governments in order to establish a settlement which they would propose in common to the other Allies, Stalin appeared reserved. He insisted, instead, on the necessity of studying each question with the United States and Great Britain, from which I inferred that he already had good reasons to anticipate Roosevelt's and Churchill's agreement with what he wanted.

Nevertheless, he asked me what guarantees France hoped for in the west. But when I spoke to him of the Rhine, the Saar Basin and the Ruhr, he declared that the solutions of these problems could be studied only in four-way negotiation. On the other hand, he answered my question as to the German frontier in the east quite categorically: "The former Polish territory of East Prussia, Pomerania, and Silesia must be restored to Poland."

"In other words," I asked, "the Oder frontier?"

"The Oder and the Neisse," he corrected. "Besides, there are rectifications to be made in Czechoslovakia's favor too."

I pointed out that we raised no objection in principle to these territorial changes which, furthermore, might permit the matter of Poland's eastern frontier to be settled in compensation. But I added: "Permit me to remark that if, in your eyes, the question of the Rhine cannot be broached at present, that of the Oder has already been discussed."

Stalin kept silence, still drawing his circles and stars. But soon, raising his head, he made the following proposition: "Let us study a Franco-Russian pact together, in order that our two countries may take common measures against a new German aggression."

"We are in favor of such a pact," I answered, "for the same reasons that led to the signing of the former Franco-Russian alliance and even," I added, with a certain malice, "of the 1935 treaty." Stalin and Molotov, pierced to the quick, exclaimed that the 1935 pact, signed by them and by Laval, had never been applied by the latter in either its spirit or its letter. I then indicated that by referring to the 1935 treaty and the 1892 alliance I intended to accentuate the fact that in dealing with the German menace, the mutual action of Russia and France was in the nature of things. As for the way in which a new pact would eventually be applied, I believed that the painful experiences of the past could serve as lessons to the leaders of both countries. "For my part," I added, "I am not Pierre Laval." It was agreed that Bidault and Molotov would elaborate the text of a treaty.

During the following days, the two ministers met several times. They exchanged drafts which, moreover, bore strong resemblances. At the same time, a series of receptions, visits and excursions were held in our honor. I recall in particular a dinner given at the Spiridonovka by Molotov, surrounded by Dekanozov, Litvinov and Lozovski, Deputy Ministers of Foreign Affairs. Stalin was present. At the dessert course, raising his glass, he toasted our imminent alliance. "I mean," he cried, "an alliance that is real, not one à la Laval!"

We had a long conversation together. To my compliments upon the success of the Russian Army, whose central sector under Tolbukhin had just completed a successful offensive in Hungary, he replied, "Pah! A few cities! We must drive on to Berlin, to Vienna!" At moments, he appeared relaxed, even playful. "It must be very difficult," he told me, "to govern a country like France, where everyone is so restless!"

"Yes," I answered. "And I cannot take you for an example, for you are inimitable."

He mentioned Thorez, whom the French government had permitted to return to Paris. Confronted by my irritated silence, the Marshal declared, "Don't take offense at my indiscretion! Let me say only that I know Thorez and that in my opinion he is a good Frenchman. If I were in your place, I would not put him in prison." He added, with a smile, "At least, not right away!"

"The French government," I returned, "treats the French according to the services it expects of them."

On another occasion, our hosts took us to a splendid ballet performed at the Grand Theatre. They gave a gala reception in our honor at the Spiridonovka Palace, attended by many People's Commissars, high officials, generals, their wives and all the foreign diplomats and Allied officers in Moscow. They also escorted us to an impressive evening of songs and folk dancing at the Red Army Hall. During these ceremonies, M. Molotov never left our side, his words always precise, their object always circumspect. He assigned us other guides, however, when we attended Mass in St.-Louis-des-Français, the only Catholic church open in the capital, visited Sparrow Mountain where Napoleon had had his first views of Moscow, attended the military museum, examined the Moscow subway, and inspected several factories, a military hospital and a signal corps school. Through the cold streets, across the snow, slipped silent and preoccupied citizens; those Russians we made contact with, whether among the people or in elite circles, impressed us as being eager to show their sympathy but hampered by orders which repressed their spontaneity.

We French therefore made all the greater effort to express our friendly admiration of this great people, taking advantage of the various social festivities and occasions of protocol. At the embassy, I received at my table a throng of intellectuals and writers officially catalogued by the Soviet authority as "friends of France." Chief among them were Victor Fink and Ilya Ehrenburg, both men of great talent though determined to use the latter only in the direction and tone prescribed. General Ignatiev, who had been a count and the czar's military attaché in Paris and celebrated *émigré* for many years afterward, was among the guests, defying the years in a becoming uniform and generous with his grand manner, though hampered by his present role. Jean-Richard Bloch, "seeking refuge" in Russia, introduced them all to me with a certain cramped geniality. All, mettlesome and touchy, reminded me of hobbled thoroughbreds. One evening, we invited the whole of official Moscow to the embassy. There was no flaw in the cordiality of the remarks exchanged. But among those present could be felt the weight of a vague anxiety. As if by stereotype, each man's personality expressed itself in a grisaille which was the common refuge.

Nevertheless, the terms of the pact became increasingly complicated, though the minor divergences separating Bidault's text from Molotov's could have been settled in a moment. But gradually the Soviets revealed their bargaining intentions. They sought, first of all, to gain an advantage over us by raising the question of ratification. "Given the fact that your government is a provisional one, who among you is qualified to ratify such a treaty?" M. Molotov asked Dejean, then Bidault. Lastly the Soviet Minister of Foreign Affairs turned to me. I put an end to his scruples. "You have," I told him, "signed a pact with Beneš. Yet his government, so far as I know, is a provisional one. Moreover, it is established in London." After this, there was no further question of ratification.

Then the real stake of the discussion came to light. As we had expected, it concerned Poland. Curious to know exactly what the Russians intended to do in Warsaw when their troops entered the city, I asked Stalin directly during a conference we were having in the Kremlin on December 6. Bidault, Garreau and Dejean were with me; Molotov, Bogomolov and the excellent interpreter Podzerov were sitting with Stalin.

I remarked that France had always favored and supported Polish independence. After the First World War, we had significantly contributed to its revival. Doubtless the policy subsequently adopted by Warsaw, Beck's in particular, had displeased and ultimately endangered us, while it obliged the Soviet Union to differ with us. Nevertheless, we regarded as essential the reappearance of a Poland in control of her destiny, provided she was friendly to both France and Russia. Whatever influence we might have over the Poles—I specified "over all the Poles"—we were resolved to wield in this direction. I added that the solution of the problem of the frontiers, as Stalin himself had explained it to us—that is, the "Curzon line" in the east and the "Oder–Neisse line" in the west—was acceptable to us. But I repeated that in our eyes Poland must be a truly independent state. It was therefore up to the Polish people to choose their future government. They could do this only after the liberation, and by means of free elections. For the moment, the French government maintained diplomatic relations with the Polish government in London, which had never ceased to oppose the Germans. If it happened that France should eventually be led to change this situation, she would do so only in agreement with her three allies.

Making his statement in turn, Marshal Stalin grew heated. Hearing his words, snarling, snapping and copious, it was apparent that the Polish question was the principal object of his passion and the center of his policy. He declared that Russia had taken "a major turn" with regard to this nation which for centuries had been its hereditary enemy and which it henceforth wished to regard as a friend. But there were conditions. "Poland," he said, "has always served as a corridor for the Germans to attack Russia. This corridor must be closed off, and closed off by Poland herself." To do this, the fact of placing her frontier on the Oder and the Neisse could be decisive, once the Polish state was strong and "democratic." For, the Marshal proclaimed, "there is no strong state which is not democratic."

Stalin then broached the question of the government to be established in Warsaw. He did so harshly, his remarks full of hatred and scorn for the "London Poles," praising the "Lublin Committee" formed under the Soviet aegis and declaring that the latter was the only expected and desired government in Poland. He gave for this choice, which he asserted was the one the Polish people themselves would make, reasons that demonstrated only his own bias. "In the battle that is liberating their country," he declared, "the Poles do not see the purpose of the reactionary government in London and the Anders army. On the contrary, they recognize the presence and the action of the 'Committee of National Liberation' and the troops of General Berling. They know, moreover, that it was agents of the government in London who were responsible for the failure of the Warsaw insurrection, which had been set off quite arbitrarily, without consulting the Soviet command and at a moment when the Russian troops were not in a position to intervene. Furthermore, the Polish Committee of National Liberation has begun to carry out on liberated territory an agrarian reform which has won it the enthusiastic adherence of the people. The lands belonging to the reactionary *émigrés* have been distributed to the farmers. It is here that tomorrow's Poland will derive her strength, as Revolutionary France derived hers from the sale of the national assets."

Then Stalin challenged me. "You have said that France has some influence over the Poilsh people. That is true! But why don't you use that influence to recommend the necessary solution? Why do you take the same sterile position which America and England have hitherto adopted? I should tell you that we expect you to act realistically and in the same direction as we do." He added, under his breath, "Especially since London and Washington haven't said their last word."

"I am taking account," I replied, "of your position. I discern its vast consequences. But I must repeat that the future government of Poland is the business of the Polish people and that the latter, we are convinced, must be able to express themselves by universal suffrage."

I had expected some violent reaction on the Marshal's part, but he merely smiled and murmured softly, "Bah! We'll understand each other anyway."

Eager to conclude this exploration, I asked Stalin what fate he envisaged for the Balkan States. He replied that Bulgaria, having accepted the Allied armistice conditions, would keep her independence, but that "she would receive the deserved punishment" and that she too must become "democratic." The same would apply to Rumania. Hungary had been on the point of surrendering to the Allies. But the Germans, having learned of this—"I don't know how," Stalin said—had arrested the regent, Horthy. "If a democratic government forms in Hungary," the Marshal added, "we will help it to turn against Germany." There was no such problem in the case of Yugoslavia, "since the country had united and risen against fascism." Stalin spoke violently against Mikhailovitch, whom he seemed to believe the British were concealing in Cairo. As for Greece, "the Russians have not penetrated there, leaving it to the British troops and ships. To know what is happening in Greece, you should therefore address yourself to the British."

From this conference, it was evident that the Soviets were resolved to deal just as they chose with the states and territories occupied or about to be occupied by their forces. There was therefore every reason to expect, on their part, a terrible political oppression in Central and Balkan Europe. It appeared that in this regard Moscow put no credence in any determined opposition from Washington and London. Finally, it was apparent that Stalin was going to try to sell us the pact in exchange for our public approbation of his Polish operations.

As in any well-made play, in which the plot remains unsolved while the peripities mingle and multiply until the moment of denouement, the problem of the pact suddenly assumed an unexpected aspect. Mr. Churchill had shown his hand. "I presume," he had telegraphed, in substance, to Marshal Stalin, "that on the occasion of General de Gaulle's visit you are contemplating the signing of a security treaty including Russia, Great Britain and France. For my part, I am in favor of such a plan." The Soviets informed us of the British proposition, which they apparently found satisfactory. But this was not my opinion.

First of all, we could not accept the form Churchill employed. Why did he address himself exclusively to Stalin in a matter concerning France as much as London and Moscow? Above all, I considered that in regard to the German danger, Russia and France must establish a private agreement, since they were the states most directly and immediately threatened. Events had proved as much, and at what cost! In case of a German threat, chances were that British intervention would occur neither in the time nor on the scale required. Particularly since England could do nothing without the—problematical—consent of the other Commonwealth states. Must Paris and Moscow wait to act until London was ready to do so? Lastly, if I eventually wished to renew and sharpen the existing alliance between France and England, I wished to do so only after having settled certain fundamental questions with London—the fate of Germany, the Rhine, the Middle East, etc.—as to which there were as yet no agreements. In short, we were not going to consent to the scheme of a tripartite pact. Furthermore, we considered that the moment had come to bring transactions with the Russians to an end, whether positive or not. Accompanied by Bidault, Garreau and Dejean, I presented myself at the Kremlin on December 8 to have a last session of negotiation with Stalin, Molotov and Bogomolov.

I began by remarking how France envisaged the settlement of Germany's fate: no further sovereignty of the central German State on the left bank of the Rhine; the territories thus separated retaining their German character but receiving their autonomy and consistency, economically speaking, from the western zone; the Ruhr placed under international control; the eastern German frontier marked by the Oder and the Neisse. We regretted that Russia was unwilling to conclude, with regard to these conditions, an immediate agreement with France which would then be proposed to England and the United States. But our position would not be modified.

As for alliances, we considered that they must be constructed "in three stages": first a Franco-Russian treaty providing for initial security; the Anglo-Soviet pact and an agreement still to be made between France and Great Britain constituting a second degree; the future United Nations pact, in which America would play a decisive role, crowning the entire edifice and serving as an ultimate recourse. I repeated the reasons which determined us not to adopt

Churchill's proposition of a single Anglo-Franco-Russian pact. Finally, I confirmed the fact that we would be leaving Moscow on the morning of December 10, as previously arranged.

Stalin challenged nothing of what I once again formulated in regard to German frontiers. He emphasized the advantages which he believed a tripartite pact would have. But suddenly, shifting the direction of his interests, he exclaimed, "After all, you're right! I don't see why the two of us shouldn't make a pact. But you must understand that Russia has a fundamental interest in the matter of Poland. We want Poland to be friendly to the Allies and resolutely anti-German. This is not possible with the government in London, which represents an anti-Russian spirit as virulent as ever. On the contrary, we could come to an understanding with another Poland, a Poland great, strong and democratic. If you share this view, recognize the Lublin Committee publicly and make an official arrangement with it. Then we can sign a pact with you. Notice, furthermore, that we Russians have recognized the Polish Committee of National Liberation, that this Committee is governing and administrating Poland as the enemy is driven out by our troops, and that consequently it is to Lublin that you should address yourself for everything that concerns your interests in the country, particularly the fate of prisoners and French deportees whom the retreating Germans are leaving on the spot. As for Churchill, I shall telegraph him that his project has not been accepted. He will be offended, of course. Once again. But he's offended me often enough."

Henceforth, everything was clear. I declared openly to Stalin that France was ready to conclude a security pact with Russia, that she bore no ill will toward the Lublin Committee, but that she had no intention of recognizing it as the government of Poland or dealing with it officially. The practical questions relative to the French prisoners could be settled, as they came up, by a delegate we would send to Lublin without his having the character of a diplomatic representative. I added: "France and Russia have a common interest in seeing an independent, united and genuine Poland on the scene, not an artificial Poland in which France, for her part, would have no confidence. In our eyes, the question of the future Polish government can be settled only by the Poles themselves, after the nation's liberation and with the agreement of the four Allies."

Stalin made no further observation on this statement. He merely said, good naturedly enough, that he was happy to be seeing us again the next day at the dinner he himself was giving in our honor.

The atmosphere was strained on December 9. Molotov had confirmed to Bidault the condition set by Stalin for the pact's conclusion. Moreover, he had gone so far as to give him the draft of an agreement between the French government and Lublin, by virtue of which Paris officially recognized the Polish Committee of Liberation. The Russians extended their good offices to the point of proposing to us, at the same time, the terms of a communiqué announcing the news to the world. The French Minister of Foreign Affairs, naturally, informed the Commissar of the Soviet People that this suggestion was unacceptable. As for me, I attributed our partners' attitude not only to their desire to see France associated with their Polish policy, but also to their estimation of our intentions. To proceed in this manner, they must have imagined, despite what I had said, that we were interested in signing the pact at any price, lest General de Gaulle find a difficult situation waiting for him in Paris. But this was an error on their part, and I was determined to prove as much.

Nevertheless, the chief members of the Lublin Committee, arriving from Galicia a few days before, increased their efforts at the French embassy to be received "on matters of intelligence" by General de Gaulle. Two months before, they had been received by Messrs. Churchill and Eden during the British ministers' trip to Moscow. They had also encountered M. Mikolajczyk, head of the Polish government in London, and several of his ministers who had come to the Russian capital on the joint request of the British and the Soviets. I saw no reason to refuse their visit. Invited to the embassy, they were shown into my offices on the afternoon of the ninth.

Chief among them were M. Bierut, their president, M. Osuska-Morawski, in charge of "Foreign Affairs," and General Rola-Zymierski, responsible for "National Defense." During the conversation I was not greatly impressed with their group. When I expressed France's deep sympathy for their country, which despite its ordeal had never ceased to take part, everywhere in Europe, in the struggle against Germany; the French government's desire to see Poland reappear independent and friendly to France and her allies; the fact that, without wishing to intrude in their own affairs, we hoped that the Poles would reach an agreement among themselves in order to re-establish their government—they replied in the most partisan tone, insistent upon their faction and their ambitions, subject to an obvious Communist allegiance and obliged to speak lines prepared for them in advance.

M. Bierut said nothing of the war. He spoke of the agrarian reform, explained what he expected from it politically and lavished bitter reproaches upon the *"émigré"* government in London. M. Osuska-Morawski resoundingly declared that Poland, traditionally friendly to France, was now more so than ever. Therefore he asked, in the same terms Molotov and Stalin had used in this regard, for the signing of an agreement between the Polish Committee and the French government, the exchange of diplomatic representatives, and the announcement of this fact by publication of a mutual communiqué. General Rola-Zymierski declared that the Committee of Liberation had ten well-equipped divisions at its disposal and expressed his total confidence in the Soviet command. Despite my requests, he made no allusion to what the Polish Army had accomplished in Poland in 1939, in France in 1940, in Italy, France and the Low Countries in 1944, or to the battles fought by the national resistance. Between my interlocutors' hackneyed phrases and the way in which *Pravda* daily dealt with Polish affairs, there was too close a resemblance to incline me to recognize the Lublin Committee as an independent Poland.

I informed Messrs. Bierut, Morawski and Zymierski that the French government was willing to delegate to territory in their control an officer, Captain Christian Fouchet, to settle practical questions involving French nationals, particularly with regard to our prisoners. We did not oppose the presence in Paris of a member of their organization to deal with analogous affairs, should there be any. But we remained on official relations, as did virtually all the Allies, with the Polish government in London and we contemplated neither agreement nor protocol nor exchange of diplomatic representatives with the Committee of Liberation. I must say that M. Osuska-Morawski then declared, with some dignity, that under these conditions it would be better to postpone the assignment to Lublin of Commandant Fouchet. "As you wish!" I replied. My visitors took their leave.

Meanwhile, Messrs. Averell Harriman, United States Ambassador to Russia, and John Balfour, England's chargé d'affaires, had come to see me upon my invitation. I was determined, as a matter of fact, to keep them informed of our transactions with the Soviets and to let them know that we were not agreeing to recognize the Lublin Committee. They seemed satisfied with this news. Harriman nevertheless told me, "For our part, we Americans have decided to behave with the Russians as if we trusted them." Hearing this remark and, further, bearing in mind what Stalin suggested as to America's and England's imminent reversal of attitude on the Polish problem, I requested the two diplomats to inform Messrs. Roosevelt and Churchill in my behalf that if they were to modify their position, I expected them to inform us of the fact with the same diligence I had shown toward them.

In this day devoted to diplomatic fencing, there was one affecting hour, when 1 passed in review the aviators of the "Normandie-Niémen" Regiment. It had originally been agreed with the Russians that I would inspect the regiment in the Insterburg region, where it

was in operation. But, as had occurred in regard to the Baku–
Moscow trip, our allies asked me to forgo a trip by air because of
the bad weather. Besides, the round trip by road or rail would
have taken three days and three nights. But Stalin, informed of the
fact, then had the entire regiment brought to Moscow by train.
I could thus salute this magnificent unit—the only western force
fighting on the Russian front—and make contact with each man of
all those serving France so valiantly. I took advantage of their
presence to decorate, along with several of their number, those
Russian generals and officers who had come from the front for the
occasion.

But when we attended the dinner given by Stalin, negotiations
were still deadlocked. Until the last moment, the Russians had
insisted upon obtaining from us at least a communiqué which would
proclaim the establishment of official relations between the French
government and the Lublin Committee, a communiqué which
would be made public at the same time as the announcement of the
Franco-Russian security pact. We had not consented to this measure. If I had determined not to commit France in the attempted
subjection of the Polish nation, it was not that I had any illusions as
to what this refusal might effect from a practical point of view.
Obviously we had no means of keeping the Soviets from executing
their plans. Further, I foresaw that America and Great Britain
would let them proceed as they wished. But however little weight
France's attitude might have at the moment, it could later be important that she had adopted it at that particular moment. The future
lasts a long time. All things are possible, even the fact that an
action in accord with honor and honesty ultimately appears to be
a prudent political investment.

Forty Russians—People's Commissars, diplomats, generals, high
officials, almost all in brilliant uniform—were gathered in the
Kremlin *salon* when the French were shown in. The United States
ambassador and the British chargé d'affaires were present. We were
taken up the monumental staircase decorated with the same pictures

as in the czar's time. Terrifying subjects were represented in them: the furious battle of the Irtysh, Ivan the Terrible strangling his son, etc. The Marshal shook hands with us and led his guests to the dining room. The table sparkled with inconceivable luxury. We were served an overpowering banquet.

Stalin and I, sitting beside each other, chatted informally. M. Podzerov and M. Laloy translated our remarks word by word, as we spoke. The operations under way, the life we led in our respective functions, the opinions we had of the chief enemy and Allied leaders, were the subjects of our conversation. The pact was not mentioned. The nearest we came to it was when the Marshal asked me, in a detached tone of voice, my impression of the members of the Lublin Committee. To which I replied that they seemed to me a group capable of being turned to account, though they were certainly not "independent Poland." Stalin's remarks were direct and simple. He assumed the manners of a peasant of rudimentary culture, applying to the vastest problems the judgments of rough good sense. He ate heavily during each course and served himself copiously from a bottle of Crimean wine frequently replaced in front of him. But beneath these good-natured appearances, the fighter engaged in a merciless struggle was apparent. Furthermore, the Russians around the table, watchful and constrained in manner, never took their eyes from him. On their part, manifest submission and apprehensiveness; on his, concentrated and vigilant authority— these were, as far as could be seen, the relations of this political and military general staff with this sociably solitary leader.

Suddenly the picture changed. The time for toasts had come. Stalin began playing an extraordinary scene.

He had, first of all, warm words for France and kind compliments for me. I made similar remarks in his behalf and that of Russia. He toasted the United States and President Roosevelt, then England and Mr. Churchill, and listened solemnly to Harriman's and Balfour's replies. He saluted Bidault, Juin and each of the other Frenchmen there, the French Army, the "Normandie-Niémen"

Regiment. Then, these formalities accomplished, he put on his big show.

Thirty times Stalin stood up to drink to the health of those Russians present. One after the other he designated them. The People's Commissars—Molotov, Beria, Bulganin, Voroshilov, Mikoyan, Kaganovitch, etc.—received the master's apostrophes first. Then he moved on to the generals and officials. The Marshal solemnly described each man's task and his merit in fulfilling it. But he continually declared and exalted the power of Russia herself. He shouted, for instance, to the Marshal of Artillery: "Voronov! To your health! You are the man in charge of deploying the system of our large- and small-bore guns on the battlefields. It is thanks to this system that the enemy has been overwhelmed all along the line. Go to it! Bravo for your cannon!" Then, addressing himself to the Chief of the Naval General Staff: "Admiral Kuznetzov! Not enough is known about all that our fleet is doing! Be patient! A day will come when we shall rule the seas!" Calling on Yakovlev, the aeronautics engineer who had perfected the splendid *Yak* pursuit plane: "I salute you! Your planes sweep the skies. But we need still more and better planes. It is up to you to make them!" Sometimes Stalin mingled threats with his commendations. He attacked Novikov, Chief of the Air Force General Staff: "You are the one who uses our planes. If you use them badly, you should know what's in store for you." Pointing toward one of the guests: "There he is! That is the supply director. It is his job to bring men and material to the front. He'd better do his best. Otherwise he'll be hanged for it—that's the custom in our country." As he finished each toast, Stalin shouted: "Come here!" to whomever he had just named. The latter, leaving his place, ran forward to clink glasses with the Marshal under the stares of the other stiff and silent Russians.

This tragicomic scene could have no other purpose than to impress the French by displaying the Soviet might and the domination of the man at its head. But, having witnessed it, I was all the less inclined to lend my support to the sacrifice of Poland. Therefore it was with a marked unconcern, in the *salon* after dinner, that I observed, sitting around Stalin and myself, the obstinate chorus of diplomats—Molotov, Dekanozov and Bogomolov on the one side; Bidault, Garreau and Dejean on the other. The Russians tirelessly returned to the deliberation on the recognition of the Lublin Committee. But since, for me, the question was closed, and since I had announced as much, I regarded this new discussion as futile. Knowing, furthermore, the propensity of diplomacy's technicians to negotiate in every case, even at the expense of political goals, and mistrusting the communicative warmth of an extended encounter, I was apprehensive lest our team of ministers be induced to make some distressing concessions with regard to terms. Of course the issue would not be affected, for my decision was made. But it would have been regrettable if the French delegation appeared to lack unity.

I therefore affected not to be interested by the council's arguments. Noticing this, Stalin bid even higher. "Ah, these diplomats!" he exclaimed. "What chatterers! There's only one way to shut them up—cut them all down with a machine gun! Someone get me one!" Then, leaving the negotiators and followed by his other guests, he led me into a neighboring room to see a Soviet film made for propaganda purposes in 1938. It was an extremely conformist and quite naïve affair; the Germans were shown treacherously invading Russia, but the invaders were soon forced to retreat before the energy of the Russian people, the courage of its army and the valor of its generals. They were then invaded in their turn; revolution broke out all over Germany, triumphing in Berlin where, on the ruins of fascism and thanks to the help of the Soviets, an era of peace and prosperity was prophesied. Stalin laughed and clapped his hands. "I'm afraid Monsieur de Gaulle was not pleased by the end of the story." Somewhat annoyed, I replied: "In any case, your victory pleases me. Particularly since at the beginning of the actual war, relations between you and the Germans did not turn out as we saw them in this film."

Meanwhile, I had sent for Georges Bidault to ask whether the Soviets were ready to sign the pact. The Minister of Foreign Affairs answered that everything depended on our own acceptance of a joint declaration by the French government and the Polish Committee, a declaration which would be published at the same time as the communiqué relative to the Franco-Russian security pact. "Under these conditions," I declared to Bidault, "it is useless and will become disadvantageous to continue the negotiation. I shall therefore bring it to an end." At midnight, the film over and the lights on again, I stood up and said to Stalin: "I am making my farewells. Soon the train will be taking me back to France. I cannot thank you enough for the way in which you yourself and the Soviet government have received me in your valiant country. We have informed each other as to our respective points of view. We have remarked our agreement on the essential point, which is that France and Russia shall continue the war together until complete victory. Au revoir, Monsieur le Maréchal!" At first Stalin seemed not to understand. "Stay then," he murmured. "We're going to show another film." But when I held out my hand, he shook it and let me leave. I reached the door, saluting the other guests who seemed paralyzed with astonishment.

M. Molotov rushed up. His face pale, he accompanied me to my car. To him, too, I expressed my satisfaction as to my visit. He stammered a few syllables without being able to conceal his confusion. There was no doubt that the Soviet minister was profoundly sorry to see the failure of a project that had been pursued with such tenacity. There remained little time to shift positions before the French left the capital. Obviously the attempt to obtain recognition of the Lublin Committee by Paris had failed. But furthermore, at the point where matters now stood, there was every danger that De Gaulle would return to France without having signed the pact. What effect would such an outcome have? And would it not be Molotov whom Stalin would blame for the failure? For my part, resolved to have the best of the argument, I returned calmly to the French

embassy. Learning that Bidault had not followed me, I sent someone to request him to do so. We left Garreau and Dejean behind
us. They would maintain contacts which might be useful but would
not commit us.

Fundamentally, I had few doubts as to what would happen next.
And as a matter of fact, toward two in the morning, Maurice Dejean
came to report a new development. After a long meeting between
Stalin and Molotov, the Russians had announced that they were
disposed to accept, with regard to relations between Paris and Lublin, a profoundly edulcorated text. Garreau and Dejean then felt
they could suggest a version on this order: "By agreement between the French government and the Polish Committee of National Liberation, M. Christian Fouchet has been sent to Lublin,
M. ———— has been sent to Paris." Then M. Molotov had indicated
that "if General de Gaulle accepted this conclusion in the matter of
Poland, the Franco-Russian pact could be signed at once."

I refused, of course, any mention of an "agreement" with the
Lublin Committee. The only release which, for several days, could
be in accord with French policy and with the truth as well was
quite simply this: "Captain Fouchet has arrived in Lublin." Dejean
left to inform Molotov of this, and the latter, after conferring again
with Stalin, announced that he was satisfied. He clung, however,
to a final condition as to the date Fouchet's arrival in Lublin would
be made public. The Soviet minister insisted that this announcement
be made at the same time as that of the signing of the Franco-
Russian security pact, that is, within twenty-four hours. But this
was precisely the coincidence I wished to avoid, and I sent Dejean
to say so formally. This was on December 10, which was to be the
date of the pact. Fouchet's presence in Galicia would not be announced until the twenty-eighth, at the earliest. This condition was
agreed to.

Meanwhile, Bidault had returned to the Kremlin to draw up the
definitive text of the pact with our partners. This was presented to
me and I approved it as a whole. In it was stated the commitment

of both sides to continue the war until complete victory, not to conclude a separate peace with Germany, and finally, to take in common all measures intended to oppose a new German threat. Mention was made of the participation of both countries in the United Nations organization. The treaty would be valid for a period of twenty years.

I was informed that the final negotiations had been made in the Kremlin, in a room next to those where the evening's guests continued to come and go. During these difficult hours, Stalin kept himself continually informed of the negotiations and arbitrated them, as they went on, on the Russian account. But this did not keep him from passing through the *salons* to chat and drink with one man or another. Colonel Pouyade, commander of the "Normandie" Regiment, was the object of his particular attention. Finally, I was informed that everything was ready for the signing of the pact. This would take place in M. Molotov's office, which I went to at four in the morning.

The ceremony assumed a certain solemnity. Russian photographers, silent and without making any requests for poses, took pictures. The two Ministers of Foreign Affairs, surrounded by the two delegations, signed the copies drawn up in French and in Russian. Stalin and I stood behind them. "Thus," I said to him, "the treaty has been ratified. On this point, I imagine, your anxiety has been dissolved." Then we shook hands. "We must celebrate this!" the Marshal declared. In an instant, tables were brought and we sat down to supper.

Stalin was a good sport. In a low voice, he complimented me: "You have played well! Well done! I like dealing with someone who knows what he wants, even if he doesn't share my views." In contrast with the fierce scene he had played a few hours before, raising toasts to all his collaborators, he now spoke of everything in a detached way, as if he regarded the other man, the war, history, and himself from a pinnacle of serenity. "After all," he said, "it is only death who wins." He pitied Hitler, "a poor wretch who won't escape from this one." To my invitation, "Will you come see us in Paris?" he answered, "How can I? I'm an old man. I'm going to die soon."

He raised his glass in honor of France "who now possessed resolved, intractable leaders, and whom he desired great and powerful because Russia needed a great and powerful ally." Finally he drank to Poland, though there was no Pole present. It was as if he were insisting on making me take note of his intentions. "The czars," he said, "had a bad policy of trying to dominate the other Slavic peoples. We have a new policy. Let Slavs everywhere be independent and free! It is then that they will be our friends. Long live a strong, independent and democratic Poland! Long live the friendship of France, Poland and Russia!" He looked at me. "What does Monsieur de Gaulle think of that?" Listening to Stalin, I measured the abyss separating words from deed in the Soviet world. I replied, "I am in complete agreement with what Monsieur Stalin has said about Poland," and I emphasized, "Yes, in agreement with what he has said."

The farewells, on his part, assumed an effusive quality. "You can count on me!" he declared. "If you or France needs us, we will share what we have with you down to our last crumb!" Suddenly, calling over Podzerov, the Russian interpreter who had attended every meeting and translated every exchange, the Marshal said to him, his expression grim, his voice harsh, "You know too much! I'd better send you to Siberia." I left the room with my ministers. Turning back at the door, I saw Stalin sitting, alone, at the table. He had started eating again.

Our departure from Moscow took place that same morning. The return trip, too, was made by way of Teheran. On the way, I wondered how French public opinion would receive the Kremlin pact, given the avatars of the Franco-Russian alliance during the last thirty years and the propaganda battles which, because of the development of Communism, had long distorted the problem. On our way through Cairo, I had a first indication. Ambassador Lescuyer presented to me the French colony, this time united in its enthusiasm, whereas on the occasion of my earlier visits, in 1941 and 1942, the colony had been divided. Here, as elsewhere, it was apparent that of all influences, the strongest is that of success.

The visit to Tunis was distinguished by an impressive reception the Bey insisted on giving me at Palais du Bardo. Alongside this wise sovereign, meeting Tunisians of the highest quality, in this residence with echoes of history, I discerned the elements necessary for the functioning of a state. The latter, prepared by our protectorate, seemed about ready to take to its own wings, with France's assistance. On December 16 we were in Paris.

The general reaction to the signing of the pact was indeed satisfactory. The public saw in the occasion a sign of our return to the concert of great powers. Political circles appreciated it as a reassuring link in the chain that held the United Nations together. Certain professionals—or fanatics—of faction whispered that the treaty had been effected only by concessions to the French Communist party, allowing it to moderate in the political and social struggle and participate in the nation's recovery. But on the whole, for various reasons, response to the Moscow agreement was distinctly favorable. The Consultative Assembly, too, expressed its approbation. Bidault opened the session on December 21 by discussing the stipulations the pact actually involved; I closed it by explaining "what had been, what was, and what would be the philosophy of the Franco-Russian alliance we had just concluded."

Nevertheless the general euphoria did not distract my attention from the disturbing probabilities revealed by the Moscow discussions. We must expect that Russia, America and England would conclude a series of bargains from which the rights of France, the liberty of peoples, and the equilibrium of Europe had everything to lose.

As a matter of fact, since the beginning of January, without any diplomatic communication having been made to us, the Anglo-American press announced that Messrs. Roosevelt, Stalin and Churchill were to have a conference. The "Big Three" would decide what was to be done in Germany after the Reich's "unconditional surrender." They would determine their behavior with regard to the people of Central and Balkan Europe. They would, finally, prepare the convocation of an assembly with a view toward organizing the United Nations.

Naturally I was offended that we were not invited, but I was not at all surprised. Whatever the progress we had made along the road that would lead France to her place, I knew the starting point too well to believe we had reached our goal already. Moreover, there was every evidence that our present exclusion would provoke a demonstration greatly to our advantage. For matters had ripened sufficiently so that we could not be kept out of what was to be done. Although Messrs. Roosevelt, Stalin and Churchill could reach decisions regarding Germany and Italy, they would be obliged, in order to apply them, to ask for General de Gaulle's co-operation. As for the Vistula, the Danube and the Balkan States, America and England would doubtless abandon them to the discretion of the Soviets. But in that case the world would discover that there was a correlation between France's absence and Europe's new laceration. Finally, judging that the time was ripe to indicate that France did not sanction the way she was being treated, I decided to take this exceptional occasion to do so.

Actually, among the "Big Three," only one state was opposed to our presence. To emphasize this fact, the British and Russians immediately had recourse to semiofficial informants. Naturally I had no illusions that Marshal Stalin, who knew my position with regard to Poland, and Mr. Churchill, who expected to obtain carte blanche in the Middle East from his partners, had stipulated that De Gaulle sit beside them at the council table. But I could not doubt that the explicit refusal came from President Roosevelt. Moreover, he himself felt he must make his attitude explicit. For this purpose, he delegated his closest adviser and intimate friend, Harry Hopkins, as his "special envoy" to Paris.

Hopkins arrived several days before the Yalta Conference began.

I received him on January 27. Accompanied by Ambassador Caffery, Harry Hopkins was supposed to "sugar-coat" the pill. But since he was a high-minded as well as a skillful man, he approached the matter from its most significant aspect and asked to discuss the fundamental question of Franco-American relations. It was in this way, certainly, that matters could best be illuminated. Hopkins expressed himself with great frankness. "There is," he said, "a discomfort in relations between Paris and Washington. Yet the war's end is approaching. To a certain degree the world's future will depend on the concerted action of the United States and France. How can we bring their relationship out of the impasse in which it is lodged?"

I asked Hopkins what, in American eyes, was the cause of the unfortunate state of relations between the two nations. "The cause," he replied, "is above all the stupefying disappointment we suffered when we saw France collapse and surrender in the disaster of 1940. Our traditional conception of her value and her energy was overthrown in an instant. Add to this the fact that those French military or political leaders in whom we successively placed our trust because they seemed to symbolize that France we had believed in did not show themselves—and this is the least that can be said—worthy of our hopes. Do not seek elsewhere for the true source of the attitude we have adopted toward your country. Judging that France was no longer what she had been, we could not trust her to play one of the leading roles.

"It is true that you yourself, General de Gaulle, appeared on the scene; that a French resistance movement formed around you; that French forces have returned to combat; that today all France acclaims you and recognizes your government. Since at first we had no motive for believing in this prodigy, since you then became the living proof of our mistake, since you yourself, finally, have not dealt sparingly with us, we have not favored you up to the present. But we acknowledge what you have accomplished and are delighted to see France reappear among the Allies. Yet how could we forget what we have lived through on her account? Furthermore, knowing the political inconsistency that riddles your country, what reasons have we to suppose General de Gaulle will be in a position to lead her for long? Are we not then justified in using circumspection as to the share we expect of France to bear of the burden of tomorrow's peace?"

Listening to Harry Hopkins, I felt I was hearing again what President Roosevelt had said to me about France in Washington, six months before. But at that time the liberation had not yet taken place. I and my government were still established in Algeria; there was still some excuse for American doubts as to the mind of Metropolitan France. But at present, everything was decided. It was known that our people wanted to take part in the victory. It was apparent what our reviving army was worth. It was recognized that I had been installed in Paris at the head of a government surrounded and supported by national fervor. Yet was the United States any more convinced that France was capable of becoming a great power once again? Did it truly wish to help her? These were the questions which, from the French point of view, dominated the present and future of our relations with the United States.

I declared as much to the President's special envoy. "You have told me why, on your part, our relations are flawed. I am going to show you what, on our side, contributes to the same result. Let us pass over the episodic and secondary frictions provoked by the abnormal conditions under which our alliance is operating. For us, this is the essential matter: In the mortal dangers we French have survived since the beginning of the century, the United States does not give us the impression that it regards its own destiny as linked with that of France, that it wishes France to be great and strong, that it is doing all it can to help her to remain or become so once again. Perhaps, in fact, we are not worth the trouble. In that case, you are right. But perhaps we shall rise again. Then you will have been wrong. In either case, your behavior tends to alienate us."

I reminded him that the disaster of 1940 was the result of the excessive ordeals the French had endured. Yet during World War I the United States intervened only after three years of combat in which we had exhausted ourselves repulsing German aggression. America, moreover, had entered the conflict solely because of the damage to her commerce by German submarines and after attempting to effect a peace by compromise, according to the terms of which France would not even have recovered Alsace and Lorraine. Once the Reich was conquered, America had refused France the security pledges formally promised her, had exercised a stubborn pressure upon her to renounce the guarantees and the reparations due to her, and lastly had furnished Germany all the aid necessary for a return to power. "The result," I said, "was Hitler."

I recalled the immobility the United States had observed when the Third Reich attempted to dominate Europe; the neutrality she had clung to while France suffered the disaster of 1940; the rejection Franklin Roosevelt had offered Paul Reynaud's appeal, when a mere promise of aid, even secret and long-term, would have been enough to persuade our government to continue the war; the support granted for so long by Washington to those French leaders who had subscribed to capitulation and the rebuffs continually offered to those who had continued the combat. "It is true," I added, "that you were obliged to enter the conflict when the Japanese, as Germany's allies, attacked Pearl Harbor. The colossal war effort you have since mustered is about to render victory a certainty. Rest assured that France is thoroughly aware of the fact. She will never forget that without you her liberation would not have been possible. Still, while she is slowly recovering, it cannot escape her notice that America is counting on her only as a subordinate, as is proved by the fact that Washington is furnishing only a limited supply of arms for the French Army, as well as by what you yourself have just told me."

"You have explained the past," remarked Mr. Harry Hopkins, "in an incisive but accurate manner. Now America and France face the future. Once again, how shall we act so that henceforth they may act in agreement and in full mutual confidence?"

"If this is really America's intention," I replied, "I cannot understand how she can undertake to settle Europe's future in France's absence. Especially since after pretending to ignore her in the imminent 'Big Three' discussions, she must ask Paris to consent to whatever has been decided."

Messrs. Hopkins and Caffery agreed. They declared that their government now attached the highest importance to France's participation in the London "European Commission," on equal footing with America, Russia and Great Britain. They even added that so far as the Rhine was concerned, the United States was more disposed than our two other great allies to settle the question in accord with our wishes. As for this last point, the question of the Rhine would not be settled by America any more than by Russia or Great Britain. The solution, if there was one, could eventually be found only by France or by Germany. Both had long sought for it, one contending against the other. Tomorrow, they would perhaps discover it in association.

To conclude the meeting, I said to the two ambassadors: "You have come in behalf of the President of the United States to discuss the profound problems of Franco-American relations. I think that we have done so. The French have the impression that you no longer consider the greatness of France necessary to the world and to yourself. This is responsible for the coolness you feel in our country and even in this office. If you want relations between our countries to be established on a different footing, it is up to you to do what must be done. Until you reach a decision, I send President Roosevelt the salute of my friendship on the eve of the conference that will bring him to Europe."

While the "Big Three" were conferring at Yalta, I felt I must publicly call France to their attention, if indeed they had forgotten her. On February 5, speaking on the radio, I formulated this warning: "As for the future peace settlement, we have informed our allies that France will of course be committed to absolutely nothing she has not been in a position to discuss and approve in the same capacity as the others. . . . I specify that the presence of French forces from one end of the Rhine to the other, the separation of the territories on the left bank of the Rhine and of the Ruhr Basin from what will be the German state, the independence of the Polish, Czech, Austrian and Balkan nations are conditions which France judges essential. . . . We are not distressed, moreover, by the like-lihood that it will be up to us to bring some of them to realization, for we are 106 million men, united under the French flag, in im-mediate proximity to what concerns us most directly."

On February 12, the "Big Three," concluding the conference, published a communiqué which proclaimed the principles on which they had agreed. They declared that the war would be continued until the Reich surrendered unconditionally; that the three great powers would occupy its territory, each in a different region; that the control and administration of Germany would be exercised by a military commission formed of the commanders in chief, with headquarters in Berlin. But in the terms of the communiqué, France was invited to join America, England and Russia in occupying a zone of German territory and in being the fourth member of the German government. Further, the communiqué declared the inten-tion of the "Big Three" to dissolve all German armed forces, to destroy forever the German general staff, to punish the war criminals, and lastly to make Germany pay reparations, to what-ever degree possible, for the damages she had caused.

To maintain peace and security throughout the world, a "General International Organization" was to be set up. For this purpose, a conference of all the states which had signed the Atlantic Charter would be held in San Francisco on April 25 and would take as the basis of the "Organization" those principles which had been defined at the Dumbarton Oaks Conference. Although France had not taken part in this last, it was specified that she would be consulted immediately by the three "great powers" in order to determine all final arrangements with them, which obviously meant that she would sit with them on the "Security Council."

The communiqué also included a "Declaration Regarding Liberated Europe." This actually concerned Hungary, Rumania and Bulgaria, who had marched with Germany and were now occupied by Russia. The declaration proclaimed the right of all peoples to settle for themselves the re-establishment of democracy, the freedom of the elections which would create their governments, but remained vague as to the practical measures to be applied, which came down to leaving the Soviets to their own devices. The three great powers expressed their hope that "the government of the French Republic would associate itself with them in regard to the proposed procedure."

The "Big Three" lastly announced that they had "come to an agreement" regarding the Polish question. They decided that Poland would be bounded, on the east, by the Curzon line and would receive, in the north and west, "a substantial increase of territory." As for the political regime, no allusion was made to free elections. A government, referred to as one of "national unity," was to be formed "starting from the provisional government already functioning in the country," that is, the Polish Committee of Liberation, known as the "Lublin Committee." Doubtless, it was indicated, the latter would be enlarged "to include democratic leaders residing in Poland and abroad." But since there was no reference to the London government-in-exile, since the composition of the new government remained quite unspecified, since no control on the part of the western powers was provided for, there could be no doubt as to the kind of government Poland would receive. Nor as to the authority that would be established in Yugoslavia. Although in regard to this country the Yalta communiqué referred to the ratification by a future "National Assembly," as a matter of fact Tito's dictatorship was recognized unconditionally. Thus Stalin was granted all he demanded in regard to Warsaw and Belgrade. To this, and this only, France was not—and for good reason—invited to accede.

In the course of the same day that the American, British and Russian leaders published their communiqué, Ambassador Jefferson Caffery brought me, on their behalf, two "communications." The first was the formal invitation addressed to France to join the three allies at the council table in regard to Germany. The second, imputing to "circumstances" the fact that France had not been able to discuss the terms of the "Declaration Regarding Liberated Europe," expressed the hope that the French government would nevertheless agree to assume in common with the other three powers the eventual obligations which this declaration implied. At the same time, Mr. Caffery handed me a memorandum from the President of the United States in the name of the "Big Three." The President asked France to be a "sponsoring power," along with America, Great Britain, Russia and China, at the next United Nations conference and to participate in the deliberations which the Moscow, Washington, London and Chungking governments were going to institute in order to further the organization established at Dumbarton Oaks.

In other words, if it remained inadmissible, from our point of view, that our three allies should have held their Crimean conference without us, the steps they were now taking in our behalf were in no way offensive. Certainly several of their conclusions might seem irritating to us, and the propositions by which they sought to attract us would have to be studied carefully before we accepted them. But on certain essential points, their communications included important satisfactions for us. This is what I decided on examining the documents brought by Mr. Caffery February 12.

But during the course of the afternoon, the ambassador asked for another audience. He brought me a personal message from President Roosevelt. The latter informed me of his wish to confer with me. He himself fixed the site of our meeting, which was to take place in Algiers. If I agreed to go there, he would also set the date.

Roosevelt's invitation seemed to me inopportune. To Mr. Harry Hopkins, who had referred to its likelihood during his visit to Paris, Georges Bidault had made it clear that it would be better not to extend it at all. To meet with the President immediately after a conference at which he had opposed my presence was scarcely a suitable move on my part. All the less so since my visit would offer no practical advantage, the Yalta decisions being made, though on the other hand it might lead others to believe that I agreed to everything that had been settled there. As a matter of fact, we did not approve the fate arbitrarily imposed not only upon Hungary, Rumania and Bulgaria, who had joined the German cause, but also upon Poland and Yugoslavia, who were our allies. Further I suspected that in regard to certain questions—Syria, Lebanon, Indochina—of direct interest to France, the "Big Three" had reached some agreement among themselves which was incompatible with our interests. If Roosevelt wanted to see De Gaulle for good reasons, why had he not permitted him to come to the Crimea?

And then, how was the American President qualified to invite the French President to visit him in France? I myself had invited him early in November to meet with me in Paris. Although he had not come, he could either do so now or ask me to choose another site. But how could I agree to be summoned to a point on the national territory by a foreign chief of state? It is true that, for Franklin Roosevelt, Algiers perhaps was not France. All the more reason to remind him of the fact. Furthermore, the President was beginning his journey home through the Middle Eastern Arab states. On board his cruiser passing through their waters, he summoned their kings and chiefs of state, including the presidents of the Syrian and Lebanese republics placed under French mandate. What he was offering General de Gaulle was to receive him on the same ship and under the same conditions. I regarded such treatment as an affront, whatever the present relationship of forces. The sovereignty, the dignity of a great nation must not be touched. I was responsible for those of France.

After having consulted with the ministers on February 13, I requested Mr. Jefferson Caffery to inform the President of the United States on my behalf "that it was impossible for me to come to Algiers at this time without preparation and that, consequently, I could not, to my great regret, receive him there; that the French government had invited him, last November, to come to Paris and greatly regretted that he could not do so at that time, but would be happy to welcome him in the capital should he wish to make a visit at any time whatsoever; that, if he wished, during his trip, to make Algiers a port of call nevertheless, would he be so kind as to inform us of the fact, in order that we might address the necessary instructions to the Governor General of Algeria for everything to be done in accordance with his wishes."

This incident provoked a considerable reaction in public opinion the world over. Personally, I should have preferred to avoid any such outbreaks. But the American newspapers, obviously trimming their sails to catch the prevailing wind, took pains to present the episode as an affront which General de Gaulle had deliberately inflicted upon the American President. The latter, moreover, felt no need to conceal his mortification. Upon his return to Washington, he published, in regard to the meeting which had not taken place, a communiqué betraying his acrimony. In the speech he made to Congress on March 2 to reveal the results of the Yalta Conference, he made a transparent allusion to De Gaulle, referring to certain "prima donnas" whose whims had prevented a valuable discussion. For my part, I was content to provide the press a note explaining the facts.

Roosevelt's bitter remarks could offend me, of course. But I was persuaded that they indicated his bad humor rather than any profound feeling he entertained in my regard. Had he lived longer, and had we had an occasion, once the war was won, to discuss matters at our leisure, I believe he would have understood and appreciated the reasons that determined my actions as chief of state. As for myself, no incident could ever have brought me to ignore the range of his mind, his talents or his courage. When death tore him from his gigantic task, at the very moment when he was about to see its victorious conclusion, it was with all my heart that I saluted his memory with regret and admiration.

In France, however, a large proportion of the elements organized to understand one another did not fail to disapprove the way in which I had received the President's "invitation" to come to Algiers. A number of "politicians" professing to see in Roosevelt the infallible champion of democracy and inhabiting a universe quite unrelated to the motives of superior interest and national dignity which I had served, took offense at my attitude. The Communists condemned it because it characterized my reserve toward the excessive concessions Roosevelt had made to the Soviets. Many businessmen were distressed by my gesture because it affected their hopes of American assistance. Prominent citizens were generally inclined to favor the foreigner, provided he was rich and strong, and to criticize any French action which appeared to indicate a policy. Furthermore, and despite formal precautions, all these categories had begun to withdraw from me in proportion as they foresaw the possibilities of returning to the pleasant tactics of illusion and denigration.

I was therefore forced to recognize that the notion I had formed of France's status and rights was shared by few of those who shaped public opinion. To support my policy, that of national ambition, I could count less and less on their voices, their pens, their influence. I must confess that I was profoundly affected by this initial dissension, which with increasing effect would compromise all my efforts to come.

But what was won was won securely. No foreign opposition, no internal discord could henceforth keep France from resuming her proper status. After all, the Yalta Conference itself had just demonstrated the fact: if we were invited to become, at once, a member of the council formed by the great powers to settle the fate of our enemies and organize the peace, it was because we

were regarded as one of the chief belligerent—and, shortly, victorious—powers. In world politics, soon nothing would remain of
the conquered-nation status which France had appeared to stoop
to, nor of Vichy's legitimacy which had inspired a pretense of
support. The success of the undertaking begun on June 18, 1940,
was assured in the international order as it had been in the domain
of arms and in the soul of the French people. The goal would be
achieved because the action had been inspired by a France which
would remain France for its sons and for the world. In spite of the
misfortunes endured and the renunciations paraded, this was the
truth of the matter. There is no success save starting from the
truth.

CHAPTER 3

ORDER

IF the sources of style, as Buffon says, are order and movement, the same is true of politics. Now the winds of change were sweeping over liberated France, but order had to be enforced or all would be lost. Yet so serious were the wounds our country had endured, so painful the living conditions in which the war's damages and continuation had kept us, so great the upheaval of established values—within the state, social hierarchies, families and tradition—that we were plunged into a general crisis affecting the life of every citizen at some point. The joy the French took in their liberation may have momentarily concealed the true state of affairs from them. Now, the realities appeared all the more bitter. For myself, when I looked into the distance I could see blue sky on the horizon. But close at hand, observing the terrible elements of chaos seething in the crucible of public affairs, I reminded myself of Macbeth before the witches' cauldron.

First of all, we lacked food to satisfy the barest needs of existence. Twelve hundred calories a day was all the official rations granted for each individual's alimentation. The indispensable complements could be procured only by recourse to the black market, both ruinous and demoralizing. Since there was no wool, no cotton and scarcely any leather, many citizens were wearing threadbare clothes and walking on wooden shoes. There was no heat in the cities, for the small amount of coal being mined was reserved for the armies, railroads, power plants, basic industries and hospitals. Nothing filtered through to private citizens. Yet the first winter of the liberation happened to be one of the severest ever known. At home, at work, in offices and in schools, everyone shivered with cold. Save for an occasional hour, gas pressure was low, electricity interrupted. Since trains were rare, streetcars out of commission and gasoline unheard of, city dwellers prolonged their workday by hours of walking or at best of bicycling, while rural citizens stayed close to their villages. The resumption of normal life was further retarded by the absence of four million young men—either mobilized or prisoners deported to Germany— and by the uprooting of a quarter of the population—displaced persons or refugees camping in the ruins or in shanties.

Many Frenchmen were astonished and irritated by so much hardship and privation, particularly since they had supposed it would vanish as if by magic with the coming of the liberation. Nevertheless, the moment was at hand when these aggravations would begin to diminish. It was expected that hostilities would terminate in a few months, imports resume immediately afterward, the men deported to Germany and many of those under mobilization return to work, communications gradually be re-established, and production develop again. Of course, it would take years before we returned to prewar living standards. Yet in spite of everything, the end of the tunnel was in sight. Considering what we had survived, the remaining ordeals could not be so harrowing or protracted as to put the future in doubt. But what made the situation a serious one was that they contributed to the profound social, moral and political upheaval the country was suffering.

This national crisis filled my life from day to day. Not that I let myself be absorbed by problems of detail, advice, condolences, and the criticisms which flowed in upon me from all sides. Though as sensitive as anyone else to the daily trials of the French people, though making every effort to restore all public services, I knew that our dilemmas were not immediately solvable. But if the present still suffered from the aftereffects of disaster, the future was ours to build. To do so, we must have a policy. I attempted to make mine equal to the demands and the dimensions of the subject—to revise social conditions so that work could begin again and subversion miscarry; to prepare for the moment when the people would receive the power to speak, without permitting anything to breach my authority until then; to assure the action of justice, so that crimes would be quickly punished, repression would be taken out of partisan hands and, once sentences were pronounced, nothing would stand in the way of rehabilitation; to restore freedom of the press, while liquidating those organs which had served the enemy; to guide the country toward economic and financial equilibrium, encouraging its activity and averting excessive upheavals; to govern by bold and arduous efforts, and despite all disadvantages. This was to be my program.

As I saw it, the stake of the conflict was not only the fate of nations and states, but the human condition as well. This was only natural, for war in its technical aspect is always a movement of societies. The passions that animate it and the pretexts it invokes unfailingly cloak a dispute over the material or spiritual destiny of men. Alexander's victories were those of a civilization. It was the barbarian's passionate hunger which caused the fall of the Roman Empire. There would have been no Arab invasion without the Koran. No crusades without the Gospels. The *ancien régime* in Europe rose against France when the Assembly proclaimed, "Men are born free and equal by law."

Like everyone else, I remarked that in our time technology dominated the universe. This was the source of the century's great debate, Would the working classes be the victim or the beneficiary of technical progress? This was the source of those recently formed

huge movements—socialism, communism, fascism—which dominated several great peoples and divided all the rest. This was the reason that various banners—Liberal, Marxist, Hitlerian—were now
located over the battlefields and that so many men and women,
swept on by cataclysm, were haunted by fears of what would become of themselves and their children. How unquestionable the
evidence that the flood of passions, hopes and griefs that now
broke over the belligerent powers, the enormous human mass to
which they found themselves subject, the effort required by reconstruction, placed the social question first among all those the
government had to resolve. I was convinced that without profound
and rapid changes in this realm, there would be no lasting order.

How true this was for France! The war had fallen upon her at
the height of the class struggle, the latter all the more intense in
that our economy, desperately out of date, rejected changes and
our political regime, lacking vigor and faith, could not impose
them. Doubtless there were unavoidable causes for such stagnation.
Unlike other nations, we were not fortunate enough to possess
sufficiently abundant sources of coal and petroleum to develop our
heavy industries. Before World War I, the armed peace had
obliged us to devote a large part of our resources to the military
establishment; after it, since we did not obtain reparations, we
had been overwhelmed by the burden of reconstruction. Lastly,
before the renascent German threat, we had had to resume the
effort of armament. Under such conditions, productive enterprises
remained too often neglected, the manufacture of equipment was
rarely converted to civilian needs, wealth remained inert while
public budgets were balanced with difficulty and the currency lost
its value. So many delays and hardships, so many sacrosanct
routines and egotisms, had a bad effect on the economy and also
on the powers willing to undertake the reforms which might have
given the workers their share. It is true that in 1936 popular
pressure imposed a few concessions, but the impulse was soon

sucked under by the parliamentary quicksands. When France entered the war, an ominous social unrest divided her citizens.

During the catastrophe, beneath the burden of defeat, a great change had occurred in men's minds. To many, the disaster of 1940 seemed the failure of the ruling class and system in every realm. There was therefore a tendency to seek their replacement. Particularly since the collaboration of certain business circles with the occupiers and the contrast between the almost universal penury and the immense prosperity of a small group exasperated the mass of the French people. Then too, a war in which Hitler was simultaneously opposing democrats and Soviets threw the entire working class on the side of the resistance. The nation saw its workers reappear as patriots and revolutionaries too, which had been the case during the Revolution, in 1830, in 1848, and under the Commune. But this time, it was against the enemy that French workers were striking or joining the maquis, and the idea that they might again withdraw from the national community was distasteful to the country at large. In short, to renew the economy so that it served the collectivity before furnishing profits to private interests, and, at the same time, to raise the condition of the laboring classes—that is what was on the nation's mind.

The Vichy regime had attempted to accomplish these goals. If, in the financial and economic realm, its technocrats had despite all setbacks shown incontestable skill, it was also true that the social doctrines of "national revolution"—corporate organization, a labor charter, family allowances—embodied ideas which were not without their attractions. But the fact that this enterprise was identified with the capitulation could only influence the masses toward an entirely different mystique.

That of Communism offered itself to their rage, and to their hopes. Their aversion for the structure of the past was exasperated by poverty, concentrated in the resistance, exalted with the liberation. Here, then, was an extraordinary opportunity for the "party." Deliberately confusing resistance with the class struggle and posing as the champion of both varieties of revolt, the Communist party had every likelihood of seizing control of the country, even when it could not do so by means of the Council of the Resistance, the committees and the militias—unless De Gaulle, assuming the initiative, realized a number of reforms by which he could regroup allegiances, obtain worker support and assure economic recovery on a new basis.

This was the immediate task on which I set the government to work. The program had long since been determined. For I had prepared the realization of my original intents at the start, while the resistance fighters, of whatever tendency, were unanimous in their intentions. The various movements had taken up their positions. The study committees working clandestinely in France, or openly in London and in Africa, had prepared the drafts. The delegates, particularly those sitting in the Consultative Assembly in Algiers, had approved the main outline of these drafts. It could be said that an essential characteristic of the French resistance was its desire for social reform. But this desire had to be translated into acts. Now, by virtue of my powers and the credit public opinion had granted me, I had the means to do so. In the course of one year, the decrees and laws passed under my responsibility involved changes of an enormous significance for the structure of the French economy and the condition of the workers, changes the prewar regimes had vainly deliberated for more than a half century. The new edifice was apparently a solid one, since nothing subsequently was either added or taken away.

Thus the principal sources of energy were put in the state's hands. In 1944 the National Coal Group of the Nord and Pas-de-Calais departments was instituted, to which the Loire group was added soon afterward. A short while later, the government determined to put the production and distribution of electricity and gas under its control. This decision was carried out as soon as the terms could be specified. In 1945 the "Petroleum Bureau" was created, its object being to encourage, regulate and co-ordinate all matters concerning the fuel and oil industry. At the year's end, the High Commission on Atomic Energy was created. Given the fact that the country's activity depended on coal, electricity, gas and petroleum, and would eventually depend on atomic fission; that in order to bring France's economy to the level that progress demanded, these resources must be developed on the largest scale; that expenditures and efforts were necessary which only the collectivity was in a position to realize—nationalization was a necessity.

Proceeding on the same principles, credit regulation also was arrogated to the state. As a matter of fact, once the state had assumed the responsibility of financing large-scale projects itself, it would need to receive the means directly. This would be accomplished by the nationalization of the Bank of France and the major credit establishments. Since the development of the territories within the French Union had become one of France's chief and perhaps supreme opportunities, the old "Caisse centrale de la France Libre" was converted into the "Caisse centrale de la France d'outre-mer," providing for state participation in the development of these new countries. A similar intention inspired the decision to group into a single network—Air-France—the airlines operated on state subsidies before the war. By the end of 1945, our transport planes were flying over all the continents of the world. As for the transformation of the Renault works into a national trust, its consequence, not on principle but as a sanction, was to place this "pilot factory par excellence" under state control. Finally, to encourage the new economy to invest, that is to levy on the present in order to build the future, the "High Commission on Plans for Equipment and Modernization" was created during this same year.

But true progress can be made only if those who create it with their own hands find their reward within it. The government of the liberation intended to bring this about, not only by wage increases, but more particularly by institutions which profoundly modified working conditions. During 1945 the social security program was entirely recast and extended to many areas it had not previously covered. Every wage earner would be obligatorily covered. Thus vanished the fear, as old as the human race, that sickness, accident, old age or unemployment would fall with crushing weight upon the workers. "The poor are always with us," but not the wretched, the starving, the hopeless. Further, a complete system of family allowances was implemented. The nation supported its families in proportion to the number of their children, the support lasting from the day of the child's birth until the day he became capable of providing for his own needs. This provision was to revive the French birth rate, once so high it had nourished the spirit of enterprise and the greatness of our nation, but which, in a hundred years, had declined until France was no more than a static and sparsely populated country. At the same time, tenant-farming status was entirely revised; henceforth, a man working a rented farm was assured he could stay on the land as long as he wished, provided that he filled the conditions of his lease. Furthermore, he had right of pre-emption, if the land should be offered for sale. In this way a remedy was provided for one virulent cause of farm agitation and the desertion of our countrysides.

Furthermore, the program I had drawn up proceeded far beyond these material reforms. It aimed at granting the workers in the national economy responsibilities which raised them far above the role of instruments to which they had hitherto been confined. That they should be associated with the progress of industry, or their labor enjoy the same rights as those accorded to capital, or their remuneration be linked, like the revenue of stockholders, to the results of the industry's developments was the goal I proposed to realize. In order to prepare this promotion of labor, the Committees of Enterprise were created in February 1956. Each committee included the director of the establishment, the workers' representatives, the employees, and the executives. It was kept informed of the common activity. It formulated advice in all matters concerning production. It administered its own funds which were devoted, over and above wages and salaries, to the material and social life of the personnel. By more closely uniting all who, in whatever capacity, participated in the same concern, by encouraging them to study together the functioning, progress and inadequacies of their enterprise, by inspiring the consciousness and organizing the practice of their solidarity, I intended to take a major step toward the association of capital, labor and technology; in this I saw the human structure of tomorrow's economy.

These metamorphoses, extensive as they might be, were realized without serious upheavals. Of course those in positions of privilege received them sullenly enough. Some nursed their grievances in secret, planning to air them later. But at the moment, all recognized the force of the current and resigned themselves to it at once, particularly since they had feared much worse. As for the Communists, they naturally preferred to regard what was being done as inadequate and to allege that the government was prevented from going any further by its reactionary connections. Nevertheless there was no opposition to our measures. As for the "politicians," they lost no time, in accordance with the rules of their art, in formulating reservations in one direction or another, though on the whole they approved the work being done and granted it overwhelming majorities in the Assembly. Many of them favored these measures because they corresponded, generally, to old and familiar demands. Others accepted them as a concession to social harmony. All intended to take credit for them tomorrow, before the electorate. Once again I remarked that if the goal was perhaps the same for them as for myself, the motives guiding them were not identical with my own. Though they adjusted their attitudes to accord with the prejudices of their respective tendencies, such considerations did not affect me. On the other hand, I perceived that they were scarcely aware of the motive inspiring me, which was the power of France.

For today, as ever, it was incumbent upon the state to create the national power, which henceforth would depend on the economy.

The latter must therefore be directed, particularly since it was deficient, since it must be renovated, and since it would not be renovated unless the state determined to do so. This was, in my eyes, the chief motive of the nationalization, control and modernization measures adopted by my government. But this conception of a government armed to act powerfully in the economic domain was directly linked to my conception of the state itself. I regarded the state not as it was yesterday and as the parties wished it to become once more, a juxtaposition of private interests which could never produce anything but weak compromise, but instead an institution of decision, action and ambition, expressing and serving the national interest alone. In order to make decisions and determine measures, it must have a qualified arbitrator at its head. In order to execute them, it must have servants recruited and trained so as to constitute a valid and homogeneous corps in all public functions. Of these two conditions, the first was fulfilled today, and I was ready to make certain it would be so tomorrow as well; the second led me to establish the National School of Administration in August 1945. If the structure thus outlined became definitive, the new levers in the hands of the state would give it sufficient control over French activity for it to be able to make the nation stronger and happier.

Independently of the spirit of justice and opportunity, it was this same intention that led me to promote our workers to the rank of responsible associates. The unity of France demanded that her workers morally reintegrate the national community, from which, either out of direct opposition or out of discouragement, many tended to withdraw. If, further, the working class applied itself of its own accord to the development of its capacities, what resources would be added to the nation's productive activity and thereby to the power of France!

But it would take time to enable the new structure to produce its effects. Meanwhile, it was a question of survival. Yet the resumption of work in factories and mines, the reconstruction of bridges, ports, railroads, power plants and canals, the reconditioning of trains, trucks and ships, required everyone's participation. Things being as they were, I intended to use in behalf of the public welfare everyone capable of furthering it. Of course, the Communists could not be excluded in this period when the very substance of France would be seriously compromised if the whole people were not brought to the task, all the more if social upheaval lacerated the nation. Not that I permitted myself any illusions as to the "party's" loyalty. I knew it aimed at seizing total power and that if I yielded even once it would immediately rise to the attack. But its participation in the resistance, the influence it wielded over the workers, the desire of public opinion, which I myself shared, to see it return to the nation, determined me to give the "party" its place in the task of recovery. Plunging, biting, rearing, but strongly harnessed between the shafts and submitting to bit and bridle, it was to help draw the heavy wagon. It was my job to hold the reins. I had the strength to do so because of the confidence of the French people.

This policy of unity had led me, since Algiers, to invite Communists to become members of my government. I had done the same thing in Paris. In addition, one Commissioner of the Republic, three prefects and several high officials belonging to the "party" had comprised part of the experiment. In the composition of the Consultative Assembly, I had accorded the Communists a representation corresponding to their importance. And now, in November 1944, I approved the proposal of the Minister of Justice granting M. Maurice Thorez, condemned for desertion five years before, the benefit of amnesty. The latter was pronounced by the Council of Ministers. The "party's" secretary general could henceforth leave Moscow and return to his country. Moreover, for some time, now, my indulgence had been sought in his behalf from the most disparate quarters. Thorez himself had sent me many requests. However, if I felt it wise to adopt this measure of clemency, and precisely at this moment, it was per-

formed quite deliberately. Taking former circumstances into account, the events occurring subsequently, and today's necessities,
I considered that the return of Maurice Thorez to the head of the
Communist party would involve more advantages than drawbacks
at the present moment.

This was, in fact, to be the case, so long as I myself was at the
head of the state and the nation. Of course, day after day, the
Communists multiplied their intrigues and their invectives, though
they attempted no insurrectional movement. Better still, so long as
I was in office not a single strike occurred. It is true that the
"party" would spare no effort to control political, trade union and
electoral contingencies and to dominate the other groups, exploiting their secret hopes of inducing De Gaulle to withdraw and the
inferiority complex inspired by their own inconsistency. But once
the Communists adopted preponderance in a parliamentary regime
instead of revolution as their goal, society ran far fewer risks. It
is true that they greatly multiplied the obstacles in my path and
conducted a backstage campaign of denigration. Yet until my
withdrawal they were always careful not to override my authority
or to insult my person. Everywhere I appeared, their representatives were present to pay their respects, and even their militant
members in the crowd shouted *"Vive De Gaulle!"* along with the
other Frenchmen.

As for Thorez, while making every effort to advance the interests of Communism, he was to serve public interest on several
occasions. On the day after his return to France, he brought an
end to the last vestiges of the "patriotic militias" which certain of
his people insisted on maintaining in a new clandestine situation.
To the degree his party's harsh and secretive rigidity permitted,
he opposed the attempted provocations of the Committees of
Liberation and the acts of violence their gangs attempted to commit. To those—and they were numerous—of the workers, particularly the miners, who listened to his speeches, he continually
urged a maximum work effort and production at any cost as

national watchwords. Was this out of patriotic instinct or political opportunism? It was not my job to unravel his motives. It sufficed that France was served.

Basically, the leaders of the "party," provisionally renouncing domination, were particularly interested in preparing what would follow the victory. The same was true of the other political fractions, of course. As the electoral perspectives grew clearer, each group focused increasingly on its own concerns, organized in its own behalf, drew up a separate platform. We had seen, first of all, the Committees of Liberation gathering in various regions to demand the *"Etats-Generaux* of the French resistance." But the attempt failed by reason of the immediately apparent opposition between those elements which were Communist-inspired and those which were not. Subsequently, the Assembly was lacerated by the various parties. In November the Socialists had staged their shake-up. In January it was the turn of the "Movement of National Liberation," then that of the "National Front." In February the delegates of the "Republican Federation" convened, soon imitated by the old "French Socialist party," while the "Popular Republican Movement" was being constituted. During the same month, Socialists and Communists decided to function in co-operation and formed a "committee of unity" to direct their mutual action. In April the "Communist Youth Movement" held its session. During this time, the officers of the Radical party began to reorganize. In short, every sort of political organ, all of which had for years performed only *en sourdine,* now tried out its tone and timbre.

Naturally I did not mix directly with the activity of any group. But I scrupulously observed this gestation of political forces. In the immediate circumstances, it was true, the conventions and their notions had only a limited importance, since De Gaulle was governing and would continue to do so until he returned the power to the nation. But he would do so soon. What happened then would depend in large measure on what was being elaborated at this very moment. I must say I considered the ferments at work quite disappointing.

What particularly struck me about the regrouping parties was their passionate desire to accord themselves all the powers of the Republic in full at the earliest opportunity, and their incapacity, which they revealed in advance, to wield them effectively. In this respect, nothing promised any sort of improvement in regard to the futile maneuvering which comprised the regime's activity before the war and which had led the country to such fearful disaster. Verbally, the politicians jealously emulated each other in denying such practices. "Revolution!" was the watchword that echoed most loudly through their speeches. But no one defined just what this meant, what effective changes were to be made in the previous situation, and particularly what authority, and endowed with what powers, would be in a position to carry them out. As for the Communists, they knew what they wanted, but were careful not to say what it was. The groups which for all their bold phraseology were fundamentally moderate cloaked their circumspection beneath Georges Bidault's formula, "Revolution by law!" As for the groups and men of the Left, or laying claim to be such, they appeared rigorous in criticism and repudiation, but vague and querulous in every constructive issue. Receiving delegations, reading newspapers, listening to speeches, I was inclined to think that for the renascent parties the revolution was not an undertaking with definite goals implying action and risk, but rather an attitude of constant dissatisfaction toward every policy, even those they had advocated themselves.

I did not conceal the apprehensions these signs inspired in me. When governmental confusion and impotence had been the direct causes of our social and moral chaos, of our diplomatic weakness, of our strategic collapse, and lastly of our national renunciation, which had cast us into the abyss, what evil genius, what mad hallucination was leading us toward the same quicksands? Given the tremendous problems confronting France, how suppose they could be solved save under the aegis of a state both impartial and strong? But I was forced to the recognition that my notions were rarely shared.

For myself, the separation of powers, the authority of a genuine chief of state, the recourse to the people by means of referendum whenever its destiny or its institutions were in question—these were the necessary bases of democracy in a country like ours. Yet it was only too clear that everything that counted or was going to count in the political realm was tending in the opposite direction. The future governmental personnel conceived their future powers as organically identified with the discretion of parties, the chief of state—on condition such an institution existed at all—as a figurehead mandated by parliamentary groups, and universal suffrage as exclusively destined to elect deputies. As far as I myself was concerned, while everyone conceded my primacy in the provisional system, admitted my popularity and the services I had rendered France, and exhibited spectacular loyalty to me on appropriate occasions, no one concealed the impatience which such so-called "personal" power inspired. Hence, though there was as yet no direct opposition to my action, I saw the clouds gathering on the horizon and henceforth advanced in an atmosphere heavy with criticisms and objections.

This fashion of regarding De Gaulle both favorably and disapprovingly was made quite clear in the Consultative Assembly. I appeared there often, eager to receive ideas at their source and to mount the platform in order to explain my actions and my motives to all. Further, I was naturally attracted by the parliamentary body's element of profound yet thwarted life, of ardent yet evasive humanity, of constrained yet violent passions which sometimes subsided as if to belie themselves and sometimes burst into noisy explosions. For reasons of protocol, my entrance and my departure were made with a certain formality. But during the entire time I participated in the Assembly tasks, I was careful not to offend its procedures in any way, respecting its order of the day, sitting on one of its benches, speaking at the same tribunal as its members, chatting with them in the corridors. The sessions, I must admit, were frequently dull, the majority of the speakers reading off a monotonous text whose generalities wakened only scant attention. Still, from time to time, the talent of certain individuals—whether ministers or not—such as Messrs. Auriol, Bastid, Bidault, Boncour, Cot, Denais, Duclos, Hervé, Laniel, Marin, Mendès-France, Philip, Pléven, Schumann and Teitgen, gave a certain distinction to the sessions. Sometimes, on a subject of burning interest, feelings ran high and a warm collective emotion hovered over the benches. Then the eloquent sentences, melting in the strained atmosphere, provoked sudden outrage or enthusiasm.

Many times over, I addressed the Consultative Assembly. On some occasions this was in order to make explanations concerning major subjects—for example, on November 22 the government's general plans, on December 21 the Franco-Russian pact which had just been signed, on March 2 the interior policies adopted, on March 20 Indochina, where the Japanese had just opened an offensive, on May 15 the lessons to be drawn from the war, after victory. In other cases, I intervened informally during the discussion. On each of these occasions, there occurred among the members a fusing of minds which momentarily expressed an imposing manifestation of unity. The importance of the subjects under discussion, the effect of the words, the human contact with De Gaulle himself reminded the delegates of the solidarity which linked us all together and deepened the attraction of the national community. For a moment, we felt ourselves closer—that is, better—men.

But if it was agreed that De Gaulle would be applauded, there was no hesitation about criticizing his government. The bitterness of the general remarks was notable, and in certain cases it overflowed in formal attacks against one or another of the ministers. One day, Jules Jeanneney, Minister of State, was assailed with invectives regarding certain deferential words he had spoken in July 1940 regarding Marshal Pétain. Yet since then he had unceasingly supported and served the resistance. During the first months of 1945, when the budget was submitted for the Consultative Assembly's approval, there was a stormy session. When the appropriations for the Ministry of Justice were under discussion, the subject of the purges was broached. The Minister François de Menthon had to endure a running fire of implacable indictments. A huge majority attempted to punish his "criminal weakness" by refusing him a vote of confidence, a platonic manifestation, certainly, but one which showed the extent of the general agitation. Shortly after, Pierre-Henri Teitgen, Minister of Information, served as a target in his turn. The difficulties into which the paper shortage had plunged the press was imputed to him in extravagant terms. "Pornographer, protector of German agents, representative of the trusts, scorner of the Rights of Man, persecutor of the resistance press, cause of France's absence at Yalta—these are the appellations by which I am identified," Teitgen declared, answering to his accusers. When the budget for Prisoners was examined, Minister Henri Frenay was the object of furious reproaches from all sides, though since at this date the prisoners were still in enemy hands, no one could yet judge the value of the measures taken against their return.

Such acrimony and agitation actually concealed precise demands. The Assembly was not able to resign itself to being merely Consultative. It would have preferred to take the power in its own hands, and this preference was soon confirmed. On March 19 I received a delegation from all the parties. "We are here," the representatives said, "to inform you that the Assembly is extremely distressed because of the limited role to which it is confined and because the government acts without considering itself bound by our opinion and our votes. We ask that henceforth the executive power make no more decisions contrary to the positions adopted by the Assembly."

To yield to this reprimand would evidently mean to lapse into confusion. "Only the people are sovereign," I replied to the delegates. "Until the French people are in a position to express their will, I have taken the responsibility of leading them. You have been willing to help me do so by responding to my call to honor. This has been your role and it will be your glory. But my responsibility remains no less complete. Even the action you are taking at this moment proves that the government's entire power is in my charge, since it is from me that you ask to receive a share of the power. However, France's situation does not permit such a dispersion."

"All the same," exclaimed the delegates, "we represent the resistance! Is it not the responsibility of the resistance to express the will of the people in the absence of the legal powers."

"You are mandated," I said, "by the resistance movements and parties. This gives you, of course, the right to make yourselves heard. That is indeed why I instituted the Consultative Assembly and designated you to participate in it. All government issues are submitted to you there. I myself and my ministers participate in your sessions. You are associated in the government's actions by the questions you ask, the explanations the government furnishes you, and the opinions you formulate. But I will not go beyond that. Furthermore, consider the fact that the French resistance was more inclusive than these movements, and that France is greater than the resistance. It is in the name of France as a whole, not of any fragment or fraction, however valuable, that I am carrying out my mission. Until the future general elections, I am responsible for the nation's fate to the nation and only to the nation."

The delegates retired without concealing their discontent. Following their visit, there was, however, a relaxation in the Assembly's tone. Accommodating themselves to what was so clearly defined, its members returned to its tasks. As a whole, its functions were of great assistance. The study by commissions and the discussion in public session of programs of economic and social reforms, justice, administration, education and overseas territories, brought to the Cabinet not only the support of the majority of votes, but also of many good suggestions. The attention and respect paid to the action of the armies by men who were themselves familiar with many trials encouraged leaders and men alike. Abroad, the spectacle of a parliamentary prefiguration in the Luxembourg amphitheater, the ideas expressed there without restraint, the fact that the government's policy was generally approved there, reinforced the hearing France obtained throughout the world. Lastly, the impression in the public mind that the principal measures adopted by the government were openly discussed, that there was a channel of expression for requests and criticisms, that we were thus making progress toward a state of affairs where the people would be restored to its rights, certainly contributed to reestablishing that free course of ideas and feelings which is an essential condition of order.

Another is the demonstration that justice was being rendered. Yet in this regard, we were confronted by an outbreak of vindictive demands. After what had occurred, this reaction was only too understandable. The collaboration had espoused under the various forms of political decisions, of police and occasionally military action, of administrative measures and of propaganda publications and speeches, not only the character of national abasement, but even the persecution of a huge number of French citizens. With the co-operation of a considerable number of officials and a mass of informers, 60,000 persons had been executed and more than 200,000 deported of whom a bare 50,000 survived. Further, 35,000 men and women had been condemned by the Vichy tribunals; 70,000 "suspects" interned; 35,000 officials cashiered; 15,000 officers degraded under the inculpation of being in the resistance. Now resentment was beyond control. Doubtless the government's duty was to keep a cool head. But to pass the sponge over so many crimes and abuses would mean leaving a monstrous abscess to infect the country forever. Justice must be rendered here.

And it was. During the winter the courts that had been formed to judge evidence of collaboration actively performed their task. Of course the rigor of the condemnations was variable, depending on the composition of the juries. The local atmosphere made itself felt. Sometimes the sessions were disturbed by mob interventions. In several regions there were even riots to snatch the prisoners from the courts. This was the case, for instance, in Nîmes, Maubeuge, Bourges, Annecy, Alès and Rodez. In fact, some twenty unfortunate prisoners were lynched throughout the country. On several occasions the government had to repress these outbreaks. I had to urge the Ministers of the Interior and of Justice to vigilance and firmness, to impose punishments upon those officials guilty of laxity in the maintenance of order, to insist on the inculpation of those who had infringed it. Nevertheless, justice was rendered as impartially as was humanly possible, considering the passions awakened. Those judgments which were later proved to be ill-founded were extremely rare.

Two thousand seventy-one death sentences were handed down by the courts, not including those sentenced *in absentia*. The files were subsequently submitted to me, after examination by the Commission of Mercy and the warranted estimation of the Minister of Justice. I studied them all, directly assisted by President Patin, director of criminal cases and reprieves at the Chancellery, and receiving the lawyers whenever they requested it. Nothing ever seemed more painful than this procession of murders, tortures, delations and appeals to treason that thus passed in review before me. Conscientiously, I attested that with the exception of about one hundred cases, all those condemned had deserved their execution. Yet I granted pardons to 1,303 among them, commuting, in particular, the death sentences of all women, of almost all minors, and, among the men, of the majority of those who had acted upon formal orders and at the risk of their own lives. I was obliged to reject 768 appeals from condemned men whose personal and spontaneous action had caused the death of other Frenchmen or directly aided the enemy.

As for the 39,900 condemnations to detention which the courts of justice handed down, they were, on the whole, equitable and moderate. There were 55,000 such sentences in Belgium at the same time, and more than 50,000 in Holland. Again, by remission of penalties, the government mitigated the effect of a large number of decisions, particularly in the case of the unfortunate young men who had been lured into the "Militia," the "Legion of French Volunteers" or the "African Phalanx," and who were given an alternative of joining the Indochinese Expeditionary Corps. It should be added that the examining magistrates decided that there were no grounds for prosecution in 18,000 cases. By the middle of 1945, among the 60,000 guilty or suspected men arrested at the time of the liberation, there was not one individual still held unless he had been formally and legally inculpated. Considering the mass of collaboration evidence and the number of atrocities committed against the resistance fighters, and recalling the torrent of rage which spread in all directions once the enemy began to withdraw, it can be said that the judgments of the courts of justice were rendered with as much indulgence as possible.

The same was true in the realm of public office. Here, however, resentment was particularly sharp, for Vichy had cashiered more than 50,000 persons and, furthermore, in the case of certain persons in public office, had lavished an odious zeal in the service of the invader. The Provisional Government decided to consult the administrations themselves to determine what sanctions to take. Recourse to the Council of State remained open, of course. As a matter of fact, the immense majority of officials had behaved honorably. Many of them, in fact, had actually helped in the struggle against the enemy and his accomplices in the exercise of their functions. Out of a personnel of more than 800,000, only about 20,000 cases needed investigation, as a result of which

14,000 sanctions were pronounced, of which scarcely 5,000 resulted in dismissals. It was with good grounds, then, that I declared on the radio, on January 18, "Those who have the honor to serve the state do so, I am convinced, with ardor and discipline and deserve to be encouraged by the esteem of their fellow citizens."

The High Court, established to judge acts of collusion with the enemy and interference with the exterior security of the state committed in the highest positions, opened its sessions in March. It was directed by the First President of the Supreme Court of Appeals, M. Mongibeaux, assisted by the President of the Criminal Chamber, M. Donat-Guigne and by the First President of the Court of Appeals of Paris, M. Picard. The jury, drawn by lot from two lists of fifty names established by the Consultative Assembly, included twenty-four members, of whom twelve were deputies or senators in 1940. President Mornet occupied the chair of the Public Ministry. The preliminary investigations for the trial were made by an "Investigations Committee" consisting of five magistrates and six members of the Assembly.

I considered it necessary that the men who had taken responsibility, in the highest office, for the acts of the Vichy regime should appear before a jurisdiction established for this purpose. Neither the ordinary tribunals, nor the courts of justice, nor the councils of war, were in a position to deal with such cases. Since the persons concerned, either as ministers, high commissioners, residents general or secretaries general, had played a political role, the courts which would judge them must be politically qualified to do so. This condition was established for all cases of the same order, at all times, and in all sectors. It was to observe it myself that I instituted the High Court by decree on November 18, 1944.

This installation took place under juridical conditions that were indeed exceptional. Naturally, I arranged for the public powers later to be established by formal legal measures to do what was necessary. But France's internal order and the world situation de-

manded that the 1940 capitulation, the breaking of alliances and
the deliberate collaboration with the enemy be judged without
delay in the persons of the leaders who had made themselves responsible. Otherwise, how and in whose name punish the executants? How and in whose name claim for France the status of a
major belligerent and victorious power? In this matter, as in so
many others, I took it upon myself to do what had to be done. It
would subsequently be the responsibility of the reconvened National Assembly to ratify the procedure. Which it did not fail to
do. Of course, once the High Court was created, I was particularly careful not to influence the prosecution, the investigation and
the judgments, abstaining from any deposition and receiving no
judicial commission of inquiry. Since I wanted the discussions to
be undisturbed by manifestations or movements of those present,
I refused to let the High Court sit in the hall of the Palais Bourbon—as many had insisted—installing it instead in the Palais de
Justice and assuring it the security of a considerable police guard.

The first trial to come before the High Court was that of Admiral Estéva, Resident General in Tunisia at the time of the Allied
landing in North Africa. Following Pétain's orders, the unfortunate man had permitted the Germans to disembark, had ordered
the roads to be opened to them and had forbidden the French
forces in the country to join those fighting the enemy. But the occupation of the Tunisian territory, particularly of Bizerte, by Axis
troops forced the Americans, French and British to engage in an
extended battle. Furthermore, the presence of the Germans and
the Italians in the Kingdom of Tunis furnished agitators many occasions to turn the citizens against France, resulting in serious
political consequences.

Admiral Estéva was sentenced to solitary confinement. At the
close of a career which had hitherto been exemplary, this old sea-
man, misled by a false discipline, had become the accomplice and
ultimately the victim of an ill-fated enterprise.

General Dentz succeeded him on the stand. As High Commissioner in the Levant, he had in the spring of 1941 permitted German squadrons to land on Syrian territory in accord with Vichy orders, had established the points where the Wehrmacht was to disembark and had used the forces under his command against the Free French and the British. After an initial resistance which might have passed for an attempt to salvage his honor, Dentz had asked for armistice conditions. These conditions, determined by myself in agreement with the British command, involved the transmission of the Vichy's High Commission to that of Free France, and the opportunity for all French soldiers and officials to join my forces. I informed Dentz that if he accepted our terms, no judiciary prosecution would be undertaken against the High Commissioner and his subordinates.

But instead of agreeing to the terms, General Dentz had commanded bitter resistance, which could benefit only the enemy. The unfortunate man went so far as to ask the direct support of the German Air Force. Obliged to lay down his arms after heavy losses had been suffered on both sides, he had concluded with the British a cease-fire, which had suited England, of course, but not France. As a matter of fact, it was to the British and not to Free France that the Vichy High Commissioner abandoned the fate of the states under French mandate. At the same time, the troops and officers under his command were withdrawn from contact with the "Gaullistes" and immediately returned to Metropolitan France on ships sent by Vichy, acting in accord with the Germans. Thus there was no further justification for the immunity I had once been able to envisage in General Dentz's regard.

General Dentz was sentenced to death. But, taking into account the loyal and excellent services he had rendered on other occasions, and touched with compassion by the tragedy of this ruined soldier, I remitted his sentence immediately.

The prosecution of Vichy's servants soon determined the High Court to institute proceedings against its master. On March 17, that court determined that Marshal Pétain would be judged *in absentia.* This was a lamentable and inevitable issue, and though I considered it necessary, from both international and national points of view, that French justice render a formal verdict, I also hoped that some vicissitude would avert from the soil of France an accused man of eighty-nine, a leader once distinguished by the most exceptional powers, an old soldier in whom at the time of the catastrophe many Frenchmen had put their trust and for whom, in spite of everything, many still felt respect or pity. To General de Lattre, who asked me what action he should take if his troops, approaching Sigmaringen, happened to find Pétain and his former ministers, I replied that all must be arrested, but that in regard to the Marshal himself, I had no desire for such an encounter to take place.

On April 23, Pétain reached Switzerland. He had secured the agreement of the Germans to take him there and of the Swiss to receive him. When M. Karl Burckhardt, Ambassador of the Confederation, came to announce the fact to me, I informed him that the French government was not at all eager to have Pétain extradited. But a few hours later, Karl Burckhardt reappeared. "The Marshal," he declared, "asks to return to France. My government cannot oppose his wish. Philippe Pétain will therefore be conducted to your border." The die was cast. The old Marshal, of course, could not doubt that he would be condemned. But he intended to appear in person before French justice and receive the punishment, whatever it was, to which he would be sentenced. His decision was a courageous one. General Koenig took Pétain in charge at Vallorbe. Traveling by special train and protected by a strong escort against the acts of violence which some wished to commit against his person, the Marshal was interned in the fortress at Montrouge.

While justice was accomplishing its task, I wanted public opinion to be kept informed of the motives for its decisions. Of course an excessive publicity given to the trials would have been scandalous, but in questions which laid every passion bare, an objective report would have set the public mind at rest. Unfortunately, the courts were functioning at a time when the newspapers, reduced to skeletal formats, could devote only extremely summary accounts to the judicial sessions. It was the same indigence which kept the public from being adequately informed as to military operations, diplomatic transactions, the state of the economy and the reactions of opinion in Allied countries. The essential episodes of this period by and large escaped the notice or the knowledge of the average French citizen. Many believed that censorship was withholding news. But many others, relying on their imagination for a notion of the problems involved and the proceedings under way, and unaware of the steps taken to control the latter and resolve the former, mournfully concluded that France could do nothing about either.

A terrible paper shortage, as a matter of fact, was strangling the French press. Our paper industry was almost completely without raw materials, and so long as we lacked currency, we could purchase only meager supplies abroad; besides, the Allied convoys were fulfilling entirely different commitments. We therefore had to ration the newspapers most severely, which limited them to absurd dimensions. Since, furthermore, almost all expressed revolutionary tendencies, their propaganda seized on whatever it could to the detriment of the facts. How remote was this reality from the projects cherished during the days of the resistance!

To create a great press had been the dream of the clandestine fighters. They wanted it to be honest and sincere, freed from financial pressures, particularly since the indignation provoked by the occupation journals had added to the bad memory left by the prewar papers with regard to independence and veracity. Further, the majority of the resistance movements and parties had been created in the shadow of the old dailies and weeklies. They now felt entitled to appear in broad daylight, and by priority.

In Algiers, the government had prepared in advance the situation of the press at the time of the liberation. According to the decree of May 6, 1944, the newspapers published in either zone under enemy rule could no longer appear. Their accounts would be confiscated and the resistance organs receive the option of renting their installations. Since there was no question of creating a monopoly, other newspapers, new or old, were permitted to appear or reappear. Furthermore, the decree intended to safeguard the independence of the press with regard to financial groups. Therefore both press and advertising societies were closely regulated. It was also established that the selling price of the publications should be high enough to permit survival and that the accounts should be made public obligatorily.

It was on this basis that the French press had gradually reappeared. Not, of course, without upheavals. In Paris and in the departmental capitals, a generally inexperienced personnel turned out its ardent leaflets in the buildings where familiar organs of the press had once been developed. Yet so gratified were the French to recover freedom of ideas and information that the newspapers and reviews sold widely. There was an extraordinary burgeoning of publications. Each was—and with reason—tiny in size, but appeared in many numbers. Moreover, the ensemble reflected the entire scale of opinion.

Taking advantage of the arrangements of the decree, the resistance journals had leaped into prominence. Naturally the Communists had not been the last among them. Under their aegis, two Paris dailies, *L'Humanité* and *Ce Soir*, seventy weeklies, including *Action, L'Avant-Garde, La Terre, Les Lettres françaises, Le Canard enchaîné*, and fifty provincial papers, claimed to uproot fascism and its works everywhere and supported every grievance advanced against it. The Communists also played a large role in the editorial policy of the *Front national*, of *Franc-Tireur, Libération*, and so on. The Socialists, limiting themselves, in Paris, to *Le Populaire*, but with numerous local papers in the various departments at their disposal, such as *Libération-Nord, Le Provençal*, and *La République du Sud-Ouest*, applied themselves to what for them was the major concern, the reconstitution of their party. The Christian Socialists felt the wind blowing across their bows and were reveled in the influence of *L'Aube,* the wide circulation of *Ouest-France,* and the development of *Temps présent* and *Témoignage chrétien.* As for the eclectic and various papers resulting from the resistance movements themselves—*Combat, Le Parisien libéré, Résistance, Défense de la France,* and *France libre*—they prospered, as did the regional sheets of the same origin, *La Voix du Nord, L'Espoir, La Montagne,* etc.

New publications attempted to follow in the wake of the lately clandestine papers. They required authorization to do so. I intervened in their behalf whenever the journal in question had sufficient means to be able to take its chances. *Le Figaro,* which had been "scuttled" during the occupation of the Southern Zone, had resumed publication two days before the capital was liberated, though its owner had not had the right to do so. I made it possible for him to print the paper nonetheless. *L'Aurore, L'Époque* and *L'Ordre,* which had also put an end to their existence in order not to submit to enemy control, received permission to reappear, and, thereby, their share of paper. I also pronounced the *nihil obstat* in the case of *La Croix,* which had somewhat extended its survival in the Southern Zone after the German arrival, but many of those editors participated in the resistance. To several new papers— *Le Monde, Paris-Presse, Les Nouvelles du matin, La Dépêche de Paris,* etc.—I accorded the right to enter the market place, for I regarded it as desirable that the French press be accessible to new and various formulations and styles.

The same cyclone with which events had swept over the press worked havoc in literary and artistic circles as well. Writers in particular, from the very fact of their vocation to explore and express man, had found themselves solicited by this war in which so many doctrines and passions confronted each other. It must be said that the majority—and frequently the greatest among them— had taken France's side, sometimes in a magnificent manner. But

ORDER 799

others, alas, had ranged themselves in the opposite camp with all the power of their ideas and their style. Against the latter now arose a great tide of indignation. Particularly since it was all too well known toward what crimes and what punishments their eloquent agitations had impelled so many wretched, credulous men. The courts of justice condemned several notorious writers to death. When they had not directly and willfully served the enemy, I commuted their punishment, on principle; but in contrary cases I did not feel I had the right to reprieve them. For in literature as in everything talent is a bond of responsibility. Most often, the courts rendered verdicts that were less severe. But aside from the actual crimes, which were punished, certain frivolous or inconsequential acts were noisily censured in a number of writers whose very success had brought them to public attention. Naturally rivalries did not fail to inspire rumors—that is, on occasion, errors. Indeed the entire world of literature, the arts, and the theater was living under a turbulent sky.

Even the Académie Française was concerned, for it was the object of harsh attacks and its dissolution was the theme of a campaign which found echoes on all sides. Naturally, the culpable behavior of several of its members and the hearing they had found among their colleagues until the very end was widely criticized. I was urged to use my powers to renovate the Academy, in other words, to suppress it. Certainly the entire body was profoundly disturbed and distressed.

Its permanent secretary, the illustrious and courageous Georges Duhamel, came to discuss the elements of the situation with me. He described the difficulties which he himself had had to surmount, with the aid of several other members, in order to keep the Academy, during the occupation, from adopting an unfortunate attitude when the strongest pressures were exerted to induce it to do so. To resume its normal course, the body now faced severe obstacles. Should it exclude or at least suspend those of its members who were condemned or threatened with collaboration sentences? Painful discussions loomed ahead! Furthermore, a dozen academicians had died since 1939, and had not been re-placed. Of course, elections could now be held; but how reach a quorum, given the fact that certain members were not at all eager to appear? It was particularly to be feared that the institution was henceforth so shaken and divided that it would have the greatest difficulties making a recovery. But then, how could it remain the incomparable representation of French thought, language and literature which it was intended to be and which for three cen-turies had so powerfully contributed to our nation's brilliance? "Everything would be much easier," my eminent interlocutor added, "if you yourself would agree to enter the Academy."

After careful consideration, I set aside this possibility. "The chief of state," I replied to Georges Duhamel, "is the protector of the Academy. How could he become a member? And then, as you know, De Gaulle cannot belong to any category, nor receiye any distinction. This admitted, it is in the highest French interest that the Academy resume the role which it fulfills. My intention is to change nothing in the constitution Richelieu provided and, except for certain instances under way against certain members, to guar-antee the entire body independence and security. Nevertheless, I think it would be to the Academy's advantage to profit by the extraordinary circumstances in which we now are able to start afresh. Since many of its chairs are empty, why should we not institute exceptional proceedings and provisionally suspend the rule of candidacy? Why should the Academy not invite among its number several writers known to be worthy of the honor and, as they have shown during the recent ordeal, champions of freedom and of France as well? The Academy's prestige and popularity, I am convinced, would have everything to gain."

However, when I met a few days later with all the academicians in a position to appear, I discovered that if my comforting prom-ise had been favorably received, my suggested innovation had been less so. In the end, the Academy, reassured by the law and

order it saw everywhere in effect, returned to its traditional procedures. For my part, I was delighted to see this precious institution revive, though regretting that it had not been able, as a body,
to render adequate homage to the liberation of France.

Thus by the joint effect of social reforms enacted, of liberty recovered, of justice rendered, of authority restored, the nation was
regaining its spirits. After all the lacerations inflicted by the war,
this was the beginning of convalescence. The latter, however,
would be precarious if the ravaged country failed to recover its
physical equilibrium. If, at the very moment when fortune was
beginning to smile on us once more, our finances collapsed and
our economy fell apart, there would certainly be no further hope
of status, order or future for France. If on the other hand, despite
the terrible conditions we were struggling against, the government
managed to obtain a solid basis of recovery for the national
activity, everything else could gradually be restored into the bargain. There was no question, certainly, of a talisman, a magic
wand. Only categorical measures would have any effect.

The budget drawn up by the government for 1945 cast a cold
light on our finances, as they appeared after five years of war and
four years of occupation; 390 billion francs of expenditure provided for, of which 175 billion were for military needs; on the
other side of the ledger, 176 billion francs normal receipts; deficit,
55 per cent. The public debt rose to 1,800 billion francs—in other
words, four times higher than before the war. Of this amount,
short-term liabilities counted for 800 billion francs whose creditors
could demand reimbursement at any moment. Since, furthermore,
a quarter of the expenses had been settled by advances from the
Bank of France since 1939, fiduciary circulation had quadrupled.

Now this enormous inflation of expenditures, of the national
debt and of the means of payment was supported by a terribly deficient economy. At the beginning of 1945, the rate of production
did not exceed half that of 1938, and foreign trade was nonexistent. Doubtless the liberation loan, drawing on liquid assets, had

averted the catastrophe which the sudden afflux of this floating mass would have provoked in markets more than three-quarters empty. Further, the treasury had in the loan the substance enabling it to deal with the immediate situation. But salutary though the expedient had been, something more was now required—a long-range policy.

In this regard, doctrines and experts contradicted each other. Aside from the Communist system of compulsory production and controlled consumption and the extreme liberalism which would leave matters to arrange themselves, we found ourselves with two theories to choose from.

The first declared: "Confronted with inflation, let us take the bull by the horns. Let us perform a radical puncture in the liquid assets by immediately decreeing that the existing bank notes are no longer valid, that the bearers must immediately exchange them at the public banks, that they will receive in return only a quarter of their funds in new currency and that the balance will be credited to the owners but without being usable. At the same time, let us block the accounts and permit each depositor the option of withdrawing only extremely limited sums. In this way, we shall reduce the possibilities of purchase and, at the same time, the extent of the black market. As for prices, let us freeze them too, and at a level low enough so that consumers, with their means of payment controlled, can still pay for what they need. Only prices of luxury products can be raised at will. Of course we must allow for the fact that the treasury's resources will be seriously affected by such a contraction. There is only one way to prepare for this: to levy a major tax on capital. Such measures are harsh. But provided General de Gaulle gives them his authority, they will permit us to overcome the crisis."

Thus reasoned the champions of the "tough" method. They cited in support of their thesis the example of the Brussels government, where M. Camille Gutt, Minister of Finance, had effectively stabilized the Belgian franc thanks to the simultaneous freezing of bank notes, bank accounts, prices, salaries and wages.

Others said: "Inflation is not so much the cause as the effect of disequilibrium. The latter is inevitable. In a time of total war, nothing can keep production of commodities and consumer goods at normal levels, since many raw materials, tools and workers are employed to other purposes. Nothing, moreover, can keep the government from distributing vast remunerations to a large number of social categories. In every belligerent state, we therefore see the public furnished with nominal resources superior to what they were, consumer goods furnished inadequate in relation to demand, prices rising and money stocks depleted. If the situation is more serious in France than elsewhere, this is because our country has for years been cut off from the outside world, because the occupiers have made exorbitant demands upon our resources, because their presence has provoked the stoppage or the slowing down of many branches of our industry, and because the present lack of raw materials and equipment, the absence of imports, the necessity of using a large share of our remaining means in urgent reconstruction programs, retard the resumption of production. Yet everything depends on this resumption. Severe artificial devices would add to our difficulties by depriving the producers of the initiative and the means of setting to work and by ruining the state's credit as well as that of its currency. On the contrary, let us encourage the economy to function, to expand. As for the excess of liquid assets, let us eliminate it by treasury bonds which favor the spirit of thrift and foster the sentiment that every man controls what is his own. Similarly, let us avoid any systematic tax on capital. Let us merely pursue the confiscation of culpable profits. This method is not miraculous, but thanks to the nation's confidence in De Gaulle, it will lead us to recovery."

Ultimately, the decision was up to me. Therefore I was a party to the dispute through every kind of administrative report, through the advice of interested groups, through arguments in the press.

In the Consultative Assembly, André Philip, general budget liaison officer, Jules Moch and other delegates at the beginning of March made themselves the eloquent apostles of levies on monetary signs, bank accounts and capital, while René Pleven set forth an altogether different plan. It must be said that this matter divided the government. Each of the two theses had a protagonist as ardent as he was qualified. Pierre Mendès-France, Minister of National Economy, identified himself with the first. Pleven, Minister of Finance, warmly advocated the second. Since both were men of merit and ambition, since they were entrusted with equal responsibility, the former for prices and trade, the latter for currency and the budget, I regarded it as futile as it was inappropriate that they should be rivals, for the dispute concerned a problem affecting the fate of the French people. Therefore, after long consideration of the matter both with them and with myself, I advocated the progressive plan and rejected the freeze.

Not that I was convinced by theoretical arguments. In economy as in politics or strategy, there exists, I believe, no absolute truth. There are only the circumstances. It was my conception of the latter which was responsible for my decision. The country was sick and hurt. I therefore felt it was preferable not to press its subsistence and its activity at this moment particularly since the months to come would, by the force of events, improve its condition. If there were no other means of recovery than to play all or nothing, I would certainly not hesitate. But why throw the nation into dangerous convulsions, if it would recover its health sooner or later in any case?

As for the experiment which the Brussels government had conducted so successfully, I did not believe it would work in France. For material and moral conditions were profoundly different for the Belgians and for us. Belgium suffered less than France from the occupation. The demands made upon her resources had remained rather limited. By virtue of a maneuver of German propaganda, her prisoners had long since been returned. At present, the share the Belgians were taking in the war cost them little. Besides, they had not had a regime like Vichy; the Communists were not powerful in the country; the national upheaval did not reach such dimensions as in France. In this country of small size and simple structure, whose communications were re-established by the Allied armies themselves, the administration's control could be imposed without difficulties. But above all, M. Camille Gutt was in a position to keep the freezing of prices and currency from cutting off supply. Since the Brussels government had a huge reserve of currency at its disposal in America, the result of ore sales—particularly uranium ore—made to the United States by the Congo throughout the war; since the port of Antwerp was the destination of the majority of the Allied convoys; since the British and American authorities, for reasons that were both political and strategic, wanted to facilitate matters for the Belgian authorities, the Pierlot-Gutt-Spaak ministry could import large quantities of American and Canadian commodities. Thus, immediately after the freeze, when Belgian producers had suspended all deliveries, the government could supply the markets with food and goods bought in the New World and sold at regulated low prices. This is why, after many upheavals, equilibrium was re-established without hunger and chaos having appeared in Belgium.

But where were our credits? Abroad, we had only debts. The agreements recently concluded with Washington and Ottawa for "imports within six months" had only begun to be acted upon by the spring of 1945. Aside from the political motifs which determined our allies to make us dance to their tune, they were not interested in overloading their ships and sending them to our ports, which were far from the battlefields. In no respect, therefore, did the Belgian experiment convince me to adopt the system of price and wage fixing and deductions. Let the liberated nation produce as much as possible! Let the state aid and encourage it to do so! In exchange, let it furnish the state, under the form of normal assessments and savings investments, the means to cover the expenditures the latter was making for the public welfare! This was the decision taken in March 1945.

The latter was not to be changed. Until the end, this policy was to guide the Provisional Government's financial and economic policy. However, in addition to our regular burdens, we had to furnish money against the enormous deficit occasioned in the 1945 budget by war and reconstruction expenditures, by the return and relocation of prisoners and deported men, by the replacement of refugees, by the re-establishment of the demobilized men in their homes, and by the transport of our troops to Indochina. But the supplementary receipts, the confiscation of illicit profits, the conversion into 3 per cent income of the 4 per cent securities of 1917 and 1918, the 4½ per cent securities of 1932, and particularly the treasury bonds to which the public continued to subscribe, provided us means of dealing with everything. Indeed we had recourse in June to the exchange of bank notes, which rendered null and void, to the profit of the state, the old currency that would not be presented. But the operation was undertaken franc for franc. Indeed we continued, between January and December, to adjust both prices and salaries, but the government remained in control and at maximum the increases did not exceed 50 per cent. At the same time, production continued to rise, particularly since, following a series of agreements made in February and March with Belgium, Switzerland, Great Britain and the United States, imports were resumed. All in all, by the end of 1945 economic activity had doubled its level at the time of the liberation, and fiduciary circulation had not risen above the level it had attained at the time of my arrival in Paris. At a period and in a realm where there was no possibility of satisfying everyone, I did not expect this result to provoke enthusiasm. I myself considered it satisfactory, however, for after having staggered along on a path bordering one abyss after another, the nation, by the year's end, had set off upon the road to a new prosperity.

As was to be expected, Pierre Mendès-France resigned from the government, by his own request, during the month of April. He did so with dignity, and I maintained all my esteem for this colleague of such exceptional merit. Furthermore, if I did not adopt the policy he advocated, neither did I adopt an attitude preventing me from doing so eventually, should the circumstances change. But for Mendès-France to be in a position to apply it eventually, he must remain faithful to his doctrine. In this way, his resignation could actually be a service rendered to the state. I united Finance and Economy into a single ministry of which Pleven was put in charge. A long-standing colleague of broad and brilliant mind, though invariably modest, an economist equal to the complex tasks which his flexible intellect readily encompassed, Pleven acquitted himself of his functions without our poor means permitting him spectacular successes, but in such a way that the nation advanced with regard to both resources and credit. Although on occasion I considered his complications superfluous, his flexibility excessive, I accorded him my entire confidence and unceasingly supported him.

I did as much for all the ministers, obliged as I was to maintain in their regard the singular position which my function as arbitrator required, but convinced of their merit and appreciative of their friendship. Today, after many years and many reversals in attitudes, it is not without emotion that I recall the loyalty of this body and the support its members have given me in our historic task. However various my twenty collaborators may have been, the fact is that we were to have one and the same policy until the day of victory. Of course these men were, for the most part, attached to various parties, but the sufferings of France were too recent, and my powers too widely recognized, for any of them to expect to function individually, or even to contemplate the prospect of doing so. As a Cabinet member each man was responsible to General de Gaulle and to him alone. The result, in the government's action, was a unity which of itself dominated the restoration of order in the state and the nation.

I frequently consulted Jules Jeanneney, the austere and reserved senior member of our government. One of Clemenceau's ministers during the First World War, he had subsequently refused to hold such a post under anyone else; at present, he did so in my government. Utterly devoted to the public welfare, Jeanneney brought us a juridical capacity and a political experience which led me to entrust him with the preparation of the projects relative to political institutions. No one was more convinced than the former President of the Senate that the old regime must be transformed from top to bottom. I had constant dealings with the three "military" ministers. André Diethelm, than whom I cannot imagine a more faithful companion or a statesman of higher conscience, organized, staffed and equipped an Army whose morale was low, whose units were heterogeneous, whose means were insolvent, yet which was to be the Army of victory. Louis Jacquinot skillfully applied himself, despite the guns fired in the wrong direction, the ships destroyed or scuttled, the wreckage of the arsenals, to reviving the Navy. Charles Tillon, firm yet sensitive, devoted himself no less effectively to the resurrection of the aircraft factories. I worked daily with Georges Bidault, Minister of Foreign Affairs. Long experienced in the history and the criticism of the subjects confronting him but coming only lately to the practice of affairs, impatient already to try his own wings but still concerned to keep to the line I had drawn, tempted to consecrate himself to his ministerial task but at the same time heedful of the nascent political movement whose leadership he intended to assume, Bidault surmounted these contradictions by the force of an intelligent finesse. On many occasions, Adrien Tixier conferred with me with regard to public order. No vicissitude altered the intellectual tranquillity of the Minister of the Interior, though he had only inadequate forces at his disposal and was unceasingly harassed by the protests of the vengeful or the exhortations of certain groups eager to have the authorities learn nothing and forget everything. Yet Adrien Tixier, wounded in the war, suffered continual pain and was to die within a year.

At intervals, resentment was expressed against the other ministers. This was the experience of François de Menthon, Minister of Justice, one of whose responsibilities, and a burning one, was to constitute the courts, the civil chambers, the High Court, and to assure their independence; De Menthon did so with distinction. The young, idealistic, eloquent Pierre-Henri Teitgen was also frequently criticized, since he was in charge of the Ministry of Information and regulated all press affairs. Those who attacked him found that they had met their match. Nothing could mar the robust lucidity of Robert Lacoste, Minister of Production. His task, however, was an ungrateful one—whether it concerned power, equipment, or raw materials, whether it was mines, metallurgy, or the textile and paper industries that were involved, his program always consisted of deficits, impasses and bottlenecks. Yet, without advertising the fact, Lacoste accomplished an enormous amount of work and was never swamped by his problems. At the Ministry of Labor, Alexandre Parodi patiently and uncomfortably spun out the Penelope's web that constituted the French wage scale. The return of the prisoners of war was prepared by Henri Frenay. As the parties outbid each other in advance over the claims to be made in the name of these two million electors, the storm rumbled around the minister. But of all the members of my government, the man harnessed to the most arduous task, and the man most certain of being able to satisfy no one, the man least spared by critics and caricatures, was Paul Ramadier, Minister of Provision and Supply. I had appointed him to the post in November; valiantly, methodically, he applied himself to its problems and succeeded in uniting and distributing the few rations available at the time, opposing his rocklike solidity to the flood of gibes and lampoons, but sensitive to their injustice.

A few ministers were somewhat more sheltered from the censure of public opinion. This was true of Paul Giacobbi, a skillful mind and an ardent heart, who replaced Pleven as Minister of the Colonies and was responsible for Indochinese affairs; of François Billoux, who headed Public Health without conflicts but not without success; of François Tanguy-Prigent, minister and servant of French Agriculture, who made every effort to organize and confederate his charge; of the astute Augustin Laurent, who reorganized the postal services and the telegraph and telephone systems ravaged by the battle. It was also in a relatively calm atmosphere that René Capitant, René Mayer, and Raoul Dautry directed the ministries they were appointed to. The first undertook with audacity and success to renovate the structure and methods of National Education. The second, responsible for Transportation, found means of resolving the immediate problems posed by the demolition of the railroads, ports, bridges, roads, canals and naval yards. The third, fertile in ideas and familiar with every technique, set in operation the Ministry of Reconstruction which I had created in December. Upon Dautry's request, I joined the Bureau of Urbanism to his ministry, so that our cities would be restored according to a general plan. On the whole, observing how all my collaborators handled their tasks in their respective domains, I was certain that the resistance offered the country great political and administrative capacities, provided that there was a captain on board the ship of state.

Since we had many tasks of the most difficult nature to accomplish, the government functioned according to fixed rules. Except in secret matters concerning operations, or when it was a question of a diplomatic emergency, all important decisions were adopted in Council. The latter convened, on the average, twice a week. This was not too often, given the wealth of subjects and the fact that the government had to make decisions for the legislative as well as the executive branches. The sessions were prepared with the greatest possible care. The constitution of the dossiers, the liaison of the Presidency with the ministers and the

Council of State were incumbent on the general secretariat, directed by Louis Joxe. Speaking little and low, always standing in the wings, Joxe assured the smooth functioning of the mechanism upon which everything else depended.

The Council held its sessions in the Hôtel Matignon. In the bare-walled hall, the atmosphere was one of objectivity. The session, however important or affecting, proceeded according to an order established once and for all. On each of the points dealt with, the minister concerned presented his report as he saw it. Those members who felt they should formulate objections or suggestions were always heard. It was my task to clarify the debate by asking the desired questions. Then, if a serious problem were under discussion, I consulted each of the members. It happened, moreover, as I had consistently noticed for over five years, that the principles of our policy rarely gave rise to discussions. The action of the armies, the goals of the war, the attitude toward the Allies, the transformation of the Empire into the French Union, the duty to assure justice with regard to the "collaborators," the obligation to maintain order against all dangers, the necessity to accomplish a far-reaching social reform—all this provoked no protests or challenges. On these matters, everyone agreed to take the direction De Gaulle himself had pointed to. But once we approached the measures to be taken—that is, the interests involved—the sessions immediately became heated. This was particularly true in the case of projects of an economic and social order, financial arrangements production, provisioning and the terms of suffrage and eligibility. In questions concerning individuals, the controversy reached its maximum pitch.

During the discussion I insisted that opinions be expressed without reserve. Ultimately I made known my own point of view. Frequently a kind of general agreement was established among the members. I would remark as much, and the matter was settled. In other cases, I formulated the decision I felt to be the right one, and it thereby became the decision of the Council. I

SALVATION

attempted, in every case, to make our procedure clear and swift, for once the cause was heard, nothing would cost dearer than the government's uncertainty.

How short the hours, and how few! I had to prepare these government Councils, and many matters besides. National defense, economy, finances, population, Indochina, North Africa were first examined by subcommittees, over which I presided, consisting of the ministers responsible in the matter with their chief assistants. I also had to deal with one or another of the members of the government separately, frequently consulting experts, asking the advice of René Cassin, Vice President of the Council of State, determining the order of the day with Louis Joxe, and signing the ordinances, decrees and decisions which were the result.

What happened from day to day was presented to me by my direct collaborators; Palewski brought me the telegrams, letters and reports concerning policy and diplomacy, the French and foreign press and radio analyses, the messages arriving from all points of France and the world. Juin kept me informed of military events and brought me the reports and requests of our armies. I then wrote my own letters, dispatches and directives and signed the correspondence prepared by the Cabinet.

The audiences I gave were limited to the essential, which meant they were many. Aside from conferences with members of Allied governments who came to negotiate in Paris—like Messrs. Churchill and Eden in November, Mr. Hopkins in January, M. Spaak in February, M. van Kleffens and later Sir John Anderson in March, Messrs. Ford and Evatt in April—I received the ambassadors; Messrs. Duff Cooper, Bogomolov and Caffery were assiduous visitors. But Monsignor Roncalli, M. Morawski, Baron Guillaume, General Vanier, Messrs. Cerny, Burckhardt, etc., frequently visited my office as well. The chief Allied or French military leaders had permanent access to me. Periodically the Commissioners of the Republic were summoned to Paris and I met with them on each occasion to hear their reports and give them general instructions. Our representatives abroad, when they passed through France, came to report on their missions. I received, on occasion, the director of the Bank of France, the Secretary General of the Quai d'Orsay, the Prefect of Police, the director of the intelligence service. It was my duty to make contact with various eminent men of other countries, as well as with French notables— presidents of associations, academicians, prelates, leaders of the economy, trade union chiefs, etc. In addition, the members of the "Consultative Assembly," the presidents of parties and certain delegates were received when they requested an audience.

Up to the day of victory, I went to the Assembly thirty times. On twenty of these occasions I spoke there. During the same period I frequently addressed the nation by radio. Speeches, addresses and press conferences permitted me to keep the country informed of its affairs, of what I expected of it, and also to carry the voice of France abroad. In certain cases I was obliged to improvise my remarks. Then, permitting myself to be caught up in a deliberate emotion, I showered my hearers with the ideas and phrases uppermost in my mind. But often I wrote the text in advance and then spoke it by heart—doubtless this was the result of my love of exactitude and a certain oratorical vanity, but it was also a heavy burden, for, although my memory serves me well, my pen is not a facile one. My journeys were numerous— eleven visits to the armies, tours in all the provinces, a trip to Russia by way of the Near East and returning by way of North Africa. In eight months, I was away from the capital seventy days. Upon each return, I was greeted by the mountains of work that had accumulated in my offices.

It was in the Rue St.-Dominique that the latter were installed. The former Hotel Brienne is central and symbolic. From morning to evening I worked and held my audiences there. Here, too, took place the presidential receptions—presentation of credentials, acknowledgment of delegations, official dinners, etc. Here convened the interministerial committees and, occasionally, the Council of

Ministers. I had refused to establish the Palais de l'Élysée as my residence, thereby showing that I would prejudice neither tomorrow's institutions nor the place I would take in them. Moreover, the style of life which the Élysée would impose on General de Gaulle and cost the state was inappropriate at a time of national austerity. For the same reasons, I made no stay at the Château de Rambouillet. I rented a private house on the outskirts of the Bois de Boulogne, on the Route de Bagatelle, where my wife and I lived with our two daughters. Our son was in the lines. Those spring and winter evenings, agreeable French and foreign guests occasionally joined our table. After their departure, my evenings were filled with the study of reports, the writing of speeches and the conscientious examination of the appeals of condemned war criminals. On Sundays I was driven to a wood outside Paris where I took walks for several hours.

From the position I occupied, nothing that was part of France was unknown or concealed from me. Now, in reports, audiences, inspections, ceremonies, a thousand signs revealed that the country was making a recovery, and in the direct contacts I made with the people, I sensed that order was triumphing over an agitation in which the nation certainly risked dismemberment.

This was the impression I received at Nantes, where I went on January 14, accompanied by Ministers Dautry and Tanguy-Prigent, to bestow the Cross of the Liberation upon Mayor Clovis Constant. Angers, which I visited next, sounded the same note of confidence and pacification I had heard in Nantes. Presiding at the opening of the University in Paris, I was struck by the vitality of atmosphere in the Sorbonne. On January 27 and 28 I drove through the Parisian suburbs. The cities of Boulogne-Billancourt, Montrouge, Sceaux, Ivry, St.-Maur, Nogent, Neuilly, Asnières, St.-Denis, Aubervilliers, Montreuil, and Vincennes saw me pass through their vibrant and flag-decked streets on foot, and received me at their municipal buildings. The bitter cold made all the more moving the enthusiasm of the people and the homage of the municipalities, whether Communist or not. Meanwhile, I had several times paid the respects of France to Alsace. On February 11, I was in Metz; the cheers of the people, the fanfares, the speeches of Prefect Rebourset, Governor Dody, Mayor Hocquard and the bishop, Monsignor Heintz, made it apparent that it was here, as always, that French victories won the greatest acclaim. On March 4, accompanied by Tixier and Lacoste, I went to Limoges. Our reception was magnificent. Though serious disturbances had shaken the Limousin, order had prevailed. Commissioner of the Republic Boursicot now wielded the full extent of his powers. Chaintron, prefect at that time, seconded him effectively. Mayor Chaudier had created unity within his municipal council. In the name of France, I made the pilgrimage to Oradour-sur-Glane. The next day after, I traveled across the Gascony countryside. At Périgueux the trip was completed by a reception made radiant by patriotic pride.

Paris on April 2 closed the series of manifestations which had served as a prelude to the victory. In the morning, in the Place de la Concorde fairly curtained with the Cross of Lorraine, in presence of the government, the members of the state bodies, those of the Assembly, and the diplomatic corps, I formally presented the 134 flags and standards to the colonels of the newly recruited regiments. Then, from the Arc de Triomphe, where a huge flag floated, along the Champs-Élysées, the Rue Royale and the great boulevards to the Place de la République, paraded 60,000 men and a powerful show of military vehicles. These were either new units or those from the front. The enthusiasm of the people, discovering the resurrection of our military might, was indescribable.

That afternoon, on the porch of the Hôtel de Ville, André Le Troquer received from my hands the Cross of the Liberation, award.d to the City of Paris. Previously I had replied to the eloquent address of the President of the Municipal Council in a speech concerning our duties. "France," I said, "is discovering with a clear mind the efforts she must make in order to repair what this war, begun more than thirty years ago, has destroyed of her substance. . . . We will re-establish ourselves only by arduous labor, a severe national discipline. . . . Let the rivalry of parties be silenced!" Referring to "the difficult world to which our country has awakened," I declared, "It is good that the realities are rigorous and uncomfortable. To a people like ours, rejecting the infamous caresses of decadence, asperities are worth more than the soft slopes of luxury."

On that day, as always in such ceremonies, I left the official cortege now and then in order to approach the crowd and join its ranks. Shaking hands, listening to the cheers, I tried to make this contact into an exchange. "Here I am, as God made me!" is what I tried to communicate to those around me. "As you see, I am your brother, at home among the members of his family, but also a leader who cannot compromise with his duty nor bend under his burden." And beneath the cheers and behind the stares, I discerned the image of the people's soul. For the great majority, what mattered was the emotion provoked by this spectacle, exalted by this presence, and expressed with smiles and tears by "*Vive* De Gaulle!" Many revealed their anxiety that new disturbances would soon threaten their national and individual lives, and seemed to be saying, "We cheer you because you represent power, order, security." But how grave was the mute question I read on certain faces, "De Gaulle! How will the greatness you have restored to us resist tomorrow's rising tide of expedience?"

In the heart of the multitude I was imbued with its joys and its cares. I felt especially close to those who, celebrating France's salvation but conscious that her inner demons had reawakened, suffered in her behalf the lucid anxiety of love!

CHAPTER 4

VICTORY

AFTER the great spring and summer battles, the western front
was established near the Reich's border, in order to prepare
the decisive blows on both sides. Taking account of the huge offensive the Russians would soon launch, the western Allies were
regrouping in mid-autumn with a view to concluding their campaign during the course of the winter. Hitler, on his side, still
hoped to crush the Allies' assault by a supreme effort and even
regain the advantage. As for France, these imminent events
would furnish her an occasion to win her share of the victory and
restore luster to her arms. Therefore my goals were clear—I intended our forces to be co-ordinated with those of our allies. I
hoped that their new glory would revive throughout the nation the
pride it so desperately needed. I wanted their action to produce,
on the national territory, specific results of direct interest to
France.

Naturally our campaign forces were placed, for operations,
within the interallied strategic system. General Eisenhower, who
exercised the supreme command, was equal to his task, fair and
methodical, skillful enough to maintain his authority over his
difficult lieutenants and to show flexibility toward the governments

which entrusted their armies to him. For my part, I had decided not to complicate his task, so that his control of the major units we had transferred to him would be as complete as possible. But aside from our mutual interest in winning the battle, there was also the national interest of France. That was my concern; to fulfill the requirements, I would on several occasions be obliged to intervene in the strategic domain during the course of the fighting.

This would not have been the case had France been granted her rightful place in the leadership of the common effort, if the Paris government, like its great allies, had been in a position to present its war aims to the coalition, and if the French general staff had also been permitted to co-operate in the Allied military decisions. But Washington and London claimed exclusive rights to strategic leadership, and the "combined" Anglo-American command jealously retained a monopoly of the plans of operations. Given the fact that France's entire destiny was at stake, that the French Army ultimately furnished nearly a quarter of the troops under Eisenhower's orders, that the battle's base of operations was on French soil, utilizing French roads, railways, ports and communications, the insistence of the Anglo-American forces on holding all the reins of command was indeed unjustifiable. To compensate for this abuse, I would, on occasion, have to force their hand and even employ our troops outside the Allied framework.

I was assisted in the military aspects of my task by the General Staff of the Office of National Defense, constituted in Algiers and directed by General Juin, whose intelligence and assiduity had made him skillful at easing my contacts with the Allies and reducing the shocks to which my manner occasionally exposed my subordinates. Juin executed my decisions in regard to operations. In matters of administration, armament, equipment, and personnel, the Ministers of War, the Navy, the Air Force—Diethelm, Jacquinot, Tillon—with their chiefs of staff—Leyer, Lemonnier, Valin—performed the same function. But it was incumbent upon me to determine the most important measures. I did so in committee with the Office of National Defense, in the presence of the three ministers and their seconds. After which the latter went to their offices and their telephones to deal with the problems inherent in a nation stripped of its means of making war, yet which it was our task to restore to battle with its sword in its hand.

I regarded Eisenhower's general plan for the resumption of the offensive during October as well conceived. The Supreme Commander wanted to move his main force in the direction of the Ruhr, sending General Bradley's army group as far as the Rhine. Montgomery's group would advance in the Low Countries to support the American left flank while, to cover their left, the two armies in Devers' group would drive into Alsace, Patch through Saverne, De Lattre through Belfort. It would also be De Lattre's task to secure cover for these positions along the Alps.

Secondary operations were also provided for. The supply services necessary in a major battle required the landing of enormous amounts of material, and since the French and Belgian ports already liberated were in the worst possible condition, the Supreme Commander decided to raise the blockade of Antwerp. The British therefore seized the islands of the Scheldt. But since the port of Bordeaux was also relatively intact, and since its utilization would greatly facilitate the supplying of French material, I urged Eisenhower to provide us with the means to get rid of the German pockets on both sides of the Gironde. He agreed to do so on principle. The French were also to blockade—until they could capture—the other Atlantic pockets, La Rochelle, St.-Nazaire and Lorient.

In October, I had decided on a redistribution of our forces corresponding to the probable eventualities. The First Army, retaining seven divisions—the 1st "Free French," the 3rd North African, the 2nd and 4th Moroccan, the 9th Colonial, and the 1st and 5th Armored—as well as the two army corps and the reserve units which had been assigned to it since Africa and Italy, also absorbed numerous reinforcements from the resistance groups. It brought the striking force of its units to maximum strength, formed new regiments and was soon to constitute one additional division, the 14th. General de Lattre was therefore to have a total of more than eight divisions under his command, with all corresponding services, supports and flying columns, in order to reach and cross the Rhine.

The 2nd Armored Division would also take part in the battle of Alsace. Following my instructions, this division was initially reassigned to the American Seventh Army with the general mission of liberating Strasbourg. Further, the 27th Alpine Division and two mountain brigades remained in the Alps to cover the Rhone valley through which the communications services of De Lattre's and Patch's armies would pass. Along the Atlantic coast, I entrusted De Larminat with the command of the "western forces," which were attached, for munitions and fuel supply, to General Devers' army group. Larminat was facing some 90,000 solidly entrenched German soldiers. Since there were some maquis troops in the area, supported by several North African and Colonial regiments and batteries of diverse origins, he was to comprise three divisions—the 19th, the 23rd and the 25th. Moreover, as soon as the indispensable troops could be taken from the Rhine front, the western forces would assume the offensive in order to liquidate the German pockets. Lastly, two divisions now being formed—the 10th and the 1st—would temporarily remain at the government's disposal, one near Paris, the other close to Bourges. They, too, would be engaged as soon as possible. In the war's final phase, there would ultimately be more than fifteen French divisions in the line. This was actually all that was possible, considering our present ·stitution. For France, unfortunately, it was little indeed, compared with the past. "Allah! Who will restore to me my terrible army?"

All the aviation forces we possessed were to fly in the battle. On September 30, we constituted the 1st Air Corps under General Gerardot's orders. This corps, which included twenty groups divided equally between bombers and reconnaissance planes, was deployed around Dijon to support the French First Army, while actually comprising part of the air forces commanded by Air Marshal Tedder. Another seven groups remained based in England, five of these assisting in Allied operations in Belgium and Holland, while two heavy-bomber groups contributed, with those in western France, to the annihilation of Germany's industrial centers. Six groups under the command of General Corniglion-Molinier were constituted to support our western forces. Several squadrons aided our units engaged in the Alps. A few others in North Africa maintained the security of our Mediterranean bases and convoys. On the Russian front, two French groups continued the combat alongside the Soviet pursuit planes. All in all, a thousand French planes would be in the line at the same time.

As for our Navy, its escort and pursuit vessels and submarines accomplished their incessant task of protecting the convoys, destroying German submarines, scouting vessels and freighters, and laying mines along enemy-held coasts. Admiral d'Argenlieu, stationed at Cherbourg, directed their operations in the Atlantic, the Channel and the North Sea. At the same time a squadron consisting of the cruisers *Montcalm, Georges-Leygues, Gloire, Émile-Bertin, Jeanne-d'Arc, Duguay-Trouin,* of seven light cruisers, and of smaller craft, under the successive orders of Admirals d'Auboyneau and Jaujard, bombarded the shores of the Gulf of Genoa, still in the hands of Kesselring's troops, and covered the southern French coast against the raids of the last enemy ships. Another squadron, commanded by Admiral Rüe and comprising, in particular, the battleship *Lorraine* and the cruiser *Duquesne,* assured the blockade of the German Atlantic pockets until they could be taken. Several naval air squadrons were operating in the same areas. The Navy had furthermore formed three armored rifle regiments, a regiment of gunners, and several battalions of marines and commandos which took part in the land army's battles. It should be added that our minesweepers were completing the clearing of our ports and roadsteads. Lastly, in the Pacific, the battleship *Richelieu,* operating in the Allied fleet, was fighting against the Japanese. However reduced our enemy's naval power, everything, until the war's end, would depend on what happened at sea. It was therefore essential that whatever was left of our Navy maintain the honor of the arms of France.

The month of November saw the launching of the western Allies' general offensive. From north to south, the armies entered action one after the other. On the fourteenth came the turn of the French First Army. Its mission was to force the Belfort Gap and drive through into Haute-Alsace.

General de Lattre had assigned the Ist Army Corps to the major operation, while in the north the IInd Army Corps was to seize the Vosges passes. This objective was to be achieved after fifteen days of battle fought in mud, in snow, and despite the stubborn resistance of eight German divisions of the Nineteenth Army. Though Béthouart was able to bring his left wing toward Belfort quickly—the 2nd Moroccan Division, the 5th Armored Division and various resistance units crossed the Lisaine causing heavy enemy losses, including General Ochsmann, commanding the defense of this sector—then to drive his right wing, consisting of the 9th Colonial Division and the 1st Armored Division, toward the Rhine; though the river was reached on November 19, at Rosenau and at St.-Louis, by General du Vigier's tanks, so that the French were therefore the first of the Allied troops to take up a position there; though our troops liberated Mulhouse and Altkirch on the twenty-first, nevertheless the enemy lines held fast, entrenched in fortified positions around Belfort and on several occasions launching counterattacks that cut off our forces advancing along the Swiss frontier.

Finally, it was the progress of the IInd Army Corps in the Vosges which permitted the Ist Army Corps to achieve supremacy on the plain. The 1st "Free French" Division, forming Monsabert's right wing, managed to cross the southern spurs of the range at Giromagny and Massevaux. Its chief, General Brosset, a combatant worthy of legend, perished during the course of this advance. But Garbay, who succeeded him, effected his junction with Béthouart's troops in the vicinity of Burnhaupt. Thus was completed the encirclement of the last German resistance between Belfort and Mulhouse. Further north, Guillaume's 3rd North African Division was able to take Gérardmer and Cornimont, and afterward the passes of Schlucht and Bussang. In fifteen days, the French First Army killed 10,000 Germans and captured 18,000 prisoners and 120 cannons. By the end of November, De Lattre was in a position to turn the entire strength of his army toward Colmar.

While he was strongly engaged there, his neighbor General Patch penetrated into Basse-Alsace. Having broken the first German position on the Lunéville–Blamont line, the American Seventh Army was approaching the Rhine from Strasbourg to Lauterbourg. This was the occasion for the French 2nd Armored Division to liberate the capital of Alsace.

On November 18 this division received orders to advance toward Saverne in order to take advantage of the American success which had broken the enemy line. Leclerc rapidly moved up his forces. Advancing methodically, resolved to bring his soldiers to Strasbourg first, he maneuvered so as not to be checked by successive German resistance. Therefore one of his groups outflanked Sarrebourg to the north, then Phalsbourg, site of the enemy positions. But to the south he would have to cross the Vosges. The roads Leclerc chose by which to bring his cannons, tanks and trucks to the front were in the worst condition and presented the most risks, but gave him the best opportunity to pass without encountering resistance. So swift was the advance of our forces, so unexpected their lines of march, through Cirey, Voyer, Rehtal, and Dabo, that the enemy units encountered were virtually all surprised, captured, or routed, so that our columns often passed the fugitives on the road. On November 22, Saverne and Phalsbourg fell into our hands, as well as many German prisoners, including General Bruhn, the regional commander.

Now Leclerc and his men had only Strasbourg in front of them. To reach it, they must cross 35 kilometers of open country, then reduce the approaches and, in the interior of the position, the resistance of a garrison whose fighting strength was greater than their own and which was entrenched in secure positions. But our men felt the wind of victory rising. Leclerc asked for orders to march on Strasbourg. General Patch knew why the French 2nd Armored Division had been attached to his army; he also understood the importance of striking while the iron is hot—he assigned Leclerc to the deserved objective.

On November 23, one of the most brilliant episodes of our military history was brought to its conclusion. In five columns—one for each road—the 2nd Armored Division charged on Strasbourg. The Germans, surprised on all sides, were not able to organize their defense. Only the position they had established before the Kehl bridges held fast, and their men retreated lost in disorder, with our combat vehicles in pursuit. The barracks and public buildings, occupied by 12,000 soldiers and 20,000 German civilians, surrendered almost immediately. By the middle of the afternoon, our troops had restored the entire city to France. The inhabitants exulted in the streets. The exterior fortifications were taken within forty-eight hours. General von Vaterrodt, the German governor of Strasbourg, after retreating to Fort Ney, capitulated on November 25. Leclerc's success was complete, having been established by forethought, masterful execution and the attraction which Alsace and its capital holds over the French spirit properly translated as an irresistible effort on the part of our soldiers.

A message from General Leclerc informed me of our troops' entry into Strasbourg when they had scarcely penetrated the city. At the beginning of that day's session, I arrived to announce the news to the Consultative Assembly. A single impulse ran through those present, suddenly raised above any partisan consideration. Arms, on occasion, may have the virtue of creating French unanimity.

Yet the success of the French and American forces in the Haut-Rhin and around Strasbourg did not persuade the enemy to abandon Alsace. On the contrary, the Germans made enormous efforts to hold fast in the south, the west and the north of Colmar, until they could resume the offensive and regain what had been lost. Hitler intervened, ordered Himmler to assume political, military and police command in Alsace, reinforced the seven divisions of his Nineteenth Army with a mountain division from Norway, a Panzer division equipped with new "Panther" tanks that outmaneuvered the Shermans of our own units, and with many contingents hurriedly sent from the interior. The Colmar pocket offered him good defense conditions. The Germans immediately installed their right wing there, south of Strasbourg in a region which the Ill, the Rhine and the canal between the Rhine and the Rhone made difficult of access; on their left they were covered by the dense Hardt forest, while in the center, the rampart formed by the crest and the slopes of the Vosges was still in their hands. While French matériel brought up to the lines had to move around the mountains by long and rough roads, the Germans, in order to shift troops and material north or south, could do so over flat ground along the chord of the arc. In their rear, along the Baden bank, the heights of the Black Forest provided emplacements for their artillery and excellent observation points over the plain below. During the first days of December, there was every reason to suppose that our First Army would not seize Colmar without new and arduous battles.

Furthermore, the Allies were meeting the same fierce resistance along the entire front. In the Montgomery group, Crerar's Canadian and Polish army succeeded in clearing Antwerp only with great difficulty, and Dempsey's English army made the same inchworm progress around Nijmegen. In Bradley's group, the Simpson and Hodges armies advanced only step by step in the north and south of Aix-la-Chapelle. Patton's army, having liberated Metz, slowly pushed on to the Saar. Devers succeeded in advancing Patch as far as Lauterbourg. Obliged, however, to act on his left in order to aid his northern flank, he extended De Lattre's front without reinforcing it proportionately, which rendered the French First Army's progress still more difficult. Moreover, the winter, which was exceptionally harsh this year, exhausted the troops, froze and blocked the roads and slowed all circulation of material. Supply services, maneuvers, and attacks all suffered in consequence. At sea, the German submarines' desperate efforts still decimated the Allied convoys and material was unloaded in the ruined ports late and with great difficulty.

In spite of everything, the First Army attempted to accomplish its mission by completing the liberation of Alsace. Its zone of action was now extended, in an arc, from the Swiss frontier to the approaches to Strasbourg, the Alsatian capital being still included in the American Seventh Army's sector, though the garrison there was formed by the "Alsace-Lorraine" Brigade. General de Lattre's army was joined by the Leclerc division regrouped south of Strasbourg and by the American 36th Division. On the other hand, Devers withdrew the 1st "Free French" Division, which was shifted toward Royan.

At the beginning of December, the First Army began to advance on Colmar. Fifteen days of stubborn fighting achieved some success to the north toward Thann, which it liberated, and in the region of Sélestat and Ribeauvillé. At the same time, along the crest of the Vosges, it attacked the Hohneck and the Bonhomme pass. But in an advance of this nature, deployed simultaneously at every point along a huge front, De Lattre did not possess the means to win a decisive victory.

Suddenly the Germans launched a powerful offensive in the Ardennes. As a consequence, the Allied munitions supplies and air support, always granted extremely sparingly, were almost completely withdrawn and transferred to the sector of the German attack. The French First Army was therefore obliged to suspend its advance. Seeing the victory they had glimpsed fade before their eyes, leaders and soldiers alike were bitterly disappointed. After expending so many efforts, their present uncertainty doubled their exhaustion.

It was upon my return from Russia, in the middle of December, that I realized what was happening to our army's morale in Alsace. I was concerned, though not surprised. Knowing the martial energy Germans are capable of, I had never doubted they could hold the western powers in check for months to come. I should add that from the national point of view, I did not deplore these setbacks in which France's importance could make itself increasingly felt among our allies. Yet it was essential that our men's morale be maintained.

Matters would soon be under control if the Army felt supported by public opinion. But in this regard, there was much to be desired. Not that the French people were theoretically unaware of the merits of the men fighting in its service. But the latter too often seemed remote and almost alien to them. For many, the liberation meant the war's end, and what happened afterwards in the realm of arms offered no immediate interest. Moreover, it was the Allies who exercised the command and furnished the majority of the forces. Many Frenchmen, deeply wounded by our collapse of five years before, were scarcely enthusiastic over battles in which the French Army no longer played the leading role. Then too, the disaster of 1940, the military character of the regime of capitulation, Vichy's abuse of conformism and discipline, had provoked a certain disaffection with regard to professional soldiers in general. Finally, in the world of politics, public interest, the press and the majority of the leaders focused their concern on other subjects than a campaign which they regarded as won in advance and which would certainly lead to disarmament. Remarking what limited space and what insipid commentaries the newspapers devoted to our troops, I called a meeting of the directors of the press to encourage them to give more prominence to events at the front. Their answer was: "We'll do our best. But we must take the public's tastes into account. And military subjects aren't of much interest now."

Indeed, on December 18, General de Lattre informed me of his concern for his army's morale. He wrote that he had asked General Devers to put at least two new divisions at his disposal, to furnish him air support and to allot him additional munitions, for otherwise his troops could not take Colmar. But at the same time, the First Army's commander described the depression prevalent among his subordinates, attributing it less to losses, fatigue and the hardships caused by the winter than to a spiritual isolation from the French nation. "From one end of the hierarchy to the other, particularly among the officers," he wrote, "the general impression is that the nation has neglected, has abandoned us." De Lattre continued, "Some have even gone so far as to imagine that the regular overseas army is being deliberately sacrificed." He added, "The real source of this problem is the nation's non-participation in the war."

Though I made every allowance for the disappointments General de Lattre and his army were encountering, following upon a phase of operations in which victories, trophies, and recognition had been the rule; though I assured him that his troops would in no way be abandoned and urged him to make this known to them; though I indicated confidence and my encouragement by this message—"Like all the Allied armies, you are going through a difficult period, but you will emerge from it to your glory"—I nevertheless took steps to reinforce the First Army in view of the coming strategic crisis.

On December 18, orders were given to incorporate into the front units the 10,000 young soldiers training in the military depots. On the nineteenth, I informed the Allied command that because of the new German offensive in Belgium, I was approving the suspension of the Royan drive, enabling the 1st "Free French" Division to return to Alsace at once. These orders were carried out at once. A few days afterward, I went to inspect the 10th Division, a large new unit in training near Fontainebleau. Under General Billotte's command, this division consisted largely of Parisians who had fought in the streets of the capital during the liberation. Reviewing them, I was once more reminded that skillful gardeners can always restore the military stalk to bloom. Although the 10th Division's training and equipment were still incomplete, I decided to send it to the front and announced this news to the division on the spot. Then its young regiments paraded across the frozen snow; fifteen thousand proud pairs of eyes met mine, one after another.

Christmas Eve and Christmas Day, accompanied by Diethelm and Juin, I spent with the First Army. Following the lines, I entered Alsace, proceeding first to Strasbourg. The great city hailed my arrival, though it was in a virtual state of siege—for the Germans still held Kehl and maintained a constant bombardment— and though the garrison, under General Schwartz's orders, was extremely reduced and badly armed. Commissioner of the Republic Blondel, Prefect Haelling and Mayor Frey discussed with me their difficulties in re-establishing a French administration. To accomplish what was necessary, it was evident that the future would have to be assured. And it was just as evident that this was not the case.

I next visited the IInd Army Corps. After hearing Monsabert's report, I decided that all his ardor was no substitute for what he lacked in order to take the enemy positions between the Rhine at Rhinau and the Vosges at La Poutraye. Then I joined the 2nd Armored Division. For weeks on end it had been thrown back, around Wittenheim, by defenses it could not penetrate; its units were exhausted; the local inhabitants anxious. At Erstein, with Leclerc and many soldiers, I attended midnight Mass. The atmosphere was one of hope, not joy. The next day I inspected the valiant American 3rd Division, which had relieved the 36th; O'Daniel, its lively and sympathetic general, informed me of the slow progress his troops were making around Kaisersberg. On my visit to the 3rd North African Division, Guillaume reported on his painful advance in the vicinity of Orbey.

By way of Gerardmer and Belfort, I reached the Ist Army Corps' sector, where Béthouart explained to me that, given the morale of his men, he was paralyzed along his entire front as far as Cernay. Near Thann, then at Altkirch, Generals Carpentier and Sudre presented to me the units of their respective divisions—the 2nd Moroccan, the 1st Armored. Both men informed me that their means were insufficient for them to advance. At Mulhouse, Magnan's division paraded before me. But the Germans were still holding the northern edge of the city, and there seemed to be no means of driving them back.

Yet here as elsewhere, the people were vehement in their demonstrations of patriotism, and their expressions of faith made it impossible to forget how severely the war had chastened every Alsatian hearth. Receiving the authorities and delegations presented by Prefect Fonlupt-Esperaber, I remarked on the seriousness of the ordeals imposed by the occupation, the establishment of the enemy's laws, the impressment of so many men into the Reich's armies, the loss of many among these, and the agony which the fate of those now in Soviet captivity inspired. Further, I noticed considerable concern over the possible results of an enemy advance from positions that were still quite near. Returning to Paris, I drew up a balance sheet of my impressions: The Army was firm, but fatigued; Alsace loyal, but alarmed. I concluded that in the case of any regrettable incident, I should have to intervene vigorously and immediately in order to forestall the gravest consequences.

And it was precisely at this moment that the regrettable incident occurred—after the German breakthrough in the Ardennes, the

Allied command decided to evacuate Alsace, withdrawing Patch's and De Lattre's armies to the Vosges.

Marshal von Rundstedt's offensive, launched between Echternach and Malmédy with twenty-four divisions, ten of which were Panzers, had in fact made considerable progress. By December 25, the Germans had almost reached the Meuse on either side of Dinant. They were then in a position to break through the rear lines of the Low Countries front by way of Namur and Liége. Therefore General Eisenhower decided that everything must be subordinated to the necessity of stopping and driving back the enemy advance, which was already eighty kilometers deep. He ordered Montgomery to take command of the defense of the Allied lines on the northern flank and in the Colmar pocket, and directed Bradley to launch Patton's counterattack on the southern flank. But Patch's army on Patton's right gave signs of weakness in the region around Forbach, obliging Devers to bring in support in the form of the French 2nd Armored Division, withdrawn from De Lattre's forces. Further, the enemy gave signs of new offensive activity around the Colmar pocket. The situation in Alsace was perilous, and the Supreme Commander supposed that if the enemy attacked here as well, there was nothing else to do but retreat to the Vosges. And it was Strasbourg which would be abandoned first of all. Eisenhower issued directives to this effect.

The evacuation of Alsace, and particularly of its capital, might appear logical from the point of view of Allied strategy, but to France it was not acceptable. That the French Army should abandon one of our provinces, and this province in particular, without even engaging in a battle to defend it; that the German troops, followed by Himmler and his Gestapo, should return in triumph to Strasbourg, to Mulhouse, to Sélestat, would be a terrible wound inflicted on the honor of our country and its soldiers, a terrible cause for the Alsatians to despair of France, a profound blow to the nation's confidence in De Gaulle. Naturally, I did not consent to it. The excuse a policy of resignation might find in the fact that the Allied command was responsible for military operations had, in this case, no validity. For if the French government could entrust its forces to the command of a foreign leader, it was on the formal condition that the use made of those forces be in accord with the nation's interest. If not, the French government was obliged to resume command of its forces. This is what I determined to do, with all the less scruple since Allied headquarters had not even deigned to inform me of a matter which touched France to the quick.

Actually, despite the silence maintained in my regard by the Allied command, various indications had alerted me to what was occurring. On December 19, it was reported that Devers had replied to De Lattre, who had asked him for reinforcements in order to resume the attack on Colmar, that he had none to give, that the entire army group was in danger and that consequently it was retreat which should be considered, not advance. On Christmas, during my inspection of the front, I had learned that De Lattre, upon orders from the command, had ordered the preparation of a retreat position opposite Giromagny across the Belfort Gap, and had withdrawn the 4th Moroccan Division toward Luxeuil. On December 27, it came to my knowledge that General Devers was withdrawing his command post from Phalsbourg and establishing it at Vittel, 120 kilometers to the rear. The next day, Devers sent the forces under his command a directive requiring them to fall back to the Vosges in case of enemy attack. Consequently, on December 30, General de Lattre ordered the First Army "to establish successive lines of defense in order to retard the enemy as much as possible, in case he manages to break through the initial position . . ."

As a matter of fact, our information services indicated enemy preparations for a drive on Saverne between Bitche and Wissembourg. Our liaison officers assigned to general headquarters observed that the German offensive was producing concern if not dismay there. On the front, in the rear, in Paris, circulated alarming rumors as to the progress of Rundstedt's troops, reports of Darnand's militiamen and enemy commandos being parachuted into various regions of France, and Hitler's boasts of returning to Brussels and restoring Strasbourg to the Reich by the New Year.

It was time to act. On December 30 I ordered General du Vigier, who had been appointed governor of Strasbourg and was about to return to his post, to proceed at once to De Lattre at Montbéliard and to Devers at Vittel, and to inform both in my behalf that whatever happened, Strasbourg must and would be defended. He was to notify them of the imminent arrival of the 10th Division, which I was assigning to the French First Army. At the same time, I ordered General Dody, governor of Metz and commander of the northeast sector, to hold the Meuse crossings at Givet, Mézières and Sedan, so that in case of a sudden retreat on the part of the American forces operating in the area, French territory would nevertheless be protected. Units furnished from the interior, summarily armed, it was true, but totaling 50,000 men, were immediately sent to Dody for this purpose.

On January 1, with Du Vigier on his way, Juin came to discuss the immediate dangers that threatened Alsace. The National Defense Chief of Staff had been informed by Supreme Headquarters in Versailles that the immediate transfer of all Allied reserves to the Ardennes was obligatory, and that consequently the German attack on Saverne was greatly endangering Devers' army group, and that General Eisenhower was therefore ordering him to fall back to the Vosges in order to shorten his front. This decision had been made because of a successful enemy air operation. Dozens of swastikaed rocket planes—the first in the world—had appeared that very day in the Ardennes sky, had swept the American pursuit planes from the sky and destroyed many planes on their bases. Incidental though it was, the episode inclined headquarters to a pessimism which might demand the sacrifice of Alsace. I would have to intervene.

My first task was to make certain Strasbourg was protected. To guarantee such defense, I had no other recourse than to assign the French First Army there myself. Such an action would contradict the instructions of the interallied command and, moreover, extend the First Army's sector northward to include Strasbourg, which belonged to the American Seventh Army zone. If, as I hoped, Eisenhower wished to maintain the military unity of the Allied forces under his command, he would agree to adopt the modification I had wrought in the measures he had described. On the afternoon of January 1 I sent my orders to General de Lattre. Referring to the High Command's decision to fall back along the Vosges front, I wrote: "Naturally the French Army cannot consent to the abandonment of Strasbourg. . . . In case the Allied forces retire from their present positions north of the French First Army lines, I order you to take matters into your own hands and to assure the defense of Strasbourg."

At the same time, I sent an explicit letter to General Eisenhower. I indicated to the Supreme Commander that the strategic reasons for his retreat had not escaped me. But I declared that "the French government, for its part, obviously cannot let Strasbourg fall into enemy hands again without first doing everything possible to prevent it." I formulated the notion that, in case the Americans did not hold the Wissembourg salient, "Strasbourg, at least, could be defended by holding the line along the canal from the Marne to the Rhine," and I declared myself ready to "push all French forces that were being mustered in this direction, first of all the 10th Division under General Billotte.

"Whatever happens," I wrote in conclusion, "the French will defend Strasbourg." Furthermore, I telegraphed Roosevelt and Churchill to keep them informed of the High Command's views as to the evacuation of Alsace, to draw their attention to the extremely serious consequences which would result for France, and to inform them that I was not in agreement with such views.

On the morning of January 2 I confirmed to De Lattre by telegram the order I had sent him by letter the night before. Toward noon, Du Vigier, having flown back to Paris, gave me an account of his mission: Three hours before he had been in Vittel, general headquarters of the Southern Army Group; there, Devers had told him that since the enemy was attacking around Saverne, the order of retreat had been given to De Lattre and Patch, and that the American troops had already begun moving. Upon which I ordered Juin to confirm to Eisenhower that France alone would defend Alsace with all the means she had at her disposal. Juin was also to announce to general headquarters that I would pay a visit the next day.

I knew as well as anyone else that the mission I had assigned General de Lattre involved great risks. Moreover, the fact of withdrawing in the middle of battle from the interallied ensemble could only be painful to the First Army commander, who naturally perceived the risky character of such a maneuver and who disliked seeing the rupture of the strategic solidarity which had hitherto distinguished his service. Nevertheless, he was forced to admit that in such a conflict of duties, that of serving France directly—in other words, of obeying me—was far more urgent than the other.

Moreover, of his own accord he had already mentally prepared himself to do what I ordered. General du Vigier's visit on the night of December 31, the messages from the Commissioner of the Republic and the Mayor of Strasbourg, and above all his own reactions, had made him aware of the disastrous nature of the envisaged retreat. On the morning of January 2, he had written to General Devers to express his point of view: "Because of the extent of its sector and the weakness of its means, the French First Army is not in a position to defend Strasbourg directly. But it has determined to do everything in its power to cover the city on the south." And he went on to urge Devers to have "the American Seventh Army defend Strasbourg down to its last resources." Therefore, when De Lattre received my letter of January 2 assigning him his mission, he found nothing in it that was not in accord with his own feelings. Yet there remained General Devers' imperative order to fall back along the Vosges front and to establish new lines there by the morning of January 5.

General de Lattre answered my letter on January 3. He communicated to me the text of the order of retreat that Devers had given him. He discussed his intention to shift the 3rd North African Division to Strasbourg, moving the 10th Division into its present position. However, he appeared to think that the execution of what I had ordered him to do should be suspended until the Allied High Command had given its consent, alleging "the necessity to be covered on his left by the American Seventh Army" and also "the pivotal role played by the French First Army in the Allied position."

I was, of course, extremely eager to have Eisenhower share my views. But whether he did so or not, I intended the French Army to do what I had ordered. A new letter, telegraphed by me to General de Lattre on the morning of January 3, clearly established what was to be done. "I cannot accept your last communication . . ." I wrote. "The First Army under your command comprises part of the Allied positions for the single reason that the French government has ordered it to, and only until it may decide otherwise. . . . Had you been obliged to evacuate Alsace, the government could not admit your doing so without a major engagement, even—and I repeat—even if your left wing were exposed by the retreat of the troops in the adjoining position."

The responsibilities of the government being thus assumed and its will made known, De Lattre immediately undertook to carry out what I expected of him. He would do so with all his heart and all his ability. The evening of that same day, he telegraphed me that an infantry regiment would occupy Strasbourg during the night and that the Guillaume division would be in a position to defend the city on January 5.

During the afternoon of January 3, accompanied by Juin, I went to Versailles. Mr. Churchill, alerted by my message, had also decided to come, apparently disposed to provide his good offices.

General Eisenhower explained the situation, which was certainly a serious one. He did not conceal that the extent and the energy of the German offensive in the Ardennes as well as the sudden appearance of new enemy arms—robot planes, "Panther" tanks, etc.—had morally shaken the Allied forces and even surprised himself. "At the present time," he said, "the greatest danger seems to have been averted. But we must regain the ground we have lost and then resume the initiative. I must therefore reconstitute reserve units. Now in Alsace, where the enemy has extended his attack for two days, the Colmar pocket makes our position a precarious one. That is why I have ordered the troops to establish another line, further back and shorter."

"If we were at Kriegspiel," I declared to Eisenhower, "I should say you were right. But I must consider the matter from another point of view. Retreat in Alsace would yield French territory to the enemy. In the realm of strategy, this would be only a maneuver. But for France, it would be a national disaster. For Alsace is sacred ground. Since, furthermore, the Germans claim that this province belongs to them, they will not hesitate to seek revenge, should they retake it, for the patriotism its inhabitants have so tirelessly revealed. The French government does not wish to permit the enemy to return to Alsace. At the present moment, we are concerned with Strasbourg. I have ordered the French First Army to defend the city. It will therefore do so, in any case. But it would be deplorable if this entailed a dispersion of Allied forces, perhaps even a rupture in the system of command. That is why I urge you to reconsider your plan and to order General Devers to hold fast in Alsace."

The Supreme Commander seemed impressed. Nevertheless he felt it his duty to formulate an objection of principle. "You give political reasons," said this excellent soldier, "for me to change military orders."

"Armies," I replied, "are created to serve the policy of states. And no one knows better than you yourself that strategy should include not only the given circumstances of military technique, but also the moral elements. And for the French people and the French soldiers, the fate of Strasbourg is of an extreme moral importance."

On this point, Mr. Churchill expressed a similar opinion. "All my life," he observed, "I have remarked what significance Alsace has for the French. I agree with General de Gaulle that this fact must be taken into consideration."

Before agreeing to what I wished, General Eisenhower asked me to consider the situation of the French First Army were it to operate independently of the Allied armies. He went so far as to imply that in such a case, the Americans might cut off our fuel and munitions supply services. I pointed out, in return, that by permitting the enemy to defeat French troops in an isolated sector, the High Command would provoke a rupture in the balance of forces that would perhaps be irreparable, and that by depriving our lines of the means of combat he exposed himself to the risk of seeing the outraged French people forbid the use of its railroads and communications which were indispensable to operations. Rather than contemplate the consequences of such possibilities, I felt I should rely on General Eisenhower's strategic talent and on his devotion to the service of the coalition of which France constituted a part.

Finally the Supreme Commander came round to my point of view. He did so with the frankness which was one of the most appealing qualities of his sympathetic character, telephoning to General Devers that the retreat was to be canceled at once and that new orders would be sent. These orders were taken to Devers during the following day by General Bedell Smith. I agreed with Eisenhower that Juin should accompany Bedell Smith, which would be an additional guarantee for me and, for the executants, proof that agreement had been reached.

While we were taking tea together after this warm discussion, Eisenhower confided to me how greatly his task was complicated, during the worst of the crisis the armies were passing through, by the requirements of various governments in the coalition, by the touchy claims of the different categories of forces—the armies, navies and air forces of several countries—and by the personal susceptibilities of their chiefs. "At this very moment," he said, "I am having a lot of trouble with Montgomery, a general of great ability, but a bitter critic and a mistrustful subordinate."

"Glory has its price," I replied. "Now you are going to be a conqueror." We parted good friends at the door of the Hotel Trianon.

The following two weeks were filled with the vicissitudes of a fierce battle for Strasbourg. The German First Army developed its offensive, driving through the Haguenau forest toward Saverne, while the Ninth Army crossed the Rhine north and south of the Alsatian capital. In the Haguenau sector, the Americans yielded to the German impact but finally halted the attack along the Moder. At Gambsheim, the Guillaume division, and at Erstein the Garbay division and the Malraux brigade also gave ground before re-establishing their lines. But Strasbourg remained in our hands. By January 20, the enemy seemed to have reached the end of his strength, and of his hope as well. The same was true in the Ardennes, where all that the Germans had gained was won back again. On the eastern front, the Russians were launching their winter offensive. Over the entire German territory, Allied bombers were sowing loads of destruction. At sea, the damages inflicted on Allied convoys began to diminish. Hitler could probably prolong the resistance of a great people and of a great army another few months, but the decree of fate had evidently been rendered and the necessary seals affixed. It was in Alsace that France had attached hers.

Yesterday, the defeat before Colmar had shaken the First Army's morale; today, satisfaction at having saved Strasbourg rekindled every heart. General de Lattre, in particular, felt inclined to take an optimistic view and consequently the offensive. By mid-January, he had made his arrangements to resume the effort against the German pocket in Alsace.

At the same moment, the Allied command determined to begin decisive operations on the other side of the Rhine. Before crossing the river, however, they would have to reach it, and this had no-where been accomplished save in the French sector near Stras-bourg and St.-Louis. Eisenhower therefore ordered Montgomery and Bradley to advance and seize the entire left bank along the Wesel–Coblenz–Mainz line. Naturally, he approved the intention of taking Colmar as well. But the First Army zone now extended over two hundred kilometers, in other words, a quarter of the total Allied front. To put De Lattre in a position to achieve his objective, and also perhaps to counteract the effect of the recent crisis in relations, the Supreme Commander decided to reinforce the French First Army. The Leclerc division, transferred from the Saar border, as well as several American divisions and a consider-able complement of artillery, joined its ranks.

Yet such was the enemy's fury that it took the First Army three weeks of constant combat to bring its task to completion. After January 19, the French Ist Army Corps advanced step by step against the pocket's southern flank. On February 4 it reached Rouffach, near Colmar, having engaged a large part of the German units in many hard-fought battles. On the northern flank, the IInd Army Corps had also advanced. But by the end of January it had moved closer to the Rhine in order to make room on its right for the American XXIst Army Corps, for it was to General Milburn's large unit that De Lattre ceded the principal effort. This time there was to be a sufficient concentration of forces at the right time and in the right place. On January 30, Milburn, commanding the 3rd, 28th, and 75th American infantry divisions and three armored divisions—the 12th American and the 2nd and 5th French—and operating in a narrow sector, penetrated the enemy lines northeast of Colmar. On February 2 he ordered the city to be liberated by General de Vernejoul's tanks. On the fourth, he reached Breisach. During this period, the French Ist and IInd Army Corps, supported by a well-equipped artillery under Chaillet's able command, liquidated the enemy slopes of the Vosges. On the ninth, our troops completed the conquest of the Hardt forest and seized Chalempé. Consequently, save in the Haguenau and Wissembourg regions, there remained no Germans in Alsace other than the 22,000 prisoners captured there.

On February 11 I visited Mulhouse and then Colmar. I cannot begin to describe the joy and the emotion all of us felt, whether administrators, officers, soldiers or populace. But with that day's patriotic zeal was mixed another element of enthusiasm—the French and American soldiers' comradeship in arms. It was evident that this brotherhood had been raised to its highest pitch by the mutual success won within the framework of our army and on this very terrain. Beneath the regiments' motionless silence I sensed the pulse of friendship that links our two peoples. In the center of the Place Rapp, now choked with tricolors and star-spangled banners, before our troops and those of our allies ranged proudly side by side, beneath the cheers of the Alsatian people, more responsive than all others to military spectacles and apter to grasp the significance of such events, I decorated General de Lattre, the victor of Colmar; then it was the turn of Generals Milburn, Leclerc and Dahlquist. During the evening, Strasbourg celebrated the liberation of Alsace in my presence and sang in its cathedral the *Te Deum* intoned by Monsignor Ruch. The following day, in Saverne, Generals Devers, Bradley and Patch received from my hand the symbols of the honors I had granted them.

In this way, and temporarily, we surmounted the obstacles which had damaged our strategic relations with the Americans. But we had to anticipate encountering still others. In the immediate future one ticklish and crucial question was to arise, that of French participation in the German campaign. I wanted our army to enter enemy territory, to have its own sector of operations there, to conquer cities, land and trophies, and to receive the surrender of the vanquished. This was, of course, a condition dictated by my concern for our prestige. But it was also the only means we had of being included in the capitulation, the occupation and the administration of the Reich. Once a zone of German soil was in our hands, the fate of Germany itself could not be decided without us. If this were not the case, our right to participate in the victory would remain at others' discretion. In short, I intended that we should cross the Rhine and advance the French military machine as far as possible into the southern German states.

Early in March the Montgomery and Bradley army groups penetrated the Reich at various points. The moment of crossing the frontier would therefore soon be at hand for us. Naturally I was keeping a vigilant eye on the sequel, for, knowing that the Allies' chief effort was being made toward the Ruhr and would move downstream from Coblenz, I suspected that the Supreme Commander would scarcely be interested in launching the French First Army into the Black Forest in isolation. It seemed more likely to me that he would leave it on the bank of the Rhine, which, perhaps, seemed a justifiable solution to the general staffs, but suggested to me that if we accepted it the French Army would play only a passive role in the final battle. Since my policy was unable to accept this strategy, I made my own decisions. Our troops, too, would have to cross the border. They would do so, if possible, within the interallied framework. If this was not possible, they would do so on our own account. In any case, they would seize a French zone of occupation on the right bank of the Rhine.

We soon learned that the Allied command's intentions justified all our apprehensions. Under the title "Operation Eclipse," which seemed peculiarly significant as far as we were concerned, Eisenhower's plans for the crossing of the Rhine and the advance into Germany accorded the French First Army a strictly defensive mission. At best it was presumed, in case of the Wehrmacht's total collapse, that one of our army corps could reach the right bank behind the American Seventh Army in order to second the latter in its task of occupying Württemberg. But the First Army's crossing of the Rhine in its own sector was not provided for. Reports from the front indicated further that the interallied command had withdrawn the bridgehead crews from the French armored division for use elsewhere, which meant depriving our forces of a large part of their autonomous means of crossing the river into Germany.

On March 4 I received General de Lattre in Paris and explained that for reasons of national order his army must cross the Rhine. De Lattre asked nothing better but observed—and rightly—that his sector, lying opposite the mountainous Black Forest region for its entire length along the right bank, was poorly equipped to effect a crossing by force. The operation would be a hazardous one against an enemy occupying the fortifications of the Siegfried line in the valley and entrenched in dominating positions further to the rear; particularly since the Allied command was going to allocate the French forces only a minimum of munitions. Furthermore, even if our men succeeded in surmounting this first obstacle, they would then have to penetrate a most difficult region, rising in successive ramparts of peaks and forests and ill suited for maneuvering and strategy.

"On the other hand," De Lattre pointed out, "once the French front is enlarged toward the north to include both Lauterbourg and Speyer along the Rhine, then we have better prospects. Actually, my army would find an advantageous base in this area, the right bank would be relatively easy to reach, and once the river was crossed, my left wing would be able to drive through the Pforzheim gap toward Stuttgart and bypass the natural fortress of the Black Forest on the north and east." Preparing in advance arguments which he drew from comradeship as well as from tactics in order to convince the Allied command, De Lattre assured me that in the next few days he would extend his sector as far as Speyer.

Furthermore, as frequently happens in arguments among allies, the enemy himself was to make matters easier for us. On March 7

General Bradley's troops had seized the bridge at Remagen, between Coblenz and Bonn, astonishingly enough still intact, and had immediately assured a bridgehead on the right bank. Consequently the Germans now opposed us on the left bank below Coblenz with only scattered resistance, and by the twelfth the Allies had reached the Rhine everywhere north of the Moselle. But south of this river the situation was not the same. The vast Saar salient remained in German hands. The enemy, covered on his right by the course of the Moselle, held the Siegfried line along the Treves–Saarbrücken–Lauterbourg front, which was deeper and better fortified in this sector than any other. Before he could bring his army groups to the right bank, General Eisenhower would first have to liquidate this pocket. The battle was to be a hard one; although the French First Army was not asked to do so, since the engagement occurred outside its normal zone, it nevertheless found means of participating, operating along the Rhine on the Americans' right and also seizing on the river's Palatine bank, the desired base of operations from which to invade Baden and Württemberg.

Nevertheless, according to the Allied command's orders, the attack on the Saar salient was exclusively the responsibility of Patton's army forming Bradley's right wing on the one hand, and of Patch's army forming Devers' left on the other. But Patch's task was particularly difficult, for his forces were directly opposite the fortifications of the Siegfried line. Therefore De Lattre had no difficulty persuading Devers that the assistance of the French forces would have its value. Our IInd Army Corps therefore took its part in the offensive. Between March 15 and 24, Monsabert, advancing along the Rhine, penetrated into German territory, forced the Siegfried line north of Lauterbourg, and reached Leimersheim. At the same time, our allies had pushed as far as Worms and liquidated the last German resistance on the left bank of the Rhine.

Henceforth, in order for our First Army to have the necessary crossing area in the Palatinate at its disposal, it had only to extend its front as far as Speyer. I had taken care to make several insistent representations to General Eisenhower as to the price my government attached to seeing the French Army satisfied on this point. Moreover, General Devers, a good ally and a good comrade, sympathized with General de Lattre's desires. And besides, it was at Worms that the American Seventh Army was effecting its crossing; Speyer was of no use in the operation, why not let the French enter the city? On March 28 the matter was decided, Speyer and its vicinity being incorporated into our First Army's sector. Thus the necessary base of operations was acquired, and all that remained to be done was the one essential thing—that is, to cross the Rhine.

I was impatient to see this accomplished, for the British and Americans were already rushing their forces onto the right bank. This was a tremendous operation; since March 21, Allied aviation had crushed the enemy's communications, supply dumps and air fields throughout western Germany, functioning with all the greater accuracy since pursuit planes, now able to use advance bases in the north and the east of France, were in a position to accompany the bombers on all missions. The raids were therefore made by daylight without meeting any opposition in the air. On the twenty-third, beneath a colossal air protection, Montgomery crossed the Rhine below Wesel. A few days later, Bradley advanced over the Remagen bridge and others built further south. On March 26, the American Seventh Army established a bridgehead in the vicinity of Mannheim.

I was eager to see our men on the other side too, not only in a spirit of national emulation, but also because reasons of high policy made it essential that De Lattre have time to drive as far as Stuttgart before his neighbor Patch reached the city himself. A personal telegram which I sent on the twenty-ninth to the commander of our First Army urged him to make all possible haste. "My dear General," I wrote, "you must cross the Rhine, even if the Americans do not help you and you are obliged to use boats.

The matter is one of the highest national interest. Karlsruhe and Stuttgart expect, even if they do not desire you . . ."

De Lattre answered at once that I would be satisfied, and in fact, on the evening of March 30, elements of the IInd Army Corps began to effect the crossing—the 2nd Moroccan Division at Germersheim, which it had reached only the night before. At Leimersheim, on April 1—Easter Sunday—the 9th Colonial Division undertook the crossing in its turn. The air support provided for all our units was meager, and they had at their disposal only an extremely reduced amount of special apparatus for the crossing. But by ingenious planning, several boats proved to be enough to move the advance guards across. As for bridges, General Dromard, in command of the Army Engineers, had prepared them far in advance. Foreseeing that he would have to construct them eventually and that when the occasion arose he could count only on himself, Dromard had collected the necessary material beforehand on our own territory. At Speyer, a French ten-ton bridge was opened. On the fourth, 130,000 French troops and 20,000 vehicles were already on the right bank. Karlsruhe was taken the same day. On April 7, accompanied by Diethelm, De Lattre, Juin and Dromard, I had the proud duty of crossing the Rhine and driving through the ruined capital of Baden.

The eruption into central Germany of some eighty American, British, French, Polish and Canadian divisions, supported by 12,000 planes, supplied by convoys totaling 25,000,000 tons and navigating on seas dominated by 1,000 combat vessels, could no longer leave the Reich's master any illusion as to his chances of escaping disaster. Particularly since by the beginning of April the Russians, too, were advancing steadily, crossing the entire length of the Oder, already threatening Berlin and about to enter Vienna. Should Hitler prolong hostilities, it would mean further losses, ruin and suffering for the German people without any compensation other than the satisfaction of a desperate pride for a few more weeks. Yet the Fuehrer continued to demand the supreme resistance of his people, and, it must be said that he obtained it. On the battlefields of the Rhine, the Oder, the Danube or the Po, the wreck of the German armies, badly supplied, scattered, hastily incorporating barely trained men, boys and even invalids, alongside the last veterans, still fought on under a sky thick with enemy aircraft, and in a battle which had no other issue save death or captivity. In the ruined cities and the panic-stricken villages, the populace maintained perfect discipline in the execution of a labor which henceforth would have no effect upon its fate.

But since it was damned, the Fuehrer probably preferred his creation to meet its destruction in apocalypse. Whenever I happened to listen to the German radio during this period, I was struck by the frenzied character of its broadcasts. Heroic and funereal music, senseless accounts made by soldiers and workers, mad speeches by Goebbels proclaiming to the end that Germany would triumph—all enveloped the German catastrophe in a kind of phantasmagoria. I regarded it necessary, for history's sake, to record the sentiments such a spectacle inspired in France. In a broadcast on April 25, I declared:

"Philosophers and historians will some day argue over the motives for this desperation which is leading a great people to complete ruin—a guilty people, certainly, and one that must be punished as justice demands, but whose destruction the higher rationality of Europe would deplore. As for France, for the moment she can do nothing better than to redouble her efforts, side by side with her allies, in order to bring the conflict to an end as soon and as completely as possible."

Moreover, there was justification for wondering if the Nazi leaders would not attempt to prolong the struggle in the natural redoubt offered by the Bavarian and Austrian Alps. According to our information, they had already set aside huge amounts of material. Reports of certain movements of their pathetic columns seemed to indicate that they were concentrating the mass of prisoners, deported men and forced labor in the interior of this fortress. It was not inconceivable that the Fuehrer would attempt here a supreme strategic and political maneuver.

How long would a defensive battle last in these mountains, one waged under his command by all the forces he still possessed? Long enough to force the eastern and western Allies, no longer operating on two fronts, but side by side on the same terrain, to inflict upon each other all the friction inherent in such contiguity? If the fighting dragged on, would not the behavior of the Soviets in the states of the Vistula, the Elbe and the Danube, that of the Americans in the Pacific, in Indochina and in Indonesia, and that of the British in the Middle East, provoke many dissensions among the Allies? Would not the postponement of the reconstruction of France, of the Low Countries, of Italy, caused by the continuation of the war and of the misery that gripped the German, Czech and Balkan peoples, result in social upheavals which might hurl the entire Western world into revolution? Universal chaos would therefore be Hitler's last chance of at least his supreme vengeance.

While the First Army was advancing in Germany beside our Allies, other French forces were executing autonomous operations on the Atlantic coast. Here it was a matter of capturing the enclaves where the enemy was still entrenched. After months of waiting, I now was eager to see the task soon accomplished, for the war's days were numbered.

The spirit of facility, of course, might counsel us to remain inactive on this front, for once the Reich had capitulated the fruits would fall from the tree of themselves. But in war, the policy of least exertion always risks being paid for dearly. Here, as everywhere, we had to strike. The blows we would inflict upon the Germans in this theater would have their repercussions elsewhere. Besides, should Hitler continue the struggle in the mountains of Bavaria and Austria, our army would have to fight there with all its forces; which made the prior liquidation of the inopportune pockets essential. In any case, I would not permit German units to remain intact until the war's end upon French soil jeering at us behind their ramparts.

My feelings were shared by the troops of the "Atlantic Army Detachment." These 70,000 former maquisards, like the regiments from Algeria, the Antilles, Equatorial Africa and Somaliland, which had come to support them, were eager not to lay down their arms before they had won some distinguished victory. Their leader, General de Larminat, outstripped all others in this regard. Since October 14, when I had appointed him to the command of the western forces, he had devoted himself to organizing, training and equipping the ardent but chaotic and badly supplied military group out of which he was to forge an army. He had succeeded in doing so insofar as this was at all possible. Knowing what he wanted, and wanting it with determination and method, experienced at his task yet burning with inspiration, an authoritative yet human and generous leader, a difficult yet unshakably loyal subordinate, he had created, out of miscellaneous bits and pieces, three divisions, reserves, artillery, an air group and supply services —all, as they now proved, ready to give battle.

Yet whatever De Larminat had accomplished, his group was not in a position to take the steel-and-concrete–clad fortifications in which the Germans were entrenched. We needed the reinforcement of at least one army. In October I had requested the interallied command to send our 1st "Free French" Division to the Atlantic at its first opportunity. The interallied command had agreed to this arrangement, but only after tergiversations which delayed the move until December—that is, too late or too soon for the occasion to be profitable. No sooner had the Garbay division reached the Gironde, in fact, than it had had to be recalled to the east because of the German offensive in the Ardennes and in Alsace. The crisis over, this large unit had been assigned to the Alps on operations which also concerned me deeply. Finally, I chose the 2nd Armored Division to participate in the seacoast offensive. Headquarters made no objection to this, and was even willing to provide our Western Army Detachment with a brigade of American artillery. During the first days of April, all the forces selected for the attack were brought to fighting strength and prepared to begin the campaign.

General de Larminat had taken the enemy positions at the mouth of the Gironde for his first objective. On the right bank Royan and its environs, on the left the Pointe de Grave, and offshore the Île d'Oléron formed a powerful and solidly held complex. It was true that three months before, the American bombers had come on orders of their own to inflict heavy damages throughout the area in a single night. But this hurried operation, while ravaging the houses and property of Royan, had left the military installations virtually intact. At the time of the attack, 15,000 Germans, commanded by Admiral Michahelles, were entrenched in the fortifications supported by 200 cannons. If his offensive succeeded, De Larminat would turn his forces toward La Rochelle, while we undertook to open the port of Bordeaux.

On April 14 our troops came under fire, supported on the ground by Jacobson's three hundred artillery pieces, in the air by Corniglion-Molinier's one hundred planes, and offshore by Rüe's ships. General d'Anselme was in charge of the attack, commanding his 23rd Division, a large part of the 2nd Armored Division and reinforcement units. On every level our men conducted the campaign skillfully and with great spirit. On the eighteenth, after bitter fighting, the enemy's major resistance center, located between the Seudre and the Gironde, was entirely in our hands, including the Coubre redoubt. Simultaneously, on the other bank, Milleret's troops attacked the Pointe de Grave, which was stubbornly defended. But by April 20 they had reached the end of the last islets. Immediately the landing on the Île d'Oléron was prepared and on the thirtieth General Marchand's army group, supported by the naval squadron, gained a foothold there. By the following day, the battle was finished, though the enemy had struggled bitterly to the very end. Thousands of Germans were killed; 12,000 more were taken prisoner, including Admiral Micha-helles. The operation in the Gironde was a French victory; I lost no time consecrating it as such, visiting Royan and the Pointe de Grave among its beaming conquerors on April 21.

Nevertheless, Larminat did not rest on his laurels, but moved on to strike at the La Rochelle pocket which, with the island of Ré, formed a huge defensive complex. During the last days of April, d'Anselme established positions for the attacking troops. On the thirtieth, the assault was begun. In three days, our men took the line of peaks—Pointe du Rocher, Thairé, Aigrefeuille—and threw back the German garrison to the outskirts of the city. Admiral Schirlitz then opened negotiations for the surrender of his 18,000 men. Soon afterward I hastened to La Rochelle to congratulate the victors, greet the cheering populace and inspect the port, which the Germans had left intact.

Once Charente was liberated, positions were established to take the fortified zones of St.-Nazaire and Lorient. But the Reich's capitulation occurred before this operation could be concluded, and General Fahrenbacher laid down his arms. Ahead of the Borgnis-Desbordes and Chomel divisions which had besieged the two areas for months, and the 8th American Division maintained in Brittany since the fall of Brest, paraded long files of prisoners. Of the 90,000 Germans who manned the western pockets, 5,000 were dead, the rest in French captivity. This chapter of the great battle had come to a suitable close.

The same was true, and at the same time, of events in the Alps. Here too, I was extremely eager that the hostilities should not end indecisively; before the cease-fire, it was necessary that we obliter-ate the outrages lately endured on this terrain, recover in combat the fragments of our territory which the enemy still held, and seize the enclaves in Italy's possession along the Little Saint Bernard, Iseran, Mont Cenis and Genèvre passes, as well as the cantons of Tende and La Brigue that had been artificially detached from Savoy in 1860. Afterward, our Alpine troops would be free for other assignments. Should Hitler then intend to prolong the conflict in his "National Redoubt," these forces would be in a position to provide highly qualified reinforcements for the First Army.

In March, we had in the Alps the 27th Division, a large and spirited unit including a number of mountain resistance fighters, particularly the survivors of Les Glières and the Vercors Massif, who formed its nucleus but who had received only haphazard arms. Under General Molle's orders, this division engaged the enemy along the approaches to the passes from Lake Leman to Mont Thabor. Farther south, an incompletely-equipped brigade held the high valleys of the Durance and the Ubaye. The region around Nice was held by an American brigade, but the latter, summoned to the Rhine, was preparing to withdraw.

For our men to assume the offensive, they would have to have a command and reinforcements. On March 1 I created the "Alpine Army Detachment" and placed General Doyen at its head. The latter, experienced in mountain warfare, was to conduct battle with great ability. Aside from the units already in the region, I put under his orders the 1st "Free French" Division, which I had restored to my command after the Colmar incident. I added to it two African regiments—unfortunately quite badly equipped—artillery, engineering and supply service units. In agreement with Eisenhower's arrangements, the Doyen army detachment, like De Larminat's, was theoretically attached to the Devers army group. But the latter, engaged in an altogether different theater, paid little attention to their operations, though it did furnish them a minimum supply of ammunition and fuel.

The attack began at the end of March. General Doyen was facing four divisions. The 5th Mountain Division was holding the Little Saint Bernard, Iseran and Mont Cenis passes; the 34th was occupying the fortified Aution Massif above Nice and blockading the Corniche road along the coast; both these divisions were German. Two Italian Fascist divisions, "Monte Rosa" and "Littorio," garrisoned the intervening areas. Doyen wanted to engage the

German 5th Division, which included the best enemy troops, and then storm the Aution Massif. Taking advantage of the advance of Alexander's armies, which were to take the offensive in Lombardy, he then intended to drive ahead into Italian territory.

At more than 2,000 meters above sea level, in the snow and cold which still enveloped the mountains, General Molle's division engaged the installations of the Little Saint Bernard and Mont Cenis passes. Several fortifications were taken; others were not. But the German garrisons, distracted and decimated, could not go to the aid of the Aution defenders. It was the 1st "Free French" Division which was assigned the mission of taking this massif. The task was difficult and ungrateful, for the officers and soldiers of this exemplary division found it painful to abandon to others the laurels which strewed the soil of Germany and to conclude in this isolated sector the epic combat they had waged since the darkest days on the most brilliant battlefields.

On April 8, leaving the Rhine, I reached the Alps. Receiving General Doyen's report at Grenoble, then reviewing part of Molle's troops at St.-Pierre d'Albigny, I finally reached Menton where Garbay's men were stationed. To these comrades, the first to answer my call to honor and subsequently indefatigable in their loyalty, I stressed the importance which this last effort asked of them assumed for France. Then, wishing to give a national resonance to their operation, I went to Nice on the ninth and from the balcony of the *hôtel de ville* announced to the crowd that "our arms are about to cross our Alps." The voice of the people acclaimed this decision. On April 10, our troops began the assault of the Aution Massif.

They fought there for seven days, scaled the steepest slopes, seized La Forclaz, Mille Fourches, Sept Communes and Plan Caval forts dominating the mountain, and cleared the slopes above the La Roya pass. The Larche and Lombarde passes were also taken after fierce fighting, and the French entered Tende and La Brigue, where the inhabitants cheered for joy. Shortly afterward, a virtually unanimous plebiscite was to consecrate their annexation to France. On April 28, the Alpine Army Detachment announced a general advance: while its left drove toward Cuneo and dashed through the Val d'Aosta, brilliant with tricolors, its center descended from the Mont Cenis and Genèvre passes, and its right pushed through the Stura and along the Corniche. By May 2, the day when the German forces and the Italian Fascists laid down their arms, our soldiers were nearing Turin at Ivrea, Lanzo and Bussoleno, had reached Cuneo and occupied Imperia. In this war it was established that the battles in the Alps, begun in 1940, later continued by the resistance, and finally resumed by our revived army, concluded in a French victory.

War resembles certain plays in which, as the denouement approaches, all the actors appear on the stage at once. While the French forces were heavily engaged in the Alps and on the Atlantic, as well as on the Rhine and the Danube, combat began in Indochina. On March 9 the Japanese troops which had occupied Tonkin, Annam and Cochin China attacked our garrisons.

This event was inevitable. The Nipponese, driven out of the Philippines and Indonesia, hard pressed in Burma, powerless to reduce China and in no condition to maintain their communications by sea, could no longer tolerate the presence in the midst of their positions of an alien force which threatened to become hostile. Despite the Tokyo-Vichy agreement on the "common defense of Indochina," Japan had no doubt that if the Allies approached the Union's territory, the French there would join them. Moreover, Vichy had disappeared. De Gaulle was head of the government in Paris. On the first occasion, he would certainly give orders to attack the Nipponese invader. Although the Indochinese government had not officially rallied to the Republic, and although at Saigon an apparent "collaboration" was maintained, the Japanese could no longer rely on such fictions. We could be sure that from one day to the next they would begin the liquidation of the French forces and administration, and that they would do so in the most sudden and brutal manner imaginable.

Yet, however painful the immediate results of such issue, I must admit that from the point of view of national interest, I was not distressed by the prospect of taking up arms in Indochina. Measuring the shock inflicted on France's prestige by Vichy's policy, knowing the state of public opinion throughout the Union, foreseeing the outbreak of nationalist passions in Asia and Australasia, aware of the hostility of the Allies—particularly the Americans—in regard to our Far Eastern position, I regarded it as essential that the conflict not come to an end without our participation in that theater as well. Otherwise every policy, every army, every aspect of public opinion would certainly insist upon our abdication in Indochina. On the other hand, if we took part in the battle—even though the latter were near its conclusion—French blood shed on the soil of Indochina would constitute an impressive claim. Since I was certain the Japanese would fight to the very end, I wished our troops to join battle despite the desperate nature of their situation.

In order to lead this resistance, the government could not, of course, turn to Admiral Decoux. Doubtless the Governor General had secretly altered his allegiance since Vichy's collapse; doubtless his orders, his observations, the tone of his radio broadcasts, bore no resemblance to what they had been previously. But for four years, he had so stubbornly vilified Fighting France that he was now too compromised to return to command. Furthermore, the Admiral, unable to rouse himself from his old-man's complacency, refused to believe in a Japanese aggression. Therefore in 1943 I had entrusted to General Mordant, High Commander of the Troops, the task of eventually leading the action. Admiral Decoux, moreover, had been notified to this effect; discreet telegrams, as well as the instructions which Governor de Langlade, twice parachuted into Indochina, had brought him in my behalf, informed him what was expected of him.

In order not to provoke the Japanese attack too soon, Decoux was apparently to remain in office, but Mordant would become the man in power once the battle was engaged. Although Vichy in the spring of 1944 had replaced Mordant as Commander of the Troops with General Aymé—which made matters more complicated—I had left Mordant his service letter as delegate general. Aymé, moreover, shared his views. Furthermore, in Calcutta, General Blaizot and the personnel of our special services, whose presence in the East Indies the British had agreed to, had been able to organize the many loyalties available to us in Indochina into clandestine networks of information and action. For months, it was our services that provided information for the American air action launched from Chinese territory and for the British raids from Burmese bases against Japanese installations, ships and planes.

The French troops in Indochina comprised some fifty thousand men, including about 12,000 Europeans. Numerically this force was weak, though it was actually much more so than the figures indicated, for the native troops, often capable of holding positions to the degree their loyalty remained certain, could generally not be used in the field. As for the French units, unrelieved in six years, they were more or less devastated by the difficult climate. Moreover, our men had only worn and outdated arms and equipment and were almost totally without planes, armored pieces and trucks. Lastly, they were scattered throughout a tremendous territory without being able to change their positions, watched as they were by an enemy ready to assail them at any moment.

My instructions to General Mordant as to the steps to take in case of an attack were intended to prolong the resistance of French troops on Indochinese territory as much as possible. Those meager forces garrisoned in Annam, Cambodia and Cochin China were too isolated to operate in the field; they would therefore defend their posts as long as they had the means, then fall back in small groups to difficult terrain in order to form guerrilla units there. But the principal force, stationed in Tonkin, received orders to retreat toward the Chinese frontier along the Hanoi–Lai-Chau line, continu-

ing the battle as long as possible. During these operations, they
might be supported, or at least given supplies, by the American
aviation deployed in Chinese territory and assigned to Chiang Kai-
shek's troops. On the basis of these instructions, General Mordant
had explained to his subordinate commands the eventual orders for
the alert and for operations. On February 21 I renewed my directives and admonitions by telegram.

This was how matters stood when, on the evening of March 9,
the Japanese ordered Admiral Decoux in Saigon and General Aymé
in Hanoi to surrender their commands and to place all French forces
under immediate Japanese control until they were disarmed. Upon
the High Commissioner's and the High Commander's refusal, they
were immediately arrested and our garrisons attacked.

Unfortunately, General Mordant was discovered and taken
prisoner almost at once. This decapitation of the resistance greatly
compromised its functioning; yet almost everywhere, our officers
and our soldiers, knowing that they were fighting a hopeless battle,
in some cases abandoned by the native auxiliaries or deciding to
release them, courageously did their duty. In particular the citadels
of Hanoi and Haiphong, the garrison of Hué, and the posts of
Langson, Hagiang, Laokay and That Khé defended themselves
with great energy. At Moncay, the attacks inflicted by the Japanese, at a high cost in human life, were repulsed for over fifteen
days. Vinh fought on until March 24. In the Bassac region, the resistance did not stop until April 1. Columns, formed in various
parts of upper Tonkin, reached Chinese territory; a few small ships
and customs vessels reached the Kwangsi coast. But above all, an
important group, constituted ahead of time in the Sontay region
under General Alessandri's orders with the Foreign Legion as its
core, valiantly carried out its mission. These few thousand men,
maneuvering and fighting first between the Red River and the
Black, then to the west of the latter, resisted the Japanese for fifty-
seven days before falling back, with their wretched arms, to join
the Allied forces in China.

On the occasion of these operations, the American prejudices were clearly revealed. Despite the incessant representations of the French government, Washington still opposed sending to the Far East the troops we were training in Africa and Madagascar. The battles waged in Indochina wrought no change in the United States attitude. Yet the presence in Burma of a French Expeditionary Corps would certainly have encouraged Indochinese resistance, and air transport of detachments to our Tonkin and Laos columns would have been of great assistance there. But even the American aviation based in China, within immediate reach of the Alessandri group, offered it no assistance. General Sabattier, who had been appointed delegate general after Mordant's disappearance from the scene and had been able to escape from Hanoi, reach Lai-Chau and make contact with the American command in China, was refused all support. Having long discerned the stakes of the game, I felt no surprise at discovering what others' intentions were. But I was all the more resolved to bring France back to Indochina when, once the victory was assured, our hands would be free in regard to the Allies.

In any case, it was henceforth certain that the French forces in Indochina would also have contributed to this victory. Two hundred officers and four thousand soldiers had been killed by the enemy. During the month of May, six thousand soldiers, mostly Europeans, were regrouped in Yunnan. The battles, suddenly yielding to a prolonged period of doubts, disappointments and humiliations, had been waged under the bitterest of circumstances —surprise, isolation, lack of supplies, the impression that God was too high and France too far. But such efforts and sacrifices were only all the more meritorious; in the moral capital of a people, the efforts of its soldiers are never wasted.

Despite my attention to the development of affairs along the Atlantic, in the Alps and in Indochina, it was what was happening in Germany that particularly concerned me. Here, in fact, destiny was in the making, fate was being sealed. Then too, the operations of the various Allied armies on German soil, their objectives, their directions, the limits of their sectors, created a succession of *faits accomplis* which were to wield a practical influence on the period following the armistice. It was my responsibility to be sure that the role of the French Army, the relative dimension of its successes and the extent of the territory it would be allowed to conquer were large enough so that France could assert herself in the discussions and decisions that would follow hostilities. In order that no one should be unaware of this, I proclaimed it on the occasion of a ceremony organized in Paris on April 2 in the Place de la Concorde during which the colonels of the new or reconstituted regiments received their flags and standards from my hands.

Yet in the mind of the Allied command, obviously oriented by Washington, it was the American forces which were to assume for themselves almost all the action in this last phase of the conflict. Supreme Headquarters entrusted to the Americans alone the task of seizing the Ruhr, a region more essential than any other, then of driving toward the Elbe as well as toward the Danube in order to submerge the body of Germany, and finally of making contact, near Berlin, Prague and Vienna, with the Soviet troops. The British were permitted to devote themselves to the coast of the North Sea. As for the French, an initial effort was made to keep them on the left bank of the Rhine. Since they nevertheless found means of crossing the river, attempts were now being made to keep them as close to it as possible. Naturally at the very moment when perspectives were widening before us, we would not consent to such a diminution.

While General Bradley's army group encircled Marshal Model's German forces in the Ruhr Basin and brought them to capitulation, then crossed the Weser in the central Reich, that of General Devers advanced southward from the Main. But Devers, instead of marching east as well, tended to bear toward the south. If the French let him continue, this movement would press Patch's army against De Lattre's, block the latter close to the Rhine, and limit the German territory we occupied to a few shreds of Baden. Here, operations also had a direct bearing on the political realm. Therefore I immediately informed De Lattre, even before his troops began to cross the Rhine, to what extent his army's action would be serving the national interest. We had agreed that in any case the First Army should seize Stuttgart. The capital of Württemberg would be, in fact, the open door to the Danube, Bavaria and Austria for our troops. Its possession would assure us, furthermore, an important pledge to support our intentions as to the French zone of occupation.

But we also had to consider the enemy, whose Nineteenth Army was energetically fighting in the Black Forest massif. It was therefore in this difficult region, and not toward Stuttgart, that the brunt of the French Army's effort was turned during the first two weeks of April. It was true that the IInd Army Corps had crossed the Rhine in the Palatinate, had taken Karlsruhe and on April 7 invested Pforzheim. But before crossing the Neckar and driving toward the Danube, De Lattre felt he must assemble his army in the Black Forest and clear this natural fortress of Germans. He therefore moved Monsabert southward to penetrate into the heart of the massif and open a passage for Béthouart from the Rhine to Strasbourg; thus Rastatt, Baden-Baden, Kehl, and Freudenstadt were captured and the German Nineteenth Army was driven into the wooded heights of the Black Forest. But the capital of Württemberg remained in enemy hands and within reach of our Allies— it was high time for us to seize it. Without interfering in the arrangements of the First Army's commander, I informed him again, on April 15, that the government expected him to take Stuttgart.

And indeed on the very next day, General Devers addressed his army group a "directive" of contrary import; according to his instruction it was the American Seventh Army, hitherto engaged further north, which was to seize Stuttgart and, later driving up the Neckar, reach the Swiss frontier near Schaffhausen. The French would be confined to mopping up the Black Forest and cut off from all the roads that might take them further east. "I must warn you," Devers wrote De Lattre, "against a premature advance of the French First Army."

General de Lattre realized that it was urgent to change direction. He gave orders to the IInd Army Corps in accord with this realization. Monsabert therefore turned toward Stuttgart and Ulm, then Pforzheim and Freudenstadt, Guillaume's 3rd North African Division, Linares' 2nd Moroccan Division, and Hesdin's and Vernejoul's 1st and 5th Armored Divisions. On April 20, French tanks entered the capital of Württemberg, a huge city where 800,000 inhabitants awaited them in silence among the ruins. But while this part of the army drove swiftly eastward, another, led by Béthouart, advanced directly southward. Carpentier's 4th Moroccan Division, Vaulluy's 9th Colonial Division and Callies', Billotte's and Salan's 1st, 10th and 19th Divisions were employed to complete the conquest of the Black Forest.

As a matter of fact, General de Lattre, while seizing the objectives I had assigned him on the Neckar and the Danube, did not want to leave behind him any enemy forces of any size. Moreover General Guisan, Swiss commander in chief, fearing that the Germans, in their last extremity, might penetrate Swiss territory in order to seek passage or refuge, had urgently requested the First Army's command to send French troops along the Rhine frontier from Basel to Lake Constance. At another period, the uncoupling of our forces along two different axes, one to the east, the other to the south, might have involved great risks; but the enemy had now reached such a point of disorganization that every step taken against him succeeded and justified itself. The report De Lattre gave me on April 21 was a bulletin of victory. "Complete success of operations engaged the last fifteen days in Württemberg, in the Black Forest and in Baden. The Danube has been crossed along a line of over sixty kilometers below Donaueschingen. We have entered Stuttgart from the south, completing the encirclement of important enemy forces. In the plain of Baden, Alt Breisach and

Freiburg are in our hands. The Black Forest is completely surrounded."

It was, however, only a week later that the French First Army
managed to defeat the German Nineteenth Army. The latter, although surrounded, had grouped in the heavily wooded massif
east of Freiburg and was desperately attempting to clear a passage
to the east. Unable to manage this, the fractions finally laid down
their arms. While this affair was being settled, our advance guards
were reaching Ulm and Konstanz. By the end of April, there was
no further organized resistance ahead of the French forces. Since
they had crossed the Rhine, 110,000 prisoners had fallen into
their hands. Every day, thousands more were to surrender before
the conclusion of hostilities.

But in the coalition, the roses of glory grew thorns as well. As
we expected, the interallied command opposed the presence of our
troops in Stuttgart. On April 24 General Devers reminded the
First Army that the city was not in its zone and that this communications center was necessary for the American Seventh Army. On
the twenty-eighth, he gave De Lattre formal orders to evacuate the
city. I informed the latter, when he referred the matter to me, that
none of my decisions had been altered. "I order you," my telegram
specified, "to maintain a French garrison in Stuttgart and to establish a military government there at once. . . . To any possible
American observations, you will reply that your government's
orders are to remain in the city and administer the territories conquered by your troops, until the French occupation zone has been
established by agreement among the governments concerned." De
Lattre therefore answered Devers that the question went beyond
the two of them, since it was in the domain of governments. Without opposing the passage of Allied columns and convoys through
Stuttgart, De Lattre maintained in the city the garrison he had established there with General Chevillon as military governor.

The controversy, therefore, moved to a higher level. In doing so
it lost a good deal of its sharpness. On April 28, General Eisen-

hower sent me an acquiescent letter. Of course, he declared, by
intervening in strategic matters for political reasons, my government, in his opinion, was violating its agreements with regard to
the rearmament of the French forces. However, he agreed that
"speaking personally," he could do nothing but accept the situation, for he rejected the notion of suspending the supplies furnished
by his services to the French First Army and wished to do nothing
which might alter "the exemplary spirit of co-operation between
French and American forces in battle."

Well and good! I replied in friendly tones to the Supreme Commander that the difficulty just encountered derived from a situation not at all of his making—"the lack of agreement between the
American and British governments, on the one hand, concerning
the policies of the war in general and the occupation of the German
territories in particular." On May 2, Eisenhower wrote me that he
understood my position and was pleased to discover that, on my
side, I understood his. As the last echo of the affair I received from
President Truman—three weeks in office at the time—a message
stamped with a certain acidity, that "questions concerning France
as closely as the occupation of German territory should be discussed with her, which, unfortunately, has not been the case." The
French remained in Stuttgart.

Like waves breaking one after another over a foundering ship,
the Allied forces submerged a wrecked Germany. Their advance
further cut off the enemy fractions, which circled in confusion.
Pockets of resistance still courageously resisted; in certain completely isolated zones, unorganized troops accumulated by virtue
of their very exhaustion. In many places, large or small units surrendered on their own account. If the appearance of the western
powers was regarded by the populations as a kind of deliverance,
where the Russians advanced panic-stricken crowds fled before
them. Everywhere, the conquerors received groups of Allied prisoners who had liberated themselves. Here and there, stupefied
with horror and indignation, they discovered the survivors and the

charnel houses of the extermination camps. In blood and ruins, with a profound fatalism, the German people yielded to its destiny.

At the end of April, Bradley reached the Elbe and there established contact, around Torgau, with Zhukov's troops, which had just taken Berlin. To the north, Montgomery had seized Hamburg and early in May took Kiel and Lübeck, within reach of Rokossovsky, who had succeeded Marshal Chernyakhovsky, killed in February, in the East Prussian theater. Thus the German occupation forces in Denmark were cut off from the Reich, as were those who had remained in Holland under Blaskowitz. To the south, three Allied armies were marching on the redoubt of the Bavarian and Austrian Alps where the enemy might have hoped to hold fast. Patton penetrated into Czechoslovakia, where he seized Plzeň, and, in Austria, reached Linz, close by Tolbukhin's Russians, who had taken and passed Vienna; Patch seized Munich and drove as far as Innsbruck; De Lattre launched his armored units and his Moroccan divisions into the Tyrol, one column driving up the Iller, another bordering Lake Constance. In the Vorarlberg, the French advance guards engaged the German Twenty-fifth Army, new in the order of battle but formed from a host of fragments and whose leader, General Schmidt, immediately offered to surrender. On May 6, the French flag was floating over the Arlberg pass. Meanwhile, Leclerc's division, hurriedly returning west and put at the head of Patch's army, had reached Berchtesgaden.

This was the end. The Axis was defeated. Its leaders capitulated. On May 1 the last broadcasts of the German radio announced the news of Hitler's death. A few days before, Mussolini's murder had been made known.

The latter, though he had persisted in the conflict until the very end, had already been effaced by events. Yet how much sound and fury had this "Duce" caused in the universe, this ambitious, audacious, vainglorious statesman with broad views and dramatic gestures, this grandiloquent and excessive orator! He had seized Italy when the country was slipping into anarchy. But for him it was not enough to save and restore his country to order; he wanted to make it into an empire. Exiling liberty in order to do so, constructing his own dictatorship, he made his country look united and resolute by means of parades, fasces and lictors. Then, relying on appearances, he became a great star of the international stage.

His demands, at the time, were oriented toward Africa. Along the shores of the Mediterranean and the Red Sea, he claimed, or would have conquered, the lion's share. Soon it was in Europe too that he aspired to enlarge his territory. Savoy, Nice, Corsica, Croatia, Slovenia, Dalmatia, Albania—all these were to be his! Then he roused "Fascist and proletarian Italy" against the decadent French, the impotent Yugoslavs. Lastly, while he saw the Panzer divisions roaring across France, while England fell back to her island, while Russia leaned on her guns and waited, while America remained neutral, the Duce joined the Fuehrer and rushed into the war, supposing it was about to end.

At the moment when a partisan's machine gun shot him down, Mussolini had lost his reasons for living. Having tried to grasp too much, he now had nothing left to hold on to. Certainly, at the time of the Fascist apogee, his dictatorship had seemed a firm one. But fundamentally, how could it be, when within it subsisted the monarchy, the Church and the interests of capitalism, and when its people, jaded by the centuries, remained what they had always been despite his fetishes and his rituals? Certainly there was some grandeur in claiming to revive the ancient primacy of Rome. But was this a realizable goal when the world was as large as the earth itself, and machine-made at that? To oppose to the west an Italy which was the mother of its genius, to associate the homeland of Latin culture with the explosion of German oppression, in short, to hurl an entire people into battle for a cause not its own—was this not to contradict its very nature? As long as Germany appeared to triumph, the Duce succeeded in bringing his ill-assured armies to the battlefields. But once his mighty ally began to weaken, the tie became indefensible and the tide of denials swept Mussolini away.

As for Hitler, it was suicide, not treason, that brought his enterprise to its end. He himself had incarnated it, and himself terminated it. So as not to be bound, Prometheus cast himself into the abyss.

This man, starting from nothing, had offered himself to Germany at the moment when she awakened to a desire for a new lover. Tired of the fallen emperor, of beaten generals, of absurd politicians, she gave herself to this unknown man-in-the-street who represented adventure, promised domination, and whose hysterical voice stirred her secret instincts. Moreover, despite the defeat recently inflicted at Versailles, this daring couple saw a long career opening before them. During the thirties, Europe, obnubilated here by the lure and there by the panic of Communism or Fascism, exasperated with democracy and encumbered with old men, offered many opportunities to German dynamism.

Adolf Hitler hoped to realize them all. Fascism combined with racism furnished him a doctrine. The totalitarian system permitted him to act without check or curb. Technological progress put into his hands the trump card of shock and surprise. Certainly the system led to oppression and oppression led to crime. But, for Moloch, all things are justified. Moreover, if Hitler was strong, he was no less cunning. He knew how to entice, and how to caress. Germany, profoundly seduced, followed her Fuehrer ecstatically. Until the very end, she was to serve him slavishly, with greater exertions than any people has ever furnished any leader.

Yet Hitler was to encounter the human obstacle, the one that cannot be surmounted. He based his colossal plan on the strength he attributed to man's baseness. Yet men are made of souls as much as of clay. To behave as if everyone else will never have any courage is to venture too far. According to the Fuehrer, the Reich, first of all, had to tear up the Versailles Treaty, counting on the democracies' fear of war. It would then proceed to the annexation of Austria, of Czechoslovakia, of Poland, assured of the cowardly solace of Paris and London and the complicity of Moscow. After which, depending on the occasion, the French would be over-powered in the presence of the motionless Russians, or else Russia struck down before a terrified France. This double goal realized, England would be drawn beneath the yoke, thanks to the sybaritic neutrality of the United States. Then, Europe entirely grouped willy-nilly under the ferule of the New Order, and Japan serving as an ally, America outflanked and isolated would yield in her turn.

At first, everything proceeded as planned. Nazi Germany, en-dowed with terrible weapons and armed with pitiless laws, marched from one triumph to the next. Geneva, Munich, the Germano-Soviet pact, justified Hitler's contemptuous reliance on his neigh-bors. But then, suddenly, courage and honor flamed forth among the latter. Paris and London did not accept the murder of Poland. An even at that very moment it seemed as if the Fuehrer, in his lucid moments, knew the charm was broken. Doubtless his armor-clad army thundered across a France without a state and without a command; but England, behind the Channel, refused to yield, and the flame of resistance was lit among the French. Henceforth, the struggle spread from ocean to ocean, to Africa, to the Middle East, and to the clandestine recesses of France. When the Wehrmacht attacked Russia, it lacked precisely those German troops needed to reduce the Soviets because they were engaged elsewhere. There-after, America, flung into the war by Japan's aggression, could de-ploy her forces to certain effect. Despite the phenomenal energy of Germany and her Fuehrer, their fate was sealed.

Hitler's attempt was superhuman and inhuman. He maintained it without stint, without respite. Until the final hours of agony in the depths of a Berlin bunker, he remained unquestioned, inflex-ible, pitiless, as he had been during his days of supreme glory. For the terrible greatness of his conflict and his memory, he had chosen never to hesitate, compromise or retreat. The Titan who tries to lift the world can neither bow nor bend. But conquered and crushed, perhaps he becomes a man again, just long enough for one secret tear at the moment when all is at an end.

The German capitulation was now no longer anything but a matter of formalities. Still, they had to be executed. Even before Hitler's death, Goering, whom he had designated as his possible heir and who believed the Chancellor could no longer make himself obeyed, attempted negotiation, but was immediately condemned by the Fuehrer. Himmler, second in the order of succession, made contact with Count Bernadotte, President of the Swedish Red Cross, and through Stockholm sent an armistice proposal to the western governments. Apparently Himmler hoped that if hostilities ceased on the western front and continued in the east, a fissure would be created in the Allied bloc of which the Reich could take advantage. The master of the Gestapo's action was accompanied by some gestures intended to reduce the abominable reputation his crimes had won for him. It was thus, *in extremis,* that he authorized the International Red Cross to distribute supplies to the deported prisoners. As soon as we were notified by this organization, we sent foodstuffs on our own trucks, driven by Swiss chauffeurs starting from Berne and Zurich, to the concentration camps and the starving columns the Germans drove along the roads of southern Germany.

To myself, Himmler sent a semiofficial memorandum which betrayed its guile beneath its anguish: "Agreed! You have won," the document admitted. "Considering where you started from, one bows low indeed to you, General de Gaulle. . . . But now what will you do? Rely on Americans and the British? They will deal with you as a satellite, and you will lose all the honor you have won. Ally yourself with the Soviets? They will restore France to their laws and liquidate you. . . . Actually, the only road that can lead your people to greatness and to independence is that of an entente with defeated Germany. Proclaim it at once! Lose no time to enter into relations with those men in the Reich who still possess *de facto* power and are willing to lead their country in a new direction. . . . They are ready to do so. They invite you to command them. . . . If you overcome the spirit of vengeance, if you seize the opportunity history offers you today, you will be the greatest man of all time."

Apart from the flattery in my behalf that decorated this message from the brink of the grave, there was certainly an element of truth in the picture it sketched. But the desperate tempter, being what he was, received no reply from me, nor from the Washington and London governments. Moreover, he had nothing to offer. As a matter of fact, Hitler, who probably got wind of these schemes, disinherited Himmler in his turn. It was to Admiral Doenitz that the Fuehrer ordered his powers transmitted after his own suicide. The Admiral was therefore invested by an ultimate telegram sent from the subterranean refuge of the Reich's chancellery.

Until the end, the last possessors of the Reich's authority made every effort to obtain some separate arrangement with the western powers. In vain! The latter excluded any issue save unconditional surrender received simultaneously by all the Allies. It was true that on May 9 Admiral Friedeburg surrendered the northwest armies, as well as those of Denmark and Holland to Montgomery; but this was merely a convention between local military leaders, not a surrender binding the Reich itself. Finally, Doenitz capitulated. General Jodl, sent by Doenitz to Reims, brought Eisenhower the unconditional surrender. The latter was signed on May 7 at two in the morning. The cease-fire was set for midnight the following day. Since the act was signed in the headquarters of the western commander in chief, it was understood that a corresponding ratification would occur on May 9 at the Soviet command post in Berlin.

Naturally, I had arranged with our allies for the French to participate in the signing of these two documents. The text, of an extreme and terrible simplicity, occasioned no objection on our part. I must say that the Allies asked us to do so of their own accord, with no circumlocutions. At Reims, as had been agreed, General

Bedell Smith, chief of General Eisenhower's general staff, presided
at the ceremony in the name of the Supreme Commander and
signed, first, with Jodl as Doenitz's representative. Next, for the
Russians, General Suslaparov, for the French, General Sevez, Assistant Chief of the General Staff of National Defense—Juin being
at San Francisco—affixed their signatures. The Berlin surrender
was to involve a greater degree of formality—not that it added
anything to the one signed at Reims, but the Soviets were extremely
eager to give it prominence. I designated General de Lattre to
represent France at the signing.

The latter, received by the Russians with all suitable regard,
nevertheless ran up against an objection of protocol. Marshal
Zhukov being the delegate of the Soviet command and the British
Air Marshal Tedder that of the western command, the Russians
declared that in principle they were in agreement that General
de Lattre should also be present. But since the Americans had sent
General Spaatz to sign with De Lattre, the highhanded M. Vishinsky, rushing forward to "advise" Zhukov, pointed out that the
American general was duplicating Tedder's function and could not
participate. The French would consequently be excluded. With
skill and firmness De Lattre claimed, to the contrary, the right to
fulfill his mission. The incident was soon settled. On May 9 General de Lattre took his place alongside the military delegates of the
major Allied powers beneath a panoply in which the tricolor figured among the other flags. At the final act of the German capitulation, the representative of France was a signatory with those of
Russia, the United States and Great Britain. Field Marshal Keitel,
exclaiming, "What? The French too!" thereby paid tribute to the
tour de force which had brought France and her army to such a
recovery.

"The war is won. Victory is ours! It is the victory of the United
Nations and the victory of France!" I broadcast this announcement
on May 8 at three in the afternoon. In London Winston Churchill,
in Washington Harry Truman spoke at the same time. A little

later, I went to the Place de l'Étoile; it was filled with a crowd which became enormous a few seconds after my arrival. No sooner had I paid my respects to the Tomb of the Unknown Soldier than the throng thundered its cheers as it pressed against the barricades. With difficulty, I extricated myself from the torrent. Yet this manifestation, the parades, the sound of bells, the salvos of artillery and the official speeches did not prevent the people's joy, like my own, from remaining sober and contained.

It was true that for months, now, there had been no doubt of the issue and that for weeks it had been considered imminent. There was nothing surprising about the news that could provoke an explosion of feeling. The latter, moreover, had already been given free rein on the occasion of the liberation. Then too, the ordeal, if it was marked for the French by a glory won from the depths of the abyss, had nevertheless involved disastrous lapses at its start. For all the satisfaction of its denouement, it had left—and forever! —a secret grief in the depths of the national conscience. Elsewhere, from one end of the world to the other, the salute of guns was of course heard with an enormous relief, since death and misery were fading away with them, yet it was heard without transports of joy, for the struggle had been sullied with crimes that shamed the human race. Every man, whoever or wherever he was, felt anew the hope that springs eternal, but feared once again lest "war, the mother of all things," had given birth to peace.

The mission to which I was prompted by France's distress was now accomplished. By incredible luck, it had been granted to me to lead my country to the conclusion of a combat in which it had risked everything. Now France was revived, respected, recovering her territory and her status, engaged alongside the greatest powers in settling the world's fate. With what dazzling light the day, now ended, was gilded! But how dim were the future dawns of France! And already all was settling, slackening, sinking. How would we keep alive the flame of national ambition, relit beneath the ashes by the storm, now that the wind had fallen?

CHAPTER 5

DISCORD

No sooner had the sound of gunfire faded than the world's appearance changed. The strength and spirit of the peoples mobilized for the war suddenly lost their unifying object, while the ambition of states reappeared in all its virulence. The Allies revoked those considerations and concessions they had necessarily granted each other in time of peril, when they were confronting a common enemy. Yesterday was the time for battle; the hour for settling accounts had come.

This moment of truth revealed France's continuing weakness in relation to her own goals and to the partisan calculations of other states. The latter, of course, would take advantage of the situation to try to force our hand on those issues still undecided, or else to relegate us to a secondary place among nations responsible for constructing the peace. But I had no intention of letting this happen. Considering, in fact, that Germany's collapse, Europe's laceration, and Anglo-American friction offered a miraculously saved France exceptional opportunities for action, it seemed likely that the new period would permit me to achieve the great plan I had conceived for my country.

I intended to assure France security in western Europe by preventing the rise of a new Reich that might again threaten its safety; to co-operate with East and West and, if need be, contract the necessary alliances on one side or the other without ever accepting any kind of dependency; to transform the French Union into a free association in order to avoid the as yet unspecified dangers of upheaval; to persuade the states along the Rhine, the Alps, and the Pyrenees to form a political, economic, and strategic bloc; to establish this organization as one of the three world powers and, should it become necessary, as the arbiter between the Soviet and Anglo-American camps. Since 1940, my every word and act had been dedicated to establishing these possibilities; now that France was on her feet again, I would try to realize them.

The means were poor indeed! Yet if France had not yet taken into her hand the trump of her ultimate power, she still held a number of good cards: first of all, the singular and century-old prestige which her miraculous return from the brink of the abyss had partially restored; then the fact that her co-operation was no longer to be despised amid the disequilibrium that burdened the entire human race; and lastly, the solid units constituted by her territories, her people and her overseas extensions. Even before we had recovered all our strength, these elements put us in a position to act and to make ourselves respected.

On condition we put them to good use. Here, indeed, lay my task. But to compensate for all we lacked, I required bold support from the nation. This granted, I could promise that no one would ignore or defy the will of France. Naturally, our allies expected the situation to be otherwise; whatever their regard for General de Gaulle, they oriented their nostalgia toward the old, political France, so malleable and so convenient, and watched for the inevitable discords to appear between myself and those who anticipated a return to yesterday's regime.

Immediately after the victory, a serious incident occurred regarding the establishment of our Alpine frontier. Our government had long since clarified its intentions in the matter; we intended to extend the boundary of our territory to the very crest of the range, the several Italian enclaves on the French side near the passes; we also intended to incorporate the formerly Savoyard cantons of Tende and La Brigue, and perhaps Ventimiglia as well, according to the wishes of the latter's inhabitants. As for the Val d'Aosta, we certainly had every ethnic and religious justification to claim it, particularly when our advancing troops encountered an almost unanimous desire to join the French camp. But for eight months of the year the snows of Mont Blanc cut off all communications between France and the Valdôtains, whose existence was consequently linked to Italy's; we decided not to claim possession of the valley; we would be satisfied with Rome's recognition of its autonomy. Further, the government of Messrs. Bonomi and Sforza indicated to our representatives it was willing to accept our considerations. The latter, indeed, could seem only moderate in relation to the ordeals Italy had inflicted and to the advantages she would acquire from reconciliation.

The final offensive launched in the Alps by General Doyen's troops had reached its assigned objectives. The enclaves, the Val d'Aosta and the cantons of La Roya were in our hands by May 2, when the German and Fascist forces in Italy surrendered. From the administrative point of view, Tende, La Brigue and Ventimiglia were at once reattached to the Alpes-Maritimes Department, while at Aosta we transferred the administration to local committees.

This was how matters stood when, during the month of May, the Americans expressed their desire to have our troops withdraw within the 1939 frontier and be replaced in the evacuated territories by Allied forces. The Quai d'Orsay was informed of this intention by Mr. Caffery; General Doyen was notified by General Grittenberg, commanding the American Occupation Corps in Piedmont, and Bidault was told as much by Truman during the former's visit to the American President in Washington. In demanding our retreat, the Americans could instance no agreement drawn up with us, nor henceforth allege any military necessities.

They merely referred to their own decision not to permit the settlement of any territorial questions with regard to prewar boundaries before the signing of the final peace treaties. Of course, Washington formulated this claim with regard to the French alone, and only for the Alpine communes.

To a certain degree, the source of this affair was the United States' desire for hegemony, which they readily manifested and which I had not failed to discern on every occasion. But above all, I perceived in their demand the effect of British influence. For at the same moment, England was preparing her decisive maneuver in the Levant. For London, to inspire Washington to find a source of friction with Paris was a strategic move. Various facts indicated that this was indeed the case.

General Alexander, Commander in Chief in Italy, obeying Mr. Churchill's orders, sent to Tende, La Brigue and Ventimiglia those Italian troops under his orders which, if we permitted them to do so, would effectively re-establish Rome's sovereignty there. Since harsh exchanges had taken place between Grittenberg, who wished to replace us, and Doyen, who would not agree to such a move; and since the French general, more experienced in combat than in such contentions, had notified his interlocutor in writing that "if need be he would extend his refusal to the extreme consequences, in accord with General de Gaulle's orders," Allied headquarters in Italy lost no time in informing the correspondents of every newspaper that French troops were preparing to fire on American soldiers by my orders. Lastly, secret observers obtained copies of the telegrams the Prime Minister was sending to the President. In them, Mr. Churchill characterized me as "enemy of the Allies," urged Mr. Truman to behave toward me, politically speaking, in the most intransigent manner, and declared to him "on the basis of information obtained in French political circles, that such behavior would be enough to provoke the immediate fall of General de Gaulle's government."

Although Truman had less passion and more discretion he de-

cided to intervene. On June 6, Ambassador Caffery delivered a
note to the Ministry of Foreign Affairs expressing the concern of
his government as to the maintenance of French forces in certain
parts of Northwest Italy, protesting against Doyen's attitude, and
demanding the retreat of our troops. Upon which Duff Cooper appeared in his turn to say that "His Majesty's government are entirely in agreement with the position taken by the United States."
The next day, a personal message from the President reached me,
expressing the distress General Doyen's threat had occasioned
him; he urged me to order the evacuation of our forces "until the
settlement of the claims which the French government wishes to
formulate with regard to the frontier can be effected normally and
rationally." Unless I was willing to act in accordance with his requests, he would be obliged "to suspend the distribution of equipment and munitions allocated to the French Army by the American
services. . . . However," he added, oddly enough, "the food supplies will continue to be furnished."

I did not take Truman's communication too seriously. However,
it seemed wise to lubricate the machinery of Franco-American
relations at the very moment the British were officially letting it be
known that they were ready to attack the French troops in Syria. I
replied to the President that "of course neither the French government's intentions nor General Doyen's orders had ever opposed
the presence of American troops in the Alpine zone," that there
were American troops in this zone as well as French forces, and
that both were living together there, "as everywhere else, on extremely good terms." What was in question was not the coexist-
ence of the French and their Allies, but indeed "the eviction of the
French by their allies from a territory conquered by our soldiers
against the German and Italian Fascist enemies and where, furthermore, several villages have populations of French origin." I informed Harry Truman that "our compulsory expulsion from this
region, coinciding with the British treatment of our interests in
Syria, would have the gravest consequences as to the sentiments of

the French people." Lastly, I wrote that to give Truman himself "satisfaction insofar as was possible," I was sending Juin to Alexander so that they would reach a solution together.

Ultimately, this solution provided that we remain in possession of what we wished to have. At first, of course, a draft of an agreement between Alexander's general staff and General Carpentier, Juin's representative, provided that our troops would gradually retire to the 1939 frontier. But save for the Val d'Aosta, which we had no intention of keeping, I refused to consent to such an arrangement, conceding only that small Allied detachments have access to the contested communes without in any way participating in their administration or government. Furthermore, while the deliberations were proceeding, we created several *faits accomplis:* The cantons of Tende and La Brigue elected municipalities which proclaimed their reattachment to France; in the formerly Italian enclaves of the Little St. Bernard, Iseran, Mont Cenis and Genèvre passes, we accorded woods and fields to the nearest French villages. The Valdôtains, supported by the liaison officers we had sent them and a militia they had formed themselves, instituted an autonomous government by the intermediary of their "Committee of Liberation." It was only in Ventimiglia that we let matters take their own course, for here feelings seemed to be mixed. Besides, the few American and British soldiers present on the disputed territory withdrew at once after Mr. Churchill's electoral defeat at the end of July. When, on September 25, M. Alcide de Gasperi, appointed Minister of Foreign Affairs in Rome after Count Sforza's death, visited me in Paris, he urged me to specify what conditions we would stipulate at the imminent signing of the peace treaty. I could tell him, as I had informed Ambassador Saragat, that we wished to see recognized by law only what had been realized in fact. Gasperi agreed, with a few sighs, that the treaty might include such clauses and that Italy would subscribe to them without rancor. Which was, in effect, what occurred.

While these difficulties were looming and consequently subsiding like a sort of side show, a major crisis exploded in the Levant. For some time the frenzy of the Arab nationalists and the desire of the British to remain the exclusive Western power in the Middle East had been uniting against us there. Hitherto, our adversaries had been obliged to take precautions; now it was no longer worth their while to do so. Once the Reich had capitulated, they united to assault France's position.

It was Syria which was to be the theater of their operations. After the 1943 elections, M. Choukri Kouatly, President of the Republic, and his successive cabinets increased their aggressive claims in our regard, all the more virulently since, in this unstable country subject to the chronic agitation of politicians, the government constantly tended to turn the flood of discontent against us. Yet in 1941 we had proclaimed Syria's independence of our own accord. Quite recently, the country had been invited to the San Francisco conference as a sovereign state as a result of France's intervention. For four years, the attributions of our authority—administration, finance, economy, police, diplomacy—had gradually been transferred to the state. But since we still remained the mandatory power and consequently responsible in the realms of defense and the maintenance of order, we had kept the local troops under our command and left minor French garrisons at several points. Thanks to which there had been no upheavals in Syria since 1941, whereas serious disturbances had occurred in Egypt, Palestine, Transjordan and Iraq, which were all under British domination.

Nevertheless, we were eager to establish France's relations with Syria and Lebanon on a secure basis. Supposing that the United Nations would soon establish a system of world security, we intended to transfer the mandate the old League of Nations had entrusted to us, to maintain two military bases in the area, to withdraw our troops from the territory, and to leave to the Damascus and Beirut governments the control of their own troops. Further, agreements with both states would determine the aid we were to furnish them and the fate of our remaining economic and cultural interests. This was the plan I had originally conceived, which I had subsequently pursued in all weathers, and which seemed close to realization, had not England's sudden intervention brought all my efforts to nothing. And it was at this very moment this intervention occurred.

I had always expected it, for the national ambitions masked by the world conflict included the British plan to dominate the Middle East. How many times I had already confronted this passionate resolve that was prepared to shatter any barrier that stood in its way! With the war's end in Europe, its occasion had come. In an exhausted France, the invasion and its consequences had obliterated our former power. As for the Arabs, a political program as subtle as it was costly had rendered a number of their leaders accessible to British influence. Above all, the economic organization established by Great Britain, with the help of the blockade, the mastery of the sea, and the monopoly of shipping, had put at her discretion the trade, in other words, the existence of the Middle Eastern states, while 700,000 British soldiers and many air squadrons dominated land and sky alike. Lastly, during the bargaining at Yalta, Churchill had managed to persuade Roosevelt and Stalin to leave him a free hand at Damascus and Beirut.

I could permit myself no illusions as to the means we possessed for weathering the storm. In Syria and Lebanon, our forces were reduced to 5,000 men—that is, five Senegalese battalions, a nucleus of service groups and one squadron of eight planes. In addition, the "special" troops—18,000 native soldiers and officers— were under our command. This was enough to maintain and, if need be, re-establish order, for the great majority of the population was not at all hostile to us. But if these minor units should be engaged by riots in various parts of the country and simultaneously assailed by the British forces, there could be no doubt as to the result. Confronted by this evidence, I had already clarified my intentions: Should such a situation arise, we would not combat both revolution and the English unless absolutely forced to do so.

But if I wished to avoid any conflict between ourselves and our allies, I had no intention of subscribing to a policy of renunciation. Such a refusal would be enough to oblige the London government to come to terms. On condition, of course, that I was supported by my own country. If France seemed as determined as I was not to yield to intimidation, there was every likelihood that Great Britain would not push matters to extremes, for the exposure of her ambitions and the threat of a break with France would soon have made her position untenable. I therefore hoped that in case of a crisis, public opinion would support me. Conversely, the British, particularly Churchill, counted on the anxiety and interests of influential French circles to frustrate De Gaulle and perhaps cause his fall. And, as a matter of fact, I was to find in political, diplomatic and press circles alike an extremely inconsistent policy of support, or else one of outright disapproval.

In Syria, at the end of April, many signs indicated that agitation was brewing, particularly in Damascus, Aleppo, Homs, Hama and Deir-ez-Zor. At the same time, the Syrian government grew more insistent in its protests, demanding the return of the "special" troops and encouraging the demands of agitation. Our Council of Ministers, upon the request of General Beynet, decided to send three battalions to the Levant, two of which would relieve an equivalent force of Senegalese Rifles which were to be repatriated. The cruisers *Montcalm* and *Jeanne d'Arc* undertook to transport them, since we had not yet been able to recover our steamers and freighters that had been lent to the interallied "pool." This minor rearrangement of troops was all the more justified in that a British division stationed in Palestine had just received orders to proceed to Beirut, whereas an entire English army, the Ninth, was already stationed on Syrian and Lebanese territory.

No sooner had the movement of French reinforcements started than the English ambassador called on me, on April 30. He was obliged to ask me, in his government's behalf, to stop sending our

obliged to ask me, in his government's behalf, to stop sending our troops into the area because "General Paget, the British Commander in Chief in the Middle East, regarded such movements as likely to cause difficulties." London proposed that our reinforcements be sent not to Beirut but to Alexandria, on merchant ships to be furnished by British services. It was evident that under these conditions our units could not reach their destination.

"We feel more secure," I replied to Duff Cooper, "transporting our troops ourselves. Furthermore, you know, the maintenance of order in the Levant is incumbent upon the French and upon them alone. Neither the British command in the Middle East nor the London government are qualified to intervene in the matter."

"However," the British ambassador said, "General Paget commands all the Allied forces in the Middle East, including yours."

"We have consented to this organization," I declared, "only in the case of further question of such operations, and moreover the common enemy was driven out of the Middle East over two years ago. Our Levant troops are therefore no longer subordinate to the British command in any way."

"The situation in Syria," Duff Cooper objected, "is linked to that of the entire Arab world in which the British have a superior responsibility."

"In the states of the Levant," I told him, "no responsibility is superior to that of France as mandatory power. Your conduct proves that despite the assurances lavished by your government and despite Spears's departure after his recall in December, British policy has not changed. You persist in interposing yourselves between France and the states under her mandate. We are therefore justified in supposing that your purpose is our eviction." Shrugging and murmuring that he feared complications were inevitable, Duff Cooper withdrew.

The complications, as a matter of fact, developed in the expected order. On May 5 Mr. Churchill sent me a message conforming in both style and spirit with those he had issued on the same subject over the last four years. The Prime Minister declared, once again, that he "recognized France's special position in the Levant." But having said as much, he let it be understood that England must nevertheless concern herself with matters in the area, "by reason of her commitments and duties." Since Mr. Churchill could no longer, as once before, justify this interference by alleging his obligations to defend the Suez Canal zone against Hitler and Mussolini, he now invoked the necessities of the war with Japan and declared: "This struggle obliges that the Allied land, sea and air communications, as well as the free passage of oil, be protected in the direction of the Indian and Pacific theaters of war. . . . The British must therefore remain on guard with regard to any disorders likely to occur at any point in the Middle East."

Then, specifying his demands, Mr. Churchill urged me to stop sending reinforcements to our bases, to restore the "special" troops to the Damascus and Beirut governments, and to make an immediate declaration on this point. He concluded by expressing the hope that I would help him "to prevent a new trial from being added to our difficulties."

I could not deceive myself as to what the sequel would be. If Mr. Churchill sent me a reprimand with regard to a reinforcement of 2,500 French soldiers sent into a region in which 60,000 British soldiers were stationed and about to be joined by 15,000 others, and 2,000 combat planes were ready to support, it was because the English were about to provoke a tremendous upheaval.

In replying to the Prime Minister, I felt it wise to expose the responsibility England was assuming by intervening in our affairs and the obstacle she herself was raising against any possibility of an accord between London and Paris. "We have recognized," I wrote, "the independence of the Levant States, as you have done in Egypt and Iraq, and we seek only to reconcile this independent regime with our interests in the region. These interests are of an economic and cultural order. They are also of a strategic order.

. . . Like you, we are interested in communications with the Far East. We are also interested in the free control of our share of Iraq oil." I added that once these various points were settled, we would terminate the mandate.

Then, assuming the offensive on this epistolary battlefield, the only one where I possessed the means to do so, I declared to Churchill: "I believe this matter could have been settled long since if the Damascus and Beirut governments had not been led to suppose they could avoid all commitment by relying on your support against us. The presence of your troops and the counsel of your agents is encouraging them in this unfortunately negative attitude." I continued, with some insistence: "I must tell you that the entry into Lebanon of a new British division from Palestine is, from our point of view, extremely regrettable and inopportune." Lastly, informing the Prime Minister that General Beynet was opening negotiations in Damascus and in Beirut, I asked him "to assure us that the situation would not be complicated, during this period, from the English side. . . . This," I concluded, "is one of the items which, from our point of view, keeps the two countries from establishing the harmony in their policies which in my opinion would be extremely useful to Europe and to the world."

Thus everything was clear, and ill-omened. What followed was no less so. Two days after this exchange, the trial by strength was begun. It opened on May 8, in Beirut, during the celebrations of victory. Troops of Arab soldiers attached to the British Division from Palestine paraded through the streets, insulting France. During the days that followed, many outrages were committed against the French in Syrian localities without the police taking any steps to prevent them. It must be added that this police force, which had proved exemplary while attached to French authority, had entirely altered since we had transferred it to the Syrian government two years before. Since the British command had continued to furnish arms to the police despite our representatives' repeated admonitions, M. Choukri Kouatly and his ministers had some 10,000 men equipped with the latest weapons at their disposal. They were to use them to foment and support disturbances. Naturally, the negotiations General Beynet attempted to open in Damascus came to nothing.

Nevertheless, on May 27, the French forces and special troops had quelled the upheavals in every region of the country save Jebel Druze, where we had only a few isolated forces. It was then that the Syrian ministers and their British advisers, seeing that the game was turning to their disadvantage, laid their trump cards on the table. On May 28, in Damascus, all our posts were attacked by bands of rioters and units of the Syrian police, all armed with machine guns, automatic rifles and British grenades. For twenty-four hours, the sound of gunfire crackled through Damascus. But on the twenty-ninth, it appeared that our men had held fast. In fact, the rebels, hard pressed, had had to take refuge in such public buildings as the House of Parliament, the Hôtel de Ville, the Police Headquarters, the Seraglio, the Bank of Syria, etc. To bring the matter to a close, General Oliva-Roget, French delegate in Syria, ordered these centers of insurrection to be captured. This was accomplished in twenty-four hours by our Senegalese troops and several Syrian companies; two cannons and one airplane were also used. By the evening of May 30, the French authority was in control of the situation and the Syrian ministers, taken in automobiles from the British legation, prudently withdrew outside the capital.

During these three weeks of rioting, the British had not stirred. In Cairo, Sir Edward Grigg, Secretary of State in charge of Middle Eastern Affairs, and General Paget, Commander in Chief, had remained impassive. In the Levant, General Pilleau, commanding the British Ninth Army, had made no move to alert the considerable forces at his disposal throughout the region. In London, silence reigned. In Paris, on the twenty-seventh, the reception given by the city and myself to General Montgomery, whom I formally decorated in Les Invalides, took place quite without incident. Everything indicated, in fact, that our "allies" were merely marking time while they supposed the "special" troops would refuse to obey us and we would therefore lose control of events. For twenty-three days, the reasons which, according to Churchill, would have justified the British in halting the conflict—"the necessities of the war with Japan," the obligation to protect "Allied communications as well as the passage of oil, in the direction of the Indian and Pacific theaters of war," and even the duty of preventing "any disorders likely to occur at any point in the Middle East"—did not determine them to abandon their passivity. We, moreover, did not ask them to take any such steps. But once they saw that the uprising had collapsed, their attitude suddenly changed. Britannia Militant pitted herself against France.

On the evening of May 30, Massigli, our ambassador to London was summoned by Mr. Churchill, in the presence of Mr. Eden, to receive a serious communication. Through the lips of the Prime Minister, the British government asked the French government to order a cease-fire in Damascus and announced that if the fighting continued His Majesty's forces could not remain indifferent.

When I learned of this, I was obliged to recognize that our men, simultaneously attacked by British troops and Syrian insurgents, would be in an untenable position. Moreover, Beynet's report, received at the very moment the British maneuver came to our knowledge, specified that French troops had occupied all the points in the city of Damascus from which shooting had been directed against our establishments. Our military action had therefore achieved its purpose. Whatever my indignation, I decided I must agree to a cease-fire insofar as there was any shooting still going on and, while maintaining our present positions, not oppose any movements the British troops decided to make. Georges Bidault, who was in charge of our delegation to the Levant and who ardently hoped that matters would not move toward catastrophe, telephoned this information to Beynet at eleven at night on May 23, with my consent. The British embassy was informed and Massigli received instructions to inform Eden of the fact at once.

If, on the British side, action had been taken only to obtain the cease-fire, the affair would have ended here. But an altogether different goal was envisioned; hence London, learning that the French had decided on a cease-fire, hastened to stage a tableau prepared in advance in order to inflict a public humiliation upon France. Mr. Churchill, apparently informed that the fighting was over in Damascus, subsequently launched a threatening ultimatum, certain that we could not respond to it by the appropriate means, eager to put himself up in a favorable light as protector of the Arabs, and hoping that in France the shock would involve a political defeat and perhaps even a loss of power for De Gaulle.

At four in the afternoon on May 31, Mr. Eden read to the House of Commons a message which I had apparently received from the Prime Minister. Yet the British Foreign Minister knew that at that hour I had received no such thing. "Because," Mr. Churchill informed me over the Commons benches, "of the grave situation now obtaining between your troops and the Levant States and the resulting conflicts, we have the sad duty of ordering the Commander in Chief in the Middle East to intervene in order to prevent further bloodshed. We do so in the interest of security over the entire area and of communications in the war against Japan. With a view to avoiding any conflicts between British and French forces, we request you to give the French troops immediate orders to cease fire and to retire to their posts. When the fighting has stopped and order is re-established, we will agree to begin tripartite discussions in London."

Thus the British government displayed to the world not only the conflict which it had instigated against us, but also the insult it offered to France in a moment when she was not in a position to accept the challenge. It had also taken every possible occasion to ignore our official notification of the cease-fire before its own outrageous orders had been broadcast. In London, Mr. Eden had managed not to receive Massigli before the Commons session, despite the requests for an audience which our ambassador had been making since that morning. As for Mr. Churchill's message, it was delivered to me at five—that is, an hour after it had been read to the British members. This delay, which added a breach of all normal usage to the insolence of the text, could have no other purpose than to keep me from making known in time that the fighting had stopped in Damascus and that there was no excuse for the British "ultimatum." I should say that Mr. Duff Cooper, unwilling to associate himself with such a maneuver, abstained from delivering his Prime Minister's statement himself; it was brought to me by the Counselor of the British embassy, who addressed himself to Gaston Palewski.

I naturally made no reply whatever to the British Prime Minister. During the course of the night, I sent Beynet explicit instructions relative to the future conduct of our troops: "Do not resume combat unless forced to; retain positions in any eventuality; do not in any case accept the orders of the British command." On June 1, our Council of Ministers convened and was informed of all dispatches and information received and sent during the preceding days. The Council unanimously approved what had been done and prescribed. I might add that the feeling among the ministers was not at all one of fear that we might be drawn into an armed conflict, since we were disposed to avoid any such likelihood and since the degree of bluff in the British threats was evident. But all shared the irritation and regret that I myself suffered at seeing Great Britain spoil—perhaps forever—the foundations of our alliance. Soon afterward, I made public what had happened, in Damascus as well as in London and Paris. My communiqué revealed the fact that the cease-fire had been ordered on the evening of May 30 and executed several hours before the British adopted their policy of intimidation. I pointed out that I had deliberately been informed of the latter only after it had been announced in London. Lastly, I repeated that the British government had ordered the French troops to maintain their positions.

During the course of that same day, General Paget came to Beirut and delivered a detailed ultimatum to General Beynet. According to the terms of this document, the Englishman who called himself "Supreme Commander in the Middle Eastern Theater," though for an area of 10,000 square miles there was no longer a single enemy soldier within this "theater," declared that he had received orders from his government "to assume command in Syria and Lebanon." He therefore ordered the French authorities "to execute without opposition" any orders he would give them. To begin with, he directed our troops to cease fighting and to withdraw to their barracks. On the occasion of this visit, General Paget employed an outrageous military display. Several pursuit squadrons escorted the plane that brought him to Beirut; between the airport and the residence of the French delegate general, he was preceded by a column of tanks and followed by a long line of combat vehicles whose occupants, as they crossed the city and passed our posts, held their guns in firing position.

General Beynet informed General Paget that with regard to orders, he had none to receive save from General de Gaulle and his government. He pointed out that the cease-fire had already been executed on the orders he himself had given in accord with my instructions. At present, our troops would remain where they were. As for the British forces, they could come and go as they chose, now as previously; we raised no objection to that. The Delegate General added, however, that he trusted Paget and his men would refrain from any attempt to force our troops and from taking responsibility for a deplorable conflict. For his part, he remained ready to settle, as previously and in agreement with the British command, all questions of cantonments, of supplies and of traffic common to the two armies. General Paget, his tanks, his combat vehicles, and his air squadrons then withdrew without disturbance.

Beynet was soon informed that he was supported; when I discovered the communication that had been made to him, I immediately reassured him. "I reiterate the orders I have given you.
. . . Our troops are to be concentrated in the positions fixed by
the French command and to remain there on the alert. Under no
conditions can they be subordinated to the British command. . . .
We hope that the necessity to oppose the British troops by force
will not arise. But not to the point where we would lose the possibility of employing our arms, which the behavior of the British
may render necessary. If they threaten to fire on us, in whatever
circumstances, we must threaten to fire on them. If they do fire, so
must we. Indicate this very clearly to the British command, for
nothing could be worse than a misunderstanding in this matter."

In order that there should be no misunderstanding in world-wide
and in national public opinion, I held a press conference on June 2.
Never before had the crowd of French and foreign journalists been
so large. I explained matters objectively, but without mincing any
words, in regard to our former allies. Then, on June 4, I sent for
the British ambassador, asked him to sit down, and said, "We are
not, I admit, in a position to open hostilities against you at the
present time. But you have insulted France and betrayed the West.
This cannot be forgotten." Duff Cooper stood up and walked out.

Mr. Churchill, stung to the quick, spoke the next day in the
House of Commons, declaring that he would answer me. He insisted that his government sincerely wished to maintain the alliance between England and France, as if the abuse of force it had
just perpetrated did not inflict a festering wound upon the amity
the French felt toward the British nation. He claimed, once again,
that the British intervention in the Levant was justified by the responsibility which his country, he declared, assumed in the entire
Middle East. But he did not say a word about the formal commitment made by Great Britain on July 25, 1941, under the signature
of her Minister of State, Oliver Lyttelton, to respect France's position in Syria and Lebanon, not to interfere in our political situation

there, and not to play any part in the administration of public order. He admitted that the Syrian police had received the arms they were now using against the French from the British, but felt he must point out—absurdly enough—that the French government had approved this British initiative. He expressed regret at not having known that the Paris government had ordered a cease-fire before London launched its ultimatum, and offered his apologies for not having sent the text to me until an hour after reading it to the House of Commons. But he gave no explanation whatever for this delay, and with good reason! Moreover, if the Prime Minister might claim to have been unaware until four in the afternoon of May 31 that the battle was over, this lacuna in his information services was certainly remedied by June 1. Yet it was on June 1 that Paget, on Churchill's orders, had come to notify Beynet, with all the support of a military demonstration ready to be transferred into action, of the details of his "diktat."

It was true that if the Prime Minister had counted on the crisis to isolate De Gaulle from leading French circles, he had been quite justified in doing so. As in the case of Roosevelt's summons to me immediately after the Yalta Conference, the Levant incident left me no effective support among the majority of the men who held public office. Masked by the precautions still considered necessary in dealing with me, it was either distress or downright disapproval which my action provoked among almost every influential man and articulate public figure.

First of all, the personnel of our diplomatic corps concurred only remotely with the attitude I had adopted. For many of the men in charge of our foreign relations, concord with England was a kind of principle. When on the British side, this concord was broken, it seemed essential to them to re-establish it by negotiating at any price to reach a favorable conclusion. The Levant question was therefore regarded by these specialists as a kind of explosive which must be handled with particular care in order to avoid a rift with Great Britain. But between the impulse I was trying to transmit and the behavior of those who actually wrote the notes, maintained the contacts and established the communications, the discrepancy was too apparent to escape our associates, thereby weakening the effect of my own determination.

The same was true of the tone adopted by the French press. I confess that in this crisis, convinced as I was that a categorical attitude on the part of French public opinion would have made the British retreat, the tone of our newspapers greatly disappointed me, for instead of evincing national resolution, they revealed only their inclination to diminish the affair's significance. The articles they devoted to it, brief and of little prominence, made it clear that for the French journalists the matter was settled—that is, lost—and that they were therefore eager to move on to something else. Resentment was occasionally expressed, but in regard to General de Gaulle, whose tenacity appeared temerarious and ill-advised.

The Consultative Assembly offered no greater support. It was only on June 17—three weeks after the British intervention—that it broached the subject. The Minister of Foreign Affairs explained the series of events before a small group of its members; then several speakers took their turn on the tribunal. Maurice Schumann and Father Carrière condemned the riots agitators had provoked against us, praised France's accomplishments in the Middle East and deplored in explicit terms the attitude adopted by Great Britain. However, they obtained only a relative success. Georges Gorse also referred to the unacceptable character of the British intervention, but addressed no fewer reproaches to the government. After which, Messrs. Florimond Bonte, André Hauriou, Marcel Astier and particularly M. Pierre Cot bitterly criticized both France and myself and received the approval of almost the entire audience.

Judging from their remarks and from the applause lavished upon them, what was happening in Syria was the consequence of an abusive policy we pursued from the start. To modify its excesses, our only recourse was to present ourselves to the peoples of the Levant in the guise of liberating, educating and revolutionary France, while leaving them to govern themselves. There was a contradiction here which these peculiar Jacobins were not concerned to resolve, nor would their ideology take into account the realities of the riots, the murder of our nationals, the obligations of the mandate and the British intention to drive us out of the region. They had no favorable word for the civilizing function France had fulfilled in Syria and Lebanon, the independence which I myself had accorded both states, the place my government had just obtained for them in the United Nations, and the efforts of our soldiers who during the First World War had helped liberate them from the yoke of the Ottoman Empire and during the Second had protected them against Hitler's domination.

Personally, I had anticipated that out of this entire gathering of men devoted to political affairs, someone—if only one man— would stand up and declare: "The honor and the interest of our country are at stake; now in a region where both are endangered, it is true that we are not immediately the stronger. But we shall not renounce our rights. Let those who have contravened them know that they have also gravely offended the alliance which united us. Let them know that France will come to the appropriate conclusions when she recovers her power and her influence."

But no one spoke such words, save myself, at the session's conclusion. The Assembly listened to me with close attention; it applauded me, as usual, when I left the tribunal; after which, it voted a motion lacking all vigor and expressing nothing but renunciation. I was obliged to declare that the text was not binding on the government's policy. This occasion led me to realize the profound lack of accord which, beneath appearances, separated me from the political factors in regard to foreign affairs.

Meanwhile, the British intervention in Syria had succeeded in unleashing a new wave of anti-French agitation, but our few forces, threatened as they were by the British, were on this occasion unable to control the situation. General Beynet therefore decided to regroup them outside the large cities, whereupon the latter were immediately occupied by the British. This resulted in many and bloody attacks, whose victims were our nationals. Upon which our "allies," on the pretext of avoiding further incidents, expelled all remaining French citizens from Damascus, Aleppo, Homs, Hama and Deir-ez-Zor. Further, our inability to assure the maintenance of order as well as the general agitation, risked throwing the Syrian troops into chaos too. The French authority therefore renounced its command of these units.

During the summer, a state of fragile equilibrium was established in the Syrian territory between the French, who still held certain points—the regions around Aleppo and Damascus, the port of Latakia, the air base of Rayak—the English, who had established themselves in most of the cities and were unsuccessfully trying to restore calm there, and the nationalists, who had now turned on the British and were demanding the withdrawal of all foreign forces. In Lebanon, on the other hand, the populace remained calm, though at Beirut the leaders added their claims to those of the Damascus government.

Under such conditions, I felt no haste in proceeding to a settlement. Therefore Mr. Churchill's proposition of a tripartite conference involving France, England and the United States received no reply from us. But the way in which the Anglo-American powers were behaving toward us justified our throwing a pebble in their diplomatic pond. Since on June 1 Soviet Russia had sent us a note expressing concern over the incidents in the Levant, as well as those in Egypt, Palestine and Iraq, all of which were eager to be free of the British, I publicly declared on June 2 that the question should be studied by a conference of the five "great powers"— France, England, the United States, the Soviet Union and China. The note we sent on this subject pointed out that these five states had just been recognized as permanent members of the United Nations Security Council and that, until this organization was set in operation, it was the responsibility of these nations to settle a problem which concerned the peace of the entire world. Our program was, of course, rejected by the British and the Americans with sullen resentment. The same reaction was accorded our next proposal to bring the entire Levant affair before the recently constituted United Nations.

Everything, therefore, remained in suspense. As matters stood, this was the most favorable situation for us. I was, indeed, convinced that the British attempt to replace us in Damascus and Beirut would end in failure. Moreover, the day would soon come when a functioning United Nations would assume the responsibility the League of Nations had previously entrusted to France in Syria and Lebanon. We would then be justified in removing the last vestiges of our authority from the Levant, without having abandoned this area to any other power. Of course, and in any case, our troops would not leave the area so long as the British forces remained there. As for what would happen then, I did not doubt that the agitation supported in the Levant by our former allies would spread through the entire Middle East to the detriment of these sorcerer's apprentices, and that eventually the British and Americans would pay dearly for the enterprise they had launched against France.

But while the British were abusing us in the Levant, the general consent of nations nevertheless restored France to the place she had once occupied among the primary states. It was as if the world hailed our resurrection as a kind of miracle, hastened to take advantage of it to accord us once more the place we had always had, and believed that with all its new anxieties it would need us. The demonstration took place in San Francisco, where the conference, convened on April 25, ended on June 26, after adopting the United Nations Charter. Franklin Roosevelt had died two weeks before its opening. (What man ever lived to see his triumph complete?) But the plan which the unanimous delegations had adopted was that of the great American leader.

Reviving an idea which had haunted the minds of many philosophers and several statesmen, had given birth to the League of Nations and then had foundered because of the defection of the United States and the weakness of the democracies, Roosevelt had wanted a world peace organization to emerge from the conflict. In our conversations in Washington the year before, the President had made me understand how close this monumental edifice was to his heart. In his ideology, international democracy was a sort of panacea; he felt that the nations, thus confronting each other, would examine their grievances and in each case take the measures necessary to keep matters from reaching a state of war. They would also co-operate in behalf of the progress of the human race. "Thanks to this institution," he told me, "the old American isolationism will come to an end and we will also be able to associate Russia, long isolated from us, with the rest of the Western world." Besides, although he did not mention it, Roosevelt expected that the crowd of small nations would force the hand of the "colonialist" powers and assure the United States an enormous political and economic clientele.

First at Dumbarton Oaks and later at Yalta, America, Great Britain and Russia had reached agreements on a constitution for the United Nations. China's consent had been obtained. When the Crimean conference was over, France's approval was asked, and Paris was invited to join Washington, London, Moscow and Chungking in issuing invitations to the San Francisco Conference. After careful consideration, we declined the offer the other four "big powers" had made to us to be a sponsoring power along with them. It was not suitable for us to recommend to fifty-one nations that they subscribe to articles drawn up without our participation.

On my part, it was with sympathy but not without circumspection that I envisaged the nascent organization. Of course its universal object was highly estimable in itself and consonant with the genius of France. It could appear salutary that cases of imminent conflict be referred to international intervention, and that the latter be

employed to effect compromises. In any case, it was good that the
states make contact with each other periodically, in full view of
world-wide opinion. Nevertheless, despite what Roosevelt thought,
what Churchill implied, what Stalin appeared to believe, I did not
permit myself to exaggerate the value of the "United Nations."

Its members would be states, that is, the least impartial and the
most partisan bodies in the world. Their meeting could, assuredly,
formulate political motions, but not render decisions. Yet it was inevitable that such an organization would claim to be as qualified
for the one endeavor as for the other. Furthermore, its more or less
tumultuous deliberations, developing in the presence of innumerable transcribers, broadcasters and cameramen, ran every risk of
balking genuine diplomatic negotiation, which is almost always
fruitful only when characterized by precision and discretion. Lastly,
it was to be presumed that many small countries would automatically oppose the great powers, whose presence and territories
extended the world over, touched many frontiers and inspired
frequent envy or anxiety. America and Russia certainly had
strength enough to inspire more than respect. England, relatively
intact, retained its maneuverability. But France, terribly damaged
by the war and assailed by all kinds of claims from Africa and
Asia—what hearing would she obtain on the occasion of her difficulties?

This was why I instructed our delegation not to give way to high-
sounding declarations, as many of our representatives had once
done in Geneva, but instead to observe an attitude of restraint. This
was done, and done well, under the successive direction of Georges
Bidault, participating for the first time in an international council,
and President Paul Boncour, whose experience with the League of
Nations made him a master of such subjects. The discretion shown
by our representatives did not, of course, keep France from taking
her place in the Areopagus of the five "big powers" which conducted the affair. It achieved, in San Francisco, all that we were
most eager to obtain. Thus, despite a certain amount of opposition,

French was recognized as one of the three official languages of the United Nations. Further, beyond the right of veto appertaining to France as to the other great powers, the Charter's original draft was amended so as to make the "General Assembly" counterbalance the "Security Council" and, at the same time, to control the tendencies of the Assembly by requiring a two-thirds majority for its motions. It was further specified that the examination of litigations by the organization would in no way impede the drafting and signing of treaties of alliance. Lastly, the system of "trusteeships," under which malevolent intentions with regard to the French Union were apparent, would be subject to severe restrictions.

The United Nations was born; but its first session, devoted to its constitution, did not deal with the problems raised by the war's end. Americans and British rushed without us to Potsdam intending to meet with the Russians there and to establish what must be done in the practical sphere. The conference began on July 17. In Truman's mind and Churchill's, it was a matter of concluding with Stalin what had been proposed at Teheran and decided at Yalta in regard to Germany, Poland, Central Europe and the Balkans. The Americans and British hoped to recover in application what they had conceded in principle. The "Big Three" would also confer on the conditions under which Soviet Russia would participate *in extremis* in the war against Japan.

That our allies of yesterday should convene yet again in our absence—for the last time, moreover—could only cause us renewed irritation. Yet fundamentally we considered it preferable not to be introduced into discussions which could henceforth be nothing but supererogatory.

For the facts were decided. The enormous chunk of Europe which the Yalta agreements had abandoned in advance to the Soviets was now in their hands. Even the American armies, after having overrun the frontiers established for them in Germany during the last days of the fighting had fallen back 150 kilometers. The Russians alone occupied Prussia and Saxony. Without further delay they had annexed all of Poland east of the "Curzon line," transferred the inhabitants along the Oder and western Neisse, and driven the German population of Silesia, Poznan and Pomerania west. Thus all question of frontiers was decided quite simply by the Soviets. Furthermore, in Warsaw, Budapest, Sofia, Belgrade and Tirana, the governments that had been installed were at their discretion and almost all at their beck and call. Yet the rapidity of this Sovietization was only the inevitable result of what had been agreed upon at the Crimea conference. The regrets the British and Americans now expressed were quite uncalled for.

As for the Soviet intervention in the Pacific theater, what purpose could it serve? The atom bombs were ready. Arriving in Potsdam, Truman and Churchill announced the success of the New Mexico experiments. From one day to the next, Japan was to suffer the terrible explosions and consequently surrender. Any commitments the Russians now made as to the war in the Pacific would involve no consequences from the military point of view, but result in the Kremlin's recognized right to participate as a victor in Far Eastern affairs. For Asia and for Europe, there was every reason to foresee that on no issue would the Potsdam conference realize any durable entente, but instead provoke unlimited friction between the Soviet and the Anglo-American participants.

This prospect convinced me that it was wiser not to climb on the band wagon at this point. Naturally I regretted that I had not been present at Teheran. There, as a matter of fact, I would have defended the equilibrium of Europe when there would still have been some point in doing so. Subsequently, I was sorry not to have been permitted to take part in the Yalta Conference, since there still remained some opportunities of preventing the iron curtain from cutting Europe in two. But now everything had been arranged—what could I have done at Potsdam?

Once the communiqué published by the conference appeared, we learned that it had concluded in a kind of uproar. Despite the wealth of conciliation lavished by Mr. Truman, despite Mr.

Churchill's vehement protest, Generalissimo Stalin had agreed to no compromises of any kind. In Poland particularly, the appearance of Messrs. Mikolajczyk, Grabski, Witos and Stanczyk in the cabinet formed on the basis of the Lublin Committee had induced Washington and London, and obliged Paris as well, to recognize the government directed by Messrs. Bierut and Osuska-Morawski, but it was soon apparent that the totalitarian character of the Warsaw government was in no way diminished thereby. In regard to Asia, Stalin, in exchange for his promise to declare war on Japan, managed to obtain for Russia the Kurile Archipelago and half of Sakhalin, induced the Allies to accord Korea to the Soviets north of the 38th parallel, and forced Chiang Kai-shek to withdraw from Outer Mongolia. The latter became a "People's Republic." For this price the Generalissimo promised not to intervene in China's internal affairs, but he was nonetheless to furnish the support and arms to Mao Tse-tung's Communists which were soon to permit them to seize the country. On the whole, far from consecrating the world-wide co-operation of America and Russia, to which Roosevelt had sacrificed the equilibrium of Europe, the Potsdam conference whetted their opposition.

Mr. Churchill left before the end, thrust from power by the British electors. Upon the Reich's surrender, Great Britain had broken up a national coalition which had lasted for over five years. Elections had been held and on July 25, a breakdown of the votes gave the Labour Party a majority in the House of Commons. The Prime Minister, head of the Conservative Party, was therefore obliged to resign.

To minds inclined toward the illusions of sentiment, this sudden disgrace inflicted by the British nation upon the great man who had led it to salvation and glorious victory might seem surprising. Yet there was nothing in the occasion which was not in accord with the order of human affairs. For, once the war was over, public opinion and policy alike cast off the psychology of union, energy and sacrifice and turned once more to interest, prejudice and antagonism. Winston Churchill lost neither his glory nor his popularity thereby, but only the general adherence he had won as a guide and symbol of the nation in peril. His nature, identified with a magnificent enterprise, his countenance, etched by the fires and frosts of great events, had become inadequate to the era of mediocrity.

In some respects, Churchill's departure facilitated the conduct of French affairs; in others, it did not. In any case, I observed it with melancholy. Certainly within the alliance itself Churchill did not deal gently with me, and latterly, with regard to the Levant, his behavior had been that of an adversary. In general, he had supported me as long as he took me for the head of the French minority which favored him and which he could put to good use. Moreover, this great politician had always been convinced that France was necessary to the free world; and this exceptional artist was certainly conscious of the dramatic character of my mission. But when he saw France in my person as an ambitious state apparently eager to recover her power in Europe and the world, Churchill had quite naturally felt something of Pitt's spirit in his own soul. Yet in spite of everything, the essential and ineffaceable fact remained that without him my efforts would have been futile from the start, and that by lending me a strong and willing hand when he did, Churchill had vitally aided the cause of France.

Having seen a great deal of him, I had greatly admired though quite as often envied him. For if his task was colossal, at least he found himself invested by the regular instances of the state, furnished with all the powers and provided with all the levers of legal authority, set at the head of a unanimous people, of a territory still intact, of a tremendous Empire, and of formidable armies. Whereas I, at the same time, condemned by apparently official powers, reduced to nothing but the fragments of an army and the vestiges of national interest—I had had to answer, alone, for the destiny of a nation in the enemy's hands and torn to its vitals. Yet different though the conditions were under which Churchill and De Gaulle had had to accomplish their tasks, fierce though their disputes had been, for more than five years they had nonetheless sailed side by side, guiding themselves by the same stars on the raging sea of history. The ship that Churchill had captained had not been moored fast. And even as I stood at the helm of mine, we had come in sight of port. Learning that England had asked her captain to leave the command to which she had called him when the tempest fell, I foresaw the moment when I would relinquish the helm of France, of my own accord, as I had taken it.

During the final sessions of the Potsdam Conference, Mr. Churchill's replacement by Mr. Attlee, who had become Prime Minister, resolved none of the hostile tensions among the Big Three. Settlements concerning Europe and, above all, the Reich could therefore not be concluded. For my part, I was convinced that this would be the case for a long time. For Germany would henceforth be the object of Russo-American rivalry, until, perhaps, it became the stake of their future conflict. For the moment, no arrangement appeared practicable save some sort of *modus vivendi* relative to the occupation and the administration of the national zones, the feeding of the inhabitants, the trials of the war criminals. Before separating, Truman, Stalin and Attlee, admitting their impotence, had arranged for their foreign ministers to convene in London, under less intensive circumstances, and attempt to determine the bases of the peace treaties. This time, France was invited to participate. We accepted—on principle, but without illusions.

It should be said that at this point one matter was settled in a manner which afforded relative satisfaction. In July the London "European Commission," on which France was represented along with Great Britain, the United States and Russia, had established the boundaries of the French zones of occupation. I myself had determined the territories we would control: In Austria, where Béthouart was in command, it was the Tyrol which fell to us, as well as the responsibility of Vienna one month out of every four; in

Germany, it was the left bank of the Rhine from Cologne to the Swiss frontier and, on the right bank, the state of Baden and a sector of Württemberg; we were to be as responsible for the occupation of Berlin as the other powers. The Allies had subscribed to these conditions save for Cologne, which the British held and insisted on keeping. In regard to our status, the future of Europe and the human relations between French and Germans, the occupation of the zone was an extremely essential but delicate task, since the reactions which the German atrocities risked provoking among our men were the responsibility of the French Army. Yet that Army was to acquit itself with a dignity, a moderation and a discipline which were an honor to France.

Immediately after the Reich's surrender, I had gone to salute this Army in the terrain of its victory, to decorate General de Lattre and several of his lieutenants, and to give them instructions. On May 19 and 20, in a totally ruined though still heavily populated Stuttgart, later at the foot of the Arlberg, and finally under the walls of Konstanz, the commander of the "Rhine and Danube" offered me splendid reviews of his troops. Among the victorious Frenchmen filing before De Gaulle, there subsisted, certainly, differences of outlook. But unity was now assured regarding the subject that had lately provoked so many divisions; today every soldier was certain that it had been his duty to oppose the invader and that, if France now had a future, it was because he had fought for her.

During my inspection, I visited, in particular, the 2nd Armored Division. Across the Augsburg plain, this entire great unit paraded swiftly before me in battle array. Before this spectacle, I was proud to realize that thanks to such units, this war and my undertaking had reached their end in honor. But at the same time I recalled—*infandum dolorem!*—that if we had only had seven such divisions at our disposal six years before, and a command capable of putting them to use, the arms of France would have changed the face of the world.

The countenance Germany showed us was certainly lamentable in any case. Observing the mountains of ruins to which the cities were reduced, passing through flattened villages, receiving the supplications of despairing burgomasters, seeing populations from which male adults had almost entirely disappeared made me, as a European, gasp in horror. But I also observed that the cataclysm, having reached such a degree, would profoundly modify the psychology of the Germans.

It would be a long time before we would see again that victorious Reich which thrice during one man's lifetime had rushed to domination. For many years, the ambitions of the German nation and the aims of its policy would necessarily be reduced to the level of survival and reconstruction. Moreover, I scarcely suspected that it must remain severed and that Soviet Russia would insist on keeping at its disposal those very German territories which had nourished the impulses toward *"Lebensraum."* Thus, amid the ruins, mourning and humiliation which had submerged Germany in her turn, I felt my sense of distrust and severity fade within me. I even glimpsed possibilities of understanding which the past had never offered; moreover, it seemed to me that the same sentiment was dawning among our soldiers. The thirst for vengeance which had spurred them on at first had abated as they advanced across this ravaged earth. Today I saw them merciful before the misery of the vanquished.

But with the Reich annihilated and the Allies not yet in agreement as to its destiny, each of us would have to assume the administration of his own zone. According to the instructions of their governments, this was what Eisenhower, Zhukov, Montgomery and De Lattre had agreed upon, meeting in Berlin to settle matters as soon as possible. Further, it was agreed that the four commanders in chief would constitute an Allied Control Commission for the whole of the German territory. At the end of July, our troops occupied Saarbrücken, Treves, Coblenz, Mainz, Neustadt and their environs, from which the Americans withdrew and in exchange for the French evacuation of Stuttgart. On the right bank of the Rhine, we remained in the regions of Freiburg, Konstanz and Tübingen.

General de Lattre then regretfully left his command to assume the highest post in our Army, that of Chief of the General Staff. General Koenig replaced him as Commander in Chief in Germany. An administrative staff was constituted under his orders; Émile Laffon was appointed adjutant to the Commander in Chief and to the French delegates in charge of the various territories —Grandval in the Saar, Billotte in the Rhineland and Hesse-Nassau, Boulay in the Palatinate, Widmer in Württemberg, Schwartz in the state of Baden. They would choose administrators and officials among those German citizens who appeared qualified.

Before the opening of the London conference, where the ministers of foreign affairs were to seek a basis of understanding, I went to Washington. For three months, Harry Truman had asked me. Probably the new President wanted firsthand information as to France's intentions in this early phase of a difficult peace.

The collapse of Germany, soon followed by that of Japan, placed the United States in a kind of political void. Hitherto, the war had dictated its plans, its efforts, its alliances. All had had no other object beyond victory. Now the universe was changing, and at an ultrarapid tempo. Yet America, the only one of the great powers completely intact, remained invested during the peace with the same responsibility she had finally had to assume in the conflict, for she was to enter a national and ideological rivalry with a state that was her equal in size and power. Confronting the Soviet Union, the United States wondered which course to take, which foreign causes to espouse or reject, which peoples to aid or ignore. In short, isolationism had become impossible. But when one is powerful and undamaged, one must accept the encumbrances of a great policy.

It was natural for President Truman to lose no time consulting France. The latter, despite the ordeals she had just survived, was the only nation on the European continent on which Western policy could count. She remained, moreover, a major African reality. Her sovereignty attended as far as the territories of America and Oceania. She had not left the Middle East. Nothing could keep her from returning to the Far East. Her prestige and her influence were gaining all over the world. Whether America tried to organize the peace by the collaboration of nations, attempted to institute balance of powers, or was merely obliged to prepare her own defense, how do so without France?

This was why, at the end of May, Truman had requested Georges Bidault, whom the San Francisco Conference had brought to the United States, to tell me that he hoped for a meeting with me soon. My reply was favorable. I invited Truman to come to France if he was able to. Otherwise, I would gladly pay him a visit in the United States. But since the Potsdam Conference was already under discussion, I indicated to the President that because of the reactions of French public opinion, his arrival in Paris or mine in Washington should not immediately precede or follow the meeting which the "Big Three" were to hold in my absence. Truman agreed that it would be better if he did not stop in France on his way to Berlin or upon his return. On July 3 he telegraphed me that he proposed our meeting take place in Washington at the end of August. I replied: "I accept your kind invitation with pleasure. . . ."

I flew to Washington on August 21, accompanied by Bidault, Juin, Palewski and several diplomats. Stopping in the Azores and in Bermuda, we reached the capital of the United States on the afternoon of the twenty-second. Mr. Byrnes, the Secretary of State, General Marshall and Mr. Caffery met us at the airport among a large crowd of officials, onlookers and journalists. Along the road leading to the White House, Washington lavished its cheers upon us. We immediately commenced a series of talks, our evenings given over to a round of receptions and ceremonies, notably that during which I made Generals Marshall, Arnold and Somervell and Admirals King and Leahy (the latter somewhat embarrassed at being decorated by De Gaulle) dignitaries of the Legion of Honor. Going through the same rituals in which I had figured a year before, listening to the remarks of the same statesmen, influential leaders and officials, being interviewed by the same press representatives, I realized to what a degree France had recovered in the world's eyes. During my previous journey, she was still regarded as an enigmatic captive. Now she was considered as a great ally, wounded but victorious, and above all, needed.

This, certainly, was President Truman's sense of the situation. For seven hours on August 22, 23 and 25, I conferred with him, attended by James Byrnes and Georges Bidault and Ambassadors Jefferson Caffery and Henri Bonnet. Mr. Truman, for all his simplicity of manner, proved to be an extremely positive man. His speech suggested an attitude remote from the vast idealism which his illustrious predecessor had developed in the same office. The new President had abandoned the plan of a world harmony and admitted that the rivalry between the free world and the Soviet bloc now dominated every other international consideration. It was therefore essential to avoid dissension and revolutionary upheaval, so that states not yet Communist would not be led to become so.

As for the complex problems of the Old World, they in no way intimidated Harry Truman, who regarded them from a position which simplified everything: For a nation to be happy, it need only institute a democracy like that of the New World; to put an end to the antagonisms which opposed neighboring countries, for instance France and Germany, all that was necessary was to establish a federation of rivals, as the states of North America had done among themselves. There existed one infallible formula to influence the underdeveloped countries to favor the West, independence; the proof, America herself, who once free of her former possessors had become a pillar of civilization. Finally, confronted with its present danger, the free world could do nothing better, and nothing else, than adopt the "leadership" of Washington.

President Truman, as a matter of fact, was convinced that the mission of serving as guide fell to the American people, exempt as they were from exterior shackles and internal contradictions that encumbered all other states. Moreover, to what power, to what wealth could America's be compared? I must admit that by the end of the summer of 1945, one was struck, at first contact with the United States, by the impression of an overpowering activity and an intense optimism that swept all before them. Among the former belligerents, this nation was the only one still intact. Its economy, based on apparently unlimited resources, quickly emerged from the wartime regime to produce enormous quantities of consumer goods. The avidity of the buyers and, abroad, the needs of a ravaged world guaranteed an outlet to the greatest enterprises, and full employment to the workers. Thus the United States was assured of being the most prosperous nation for some time. Then, too, it was the strongest! A few days before my visit to Washington, the atom bombs had reduced Japan to capitulation.

The President, therefore, did not expect that Russia could risk an actual war for a long time to come. This was why, he explained to me, the American forces were entirely withdrawing from Europe, with the exception of occupation forces in Germany and in Austria. But he considered that in many areas an extreme of devastation, poverty and disorder could result in the succession of Communism and afford the Soviets so many victories without the need for battle. The peace problem, according to Truman, was therefore of a largely economic order. The nations of western Europe, whether they had won or lost the war, had to resume the normal course of their existence as soon as possible. In Asia and Africa, the underdeveloped peoples should receive the means of raising their standard of living. This was what mattered, not frontiers, grievances and guarantees!

It was with these convictions that President Truman examined with me the problems raised by the victory. He listened to me explain how we French envisaged the fate of the German territories and made no direct objection to any of our proposals—termination of the centralized Reich, autonomy of the left bank of the Rhine, international government of the Ruhr. But he remained reserved on these points. On the other hand, he was categorical as to the necessity of materially aiding Germany. While eager—like myself —to assist the Westphalian basin to resume its coal production on a large scale and at once, he did not favor the notion of handing over certain quantities of its output to France, Belgium and Holland in compensation for the devastation of which they had been the victims. At best, he suggested that these nations buy—in dollars —a share of the fuel. Similarly, the President opposed the withdrawal from Germany of raw materials, machinery and manufactured objects. Even the recovery of the machinery which the Germans had taken from France disturbed Harry Truman. On the other hand, he was quite favorable to the reattachment of the Saar to France, since her coal and steel production would certainly be increased thereby.

I explained to the President why France conceived of the world in a less abstract manner than the United States. "You Americans," I said, "have taken part in two world wars with an effectiveness and a courage which one must certainly salute. Nevertheless, invasion, devastation and revolution are for you unknown ordeals. But in France, an old man has seen our nation thrice invaded during his own lifetime, the last time completely. The resulting amount of human loss, destruction and expense is actually incalculable. Each of these crises, particularly the last, has provoked in our people divisions whose profundity cannot even be estimated. Our inner unity and our international status will long be compromised. My government and I must therefore take the necessary measures to prevent the German threat from ever reappearing. Our intention, of course, is not to drive the German people to despair. On the contrary, we desire that people to live, to flourish and even to draw closer to us. But we must have guarantees. I have specified which ones. If, later on, it appears that our neighbors have changed their ways, we could modify these initial precautions. But at present, the armature Germany is to be given must be pacific and it must be forged while the Lord's fire has rendered the iron malleable."

I observed to Mr. Truman that here lay the hope of one day re-establishing European equilibrium. "This equilibrium has been shattered," I said, "because with the consent of America and Great Britain, the states of Central Europe and the Balkans are forced to serve as satellites to the Soviet Union. If these states have in common with their 'protector' the same national dread of seeing an ambitious Germany reappear, the bonds which link them by force to the Soviet policy will be all the stronger. If they realize, on the contrary, that the German menace no longer exists, their national interest will not fail to develop within the Soviet camp. Whence, between them and their suzerain, the inevitable discords which will turn the Kremlin from belligerent enterprises, particularly since Russia herself will be profoundly less inclined to such adventures. Even Germany will be able to take advantage of the new structure which must be established, for a truly federal regime would be her unique opportunity to induce the Soviets to permit the Prussian and Saxon territories to rejoin the common body. The road France proposes to the former Reich is the only one which can lead to European reorganization and regrouping."

At the end of these exchanges between Truman and myself on the subject of Germany and of the complementary discussions between Byrnes and Bidault, it was agreed that at the London conference, the American delegation would recommend that our proposals be taken into consideration. Without prejudice to the eventual decision relative to the Ruhr's status, it was agreed that a Franco-Anglo-American commission would immediately be established in the Basin to promote the rapid recovery of the mines and determine that France received a significant share of the coal produced, the terms of payment to be settled at the same time as those of reparations. The Americans announced that they would not oppose the measures we wished to adopt relative to the Saar. Finally, my trip to Washington was made the occasion to conclude negotiations, conducted for several months, by Jean Monnet, with regard to a long-term loan of 650 million dollars which America was making to us at the moment she was bringing "lend-lease" to an end.

As for the more or less "colonial" countries of Asia and Africa, I declared that in my opinion the new era would mark their accession to independence, though the means would inevitably be varied and gradual. The West should understand and even desire this. But it was essential that these changes be made with, not against us, or else the transformation of peoples still primitive and ill-assured states would launch a wave of xenophobia, poverty and anarchy. It was easy to predict who would be in a position to take advantage of such a situation.

"We have determined," I told the President, "to forward those countries which depend on ours toward self-government. In some cases, we can proceed rapidly; in others, less so. Evidently, that is France's affair. But in this domain nothing is so deplorable as the appearance of rivalry among the Western powers. Unfortunately, that is precisely what is happening in the Levant." And I expressed my irritation over the support America had just given the British intervention there. "Ultimately," I declared, "I predict that the West will have to pay for this error and this injustice."

Mr. Truman agreed that Washington had accorded disproportionate credit to the British claims. "In any case," he said, "my government offers no opposition to the return of the French Army and authority in Indochina."

I replied, "Although France need ask no permission or approval in an affair which is hers alone, I note with satisfaction the intentions you express. The enemy recently seized Indochina. Thanks to the victory in which America has played an incomparable part, France is about to return there. She does so with the intention of establishing a regime in harmony with the will of the people. Nevertheless, in this area too, we find ourselves hampered

by the arrangements our allies are making without consulting us
first."

I indicated to Mr. Truman that we were not eager to see British
troops replace the Japanese in the southern part of Indochina or
Chinese troops in the north. Yet this was what was about to happen, according to an agreement concluded in Cairo in 1943 between Roosevelt, Churchill and Chiang Kai-shek and recently confirmed by the Potsdam Conference. We were not unaware, further,
that American agents, under General Wedemeyer, United States
delegate to the Chinese command, were preparing to infiltrate into
Tonkin in order to establish contact with the revolutionary power.
All this, I pointed out, was not of a nature to facilitate matters for
us. Thereupon the President felt he should inform me once again
that, from Washington's point of view, there would be absolutely
no attempt to hamper our undertakings in the Far East.

We parted on good terms. Doubtless between our two states
there could not have been either understanding or confidence without some reservations. The Washington talks had shown that if
necessary America would follow a road which was not the same as
ours. But at least Harry Truman and I had discussed this frankly
with each other. As Chief of State, Truman impressed me as equal
to his task, his character firm, his mind oriented toward the practical side of affairs—in short, a man who doubtless promised no
miracles but who could be counted on in a crisis. He certainly
showed every consideration for me, and his statements following
my visit went far beyond official praise. During our last meeting,
he suddenly opened the doors of his office, behind which were
standing some twenty photographers, and slipped a decoration
around my neck, knowing that I would have declined any distinction had I been informed beforehand; he then decorated Bidault
as well. Upon my departure Truman, in the name of the United
States, presented me with a magnificent DC4. On subsequent occasions no bitter word ever passed between us.

To receive De Gaulle and his colleagues, New York lavished its torrential friendship upon us. We drove there on August 26, by way of West Point, where I inspected the Military Academy, and Hyde Park, where I saluted Roosevelt's tomb. It was Sunday and happened as well to be the first day when gasoline could be sold without ration cards. The roads were jammed and a tremendous row of cars parked along the curb for about one hundred kilometers hailed our passage with an incredible racket of horns. Mayor Fiorello La Guardia, a marvel of energy and sympathy, received us as we entered the city. That evening, after various ceremonies, he took me to Central Park where Marian Anderson was to sing the "Marseillaise." There, in the darkness, twenty irresistible arms drew me onto the stage of the huge amphitheater. The spotlights came on and I was revealed to the crowd sitting in the theater. Once the storm of cheers had died away and the singer's superb voice had rendered our national anthem, I saluted the great city with all my heart.

The next day was the occasion for the "Victory Parade." We drove through the city in state, the mayor beside me exultant with satisfaction while cheers filled the air and flags and banners fluttered at every window. We reached lower Broadway amid an indescribable storm of "Long Live France!" "Hurrah! De Gaulle!" "Hello, Charlie!" beneath thick clouds of confetti and ticker tape thrown from 100,000 windows. At City Hall took place the reception. I decorated La Guardia, who since June 1940 had proved one of the most ardent and effective advocates Fighting France had in the United States. Then I was awarded honorary citizenship of New York, and at the colossal banquet which followed, the mayor declared in his toast, "In raising my glass to the glory of General de Gaulle, I wanted to salute him as New York's youngest citizen, for we inscribed his name on the city register only an hour ago. But since then, the birth of forty-five other babies has been announced!"

New York State's Governor Thomas Dewey declared, "Calm though I might have seemed, I was overwhelmed by the city's emotion." Certainly this quality of the picturesque in the colossal is characteristic of American public manifestations. But the explosion of enthusiasm which had marked this occasion revealed the extent of the city's extraordinary love of France.

Chicago gave token of the same emotion. Unlike New York, however, Chicago is not oriented toward Europe, and its population derives from the most various nations of the world. "Here," Mayor Edward Kelly told me, "you will be cheered in seventy-four languages." And in fact that evening going to the municipal banquet, and the next day when we drove through the avenues of Chicago to visit the New Deal buildings, when we were received at the city hall, or driving to a monster banquet given by the Chamber of Commerce and the American Legion, we were surrounded by a tremendous crowd which mingled all the races of the earth, unanimous in their cheers.

Canada, in its turn, gave us a warm welcome. My hosts, Governor General the Earl of Athlone and his wife, Princess Alice, declared to me upon my arrival, "When you were here last year, you could see what feelings public opinion in this country entertained toward you. But since then, France and you have risen about three hundred per cent."

"Why?"

"Because then you were a question mark; now you are an exclamation point."

In Ottawa, authorities and people alike lavished upon us every imaginable evidence of their enthusiasm. "Premier" Mackenzie King, assisted by Minister of Foreign Affairs St. Laurent and Ambassador Vanier, and myself, accompanied by Bidault and our Ambassador Jean de Hauteclocque, found we could discuss major issues with great candor, since France's interests were quite separate from those of Canada.

Mackenzie King, a veteran of Canadian politics and a resolute advocate of an independent Canada, told me quite candidly, "This is our situation: Canada adjoins the United States for over five thousand kilometers—a frequently overwhelming contiguity. It is, besides, a member of the Commonwealth—an occasionally onerous responsibility. But we intend to act in complete independence. We are a nation of unlimited space, endowed with great natural resources. Our ambitions are to exploit these, and therefore they are oriented internally. We have no interest in opposing France in any of her fields of action. On the contrary, we have every reason to lend her our good offices to whatever degree that we can, whenever France feels the necessity of calling upon us."

"As for us," I said to Mackenzie King, "two world wars have shown us the value of your co-operation. Certainly we shall need to rely on your friendship during the peace. What you have just said convinces me that France was quite right in coming here long ago and planting the seed of civilization."

We passed through Newfoundland in order to fly back to Paris. During the stopover at the American base at Gander, in the midst of a normally almost desert country, I heard my name shouted by a crowd of cheering men gathered along the fences. I walked over to them; they were inhabitants assembled from various parts of the island to greet General de Gaulle. Faithful to their Norman, Breton and Picardy ancestors who first settled Newfoundland, all spoke French. All, too, seized by an ancestral emotion, shouted *"Vive la France!"* as they held out their hands.

Almost immediately after our journey, the London conference convened, a last chance for agreement among the four allies. From September 11 to October 3, Byrnes, Molotov, Bevin and Bidault examined the problems of Europe together. Yet the Big Four's discussions did nothing but sharpen the antagonism between Russians and Anglo-American powers. It was with the greatest difficulty, in regard to Italy, that we were able to conceive the possibility of an agreement as to the fate of Istria and Trieste. Georges Bidault further specified the minor changes we expected to be made in our Alpine frontier, and obtained the approbation of his three colleagues on this point. But when the question of the former

Italian colonies was broached, when the British and American ministers spoke of making Libya into an independent state, while the French Minister proposed placing the territory under United Nations control with Italy as "trustee," Messrs. Bevin and Byrnes, outraged, broke off the conversation and the Italian question stood at an impasse.

The same was true of the projected treaties with Hungary, Rumania and Bulgaria. The Soviets let it be understood that it was their responsibility to establish the terms and that they had the means to do so, since they were the sole occupiers; British and American ministers protested against the political oppression all three states were suffering, as if the latter were anything but the consequences of the Teheran, Yalta and Potsdam agreements. The problem of Germany, however, made the four powers' inability to reach any solution particularly manifest.

France, however, and France alone had formulated one. On the eve of the London conference, I had made public, in an interview with Gerald Norman, Paris correspondent of the London *Times,* what our conditions for peace with Germany were. Then, during the conference, a memorandum from our delegation and a report by Bidault specified our position. The conference did not give the French program a negative reception. The notion of replacing the Reich by a federation of states was apparently regarded as extremely reasonable; the conception of a Franco-Saarois economic union provoked no objection; the projected transformation of the Palatinate, Hesse and the Rhineland into autonomous states and their integration into a western economic and strategic system did not appear unacceptable. At first our partners even sanctioned our proposition to put the Ruhr under international control. But after M. Molotov insisted that Russia participate in such a regime and that Soviet troops join the detachments of western forces in Düsseldorf, Mr. Byrnes strongly objected and Mr. Bevin took up the refrain. The conference advanced no further in its examination of our solution; no one, moreover, proposed any other, and the minis-

ters separated after twenty-three days of discussion as futile for
the present as they were unpromising for the future.

Each power was consequently inclined to proceed in its own
zone as it judged best. In the east, the Soviets were to impose
their now familiar political and social system upon Prussia and
Saxony. In the west, the Americans, opposing certain "autono-
mist" tendencies appearing in Bavaria, Lower Saxony and Württemberg, and the British, who were finding the direct responsibility
for the Ruhr and the major North Sea ports a heavy one, proceeded to the kind of organization they found easiest—they merged
their two zones into a single unit delegating authority to a college
of German secretaries general. Thus a Reich government was created after all, at least until general elections could be held. The
prospect of a true German federation vanished in the hard light
of the facts. Later the British and Americans urged us to unite the
territories we occupied to the zones where they were rebuilding
the Reich, but I would not agree to this step.

For the moment, in any case, our zone was our own responsibility. Early in October, I visited the area to make contact with
the German authorities and the people, and to determine the possibilities of realizing the policy to which I had committed France.
Diethelm, Capitant, Dautry, Juin and Koenig accompanied me.
Our first visit was to the Saar. On October 3, in ruined Saarbrücken, Dr. Neureuther, president of the government, and M.
Heim, the burgomaster, informed me of the difficulties they were
struggling against. To them and to the other Saar officials and
prominent citizens, all evidently devoured by apprehension and
curiosity, I declared: "I shall deliberately not refer here to the
past events. But for the future's sake we must understand each
other, for there is much for us to accomplish together." Then I
indicated that our task consisted in re-establishing normal life and
eventually prosperity in the Saar. I concluded by expressing the
hope that "with the passing of time and the results of our collaboration, we French will discover excellent reasons for esteem

and confidence in the people of the Saar, and that the latter will realize, humanly speaking, how close we are to them. If this is the case," I added, "so much the better for the West and for Europe, of whom you, like ourselves, are the children." When I finished my address, I saw tears in the eyes of my auditors.

In Treves, I encountered the same spectacle of mute resignation and mountainous rubble. Yet the ancient Moselle city had preserved its characteristic aspect around the "Porta Nigra," which had emerged intact from the cataclysm. The local dignitaries, including the bishop, Monsignor Bornewasser, disclosed to me the extent of their demoralization. I delivered the same kind of speech I had made in Saarbrücken. "France," I said, "is not here to crush but to create a resurrection." That same evening, I visited Coblenz. M. Boden, president of the government, and the prominent citizens who surrounded him received from my lips the encouragements of France. Here, as elsewhere, these words were received with respect and emotion.

This was the case, the following day, in Mainz, where the crowd that received Charles de Gaulle was a large one. It was as if after centuries of terrible ordeals the souls of their Gallic and Frankish ancestors lived again in those present. The president of Hesse-Nassau, Dr. Steffan, the burgomaster, Dr. Kraus, and the bishop, Monsignor Stohr, alluded to this phenomenon in their speeches. I replied with words of hope, adding: "As we stand here, we proceed from the same race. And as we stand today, we are Europeans, men of the West. How many reasons for us to stand by one another henceforward!"

Reaching the terribly ravaged Palatinate, I was given a striking reception in Neustadt. Around the president, Dr. Eisenlaub, his adjutant, Dr. Koch, and the bishop, Monsignor Wendel, crowded district councilors, burgomasters, curés, pastors, professors, representatives of the bar, labor and management; all warmly applauded the head of their government when he declared that the territory desired to become what it had once been, that is, the Palatine

State, to take its destiny into its own hands and to ally itself with France.

Freiburg, in the Black Forest, received De Gaulle with every element representative of the regions we occupied on the right bank of the Rhine. On October 4, Dr. Wohleb presented to me the prominent citizens of Baden. On the morning of the fifth, M. Carlo Schmitt introduced those of Württemberg. Monsignor Groeber, Archbishop of Freiburg, as well as Monsignor Fisher of the diocese of Rotthausen, were among the visitors. Then these distinguished men, full of good will, gathered to hear me discuss "the bonds which once linked the French and the southern Germans and which must now reappear in order to reconstruct 'our' Europe and 'our' West." Upon which the hall burst into the most ardent cheers. In this surprising atmosphere I began wondering if so many battles fought and invasions endured for so many centuries by the two peoples struggling against each other, as well as so many fresh horrors committed to our detriment, were not merely bad dreams. How believe that the Germans had ever entertained toward the Gauls anything but this cordiality of which I was being offered such striking proofs? But when I left the ceremony to find myself again in the ruined streets amid a grief-stricken crowd, I could see what disaster this nation had had to endure in order to heed the counsels of reason at last.

Later that day, I went to Baden-Baden, where General Koenig had his headquarters. Here, all who directed some branch of the French administrative organization described the eagerness of the Germans to obey our directives and their desire for a reconciliation. One of the signs of this state of mind was the extraordinary success of the Franco-German University of Mainz, as well as the schools, *lycées* and study centers which we had just opened at various points. Leaving Germany that afternoon, I reached Strasbourg, intending to reveal from that city toward what great goal I was leading the French nation, provided it would follow me. Émile Bollaert, Commissioner of the Republic, Bernard Cornut-Gentille,

Prefect of the Bas-Rhin, and General du Vigier, the governor, escorted me here by the river. Having crossed the harbor, our boats entered the city through the canals whose banks and bridges were covered with a crowd manifesting incomparable spirit. I presided at the reopening of the University of Strasbourg, received the Alsatian authorities at the Palais du Rhin and finally, in the Place Broglie, from the balcony of the *hôtel de ville,* I addressed the populace.

"I am here," I said, "to proclaim the great task of the French Rhineland. Yesterday, the River Rhine, our river, was a barrier, a frontier, a line of battle. Today, now that the enemy has fallen as a result of our victory, now that the fevered affinities which once united the German states to such evil purpose have disappeared, the Rhine can resume the role which nature and history have assigned it. It can again become a western bulwark." And I exclaimed: "Consider this river! It bears upon its waters one of the greatest destinies in the world. From its source in Switzerland, through Alsace, the Moselle region, Baden, the basins of the Main and Ruhr, which are situated on its banks; across the Low Countries, where it flows into the seas not far from the coasts of England, ships can henceforth ply up and down upon it, and wealth spread freely from one end to the other. The same is true of ideas and influences, of all that proceeds from the mind, the heart, the soul . . . Yes, the link of western Europe is here, in the Rhine, which flows through Strasbourg!"

This conception of an organized group of western nations found an ardent hearing in Belgium. I realized this upon my visit. The Prince Regent had invited me there, and I reached Brussels in his own train on October 10, accompanied by Georges Bidault. At the station, where the Prince had come to meet me, I was struck by the popular acclaim which rolled over me like a tide. For two days in Brussels, which we spent visiting the royal palace, the Tomb of the Unknown Soldier, Ixelles, and Laeken—where we were received by the Queen Mother Elizabeth—the city hall, the

University, the Ministry of Foreign Affairs, the French *lycée,* and the French embassy, where Raymond Brugère was our host, each of our comings and goings was the occasion for enthusiastic ovations. It was evident that the Belgians identified their joy and hope with those of the French people.

Prince Charles told me as much, and I received his remarks with great consideration, in proportion to my esteem for him. Amid the bitter divisions which the question of the King—at the moment absent in Switzerland—provoked among the people and which rendered the Regent's situation extremely delicate, I saw this clear-thinking prince, firm in the exercise of his duties, safeguarding the throne and national unity, yet certain, though he made no mention of it, that he would not be given credit for it in any of the opposing camps. The ministers, particularly the robust Premier, M. van Acker, and the always well-informed and enterprising Minister of Foreign Affairs, M. Spaak, as well as the Presidents of the Assemblies, Messrs. van Cauwelaert and Gillon, and Cardinal van Roey, all addressed me in similar terms, for all believed that Europe would have been lost if France had not been present at the victory. As for the future, the vital interest of the establishment of close relations among the states of western Europe dominated every hope.

The next day, at the *hôtel de ville,* where Burgomaster Vandemeulebroek received us while a huge crowd filled the splendid square, and then at the University of Brussels, whose President Fredrichs and Dean Cox made me a *Doctor Honoris Causa,* I proclaimed my faith in the efficacy of an eventual association of all the peoples of Europe and, in the immediate present, "a western grouping having as its arteries the Rhine, the Channel, and the Mediterranean." On each occasion, this great French project was received by my audiences with transports of joy. Upon my return to Paris, I discussed it again at an enormous press conference.

Thus the idea was launched. Once the elections which were to take place in fifteen days had decided the question of our insti-

tutions and thereby of my future role, the appropriate proposals
would either be addressed by me to the other powers or would not.
But if this immense plan seemed to provoke the passionate attention of the other interested nations, I had the impression that the
French political leaders did not, in fact, greatly favor it. From the
day of the victory to that of the elections, not a single discussion
in the Consultative Assembly referred to these problems. Except
for vague formulas, the many congresses, party motions, and meetings mentioned virtually nothing relating to France's effect and influence on other nations. The press, of course, reported General
de Gaulle's speeches and journeys. But the goals the latter proposed gave rise to no campaign, nor even to any commentary, as
if what was at stake were beyond national interest. Everything
occurred as if my conviction that France had the opportunity to
play an independent role and my effort to lead her to do so received, among those preparing to represent the nation, an unex-
pressed esteem but a universal doubt.

I could not, moreover, overlook the fact that in order to realize
such a European policy we must have our hands free elsewhere.
If overseas territories cut themselves off from Metropolitan France,
or if our forces were engaged there, what consequence would we
have between the North Sea and the Mediterranean? Conversely, if
those territories remained associated with us, we would have every
opportunity for action on the continent! The age-old destiny of
France! Yet after what had happened on the soil of our African
and Asian possession, any attempt to maintain our Empire there
as it had been would be perilous, particularly when new nationalist
movements were springing up all over the world, with Russia and
America competing for their adherence. If the peoples for whom
we were responsible were to remain with France tomorrow, we
must take the initiative and transform a relation which at present
was merely one of dependency for them. On condition, of course,
that we remain firm, but insisting on loyalty to the word given it

as well. I had inaugurated this policy in Brazzaville. Now we would have to apply it in Indochina and in North Africa.

In the Maghreb, matters could still be arranged peacefully and gradually. Although signs of agitation were already appearing there, we were still in control of the situation. In Tunisia, the popularity of the former Bey Moncef provoked little beyond Platonic regrets; the two experienced "Destours" kept on the alert and Resident General Mast maneuvered readily between plans for reform and authoritative action. In Algeria, an insurrection begun in the Constantinois and synchronized with the Syrian riots in May was put down by Governor General Chataigneau. In Morocco, the proclamations spread by the "Istiqlal" and the parades it organized had little effect on the people; moreover, Sultan Mohammed V, after some hesitations and upon the pressing request of Resident General Puaux, had moreover repudiated such manifestations. But if we still had time, it was not time to waste. I took immediate action.

Sovereignty in the Empire of Morocco and in the Regency of Tunis was identified with their sovereigns. I therefore wished to deal with them directly. I invited the Sultan of Morocco to France and received him as a chief of state entitled to great honors and a loyal friend who had shown his worth in the most trying circumstances. In addition to the usual receptions, I requested him to stand beside me during the great military ceremony of June 18 in Paris, and awarded him the Cross of the Liberation. Later he accompanied me on a trip to Auvergne, receiving the cheers of enthusiastic crowds in the cities and the heartfelt welcome of the country people. He then visited Germany with the First Army and reviewed its splendid Moroccan troops. Finally, he visited our great hydroelectric installations. He was universally acclaimed, which created a favorable atmosphere for our personal encounters.

I asked the Sultan to express quite frankly his considered opinion as to the relations between France and Morocco. "I am profoundly aware," he declared, "that the protectorate has brought my country order, justice, a basis of prosperity, elementary education for the masses and the formation of an elite. But this regime was accepted by my uncle, Moulay-Hafid, then by my father, Moulay-Youssef, and is accepted today by me as a transition between the Morocco of the past and a free and modern state. After the recent events of this war, and before those that will occur tomorrow, I believe this is the moment to take a further step along this road. That is what my people are waiting for."

"The objective you envisage," I said, "is the one which France has adopted, which the Treaty of Fez and the Act of Algeciras formulate, and which Lyautey, the founder of modern Morocco, never ceased to pursue. Like yourself, I am convinced that we must modify in this direction the bases of our relationship. But as things stand now, such liberty can be only relative for anyone. Is this not particularly true of Morocco, which has still so much to accomplish before it can exist by its own means as a nation? It is France's duty to lend you her assistance, in return for your loyalty. Who else could do so honorably? When President Roosevelt jingled the marvels of independence before your Majesty at Anfa, what did he offer you beyond the cash and a place among his customers?"

"It is quite true," Mohammed V declared, "that the progress of my country must be accomplished with France's aid. Of all the powers that can lend us their support, France, best situated and best endowed, is the one we prefer. You have learned, during the war, that our aid, too, is not without its value. The result of the new agreements we could negotiate would be the contractual association of our countries from economic, diplomatic, cultural and military points of view."

I indicated to the Sultan that, pending actual terms, which must be closely studied, I agreed with him on all essential matters. As to a suitable date for opening negotiations, I proposed the day following the Fourth Republic's adoption of its own constitution. For surely the latter could not fail to define the federal or confederated links applicable to certain territories or states whose self-government and participation in a common structure must be provided for. I proposed to Mohammed V that we keep in personal touch concerning all matters that related to the union of our two countries, assuming, of course, that I remained in office. He acquiesced immediately and, I believe, enthusiastically. To begin with, the Sultan indicated his approval of my government's initiative in re-establishing at Tangier the Sherifian authority and the international status abolished in 1940 by a Spanish *coup de force*. This was achieved in September, following a Paris conference of French, English, American and Russian representatives whose settlements the Madrid government agreed to recognize.

In his turn, the Bey of Tunis came to France on my invitation. Sidi Lamine was the object of a reception as brilliant as the circumstances permitted. In Paris, on July 14, he attended the imposing review of our victorious Army. Many receptions and gatherings gave him the opportunity to see French leaders of all circles. During our conversations the sovereign made clear to me what, in his opinion, the Regency should become in order to correspond to the aspirations of its people and the demands of the times. In general, the Bey's notions coincided with the Sultan's. Sidi Lamine's tone, of course, was less clarion than that of Mohammed V because of a difference in age and temperament, as well as of a less assured popularity and the fact that he was speaking in the name of a kingdom weaker than Morocco. But the general tenor was the same, as was that of my reply. The Bey received it with great amity.

From the remarks exchanged with the Maghreb sovereigns, I drew the conclusion that it was possible and necessary to reach agreements of co-operation with both states that accorded with the demands of the time, agreements which, in a changing world, would settle the relations among our countries for at least a generation.

If North African questions appeared in a more or less encouraging light, affairs in Indochina offered the greatest difficulties. Since the liquidation of our military posts and our administration by the Japanese and the retreat into Chinese territory of our remaining free detachments, nothing was left of France's authority in Cochin China, Annam, Tonkin, Cambodia and Laos. The surviving soldiers were in captivity; the officials, interned; the private citizens, closely watched; all were subject to the most odious treatment. In the states of the French Union the Japanese had supported the native governments under their sway, while a resistance movement appeared, directed by Communists resolved to seek eventual independence. This league organized a clandestine government which was preparing to become public. The French were reduced to sending a small advance guard to Ceylon in view of the possibility that the Allies would agree to transport our expeditionary corps; we also organized a skeleton information service operating throughout Indochina and attempted to persuade the Chungking government and its American military advisors to facilitate the regrouping of our detachments retreating from Tonkin and Laos.

But the German capitulation determined the United States to bring an end to the Japanese conflict as well. In June their forces, advancing from island to island, had come close enough to Japanese territory to be able to effect a landing there. The Japanese fleet was swept from the seas by Nimitz's warships, and their aviation was too far reduced to hold its own against MacArthur's. In Tokyo, however, the party favoring war retained its influence. Yet it was with apprehension that the American President, military command and Congress envisaged the bloody conquest, foot by foot, cave by cave, of the territory of a people both valiant and made fanatical by its leaders. Consequently, we witnessed a singular reversal of Washington's attitude toward the value of French military aid. Early in July the Pentagon even asked us if we would be disposed to send two divisions to the Pacific. "It is not out of the question," I replied. "But in that case, we should also want to send the necessary forces to Burma to take part in the Indochinese offensive."

On June 15 I determined the composition of our Expeditionary Corps. General Leclerc was to take command, though I was obliged, on this occasion, to contravene his wishes. "Send me to Morocco," he asked me once. "You will go to Indochina," I told him, "because that is more difficult." Leclerc began to organize his units. By the beginning of August they were ready. It was with great enthusiasm that soldiers and officers alike prepared to restore the flag of France to the only one of her territories from which it had not yet reappeared.

Then, on August 6 and 10, the atom bombs were dropped on Hiroshima and Nagasaki. As a matter of fact, the Japanese had given indications, before the cataclysm, that they were prepared to make peace negotiations. But it was unconditional surrender the Americans demanded, certain as they were, following the success of the experiments conducted in New Mexico, that they would obtain it. Emperor Hirohito capitulated immediately following the destruction of the two cities. It was agreed that the treaty by which the Empire of the Rising Sun would surrender to its conquerors would be signed on September 2, in Yokohama harbor, on the battleship *Missouri*.

I must say that the revelation of the terrible weapons stirred me deeply. Certainly I had long been aware that the Americans were in the process of perfecting irresistible explosives by smashing the atom. But though I was not surprised, I was no less tempted to despair at the birth of means that made possible the annihilation of the human race. Yet these bitter visions could not keep me from taking advantage of the situation created by the bombs' effect. For the capitulation collapsed both the Japanese defense and the American veto which had kept us out of the Pacific. Indochina from one day to the next became accessible to us once again.

We were to waste no time returning there. Still, it was essential to do so as acknowledged participants in the victory. As soon as

Tokyo had shown its intention to negotiate, we had not failed to insist, in Washington, that the Allied reply bear the seal of France as well, which had been agreed to. Then, when Emperor Hirohito capitulated, it was agreed that the French command would receive the surrender along with the Allied chiefs. I delegated General Leclerc to the ceremony, and he signed the agreement on board the *Missouri*. Previously, on August 15, I had appointed Admiral d'Argenlieu as High Commissioner in Indochina.

The sending of troops was the condition on which everything else depended. Seventy thousand men had to be transported along with a great deal of material. This was a considerable undertaking, for we had to begin it in a period of demobilization and while we were maintaining an army in Germany. But it was essential, after yesterday's humiliating liquidation, that the arms of France give an impression of force and resolution. Moreover, a squadron consisting of the battleship *Richelieu,* already in those waters, the cruisers *Gloire, Suffren, Triomphant,* the transport vessel *Béarn,* and several smaller craft, all under Admiral Auboyneau's orders, would cover the Indochinese coast. Some hundred planes would operate in the skies over the Peninsula. Since the war's end permitted us to recover the freighters we had lent to the interallied pool, we could control their movements, despite generally inadequate tonnage, in such a way that in three months the entire Expeditionary Corps reached its destination 14,000 kilometers away. Yet however rapidly it had arrived, the situation was to be no less difficult.

There were one hundred thousand Japanese soldiers in Indochina. They had ceased fighting and were waiting to be reembarked. But at present they were fraternizing with the units of the league that was to become the "Vietminh." The latter emerged from the brush, proclaimed its independence, demanded the union of the "Three-Ky" and issued propaganda against the re-establishment of the French authority. In Tonkin, their political leader Ho Chi Minh and their military leader Giap, both Communists, formed a committee which assumed the appearance of a government. The Emperor Bao Dai had abdicated and now figured beside Ho Chi Minh as an "adviser." Our delegate to Tonkin, Jean Sainteny, landing at Hanoi on August 22, found the Vietminh authority established in the capital and on good terms with the Japanese there. Throughout Indochina the population which had recently seen the French lose face now appeared hostile toward our compatriots there. In Saigon on September 2, several of the latter were massacred despite the pacific efforts of Governor Cédile, who had been parachuted in on August 23. Famine complicated the political difficulties; for, since the disappearance of the French authority, supply services had been paralyzed. Lastly, the Allies, applying their pre-established plan for the occupation of the country—Chinese north of the 16th parallel, British south, American missions everywhere—had fatally compromised the effect which the immediate arrival of French troops and officials and the disarmament of the Japanese by our forces might have produced.

Naturally we did not consent to this triple foreign intrusion. Not that the presence of the British in Cochin China concerned us particularly, for we would manage to arrive there at the same time as they. Furthermore, the British Empire had its hands full in India, Ceylon, Malaya, Burma, Hong Kong, and it was so eager to allay the resentment provoked by the recent crisis in the Levant that we had every reason to believe it would agree to an imminent withdrawal of its forces. Which proved, as a matter of fact, to be the case. Then too, we regarded the presence in the area of United States personnel for the combined task of economic prospecting and political indoctrination as ungracious but, generally speaking, without great effect. On the other hand, the occupation of Tonkin, as well as of a large part of Annam and Laos, by General Lu Han's Chinese army threatened to have the gravest consequences; our political and administrative action would thereby be hampered for a long period; once the Chinese were established, when would they leave, and at what price?

Nevertheless, the Chungking government unceasingly lavished its assurances of good will upon us. In October 1944 Marshall Chiang Kai-shek, receiving Ambassador Pechkoff, assured him: "I promise you that we have no interest in Indochina. And if at any time we can help you restore French authority there, we shall do so gladly. Tell General de Gaulle that this is our policy. But let him also consider it as a personal commitment to him on my part." During my stay in Washington, in August, I received Mr. T. V. Soong, who happened to be in the city at the time. The Minister of Foreign Affairs of the Republic of China also made me formal declarations. On September 19, when the same Mr. Soong visited me in Paris, accompanied by Ambassador Tsien-Tai, and referred to the unfortunate behavior of General Lu Han's troops, the minister promised me that his government "would bring this state of things to a halt and withdraw its forces from Indochina." But whatever the intentions, not to mention the orders, of the central government, the fact of the matter was that Lu Han had established himself as master of Tonkin.

The arrival of our soldiers, the departure of the Japanese, the withdrawal of foreign troops—these conditions would have to be fulfilled for France to recover her status in Indochina. But above all, she had to know what she wanted to accomplish there. I could not, of course, determine my policy as long as the situation in the area remained as confused as it was. But I knew enough to be certain that our direct administration could not be re-established. Henceforth, our goal would be the association of the French Republic with each of the countries which constituted the Union. The agreements should be negotiated by accepting as interlocutors those who seemed best to represent the states and the population and without the exclusion of any member. This was the plan I had settled on.

In regard to Laos and Cambodia, the presence of solid dynasties dispelled all incertitude. But in Vietnam matters were much more complicated. I decided to proceed step by step, ordering Leclerc to gain footholds first in Cochin China and Cambodia. He would not proceed into Annam until later. As for Tonkin, his forces would not enter the area except on my orders, and I had no intention of giving them until the situation was clarified, the population thoroughly exasperated by the presence of the Chinese, and relations settled between Sainteny and Ho Chi Minh. High Commissioner d'Argenlieu received my instructions to proceed first to French India. It was from Chandernagor that he would gain an adequate perspective of the situation. Then, when the presence of our troops had produced some effect and his adjutants had returned to the various territories, he would install himself in Saigon, making all the necessary contacts from there.

Meanwhile, I was developing a secret plan which might prove effective. This was to provide the former Emperor Duy Tan means to reappear if his successor and relative Bao Dai proved, as seemed to be the case, a victim of the turn of events. Duy Tan, dethroned in 1916 by the French authority, retitled Prince Vin Sanh and transferred to Réunion, had nevertheless insisted during the Second World War on serving in our army, in which he received the rank of commander. The man possessed a strong character, and some thirty years of exile had not obliterated this sovereign's image from the soul of the Annamite people. On December 14, I received him in order to discuss with him, as one man to another, what we might accomplish together. But whoever the persons my government was obliged to deal with, I intended to go to Indochina myself to settle matters in due form when the time came.

But it was still far away. At present, our problem was primarily of a military order. On September 12, the first French troops, and on the thirteenth a British unit arrived in Saigon. Riots broke out in the city on the twenty-third, and several Europeans and Americans were killed by fanatics. Nevertheless, Allied forces, including a regiment of French soldiers and officers who had recently been prisoners of war, finally gained the upper hand. Jean Cédile obtained a truce and on October 5 General Leclerc entered the capital, acclaimed by 10,000 Frenchmen who had been exposed to many threats and insults for seven months. As the forces of our Expeditionary Corps landed, matters improved in Cochin China, where swift operations re-established law and order, and in Cambodia, where the ministers installed by the Japanese were replaced by appropriate officials. Moreover, the Japanese troops were gradually leaving the country, and Admiral Mountbatten was withdrawing the British forces as well. On October 31, the French High Commissioner was installed in the Norodom Palace.

In Indochina, France was now reappearing with suitable dignity. The problems, certainly, remained thorny ones, in a territory strewn with obstacles and beneath a sky heavy with storm clouds. But already there had been a complete change in regard to the terrible indigence that had damaged our prestige. Yesterday, we had apparently been definitely expelled from Hanoi, Pnompenh and Luangprabang. Today, no one doubted any longer that what had to be done could be done only with our co-operation.

In Europe, in Africa, in Asia, where France had suffered an unprecedented abasement, an astonishing recovery and an extraordinary combination of circumstances already offered her the opportunity to play a role in accord with her genius. Were these the beams of a new dawn or the last rays of the setting sun? The desire of the French themselves would decide that. For, if we were weakened, on the other hand the fall of our enemies, the losses suffered by our former competitors, the rivalry which opposed the two greatest states in the world to each other, and the universal desire to see France fulfill her mission, left us, for a time, a clear field.

As for myself, only too well aware of my limitations and my failings, certain that no man can substitute himself for a people, how I longed to implant in every Frenchman the same convictions that inspired me! The goals I proclaimed were difficult, but worthy of us. The road I pointed to was rough, but rose to the summits. Having made my appeal, I listened for the answering echoes. The murmurs of the multitude remained enthusiastic but confused. Perhaps the voices that were making themselves heard in the forum, from the tribunal of assemblies, the pulpit and in faculties and academies would support my own? In that case, there could be no doubt that the people were in accord with the spirit of their elite. I listened, but only to hear the scuffles of their circumspection. Yet what were these peremptory and conflicting cries that now resounded so noisily throughout the nation? Alas, nothing but the clamor of partisans.

CHAPTER 6

DISUNION

THE road to greatness lay open before us, but what condition France was in to follow it! While the reactions from every part of the globe, the conversations with statesmen, the ovations of foreign crowds conveyed the world's appeal to France, the graphs and statistics laid on my desk, the reports furnished by our services, the spectacle of devastation offered by our territory, the councils, where I heard our ministers describing the extent of our misery and the penury of our means, gave me the measure of our debilitation. No power now contested our right to play a major role in the world's destiny. But at home, France's condition was expressed in a balance sheet of ruins.

One third of our nation's wealth had been annihilated. In all forms, in all regions, devastations covered our territory. Naturally, that of buildings was the most spectacular. As a result of the battles of 1940, later the Allied bombings and finally the liberation itself, 500,000 buildings had been completely destroyed, 1,500,000 seriously damaged. It was the factories which had chiefly suffered, causing an additional delay in our economic recovery. We also lacked housing for six million Frenchmen. And what could be said of the ruined railway terminals, the lines cut, the bridges exploded,

933

the canals blocked, the harbors choked? The engineers whom I asked for an estimate of the time necessary to restore our edifices and communications replied, "It will take twenty years!" As for the land, a million hectares had been reduced to nonproductivity, spoiled by explosions, strewn with mines, pitted with entrenchments; fifteen million more yielded scarcely anything, since our farmers had been unable to cultivate them properly for five years. Everywhere there was a shortage of tools, fertilizers, plants and seeds. The livestock was reduced by half.

Though less apparent, the damages caused by theft were heavier still. We had been pillaged, so to speak, regularly. In the text of the "armistice," the Germans had specified that the "expenses of the occupation troops will be met by the French government." Under this rubric the enemy had laid hold of exorbitant sums, thanks to which he not only supported his armies, but also purchased (with our money) and shipped to Germany huge quantities of machinery and consumer goods. Further, a so-called "compensation agreement" had imposed on the French treasury the settlement of the differences between the value of the exports "freely made" to Germany and the cost of imports of coal and raw materials the Reich sent to France to supply the factories it was maintaining in operation for its own advantage. Since there were virtually no such exports and, on the other hand, such imports continued to be considerable, the "agreement" had been a terrible burden for us. In addition, all kinds of German purchases on the black market, partial requisitions, local fines, and qualified thefts had completed the spoliation of France. And how evaluate the millions of days of labor imposed on French workmen to the enemy's profit and diverted from our production, the lowering of physical value inflicted on our people by undernourishment, the fact that during five years everything in France had deteriorated without our being able to maintain, repair, renew? All in all, the occupation cost us more than 2,000 billion 1938 francs, that is, 80,000 billion today. Peace found our economy deprived of a large part of its means of production, our finances crushed beneath a colossal public debt, our budgets condemned to bear the enormous expenses of reconstruction for a long time.

This disappearance of our resources and instruments of labor was all the more ruinous in that it followed close upon the ravages of the First World War. The interval of twenty years between the end of the First and the start of the Second had not been long enough for us to recoup our lost wealth. In particular, the accumulated capital the French possessed in France and abroad before 1914 had evaporated, while the 500 million shells we fired from the Somme to the Vosges exploded over a period of fifty-one months. To reconstruct, afterward, all that had been destroyed, to pension off the wounded, widows and orphans, to pay the war's innumerable expenses, we had been forced to borrow continually, to devaluate our currency, to abandon renovation and modernization projects. In 1939, it was a poverty-stricken, outmoded France who entered the conflict; and in the course of the latest ordeal, a large share of what remained had been engulfed. To bind up her wounds and repair her ruins once again, she had only minimum reserves at her disposal and a cruelly reduced credit. How manage if we were reduced to our own poor means? How maintain independence if we had recourse to others?

In this as in all domains, what we lacked could be compensated for, up to a point, by human values. But our losses were heavy here too. More than 635,000 Frenchmen had died as a result of enemy action, 250,000 in combat, 160,000 in bombardments or executed by the occupiers, 150,000 victims of maltreatment in concentration camps, 75,000 as prisoners of war or forced laborers. Further, 585,000 men had become invalids. In relation to the total population, the percentage of French losses had not reached that of the Germans or the Russians. But it was higher than that of the British, the Italians, or the Americans. Most important, the losses suffered by our nation were relatively higher than the figures indicated. For it was among our scant youth that death had reaped this harvest. Again, during the First World War, twice the number of victims had fallen—that is, the highest proportion among all the belligerents—and at a period when our birth rate was the lowest in the world. In sum, the French people, their average age the highest among nations and their death rate the only one to exceed the birth rate since the beginning of the century, not yet having made good the losses of the preceding hecatomb, had just suffered an extremely critical amputation of its rare active elements. Indeed those it had lost were the most enterprising, the most generous, the finest of its number.

In addition, the diminution of substance and consequently of power inflicted upon France during two world wars had only accentuated the abasement she had suffered in the space of two human lifetimes. At the beginning of the last century—quite recently, in historical terms—our country was the most populous in Europe, the strongest and richest in the world, and her influence unequaled. But disastrous causes had combined to drive her from this dominant position and to start her down a slope where each generation saw her stumble lower. Mutilated of the territories nature intended her to have, grotesquely costumed in artificial frontiers, separated from a third of the population springing from her stock, France had been living for a hundred and thirty years in a chronic state of infirmity, insecurity and acrimony. When the economic capacity of the great nations depended chiefly on coal, France had virtually none. Subsequently, when petroleum controlled everything else, France had been without any supply of her own. During the same period population doubled in England, tripled in Germany and in Italy, quadrupled in Russia, decupled in America; in France it remained stationary.

This physical decline went hand in hand with a moral depression. The disasters which put an end to Napoleon Bonaparte's attempt at hegemony and later the defeat inflicted upon the nation by the might of Prussia and her German satellites had submerged the French beneath such waves of humiliation that henceforth they were to doubt themselves. Certainly the 1918 victory revived their faith, for a moment. But it cost so dear and bore fruits so bitter that such hopes died at once under the shock of 1940. The soul of France died a little more. Thanks to the wakening of the resistance and to the miracle of our victory, it still survived, but lame and, so to speak, sclerotic. Moreover, so many disasters had not failed to inflict terrible wounds upon national unity. Fifteen regimes had supervened since 1789, each in turn installed by revolution or *coup d'état,* none succeeding in insuring equilibrium, all swept away by catastrophes and leaving ineffaceable divisions behind them.

And today I was at the head of a ruined, decimated, lacerated nation, surrounded by ill will. Hearing my voice, France had been able to unite and march to her liberation. She had subsequently accepted such order until the war was over. Meanwhile, the nation had gladly received the reforms which spared it social strife and permitted its recovery. Lastly, it had permitted me to carry out the foreign activity which assured the recovery of its status. This was a great step, in relation to the disasters that had almost engulfed us. But it was minuscule in comparison to all that we must achieve before recovering our power, without which we would ultimately lose even our reasons to exist.

I had conceived a plan which was nothing more than common sense. First, we must procure what we had so long lacked in respect to sources of energy. As for coal, union with the Saar, now virtually accomplished, and the annual fifty million tons we were about to obtain from the Ruhr would afford us twice what our own mines produced. As for petroleum, there was every likelihood that the research group we had just established would discover reserves in the immense French possessions, since we had territories in each of the world's major geographical groups. As for the nascent atomic energy production, the resources of uranium which seemed abundant in our territories, as well as our scientific and industrial capacities, offered us an opportunity of reaching an exceptional level. The High Commission created to this effect was to get the project under way. Further, and whatever our actual penury, a careful policy of modernization and supply would replace our outmoded machinery. The High Commission on Planning had charge of this task. But of all our projects, those tending to increase the population were the most necessary; the measures already taken—assistance to families, allowances—would henceforth produce their effects. Finally, the social harmony to be established by the association of capital, labor and technology, the national independence maintained in any event, could cause a climate favorable to pride and effort to prevail in France.

Our country was in a position to achieve these goals if it remained united and the state led it forward. For how could it advance if it were divided against itself, if it were not guided in its progress by an authentic government? Yet, as France became free again, I realized with chagrin that her political forces were making great efforts to divide her and that on various levels everything was attempting to sever the nation from me.

I had every apparent justification for prolonging the sort of monarchy which I had recently assumed and which the general consent had subsequently confirmed. But the French people was itself, and not any other; if it did not desire such a regime nothing could impose it. To what upheavals would I condemn France by claiming to impose my absolute authority officially and for an unlimited period, once the danger which had put it into my hands had vanished? During the conflict, my declarations had deliberately left no doubt as to my resolution to restore its power to the French people once events would permit elections. If my power had been increasingly recognized, it was to a large degree because of this commitment. To refuse to fulfill it now would stamp my mission with a fraudulent seal. But it would also gradually turn against me the nation which would no longer distinguish the reasons for this despotic action; the Communists, then at the peak of their energy and influence, would gain control of the opposition and simultaneously designate themselves as my necessary successors.

Opposition would be all the more certain since, save in periods of public danger, there can be no such thing as a lasting dictatorship, unless a single faction, resolved to overpower the rest, supports it against all comers. As the champion of France rather than of any class or party, I incited hatred against no one and had no clientele who favored me in order to be favored in return. Even the men of the resistance, if they remained emotionally loyal to the ideal that once united them, had already, to a large degree, abandoned me politically and split into various factions. Only the Army could furnish me the means of controlling the country by constraining the recalcitrant elements. But this military omnipotence, established by force in peacetime, would soon appear unjustifiable to adherents of every tendency.

Fundamentally, what was, what could be dictatorship's resource if not great national ambition or the fear of a people imperiled by foreign powers? France had had two empires. She acclaimed the first when she felt capable of dominating Europe and when she was exhausted by disorder and confusion. She consented to the second in her desire to efface the humiliation of treaties which had sealed her defeat and in the agony recent social upheavals had forced upon her. Yet how had each of these Caesarean regimes ended? Today, no conquest, no revenge tempted our citizens; the mass of the people feared neither invasion nor revolution. Public safety was now a *fait accompli,* and I had no desire to maintain the momentary dictatorship which I had exercised in the course of the storm and which I would not fail to prolong or resume if the nation were in danger. Therefore, as I had promised, I would let the people make their choice in a general election.

Yet even as I dismissed the notion of my own despotism, I was no less convinced that the nation required a regime whose power would be strong and continuous. The parties were evidently unqualified to provide such power. Apart from the Communists, who intended to dominate by any means whatever, whose government would ultimately be infiltrated by an alien organization, who would find in France the resolute support of a portion of the population and of the Soviets abroad, but who would bring France to servitude, I observed that no political formation was in a position to assure the leadership of the nation and of the state. Although some among them could obtain the votes of an important fraction of the citizens, not a single one was thought of as representing public interest as a whole. Each would gather only the voices of a minority, and many electors would vote not so much *for* one party as *against* the others. In short, no organization commanded either the power or the credit which would permit it to lay claim to national authority.

To the parties' fractional character, which infected them with weakness, was added their own decadence. The latter was still concealed beneath rhetoric, but the doctrinal passion which was once their source, their attraction and their greatness could not be maintained in a period of materialism so indifferent to ideals. No longer inspired by principles, no longer ambitious to proselytize since they found no audiences on these grounds, they were inevitably tending to degradation, shrinking until each became nothing more than the representation of a category of interests. If the government fell into their hands again, it was certain that their leaders, their delegates and their militant members would turn into professionals making a career out of politics. The conquest of public functions, of influential positions, of administrative sinecures would henceforth absorb the parties and limit their activities to what they called tactics, which was nothing more than the practice of compromise and denial. Since all were minority representatives, they would have to share the positions of command with their rivals in order to accede to them at all. As a result they would proceed by giving themselves the lie in relation to the electorate. While the constant juxtaposition, within the government, of conflicting groups and men could result only in impotence.

As for me, considering France's immediate political realities and the extent and difficulty of the state's task, I had determined what the desirable institutions had to be; to realize them, I had naturally taken into account the lessons of our recent disaster, still so painful, as well as my experience of men and affairs, and lastly the role which events enabled me to play in the establishment of the Fourth Republic.

As I saw it, the state must have a head, that is, a leader in whom the nation could see beyond its own fluctuations, a man in charge of essential matters and the guarantor of its fate. It was also necessary that this executive, destined to serve only the national community, not originate in the parliament which united the delegations of particular interests. These conditions implied that the chief of state not belong to a party, that he be designated by the people, that he be empowered to appoint the Cabinet, that he possess the right to consult the nation, either by referendum or by election of assemblies, that he receive, finally, the mandate of insuring the integrity and independence of France in case of danger. Beyond those circumstances when it would be the President's duty to intervene publicly, government and parliament would collaborate, the latter controlling the former and authorized to cause its fall, but the national magistrate exercising his arbitration and having recourse to that of the people.

I could not overlook the fact that my project contradicted the claims of every party. None among them, whether by conviction or precaution, had as yet dared to oppose De Gaulle. Some who already expressed criticism and admonishment still refrained from challenging him outright. The Communists themselves, while brandishing trumpets and drums, were careful not to cross swords with me. But it was clear that in the crucial debate that was approaching, discord was inevitable. With various qualifications, all the parties intended the future constitution to re-create a regime whose powers would depend directly and exclusively on themselves and in which De Gaulle would have no place, unless he were willing to be merely a figurehead. In this regard, the lessons of the past, the realities of the present, the threats of the future had absolutely no effect on their point of view and their demands.

That the Third Republic had constantly failed to achieve equilibrium, finally collapsing in an abyss of capitulation, gave each party reasons to attack the others in its own behalf, but not the necessity to abjure the same weaknesses. That France could not re-establish herself without the cohesion of her people, the abnegation of factions, and the leadership of a recognized and continuous authority was a principle altogether alien to their universe. For them, on the contrary, it was a matter of opposing all competitors, of provoking those passions and claims by which they could support themselves, of seizing power not so much to serve the entire nation as to fasten their own particular program to it. That De Gaulle, having succeeded in uniting the nation and leading it to salvation, should now be kept at its head was not the way they envisioned the future, though they were careful to lavish their praises upon him now. For tomorrow, they conceded, his withdrawal could not occur without certain transitions. They even attempted to create some sort of decorative position to which he could be relegated. Yet none of them supposed that leadership could long remain in the hands of a person whose mere presence was evidently incompatible with their regime.

Nonetheless, though I did not expect the spontaneous support of the parties, it seemed conceivable to me that the nation's instinct and the confidence it had hitherto accorded me were sufficiently manifest to oblige the "politicians" to swim with the current. It was my task to sound out French opinion as to whether the state should be constructed as I proposed. If they responded affirmatively, the parties would adapt themselves to it, and the new Republic would have my participation. If not, I would not fail to draw the consequences.

But if I had always intended that the people should ultimately make the decision, I felt no less doubt and anxiety as to the result.

For was this people, beneath the moving proofs of affection it lavished upon me which nevertheless expressed its distress as much as its affection—was this people not exhausted, discouraged, divided? And as for these enormous enterprises, this vigorous action, these strong institutions which I proposed to its effort, did they not exceed its means and its desires? And I myself—had I the capacity, the skill, the eloquence necessary to galvanize them, when everything was sinking into mediocrity? Yet, whatever the nation's eventual answer to the question which would be put to it, it was my duty, while I waited, to govern with all the authority it had accorded me.

Actually, during the first days after the German surrender, it was possible to believe in a renewal of political unity around me. For the moment, the press spared me no praise. On May 15 the Consultative Assembly enthusiastically cheered my speech on the lessons the war had taught us. Prominent personalities outdid themselves in demonstrative gestures in my behalf. This was particularly the case among the former presidents of the Council of State whom the Germans had held as hostages and who now returned to their country. The first action of Messrs. Paul Reynaud, Daladier, and Sarraut was to assure me of their devoted adherence. The moment Léon Blum was free, he declared: "France revives, thanks to General de Gaulle! We have had the luck to have a General de Gaulle. Deep in my prison, I have always hoped my party could support him. All of France had every confidence in him. His presence is an irreplaceable guarantee of our nation's concord."

Édouard Herriot, liberated by the Russians and passing through Moscow, broadcast a similar message: "My conviction is that the nation is concentrated around Charles de Gaulle, under whose orders I place myself without reserve." But these gestures and these words were not to have any consequences.

As a matter of fact, it was now partisan and electoral concerns which dominated French public life. The renewal of the municipalities served them as a primary aliment, for in its effort to set the democratic machinery in motion again, the government had decided to begin with the communes. The municipal councils, elected in 1937, had been subject to Vichy's arbitrary interventions and to the upheavals of the liberation. They now returned to their source, the suffrage of the citizens. Although many local contingencies influenced the ballotings of April 29 and May 13, the dominant tendencies were nevertheless evident. Those members of the strongly hierarchized parties claiming to be the "movement" —Communists, Socialists, Popular Republicans—won many votes and seats to the detriment of the various moderate and radical groups. The two categories of Marxists united for the voting. Lastly, all tendencies played up those candidates who had played an active part in the struggle against the enemy, and the electorate enthusiastically confirmed this preference.

The conflict had therefore modified the distribution of votes, without, however, changing the nature of any French party or instigating a truly new current. In general, public opinion tended increasingly to fractionate according to particular claims and disputes rather than unite for a great national undertaking. In this atmosphere of rivalry, it was of course the Communists who set the tone and gained the ascendancy. Further, the electoral campaign had shown that as far as the nation's future institutions were concerned, only two ideas interested the "politicians." Radicals and moderates advocated the return to the constitution of 1875. The others proclaimed their desire to obtain "a single and sovereign Assembly." But over and above these divergencies, all demanded that the parties control the state as before, without any restrictions. There was no observer who did not therefore conclude that such would be tomorrow's results, if necessary without De Gaulle's presence. If, as Clemenceau remarks, "the soul's worst agony is to endure cold," it was evident that the atmosphere in which I was to function, during the months that followed, would be more painful for me every day.

The municipal elections were not yet over when the prisoners of war, the deported citizens, and the forced-labor groups began to return. A great national event, charged with emotions, with joys, but also with tears! In a few weeks, the nation, its families and its cities recovered two and a half million of their sons, who were the dearer for being the most wretched. This *"grand retour"* posed many grave problems for the government. It was not simple to transport to France, then to restore to their homes such a great number of men, presenting themselves in impatient waves. It was perplexing to find means to feed and dress them decently, when the country was cruelly short of supplies and clothing. It was difficult to reintegrate them immediately and simultaneously into the national activity, still functioning at a retarded rate. It was not easy to hospitalize, nurse and re-educate all those sick, wounded or handicapped. Yet since the Reich's defeat immediately liberated all the Frenchmen held in Germany, the questions concerning them had to be settled at once.

This tremendous operation had been foreseen and prepared for. The Ministry of Prisoners, Deportees and Refugees, created in Algiers in 1943, had taken steps long in advance in order to direct it as well as possible. The men had to be regrouped in Germany and their transport organized. This was relatively easy in the French Army zone. It was less so in those of the British and American armies. It was complicated in the Russian zone, for the Russians were distant and suspicious, and insisted on the observance of every formality, for they were in the process of moving the inhabitants of whole provinces. Nevertheless, an agreement immediately drawn up in Leipzig had provided for the co-operation of the various military commands. There were serious disappointments only in regard to the young Alsatians and Lorrainers forcibly incorporated into the Wehrmacht, captured by the Russians and now classified as Germans in every prison camp in Russia. Our Ambassador General Catroux and his military mission in Moscow had difficulty making contact with these men, establishing their identity, and obtaining their repatriation. Some were not found until much later. Some did not return at all.

However, by June 1, that is, three weeks after the movements had begun, the first million of our liberated men reached the French border. A month later, the majority of the captives had returned to their country. Received as well as possible in the hospital centers, supplied with a sum of money and demobilized, they resumed their place in a country lacking in everything but whose sons had never been needed so much.

Despite these steps, the return of a group this size and in such a short time could not be accomplished without mishap. Moreover, it was occasionally disappointment and disillusion which awaited those returning after an absence of such length. Then too, life was hard, though in the miseries of captivity it had been dreamed of differently. Lastly, some of those who behind barbed wire had imagined a renewed France were saddened by the moral mediocrity and the national atony in which too many Frenchmen were steeped. To offset this acrimony was an obligation in the nation's highest interest, but partisan rivalry sought to exploit it. In this competition, the Communists naturally emerged victorious.

Utilizing calculation and rancor alike, they had taken under their influence the "National Movement of Prisoners," which opened its battle against the Minister of Prisoners, Henri Frenay. In addition to the insulting motions the "Movement" published in the papers and the speeches its orators delivered, it attempted to organize demonstrations in public places and in the hospital centers. The ceremonies inspired by the return of the prisoners, particularly the men deported for resistance activities, were so many opportunities for the "Movement" to call out its noisy gangs. In Paris itself, parades were formed, filing down the boulevards and through the Avenue Foch under the windows of the Ministry of Prisoners, marching to cries of "Down with Frenay!" In their ranks marched the men who had donned for the occasion the striped clothes of the concentration camp martyrs. Certainly the huge majority of the repatriated men took no part in such scandalous incidents. But the instigators hoped that the government would turn the police against the demonstrators and excite popular indignation, or else yield to the threat and sacrifice the vilified minister. As for the other political factions, they observed this display of demagogy without furnishing the government the slightest support.

Nevertheless, the matter was soon settled. I summoned the leaders of the "Movement" to my office. "What is happening," I told them, "is intolerable. I demand that it come to an end, and it is you who must see that it does."

"These events," they assured me, "are an explosion of the prisoners' justified outrage. We ourselves cannot prevent them."

I declared, "Public order must be maintained. Either you are impotent to deal with your own men, and in that case you must forthwith indicate the fact to me in writing and announce your resignation; or you are truly the leaders, in which case you will give me your formal promise that all agitation will be stopped today. If, before you leave this building, I have not received either the letter of resignation or the promise, you will be arrested as you leave my office. I can allow you only three minutes to decide."

The leaders conferred together in the window niche and returned at once. "We will do as you say. We guarantee that the demonstrations will cease." Which proved to be the case that very day.

This affair proved that authority remained strong so long as it was not divided, but also that the "politicians" were not inclined to support it. I made a similar discovery in regard to the financial and economic question. This rose again, and sharply, during the summer following the victory. Since it was impossible to avoid this problem, and since, too, the measures to be taken concerned the interests of the electors so closely, I expected that the parties would permit my government to do what was necessary, taking whatever advantage of the situation they could; which was, in effect, what happened.

We were faced with the simultaneous tasks of procuring ex-

ceptional resources for the treasury, opposing inflation and restraining the rise of prices. This was indeed the perpetual problem
in a period when public expenditures inevitably increased, when
the cessation of hostilities provoked among the people a general
tendency to consume more, and when production was still far
from reaching a satisfactory level. The arrangements made during
the aftermath of the liberation had permitted us to avoid the
worst. Now we must make a new effort. But in any case, there
would be many discomforts for all, and heavy sacrifice for some.
Given the imminence of the general elections, I might have postponed decisions for several weeks, so that the responsibility
would be shared by the future National Assembly. Expedients
would have sufficed, but they would have been costly. I decided
not to wait, and to take the steps leading to recovery on my government's responsibility alone.

The first of these was the exchange of bank notes. The operation's chief purpose was to reveal the wealth of each Frenchman.
Already the administration knew the value of holdings in real
estate, income stocks and bonds. It remained to discover the distribution of the mass of bonds payable to the bearer—bank notes
and short-term bonds. The owners had to present and thereby
declare their holdings. These were replaced, franc for franc, by
new notes. The currency not exchanged, particularly that which the
Germans had taken with them and that which its possessors preferred to lose rather than to admit *in toto,* immediately became
null and void. Further, the owners of immense sums in bank notes
frequently chose to convert them into bonds, since the aggregate
of their fortune would henceforth be known.

All proceeded extremely smoothly, from June 4 to 15, under
Pleven's direction. Nothing, in French economic life, offered an
analogy to the severe shock which a similar operation, though one
involving the blocking of credits, had produced in Belgium. The
fiduciary circulation, which rose to 580 billion francs at the end
of May, reached only 444 billion by July. But this "photography"

of taxable matter was also to permit the government to establish on a firm basis the extraordinary contribution it intended to levy.

Until it did so, it would have to keep prices from rising to excess. Though it had not adopted the extremely rigorous plan proposed by Mendès-France, though it had not officially suppressed three quarters of the currency and definitively frozen wages and prices—in short, though it had not attempted to achieve immediate and decisive results at the risk of breaking the nation's incentive to activity, the government was no less resolved to construct dikes against the rising flood. In any case, stabilization could not be realized before the supply of products corresponded to the demand, which would not be the case for a long time. But we had the means to prevent brutal shocks and to punish abuses. The two decrees of June 30 codified what was necessary; one established the procedure by which the authorities fixed or modified prices, the other controlled the way infractions were dealt with. These decrees, immediately applied, are still in effect today.

Whatever my government's concern to spare the scarcely convalescent nation and to effect changes gradually, we had to establish the 1945 budget and provide means of maintaining that of 1946. Since it was impossible to renew the "liberation loan" and dangerous to increase our short-term debt, we decided to have recourse to a special levy. The decree of August 15 instituted the "solidarity tax," intended to meet the exceptional expenses involved in the return of the prisoners, the demobilization and repatriation of the troops, the transport of the Expeditionary Corps to Indochina, and the initial reconstruction costs. We had set at 80 billion francs—900 billion today—the resources to be obtained, and determined that they would be furnished by those who possessed capital. Who else could do so? Were they not, moreover, those chiefly interested in the equilibrium of the nation's finances, as they had been in the re-establishment of law and order and the maintenance of social peace? Quite simply, the decree prescribed a levy on inheritance, a tax on war profits, a contribution from corporate funds, the whole constituting an "exceptional tax for national solidarity."

The Consultative Assembly was to give its opinion of the project. The parties, during the discussion which took place on July 15, spared us no criticism; those of the Left, by the voices of Messrs. Philip, Moch, Duclos and Ramette, proclaiming that the government was not going far enough in the direction of the amputation of private capital; those of the Right, whose grievances were expressed by Messrs. Laniel and Denais, insisting that the projected levy would do incalculable damage to the course of business. Nevertheless, when the matter was put to a vote, the text was approved almost unanimously. This was to be the last time the Assembly moved to follow the government. Soon the discussions relative to the constitution would set it openly and entirely in opposition.

Meanwhile, I had insisted that the painful affair of Pétain, Laval, and Darnand be settled, for it occupied everyone's mind and continued to inspire antagonism and anxiety. Without actually intervening in the High Court's handling of the case, the government had informed that body of its desire to see the proceedings conclude as soon as possible. The trials were therefore opened, beginning with that of the Marshal. There had been predictions on all sides that the result would provoke profound upheavals. No such thing occurred. Certainly, the men who took part in the melancholy sessions, whether as magistrates, jurors, witnesses or lawyers, could not always contain their emotion or their excitement. But the disturbances never went beyond the walls of the Palais de Justice. Certainly the public followed the sessions with tense interest, as they were reported, in abbreviated form, in the newspapers. But there was no mass demonstration of any sort whatever. The nation, in fact, considered it necessary that justice render its decision, and for the immense majority the result was inevitable.

I shared this point of view, yet what seemed to me essential in the arraignment was not regarded as such in the eyes of many. For me, the capital error of Pétain and his government had been to conclude with the enemy, in the name of France, the so-called "armistice." Certainly, at the time this was signed the battle in Metropolitan France had been indisputably lost. To cease fire between the Atlantic and the Alps, to bring the debacle to an end would have been entirely justified as a military and local action. The command of the forces concerned was responsible to the government until its leadership had changed. That government might have reached Algiers, taking with it the treasure of French sovereignty which for fourteen centuries had never been surrendered, continuing the battle, keeping its word to the Allies, and demanding their aid in return. But to have retired from the war with the Empire intact, the fleet untouched, the air force largely undamaged; to have withdrawn our African and Levantine troops without a single soldier lost; to have abandoned all those forces which, in France herself, could be transported elsewhere; to have broken our alliances; above all, to have submitted the state to the Reich's discretion—this is what had to be condemned in order to clear France of the stigma. All the faults Vichy had been led to commit subsequently—collaboration with the invaders; hostilities in Dakar, Gabon, Syria, Madagascar, Algeria, Morocco and Tunisia against the Free French or the Allies; combat against the resistance in direct liaison with the German troops and police; surrender of French political prisoners, Jews and aliens seeking refuge in France to Hitler; assistance, in the form of forced labor, raw material and propaganda, to the enemy's war machine—all flowed inevitably from this poisoned spring.

Consequently I was irritated to see the High Court, the parliamentary circles and the newspapers abstain to a large degree from excoriating the "armistice" and instead concentrate in detail and at length on facts which were accessory to it. Further, they emphasized those facts which related to the political struggle rather than to that of the nation against the enemy at its gates. Too often, the discussions assumed the nature of a partisan trial, even, on occasion, of a settling of accounts, whereas the matter should have been treated only from the point of view of national defense and independence. The old conspiracies of the Cagoulards, the dispersion of the parliament after its abdication, the detention of its members, the Riom trial, the oath demanded of the magistrates and officials, the labor charter, the anti-Semitic decrees, the persecution of Communists, the mistreatment of parties and trade unions, the campaigns led by Maurras, Henriot, Luchaire, Déat, Doriot, etc. before and during the war—all this took up more place and time, during the discussions and commentaries, than the regime's capitulation, its betrayal of our Allies, and its collaboration with the invader.

Philippe Pétain, during his trial, shrouded himself in silence. Given his age, his exhaustion, and the fact that what he had shielded was indefensible, his attitude seemed to me one of discretion. By remaining silent, he accorded a kind of final consideration to the military dignity in which his former great services had cloaked him. The facts cited, the testimonies given, the prosecution's summary and address made it clear that his had been the drama of a senility lacking the strength necessary to lead men and control events. Beneath the appearance of firmness, behind the screen of subterfuge, the Marshal was only a victim served up to servile or threatening intrigues. The court pronounced a sentence of capital punishment but at the same time expressed the decision that there be no execution. I was, moreover, determined to sign a reprieve whatever the result. Furthermore, I had taken the necessary steps to withdraw the Marshal from the insults which threatened to assail him. Scarcely was the judgment pronounced, on August 15, than he was flown to Portalet. Later he was confined on the Île d'Yeu. My intention was that after having two years' detention in fortified captivity, he would finish his days in retirement in his home near Antibes.

Pierre Laval next appeared before his judges. At the time of the

Reich's capitulation, a German plane had taken him to Spain, where he counted on finding a refuge. But General Franco had had him arrested and flown back to German territory. Perhaps the fugitive hoped for some appeal from the United States? In vain! The American Army handed him over to the French authorities, and in October the head of the Vichy government appeared before the High Court.

At first Laval attempted to account for his behavior not as a deliberate collaboration with the Reich, but as the stratagem of a statesman compromising with the worst in order to limit its depredations. Since the jurors were yesterday's or tomorrow's parliamentarians, the accused could hope the discussion would turn into a political debate, opposing various professional theories, and resulting in a state of contention which would ultimately get him off with "extenuating circumstances." This tactic, however, had no effect on the tribunal. Realizing this, Laval played all or nothing, adopted a provocative attitude with regard to his judges, and manipulated them into several unfortunate name-calling sessions. Immediately taking this irregular behavior as his pretext, he refused to appear again before the Court. Thus he attempted to surround his trial with an aura of irregularity so that justice would either have recourse to some new trial or commute the sentence of capital punishment which Laval guessed was inevitable and which was, in fact, pronounced. However, he obtained neither revision nor reprieve. In a supreme attempt to avoid execution, the condemned man took poison, but was revived. Then, all avenues of escape barred, Pierre Laval stood up, walked straight to the scaffold and died bravely.

A few days before, Joseph Darnand had suffered the same condemnation and been put to death without showing any more weakness than Laval. His trial was brief. The accused bore the responsibility of a large number of crimes committed by Vichy in the name of order. The former "secretary general" invoked in his defense only the service of the Marshal. The doctrinal aspects of

National Socialism had certainly attracted Darnand's intellect, exasperated by low motives and the ideological flabbiness of his milieu. But above all, this man of energy and resolution had regarded collaboration as a thrilling adventure which justified every audacity and every means. Had the occasion presented itself, he would have accepted other inducements in the contrary direction, as was proved by his exploits at the war's beginning, at the head of his guerrilla groups, and also by the fact that even wearing the uniform of a German officer and covered with the blood of resistance fighters, he had sent me his request to join Free France. Nothing revealed more dramatically than the behavior of this great adventurer the surrender of a regime which had alienated from the nation men born to serve it.

The condemnation of Vichy in the person of its leaders detached France from a policy which had been one of national renunciation. It was still essential that the nation deliberately adopt the opposite course. During the years of oppression, it was faith and hope in France which had gradually led the French toward resistance and liberation. The same motives had later functioned to prevent subversion and make recovery possible. Today, no others would have any effect, from the moment we hoped to advance toward power and greatness. If this state of mind prevailed in the masses, the future National Assembly would certainly be influenced by it. Until the date of the elections, I was consequently to do everything possible in order to inspire the country with a quality of ardor in its effort and confidence in its destiny.

On May 9, immediately after the victory, I went to Notre Dame for the ceremonial *Te Deum*. Cardinal Suhard received me beneath the portal. The entire official body was there, while a huge throng filled the building and overflowed around it. While the hymn of victory echoed through the vaults and a kind of vibration rising from those present swept toward the portico, the quais, and the streets of Paris, as I stood in my traditional place in the choir, I was stirred by those same feelings which had exalted our fathers each time glory had crowned our nation. Unable to forget the tragedies that offset our triumphs, or the obstacles that rose in the nation's path this very day, there was, in this perenniality, substance to support our courage. Four days later, the feast day of Joan of Arc provided a similar occasion for patriotic fervor. This was the first time in five years that we were able to celebrate it according to the traditional ceremonies.

Yet on May 24 I broadcast to the French people an austere address, couched in severe terms. I spoke of our losses, our duties, the sacrifices it would cost "to become what we desire to be—that is, prosperous, powerful and fraternal." I indicated how difficult a task it would be to re-establish France "in her place in a universe not easily influenced." I declared that "our capacity to work and to produce and the spectacle of order that we must present in political, social and moral realms are the conditions of our independence and, even more, of our influence. For there is no influence in confusion, nor progress in chaos." We would therefore have to expect the government to control prices, wages, salaries, whatever the inconvenience of such steps and the opposition to them. This rigor would be accompanied, moreover, by various reforms. I announced that before the year's end, the state would "appropriate the production of coal, electricity, and the distribution of credit, levers of command which will permit it to orient the whole of the nation's activity." Further, new measures concerning the nation's population would be applied in view of the same goal —to re-establish France's power. I compared the French to Christopher Columbus' sailors who sighted land on the horizon when they were at the worst moment of their fear and their fatigue. And I exclaimed, "Only look up! Beyond the sacrifices and the mists of the present, a magnificent future is ours!"

With the same intention of charging the atmosphere with electricity, on June 10 I visited the departments of the Manche and the Orne, which with Calvados were the most ravaged of all. Accompanied by Dautry, I visited St.-Lô, Coutances, Villedieu-les-

Poêles, Mortain, Flers, Argentan, and Alençon, as well as many smaller towns. A flood of joyous recognition broke over the ruins. On June 18, all Paris was on its feet to greet the troops from Germany which paraded down the Champs Élysées with Leclerc and Béthouart at their head. Among the delighted soldiers, the people weeping for joy, and De Gaulle standing at the center of the ceremony, passed that magical current activated by a great and mutual emotion. On June 30 and July 1 I traveled through the Auvergne, which in its sober cities of Clermont-Ferrand, Riom and Aurillac, as in its scattered villages, proved as enthusiastic as the capital had been.

The national elections were approaching, having been planned for the month of October. Consequently I hastened the manifestations. The one in Paris on July 14 was suitably marked by an impressive military parade. But this time, the triumphal march took place from east to west. General de Lattre presented to me, in the Cours de Vincennes, detachments furnished by all the major units of his victorious army. Then the general and the combatants of the "Rhine and Danube" paraded beneath a storm of cheers and a riot of flags through the Avenue du Trône, la Nation, and the Faubourg St.-Antoine to march before me in the Place de la Bastille.

The following week I went to Brittany, accompanied by Pleven and Tanguy-Prigent. But it was at Brest, Lorient and St.-Nazaire, all in ruins, that popular sentiment was the most affecting. I then proceeded to La Rochelle, liberated without excessive damage and already functioning as a port.

Picardy and Flanders next demonstrated to me that their faith in the future was of a sort to surmount all obstacles. At Beauvais, then in Amiens, where I was received on August 11, accompanied by Dautry, Lacoste, Laurent, and Mayer, every voice was raised in the concert of enthusiasm. Through Doullens, St.-Pol and Bruay I reached Béthune where 50,000 miners awaited me before the *hôtel de ville*. From the balcony I addressed them and the nation.

"We have been," I declared, "among the most afflicted because we were the most exposed. But we are in the process of effecting an extraordinary recovery, and I declare with great French pride, that we are swiftly marching toward the moment when it will be said of us, 'They came through!' " Then I cited the figures. In regard to coal, during the month following the liberation of the pits, the miners of France had produced a million and a half tons; yet in the course of the last four weeks, they had mined double that amount. In regard to electricity, we had advanced from 400 to 1,350 million kilowatts a month—that is, to the 1938 level. In the same period, we had tripled our production of cast iron, steel and aluminum, and decupled the amount of iron ore mined. Immediately after the liberation, we were producing 23,000 tons of concrete a month; during the last month, the figure had risen to 120,000 tons. We had taken 40,000 tons of lime from our kilns in thirty days; now, we were producing 125,000 tons. We had filled 160,000 railway cars a month; now, we were loading 470,000. "Having my eye necessarily fixed on the dial marking the degrees of our advance, my official duty is to remark that not a day has passed without some progress over the one before."

But in speaking of the future, I rejected all demagoguery. "Whether it is a question of reforms, of prices, of wages or of elections, we know that no decision will satisfy everyone. Yet we continue on our way. We shall postpone the accounting of our grievances, our disappointments and our disillusionments. We realize that the important thing is to survive—that is, to advance. We are doing so, and we *shall* do so by effort, unity, discipline, not by internal divisions. We are doing so and we *shall* do so by gradually and logically rebuilding, not by returning to old formulas or by taking mad risks. . . . To work!"

The next day, after visiting Bergues, I went to Dunkirk. Seeing the harbors, the locks and the quais which were nothing but rubbish and wreckage, and the houses mostly ruined, it seemed unlikely that the great port could ever be resuscitated. But the huge crowd that had gathered in the Place Jean-Bart refuted all doubts.

To the words I addressed them, the people replied by such cheers that hearing them once there could be no hesitation, no half-heartedness. All together, before the great sailor's statue still miraculously standing, we sang the "Marseillaise," and then "Jean Bart! Jean Bart!" which dispelled all our misery. Next, Calais offered me a similar spectacle. If the St.-Pierre district was relatively preserved, the port was in ruins. Nothing remained of the old town except for the Watch Tower and the walls of the Église de Notre-Dame. But the people, crowded before the *hôtel de ville,* where I was received by the mayor, my brother-in-law Jacques Vendroux, made it clear by the thunderous cheers that the future was in their hands. At Boulogne, in the lower town all was ruin and desolation, which did not keep the populace from manifesting a ringing confidence. This was particularly the case among the sailors, fishermen, dock workers and stevedores whose spokesman declared, "Here we are! There is the sea! The two of us must come to terms!" Amid the general ardor, the crowds of workingmen were, as always, the most vibrant and spontaneous. My visit to Portel, reduced to a heap of rubble but determined to revive, concluded the final trip.

But while the people's sentiment showed they were ready to rise above all divisions, to follow De Gaulle on the road to national recovery, and to approve his intention of instituting a strong state, political activity took a contrary direction. All my government's decisions and attitudes were now received with criticism or resentment on the part of the various factions. The "politicians" exhibited mounting caution in my regard.

During the month of June, the parties raised their shields. It should be said that on the third I myself had indicated in a press conference how I regarded the problem of the Constituent Assembly. "Three solutions," I remarked, "are conceivable. Either return to yesterday's ways and weaknesses, separately elect a Chamber of Deputies and a Senate, and then unite them at Versailles in a National Assembly which either will or will not modify the 1875 constitution. Or else regard this constitution as extinct and proceed to elections for a Constituent Assembly which will do what it thinks best. Or finally, consult the country on the terms which would serve as a basis for determining its wishes and to which its representatives would have to conform." I did not specify which was my own choice, but it could be guessed from the very fact that I invoked the hypothesis of a referendum. This was enough to provoke formal opposition or at the least strong reservations on all sides.

My referendum project had a triple end in view. Since the 1875 system had been swept away by 1940's disaster, it seemed to me that it would be arbitrary either to re-establish it myself or to forbid its return. After all, the sovereign nation was there to decide the matter. Although I had no doubt as to its response, I would ask the people if it desired to return to the Third Republic or to create another. Further, when the people's vote had obliterated the old constitution, the new one would have to be elaborated by the Assembly which would emerge from the elections. But must this Assembly be omnipotent, determining the national institutions exclusively and finally, possessing all rights without exception, restraint or appeal? No! Thanks to the referendum, a balance could be set up between its powers and the government's, so that the constitution subsequently elaborated would be subject to approval by universal suffrage. The referendum, then instituted as the first and the last act of the constitutional undertaking, would provide me the opportunity to speak directly to every Frenchman and would furnish the latter the occasion to approve or disapprove of my attitude on a subject affecting the nation's destiny for generations. My intention, once it was realized, provoked stubborn opposition from every party. On June 14 the Politburo of the Communist party let it be known that it had determined to pursue its "campaign for the election of a sovereign Constituent Assembly"; that it opposed "any plebiscite, avowed or not, in the form of a referendum"; that it rejected "any consideration of a presidential character." The Confédération Générale de Travail (CGT) immediately adopted a similar resolution. On June 21 the Socialists, in their turn, formally announced, by the organ of their executive committee, their desire to obtain "a constituent and legislative assembly" which nothing must hamper. They further declared themselves "resolutely opposed to the method, contrary to democratic traditions, which would consist in asking the electorate to express its wishes by means of a referendum on a constitutional draft prepared by restricted commissions." The committee for Socialist-Communist understanding convening on June 22; the executive committee of the Popular Republican Movement (MRP) in a communiqué on June 24; the Democratic and Socialist Union of the Resistance declared from its inception on June 25; the National Council of the Resistance convening on June 29; the central committee of the League of the Rights of Man in a motion on July 1—all demanded the renowned single and sovereign Assembly and expressed their disapproval of the notion of a referendum.

Those who had held office under the prewar system expressed resentment that a referendum should even be discussed. Since 1940, whether they had sided with Vichy or with the resistance, they had applied their efforts to the restoration of what had been. To their mind, De Gaulle need only ask the electorate to indicate deputies, and the formally qualified colleges to appoint senators, in order that the parliament reappear in its old form. That the nation evidently condemned the Third Republic's vacillations was in their eyes a further reason for not permitting the former to judge the latter. The various moderate groups therefore came out in favor of the election of a Chamber and a Senate, according to yesterday's procedures. On June 18, the executive committee of the Radical-Socialist party demanded the "re-establishment of republican institutions" as they had been before the conflict, and declared itself "opposed to any plebiscite and any referendum."

Thus the political factions, divided as they were between the

creation of an omnipotent Assembly and the return to the old system, were unanimous in rejecting my own conceptions. The prospect of a direct appeal to the nation seemed scandalous to all of
them. Nothing showed more clearly to what distortion of the
meaning of democracy the spirit of faction led. According to the
parties, the Republic should be their property, the nation being
sovereign only to delegate its rights and even its free will to the
men which they selected for it. Further, my concern to assure the
government's authority and effectiveness conflicted with their fundamental nature. They instinctively believed the state should be
weak so they could manipulate it more readily and win from it
not so much the means of action as office and influence.

Thoroughly aware that party tendencies might lead us to adopt
a disastrous constitution, I clung to my intention of submitting the
result for the nation's approval. But before crossing swords with
the parties, I attempted to obtain the assistance and co-operation of
qualified men variously situated in the political array and whom I
regarded as likely to influence public opinion. I called on President
Léon Blum, Édouard Herriot and Louis Marin, upon whom the
years and the events they had lived through had perhaps conferred
serenity.

Léon Blum, as a matter of fact, had just emerged from the long
detention which Vichy and then the Third Reich had inflicted upon
him. He was, as I knew, more attached to socialism than ever. But
I also knew that during his ordeals, certain scruples had troubled
him as to the convictions professed and the policies lately advocated by his party. He had re-examined them in the light of that
lucidity which a prison affords a noble soul. The question of political power in particular had appeared to him in a new light. In
his captive meditations, which he published under the title *On the
Human Scale,* he remarked that "parliamentary government is not
the unique nor even the pure form of democracy." He indicated
that the presidential regime was, in his eyes, the best. "Personally," he wrote, "I incline toward a system of the American

type, based on the separation and the balance of powers." No sooner had his freedom been restored, than Léon Blum publicly expressed his confidence in me. To assist me in my first project of renovating the Republic, I intended to rely on his support first of all.

I was soon obliged to abandon this hope. As a matter of fact, Léon Blum was quickly caught up again in the habitual inclinations of the Socialist group. At our first meeting, he refused to enter the Provisional Government as Minister of State, alleging as an excuse his poor health but also his desire to devote himself entirely to his party. On May 20, that is, ten days after his return to France, he declared at a meeting of Socialist Federation leaders, "No man has the right to power. But *we* have the right to ingratitude." In the daily articles he wrote for *Le Populaire,* influential by their qualities of form as well as their subject matter, Blum substantially supported the notion of the single and sovereign Assembly. He did not reject the principle of the referendum, provided that it determine only whether the prewar regime was to be re-established. But for Léon Blum the question was much less one of rendering the state stronger and more effective than of preventing the reappearance of the Senate of recent years, against which he nursed stubborn personal grievances. Nothing, according to Blum, should offset the Assembly's powers. It was from the same viewpoint that he considered what he called "the De Gaulle case." He lavished his esteem upon my person, but in proportion to his kind words in this regard, he raised his guard against my authority and bitterly opposed any attempt to designate the chief of state by an enlarged suffrage. In short, he too had again adopted the fundamental principle of the French parliamentary regime: "Let no head show above the trenches of democracy!"

Shortly before the elections, I requested a meeting with Blum, during which I said, "My task of national defense and public safety is reaching its conclusion. The nation is free, victorious and in order. It will speak with complete sovereignty. For me to reach a new stage at its head, its elected representatives must support me, for in the realm of politics, no one can govern against all the rest. Yet the party spirit leads me to doubt that I will be able to conduct the affairs of tomorrow's France as I believe proper. I therefore plan to withdraw. In that case, I believe you are the man to assume the burden of leadership in consideration of your merits, your experience, and the fact that your party will be one of the most numerous in the imminent Assembly as well as situated in the center of the preponderant wing. You can be sure that I will facilitate matters for you at that time."

Léon Blum made no objections to my eventual withdrawal, which gave me to understand that he gladly accepted the notion. But he declared in response to my plans regarding himself, "No, I can't accept that, for I have been so long excoriated and criticized by a section of the public opinion which I loathe, that now I cannot honestly entertain the idea of holding power. Then too, I cannot accept because the functions of the chief of state are terribly demanding and my strength will not permit me to support the burden." I then asked him, "If, after my retirement, you were to decline, who do you think could continue in my place?" "Gouin is the only one!" Blum told me. And referring to Churchill's replacement by the Labour leader, he added, "Gouin is the man most like Attlee." Evidently Blum considered the great national problem we were discussing only from the Socialist viewpoint. I must admit that in view of the experiences the country had just survived and of which Blum himself had been a victim, I felt considerable discouragement.

I had still less success with Édouard Herriot. Despite the shifting attitude he had exhibited regarding Laval and Abetz when the latter, on the eve of the liberation of Paris, proposed that he reconvene the 1940 "National Assembly" and form a government which would not be mine, I had made every effort to receive cordially this veteran of the sessions, the rites and the honors of the Third Republic, this still-affecting bard of the contradictory impulses between which yesterday's regime had vacillated, this patriot in whom the sorrows of France had wakened despair rather than resolution, but who had nonetheless courageously endured the ordeals inflicted upon him by Vichy and by Hitler. When Herriot returned by way of Russia and the Middle East from his detention in Germany, I sent my own plane to Beirut for him. Upon the first visit he paid me, I restored his Cross of the Legion of Honor which he had returned to Pétain during the occupation. I invited him, in his turn, to participate in my government. If he consented to do so, he would be Minister of State in charge of United Nations affairs. I expected to find him cordial beneath the frankness of his good will, but he proved, on the contrary, full of grievances and malevolence.

Herriot was most annoyed by the reversal in the general attitude toward himself. He spoke acrimoniously of the rather indifferent reception he had been given at Moscow, so different from the treatment he had enjoyed there on other occasions. He did not conceal his vexation at the meager enthusiasm the city of Lyons had just shown in his behalf. When he asked me to let him return to the presidential palace of the Chamber of Deputies, his former residence, and when I made the impossibility of such a step clear to him, he expressed his dissatisfaction in the strongest terms. Finally and above all, the relative and moreover rather unjustified collapse of the Radical party with which he identified himself caused him great distress. As for institutions, Édouard Herriot insisted upon a return to those he had been accustomed to; he therefore advocated the immediate election of a Chamber of Deputies and a Senate which would appoint their presidents, send a policy without character to the Élysée and furnish a series of cabinets composed of interchangeable parliamentarians! He regarded all that had happened and particularly the collapse of the regime so dear to him as a horrible episode, but saw no lesson in it. Édouard Herriot declined my invitation to join the government. I asked him to help in the reconstruction of France; he declared he would devote himself to rebuilding the Radical party.

Louis Marin also showed me that his principal concern was to revive a political grouping in accord with the ideas he had served throughout his career. He was employing his influence and his activity to unite the Moderates in view of the forthcoming elections. As long as it had been a question of driving the Germans from the national territory, this old Lorrainer had given me his unreserved loyalty and adherence. Now he insisted on his autonomy in relation to me. A parliamentarian of wide experience, moreover, deeply attached to the life of Assemblies, relishing the acrimonious and heady ferments and in fact hoping for nothing better than to see them reappear as he had practiced them. Hence my intention of limiting their powers was of little interest to him. Like Blum and Herriot after him, he refused to enter the Provisional Government. However he strongly assured me that in regard to my policy of national security, he would support me with all the means in his power.

Without having in my camp these three personalities who could have helped mark the accession of the Fourth Republic with the signs of unity and publicity, I approached the constitutional discussion surrounded by the government I had reconstituted during the aftermath of the liberation of Paris. However, so that the same men need not constantly serve as targets, at the end of May I replaced Paul Ramadier as Minister of Supplies with Christian Pineau, recently returned from Buchenwald, and appointed Pierre-Henri Teitgen to the Ministry of Justice, while François de Menthon represented France on the Nuremberg tribunal. Teitgen relinquished the Ministry of Information to Jacques Soustelle. Shortly afterward, Augustin Laurent left the Ministry of Postal Services for reasons of health, and I entrusted this post to Eugène Thomas, recently returned from deportation.

On July 9 I informed the Council of the projected statute which I had established with the devoted collaboration of Jules Jeanneney.

The deliberation was calm and searching. Since the majority of the ministers belonged to parties and since the latter had all manifested their disapproval, I let it be known that I accepted in advance the resignations which would be tendered. None, however, was sent in. The Council adopted the text unchanged and in unanimity.

The election of an Assembly was set for the month of October. The nation was to decide by referendum whether the Assembly would be a Constituent Assembly. The reply, by yes or no, to this question would mean either the accession of the Fourth Republic or a return to the Third. If the Assembly was to be Constituent, its powers would be determined by the second question of the referendum; either the nation would adopt the government's plan (limiting the duration of the Assembly's mandate to seven months, restricting its powers, in the legislative domain, to voting on budgets, structural reforms and international treaties, according it no initiative in the matter of expenditures but granting it power to elect the President of the Government, who would remain in office as long as the deputies, and lastly —and most important—subordinating the adoption of the constitution to its ratification by universal suffrage); or, if the nation refused the government's proposal, the Assembly would be omnipotent in all matters and for as long as it chose to exist. The reply, by yes or no, would establish, or not establish, the balance of the executive and legislative powers for the "preconstitutional period."

During the same session, the Council further decided that the cantonal elections would take place in two ballotings on September 23 and 30. In this way, the general councils would be constituted before the referendum. If, contrary to every expectation, the referendum favored the re-establishment of former institutions, the Senate could then be elected by limited suffrage, as had been previously the case.

On July 12, I made a nationwide broadcast, discussing the points on which the people were to be consulted and what I asked them to do. After reading the text of the questions the referendum would ask, I declared, "As for my opinion, I shall express it in this way: I hope and trust that the French people will answer Yes to both questions."

Then it was the Consultative Assembly's turn. I foresaw an animated discussion, as acrimonious as it was inconclusive, which proved to be the case. The delegates expressed their virtually unanimous opposition to the government's text, but could frame no constructive proposition of their own.

In the name of the Radicals and certain Moderates, Messrs. Plaisant, Bonnevay, Labrousse, Bastid, and Astier passionately demanded the restoration of the old constitution and, first of all, the election of a Senate at the same time as that of a Chamber of Deputies. To strengthen their position, these delegates did not abstain from likening General de Gaulle's referendum to Bonaparte's and the Prince-President's plebiscite. The Communists and those members of the Assembly who had taken their stand with them, represented by Messrs. Cogniot, Duclos, Cot and Copeau, pointed to the same bogey, but contrary to the preceding speakers concluded that the Constituent Assembly must be permitted to decide of its own free will on all matters, particularly the nation's institutions. The Socialists, Popular Republicans, and representatives of the new Democratic Union of the Resistance, as well as some Moderates, probably calculating that there would be an electoral advantage in not breaking with me, adopted a middle position. These factions now accepted the principle of a referendum, but nonetheless proclaimed their desire to achieve a single and sovereign Assembly and their opposition to the restriction of the latter's powers.

Thus the Consultative Assembly split among three tendencies, none of which was in a position to achieve a majority. But without being able to agree on tomorrow's institutions, or on the means to do so, they were unanimous in demanding the absolute primacy of the parties. Further, none made any concession or even allusion to the crucial necessities of separation of powers or the effectiveness of the state's powers.

Yet it was these very conditions that I particularly stressed when I mounted the tribunal at the end of the discussion. In my opinion, it was in order to fulfill them that the nation must assign limits to the Constituent Assembly's duration, impose restrictions upon its powers and attach regulations to its relations with the executive power. It was the responsibility of the Provisional Government to propose these limits, restrictions, and regulations to universal suffrage. But I urged the delegates to join with the government in order to do so. I characterized as spurious all comparisons between my referendum and the Napoleonic plebiscite. Pretending to fear I would stifle the Republic when I was releasing it from its tomb was simply ridiculous. When the parties and the parliament had betrayed and denied the Republic in 1940, I had "taken up its arms, its laws, and even its name." Now I was doing what was essential to bring to these elections an Assembly to which I would hand over my powers, hardly the procedure employed on December 2 or the 18 Brumaire. But tomorrow the Republic must have a true government, and must not revert to yesterday's deplorable practices.

Insisting on this point, which for me was a crucial one, I declared: "What this perpetual threat hanging over the men who had the task of governing, this almost chronic state of crisis, these bargainings with foreign powers, their intrigues within the Council, all consequences of such a situation—what this will have cost the nation is probably incalculable." I reminded my audience that from 1875 to 1940, we had had one hundred and two governments, while Great Britain's numbered twenty and America's fourteen. What, consequently, could be the authority, at home and abroad, of the cabinets formed under such conditions in comparison to that of the ministries functioning in other countries? I indicated what Franklin Roosevelt had told me: "Even I, the President of the United States, would sometimes find myself incapable of remembering the name of the current head of the French government."

"Tomorrow, still more than yesterday," I declared, "the state can take no effective action and—I say it categorically—French democracy can have no future if we return to a system of this order." And I added, "In the disaster of 1940, the abdication of the Republic and the accession of Vichy, how much was directly accountable to the nation's disgust with this absurd game it had watched so long and which so badly conducted its affairs."

But these considerations were hardly those which preoccupied the parties. The Consultative Assembly listened to me deferentially; then it indicated that my concerns were not its own. By a vote of 210 to 19 it rejected the government's entire proposal. An enormous majority subsequently rejected an amendment providing for the election of a Senate and thereby a return to prewar institutions. When, to conclude, Messrs. Vincent Auriol and Claude Bourdet defended a compromise proposition accepting a referendum but greatly reducing the government's proposal, their text was defeated by a vote of 108 to 101. The session therefore terminated without the Consultative Assembly's having managed to formulate any positive opinion.

Once again, I had to intervene decisively. On August 17 the Council of Ministers adopted the definitive terms of the statute relative to the referendum and the elections. In relation to the original text, the only modifications were specifications intended to avert a possible ministerial crisis for the duration of the Constituent Assembly's mandate. The latter could, as a matter of fact, overthrow the government only by a special vote of absolute majority and after a delay of at least forty-eight hours. No change was made in the two essential points. The French people were to settle the final destiny of the Third Republic. The sovereignty of the people formally established despite the Consultative Assembly's opposition, would ultimately determine the nation's institutions.

The August 17 statute, at the same time that it formulated the text of the referendum's two questions, determined the means of balloting. But on this last point too, the decisions reached also constituted the object of vehement protests.

Two opposing and, in my opinion, equally distressing conceptions divided the political factions. The partisans of prewar institutions advocated a return to the former electoral regime as well, that is, to voting for only one candidate in each arrondissement. All principles aside, Radicals and Moderates inclined to think that the prominent men they had formerly put up for office would again find the approval of electors in the old constituencies. On the other hand, Communists, Socialists and Popular Republicans, who expected to obtain votes thanks to the attraction of their platforms rather than by the personal fame of their candidates, insisted on "integral" proportional representation. According to these doctrinaires, equity could be arithmetically and morally satisfied only if each party, proposing a single list of all candidates to all of France, was granted a number of seats exactly proportional to the total of votes received throughout the nation. Should this "perfect" system fail and if, more modestly, proportional representation functioned in multiple constituencies (such as the departments), they insisted that the votes not comprising part of the local quotients be added on the national scale. Thanks to these returns, which would obtain additional seats, each party would be sure of bringing in some of its leaders who would have bitten the dust in the provinces or not even have stood for election anywhere. In short, a representation by arrondissement that was too narrow and a proportional representation that was too wide were advocated and argued over by

impassioned and partisan apostles. I did not favor or even discuss
the arguments of either camp.

Yesterday's means of balloting did not have my approval. First
of all, I considered it somewhat unfair, given the great differences
in population among the arrondissements. In the past, Briançon
with 7,138 electors, Florac with 7,343 and a part of the Sixth
Arrondissement of Paris with 7,731 elected a deputy, just as did
Dunkirk, Pontoise, or Noisy-le-Sec, which included respectively
33,840, 35,199, and 37,180 electors. To introduce more equity
into this system, we would have to institute throughout the entire
national territory, a hasty remodeling of the constituencies, amid
innumerable and fierce contestations. But what now particularly
discouraged me about balloting by arrondissement was the prospect
of the effect it would have on the nation's future by assuring the
primacy of the Communist party.

If the election was determined by a single balloting, as many
advocated, by analogy with the British practice, there was no
doubt that a Communist would be returned in most constituencies.
For confronting the "party's" candidate in each arrondissement
would be at least one Socialist, one Radical, one Popular
Republican, one Moderate, and one exemplary resistance fighter,
not to mention several dissidents and various theoreticians. Given
the number of votes which the Third International would garner
throughout the country and which gave a good indication of the
imminent results of the municipal and cantonal elections, it was
the Communist candidate who would most frequently be elected.
If there were two ballotings, Communists and Socialists, provisionally united by their contractual understanding and by their
basic tendencies, would combine their votes in all ballotings,
which would obtain the greatest number of seats for their coalition
and also yoke together, by common electoral interest, both sorts
of Marxist. In any case, balloting by arrondissement would bring
to the Palais Bourbon a majority that would vote as the Communists wished. This consequence doubtless escaped the adherents

of the old formula. But being responsible for the destiny of France, I could not run such a risk.

The concept of "integral" proportional representation was no more to my liking. To propose to some 25 million electors an unlimited number of lists, each consisting of 600 names, would characterize almost all the mandataries by anonymity and eliminate all human *rapport* between those voting and those elected. Yet by common sense, by tradition and by public interest, the various regions of the nation should be represented as such within the Assemblies, and should be represented by men who would maintain their contacts with the local voters. Moreover, only the chief of state should be elected by the nation as a whole. If, however, each party used the remaining votes it would obtain in the constituencies on the national level, this would mean instituting two kinds of deputy—those elected by departments, and those put into office by a mythical collection of votes, though the citizens had not actually voted for them. I was flatly opposed to this procedure.

The Provisional Government therefore adopted balloting by list and proportional representation on the departmental scale. Further, the most densely populated departments were also subdivided. No constituency would have more than nine deputies. None would include less than two. All in all, the Assembly would include 522 elected representatives from Metropolitan France and 64 from the French Union. The electoral system instituted by my decree subsequently remained in effect. The parties made only one—hardly suitable—modification in it later on: that of party alliances.

At the moment, a violent outcry was raised on all sides against the decision taken. Since the Consultative Assembly had disbanded on August 3, a "Delegation of the Left" was constituted, intended to organize the ensemble of protests. On the initiative of the Confédération Générale de Travail (CGT), totaling some four million adherents under the leadership of its Secretary General

Léon Jouhaux, the mandatories of the Communist, Socialist and Radical parties, and of the League of the Rights of Man united; although the members of this delegation were not in agreement among themselves as to the means of balloting, they unanimously disapproved of the solution adopted by the government and agreed to take spectacular action with regard to General de Gaulle in order to indicate their opposition. On September 1, Jouhaux asked me to receive him along with several other delegates.

I felt a great deal of cordial respect for Léon Jouhaux. This eminent trade unionist had divided his life to the service of the working classes, applying his great intelligence and skill to clearing a path for labor's well-being and dignity. Under the occupation, he had immediately adopted an attitude of marked opposition to the "national revolution" and had shown that he regarded the enemy as the enemy. Imprisoned by Vichy, then deported to Germany, he had now resumed the leadership of the Confederation, insofar as the growing influence of the Communists permitted him to do so. I had frequently discussed various social problems with him. But on this occasion, my duty to the state prevented me from receiving him. According to law, the Confederation's exclusive object was "the study and the defense of economic interests." I had no intention, now less than ever, of admitting the trade union's qualifications to mingle in political and electoral questions. I replied to Jouhaux's letter that I could not accede to his request for an audience. Then, despite the indignation which every faction and every newspaper chose to express, I refused to modify my position, and as a result each group decided to adapt itself to it as well as possible. On the bases established by the statute, the parties prepared themselves to confront universal suffrage.

The electoral campaign was extremely animated, not so much as a consequence of the opposing candidate lists as because of the passions provoked by the referendum questions De Gaulle had insisted upon. Actually, the nation's response to the first was known in advance. It was only a matter of discovering how large a proportion of Frenchmen would ask for something else than the Third Republic. As to the second question, a passionate debate began throughout the nation.

The Communists, imitated in many areas by Socialist elements and indirectly aided by the Radicals and some Moderates, made great efforts to obtain a negative majority in order to put me in check. Thus the French section of the Third International openly showed whom it regarded as the chief adversary. As a consequence the Popular Republican Movement (MRP), the Democratic Union of the Resistance and several rightist groups championed the positive reply to the referendum. As for the Socialist party, it had finally and officially subscribed to my cause. But rather than fight in behalf of a cause that was not of its own making and that divided its own militants, it left the "questions" in obscurity and applied itself to publicizing its own platform, which was not receiving much attention from the public. All in all, the electoral battle, waged with a great many posters, tracts, and slogans painted on walls, had at stake the "Yes" asked by De Gaulle and the "No" insisted on by the Communist party. While refraining from appearing at meetings or ceremonies during the three weeks the campaign lasted, I insisted on reminding the French, on October 17, how much depended on this balloting and what my own opinion was.

On October 21, the voting offices received the ballots in two urns, one for the referendum, the other for the election of deputies. Out of 25 million registered voters, there were about 20 million votes cast. Of the five million abstainers, the majority were women avoiding unfamiliar formalities. Once the results were tallied for both Metropolitan France and North Africa and a certain number of obscure tickets were cleared up, it was found that the Communists had 160 elected representatives, the Socialists 142, the Democratic Union of the Resistance 30, the Popular Republicans 152, the Radicals 29, the Moderates 66.

Thus the Communist party, although it had obtained a quarter of all the votes cast, did not carry the great mass of the nation's votes. However, the events from which France had just emerged had provided it exceptional opportunities for victory. The disaster of 1940, the national failure of many elite elements, the resistance in which it had played a leading role, the long misery of the people during the occupation, the political, economic, social and moral upheavals the country had endured, the victory of Soviet Russia, the abuses committed in our regard by the western democracies—all were so many favorable conditions for its success. If, indeed, the "party" had not been able to seize its opportunity, it was because I had been there to incarnate France as a whole. Conversely, by associating the Communist party with the liberation of the country and subsequently with its recovery, I had given it the means to integrate itself in the community. Now the people accorded it a considerable hearing, but not the right to domination. Would it choose to be a functioning element of French democracy or merely a separate group manipulated by foreign masters? The answer would in part depend on the nature of the Republic itself. Strong, proud, fraternal, it would perhaps offset such dissidence. Impotent and motionless, it would surely incline this power to become centrifugal once again.

But would the other political factions be willing to unite around me to reconstruct the state? The referendum proved that this was the nation's profound desire. By more than 96 per cent of the votes, the people had answered Yes to the first question, testifying that they condemned almost unanimously the regime without a leader and consequently without direction or authority which had collapsed in the disaster. Further, they expressed their confidence in me personally by a more than 66 per cent vote approving my proposal reducing party omnipotence. This evidence was confirmed by the electoral results among the various political formations, depending on the attitude they had adopted toward me. The hostility the Communists showed me certainly cost them a degree of popular suffrage. The Radicals were crushed as much because their leaders opposed Charles de Gaulle as because they symbolized and advocated the old system. For lack of having adopted a favorable position in my regard, the Moderates lost almost two thirds of the seats that had once been theirs. If the Socialists, surprised and disappointed as they were by the results, did not come in first, the growing remove which they indicated in regard to me, though so many of their men had remained so close to me for so long, sufficed to explain the fact. On the other hand, the Popular Republican Movement (MRP), scarcely out of its cradle but declaring for the moment, a "resolute Gaullism," came in ahead of all other groups in regard to votes and seats.

Certainly the referendum had not revealed a great national renewal, yet it afforded me the impression that the country as a whole desired me to lead it, at least until it had ratified its new institutions. It seemed to me essential, moreover, both historically and politically, that this ratification be accomplished with my approval and accord, considering what it was that events had led me to represent.

But I had to admit that at this point in my journey, the support the nation offered me was growing slight and uncertain. Now the rudimentary powers which it had lately provided me for battle were fading; the dispersion of the resistance forces was a *fait accompli*. Further, the current of popular ardor which had been poured out so generously upon me was now channeled in various directions. As for the voices which traditionally expressed the nation's conscience, I received little encouragement from them. As a matter of fact, the nation no longer delegated anything but parties around me. And the latter, after the elections, whether they were pleased or disappointed by the results, were less concerned than ever to follow me. Particularly since, though the distant horizon was still dark with clouds, there were no immediate threats discernible. France had recovered her integrity, her status, her equilibrium, her overseas extensions. Here was substance to nourish for a while the strategies of party politicians, their desire to control the state, their opinion that the "man of the storm" had now played his part and must step aside.

For myself, having summed up my possibilities, I had determined my conduct. It was my task to be and to remain the champion of an orderly and vigorous Republic, and the adversary of the confusion which had brought France to the abyss and risked casting her into it once again tomorrow. As for my government's power, I should in any case be able to withdraw from events before they withdrew from me.

CHAPTER 7

DEPARTURE

N ow it was November. The war had been over for two months, the nation's attention was flagging and great actions no longer held the stage. Everything pointed to the reappearance of yesterday's regime, less adapted than ever to the nation's needs. If I was still in power, it could only be provisionally. But to France and the French, I owed something further—to take my leave as a man morally intact.

The Constituent Assembly convened on November 6. Cuttoli, a Radical deputy and the senior member, presided. Although this first session was a purely formal one, I had insisted on being present. Some may have felt that the transmission of public powers from De Gaulle to the national representation should be made with some formality. But the notion that my visit to the Palais Bourbon might involve a degree of ceremony antagonized the provisional committee and even the men of protocol. So everything was accomplished without a show of state and, on the whole, in a mediocre manner.

Cuttoli made a speech paying homage to Charles de Gaulle but lavishing criticisms on his policy. The praises found few echoes among those present but the disparagements received strong applause from the Left, while the Right abstained from any manifestation whatever. Then the presiding officer read aloud my letter announcing that the government would resign once the Constituent Assembly had elected its committee. There was no particular reaction. As for myself, sitting in a lower row of the arena, I sensed converging upon me the ponderous stares of six hundred parliamentarians and I felt, almost physically, the weight of the general uneasiness.

After the Assembly had elected Félix Gouin as its president, its next task was to elect the President of the Government. Naturally I abstained from submitting my candidacy or making any reference to my eventual platform. They would take me as I was or not take me at all. During an entire week, there were many trying conferences among the various groups. Meanwhile, on November 11, I presided over the ceremony in the Place de l'Étoile. Fifteen coffins, brought from every battlefield, were arranged around the Tomb of the Unknown Soldier, as if the combatants had come to pay the final homage of their own sacrifice before being transferred to a casemate of the Mont Valérien military cemetery. Speaking a few words at the foot of the Arc de Triomphe, I appealed for unity and fraternity in order to cure wounded France. "Let us walk together," I said, "on the same road, at the same pace, singing the same song! Let us look toward the future with the eyes of a great united people!" Around the circumference of the Place de l'Étoile, the crowd was as enthusiastic as ever; but at my side the official faces indicated that the government was about to change its nature.

Nevertheless, two days later, the National Assembly unanimously elected me President of the Government of the French Republic and proclaimed that "Charles de Gaulle had deserved well of his country." Although this demonstration occurred only after eight days of disagreeable palavers, it might be interpreted as expressing a conscious intention of assembling around me in order to support my policy. This was what Mr. Winston Churchill, for example, appeared to believe after passing through Paris on November 13, dining at my table and subsequently hearing the election results, Churchill expressed his enthusiasm in a generous letter. Recalling Plutarch's remark, "Ingratitude toward men is the sign of a strong people," which had recently been taken as an epigraph for a celebrated book, he wrote, in his turn, "Plutarch lied!" But I knew that the vote was a form of homage addressed to my past action, not a promise that engaged the future.

This was immediately brought home to me. On November 15, undertaking to constitute the government, I was to step in one wasp's nest of intrigue after another. The leftist groups, who formed a considerable majority in the Assembly, raised many objections. The Radicals informed me that they would not participate in any government of mine. If any of their members accepted a portfolio nevertheless, it would be against the explicit will of the entire party. The Socialists, suspicious and anxious, made inquiries as to my platform, multiplied their conditions and declared that in any case they would grant their votes only to a Cabinet that had the support and the participation of the Communists. The latter were playing for high stakes; for them Maurice Thorez demanded at least one of the three ministries they regarded as most important: National Defense, Interior, or Foreign Affairs. This was indeed the question. If I should yield to their demands, the Communists would hold one of the state's essential powers and thereby have means of taking control in a moment of confusion. If I should refuse, I ran the risk of finding myself powerless to form a government. But then the "party," having demonstrated that it was stronger than De Gaulle, would become the master of the hour.

I decided to take a decisive step; I would oblige the Communists either to enter the government under my conditions or to leave it altogether. I informed Thorez that neither the Ministry of Foreign Affairs, nor that of National Defense, nor that of the Interior would be assigned to any member of his party. To the latter I offered only "economic" ministries. As a result of this move, the Communists published furious diatribes, declaring that by refusing to give them what they asked I was "insulting the memory of the war dead," and invoking their "75,000 assassinated men," an entirely arbitrary figure, moreover, for happily the total number of their adherents who had fallen before the firing squads did not amount to a fifth of this number, and furthermore those Frenchmen who had sacrificed their lives had done so— Communists included—for France, not for a party.

Thereupon I was flooded by the alarmed reproofs of various men of the Left who urged me to yield in order to avoid a fatal crisis, while the other factions remained silent and withdrawn. But my resolution was firm. I intended to oblige the National Assembly to support me against the Marxist Left, and on November 17 I therefore wrote to the President of the Constituent Assembly that since I was unable to create a unified government, I was restoring to the national representation the mandate it had entrusted to me. The following day, speaking on the radio, I called the people to witness the abusive demands which partisan groups claimed to impose upon me. I announced that for obvious national and international reasons, I refused to put the Communists in a position to dominate our policy by surrendering to them "the diplomacy which expresses it, the Army which sustains it or the police which protects it." This being so, I would form a government with the support of those who chose to follow me. Otherwise, I would resign from office immediately and without bitterness.

Moreover, however threatening the atmosphere, every intangible factor, the expression of every apprehension, led me to believe that I would succeed in my design. And indeed, after a debate I did not attend, the Assembly re-elected me President of the Government by every vote save those of the Communists. It is true that André Philip, spokesman for the Socialists, had tried to explain his party's reluctant adherence by proclaiming that the Chamber was conveying to me the "imperative charge" of setting up a Ministry in which the extreme Left would be represented. This formulation deceived no one. It was clear that the Communists had not been able to impose their will. Not a single deputy, outside their own group, had supported them, and in the decisive vote, they were isolated against all others, without exception. Thus was broken, from the start, a spell which had indeed threatened to become calamitous.

The Communists drew the appropriate conclusions at once. The next day, their delegation called to inform me they were willing to enter my government without stipulating conditions, and asserted I would find no support firmer than theirs. Without deluding myself as to the sincerity of this sudden reversal, I accepted their support, considering that for a while at least their rallying to my cause could further the social harmony of which the nation stood in such need.

On November 21 the government was constituted. Four portfolios went to Communist deputies—Billoux, Croizat, Paul and Tillon; four to Socialists—Moch, Tanguy-Prigent, Thomas and Tixier; four to Popular Republicans—Bidault, Michelet, Prigent and Teitgen; two to resistance leaders of the Democratic Union —Pleven and Soustelle; one to Giacobbi, a Radical; one to Dautry and one to Malraux, neither of whom was a parliamentarian or had any party affiliation whatever; the entire structure was surmounted by four Ministers of State—a Socialist, Auriol; a Popular Republican, Gay; a Moderate, Jacquinot; a Communist, Thorez. As expected and announced, the Marxist Left received only economic ministries—National Economy, Labor, Production and Armament Manufacture.

On November 23 I made a speech before the Assembly in which I emphasized the gravity of the nation's present circumstances, the necessity of adopting as soon as possible institutions assuring "the responsibility, the stability, the authority of the executive power," and lastly the duty of the French and their representatives to unite in order to re-create France. Once again, the national representation supported me unanimously. In the crisis which had been prolonged for seventeen days without any valid reason, only the political parties had found their sustenance and their satisfaction.

Despite the accord achieved, I could not doubt that my power hung by a thread. Nevertheless, during the month of December I had the government adopt and the Assembly pass a law nationalizing the Bank of France and four credit establishments, and instituted a National Credit Council serving under the Minister of Finance. Shortly after, another law settled the terms of transferring the production and distribution of gas and electricity to the state. In both these issues all demogogic amendments had been successfully discarded. Furthermore, on December 15 I had the satisfaction of inaugurating the National School of Administration, an important institution which would co-ordinate and standardize the recruiting and training of the principal public servants, who had hitherto come to office from various disciplines. The school, springing full-fledged from the brain and the labors of my adviser Michel Debré, saw the light of day, it was true, in an atmosphere of skepticism on the part of the major bodies of public service and the parliamentary milieus. Yet it was to see their prejudices dissolve as it gradually became, from the point of view of administrative training, attitude and action, the foundation of the new state. Nevertheless, and by a sort of ironic coincidence, at the very moment when this nursery of the future servants of the Republic was being created, the threat of a general strike of civil servants sorely tried the cohesion of the government and my own authority.

It was only too true, of course, that the standard of living of these public servants had suffered greatly from the inflation. Their wage increases were not sufficient to meet the rise of prices. But what the trade unions demanded for them could not be granted without unbalancing the budget and depleting the treasury.

Although this was acknowledged by the Council of Ministers, although I had indicated my determination not to allocate more than the reasonable increase proposed by René Pleven and my resolve to forbid the strike under threat of penalties to be imposed on the offenders, I noticed violent agitation rising within the government itself. Several Socialist members, following their party's instructions, gave me to understand that they would retire rather than send a refusal to the trade union and penalize the functionaries and employees who abstained from work. At the same time, the civil servants were convened by their federations on December 15 at the Vélodrome d'Hiver in order to stigmatize "the absurd inadequacy of the measures contemplated by the government" and to call for a general strike.

By a curious complication, at the moment when a major crisis seemed inevitable, it was Communist support that permitted me to avert it. Within the Council, which was holding another session, Maurice Thorez suddenly declared that there must be no yielding to such intolerable pressures provided a few minor modifications were made; the arrangements proposed by the Finance Minister and approved by the President should be applied. Immediately the possibility of a Cabinet checkmate vanished from sight. That afternoon, at the Vélodrome d'Hiver, when the speakers mandated by the trade unions and in conjunction with the Socialist party had requested the audience to stop work and take action against the government, the Communist representative, to the general astonishment, violently opposed the agitators. "If the civil servants go on strike," he declared, "they will be committing a crime against their country!" Then, taking advantage of the confusion produced by this unexpected outburst from the "workers' party," he caused the decision to strike to be postponed. Thereafter, in order to settle the question, there remained only the parliamentary procedures to be executed.

On December 18, at the end of the debate the National Assembly had opened on the subject, I made it clear that the government could not go beyond the measures it had adopted, whatever its regret at being unable to do more for the state workers. "We have come," I said, "to the moment when, economically and financially speaking, we may lose everything or save nothing." I added, "We must know if the present government, confronting a serious difficulty and offering its solution, has or has not your confidence. We must know too if the National Assembly will or will not be able to devote itself to the nation's general interest beyond party concerns." The order of the day ultimately voted was as confused and ineffectual as I could wish.

But this success was a temporary one. A few days later, it was shown still more clearly how precarious General de Gaulle's power had become in relation to the parties and to the Assembly.

The 1946 budget was under discussion. For form's sake the government insisted that the final vote be taken on January first. But on that day, as the discussion seemed to draw to a close, the Socialists suddenly demanded a 20 per cent reduction of the credits assigned to National Defense. It was obvious that so sudden and summary a proposition, directed against an order of expenditures which evidently could not be reduced to such proportions from one day to the next, was inspired by both electoral demagogy and hostility toward me.

Since I was detained in the Rue St.-Dominique on New Year's Day by the visits of the diplomatic corps and the authorities, the Palais Bourbon debate dragged on without reaching an outcome. Though Minister of Finance Pleven, Minister of the Armies Michelet, Minister of Armament Tillon and Minister of State Auriol followed my instructions and declared that the government rejected the proposition, the Left—Socialists, Communists and the majority of the Radicals—which together comprised the majority, was prepared to vote it through. However, and as if to prove that the real issue was De Gaulle, the Assembly postponed any conclusion until I came in person to take part in the discussion.

I did so during the afternoon. In my presence, Messrs. Philip and Gazier led the attack with passion, supported by the applause of their Socialist colleagues, the Radicals counting the blows. Actually, the challengers protested their intention was not to destroy the government; they were taking action, they said, only to oblige it to yield before the parliamentary will. The Popular Republicans made it clear that they did not approve the aggression launched against me on such grounds, while the Right voiced its anxiety, but these fractions of the Assembly were careful not to condemn the opposition in explicit terms. As for the Communists, hesitating between the immediate imperative of demagogy and their tactics of the moment, they informed me that the assault had not been made with their agreement, but that if the Socialists were to bring the matter to vote, they themselves would be obliged to deny me their support.

That evening, probing hearts and hopes, I realized that the matter was already decided, that it would be vain and even unworthy to presume to govern when the parties, their power restored, had resumed their old tricks; in short, that I must now prepare my own departure from the scene.

In two brief interventions, I indicated to the Assembly the absurdity of the constraint they hoped to impose upon me and the frivolity with which the representatives of the people were preparing to cut into the national defense in order to give themselves the advantage of a partisan maneuver. Then, proceeding to the heart of the matter, I declared that this debate posed the entire problem of tomorrow's institutions. Once the government, acting in full knowledge of the case, had assumed its responsibility in so serious a matter, was it acceptable that the parliament should now wish to oblige it to contradict and humiliate itself? Were we imitating the regime of the Assembly? For my part, I refused to do so. If the credits requested were not voted that same evening, the government would not remain in office another hour.

"I should like to add a word," I said, "which is not for the present but, even now, for the future. The point that divides us is a general conception of the government and its relations with the national representation. We have begun to reconstruct the Republic. After me, you will continue to do so. I must tell you in all conscience—and doubtless this is the last time I shall be speaking to you from this place—that if you do not take into account the absolute necessities of governmental authority, dignity and responsibility, you will find yourselves in a situation which I predict will cause you bitter regret for having taken the way you have chosen."

As if the opposition wished to emphasize the fact that its attitude had been nothing but ruse and palinode, it suddenly fell silent. The order of the day, adopted virtually unanimously by the Assembly, imposed no conditions upon me. After which, the budget was passed without difficulty. But although my defeat had not been accomplished, the mere fact that it had appeared possible produced a profound effect. My government had been breached by the majority during a threat-crammed debate. Henceforth, perhaps, the same effect could be accomplished apropos of virtually any issue. It was apparent that if De Gaulle tolerated this situation in order to remain in office, his prestige would decline, until one day the parties would either no longer tolerate him or else relegate him to some harmless and decorative function. But I had neither the right nor the inclination to lend myself to such calculations. As I left the Palais Bourbon on the evening of January 1, I had determined upon my departure from office. All that remained was to select the date, without making any concessions whatever.

Certainly it would be before the end of the month. For the constitutional debate would then begin, and I was convinced that by remaining in the nascent regime I would not have the possibility of imposing my views nor even of supporting them. The draft which the committee created by the Constituent Assembly had prepared was precisely the converse of what I considered necessary, instituting as it did the absolute government of a single and sovereign Assembly; the executive having no other role than to apply what was prescribed; the President of the Council being elected by the parliament and permitted to form his Cabinet only after passing a thorough examination as to his tendencies and platform and assuming commitments which would severely bind him beforehand. As for the President of the Republic, it was agreed, after many hesitations, that there might be one, though he must be deprived of any political role and not have the slightest effect on the machinery of state—in other words, be the prisoner of his insipid symbolic function. This was probably the position intended for General de Gaulle by those who were calling the tune. Moreover, the committeemen, as well as the parties, were careful not to have any communication with me on the subject. Once, when I summoned the chairman, M. François de Menthon, to inquire as to the progress made, I was told that the Assembly and its committee considered that I was not to participate in the debate, since I was not a member myself. Under such conditions, to attempt to pursue my goals in this crucial area as in all other respects, would be to invite impotence and insult.

The immediate dismemberment of Charles de Gaulle's government did not, of course, escape the notice of the various foreign offices. As a result, the state of relations with them, which had at first improved, now once more declined. At the beginning of December, Paris learned through the news agencies that a meeting of the British, American and Soviet foreign ministers would take place on the fifteenth, in Moscow, "in order to discuss certain questions of particular interest to all three countries." This looked like a return to the systematic exclusion of France—which the London conference, the installation of quadripartite governments in Germany and Austria, the fact that we occupied a permanent chair on the Security Council of the United Nations, our participation in the Japanese armistice, etc., had seemed to bring to an end.

It was true that the purpose of the "Big Three" meeting was to prepare the peace treaties with Bulgaria, Rumania, Hungary and Finland, and that London, Moscow and Washington alleged, in order to justify our exclusion, that since the opening of hostilities against the Reich's satellites had occurred during the Vichy regime, France had not been officially in a state of war with Sofia, Bucharest, Budapest and Helsinki. But, for the participants of the Yalta and Potsdam conferences, it was actually a question of applying their recent decisions, without consulting us, to these unfortunate states—that is, of handing them over to the discretion of the Soviets. To the notification we received from our Allies on December 26 as to the conclusion of their conference, we replied on January 3 that they did not commit us, all the less so since France had, in these various parts of Europe, primary interests which had not been taken into account. But the dilatory reception accorded our note made it clear that all three powers were waiting for an imminent change in the French government in order to get what they wanted.

The same was true of the final settlement of the complex situation in the Levant. Since the crisis of the preceding May, Franco-British relations had remained in the refrigerator, as I had recommended. In Syria and Lebanon, the weak forces we maintained and the major units the British had sent remained at their positions; political agitations continued to provoke incidents; the Damascus and Beirut governments multiplied their notes and communiqués insisting on the departure of all foreign troops; finally, the neighboring Arab states—Egypt, Iraq, Transjordan, Palestine —joined in the chorus with their "oppressed brothers," all accommodating themselves, nevertheless, to British protection and occupation.

This is how matters stood when, at the beginning of December, I was informed of a projected agreement which had just been established between the British government and our embassy in London. The text appeared to call for French and British forces to evacuate Syrian territory simultaneously, the French regrouping in Lebanon though it was not specified that the British would do the same. This would not greatly modify our situation, for the majority of our units were already stationed on Lebanese soil. But for the British, such an agreement appeared to involve considerable concessions: first of all, the end of their military presence in Syria along with ours; further, their departure from Lebanon where we would remain; and lastly, the recognition of our right to maintain a military establishment in Lebanon until the United Nations Organization was in a position to relieve us of the responsibilities of the mandate. Aware on the one hand of the British Foreign Office's skill and on the other of our own diplomacy's horror of a vacuum when our relations with England were at stake, I doubted, at first sight, that matters were as they seemed to be. But when the Quai d'Orsay in Paris and our embassy in London assured me that this was indeed the significance of the draft, I gave my consent. On December 13, Messrs. Bevin and Massigli signed two agreements in Whitehall, one relative to the regrouping of troops; the other providing for consultations between the two governments to avoid the recurrence of incidents in the Middle East.

However, it soon appeared that our diplomats' interpretation of the agreement was not shared by the British. General de Larminat, sent to Beirut to settle the details of the military measures to be taken by either side with General Pilleau, commander of the British Ninth Army, discovered at the first contact that there existed profound divergence between the instructions he had received and those sent to his colleague. The British were perfectly content to have everyone leave Syria. But they then expected that their forces, like our own, would regroup in Lebanon—in other words, about 7,000 of our men and more than 35,000 of theirs. After which they would leave that country only if we ourselves left too. In other words, the "agreement" would come down to this: The French would retire from the entire Middle East—for our troops, embarking at Beirut, could go nowhere but to Algiers, Bizerte or

Marseilles—while the British alone, remaining in force in Cairo, Baghdad, Amman and Jerusalem, would dominate that part of the world.

I immediately canceled my orders and recalled De Larminat. But regarding the steps to be taken on diplomatic grounds, either to correct this strange misunderstanding or else to cancel the "agreement," I discovered our own men had all kinds of reservations. The British, on their side, refused all the more obstinately to reconsider what they regarded as a *fait accompli,* since they realized that a little patience would permit them—once I had left the government—to realize their goal. I must say that in such a serious matter and one which was close to my heart, this proof that I no longer held the reins of command would have made the cup run over if, for many other reasons, it were not leaking on all sides already.

Before taking the decisive steps, I felt it would be wise to withdraw. Antibes offered me the refuge of Eden-Roc, and for the first time in more than seven years, I took a few days' rest. Thus I assured myself and could assure others that my departure was not to be the effect of thoughtless resentment or of depression caused by fatigue. As I meditated by the sea, I determined the fashion in which I would withdraw from public life—leaving the tribunal in silence, without attacking anyone, either in public or in private; without accepting any further function, either honorary or emeritus; lastly, without giving any indication of what I intended to do afterward. More than ever, I would hold myself above contingencies.

After eight days in the south, I returned to Paris on January 14, a Monday. My resignation would be made the following Sunday. I spent the week promulgating the laws and decrees whose texts, accumulated in my absence and needing to be put into immediate effect, required my signature. To several of my ministers, particularly those of the Interior, Justice, and the Armies, I announced my imminent retirement; I also informed the Commissioners of the

Republic, whom I had convened for this purpose. Thus those who, either in the government or locally, were responsible for public order would not be surprised by the event.

Before my withdrawal, I had one further opportunity to discover the parliamentary state of mind in my regard. M. Herriot, who was a past master at such things, considered the moment had come to take me to task personally. He did so on January 16. A few days before had been published the regularization of certain citations made in 1943 by General Giraud to soldiers, sailors and aviators killed or wounded during the unfortunate North African engagements that Darlan had ordered against the Americans. I had not wanted to efface these poor tributes, but the president of the Radical party, brandishing the list published in the *Journal Officiel,* invoked "my own justice" to condemn a measure in which he claimed to see an insult to our allies and the glorification of a battle disastrous to France. Applause and jeers, spreading over several rows, supported this intervention.

Such an attack, on such a subject, was naturally disagreeable for me. But the reception given it, in my presence, by an Assembly the majority of whose members had but lately answered my call to honor filled me, I must admit, with sadness and disgust. I answered Édouard Herriot that there was no question of snatching from the coffins of the lamented dead and from the breasts of the wretched wounded the crosses which had been awarded them three years before for having obeyed the orders of their leaders, though those orders were wrongly given. Then, taking my distance from this challenger who, on the eve of the liberation of Paris, had had the weakness to negotiate and to dine with Laval and Abetz, I added that I was the better judge of those citations since "I have never had dealings with Vichy or with the enemy save by cannon-fire." The quarrel Herriot had sought with me fell flat, but I had seen how indelibly prejudice and political resentment tainted men's souls.

On January 19, I requested the ministers to convene the next day in the Rue St.-Dominique. With the exception of Auriol and Bidault, in London at the time, and Soustelle, on tour in the Gabon, all met on the morning of Sunday, January 20, in the "hall of arms." I came in, shook hands all around and before anyone sat down, spoke these words: "The exclusive regime of parties has reappeared. I disapprove of it. But aside from establishing by force a dictatorship which I do not desire and which would certainly end in disaster, I have not the means of preventing this experiment. I must therefore withdraw. Today, in fact, I shall send the President of the National Assembly a letter informing him of the government's resignation. I sincerely thank each of you for the support you have given me and urge you to remain at your posts in order to assure the conduct of business until your successors are appointed." The ministers impressed me as being more grieved than astonished. None of them uttered a word, either to ask me to reconsider my decision or even to say that it was regretted. After taking my leave of them, I returned to my residence.

I was informed that after my departure the ministers conferred together for several minutes. M. Thorez, apparently, remarked, "A departure made with greatness!" M. Moch said, "This retirement is indeed a serious one, but good can come of evil. The General's personality stifled the National Assembly. Now the latter can reveal itself freely." M. Pleven made the voice of bitterness and anxiety heard, "Now see what your factions have brought us to!" He reproached his colleagues, whose parties had raised obstacles to my action. "We are confronting," declared Messrs. Gay and Teitgen, "the heavy responsibility of succeeding De Gaulle. Our movement will try to be worthy of it." "Come now," M. Thorez exclaimed, "since you couldn't get anywhere with the General, how will you do better without him?"

In the letter I wrote to the President of the Assembly, I made sure there was not the trace of polemics. "If I have remained," I wrote, "at the head of the government after November 13, 1945, it was to assure a necessary transition . . . Now the parties are in

a position to assume their responsibilities." I abstained from pointing out in what state the nation was when "I assumed the burden
of directing it toward its liberation, its victory, and its sovereignty."
But I remarked, "Today, after terrible ordeals, France is no longer
in a state of emergency. Certainly many sufferings still weigh upon
our people, and grave problems remain. But the very life of the
French people is, in all essential respects, assured. Our economic
activity is staging a recovery. Our territories are once again in our
own hands. We have re-established ourselves in Indochina. Public
order is not threatened. Abroad, despite the anxieties which subsist, our independence is firmly re-established. We are holding the
Rhine. We are participating, in the first rank, in the new international organization, and it is in Paris that the first peace conference is to be held this coming spring." Finally, I expressed the
"profoundly sincere hope that tomorrow's government may succeed in its task." M. Félix Gouin's reply was extremely gratifying.

But if my own soul was calm, this was not the case for the world
of politics. After being greatly disturbed by my presence, it was
equally shaken by my absence. There were even rumors that I was
plotting a *coup d'état,* as if the fact that I had resigned from power
of my own free will was not sufficient to stigmatize such alarms
with the absurdity they deserved. Without going so far as these
suspicions, others felt it was prudent to show their vigilance. Thus
M. Vincent Auriol, hurriedly returning from London in the supposition that I was going to speak on the radio to rouse popular
indignation, wrote me on the evening of January 20 to say that
by so doing "I would divide the country to the advantage and the
satisfaction of democracy's enemies." I calmed the Minister of
State's fears. As a matter of fact, had I chosen to explain the reasons for my retirement, I would not have failed to do so, and
this explanation, given to a sovereign people, would not have been
contrary to democratic principles. But I considered that my
silence would weigh more heavily than anything else, that thought-

ful minds would understand why I had left, and that the rest would sooner or later be informed by events themselves.

Where was I to go? Contemplating the prospect of my resignation from office, I had resolved to live in Colombey-les-deux-Églises, and had begun repairing my war-damaged house with this in mind. But these arrangements would take several months. At first I thought of traveling to some distant region where I could wait in peace. But the tide of insult and invective launched against me by political dens and the majority of newspapers determined me to remain in Metropolitan France so that no one could suppose such attacks had affected me. I therefore rented the Pavillon de Marly from the Service des Beaux Arts, and lived there until May.

Nevertheless, while the regime's personnel gave itself up to the euphoria of old habits regained, the mass of the French people, on the contrary, sank back into distress. Gone was that atmosphere of exaltation, that hope of success, that ambition for France, which supported the national soul. Every Frenchman, whatever his tendencies, had the troubling suspicion that with the General vanished something primordial, permanent and necessary which he incarnated in history and which the regime of parties could not represent. In the sidetracked leader, men persisted in seeing a kind of capital of sovereignty, a last resort selected in advance. They supposed such legitimacy could remain latent in a period without anxiety. But they knew it could be invoked by common consent as soon as a new laceration threatened the nation.

My attitude, through the years, would be dictated by this mission which France continued to assign me, even when, in the immediate circumstances, many tendencies did not follow me. Whatever I said or was made to say, my words, real or supposed, would pass into the public domain. All those I dealt with reacted as if, invested with the supreme authority, I had received them in the national palaces. Wherever I happened to make an appearance, those present would burst into ardent manifestations.

It was this atmosphere which enveloped me during the course

of the first public action I took once I had abandoned my official status; I made a speech in Bayeux, describing what our institutions should be. I spoke on many subsequent occasions, condemning the constitution wrung from the country's lassitude; appealing to the French people to unite in order to change the bad regime; launching ideas to deal with the future from many platforms; appearing before crowds in every French and Algerian department, at least twice in each and more in some, in order to keep the spark alight and to make contact with many affecting loyalties. It was these same tributes which were lavished upon me after 1952, when I determined to withdraw from the situation as it stood, the disease being too advanced for any remedy to affect it before the inevitable upheaval; when I occasionally presided at some ceremony; when I visited our territories in Africa and the Indian Ocean, traveling around the world from one French territory to the next, watching the oil gushers being brought in in the Sahara. At the moment of finishing this book, I feel the same countless hearts turning toward my simple house.

This is my home. In the tumult of men and events, solitude was my temptation; now it is my friend. What other satisfaction can be sought once you have confronted history? Moreover, this section of Champagne is imbued with calm—wide, mournful horizons; melancholy woods and meadows; the frieze of resigned old mountains; tranquil, unpretentious villages where nothing has changed its spirit or its place for thousands of years. All this can be seen from my village. Situated high on the plateau, near a wooded hill, it weathers the centuries among the fields cultivated by its inhabitants. The latter, though I am careful not to force myself upon them, surround me with their discreet friendship. I know their families, I respect and love them.

Silence fills my house. From the corner room where I spend most of my daylight hours, I look out far into the west. There is nothing to obstruct my view for some fifteen kilometers. Above the plain and the woods, my eyes follow the long slopes descending toward the valley of the Aube, then the heights of the slope opposite. From a rise in the garden, I look down on the wild depths where the forest envelops the tilled land like the sea beating on a promontory. I watch the night cover the landscape. Then, looking up at the stars, I steep myself in the insignificance of earthly things.

Of course letters, the radio, the newspapers bring news of our world into this hermitage. During brief visits to Paris, I receive visitors, whose remarks reveal the course of men and events. During vacations, our children and grandchildren surround us, with the exception of our daughter Anne, who left this world before us. But how many hours slip by in reading, writing, dreaming, when no illusion sweetens my bitter serenity.

Yet, on our little property—I have walked around it fifteen thousand times—the trees, stripped by the cold, rarely fail to turn green again, and the flowers my wife has planted bloom once more each spring. The village houses are decrepit, but suddenly laughing girls and boys come out of their doors. When I walk to one of the nearby woods—Les Dhuits, Clairvaux, Le Heu, Blinfeix, La Chapelle—their solemn depths fill me with nostalgia; but suddenly the song of a bird, the sun through the leaves, or the buds of a thicket remind me that ever since it has existed on earth, life wages a battle it has never lost. Then I feel a secret solace passing through me. Since everything eternally begins anew, what I have done will sooner or later be a source of new ardor after I have gone.

As age triumphs, nature comes closer to me. Each year, in the four seasons which are as so many lessons, I find consolation in her wisdom. In spring she sings: "Whatever has happened, I am in the beginning! All is bright, even the snow flurries; young, even the wizened trees; beautiful, even the stony fields. Love raises the sap within me and with it certitudes so radiant and powerful they will never end!"

And in summer she proclaims: "Consider the glory of my

fruitfulness. Striving, everything that nourishes life comes from me. Each life depends on my warmth. These seeds, these fruits, these herds the sun now floods with light are a victory nothing can destroy. Henceforth, the future belongs to me!"

In autumn, she sighs: "My task is near its term. I have given my flowers, my harvests, my fruits. Now, I retire within myself. See how beautiful I am still in my robe of purple and gold, beneath the brilliant sun. Alas, the winds and the frosts will soon tear away my vestments. But one day, upon my naked body, my youth will flower again!"

In winter, she moans: "Here I lie, barren and frozen. How many plants, animals and birds have I created and loved, who die now on my breast that can no longer feed or warm them! Then is my destiny sealed? Is death's the victory forever? No! Already, deep in my inert soil, a secret labor is being accomplished. Motionless in the heart of darkness, I foresee the marvelous return of light and life!"

Old Earth, worn by the ages, wracked by rain and storm, exhausted yet ever ready to produce what life must have to go on!

Old France, weighed down with history, prostrated by wars and revolutions, endlessly vacillating from greatness to decline, but revived, century after century, by the genius of renewal!

Old man, exhausted by ordeal, detached from human deeds, feeling the approach of the eternal cold, but always watching in the shadows for the gleam of hope!

INDEX

Aachen (Ger.), *see* Aix-la-Chapelle
Abadie, Dr., 430, 473
Abbeville (Gehring), 47
Abbeville (Fr.) operation, 43–50; map of, 45
Abdullah, Emir, 198, 529
Abetz, Heinrich Otto, 630, 634–35, 963, 992
Abidjan (Fr. W. Africa), 107, 338, 511
Abrons (tribe), 339
Abyssinia, 236; Free Fr. victories in, 171; *see also* Ethiopia
Abzac, d', 374
Académie Française, 692, 799–801
Accra (Brit. W. Africa), 386, 550
Achard, Jean, 262
Acker, M. van. 920
Aconit (Free Fr. corvette), 214, 282
Action, 797
Adam, M., 338
Addis Ababa (Ethiopia), 236–37, 367
Adeline, Colonel, 592, 684–86
Africa, 49, 79, 155–58, 165, 695, 703, 704, 726, 858, 896, 905, 907, 910, 921, 996; French, 93, 149, 181–82, 211; *See also* Camaroons, French Equatorial Africa, French Somaliland, French West Africa, Madagascar, North Africa, Réunion, Tunisia
African Conference, Brazzaville, 511–13

African Phalanx, 371, 442, 791
African army, *see* French Armed Forces under Darlan, Giraud; French Armed Forces under Vichy
Afrika Korps (Ger.), 296
Agence Française Indépendante, 154, 400
Ahmed Bey, 339
Ahne, M., 122
Aigrefeuille (Fr.), 851
Ailette River (Fr.), defensive front at, 37
Ain (Fr. dept.), 618, 700
Air force, tactical use of, 15
Air-France, 337, 777
Aisne River (Fr.), defensive front at, 37; French retreat to, 42; Ger. drive toward, 50
Aix-la-Chapelle (Ger.), 826
Ajaccio (Corsica), 463, 465–66, 468–69, 492, 677
Ajax (Vichy submarine), 127, 283
Alawis, Territory of the, 325
Albania, government in exile, 97
Albatros (Fr. destroyer), 353
Albert Canal (Belg.), strategic importance of, 28
Albert Hall (London), 677
Albertville (Fr.), 691
Alcyon (Fr. torpedo boat), 465
Alençon (Fr.), 624, 641, 956
Aleppo (Syria), 178, 198, 325, 337, 880, 893
Alés (Fr.), 790

532, 533, 596, 722, 724, 727, 817, 867, 868–69, 873, 897–99, 907, 914, 915, 924, 940, 975, 988; air force, 821; army, 534, 535, 569, 699, 734, 739, 839, 846, 859, 863, 864, 869, 870, 897–98, 915, 945; "concern" over Levant, 893; Czechoslovakia, relations with, 246; de G. visit to, 729–57; France, relations with, 8; at German surrender, 870; Germany, relations with, alliance, 28, 32, 143, 229: offensive in Russia, 187, 207, 224–25, 227–28, 267; military operations, 305, 306, 308, 309, 313, 346, 348, 624; pact with France, 729, 730, 732, 738, 744–47, 751–58; plans for Polish reconstruction, 724–25, 741–43, 745–51, 753–57, 765, 899; Poland, relations with, 28, 246–48; policy on postwar Germany, 737, 763, 897, 903, 915, 916; postwar ambitions, 530–31, 534–38, 567, 569, 573, 574; postwar rivalry with U.S., 727, 873, 901–02, 904, 906, 907, 914; program for postwar Europe, 721–22, 724–25, 728, 744, 759, 765, 898, 909, 915; recognizes de G. government, 717; relations with Fighting France, 208, 224–30, 292–94, 307, 314, 330, 345, 457–58, 516–17, 519, 520, 539, 540, 542, 585; return of French POWs, 830, 945–46; seen as postwar leader of Europe, 726–29; supports U.N. organization, 945–46; Vichy France, relations with, 87, 225–26; war, entry into, 238, 244, 246, 261; war with Japan, part in, 897, 898

United Kingdom, *see* Britain

United Nations, 213–14, 238, 239, 300, 722, 745, 756, 759, 766, 892–94, 897, 964, 990; San Francisco Conference, 764, 878, 894–97; Security Council, 722, 730, 765, 893, 897, 898; trusteeship plan for Italian colonies, 915

United States of America, 305, 307–09, 337, 392, 428, 448–49, 455, 479, 516–17, 530, 532, 533, 535–38, 573, 722–30, 745, 762, 805, 806, 848, 863, 867–69, 872, 904–07, 911, 916, 924, 988; armed forces, *see* United States Army, United States Navy; attitude toward USSR, 749; Britain, relations with, 186, 232–33; dealings with Vichy, 310, 331, 350, 352; de G. visits, 905–13; France, relations with, 61; Free France, relations with, 127, 129–30, 160–61, 182, 208, 209–17, 218, 221–24, 233, 242–43; Germany, relations with, 143; Hopkins meets with de G., 759–63; hostility to France in Far East, 855–58, 925, 928; Italian peace terms, 915; Lend-Lease aid, *q.v.;* military operations in France, 308, 312, 562, 594, 596, 621–22, 626–27, 635–37, 640–41, 651–52: in Italy, 452, 458–60, 598, 604–10: in North Africa, 308–10, 314, 317, 323, 330–31, 337, 348, 349–54, 370, 414; opposes France on Alpine enclaves, 874–77; policy on Levant crisis, 893–94, 910; policy on liberation government in France, 501, 508, 510, 543–51, 554–59, 562, 570, 579, 630, 637, 642, 643, 644, 652; policy on postwar German settlement, 763; policy toward de G., 311, 314, 329–31, 335–36, 345, 347, 350, 363–64, 368, 375–79, 386–94, 396–402, 408-13, 417, 432–39, 452, 456–57, 459–60, 486, 499, 516–17, 519–20, 525, 540, 542–48, 552–63, 565–66, 567–77, 579, 582–83, 585, 597–98, 600–01, 634, 652, 662; postwar rivalry with USSR, 727–29, 873, 901–02, 904, 906, 907; recognizes de G. government, 674, 717–18; Roosevelt invitation to de G., 767–69; sponsorship of U.N., 722, 766, 895–96; stints on aid to France, 670, 703, 704, 724, 762,

549; Free France, relations with, 139–40; de G., relations with, 102, 137–40, 173–74; Germany, relations with, 120, 139, 143–44, 171, 176, 178–79, 181, 191, 239; government, 87–89, 138–40, 146–47, 150, 155, 157, 160, 161, 169, 189–90, 196, 214, 220, 238, 240, 250, 260–63, 265–66, 278, 301, 306, 307, 315, 328, 344–48, 351, 355, 365–68, 380, 389, 394, 395, 407, 408, 414, 416, 422, 441, 448, 450, 454, 457, 503, 516–17, 567, 581, 590, 625, 630, 635, 638–40, 650, 657, 662, 664, 678, 680, 682, 687, 693, 702, 713, 770, 775, 789, 791, 792, 794, 805, 827, 854–56, 944, 951–54, 960, 961, 964, 969, 973, 989, 992; governments in exile, relations with, 244; military forces, 109, 124, 125–26, 135, 137, 165, 168, 172–73, 179, 181, 185, 186–87, 190–95, 197–98, 201–02; naval forces, 91–93, 112–14, 119–22, 124–26, 128, 129, 135, 136, 188–89; U. of So. Africa, relations with, 87; USSR, relations with, 87, 225–26; U.S., relations with, 87, 139, 177, 186, 210, 213, 214, 216, 250–51
Victor, M., 102, 160
Victor Emmanuel III, King of Italy, 452, 458, 487, 522–23, 566
Vienna (Austria), 15, 24, 26, 739, 846, 859, 864, 901
Vienne (Fr. dept.), 686
Viénot, Pierre, 274, 318, 404, 455, 518–19, 548, 550, 553, 555, 560, 561, 563, 565, 579, 674
Vietminh, 927–28
Vietnam, 929
Vigier, General du, 695–96, 822, 833, 835, 919
Vignes, M., 160
Viking (Free Fr. patrol trawler), 117, 282
Vili (tribe), 339
Villedieu-les-Poêles (Fr.), 955–56
Ville d'Oran (Fr. transport), 401
Villers (Fr.), 46

Villeurbanne (Fr.), 679
Villon, M., 632
Villoutreys, Commandant de, 185
Vincennes (Fr.), 814; Château de, 713
Vinh (Indochina), 857
Vin Sanh, Prince, 930
Violet Plan, 592
Vishinsky, Andrei Y., 228, 521, 542, 870
Vistula River, 721, 727, 759, 848
Vitry-sur-Seine (Fr.), 712–13
Vittel (Fr.), 707, 832, 833, 835
Vittori, M., 462–63
Vizille, M., 486
"Vlassov Army," 683
Voges Mountains, 586, 669, 694, 698, 704, 705, 707, 822, 823, 825, 826, 829, 831, 832, 836, 841
Voice of America, 644
Voice of the North, 267, 347
Voix de la France, La, 400
Voizart, Lieutenant, 567
Volunteer Corps (Fr. African Army), 414
Vorarlberg, 864
Vorges (Fr.), 42
Voronov, Marshal Nikolai, 752
Voroshilov, Marshal Kliment E., 752
Voyer (Fr.), 823
Vuillemin, General, 66, 91, 421

Wadai (Fr. Eq. Africa), 339
Wake Island, fall of, 220
Wallace, Henry A., 572
Wallis Islands (New Caledonia), 282
Walney (Brit. escort vessel), 354
Wane, Mac, 562
War Committee (French), 33
War Ministry, 702, 723; *see also* Diethelm, André
Warsaw (Poland), 15, 24, 535, 537, 538, 741–43, 898
Washington (D.C.), 402, 438, 439, 529, 551–52, 554–55, 561, 565, 570–73, 576, 674, 905–11
Waterhouse, Gilbert, 14 n.

Wavell, Gen. Sir Archibald Percival, 110, 155–57, 159, 170–71, 174, 176, 178–81, 186, 189
Wedemeyer, Gen. Albert C., 911
Weiss, General, 506
Weitzel, Capitaine de Corvette, 90, 284
Welles, Sumner, 211–13, 360, 385–86, 402
Welwert, General, 369, 414
Wendel, Msgr., 917
Wesel (Ger.), 840, 845
Weser River, 859
West Africa, *see* French West Africa
Westerland (Dutch liner), 117, 118–19, 123–25
Western Army Detachment (Fr.), 850
West Point (U.S. military academy), 912
Weygand, Gen. Maxime, 19, 21, 43, 50–52, 54–56, 61–62, 63, 64–65, 67, 70, 72, 85, 86, 139–40, 173–74, 181, 210, 213, 262, 289, 314–15, 356, 358, 411, 523, 663, 693
Wichita (U.S. cruiser), 354
Widmer, General, 904
Wiese, General, 699
Wietzel, Corvette Captain, 615
Wijk, M. van, 570
Wilbur, Gen. William H., 388, 397
Wilhelm II, Kaiser, 720
Wilhelmina, Queen of the Netherlands, 245, 560, 562
Williams, Colonel, 89–90
Willkie, Wendell L., 335–36
Wilson, Edwin, 540, 570, 598, 599, 718
Wilson, Gen. Sir Henry Maitland, 180, 189, 191, 195, 197–201, 205, 235, 566, 596, 600, 601, 606, 607, 613

Winant, John G., 220, 310, 312, 329, 411
Wissembourg (Fr.), 832, 834, 841
Witos, Andrej, 899
Wittenheim (Fr.), 829
Wohleb, Dr., 918
World War I, 309, 434, 535, 575, 578, 719, 735, 741, 762, 774, 808, 892, 935, 936
Worms (Ger.), 845
Württemberg (Ger.), 843, 844, 860, 861, 902, 904, 916, 918
Wybot (underground), 151
Wyoming (Fr. tanker), 401

Yakovlev, M., 752
Yalta Conference, 758–59, 763–69, 787, 879, 890, 895, 897, 898, 915, 989
Yaunde (Fr. Cameroons), 131
Ybarnegaray, Jean, 72, 262
Yeu, Ile d', 952
Yokohama (Japan), 926
Yonne (Fr. dept.), 700
Yovanovich, Slobodan, 245
Yugoslavia, 159, 176, 244–45, 305, 310, 519, 522, 531–33, 562, 594, 595, 699, 725, 744, 765, 767
Yunnan (China), 858

Zaleski, August, 118, 246
Zay, Jean, 639
Zeller, Col. Henri, 494, 624
Zhukov, Marshal Georgi K., 227, 864, 870, 903
Zinder (Fr. W. Africa), 338, 373, 513
Znaïm, Colonel, 334
Zuara (Libya), 338
Zurich (Switzerland), 868